THE ART
OF CAPITAL
RESTRUCTURING

The *Robert W. Kolb Series in Finance* provides a comprehensive view of the field of finance in all of its variety and complexity. The series is projected to include approximately 65 volumes covering all major topics and specializations in finance, ranging from investments, to corporate finance, to financial institutions. Each volume in the *Kolb Series in Finance* consists of new articles especially written for the volume.

Each volume is edited by a specialist in a particular area of finance, who develops the volume outline and commissions articles by the world's experts in that particular field of finance. Each volume includes an editor's introduction and approximately thirty articles to fully describe the current state of financial research and practice in a particular area of finance.

The essays in each volume are intended for practicing finance professionals, graduate students, and advanced undergraduate students. The goal of each volume is to encapsulate the current state of knowledge in a particular area of finance so that the reader can quickly achieve a mastery of that special area of finance.

Please visit www.wiley.com/go/kolbseries to learn about recent and forthcoming titles in the Kolb Series.

THE ART OF CAPITAL RESTRUCTURING

Creating Shareholder Value through Mergers and Acquisitions

H. Kent Baker

Halil Kiymaz

The Robert W. Kolb Series in Finance

WILEY

John Wiley & Sons, Inc.

For general information on our other products and services or for technical support,
please contact our Customer Care Department within the United States at (800) 762-2974,
outside the United States at (317) 572-3993 or fax (317) 572-4002.

Wiley also publishes its books in a variety of electronic formats. Some content that
appears in print may not be available in electronic books. For more information about
Wiley products, visit our web site at www.wiley.com.

Library of Congress Cataloging-in-Publication Data:

The art of capital restructuring : creating shareholder value through mergers and
acquisitions / H. Kent Baker and Halil Kiymaz, editors.
    p. cm. – (The Robert W. Kolb series in finance)
  Includes index.
  ISBN 978-0-470-56951-1 (cloth); ISBN 978-1-11803035-6 (ebk); ISBN 978-1-11803033-2
(ebk); ISBN 978-1-11803034-9 (ebk)
   1. Consolidation and merger of corporations.   2. Corporate reorganizations.
3. Corporate governance.   4. Corporations–Valuation.   I. Baker, H. Kent (Harold Kent),
1944–   II. Kiymaz, Halil, 1964–
  HG4028.M4A78 2011
  658.1′62

                                                                              2010047236

Printed in the United States of America

10 9 8 7 6 5 4 3 2 1

Contents

Acknowledgments

The expression "it takes a village" aptly applies to this book because it has involved a large cast of participants in which each has provided important contributions. At the heart of *The Art of Capital Restructuring* is the outstanding work of the scholars who wrote the chapters as well as the authors whose work is cited therein. Meghan Nesmith meticulously reviewed the chapters and provided many helpful edits and substantive suggestions. Thomas Bradley also provided assistance. We thank our talented publishing team at John Wiley & Sons, especially Emilie Herman and Claire Wesley, who took the manuscript to final production while demonstrating professionalism and expertise throughout the process. Bob Kolb, the series editor, deserves our appreciation for his vision in developing this series. We also want to recognize the support provided by the Kogod School of Business at American University and the Crummer Graduate School of Business at Rollins College. Finally, our friends and families, who have been silent partners in this effort, deserve our gratitude. Linda Baker deserves special thanks for editorial assistance and her endless patience and support. Nilgun Kiymaz also provided support that warrants special recognition.

CHAPTER 1

Mergers, Acquisitions, and Corporate Restructuring: An Overview

H. KENT BAKER
University Professor of Finance and Kogod Research Professor, American University

HALIL KIYMAZ
Bank of America Chair and Professor of Finance, Rollins College

INTRODUCTION

An important question in finance is whether managerial actions create market value or shareholder wealth. Neoclassical economic theory assumes that corporate management acts to maximize shareholder wealth. Studies involving mergers and acquisitions (M&As) directly examine this issue. Such studies, which are relevant to shareholders, managers, regulators, and other stakeholders, show considerable variation in their results. Thus, debate continues about both the short-term and long-term performance of M&As. As markets become more integrated, M&As continue to be a hot topic in both academia and the business world. Given the frequency of these activities, businesspeople need to understand why and how such activities take place.

Although sometimes used interchangeably or synonymously, the terms *merger* and *acquisition* mean slightly different things. A *merger* is a combination of two or more companies in which one company survives and the merged company goes out of existence. Unlike a merger, a *consolidation* is a business combination in which two or more companies join to form an entirely new firm. With an *acquisition*, one company takes controlling ownership interest in another firm, typically buying the selected assets or shares of the target company. On the surface, the distinction in meaning may not seem to matter because all of them are strategic transactions that usually change not only the control of a company but also its strategic direction. Depending on the transaction, the financial, legal, tax, and even cultural impact of a deal may differ substantially.

M&As represent a fast-paced and highly complex environment in which transactions provide unique opportunities with considerable risk. Worldwide M&A transactions involve trillions of dollars that can have a major impact on both domestic and global economies. M&As are a vital part of any healthy economy

because they force firms to use their resources efficiently and allow strong companies to grow and weaker companies to be swallowed. Further, M&As enable firms
to achieve or maintain their competitive advantage by anticipating and adjusting
to change. Through M&As a company can grow rapidly without having to create
another business entity. Consequently, M&As represent a vital business tool and
an alternative growth and expansion strategy for many companies. In short, an
M&A is an instrument of macroeconomic renewal. Yet, these complex transactions
are laden with potential problems and pitfalls. In fact, many M&A transactions
fail to realize expected benefits. Understanding how to ensure the successful consummation of these transactions is critical to the goal of maximizing shareholder
wealth.

PURPOSE OF THE BOOK

This book provides a fresh look at the current state of mergers, acquisitions, and
corporate restructuring in both developed and emerging markets. Although M&As
generally focus on corporate expansion, companies sometimes contract and down-
size their operations. *Restructuring* refers to the act of partially dismantling or
otherwise reorganizing a company for the purpose of making it more profitable.
This book considers several different forms of physical restructuring such as divestitures as well as capital restructuring, which refers to alterations in the capital
structure of the firm. This volume explains not only the financial aspects of these
transactions but also legal, regulatory, tax, ethical, social, and behavioral considerations. In short, although economics plays an essential role in understanding
M&A activity, psychology also plays a critical part. Thus, achieving "success" in
any M&A effort is a combination of both art and science.

Additionally, the latest research on M&A-related topics permeates the book.
The coverage extends from discussing basic concepts, motives, strategies, and
valuation techniques to their application to increasingly complex and real-world
situations. The book explains these methods from both a management and investor
perspective while emphasizing the wealth effects on shareholders of these different
strategies. Thus, this volume spans the gamut from theoretical to practical, while
attempting to offer a useful balance of detailed and user-friendly coverage.

DISTINGUISHING FEATURES OF THE BOOK

Given the popularity and importance of mergers, acquisitions, divestitures, and
other financial capital restructuring, the fact that many books deal with these
topics is not surprising. Yet, most do not offer the scope of coverage and breadth
of viewpoints contained in this volume. The book provides a comprehensive and
current discussion of theoretical developments, empirical results, and practice
involving M&As. Where possible, this volume avoids theoretical and mathematical
derivations unless they are necessary to explain the topic. It attempts to distill
the results of several hundred empirical studies in an understandable and clear
manner.

The book has seven other distinguishing features.

1. The book attempts to blend the conceptual world of scholars with the pragmatic view of practitioners. This volume is not a "how to" book or a simple easy-to-use-guide but instead incorporates theory and practice. It also provides a synthesis of important and relevant research studies in a straightforward and pragmatic manner and includes recent developments.
2. The book contains contributions from more than 40 scholars and practitioners from around the world who are leading experts in their fields. Thus, the breadth of contributors ensures a variety of perspectives and a rich interplay of ideas.
3. This book emphasizes best practices that lead to M&A success. Such practices focus on valuing the target, negotiating and financing the deal, and engaging in postacquisition planning and integration.
4. The book offers a strategic focus to help provide an understanding of how these decisions can affect overall value. These strategies include both takeover and defensive strategies.
5. The book has a global focus rather than being U.S.-centric. It reviews research dealing with both U.S. firms and others from around the world. Special emphasis is placed on the cross-border effects involving developed and emerging markets.
6. The book examines both technical and human aspects of M&As. The technical aspects mainly deal with legal, regulatory, and valuation issues. By contrast, the human aspects deal with issues involving corporate governance, cultural due diligence, organization and human resources, and the behavioral effects.
7. Each chapter contains a set of discussion questions that helps to reinforce key aspects of the chapter's content. A separate section near the end of the book contains guideline answers to each question.

INTENDED AUDIENCE FOR THE BOOK

The intended audience for this book includes academics, researchers, practitioners (e.g., business executives, managers, investment bankers, lawyers, and consultants), students, libraries, and others interested in mergers, acquisitions, and restructuring. Given its extensive coverage and focus on the theoretical and empirical literature, this book should be appealing to academics and researchers as a valuable resource. Practitioners can use this book to provide guidance in helping them navigate through these strategic transactions. This book should be appropriate as a stand-alone or supplementary book for advanced undergraduate and graduate business students as well as for management training programs in M&As. Finally, libraries should find this work to be suitable for reference purposes.

STRUCTURE OF THE BOOK

The remainder of this book consists of 28 chapters divided into six main parts. A brief synopsis of each part and chapter follows.

Part I. Background

This part contains six chapters (Chapters 2–7) that provide important background information that sets the stage for the remaining sections. The first three chapters focus on merger waves, takeover regulation, and corporate governance. Next, Chapters 5 and 6 examine ethical, social, and theoretical issues involving M&As. Chapter 7 focuses on the short-term and long-term performance of M&As.

Chapter 2 Merger Waves (Jarrad Harford)

The chapter surveys the vast literature on mergers with a focus on merger waves. The motives for mergers run the spectrum from a purely efficient reshuffling of assets to purely managerial driven empire-building strategies. Because merger activity clusters in time and within industries, an understanding of the causes of these merger waves is needed to comprehend the dominant motivations behind mergers. Research clearly establishes a link between aggregate economic activity, especially as reflected in the stock market, and aggregate merger activity. Further, research shows that technological, regulatory, and economic shocks to industries' operating environment, coupled with macro-level ease of financing, generate merger waves. While the primary driver of merger activity is economic efficiencies, room exists for other motives such as empire building. Nonetheless, the other motives do not dominate the activity.

Chapter 3 Takeover Regulation (Marina Martynova and Luc Renneboog)

Takeover regulation is a set of legal provisions aimed at facilitating efficient corporate restructuring, mitigating potential conflicts of interest among parties involved in the control change transaction, and protecting minority shareholders. This chapter reviews the major takeover regulation provisions present in different jurisdictions around the world that include the mandatory bid rule, principle of equal treatment of shareholders, squeeze-out and sell-out rules, ownership and control disclosure, board neutrality concerning the takeover bid, and restrictions regarding the use of takeover defense measures. The chapter shows that takeover regulation provisions vary substantially across jurisdictions, reflecting different priorities as to the goals regulators set relating to the development of the takeover market and corporate governance.

Chapter 4 Corporate Governance and M&As (Fei Xie)

This chapter surveys the body of research at the intersection of two broad literatures, corporate governance and M&As. Four major themes and findings emerge. First, M&As as a managerial disciplinary device and part of a comprehensive corporate governance system have powerful incentive effects on managers and valuation effects on shareholders and bondholders. Second, as major corporate investments, M&As generate higher returns for acquiring shareholders when acquiring managers operate in environments of better corporate governance. These environments are defined by exposure to threats of hostile takeovers, competition from the product market, effective monitoring by boards and institutional investors, a strong link between managerial wealth and performance, and the risk of financial distress and ceding control to creditors. Third, the target firm's corporate governance is also important as target shareholder gains are significantly higher when the interests of target managers and shareholders are better aligned. Lastly, as a mechanism to allocate resources to their most efficient use, M&As generate synergistic gains and efficiency improvement that increase with the difference in corporate governance between acquiring and target firms.

Chapter 5 Ethical and Social Issues in M&As (Robert W. McGee)

The press, politicians, policy makers, and some economists often view M&As negatively, as something that must either be stopped or heavily regulated. Some perceive that workers are harmed by M&As, which is sometimes the case, while others view M&As as anticompetitive, which is often not the case. From a philosophical perspective, one might raise the question of whether such activity should be regulated at all if M&As do not violate anyone's rights. Yet, this question is seldom raised. This chapter examines some ethical issues that have been raised and applies several tools of ethical analysis in an attempt to determine which acts are ethical and which are not.

Chapter 6 Theoretical Issues on Mergers, Acquisitions, and Divestitures (Abdul H. Rahman)

Value-increasing motives for corporate takeovers may be categorized as creating operational efficiencies or allocative synergies, which can create market power. Empirical findings suggest that the former category dominates managers' motives. Value-decreasing motives are based on managers' private interests such as reduction of employment risk, managerial discretion driven by excess free cash flow, and managers' overconfidence or hubris. Evidence suggests that M&As occur in waves and across industries. The level of merger activity is also positively correlated with bull stock markets. Several models, including those based on chief executive officer envy and firm size, offer explanations for this evidence. Divestitures may be viewed as managerial actions to reverse or correct previous strategic decisions such as diversification, or to establish strategic positioning. As such, while takeovers expand the boundary of the firm, divestitures do the opposite. Sources of divestiture gains include the focus hypothesis where managers attempt to eliminate business units in different industries. Divestment may also reduce information asymmetry and hence lead to a more optimal pricing mechanism for both the parent firm and the spin-off business unit. Finally, divestiture gains may arise from negative synergies when the firm is overdiversified.

Chapter 7 The Short-Term and Long-Term Performance of M&As (Shantanu Dutta and Samir Saadi)

This chapter focuses on short-term stock return performance of target and acquiring firms and long-term stock return and operating performance of acquiring firms. Evidence shows that target shareholders generally earn significantly positive abnormal returns but the acquirers' shareholders earn, on average, a zero abnormal return at the acquisition's announcement. Considerable variation exists in these results. However, various studies with non-U.S. data consistently report significant and positive abnormal returns for acquirers' shareholders around the announcement date. A set of other studies investigates the long-term stock return performance of acquiring firms. Most of these long-term studies conclude that acquiring firms experience significant negative abnormal returns over a one- to three-year period after the merger. Still, debate continues on this issue. Given a lack of consensus on market-based studies and counterintuitive results, a smaller but growing body of literature investigates the long-term operating performance of acquiring firms. Previous empirical studies in this area report mixed and inconsistent results.

Part II. Valuation

This part consists of four chapters (Chapters 8–11) dealing with valuation methods. Chapters 8 and 9 examine standard valuation methods and real options, respectively. Chapter 10 examines the adjustment needed for the implicit minority discount. Chapter 11 focuses on cross-border valuation effects in developed and emerging markets.

Chapter 8 Standard Valuation Methods for M&As (Pablo Fernandez)
This chapter describes the four main groups comprising the most widely used company valuation methods: (1) balance sheet–based methods, (2) income statement–based methods or multiples, (3) discounted cash flow methods, and (4) value creation methods using economic value added and economic profit. Conceptually correct methods are based on cash flow discounting. The chapter briefly discusses other methods that are conceptually incorrect but continue to be used in practice. The chapter also addresses the lack of agreement about ways of calculating the value of tax shields and the dispersion of the market risk premium used by professors and financial analysts.

Chapter 9 Real Options and Their Impact on M&As
(Hemantha Herath and John S. Jahera Jr.)
The use of option analysis has grown from use with financial options to the application to real options. One specific application involves the M&A process. Almost all such transactions have embedded options that can address issues ranging from the specific terms of the M&A to the timing of the M&A decision and perhaps even the later divestiture decision. The impact of real options on M&A analysis is still developing as more managers acquire the knowledge to specifically value different decisions involved in a transaction. Traditional M&A analysis followed capital budgeting techniques such as net present value. Financial economists argue that such techniques are unable to capture value associated with managerial flexibility and other elements. As M&A activity has become more global, managers not only face greater complexity but also more alternative courses of action. Real options analysis represents another dimension to be incorporated into the decision to engage in M&A activity.

Chapter 10 The Law and Finance of Control Premia
and Minority Discounts (Helen Bowers)
The adjustment for the implicit minority discount is a controversial element of Delaware court practice. The Delaware courts usually adjust the value of minority shares in appraisal action upward to reflect a perceived market inefficiency that results in a persistent undervaluation of equity relative to intrinsic value. The genesis of the implicit minority discount may arise from a misunderstanding of

the assertion that stock prices represent minority values. Although some view the adjustment for the implicit minority discount as possible minority compensation for the wealth misappropriated by the majority, a direct adjustment according to the facts of the case would lead to a more economically efficient and equitable outcome. Because the value of minority shares that is derived from comparable company analysis is a minority value only in the sense that it is the value of the equity in the absence of a controlling stockholder, the adjustment for implicit minority discount transfers wealth from the controlling stockholders to the minority.

Chapter 11 Cross-Border Valuation Effects in Developed and Emerging Markets (Wenjie Chen)

Cross-border M&As have become an integral part of the global business land-scape. In 2007, the value of cross-border M&A transactions amounted to $1,637 billion, which is a 21 percent increase from the previous record set in 2000. Histor-ically, the majority of M&As have taken place between industrialized countries. In recent years, however, emerging markets started engaging in cross-border M&A activities. Developed and emerging markets have fundamental differences in insti-tutions, legal environment, corporate governance, and factor endowments such as accessibility to relatively cheap labor. These differences have profound impacts on the participants in and outcomes of cross-border M&As. Studying these impacts is important in understanding the nature of cross-border M&As and their valuation effects on both target and acquiring firms.

Part III. The M&A Deal Process

Chapters 12–17 provide an overview of the M&A deal process. Chapters 12 and Chapter 13 offer a discussion on sources of financing and means of payments and cultural due diligence. Chapter 14 and 15 focus on the negotiation process. The final two chapters examine the postacquisition planning and integration process and issues related to organizational and human resources.

Chapter 12 Sources of Financing and Means of Payments in M&As (Marina Martynova and Luc Renneboog)

This chapter reviews the academic literature regarding an acquiring firm's choices of financing sources and the means of payment in corporate takeovers. The financ-ing and payment decisions have a significant impact on the value of the acquiring firm. Investors take into account the information signaled by the choices of both the payment method and the sources of takeover financing when estimating the possible synergistic takeover value at the announcement. The financing decision is influenced by the acquirer's concerns about the cost of capital. In particular, in line with the pecking order hypothesis, cash-rich acquirers opt for the least expensive source of financing—internally generated funds. Acquirers operating in a better corporate governance environment benefit from lower costs of external capital. That is, debt financing is more likely when creditor rights are well protected by the law and court system, and the use of equity financing increases when shareholder rights protection is high. The takeover financing decision is closely related to the acquirer's strategic preferences for specific types of payment.

Chapter 13 Cultural Due Diligence (Ronald F. Piccolo and Mary Bardes)
The due diligence process associated with evaluating the viability of a merger, acquisition, or extended partnership most often comprises a comprehensive examination of strategic, economic, and financial metrics that estimate firm fit and expectations for economic return. Despite the vast amounts of hard data that characterize this process, a high failure rate remains for M&As, due in large part to conflicts in the merging firms' organizational cultures. Managers in the due diligence process often fail to make valid assessments of the norms, values, standards, and traditions of merging firms; neglect the influence of an organization's culture on the behavior and attitudes of its members; and underestimate the challenges associated with integrating two otherwise diverse firms. This chapter presents a brief description of organizational culture with some suggestions for measuring culture in an organizational setting.

Chapter 14 Negotiation Process, Bargaining Area, and Contingent Payments (William A. Grimm)
This chapter describes the negotiation process using two hypothetical situations involving a large, publicly held company as the buyer and two types of sellers—a small, publicly held company and a small, privately held company. The major issues that are usually involved in each type of transaction are discussed. The chapter emphasizes the thorough preparation needed for the negotiation by both the buyer and the seller and discusses how the preparation differs for each. It also discusses the interaction among the issues being negotiated, which makes clearly defining the bargaining area around the price to be paid difficult.

Chapter 15 Merger Negotiations: Takeover Process, Selling Procedure, and Deal Initiation (Nihat Aktas and Eric De Bodt)
Recent literature in finance reveals that the takeover market during the deal-friendly decade of the 1990s was much more competitive than prior research had indicated. The chapter provides an analysis of the private portion of the takeover process. The results show that about half of all targets are auctioned among multiple bidders, whereas the remainder negotiates with a single bidder. The chapter documents the takeover process of 1,774 large U.S. deals announced during the period from 1994 to 2007, of which 847 negotiations (48 percent) involved no explicit competition and 927 auctions (52 percent) had multiple bidders. An empirical analysis of the sales procedure's determinants reveals that, consistent with auction theory, auctions are more frequent for smaller targets (relative to the acquirer), less diversified targets, and cases in which the number of potential acquirers is large. Finally, the chapter discloses a relationship between deal initiation and the choice of the sales procedure; auctions represent the preferred method when the seller initiates the transaction.

Chapter 16 Postacquisition Planning and Integration (Olimpia Meglio and Arturo Capasso)
The purpose of this chapter is to provide an in-depth analysis of the postacquisition process, which involves both planning and implementation processes. The integration process is a crucial part in making a merger or acquisition successful. This process can result in synergy and capability transfers that can produce real benefits

for the combined entity. This process is vital to creating value and deserves careful planning and execution because it contains potential pitfalls that can be detrimental to postacquisition performance. The analysis in this chapter focuses on setting priorities according to acquisition goals, identifying the roles and competencies of the integration manager, developing reliable integration tools, and measuring acquisition performance.

Chapter 17 Organizational and Human Resource Issues in M&As (Siddhartha S. Brahma)

Success in M&As cannot be assured because many of them fall short of their stated goals. Although the strategy and finance literature dominate this field, relatively little attention is given to the organizational and human resource aspects of M&As. This chapter reviews the literature on this subject and suggests that organizational and human resource issues play a crucial role in shaping the M&A outcome. The organizational perspective presents the literature on the organizational-fit and process school. The decision-making process and the cultural integration process constitute the two views of the process school. On the other hand, the human resource perspective covers the areas of employees' reaction, role of communication, social integration, postmerger identification, and organizational justice.

Part IV. Takeovers and Behavioral Effects

Chapters 18–21 provide an overview of takeover strategies and defensive takeover strategies in M&As. These chapters further discuss the impact of restructuring on bondholders and behavioral effects in M&As.

Chapter 18 Takeover Strategies (Shailendra Pandit)

Takeover strategies involve identifying potential takeover targets, determining the timing and terms of the offer, addressing competing bidders and target resistance, and navigating takeover negotiations to a successful conclusion. This chapter traces the antecedents of takeover strategies that include several external and internal factors such as macroeconomic and capital market conditions, taxes, regulatory environment, motivations of the involved firms, and potential competition from other firms. This material is followed by a discussion of specific forms of bidding approaches including the level of friendliness of the acquirer's approach, the form of compensation, and other contractual features that have consequences for the firms involved in both the acquisition and the actual outcome of the bid itself. Thus, the discussion in this chapter centers on the causes and effects of takeover strategies on acquirers.

Chapter 19 Defensive Strategies in Takeovers (Christian Rauch and Mark Wahrenburg)

Over the past decades, defense mechanisms against hostile takeover attempts have become both more versatile and increasingly complex. As a reaction to more sophisticated takeover strategies, M&A consultants and their clients have developed a vast array of preventive and remedial defense strategies to deter potential hostile bidders and fend off actual bids from hostile acquirers. This chapter introduces the most common and frequently used antitakeover strategies, while focusing on the economic evaluation of each strategy and examining cases that highlight the different strategies. To account for more recent developments, the chapter also provides a discussion of the current financial crisis and its effect on hostile takeovers.

Chapter 20 The Impact of Restructuring on Bondholders (Luc Renneboog and Peter G. Szilagyi)

This chapter provides an overview of the existing literature on the impact of corporate restructuring on bondholder wealth. *Restructuring* is defined as any transaction that affects the firm's riskiness by changing its underlying capital structure. Thus, restructuring extends beyond asset restructuring and includes transactions such as leveraged buyouts, security issues and exchanges, and the issuance of stock options. The chapter identifies major gaps in the literature, emphasizes the potential differences in bond performance between market and stakeholder-oriented corporate governance systems, and provides insights into methodological advances. Studies providing empirical evidence are often inconclusive and mainly focus on the U.S. data. Although the corporate bond markets in other countries are relatively less developed, findings in these markets should prove relevant.

Chapter 21 Behavioral Effects in M&As (Jens Hagendorff)

This chapter provides a synthesis of the applications introduced in behavioral finance literature regarding M&As. Most of the existing M&A literature is based on a neoclassical framework that views managers and investors as utility maximizing and rational. However, mixed findings regarding the realized performance effects of mergers are difficult to reconcile with this neoclassical view of acquisition activity. This chapter contends that having managers or investors relax the rationality assumption complements neoclassical theory and leads to a more realistic view of what causes mergers, merger waves, and merger underperformance. Further, emphasizing the potential consequences of how chief executive officer overconfidence affects executive pay offers a promising behavioral approach to why managers overinvest in the market for corporate control.

Part V. Recapitalization and Restructuring

Chapters 22–24 discuss issues related to various types of restructuring activities including financial restructuring, going private and leveraged buyouts, and international aspects of takeovers and restructuring.

Chapter 22 Financial Restructuring (Otgontsetseg Erhemjamts and Kartik Raman)

Corporate restructuring can encompass a broad range of transactions including changing asset portfolio composition through divestitures, asset sales, spin-offs, and M&As; altering capital structure; and changing the firm's internal organization. This chapter discusses financial restructuring activities that substantially change the capital structures of firms. Separate sections cover share repurchases, dual-class recapitalizations, exchange offers and swaps, and debt restructurings via private workouts and bankruptcy. While discussing the motivations and recent evidence for the financial restructuring activities, the interrelation between financial restructuring events and takeovers is examined wherever appropriate.

Chapter 23 Going Private and Leveraged Buyouts (Onur Bayar)
This chapter reviews some recent trends and motives for public-to-private leveraged buyout (LBO) transactions. The potential sources of value creation in such transactions include the following: improvements in managerial incentives and firm governance, improvements in operating performance and productivity, tax shield benefits of leverage, asymmetric information, and market timing. Value creation in these deals is also closely associated with the availability of debt financing in credit markets and general market conditions. The chapter describes the actors in the private equity industry, the key properties of a typical LBO transaction, recent private equity waves in the United States and other countries, and exit opportunities. The chapter also discusses the existing theory and evidence on the value created in going-private transactions. Lastly, the chapter offers some observations about the direction of future research.

Chapter 24 International Takeovers and Restructuring (Rita Biswas)
Cross-border M&As remain an increasingly important means of foreign expansion for firms. Firms that acquire targets in foreign countries are motivated by a wide range of factors including lower costs, better technology, expanded markets, and regulatory and tax considerations. While cross-border acquisitions offer unique benefits, they also present unique complexities in all three stages of the acquisition: (1) target identification, (2) transaction execution, and (3) integration. Acquirers consider the strategic context of the potential target when selecting the right firm from a global set of targets. While executing the transaction, acquirers decide on the form and vehicle of acquisition, manage cross-border tax planning opportunities and implications, and execute the valuation, taking into consideration the issues exclusive to multicurrency and multicultural settings.

Part VI. Special Topics

Chapters 25–29 examine special topics. These topics are joint ventures and strategic alliances, fairness opinions, the dual tracking phenomenon, the diversification discount, and partial acquisitions.

Chapter 25 Joint Ventures and Strategic Alliances: Alternatives to M&As
(Tomas Mantecon and James A. Conover)
This chapter provides an analysis of the decision to expand the boundaries of the firm with M&As or by sharing control in alliances. During the period 1990 to 2008, at least one of these deals occurred every 22 minutes. Existing research suggests that firms prefer M&As over alliances. Firms choose alliances only when full integration is too costly. Equity joint ventures (JVs) are typically less common than other alliances but more common in cross-border deals when the host country presents low levels of economic freedom. Joint ventures can foster knowledge exchange and are preferred by firms in the presence of higher levels of uncertainty, risk, and opportunistic behaviors. The evidence is unclear about which of the alternatives creates more wealth for shareholders. Event studies suggest that buyers in M&As fare worse than parents in alliances, but M&As create more combined wealth. Long-term performance studies, however, yield inconclusive results.

Chapter 26 Fairness Opinions in M&As (Steven M. Davidoff, Anil K. Makhija, and Rajesh P. Narayanan)
When evaluating a merger or acquisition proposal, boards frequently seek fairness opinions from their financial advisors. This fairness opinion ratifies the consideration being paid or received as "fair from a financial point of view" to shareholders. This chapter describes how a Delaware Supreme Court ruling and Delaware corporate law combined to institutionalize fairness opinions and how the form and content of a fairness opinion results from concerns over limiting the liability associated with delivering the opinion. It then surveys the limited finance literature examining whether fairness opinions provide value to shareholders or instead serve the interests of the board and management at the expense of shareholders. The chapter also highlights the difficulties associated with conducting such empirical tests because of the way fairness opinions are sought and provided. The chapter concludes with some conjectures about the potential value of fairness opinions and raises questions for future research.

Chapter 27 How Initial Public Offerings Affect M&A Markets: The Dual Tracking Phenomenon (Roberto Ragozzino and Jeffrey J. Reuer)
Recent research in financial economics reports a phenomenon in which firms filing to go public become acquisition targets either shortly after executing the initial public offering (IPO), or even before the IPO takes place. This phenomenon, labeled "dual tracking," raises important questions about the potential effects that IPOs may bring about in addition to their capital creation properties. Namely, at the most basic level, the question arises as to why IPOs may trigger subsequent M&A activity, especially because IPOs and M&As have been typically considered as separate corporate events and have not been studied jointly in research. Further investigation into the dual tracking phenomenon suggests the need to answer several questions: What properties of IPOs are most conducive to dual tracking and affect acquisition activities, structures, and outcomes? How might acquirers and sellers gain from dual tracking? Can entrepreneurs and venture capitalists stage their exit to include an IPO and a takeover, rather than considering either option as a substitute decision or as an independent, go/no-go decision? This chapter provides a discussion of how IPOs affect M&As to address these questions and several others.

Chapter 28 The Diversification Discount (Seoungpil Ahn)
Does corporate diversification destroy or enhance firm value? Although researchers on corporate diversification have explored this issue for decades, they are still searching for answers involving many aspects of corporate diversification strategy. In theory, corporate diversification can be both beneficial and detrimental to firm value. Much of the debate on the diversification discount is about whether the valuation impact of diversification is, on average, positive or negative. Although the cross-sectional evidence shows that this net effect of diversification is, on average, detrimental to firm value, ample evidence exists to the contrary. Therefore, the impact of diversification on firm value is not completely resolved. As with many cases in economic studies, the value of diversification is conditional on firm and industry characteristics. The value is also time-variant. Future research in the

field should identify the conditions that are associated with value-enhancing and value-destroying diversification.

Chapter 29 Partial Acquisitions: Motivation and Consequences on Firm Performance (Pengcheng Zhu and Shantanu Dutta)

This chapter reviews the literature on partial acquisitions and focuses on the impact of partial acquisitions on target firm performance. The partial acquisition sample permits investigating both target firms' structural and performance changes during the postacquisition integration process. This chapter summarizes the key motivations for undertaking partial acquisitions and reviews the empirical evidence on the short-term and long-term consequences of partial acquisitions on target firm performance. Furthermore, the chapter highlights the factors that may moderate the acquisition impact including the postacquisition governance and control change, the acquiring firms' identities and motivations, and the external information environment. Overall, the literature shows that partial acquisitions improve target firm performance because the activist acquiring firms bring increased monitoring power and improved governance mechanisms.

SUMMARY AND CONCLUSIONS

Despite many theories and voluminous research, the subject of capital restructuring has elements of both art and science. The large proportion of unsuccessful M&As suggests that those entering such deals face many challenges. One of the measures of a deal is whether it creates market value. While economics can explain some of the forces at work, psychology also plays an important role. The following chapters help to identify key factors or drivers leading to success. Nonetheless, success in M&As is uncertain. Let's now begin a journey into the fascinating world of mergers, acquisitions, and corporate restructuring.

ABOUT THE AUTHORS

H. Kent Baker is a University Professor of Finance and Kogod Research Professor in the Kogod School of Business at American University. He has held faculty and administrative positions at Georgetown University and the University of Maryland. Professor Baker has written or edited numerous books. His most recent books include *Survey Research in Corporate Finance: Bridging the Gap between Theory and Practice* (Oxford University Press, 2011), *Capital Structure and Financing Decisions: Theory, Evidence, and Practice* (Wiley, 2011), *Capital Budgeting Valuation: Financial Analysis for Today's Investment Projects* (Wiley, 2011*), Behavioral Finance—Investors, Corporations, and Markets* (Wiley, 2010), *Corporate Governance: A Synthesis of Theory, Research, and Practice* (Wiley, 2010), *Dividends and Dividend Policy* (Wiley, 2009), and *Understanding Financial Management: A Practical Guide* (Blackwell, 2005). He has more than 230 publications in academic and practitioner outlets including in the *Journal of Finance, Journal of Financial and Quantitative Analysis, Financial Management, Financial Analysts Journal, Journal of Portfolio Management*, and *Harvard Business Review*. Professor Baker ranks among the most prolific authors in finance during the past half century. He has consulting and training experience with more than 100 organizations and has presented more than 750 training and development programs in the United States, Canada, and Europe. Professor Baker holds a BSBA from Georgetown University; M.Ed., MBA, and DBA degrees from the University of Maryland; and MA, MS, and two PhDs from American University. He also holds CFA and CMA designations.

Halil Kiymaz is Bank of America Chair and Professor of Finance in the Crummer Graduate School of Business at Rollins College. Before joining the Crummer School, Professor Kiymaz taught at the University of Houston–Clear Lake, Bilkent University, and the University of New Orleans. He holds the CFA designation and has served as a grader for The CFA Institute. Professor Kiymaz maintains an extensive research agenda and has published more than 60 articles in scholarly and practitioner journals. His research has appeared in the *Journal of Banking and Finance, Financial Review, Global Finance Journal, Journal of Applied Finance, Journal of Economics and Finance, Review of Financial Economics,* and *Quarterly Journal of Business and Economics,* among others. He is the recipient of several research awards including the McGraw-Hill Irwin Best Paper Award and the Outstanding Research Award at the Global Conference on Business and Finance. He also serves on the editorial board of numerous journals. Professor Kiymaz has consulting and training experience with various governmental and public organizations such as the Central Bank of Turkey, Bankers Association, and Stalla. He has been listed in various biographies including *Who's Who Among America's Teachers, Who's Who in Business Higher Education, Academic Keys Who's Who in Finance and Industry, International Who's Who of Professionals,* and *Marquis Who's Who.* Professor Kiymaz received a B.S. in Business Administration from the Uludag University and an MBA, MA in Economics, and a PhD in Financial Economics from the University of New Orleans. Professor Kiymaz also holds visiting professor positions at the IMADEC University, School of International Business, Vienna, Austria; East Chinese University of Science and Technology, Shanghai, China; and Copenhagen Business School in Copenhagen.

PART I

Background

CHAPTER 2

Merger Waves

JARRAD HARFORD
Marion Ingersoll Professor of Finance, University of Washington

INTRODUCTION

The goal of this chapter is to provide a survey and synthesis of the literature on merger waves. Given the sheer volume of research on the subject of mergers, the chapter cannot discuss all the facets of this important topic. Thus, the chapter includes only some of the more important research on merger waves.

The chapter begins by discussing the motives for combining previously independent assets and then attempts to explain the clustering of such activity. While merger activity is motivated by a variety of factors, understanding what causes merger activity to cluster is critical. Because this clustered merger activity inside waves represents such a high proportion of all activity, understanding the drivers of clustering leads to an understanding of the main drivers of mergers.

MERGER MOTIVES

Many theories have been put forth to explain mergers. Some are rooted in the theory of the firm. Determining the right combination of jointly managed assets is clearly related to the question of the boundary between the firm and the marketplace as posited in Coase (1937), Alchian and Demsetz (1972), and others. A related strand of literature builds on Jensen and Meckling's (1976) discussion of the agency conflict between a corporation's managers and owners. Jensen (1986) lays out a theory where the agency conflict, aided by an abundance of free cash flows, results in value-destroying acquisitions. Still other theories center on behavioral issues such as hubris on the part of managers (Roll, 1986) or biases by market participants (Shleifer and Vishny, 2003). These theories are not mutually exclusive and each has some import for explaining merger activity. The following sections discuss each theory in more detail before surveying the evidence.

Theories Explaining Mergers

The major theories explaining mergers can be classified broadly into neoclassical, agency, and behavioral. Each is discussed in turn.

Neoclassical Theory

In an early survey of the evidence on mergers and acquisitions (M&As), Jensen and Ruback (1983) characterize the market for corporate control as one in which managerial teams compete to manage assets while shareholders act as mostly passive judges. In the market for corporate control, merger arbitrageurs and takeover specialists fill the role of intermediaries. In such a market, higher skilled managers who can get the most value out of an asset will gain control of that asset. Exchanges happen only because value can be created either through synergies or by replacing managers who suffer from low-skill or excessive agency problems.

The synergies could come from economies of scale or scope or from combining different technologies. Practitioners typically refer to two categories of synergies: cost reduction and revenue enhancement. Cost reduction synergies often come from economies of scale. For example, when two banks merge they do not need two headquarters, two back office operations, branches in close proximity to each other, and the like. They can provide largely the same level of service to a much greater customer base without a proportionate increase in the cost. Revenue enhancement synergies often come from economies of scope. For instance, when Oracle purchased PeopleSoft, this transaction immediately pointed to the possibilities of gaining more customers because Oracle could sell one integrated suite of software products. A similar argument was made when Delta merged with Northwest—the combined route map would connect far more city pairs, consequently attracting more customers.

Some merger-created synergies are due to market frictions. Lewellen (1971) proposes a purely financial rationale for mergers. He argues that acquiring assets with cash flows not perfectly correlated with a firm's existing assets' cash flows lowers the volatility of the combined firm's cash flows, increasing its debt capacity and ability to utilize the tax deductibility of interest.

Similarly, others such as Erickson and Wang (2007) propose that profitable acquirers can essentially buy tax shields by purchasing a target with loss carry-forwards. Here, the synergy merely comes from uniting the tax shield represented by the carry-forward with the profits of the acquirer. The government provides all the synergies through reduced taxes.

Based partly on Myers and Majluf's (1984) pecking order theory emphasizing the importance of slack, Smith and Kim (1994) and others propose that some mergers can create synergies by uniting the financial slack of one company with the growth options of another. Smith and Kim (1994) find some evidence of value creation when high-slack, low-growth companies merge with low-slack, high-growth companies.

Relying less on frictions and instead on returning to the idea of a "market" for corporate control of assets, Jovanovic and Rousseau (2002) propose a theory based on differences in target and acquirer Tobin's q, which is called the "Q-Theory of Mergers." They start with the fact that q-based investment theories predict that higher q firms should invest more than lower q firms. Jovanovic and Rousseau argue that the same prediction is applicable to mergers. The authors note that the empirical evidence supports the claim that high-q firms generally buy low-q firms. Furthermore, they conclude that mergers are a way for capital to transfer away from marginal projects and/or poor management to better projects and/or management.

Rhodes-Kropf and Robinson (2008) also use q in their explanation of merger activity but come to a different conclusion than Jovanovic and Rousseau (2002). They start by showing that high-q acquirers actually tend to buy high-q targets and likewise for low-q acquirers and low-q targets. Rhodes-Kropf and Robinson show that this "like-buys-like" result can be generated by a model based on asset complementarities and search frictions.

Agency Theory

As Jensen and Meckling (1976) point out, the separation of ownership and control in the modern corporation carries with it many benefits but also some costs. The costs stem mostly from the agency conflict resulting when ownership and management are separated. Jensen (1986) points out that this conflict—manifesting in disagreement over the optimal size of the firm, and when and how much cash should be paid to shareholders—is a particular problem when a firm has excessive free cash flows. He then applies this specifically to mergers by pointing out that maturing industries often have high free cash flows, leading to managers making potentially value-destroying acquisitions by diversifying into new lines of businesses.

Stulz (1988) follows Jensen (1986) and builds a formal model of self-interested managers with private benefits of control. When managers increase the fraction of their own stock held, there are two effects: (1) a decrease in the chance of a hostile takeover attempt, and (2) an increase in the price conditional on such an attempt occurring. Stulz shows that a unique fraction will balance the two effects. Stulz also uses the model to explain why shareholders vote for takeover defenses: Some defenses have the same effect as increasing managers' fraction of stock, resulting in a higher price should a takeover attempt occur.

In a novel application of agency theory, Gorton, Kahl, and Rosen (2009) propose a merger theory that combines agency problems with efficiency merger motives. In their model, a shock to an industry creates value-increasing merger opportunities. Managers have private benefits of control that they would like to preserve. Anticipating the possibility of being acquired in one of these mergers, some managers will undertake "defensive acquisitions" in an attempt to become too big to be bought. Other managers will undertake acquisitions designed to make their firm more attractive as a target, garnering a higher premium. The authors test and provide support for their model using data from the 1980s and 1990s.

Behavioral Theory

Roll (1986) surveys the evidence on mergers, concluding that it is consistent with a simple hubris-based explanation for merger activity. He points out that bids take place above the current market price, increasing the likelihood of bidders making positive valuation errors. Drawing from the psychology literature on overconfidence, Roll posits that managerial hubris of well-performing bidding firms suggests that bidding firms are simply overpaying for their targets. His was the first paper to suggest a behavioral explanation where a decision maker's psychological bias drives the activity. He argues that this bias matters because it takes repeated failures for people to update beliefs about themselves, but most chief executive officers (CEOs) participate in only a few acquisitions. While both agency- and hubris-based hypotheses produce value-destroying transactions, they assume different motives for the managers. Under the agency-based hypothesis, managers are aware that they are undertaking a value-destroying acquisition but do it anyway because it helps them personally. Under the hubris-based hypothesis, managers believe they are undertaking a value-increasing acquisition but are incorrect due to their overconfidence.

The paper by Roll (1986) was published before behavioral finance gained popularity and even before the debate over possible evidence of inefficiencies and persistent market mispricings. In an influential paper, Shleifer and Vishny (2003) note the strong correlation between merger activity and stock market appreciation. They propose a model of mergers driven by the stock market. Specifically, bidder managers, who are aware that their stock is overvalued, seek to use it to finance the acquisition of a target (and its real assets) before the misvaluation is corrected. The model contains two important assumptions. First, the market is inefficient in that it does not, on average, fully adjust the bidder's stock price downward upon the announcement of a stock-financed acquisition. Second, target managers must rationally accept the overvalued stock, so they are assumed to have short horizons compared to those of the bidder managers. Thus, target managers will accept the overvalued stock and sell it.

Again looking at the relation between the stock market and merger activity, Rhodes-Kropf and Viswanathan (2004) construct a model that includes market mispricings, producing over- and undervaluation. However, in their model, both bidder and target managers act rationally. Specifically, bidders and targets can be undervalued and overvalued and the valuation is driven by marketwide and firm-specific components (the managers do not know which). When marketwide overvaluation is high, targets mistakenly overestimate the synergy-based premium because they rationally believe that the bid may simply be a high synergy bid. This leads targets to rationally accept the offer even if it involves overvalued bidder stock, creating waves in M&As that are tied to value even in this rational environment.

Evidence on Mergers

The past 30 years has witnessed an explosion in research and evidence on mergers. This section briefly surveys the evidence and relates it to the theory discussed above.

Foundational Evidence

In the survey discussed earlier, Jensen and Ruback (1983) note that M&A announcement returns are clearly large and positive for the target, but are only positive for the bidder in a tender offer and are indistinguishable from zero in a merger. The target's stock price reaction represents two effects: the premium and a reassessment of the target's stand-alone value. Bradley, Desai, and Kim (1983) disentangle these two effects by looking at failed mergers. They note that in cases where no new bid emerges for the target, the target's price returns to its prebid level (on average), suggesting that the target stock price reaction is due to the expected premium.

Healy, Palepu, and Ruback (1992) study the 50 largest mergers from 1979 to 1984 and find that asset productivity improves after the merger, increasing overall operating cash flows (especially in horizontal mergers). Announcement returns are correlated with subsequent operating improvements, suggesting that revaluations at announcement are due to the pricing of these synergy gains. Research and development (R&D) and capital spending is not cut, on average. These results support efficiency arguments for mergers, as well as the efficient markets hypothesis with respect to the announcement return. They stand in contrast with Scherer and Ravenscraft (1989), who document performance declines in the 1960s wave, which was characterized by many diversifying acquisitions.

Maksimovic and Phillips (2001) take a wider view of M&As by studying plant-level data in what they call the "market for corporate assets." Their main finding is that more productive firms buy assets, while less productive firms sell assets during expansions. Firms end up buying in divisions that have high productivity and selling from low productivity divisions. Further, productivity improves at a plant postpurchase. This is largely consistent with a profit-maximizing model with scarce managerial talent and inconsistent with empire building.

Bidder Stock Price Reaction

The bidder's stock price reaction is even harder to parse than the target's price. Among other factors, the market could be reassessing the bidder's internal growth opportunities, the skill of the management, the impact of the bid's financing on the combined firm's capital and ownership structure, and of course, the premium paid relative to potential synergies created. Fuller, Netter, and Stegemoller (2002) take a novel approach to disentangling these factors. They study firms making five or more acquisitions within three years. Through this, they attempt to isolate the characteristics of the target and the specific bid from those of the bidder. The authors find that the best bidder stock price reaction comes from a public firm buying a relatively large private firm for stock. The explanation is twofold. First, when buying a private firm, the bidder generally gets better pricing because it is providing liquidity to the target owners. Second, by using stock to buy out the concentrated owners of the target, the bidder effectively creates a new set of blockholders with incentives to monitor the combined firm's management. Based on this and other evidence in their paper, Fuller et al. draw the overall conclusion that illiquidity discount, tax, and control effects exist in the merger market.

Moeller, Schlingemann, and Stulz (2004) take a different approach to understanding the bidder stock price reaction, examining 12,023 public acquisitions from 1980 to 2001, which is the largest sample to date of public acquirers. They conclude that the potential for hubris as an explanation for large firm decisions exists. That is, acquisitions by small firms are overwhelmingly value-creating (positive value for bidder and for combined firm), but large bidders on average destroy value in acquisitions. Interestingly, even though the vast majority of acquisitions create value, the aggregate effect is net value destruction because the value-destroying acquisitions are typically undertaken by large acquirers to large targets, resulting in a greater amount of destroyed value. The authors' evidence is also consistent with an agency explanation wherein managers of larger firms have smaller ownership stakes, thus making value-destroying acquisitions in order to create personal net benefits.

Agency Hypothesis

Some papers specifically examine the agency or free cash flow (FCF) hypothesis. For example, Lang, Stulz, and Walkling (1991) find evidence in favor of the FCF hypothesis by documenting a negative correlation between acquirer free cash flows and acquisition announcement returns. Harford (1999) examines cash-rich firms and finds that not only are they abnormally active as acquirers, but also they tend to destroy value with their acquisitions. Applying the more recently popular Gompers, Ishii, and Metrick (2003) governance index, Masulis, Wang, and Xie (2007) find lower returns for acquirers with high governance indexes (indicating more entrenched managers).

Market-Power and Collusion

One possible source of gain and hence motivation for merging is the desire to increase industry concentration to gain market power or enable collusion. Thus, the gains from a merger would be wealth transfers from consumers or competitor shareholders. Eckbo (1983) and Stillman (1983) examine this hypothesis explicitly. Rivals have positive returns at the horizontal bid announcement, but these returns do not decrease at government challenge announcements. This finding is inconsistent with the market power hypothesis. It is more in line with a hypothesis put forth by Song and Walkling (2000) that the share prices of firms similar to a merger target anticipate the possibility of those firms becoming targets themselves and rise at the initial acquisition announcement. Fee and Thomas (2004) and Shahrur (2005) further examine the merger impact throughout the supply chain and determine that customers and suppliers do not incur large losses. They also find evidence that mergers force upstream efficiencies, which in turn force those suppliers who cannot adapt to lose out. Again, there is little to no evidence that merger gains come in the form of wealth transfers from customers or suppliers.

Another possible source of wealth transfers is the bondholders. Research here has been hampered by a lack of daily bond prices for the target and bidder. However, the increase in data availability has permitted some studies such as the work by Billett, King, and Mauer (2004), who find that wealth-transfers are either nonexistent or at best second in importance to synergy effects on bondholders. Also, since the early 1990s, most corporate bonds carry event risk covenants that largely protect bondholders in the event of an acquisition.

Betton, Eckbo, and Thorburn (2008) undertake an exhaustive review of the mergers literature and in so doing use the entire Securities Data Company (SDC) database, finding that in all samples, targets have positive three-day cumulative abnormal returns (CARs) around the announcement day. About one-third of the target's total price appreciation happens in the preannouncement run-up when rumors and insider trading begin moving the price up. Schwert (1996) studies this prebid run-up and concludes that it is essentially a cost to bidding firms in that they must mark up the acquisition price over that run-up rather than counting that run-up as part of their overall premium.

For the bidder, Betton et al. (2008) find that the most consistent positive announcement returns are found for small bidders, cash-only deals, deals involving private targets, and deals taking place from 1991 to 1995 (early in the 1990s merger wave). Their evidence shows that the most consistent negative returns are for large bidders and stock-only deals involving public targets.

Exhibit 2.1 Announcement Returns for Public Bidders Upon Announcement of a Bid for a U.S. Target from 1985 to 2009

Panel A. Overall

	# Observations	Mean	Median
Entire sample	19,406	0.014	0.001
Method of payment			
Stock only	6,674	0.016	−0.001
Cash only	3,899	0.011	0.004
Mixed	2,877	0.007	−0.003
Other	3,710	0.021	0.002
Form of the target			
Private	9,574	0.028	0.006
Public	7,402	−0.007	−0.007
Subsidiary	2,184	0.028	0.008

Panel B. By Form of Target and Method of Payment

		Method of Payment			
Form of target		Cash	Stock	Mixed	Other
Private	Mean	0.019	0.038	0.027	0.025
	Median	0.007	0.007	0.007	0.003
Public	Mean	0.004	−0.016	−0.018	0.005
	Median	0.001	−0.013	−0.014	−0.002
Subsidiary	Mean	0.015	0.038	0.037	0.033
	Median	0.007	0.009	0.010	0.005

The table provides mean and median announcement stock returns for public firms announcing merger bids for U.S. targets from 1985 to 2009. The announcement returns are computed as three-day returns centered on the day of the announcement net of the market return for the same period. The author calculated the returns using data from the Center for Research in Securities Pricing (CRSP).

Exhibits 2.1 and 2.2 present some summary statistics for more than 19,000 bids by public bidders for U.S. targets from 1985 to 2009. The results are broadly consistent with the findings cited above and also confirm the work of Fuller et al. (2002), concluding that one cannot study the payment method in isolation from the target form.

As Panel A of Exhibit 2.1 shows, the announcement return distributions are highly skewed such that the means are generally larger in magnitude than the medians. Overall, mergers create a small amount of value for the bidders on average. The mean is greater in stock mergers (1.6 percent) than in cash deals (1.1 percent), but that relation is reversed when looking at the medians (−0.1 percent vs. 0.4 percent). Target form clearly matters: Bidders have large and positive stock price reactions to acquisitions of private firms or subsidiaries. In contrast, they have significantly negative returns, on average, to acquisitions of public targets.

Given the importance of both payment method and target form, Panel B of Exhibit 2.1 presents results detailed by both characteristics. The results confirm

Exhibit 2.2   Announcement Returns for Target Shareholders in Bids by Public Firms from 1985 to 2009

	# Observations	Mean	Median
All	6,993	0.184	0.138
Method of payment			
Cash	2,219	0.269	0.214
Mixed	1,171	0.173	0.137
Stock	2,338	0.149	0.115
Other	727	0.094	0.053

The table provides mean and median announcement stock returns for public targets in merger bids from 1985 to 2009. The announcement returns are computed as three-day returns centered on the day of the announcement net of the market return for the same period. The author calculated the returns using data from the Center for Research in Securities Pricing (CRSP).

those of Fuller et al. (2002). Stock-based acquisitions of private targets are met with a greater announcement return than cash-based acquisitions of private targets (this is the effect of creating a blockholder as discussed earlier). The reverse is true with public targets; acquisitions of public targets using all or partial stock are value-destroying for bidder shareholders. However, buying public targets with cash is value-creating.

Finally, the results in Exhibit 2.2 for the target shareholders in the subsample of public target deals are unsurprising. Target shareholders enjoy a large positive gain upon announcement due to the typical premium over the market price that the bidder offers. Cash offers have a higher reaction, possibly due to the greater value certainty provided by such offers.

Exhibits 2.1 and 2.2 present data for all bids by public firms irrespective of merger waves. Indeed, most theory and empirical work on mergers attempts to hypothesize and test motives for mergers without regard to the time-series properties of aggregate or industry-level merger activity. As discussed in the next section, there has long been a nascent strand of literature examining the clustering of merger activity. Work in that field has been more active in the last 10 to 15 years, bringing with it a far greater understanding of the drivers of merger activity.

MERGER WAVES

The fact that mergers occur in waves is well established. As Exhibit 2.3 shows, a clear clustering of aggregate activity occurs in the time series. Jovanovic and Rousseau (2002) show that this clustering extends back with peaks in merger activity taking place in the 1920s and at the turn of the twentieth century. Indeed, the merger wave around 1890 has been called the "monopolization wave," serving as the primary motivation behind the Sherman and Clayton Antitrust Acts in the United States.

Early research into merger waves advanced on several fronts. Some work set about formally establishing via statistics that merger activity does indeed occur in clusters. Golbe and White (1988) note that despite the common assertion that mergers occur in waves, no one has actually proven this to be the case. Using a

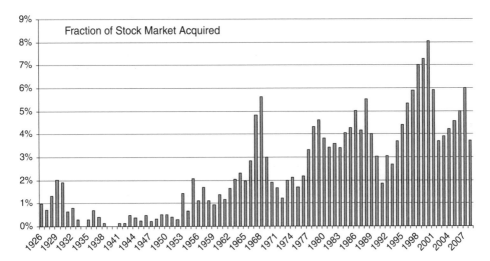

Exhibit 2.3 The Fraction of U.S. Public Firms Acquired by Year
Note: The graph displays merger activity over time.

time series that stretches from 1895 to 1989, they fit a sine wave function to the data and show that the function predicts the peaks and troughs of actual merger activity fairly accurately.

Town (1992) takes a similar purely statistical approach. He shows that objectively one can fit a two-state, Markov switching-regime model to the time series of merger activity. This confirms that merger activity is best characterized by waves or periods of unusually high activity surrounded by periods of low activity.

Melicher, Ledolter, and D'Antonio (1983) undertake an examination of the time-series relation between aggregate merger activity and macroeconomic factors. They expect to find that business conditions would have significant explanatory power for aggregate merger activity. Instead, they find a weak correlation, indicating that changes in production lag behind merger activity. They do, however, uncover a strong correlation between capital market conditions and merger activity. Specifically, aggregate increases in stock prices and, to a lesser extent, decreases in interest rates lead to merger activity. The authors conclude that since merger negotiations start about two months before announcement, negotiations begin at a time when capital market conditions indicate receptiveness and lower financing costs.

Becketti (1986) also examines the correlation between macroeconomic variables and merger activity. He focuses on the S&P 500 return, interest rates, gross national product (GNP), and capacity utilization. He finds the strongest support for interest rates and capacity utilization. Specifically, merger activity responds negatively to increases in interest rates and positively to capacity utilization, suggesting that firms attempt to add capacity quickly through acquisition when utilization is high. His results for the aggregate stock return are mixed, in contrast to Melicher et al.'s (1983) findings. However, Becketti confirms their finding of little correlation between aggregate production and merger activity.

Building on the prior work on aggregate merger waves, Mitchell and Mulherin (1996) document clear clustering of waves within industries, formally showing that the clustering is too great to be random. They further propose some explanations for clustering, tying it to various industry-level technological, economic, and regulatory shocks. The authors focus on two-year periods of activity, admitting that this is ad hoc, but that it appears to match the average length of an industry-level merger wave. Finally, Mitchell and Mulherin suggest that a systematic analysis of industry shocks and merger activity may shed light on aggregate merger waves.

Mulherin and Boone (2000) follow up Mitchell and Mulherin's (1996) original study by examining both acquisition and divestiture activity in the 1990s. They show that industry-level clustering of mergers occurs in the 1990s as well (a fact also confirmed by Andrade, Mitchell, and Stafford, 2001) and is accompanied by industry-level clustering of divestitures. According to Mulherin and Boone, the fact that both are occurring simultaneously and that the market reacts positively and symmetrically to each is supportive of an economic rationale for the activity.

Although most of the empirical investigations have relied on U.S. data, confirmatory evidence exists in other countries. Powell and Yawson (2005) examine both divestiture and merger activity in the United Kingdom. They document significant abnormal clustering of takeovers in time and industry in the 1980s and 1990s and clustering of divestitures primarily in the late 1990s. They further relate the activities to broad and industry-specific shocks: Takeovers are negatively correlated with industry growth and positively correlated with foreign competition and industry returns. Divestitures are negatively correlated with broad shocks (e.g., employment, sales, and cash flow), but positively correlated with industry concentration (as it would be the only restructuring option allowed by antitrust authorities) and deregulation.

Despite the increasing interest in documenting and understanding merger waves, no consensus exists as to why merger waves occur. The competing explanations can be broadly categorized into two groups: neoclassical and behavioral.

Neoclassical Hypothesis

Neoclassical explanations of rational merger waves are based on an economic disturbance that leads to industry reorganization. Coase (1937) is one of the earliest to argue that technological change leads to mergers. Schumpeter's (1950) theory of creative destruction can be applied to explain merger waves, but it was Gort (1969) who formally proposed an economic disturbances theory of mergers. He hypothesizes disturbances that change the valuation of different assets in ways that generate variation in merger frequencies between industries and over time. Gort argues that some kind of disturbance model is needed to explain time-series variation that standard theories (e.g., to pursue economies of scale) cannot.

Matsusaka (1993a, 1993b) studies the 1960s merger wave in depth. He finds that the bidder stock price announcement around diversifying acquisitions (during the merger wave) is positive on average. This runs contrary to typical assumptions about conglomerate mergers destroying value. Upon further investigation, he finds that the reaction turns negative if the target management is dismissed. Thus, the market is skeptical of the idea that bidder management has the expertise to manage a completely different business. Matsusaka also shows that most of the targets are performing abnormally well before the acquisition, except in the public targets, suggesting that managerial discipline may have been a factor in those acquisitions.

Evidence Supporting the Neoclassical Hypothesis

Calomiris (1999) provides some evidence in support of the neoclassical hypothesis by examining bank consolidation waves. He finds that throughout history, bank consolidation waves have produced measurably large efficiency gains. However, Calomiris also cautions that the very fact that these mergers take place in waves produces a challenge for the econometrician to appropriately measure the gains. With the industry and its constituents in flux, establishing a reasonable counterfactual benchmark against which to measure the performance of the combined postmerger firm is difficult.

As mentioned earlier in this chapter, Jovanovic and Rousseau (2002) put forth models under which technological change and subsequent increased dispersion in q ratios lead to waves of high-q firms taking over low-q ones. They further examine all waves in the United States from the 1890s through the 1990s and conclude that most merger waves coincided with profitable reallocation opportunities, with the exception of the 1960s "conglomerate" wave. Thus, a link exists between their work and Gort's (1969), in that they both rely on a technological change (or shock) that induces the dispersion of q's leading to the merger wave.

Jovanovic and Rousseau (2008) extend their idea of merger waves as reallocation waves. Specifically, they argue that merger waves reallocate assets and spread new technology. They broadly characterize two significant periods of technological change: electricity and the internal combustion engine (1890 to 1930) and information technology (1970 to 2000). Empirically, both periods are characterized by a strong increase in total economic reallocation, including high activity in both firm entries and exits from the market along with high merger activity. Both periods contain more than one merger wave and further, a graph of merger activity, firm exit, and firm entrance shows strong time series correlations in the peaks of all three types of activity. Again, note that the 1960s wave falls outside these two periods of innovation and remains hard to explain by Jovanovic and Rousseau's theories.

Maksimovic and Phillips (2001) use a novel data set to test empire building versus neoclassical theories of merger waves. Using the Longitudinal Research Database from the Department of Census that allows them to calculate plant-level performance even for plants of private firms, they assess the result of asset reallocations through the market for corporate assets. They start with the assumptions that some managers are better than others and that managers add productive assets until the marginal benefit is equal to the marginal cost of production. The authors propose that increases in aggregate output cause the marginal benefit for higher-quality managers to increase so that these firms increase their size by buying divisions and plants from lower-quality management teams. This shift in the optimal size of high-quality firms is what causes the sudden cluster of activity. Their paper draws attention to the considerable market for partial-firm assets that is rightfully part of the overall market for corporate assets that includes mergers. By also showing that plants purchased in these waves show performance improvements, their study lends strong support to the neoclassical theory.

Dittmar and Dittmar (2008) take the examination of clustering a step further and show that repurchases, equity issuances, and mergers all occur in waves related to the business cycle. This challenges valuation-based explanations of wave activity since, for example, repurchase and equity issuances are opposite transactions. They argue that the primary driver is growth in GDP, which affects firms differently and at different points in the business cycle. Hence, the optimal response for a firm can be repurchase, equity issuance, or merger, depending on the situation.

Is There a Role for a Macro Factor?
De Bondt and Thompson (1992) take issue with the neoclassical explanations by examining merger activity by industry from 1926 to 1988. They assert the fact that mergers cluster in waves poses a problem for the efficiency argument because no rational reason exists for a sudden surge in mismanaged firms or potential synergies. This leads them to conclude that while efficiency gains are a substantial motivator of merger activity, such gains cannot explain all activity, noting that most targets are not underperforming before the merger. Possible undervaluation of the target is one of the motives, in which case the gain is merely a wealth transfer as opposed to social gain.

As De Bondt and Thompson (1992) point out, one problem with the industry shocks explanation for merger waves is that it is not at all clear why various techno-logical, regulatory, or economic shocks should hit all or most industries at the same time, since the data clearly show that these industry-level merger waves cluster in time. Some of the empirical work hypothesizes aggregate output as the main cause of the shock, leaving aside the idea of industry-specific shocks as a possible cause of merger clustering. Other work presents a way to combine a macro-level factor with the industry-specific shocks. Building on some work on the importance of capital liquidity in asset reallocation, Harford (2005) suggests a role for capital liquidity in a neoclassical hypothesis of merger waves. Specifically, Eisfeldt and Rampini (2006) show that capital liquidity variation strongly affects the degree of total (industrial, household, and labor) capital reallocation in the economy and further that the degree of capital liquidity is cyclical. While Eisfeldt and Rampini do not explicitly study market valuations, Harford argues that because higher market valuations relax financing constraints, market valuations are an important component of capital liquidity.

Shleifer and Vishny (1992) make a similar argument in a study of asset liquidity, showing that in order for transactions to occur, buyers who intend to employ the asset in its first-best use must be relatively unconstrained. This allows offered prices to be close to fundamental values. Shleifer and Vishny hypothesize that the reason merger waves always occur in booms is because cash flow increases simultaneously increase fundamental values and relax financial constraints, thus bringing prices closer to fundamental values. Empirical evidence by Harford (1999) supports this argument by showing that firms that have built up large cash reserves are more active in the acquisition market.

International Evidence
Almost all empirical work on merger waves centers on the United States, the United Kingdom, or a subset of continental European countries. Makaew (2010), in contrast, examines a global merger sample from 25 developed and 25 develop-ing countries from 1989 to 2008. He finds that cross-border mergers come in waves that are highly correlated with the business cycle. Further, both acquirer and target

countries tend to be booming (as opposed to expanding economies buying firms in contracting ones). Consistent with Harford's (2005) findings on U.S. data, merger waves have both an industry productivity shock component and a country-level financial or liquidity shock component. Also consistent with neoclassical arguments and the findings of Maksimovic and Phillips (2001), acquirers tend to have above-average productivity, with targets having below-average productivity.

Summary of the Neoclassical Hypothesis and Evidence

To summarize, under the neoclassical hypothesis, once a technological, regulatory, or economic shock to an industry's environment occurs, the collective reaction of firms inside and outside the industry is such that industry assets are reallocated through mergers and partial-firm acquisitions. This activity clusters in time as managers react by competing for the best combinations of assets. Considerable empirical evidence supports a neoclassical, performance-improving motivation for this reallocation. Harford's (2005) capital liquidity argument modifies the neoclassical hypothesis to predict that only when sufficient capital liquidity exists to accommodate the reallocation of assets will an industry shock generate a merger wave. Thus, even if industry shocks do not cluster in time, the importance of capital liquidity means that industry merger waves as reactions to shocks will cluster in time to create aggregate merger waves.

Behavioral Hypothesis

Recent theoretical work addresses the observed positive correlation between stock valuations and merger activity, as noted by Golbe and White (1988) among others. Shleifer and Vishny (2003) argue that clustering occurs in merger activity because stock market valuations drive a substantial portion of such activity. They posit that bull markets lead groups of bidders with overvalued stock to use the stock to buy real assets of undervalued targets through mergers. Coupled with sufficiently high misperceived merger synergies in the marketplace, Shleifer and Vishny's model allows for (less) overvalued targets as well, relying mainly on dispersion in valuations. Target managers with short time horizons are willing to accept the bidder's temporarily overvalued equity. Overvaluation in the aggregate or in certain industries will lead to wave-like clustering in time.

Contemporaneously, as discussed earlier, Rhodes-Kropf and Viswanathan (2004) develop a model of rational managerial behavior and uncertainty about sources of misvaluation. Their model also leads to a correlation between stock market performance and merger waves. In their model, rational targets without perfect information will accept more bids from overvalued bidders during market valuation peaks because the targets overestimate synergies during these periods. The greater transaction flow produces a merger wave. Their model differs from that of Shleifer and Vishny (2003) in that target managers rationally accept overvalued equity because of inadequate information about the degree of synergies rather than shorter time horizons. Nonetheless, because both explanations rely at least partly on bidders taking advantage of temporary misvaluations and also on dispersion in misvaluations in the market, they can be grouped as behavioral hypotheses.

In a follow-up empirical study, Rhodes-Kropf, Robinson, and Viswanathan (2005) show that aggregate merger waves occur when market valuations, measured as market-to-book ratios, are high relative to true valuations. To estimate a firm's true valuation, the authors use residual income models or industry multiples. However, they note that their results are consistent with both the behavioral mispricing stories and the interpretation that merger activity spikes when growth opportunities are high or when firm-specific discount rates are low. This latter interpretation is similar to a neoclassical hypothesis with a capital liquidity component. Nonetheless, further tests lead them to conclude that while neoclassical explanations are still important, misvaluation explains a nontrivial fraction of the activity.

Dong, Hirshleifer, Richardson, and Teoh (2003) and Ang and Cheng (2006) also use accounting numbers to estimate a fundamental value and find evidence consistent with Shleifer and Vishny's (2003) overvalued equity explanation of merger activity. Although these findings are consistent with behavioral explanations and even necessary for some, they are also consistent with neoclassical explanations. While Rhodes-Kropf et al. (2005) recognize alternative interpretations of their evidence and try to distinguish between competing explanations, the other studies that examine the behavioral hypothesis tend to only provide evidence consistent with behavioral explanations, rather than first considering both neoclassical and behavioral hypotheses and then formally rejecting the neoclassical.

One exception to that general rule is Gugler, Mueller, and Yurtoglu (2006), who test both neoclassical (industry-shock) and behavioral (overvaluation and managerial discretion) hypotheses. In their paper, managers have more discretion during expansions, which contributes to increased merger activity. They conclude that both neoclassical and behavioral motives contribute to merger waves, but that the behavioral hypotheses are more important.

Finally, Goel and Thakor (2010) provide a novel explanation for merger waves. They develop a model that produces merger waves even when the shock that motivated the first merger is purely idiosyncratic. Their model is based on an assumption that CEOs envy each other's compensation, which is driven at least partly by the size and scope of the firm. When one CEO's compensation increases due to a merger, others undertake mergers to match the increased compensation.

DISCUSSION AND NEW DIRECTIONS

The last 30 years of extensive merger research begs the question: What have we learned? Following is a summary of the cumulative knowledge surrounding merger waves and what still needs further investigation.

Mergers Happen for Both Good and Bad Reasons

A reasonable interpretation of the evidence is that the majority of mergers occur due to expected synergies between the bidder and target. As Moeller et al. (2004) show, the vast majority of deals result in net combined value creation. Specifically, summing the dollar announcement return of the target with the dollar announcement return of the bidder yields a positive number. Even in many bids where the bidder's dollar announcement return is negative, it is still outweighed by the target's value increase. One characterization of these deals is that despite the existence of positive synergies, the bidder simply overpaid for those synergies.

Yet, Moeller et al. (2004) also note that the aggregate value effect of mergers by public bidders from 1980 to 2001 has been the destruction of over $300 billion in net value. How can these two facts be reconciled? Both are true—the vast majority of bids do create value, but that value creation is dwarfed in the aggregate by a minority of extremely large deals that destroy large amounts of value. Specifically, many of the largest bids for public targets at the end of the 1990s destroyed more than $10 billion in bidder value upon announcement.

The second fact suggests either mistakes that are concentrated in large bidders bidding for large targets, agency problems, or hubris. Why mistakes should be concentrated in large deals is unclear. One should expect that mistakes will be made, and clearly the value implications of a mistake are much larger when the target is large. Still, another expectation is that there should be as many positive "mistakes" as negative ones in the sense that large positive revaluations should offset large negative revaluations in the aggregate.

One possible explanation is that in large bidders, managers typically hold a very small fraction of the company's equity; thus, their personal direct cost of a mistake is small. Moeller et al. (2004) find that, controlling for a wide array of other firm and deal characteristics, smaller bidders have more positive announcement returns. Assume that small size can proxy for fewer agency conflicts due to potentially higher managerial ownership or greater product market discipline. In that case, a negative bias in announcement returns by large bidders would not be surprising.

Hubris can also produce a similar size effect because managers of larger firms might be expected to have greater hubris. As a partial control for hubris, researchers typically include prior-year stock return and market-to-book ratio for the bidder. The idea is that strong performance exacerbates hubris. Yet, even controlling for these bidder characteristics, smaller bidders still enjoyed better announcement returns. While hubris might be a part of the problem, it cannot be responsible for it all.

Shleifer and Vishny (2003) would argue that the drop in bidder value at announcement does not represent wealth destruction but rather partial correction of bidder overvaluation. In fact, their model explicitly predicts that bidding stockholders would be worse off had their managers not traded their overvalued stock for real assets. Of course, the problem with testing this prediction is that the counterfactual—how the bidder would have done had it not made a stock-swap acquisition—is inherently unobservable. Taking an innovative approach to this problem, Savor and Lu (2009) examine a sample of bids that failed to consummate for exogenous reasons. A sample of stock-swap bidders whose deals exogenously failed is the best counterfactual available to an econometrician. They find that unsuccessful stock bidders significantly underperform successful ones, lending support to the hypothesis that overvalued acquirers create value for their shareholders by acquiring companies for stock.

Structure of the Deal Matters

A cursory examination of the literature reveals that deals with certain characteristics (all else being equal) tend to be associated with higher bidder announcement returns. What kinds of deals does the market like? A partial list of these characteristics includes deals where: (1) no competition for the target exists; (2) the bidder pays with cash; (3) the target is private (especially if the bidder uses stock); (4) the bidder is smaller; and (5) the bidder increases focus. When considering why such characteristics should matter, some patterns emerge.

Intuitively, the bidder's share of the synergies should matter. Competition for the target will increase the premium required to win, decreasing the bidder's share of the synergies. Deals for private targets also result in a greater share for the bidders. The evidence suggests that bidders can buy private targets at lower valuations than public targets (Officer, 2007). One plausible reason is that when buying a private target, bidders are providing something of great value to target owners: liquidity. This forms part of the overall value provided to target owners, allowing the bidder to negotiate for a lower price. Discussions with practitioners put the value of liquidity at 20 to 25 percent of asset value.

The bidder stock price reaction is generally larger when the bidder pays with cash, except when buying a private target. The reaction is generally larger in cash deals (Travlos, 1987) because stock deals combine an investment decision with a seasoned equity offering. The fact that the bidder is willing to use its stock as a method of payment could mean that managers' private information indicates that the stock is not undervalued. The difference for private targets comes about because when a bidder buys a private target for stock, it creates blockholders—the previous owners of the private target (whose ownership was concentrated). These blockholders have incentives to monitor bidder management, creating positive externalities for the remaining bidder shareholders.

SUMMARY AND CONCLUSIONS

Counting all target forms, tens of thousands of merger transactions have occurred in the last 30 years. Certainly room exists in such a sample for all kinds of motives and associated outcomes. Nonetheless, identifying the primary drivers of merger activity is important. Understanding the catalysts of merger waves helps to identify the main drivers of merger activity.

Harford (2005) sets forth the idea that generally industry-level reasons help to explain a sudden increase in merger activity. Empirical work consistently shows that merger activity clusters at the industry level and that these clusters can be linked to technological, regulatory, or economic shocks to the industry's operating environment. However, asset exchanges are not frictionless. The right macro conditions must be in place for the shock to propagate a wave. Several characteristics of economic expansions increase the likelihood of asset reshuffling. First, capital liquidity is greater, meaning that financing for such reshuffling is generally less dear. Second, potential buyers of assets are generating high cash flows, reducing financing constraints on the first-best users of the assets. When this happens, the target can sell at a higher price, making the transaction more likely to take place. Finally, some of the same factors that drive expansions motivate asset reshuffling at the industry level. For example, technological improvements often drive both economic expansion and merger activity.

In recent work, Ahern and Harford (2010) explore how industry-level shocks can propagate waves by traveling along the economic connections created by supply-chain interactions between industries. The idea is simple: If a shock to an industry causes it to restructure, then that restructuring can be viewed as a shock to connected industries. Galbraith's (1952) countervailing power hypothesis explicitly predicts that in order to maintain bargaining power in the product market, an industry will consolidate in response to supplier or customer consolidations. Another way that shocks can travel across economic connections is by opening new avenues of vertical integration or changing optimal production technology. Ahern and Harford's results find strong support for the hypothesis that the economy can be treated as a network of interconnected industries and that merger activity in an industry can cause future merger activity in a connected one.

The result of this macro-level influence and the interconnectivity of industries is that industry-level merger waves cluster in time. Rational reshuffling of assets in response to economic expansion and industry-level shocks drive aggregate merger waves. Nonetheless, this does not rule out other explanations for merger activity. One argument is that they are part of the activity, but not the driver of the activity. This seems like a sensible interpretation of the evidence. Specifically, merger activity starts for economically motivated reasons, but the intensity of efficient merger activity provides cover for many other motivations such as empire building, hubris, or spending overvalued stock. Indeed, much evidence suggests that all of these types of mergers take place.

Several areas for further investigation exist. Some of the most promising avenues for continued research are those that explore and make use of the interconnections between industries, viewing the economy as a network where the industries are the nodes. The tools of graph theory, typically used to investigate social networks and disease spread, can be applied in such a context to provide new insights into how shocks and merger activity diffuse through the economy. Another type of interconnection is cross-country. Makaew's (2010) paper provides an important step in this direction. Understanding how merger waves in one economic zone affect merger activity in other zones is an overlooked piece of the puzzle. As the world economies become increasingly integrated, international influences on merger activity will become more important.

DISCUSSION QUESTIONS

1. Discuss the different motivations for individual mergers and their differing implications for shareholder wealth, both of the bidder firm and the combined wealth of the bidder and target shareholders.

2. Empirically, aggregate merger activity is positively correlated with the level of the stock market. The neoclassical and behavioral merger wave hypotheses each explain this fact differently. Discuss how each approach makes use of this fact with a focus on the different interpretations of the association between merger activity and stock market level.

3. If you were trying to evaluate the causes of merger waves using international data, what would you look for and what would you hope to learn?

4. Is there a place for more than one explanation for merger activity? That is, can neoclassically driven merger waves allow room for and perhaps even foster behavioral- or agency-driven mergers?

REFERENCES

Ahern, Kenneth R., and Jarrad Harford. 2010. "The Importance of Industry Links in Merger Waves." Working Paper: University of Washington.

Alchian, Armen A., and Harold Demsetz. 1972. "Production, Information Costs, and Economic Organization." *American Economic Review* 62:5, 777–795.

Andrade, Gregor, Mark Mitchell, and Erik Stafford. 2001. "New Evidence and Perspectives on Mergers." *Journal of Economic Perspectives* 15:2, 103–120.

Ang, James S., and Yingmei Cheng. 2006. "Direct Evidence on the Market-driven Acquisitions Theory." *Journal of Financial Research* 15:1, 38–51.

Becketti, Sean. 1986. "Corporate Mergers and the Business Cycle." *Federal Reserve Bank of Kansas City Economic Review* 71:5, 13–26.

Betton, Sandra, B. Espen Eckbo, and Karin S. Thorburn. 2008. "Corporate Takeovers." In B. Espen Eckbo, ed. *Handbook of Corporate Finance: Empirical Corporate Finance*, 291-430. North-Holland: Elsevier.

Billett, Matthew T., Tao-Hsien Molly King, and David C. Mauer. 2004. "Bondholder Wealth Effects in Mergers and Acquisitions: New Evidence from the 1980s and 1990s." *Journal of Finance* 59:1, 107–135.

Bradley, Michael, Anand Desai, and Han E. Kim. 1983. "The Rationale Behind Interfirm Tender Offers." *Journal of Financial Economics* 11:1–4, 183–206.

Calomiris, Charles W. 1999. "Gauging the Efficiency of Bank Consolidation during a Merger Wave." *Journal of Banking & Finance* 23:2–4, 615–621.

Coase, Ronald. 1937. "The Nature of the Firm." *Economica* 4:16, 386–405.

De Bondt, Werner F. M., and Howard E. Thompson. 1992. "Is Economic Efficiency the Driving Force behind Mergers?" *Managerial & Decision Economics* 13:1, 31–44.

Dittmar, Amy K., and Robert F. Dittmar. 2008. "The Timing of Financing Decisions: An Examination of the Correlation in Financing Waves." *Journal of Financial Economics* 90:1, 59–83.

Dong, Ming, David Hirshleifer, Scott Richardson, and Siew Hong Teoh. 2003. "Does Investor Misvaluation Drive the Takeover Market?" *Journal of Finance* 61:2, 725–762.

Eckbo, B. Espen. 1983. "Horizontal Mergers, Collusion, and Stockholder Wealth." *Journal of Financial Economics* 11:1–4, 241–273.

Eisfeldt, Andrea L., and Adriano A. Rampini. 2006. "Capital Reallocation and Liquidity." *Journal of Monetary Economics* 53:3, 369–399.

Erickson, Merle M., and Shiing-wu Wang. 2007. "Tax Benefits as a Source of Merger Premiums in Acquisitions of Private Corporations." *Accounting Review* 82:2, 359–387.

Fee, C. Edward, and Shawn Thomas. 2004. "Sources of Gains in Horizontal Mergers: Evidence from Customer, Supplier, and Rival Firms." *Journal of Financial Economics* 74:3, 423–460.

Fuller, Kathleen, Jeffry Netter, and Mike Stegemoller. 2002. "What Do Returns to Acquiring Firms Tell Us? Evidence from Firms That Make Many Acquisitions." *Journal of Finance* 57:4, 1763–1793.

Galbraith, John K. 1952. *American Capitalism: The Concept of Countervailing Power*. Boston: Houghton Mifflin.

Goel, Anand M., and Anjan V. Thakor. 2010. "Do Envious CEOs Cause Merger Waves?" *Review of Financial Studies* 23:2, 487–517.

Golbe, Devra L., and Lawrence J. White. 1988. "A Time Series Analysis of Mergers and Acquisitions in the U.S. Economy." In Alan J. Auerbach, ed. *Corporate Takeovers: Causes and Consequences*, 265–302. Chicago: University of Chicago Press.

Gompers, Paul, Joy Ishii, and Andrew Metrick. 2003. "Corporate Governance and Equity Prices." *Quarterly Journal of Economics* 118:1, 107–155.

Gort, Michael. 1969. "An Economic Disturbance Theory of Mergers." *Quarterly Journal of Economics* 83:4, 623–642.

Gorton, Gary, Mathias Kahl, and Richard J. Rosen. 2009. "Eat or Be Eaten: A Theory of Mergers and Firm Size." *Journal of Finance* 64:3, 1291–1344.

Gugler Klaus P., Dennis C. Mueller, and B. Burcin Yurtoglu. 2006. "The Determinants of Merger Waves." Working Paper, University of Vienna.

Harford, Jarrad. 1999. "Corporate Cash Reserves and Acquisitions." *Journal of Finance* 54:6, 1969–1997.

Harford, Jarrad. 2005. "What Drives Merger Waves?" *Journal of Financial Economics* 77:3, 529–560.

Healy, Paul M., Krishna U. Palepu, and Richard S. Ruback. 1992. "Does Corporate Performance Improve After Mergers?" *Journal of Financial Economics* 31:2, 135–175.

Jensen, Michael C. 1986. "Agency Costs of Free Cash Flow, Corporate Finance, and Takeovers." *American Economic Review* 76:2, 323–329.

Jensen, Michael C., and William H. Meckling. 1976. "Theory of the Firm: Managerial Behavior, Agency Costs and Ownership Structure." *Journal of Financial Economics* 3:4, 305–360.

Jensen, Michael C., and Richard S. Ruback. 1983. "The Market for Corporate Control: The Scientific Evidence." *Journal of Financial Economics* 11:1–4, 5–50.

Jovanovic, Boyan, and Peter L. Rousseau. 2002. "The Q-theory of Mergers." *American Economic Review* 92:2, 198–204.

Jovanovic, Boyan, and Peter L. Rousseau. 2008. "Mergers as Reallocation." *Economic Perspectives* 90:4, 765–776.

Lang, Larry H. P., René M. Stulz, and Ralph A. Walkling. 1991. "A Test of the Free Cash Flow Hypothesis: The Case of Bidder Returns." *Journal of Financial Economics* 29:2, 315–336.

Lewellen, Wilbur G. 1971. "A Pure Financial Rationale for the Conglomerate Merger." *Journal of Finance* 26:2, 521–537.

Makaew, Tanakorn. 2010. "A Dynamic Model of International Mergers and Acquisitions." Working Paper, University of South Carolina.

Maksimovic, Vojislav, and Gordon Phillips. 2001. "The Market for Corporate Assets: Who Engages in Mergers and Asset Sales and Are There Efficiency Gains?" *Journal of Finance* 56:6, 2019–2065.

Masulis, Ronald W., Cong Wang, and Fei Xie. 2007. "Corporate Governance and Acquirer Returns." *Journal of Finance* 62:4, 1851–1889.

Matsusaka, John G. 1993a. "Takeover Motives During the Conglomerate Merger Wave." *RAND Journal of Economics* 24:3, 357–379.

Matsusaka, John G. 1993b. "Target Profits and Managerial Discipline During the Conglomerate Merger Wave." *Journal of Industrial Economics* 41:2, 179–189.

Melicher, Ronald W., Johannes Ledolter, and Louis J. D'Antonio. 1983. "A Time Series Analysis of Aggregate Merger Activity." *Review of Economics and Statistics* 65:3, 423–430.

Mitchell, Mark, and J. Harold Mulherin. 1996. "The Impact of Industry Shocks on Takeover and Restructuring Activity." *Journal of Financial Economics* 41:2, 193–229.

Moeller, Sara B., Frederik P. Schlingemann, and René M. Stulz. 2004. "Firm Size and the Gains from Acquisitions." *Journal of Financial Economics* 73:2, 201–228.

Mulherin, J. Harold, and Audra L. Boone. 2000. "Comparing Acquisitions and Divestitures." *Journal of Corporate Finance* 6:2, 117–139.

Myers, Stewart C., and Nicholas S. Majluf. 1984, "Corporate Financing and Investment Decisions When Firms Have Information That Investors Do Not Have." *Journal of Financial Economics* 13:2, 187–221.

Officer, Micah S. 2007. "The Price of Corporate Liquidity: Acquisition Discounts for Unlisted Targets." *Journal of Financial Economics* 83:3, 571–598.

Powell, Ronan, and Alfred Yawson. 2005. "Industry Aspects of Takeovers and Divestitures: Evidence from the UK." *Journal of Banking & Finance* 29:12, 3015–3040.

Rhodes-Kropf, Matthew, and David Robinson. 2008. "The Market for Mergers and the Boundaries of the Firm." *Journal of Finance* 63:3, 1169–1211.

Rhodes-Kropf, Matthew, David Robinson, and S. Viswanathan. 2005. "Valuation Waves and Merger Activity: The Empirical Evidence." *Journal of Financial Economics* 77:3, 561–603.

Rhodes-Kropf, Matthew, and S. Viswanathan. 2004. "Market Valuation and Merger Waves." *Journal of Finance* 59:6, 2685–2718.

Roll, Richard. 1986. "The Hubris Hypothesis of Corporate Takeovers." *Journal of Business* 59:2, 197–216.

Savor, Pavel G., and Qi Lu. 2009. "Do Stock Mergers Create Value for Acquirers." *Journal of Finance* 64:3, 1061–1097.

Scherer, F. M., and David J. Ravenscraft. 1989. "The Profitability of Mergers." *International Journal of Industrial Organization* 7:1, 101–116.

Schumpeter, Joseph A. 1950. *Capitalism, Socialism, and Democracy.* New York: Harper and Brothers.

Schwert, G. William. 1996. "Markup Pricing in Mergers and Acquisitions." *Journal of Financial Economics* 41:2, 153–192.

Shahrur, Husayn. 2005. "Industry Structure and Horizontal Takeovers: Analysis of Wealth Effects on Rivals, Suppliers, and Corporate Customers." *Journal of Financial Economics* 76:1, 61–98.

Shleifer, Andrei, and Robert W. Vishny. 1992. "Liquidation Values and Debt Capacity: A Market Equilibrium Approach." *Journal of Finance* 47:4, 1343–1366.

Shleifer, Andrei, and Robert W. Vishny. 2003. "Stock Market Driven Acquisitions." *Journal of Financial Economics* 70:3, 295–311.

Smith, Richard L., and Joo-Hyun Kim. 1994. "The Combined Effects of Free Cash Flow and Financial Slack on Bidder and Target Stock Returns." *Journal of Business* 67:2, 281–320.

Song, Moon H., and Ralph A. Walkling. 2000. "Abnormal Returns to Rivals of Acquisition Targets: A Test of the 'Acquisition Probability Hypothesis'." *Journal of Financial Economics* 55:2, 143–171.

Stillman, Robert. 1983. "Examining Antitrust Policy towards Horizontal Mergers." *Journal of Financial Economics* 11:1–4, 225–240.

Stulz, René M.. 1988. "Managerial Control of Voting Rights: Financing Policies and the Market for Corporate Control." *Journal of Financial Economics* 20:1/2, 25–54.

Town, R. J. 1992. "Merger Waves and the Structure of Merger and Acquisition Time-Series." *Journal of Applied Econometrics* 7, S83–S100.

Travlos, Nickolaos G. 1987. "Corporate Takeover Bids, Methods of Payment, and Bidding Firms' Stock Returns." *Journal of Finance* 42:4, 943–963.

ABOUT THE AUTHOR

Jarrad Harford is the Marion B. Ingersoll Professor of Finance at the University of Washington's Foster School of Business. He received his PhD in Finance from the University of Rochester. Professor Harford has taught the core undergraduate finance course, Business Finance, for 12 years, as well as an MBA elective in mergers and acquisitions, and Finance for Non-financial Executives in the executive education program. He has won numerous awards for his teaching including the Wells Fargo Faculty Award for Undergraduate Teaching (2005), the ISMBA Excellence in Teaching Award (2006), and the IFC Excellence in Teaching Award (2007 and 2008). In 2008, Pearson-Prentice Hall published an undergraduate finance textbook co-authored by Professor Harford. He currently serves as an associate editor for the *Journal of Financial Economics*, *Journal of Financial and Quantitative Analysis*, and *Journal of Corporate Finance*. His primary research areas are mergers and acquisitions, corporate governance, and payout policy.

CHAPTER 3

Takeover Regulation

MARINA MARTYNOVA
Associate, Cornerstone Research and Research Fellow, Tilburg University

LUC RENNEBOOG
Professor of Corporate Finance, Tilburg University

INTRODUCTION

Mergers and acquisitions (M&As) represent an important means of corporate restructuring. Companies are keen to participate in M&As because by combining
their assets with those of another firm they can achieve operating and financial
synergies such as realizing economies of scale and scope, increased market power,
increased utilization of the management team, cheaper access to capital, and a
greater internal capital market. Some consider M&As as an important corporate
governance mechanism. Jensen (1988) defines this activity as the market for corporate control where management teams compete for the right to manage the assets
owned by shareholders. The team offering the highest value to the shareholders
acquires the right to manage the assets until another management team that is
able to realize a higher value of the assets replaces the existing management. The
high incidence and volume of M&As highlights their significance to the corporate
world (Martynova and Renneboog, 2008).

Given the high incidence of M&As and the large sums of money involved,
regulatory attention focuses on this field. The regulators have several objectives
to pursue. The first objective of regulatory intervention is to facilitate efficient corporate restructuring. More value-creating takeovers can be encouraged by a set of
regulatory rules that reduce takeover costs, allocate more of the takeover surplus
to the acquirer, and enable potential acquirers to conduct a takeover transaction.
Despite their economic importance, corporate takeovers also give rise to various
conflicts of interest among the parties involved in these transactions. Mitigating
such conflicts constitutes the second objective of regulatory intervention. In particular, takeover regulation sets rules to resolve the conflicting interests between the
target company's management and the shareholders concerning the installment
of antitakeover devices. Takeover regulation also includes provisions that provide
protection to the target's minority shareholders from being expropriated by the
acquirer.

This chapter presents a map of the takeover regulation in different jurisdictions
around the world. It shows that regulatory provisions vary across jurisdictions,

reflecting different priorities by regulators regarding the development of the takeover market, conflicts of interest among the parties involved, and the protection of minority shareholders. As recent M&A activity goes beyond the national borders and the number of cross-border M&As continues to increase, understanding the differences in legal rules across jurisdictions became essential. Therefore, this chapter focuses on identifying and discussing major differences in takeover regulation provisions across jurisdictions.

The remainder of the chapter is organized as follows. The next section discusses the takeover regulation functions in more detail. This is followed by a review of the individual legal provisions and their functions. Major regulatory provisions include: the mandatory bid rule, the principle of equal treatment of shareholders, the squeeze-out and sell-out rules, ownership and control disclosure, board neutrality regarding the takeover bid, and restrictions involving the use of takeover defense measures.

THE FUNCTIONS OF TAKEOVER REGULATION

Although takeover regulation is mainly seen as a mechanism to facilitate efficient corporate restructuring (Burkart, 1999), it is also an important tool in mitigating conflicts of interest among diverse company's constituencies such as management, shareholders, and stakeholders. Takeover regulation not only curbs conflicts of interest related to transfers of control, but also has a more general impact on the agency problems among management and shareholders, minority and majority investors, and other stakeholders. As such, it constitutes an important element of a corporate governance system (Goergen, Martynova, and Renneboog, 2005). The role that takeover regulation plays in a particular jurisdiction, however, depends on companies' corporate governance characteristics such as ownership and control.

When companies have dispersed ownership, the primary role of takeover regulation is to facilitate corporate takeovers that restrain opportunistic managerial behavior. Small shareholders cannot effectively monitor management due to coordination problems and have to rely on external monitoring via the market for corporate control. Part of the takeover activity is focused on poorly performing firms and aims to replace poorly performing management. The threat of losing their jobs and perquisites provides managers with an incentive to focus on shareholder objectives. The role of takeover regulation is then to design rules and provide instruments that minimize the costs and inefficiencies associated with the takeover mechanism and thereby facilitate a transfer of control toward more productive owners and management. Examples of measures stimulating takeover activity are the squeeze-out rule and limitations on the use of antitakeover defense measures.

For companies with concentrated ownership, takeover regulation could function as a corporate governance device for protecting minority shareholders' interests. Concentration of ownership and control can serve as an alternative mechanism that can mitigate the conflicts of interest between management and shareholders. Major investors have strong incentives to monitor and replace management in poorly performing companies. However, the presence of controlling shareholders may also be associated with their potential opportunistic behavior toward minority shareholders. Although standard company law techniques are available when resolving conflicts between the large shareholder and minority shareholders, takeover regulation plays an important role, as it can provide minority shareholders with an "exit on fair terms" opportunity. Provisions such as the sell-out right, the mandatory bid rule, or the equal treatment principle ensure such exit opportunities for minority shareholders.

Specific provisions of takeover regulation apply to control transactions to regulate conflicts of interest between the management and shareholders of the target and the acquirer. Two major conflicts of interest may emerge. First, the management of the target company may be tempted to implement unduly defense measures to obstruct the takeover, even if this clashes with shareholder interests. Second, control transfers may turn the target's incumbent shareholders into minority shareholders, creating an opportunity for the acquirer to extract private benefits of control at the minority shareholders' expense. Takeover regulation should aim at minimizing both potential conflicts. In particular, a limit on the defense measures is seen as the best way to constrain opportunistic managerial behavior. Additionally, the mandatory bid rule and the sell-out right ought to provide the target's shareholders with the right to exit the company at a fair price.

Overall, takeover regulation can have various provisions that perform corporate governance functions both in the case of a transfer of control and in terms of governance of ordinary corporate activity. There are, however, several important trade-offs. First, provisions aiming to provide an exit opportunity for the target's minority shareholders are likely to discourage the development of the market for corporate control, thereby eliminating an important external corporate governance mechanism. Takeover provisions that provide the target's minority shareholders with the right to exit at a fair price redistribute the takeover surplus from the acquirer to the target shareholders and hence make a takeover bid less attractive for the acquirer. On the other hand, regulatory provisions that allocate more of the takeover surplus to the acquirer increase the acquirer's incentive to make a bid for a poorly performing firm and replace its inefficient management upon the acquisition of control. Yet, these provisions may dilute rights of the target company's incumbent shareholders. The opposite nature of the two types of provisions gives rise to a trade-off in regulation resulting in promoting efficient corporate restructuring and facilitating the market monitoring of managers, while also providing protection for minority shareholders.

Takeover regulation also indirectly affects the incentives for a company to seek a listing on a stock exchange. If the incumbent owners value control, they will often be reluctant to take their firm public if this exposes them to an active market for corporate control. Their reluctance to take their firm public depends on the distribution of gains from a future takeover bid, which is determined by takeover regulation. Furthermore, regulation that is likely to reduce the power of the blockholders discourages listing. This constitutes another trade-off of the regulation: promoting the expansion of financial markets and supplying corporate governance devices aimed at protecting the rights of corporate constituencies.

The next section discusses in detail the main provisions of takeover regulation and the functions that they perform. Takeover regulation provisions vary substantially across countries, reflecting different priorities regulators set regarding the takeover regulation functions.

TAKEOVER REGULATION PROVISIONS

As discussed earlier, takeover regulation should ensure a well-functioning market for corporate control while protecting the interests of minority shareholders and other types of stakeholders. The regulatory devices available to achieve these aims are manifold and comprise: (1) the mandatory bid rule, (2) the principle of equal treatment of shareholders, (3) squeeze-out and sell-out rules, (4) disclosure of changes in ownership and control, (5) the target company's board neutrality concerning the takeover bid, and (6) restrictions regarding the use of antitakeover defense measures, including the one-share-one-vote principle and the breakthrough rule. This section discusses each device and its role in stimulating the efficient market for corporate control, mitigating agency problems among parties involved in control transactions, and protecting minority shareholders.

The Mandatory Bid Rule

The mandatory bid rule provides the minority shareholders with an opportunity to exit the company on fair terms once the large shareholder reaches a certain level of ownership. The rule imposes a duty on the acquirer to make a tender offer to all the shareholders once the acquirer has accumulated a certain percentage of the shares. The tender should be for all outstanding shares and not limited to the shares the acquirer intends to own. About a decade ago, a tender offer on all shares outstanding was only mandatory after an investor had acquired de facto majority control; today, thresholds are substantially lower. For instance, thresholds have decreased in Denmark and Italy. In these countries, the acquirer needs to make a tender offer to all of the remaining shareholders after accumulating one-third of the company's shares.

The mandatory bid requirement is justified on the grounds that, following the acquisition of a large block of shares, the remaining shares in the hands of minority shareholders may become illiquid and their value may plunge on the market. Anticipating this, shareholders feel pressure to accept any offer the acquirer makes, even when the offer undervalues the company. The mandatory bid rule ensures that every shareholder has the opportunity to sell his or her shares to the acquirer at a fair price, thereby protecting the target's shareholders from being pressured by the acquirer to sell their shares at unfavorable terms. The mandatory bid rule can also be justified on the grounds that an investor who obtains control may be tempted to extract private benefits of control at the expense of the minority shareholders. As a consequence of such anticipated conflicts of interest between majority and minority shareholders after an acquisition, a rule giving minority shareholders the option to exit the company at an attractive price is important.

The mandatory bid rule usually states how the minimum price for tendered shares is determined. The national regulations differ, but the price must not be lower than the highest price paid for the shares already purchased by the acquirer or must not be lower than a certain percentage of the average market share price over the previous 12 months (e.g., 75 percent). The minimum tender offer price may also be determined as the higher of the book value and past market prices in cases when shares are illiquid and their market price does not reflect the fair value. This serves as a protection against acquirers underpaying for shares relative to their fair value.

Although the mandatory bid requirement may mitigate the problem of expropriation of the target company's incumbent shareholders by the acquirer, it also decreases the likelihood of value-creating restructuring. The main reason for this is that the rule makes control transactions more expensive and thereby discourages acquirers from bidding in the first place. Several ways are available to reduce these costs: (1) increase the threshold above which the acquirer has to make a mandatory offer; (2) allow the price in the tender offer to be lower than the highest price paid for any of the shares previously purchased; or (3) grant further exceptions to the rule rather than just for financial distress of the target. However, any of the suggested modifications to the rule automatically increase the likelihood that minority shareholders will be expropriated and violate the equal treatment principle of corporate law discussed in the next section.

The mandatory bid rule has been widely adopted in European and Asian countries but not in the United States. Despite the widespread adoption of the rule, its settings vary substantially across countries both with respect to the threshold and the price at which the offer must be made. The threshold varies between 20 percent and 67 percent of the voting capital, with the majority of countries having a threshold of one-third of the voting rights. For example, the mandatory offer threshold is below 30 percent in Austria, India, and Spain; it is 30 percent or one-third of voting capital in the United Kingdom, Germany, France, China, and Hong Kong; and it is two-thirds in Finland. Still, countries such as Belgium have not specified a threshold and instead require a mandatory bid as soon as control has been obtained. Moreover, some countries allow shareholders of a potential target company to choose between having protection in the form of the mandatory bid rule set by the statutes or modifying the rule by including in the company's articles of incorporation a higher bid threshold in order to encourage changes of control, as is the case in Switzerland.

The rules of price fixing in mandatory offers also differ across jurisdictions. For example, the United Kingdom and Germany require the price to be equal to the highest price paid for pre-bid purchases. Other jurisdictions have opted for a more flexible approach. In Italy, the price has to be equal to the average market price over the 12 months before the bid announcement, whereas in Switzerland it has to be at 75 percent of the highest pre-bid market price. The rule may also set restrictions on the means of payment in the acquisition. For example, in the United Kingdom the acquirer has to offer the target shareholders a cash alternative if it makes an equity offer.

The Principle of Equal Treatment

The principle of equal treatment constitutes an important standard of corporate governance regulation. The principle requires controlling shareholders, management, and other constituencies to treat all shareholders within each individual class of shares equally. The equality of treatment requirement is particularly important in the corporate takeover context where the possibilities of violations of the rights of minority shareholders are far-reaching. Its inclusion in takeover regulation implies that the acquirer has to offer minority shareholders the opportunity to exit the company on terms that are no less favorable than those offered to the shareholders who sold a controlling block of shares. As such, the role of the equal treatment principle in takeover regulation embeds the mandatory bid rule, given that both aim at protecting the target company's minority shareholders.

The adoption of the principle of equal treatment greatly affects takeover transactions involving target companies with concentrated ownership, but has virtually no effect on the target companies with dispersed ownership. This is because a target company's controlling shareholder typically agrees to sell its controlling block at a price that includes a premium reflecting the private benefits of control. The equal treatment requirement prescribes that the acquirer has to make an offer to all shareholders to purchase their shares at a price no less than the price paid for the controlling block. Therefore, if an acquirer paid a premium to purchase the controlling block from the controlling shareholder, the acquirer has to offer the same premium to the remaining minority shareholders. Although this provides firm protection to minority shareholders by ensuring that they can exit at favorable terms, it also increases the costs of the acquisition and decreases the price that the acquirer can offer to the controlling shareholder (Davies and Hopt, 2004).

Higher costs may discourage some acquirers from participating in acquisitions, while a lower offer price may make the target's controlling blockholder pull out of the acquisition negotiations because the price does not reflect the private benefits of control. Consequently, the equal treatment principle may create an additional barrier to a more active market for corporate control for companies with a concentrated ownership structure. Only in the absence of large private benefits of control are private negotiations with the incumbent controlling blockholder likely to result in lower costs for a control transfer than an open market purchase from dispersed shareholders (Bagnoli and Lipman, 1988; Holmstrom and Nalebuff, 1990; Burkart, Gromb, and Panunzi, 1997). The presence of controlling shareholders in companies may then facilitate an active market for corporate control.

Despite the additional barriers for potential value-creating control change transactions raised by the equal treatment principle, widespread consensus exists among European countries regarding the adoption of the principle. The pan-European acceptance of the equal-treatment principle can be regarded as the result of regulatory competition among the jurisdictions. The acceptance of the principle in Europe can also be justified on the grounds that a legal guarantee of the highest price to minority shareholders when control changes should encourage investments in companies with concentrated ownership. Since companies with concentrated ownership prevail in most European countries, regulators in these countries have an interest in promoting the equal treatment principle, thereby stimulating investment activity.

Other jurisdictions, such as many U.S. states including Delaware, have opted not to adopt the general equal treatment principle to regulate takeovers. In these jurisdictions, a takeover transaction can be structured as a two-tier offer. In the first tier offer, the acquirer pays a premium above the market price for a controlling block, whereas in the second tier, the terms are less favorable. In contrast to a system with the equal treatment restriction, the two-tier offer system results in lower acquisition costs and mitigates the controlling shareholder's hold-out problem. Therefore, it stimulates the development of the takeover market. However, this system also pushes minority shareholders to tender even when they believe the bid is inadequate. To resolve this problem, all U.S. state laws grant shareholders appraisal rights that allow them to not tender shares and, after the tender has closed, demand the controlling shareholder to purchase their shares at a fair price, which is typically determined by the court. Also, nearly half of the U.S. states mandate the equal treatment of minority shareholders by prescribing the acquirer to pay the same price to minorities as the highest price it has paid for the shares purchased in the recent past.

The Squeeze-Out, Freeze-Out, and Sell-Out Rules

A typical takeover scenario involves an acquisition of a controlling block followed by a tender offer to buy out all remaining shares. However, there may be situations when all but a few minority shareholders have accepted the offer and the acquirer cannot obtain full ownership at the end of the tender process. The minority shareholders may decide not to sell their shares, hoping to negotiate for favorable terms with the acquirer after the tender has closed. Such hold-ups are especially problematic for acquirers seeking to take the target company private.

In many jurisdictions, the issue of minority hold-ups is directly addressed in takeover regulation in the form of a squeeze-out rule. The rule gives the acquirer the right to force minority shareholders, who hold out in a tender offer, to sell their shares to the acquirer at a price that is set by statute or an outside expert (Boehmer, 2002; Becht, Bolton, and Röell, 2003). The squeeze-out rule only takes effect if the acquirer has accumulated a specific percentage of the equity, usually 90 or 95 percent. The rule allows the acquirer to obtain 100 percent of the equity and frees the acquirer from having to deal with minority shareholders after the deal completion. As such, the adoption of the squeeze-out rule may encourage more control change transactions.

The squeeze-out rule affects the behavior of the target's shareholders during the tender offer as it reduces the hold-up problem and may lead to a decrease in the tender price. When a tender offer is conditional on the squeeze-out threshold, shareholders cannot gain from retaining shares. Hence, they are willing to tender at a price as low as the post-takeover value of the minority shares. Therefore, acquirers who condition their tender offers on the squeeze-out threshold should expect to pay less and, hence, earn higher returns. According to Yarrow (1985) and Maug (2004), the economic efficiency of the squeeze-out rule depends on how the price at which the minority shares are squeezed out is determined. For example, Maug's model predicts that economic efficiency worsens if minority shareholders extract higher premiums in squeeze-outs. If these premiums are higher than those offered in the tender offer, few will be tempted to tender in the first place.

The squeeze-out provision is now commonly used in the English, German, and Scandinavian law countries. However, less than two-thirds of the French law jurisdictions had adopted the squeeze-out rule by 2010. As in the case of the mandatory rule, the provisions of the squeeze-out rule vary substantially across jurisdictions. Thus, the threshold beyond which acquirers can force remaining shareholders to sell their shares ranges from 80 percent (in Ireland) to 95 percent (in Belgium, France, Germany, and the Netherlands), with a threshold of 90 percent in the majority of countries. Other countries such as the United States and Japan have more general provisions granting a majority blockholder compulsory purchase power over the minority shares, whether the majority was acquired or not. These provisions are typically referred to as a freeze-out right.

The key element of the squeeze-out (freeze-out) right is the definition of the "fair price" that should be offered for the remaining minority shares. If the equal treatment principle applies, then the fair price should be the same as the price paid for the controlling block of shares. If two-tier offers are legally allowed, then the fair price in the squeeze-out (freeze-out) purchase is typically determined as the average of past market prices. Some jurisdictions also grant minority shareholders the right to contest the purchase price in court, thereby providing shareholders with additional assurance of getting a fair price. The provisions for the fixing of the price for squeeze-out and freeze-out purchases vary across jurisdictions.

In many jurisdictions, the squeeze-out right of the acquirer is balanced by the sell-out right of minority shareholders to demand that the controlling shareholder buy their shares at a fair price. The right permits shareholders to wait for the final result of the tender offer before they decide whether to sell their shares. According to the sell-out rule, if a certain percentage of shares (typically 90 percent) are tendered, the remaining shareholders can require the acquirer to buy out their shares at a fair price to exit the company. The sell-out price is typically the same as the price paid in the tender offer. However, in some countries the sell-out price can be disputed in court, and the acquirer may be prescribed to pay a higher price to the suing shareholder upon the court's decision.

The sell-out rule is another provision that aims to protect the remaining minority shareholders, and it reduces the pressure on the target's shareholders to tender. Additionally, this rule has a negative impact on the likelihood of acquisitions occurring. Although the sell-out rule is seen as a counter-provision to the squeeze-out rule, many jurisdictions jointly use the two rules. Many European countries have adopted both the squeeze-out and sell-out rights. In the United States, similar provisions are present in the form of the freeze-out and appraisal rights, respectively.

The squeeze-out and sell-out rules are functionally very different. The squeeze-out rule mitigates potential free-riding behavior by small shareholders, thereby allocating more of the takeover gains to the acquirer. Further, the rule eliminates potential problems that may arise between the acquirer and the remaining minority shareholders after most of the target's shares have been acquired. Hence, the squeeze-out rule is expected to facilitate takeovers, and its introduction may have a positive impact on the development of a takeover market. In contrast, the sell-out rule reduces the share of takeover gains allocated to the acquirer, thereby discouraging some value-creating takeovers. The rule aims to protect minority shareholders. What the two rules have in common is how they eliminate potential conflicts between the acquirer and the remaining target's minority shareholders.

Disclosure of Changes in Ownership and Control

An important element of the takeover regulation consists of the disclosure of major changes in the company's ownership and control structure. Disclosure rules oblige companies to inform regulators and public investors when one of the shareholders accumulates a substantial share block in the company. In some countries, the "strategic intent" or purpose for which the share block was acquired also has to be disclosed. Such disclosures enable the market to learn about potential parties interested in taking control over the company well before the public announcement of the actual takeover bid.

Typically, disclosure rules prescribe thresholds above which ownership needs to be disclosed. For example, in France, companies are required to disclose a change in ownership if one of the shareholders crosses a threshold of 5, 10, 20, 33.3, 50, or 66.7 percent. Such disclosure should be made to a regulator within three to seven days of crossing the threshold. Virtually all of the jurisdictions worldwide have recently lowered the minimum threshold for mandatory ownership disclosure. Thus, in the early 1990s, the average threshold for disclosure in Western Europe and Scandinavia was about 9 percent, with the United Kingdom having the lowest threshold (3 percent), and Germany the highest threshold (25 percent). In countries such as Italy and Sweden, a mandatory disclosure of voting rights was introduced for the first time as late as 1992. By 2010, the average threshold was reduced to 5 percent, and some countries, such as Italy, require ownership disclosure starting from 2 percent. In the United States, the minimum ownership disclosure threshold is 5 percent.

Information about major share blocks allows the regulator, minority shareholders, and the market monitor large blockholders in order to avoid letting these major blockholders to extract private benefits of control at the expense of other stakeholders. In other words, transparency minimizes potential agency problems ex ante. Moreover, transparency allows the regulator to investigate, for instance, insider trading or self-dealing by large blockholders.

A higher threshold for the mandatory control disclosure improves the efficiency of the takeover mechanism (Grossman and Hart, 1980). The reason is that acquirers can make substantial profits on the toehold stake they built up before reaching the disclosure threshold. The disclosure of the acquisition of a major stake may alert the market that a bid is likely to take place. This leads to a revision of the share price that may then reflect the likely gains from the takeover. The higher the thresholds for the ownership disclosure and the mandatory bid, the lower is the number of shares for which the acquirer pays the full takeover premium. Conversely, lowering the disclosure and mandatory bid thresholds will cause a fraction of potential takeovers not to be undertaken (e.g., Shleifer and Vishny, 1986; Hirshleifer and Titman, 1990; Kyle and Vila, 1991; Burkart, 1999).

The Target Company's Board Neutrality

Although the takeover market is considered to be an external corporate governance mechanism that forces managers to act in the interests of the shareholders, it can also be a trigger for even greater divergence of interests between these two parties. In the wake of a takeover threat, the management of the target company potentially faces a conflict of interest: the transaction may create shareholder value, but also endangers management jobs and perquisites. If the management of the target company has unrestricted power, the line of actions chosen may focus on its own interests and hence on preventing a takeover even when the takeover offers a higher value to the company's shareholders. Examples of such actions are attempts to make the company less attractive to a potential acquirer, the advice to the company's shareholders to reject the bid, and the search for an alternative "friendly" acquirer, also known as a "white knight." This potential conflict of interest calls for a set of rules to govern the behavior of management and shareholders when a takeover offer is imminent. The rules deal with the issues of who decides whether to reject or accept the offer, the adoption of takeover defenses, and the bargaining strategy with the bidder.

Two solutions are available for mitigating the managerial agency problem in a takeover context (Davies and Hopt, 2004). The first solution is to transfer the decision as to the acceptance of the bid to the target company's shareholders and to remove it from the management. Currently, several jurisdictions impose a requirement for the target company's board neutrality regarding takeover offers, preventing the board of directors from taking actions that may frustrate a potential bid. For example, most European countries forbid the use of antitakeover devices such as poison pills. The main argument favoring board neutrality is that it limits the potential coercive effect of a bid (Bebchuk, 2002; Arlen and Talley, 2003). In most jurisdictions, the board should remain neutral and limit the use of antitakeover devices unless shareholders at a general meeting approve an antitakeover strategy and only after the announcement of the bid.

The second solution is to provide the management with substantial decision power, but to give the shareholders the possibility to veto its decisions. The board then has the right to negotiate with an acquirer on behalf of the shareholders and other stakeholders such as employees. This arrangement mitigates the coordination problem between small shareholders in the case of dispersed ownership and the agency problems of the other company's stakeholders. Also, due to its insider knowledge of the company's true value, the management is likely to be more successful in negotiating with the acquirer on takeover terms for the shareholders and other company's stakeholders. After the board completes negotiations with the acquirer and issues its recommendation, the shareholders are asked to approve or reject the managerial advice. Although this arrangement gives more flexibility to the target's management to act against bids that are potentially unfavorable for shareholders by setting up an anticipatory antitakeover strategy, there is also more opportunity for managers to pursue their own interests. Therefore, additional corporate governance devices should be introduced, such as strengthening the independence of the non-executive directors and using executive compensation contracts that align managerial interests with those of the shareholders.

The first solution effectively addresses the potential agency problems between target shareholders and management in the wake of a takeover. However, its weakness is that the defense tactics can only be applied once a bid has been received and not before receiving a bid. In contrast, the second solution provides management with the flexibility to prevent value-destroying takeovers ex ante. However, this mechanism may increase the agency problem between the target's management and shareholders. Both solutions are applied in the real world. The board neutrality principle is used mainly in the United Kingdom and most European countries, whereas the shareholder veto power principle is applied in the United States and some European countries such as the Netherlands. Germany has opted for a mix of the two.

Antitakeover Measures

The target company's management often has legitimate reasons to oppose a takeover bid and install antitakeover measures. One such reason is the target management's disagreement with the acquirer's intentions to restructure the company. For example, institutional raiders make many acquisitions that hunt for short-term excess gains by taking over companies and then reselling their individual assets at a higher price. These acquisitions are likely to damage the interests of the long-term–oriented shareholders of the target company; hence, undertaking defensive actions to prevent such takeovers may be a rational managerial response. The management of the target may also opt to oppose acquisitions by corporate acquirers if it believes that the proposed strategic plan underlying the acquisition is incompatible with the target company's own strategy. The use of antitakeover measures is also justified on the grounds that a takeover threat may demoralize corporate managers and directors, negatively affecting the company's investment and business development strategy. That is, managers may respond to the takeover market pressures by switching to short-term strategies to sustain growth, thereby forgoing beneficial long-term projects and investments.

The set of actions that companies employ to defend themselves against unwanted takeovers is vast. It includes but is not limited to introducing one or more poison pills, negotiating with an alternative "friendly" acquirer, also known as a "white knight," initiating a counter offer to purchase the acquirer's shares, making a major change in the capital structure, engaging in sell-offs or spin-offs, and restricting the voting rights and governance powers of shareholders. Substantial differences exist across jurisdictions in terms of the limitations with respect to these takeover defense actions. Some jurisdictions encourage companies to undertake antitakeover actions, while others set limits on when and how the actions can be applied. Some jurisdictions totally ban antitakeover actions. Some of these actions and their regulatory restrictions are discussed more fully below.

Poison Pills

A *poison pill* is a broad term used to define those types of takeover defense measures that effectively block an acquisition attempt or force the acquirer to pay a substantial premium to the target's shareholders. Besides their harmful effect on acquirers, poison pills may also harm the target's shareholders by causing dilution and devaluation of their shares. This typically happens after the takeover bid is successfully impeded and no other potential acquirers have interest in taking over the company.

One of the best-known poison pills is a shareholder rights plan that grants the incumbent target's shareholders the exclusive right to purchase a company's newly issued equity at a substantial discount. The right is conditional upon the acquisition of a certain percentage of shares by an outside investor. For example, a typical shareholder rights plan enables shareholders to exercise the right after an outside investor has acquired more than 15 percent of the target company's shares. In this case, the right-holders become eligible to purchase more company's shares at a lower-than-market price. An additional equity issue, in the wake of a takeover, dilutes the share block accumulated by the acquirer and makes the acquisition more costly and sometimes impossible. Therefore, the poison pill is considered a very effective antitakeover device.

Another poison pill device consists of "golden shares." A golden share grants a decisive vote to its holder to veto corporate decisions and overrule the voting outcome of all other shareholders. Golden shares are typically held by a government, and its veto power is implemented through clauses in the company's articles of incorporation. The veto power allows the government to interfere in major corporate actions when it believes that the actions are against the national interest. For example, when a foreign investor attempts to take control of a strategically important national company, the government may use its veto power to prevent such a takeover.

Poison pill devices may also involve the target company's employees, suppliers, and customers. For example, the target may grant its employees stock options that can be vested when control changes. Or employment contracts may include a so-called "golden parachute" clause granting an employee substantial benefits if employment is terminated as a result of a takeover. Target companies may also use poison pill tactics in order to prevent the acquirer from changing the company's business policy after the takeover. For example, targets may promise their customers a guaranteed refund if the company changes its service policy after an acquisition.

Poison pills in the form of shareholder rights plans are considered illegal in most jurisdictions around the world (e.g., the United Kingdom). However, they are commonly used in the United States, particularly for companies incorporated in Delaware. The widespread adoption of poison pills in the United States in the 1980s was a response to frequent incidences of takeovers by institutional raiders hunting for short-term gains. Regulators allowed managers to adopt poison pills at their own discretion whenever they considered such adoption necessary. Today, an increasing number of U.S. companies have amended their articles of incorporation to require management to get shareholders' ratification for the poison pill. Golden shares have been frequently employed to prevent unwanted acquisitions by the governments of many European countries such as France, Spain, and Germany. Today, the use of golden shares in Europe is declining due to the European court ruling on the legality of these devices as their use contradicts the principle of free capital circulation in the European Union.

Changes in Capital Structure and Asset Sell-Offs and Spin-Offs

Another way for companies to prevent a takeover is to make a major change in their capital or assets structure. For example, a company can take on larger debts and use the borrowed money to buy back its shares. Some companies may even initiate a full-scale leveraged buyout (LBO) to prevent an unwanted takeover by using the borrowed money to buy back all of their shares and go private. Higher leverage may make companies less attractive as takeover targets because acquirers would ultimately have to pay these debts. However, not every company can afford such defense tactics due to the limited access to and high costs of debt financing.

Alternatively, companies facing an unwanted takeover bid can avert it by increasing their market capitalization by issuing more equity, which makes it more expensive to take over the company. In many jurisdictions, corporate law sets restrictions on equity issues by companies subject to a takeover bid. For example, some jurisdictions such as India and Singapore require a shareholder vote to approve a defensive equity issuance. In jurisdictions such as the United States and Japan, a defensive equity issue typically does not even require a shareholder vote, conditional upon leaving the number of issued shares below the charter's authorization limit. Other jurisdictions such as the United Kingdom and Bulgaria forbid an equity issuance when a company faces a takeover bid.

Target companies can also avert unwanted takeover attempts by initiating mergers with other companies by means of share swaps. This way, the target company dilutes the acquirer's accumulated block so that it will need to bid for the entire merged company if it wants to get the desired assets of the target company. However, takeover regulation can grant shareholders the right to oppose such mergers. A common practice across jurisdictions is to require a supermajority shareholder authorization for a merger. In other words, a merger can take place only when the supermajority of the company's shareholders approves it. The definition of supermajority is set in national corporate laws and, thus, varies from country to country. For example, Germany and the United Kingdom require that 75 percent of voting shareholders ratify a merger. France and Japan require at least two-thirds. U.S. jurisdictions, including Delaware, require a simple majority of outstanding shares to approve a merger, which may easily translate into 70 percent or more of voting shares.

Assets sell-offs and corporate divisions (spin-offs) are takeover defense tactics inverse to mergers. Instead of expanding by merging with another company, a target company can also avert a takeover bid by selling off or spinning off some of its assets, without which it would appear less attractive to the acquirer. Since sell-offs and spin-offs are "smaller" transactions than most mergers, regulatory requirements with respect to these actions are also less strict. As many antitakeover measures, sell-offs and spin-offs may require shareholder approval if prescribed by statute. Some jurisdictions such as Germany and France design additional rules for sell-off and spin-off procedures, but in most jurisdictions, these rules are avoided, as in the United States and Japan. However, if successful, sell-offs and spin-offs may leave the target company worse off when compared to its pre-defense condition and hence may harm the target's long-term shareholders.

Voting Rights Restrictions
Deviation from the "one-share-one-vote" principle by means of voting restrictions such as shares with multiple voting rights, non-voting shares, and voting caps, represents effective antitakeover measures that discourage potential acquirers from making a takeover offer. Many jurisdictions allow the issue of non-voting shares that embed cash flow rights but no voting rights. Holders of such shares are eligible to receive all cash distributions initiated by the company but cannot participate in corporate decision making and governance. Other jurisdictions such as Scandinavian countries forbid non-voting shares but allow companies to issue multiple-class shares that each bear a different number of votes. For example, the votes from B-class shares in Sweden are typically one-tenth of the votes from A-class shares. Corporate takeovers are effectively prevented if the only shares traded on the stock exchange are those that bear no (or a minimum number of) votes, while the majority of voting shares are controlled by the management (as is frequently the case in the Netherlands) or by major shareholders (which often

occurs in Sweden). If differentiated voting rights facilitate the control by a few owners, takeovers are virtually impossible.

The potential benefit from introducing shares with differentiated voting rights is that more firms may seek a stock exchange listing and, hence, get access to additional financing sources. Company owners who value control are often reluctant to take their firm public if they risk losing control in the process. The possibility of issuing shares with multiple voting rights allows owners to minimize the risk of losing control. Hart (1988) argues that multiple voting shares are unlikely to hurt minority shareholders as the lack of control rights is compensated by the lower offer price at the flotation. However, in spite of these advantages and in contrast to the wide acceptance of non-voting shares, the use of shares with multiple voting rights is declining worldwide.

The use of voting caps is another way to impose restrictions on voting rights. Voting caps set a limit on the number of votes that a single shareholder can control, regardless of the size of his or her shareholding. For example, U.K. companies frequently employ a "voting by hands" procedure to authorize major corporate actions. According to this procedure, each shareholder is assigned one vote, no matter whether he or she has only one or millions of ordinary shares. The introduction of voting caps makes gaining control over the company without amendments to the company's articles of incorporation virtually impossible. This discourages potential acquirers from making takeover offers. Regulators see the benefits of allowing voting caps in their ability to curb the voting power of the large blockholder and hence reduce his or her influence on managerial actions, leaving more scope for minority shareholders to participate in corporate governance. This provides greater protection to minority shareholders. Nonetheless, many jurisdictions such as countries of the French legal origin have opted to abolish voting caps.

The effects of a deviation from the one-share-one-vote principle by means of dual class shares, non-voting shares, or voting caps can be undone if corporate law allows for a breakthrough rule. This rule enables a bidder who has accumulated a certain percentage of equity to break through the company's existing voting arrangements and exercise control as if the one-share-one-vote principle is upheld. For example, a recently acquired block consisting of a majority of non-voting rights may be converted into a voting majority by means of the breakthrough rule. The rule facilitates corporate restructuring as it allows the acquirer to bypass antitakeover devices and redistribute the takeover gains from the incumbent shareholders to the acquirer. Thus, the breakthrough rule makes transfers of control feasible that would otherwise have been impossible.

However, the breakthrough rule also has some major disadvantages. First, there is inconsistency between the breakthrough rule and the mandatory bid rule. The breakthrough rule yields control by circumventing the provisions in the articles of incorporation rather than by acquiring a certain percentage of voting shares. As such, the breakthrough rule violates the principle of shareholder decision making. Second, besides making value-increasing takeover bids possible, the breakthrough rule also facilitates takeover attempts by inefficient bidders who would otherwise be discouraged by the mandatory bid requirement. Third, the rule not only makes inefficient acquisitions possible but also frustrates attempts by the incumbent shareholders to prevent such bids. Finally, the main concern is that the breakthrough rule may induce the creation of even more complex voting rights restrictions via pyramids and cross-holdings (Bebchuk and Hart, 2002). Such voting structures are not covered by the breakthrough rule, which only targets voting caps, non-voting shares, and multiple-voting shares. Technically, potential shifts toward pyramidal ownership structures could disable most of the advantages of the breakthrough rule. Not surprisingly, only a few jurisdictions, such as Italy and some Eastern European countries, have adopted the breakthrough rule.

SUMMARY AND CONCLUSIONS

This chapter reviews takeover regulation in different jurisdictions around the world. The major regulatory provisions include the mandatory bid rule, the principle of equal treatment of shareholders, the squeeze-out and sell-out rules, ownership and control disclosure, board neutrality concerning the takeover bid, and restrictions regarding the use of takeover defense measures. Important differences exist across jurisdictions in terms of the adopted regulatory provisions. Such differences reflect the different priorities of the regulators with respect to developing the takeover market, mitigating conflicts of interest among the involved parties, and protecting minority shareholders.

In particular, European countries such as the United Kingdom have opted for takeover regulation that facilitates the market for corporate control. For example, the City Code on Takeovers and Mergers in the United Kingdom prohibits the target management from taking any actions against a takeover without shareholders' consent and limits the number of allowable antitakeover tactics to virtually none. In contrast, Delaware allows management to install antitakeover devices, such as a poison pill, following its own judgment and without asking for shareholders' consent. This effectively prevents any undesired takeover attempts by the target's management and, therefore, creates a barrier for the development of an efficient market for corporate control.

However, even jurisdictions that prohibit antitakeover measures and require the board's neutrality in relation to actual or threatening takeovers do not solely focus on the objective to promote the market for corporate control. This is because takeover regulation in these countries also includes provisions aimed at protecting target companies' shareholders against opportunistic acquirers. This restricts acquirers' freedom to structure their bids and makes acquisitions more costly. Such provisions include the mandatory bid, equal treatment requirements, and a squeeze-out right. While many jurisdictions in Europe and Asia make these provisions the core of their takeover codes, this is not the case in the United States.

DISCUSSION QUESTIONS

1. What are the corporate governance functions of takeover regulation?
2. What is the mandatory bid rule? What regulatory function does the mandatory rule perform?
3. What are the major takeover regulation provisions in the United States?
4. What are the major takeover regulation provisions in the United Kingdom?
5. Explain how specific takeover defense measures avert potential takeovers.

REFERENCES

Arlen, Jennifer H., and Eric L. Talley. 2003. *Unregulable Defenses and the Perils of Shareholder Choice*. Working Paper, New York University Law School.

Bagnoli, Mark, and Barton L. Lipman. 1988. "Successful Takeovers without Exclusion." *Review of Financial Studies* 1:1, 89–110.

Bebchuk, Lucian. 2002. "The Case Against Board Veto in Corporate Takeovers." *University of Chicago Law Review* 69: July, 973–1035.

Bebchuk, Lucian, and Oliver Hart. 2002. "A Threat to Dual-class Shares." *Financial Times*, May 31.

Becht, Marco, Patrick Bolton, and Ailsa Röell. 2003. "Corporate Governance and Control." In George Constantinides, Milton Harris, and René Stulz, eds. *The Handbook of the Economics of Finance*, 1–109. North-Holland: Elsevier.

Boehmer, Ekkehard. 2002. "Who Controls German Corporations?" In Joe McCahery, Piet Moerland, Theo Raaijmakers, and Luc Renneboog, eds. *Corporate Governance Regimes: Convergence and Diversity*, 268–286. Oxford: Oxford University Press.

Burkart, Mike. 1999. "Economics of Takeover Regulation." *SITE Working Paper* 99/06, Stockholm School of Economics.

Burkart, Mike, Denis Gromb, and Fausto Panunzi. 1997. "Large Shareholders, Monitoring, and the Value of the Firm." *Quarterly Journal of Economics* 112:3, 693–728.

Davies, Paul, and Klaus Hopt. 2004. "Control Transactions." In Renier Kraakman, Paul Davies, Henry Hansmann, Gerard Hertig, Klaus Hopt, Hideki Kanda, and Edward Rock, eds. *The Anatomy of Corporate Law*, 157–191. Oxford: Oxford University Press.

Goergen, Marc, Marina Martynova, and Luc Renneboog. 2005. "Corporate Governance Convergence: Evidence from Takeover Regulation Reforms in Europe." *Oxford Review of Economic Policy* 21:2: 243–268.

Grossman, Sanford. J., and Oliver Hart. 1980. "Takeover Bids, the Free-rider Problem, and the Theory of the Corporation." *Bell Journal of Economics* 11:1, 42–64.

Hart, Oliver. 1988. "On SEC's One-share-one-vote Decision." *Wall Street Journal*, July 14.

Hirshleifer, David, and Sheridan Titman. 1990. "Share Tendering Strategies and the Success of Hostile Takeover Bids." *Journal of Political Economy* 98:2, 295–324.

Holmstrom, Bengt, and Barry Nalebuff. 1990. "To the Raider Goes the Surplus: A Reexamination of the Free-rider Problem." *Journal of Economics and Management Strategy* 1:1, 37–62.

Jensen, Michael C. 1988. "Takeovers: Their Causes and Consequences." *Journal of Economic Perspectives* 2:1, 21–48.

Kyle, Albert S., and Jean-Luc Vila. 1991. "Noise Trading and Takeovers." *RAND Journal of Economics* 22:1, 54–71.

Martynova, Marina, and Luc Renneboog. 2008. "A Century of Corporate Takeovers: What Have We Learned and Where Do We Stand?" *Journal of Banking and Finance* 32:10, 2148–2177.

Maug, Ernst G. 2004. "Efficiency and Fairness in Minority Freezeouts: Takeovers, Overbidding, and the Freeze-in Problem." Available at http://papers.ssrn.com/sol3/papers.cfm?abstract_id=610582.

Shleifer, Andrei, and Robert Vishny. 1986. "Large Shareholder and Corporate Control." *Journal of Political Economy* 94:3, 461–488.

Yarrow, Greg. 1985. "Shareholder Protection, Compulsory Acquisition and the Takeover Process." *Journal of Industrial Economics* 34:1, 3–16.

ABOUT THE AUTHORS

Marina Martynova is an Associate at Cornerstone Research, the leading company in economic and financial litigation consulting in the United States. Before moving to the United States, Dr. Martynova held posts as an Assistant Professor of Finance at Sheffield University (United Kingdom) and a Research Fellow at Tilburg University (The Netherlands). She also participated in the European Commission research project "New Forms of Governance." Her expertise is in corporate finance and corporate governance. She specializes in mergers and acquisitions, leveraged financing, equity issues, financial and accounting reporting, corporate governance regulation, and applied econometrics. Her research has been published in highly ranked academic journals such as *Journal of Corporate Finance, Journal of Banking and Finance,* and *Oxford Review of Economic Policy.* Dr. Martynova has been invited to give presentations at numerous conferences and seminars including annual meetings of the American Finance Association and European Finance Association. She also acts as a referee for major journals in the field of finance. She holds a PhD in financial economics from Tilburg University

Luc Renneboog is Professor of Corporate Finance at Tilburg University and a research fellow at CentER and the European Corporate Governance Institute (ECGI, Brussels). He graduated from the Catholic University of Leuven with degrees in management engineering (MSc) and philosophy (BA), from the University of Chicago with an MBA, and from the London Business School with a PhD in financial economics. He held appointments at the University of Leuven and Oxford University, and visiting appointments at London Business School, University Paris-Dauphine, University of Venice, University of Cardiff, and HEC (Paris). He has published in the *Journal of Finance, Journal of Financial Intermediation, Journal of Law and Economics, Journal of Corporate Finance, Journal of Banking and Finance, Oxford Review of Economic Policy, Cambridge Journal of Economics,* and others. He has co-authored and edited several books on corporate governance, dividend policy, and venture capital with Oxford University Press and Elsevier. His research interests are corporate finance, corporate governance, takeovers, dividend policy, insider trading, law and economics, and the economics of art.

CHAPTER 4

Corporate Governance and M&As

FEI XIE
Assistant Professor of Finance, George Mason University

INTRODUCTION

Corporate governance and mergers and acquisitions (M&As) have been among the most fertile areas of finance research for more than 30 years. Multiple attempts have been made to summarize the two literatures at various stages of their development. For example, Jensen and Ruback (1983) and Andrade, Mitchell, and Stafford (2001) provide a synthesis of the M&A literature and Shleifer and Vishny (1997) present a review of the corporate governance literature. Rather than repeating much of the earlier work, this chapter surveys the research that falls at the intersection of these two broad literatures. Studies that fit this profile primarily address one or more of the following questions. First, do takeovers play a managerial disciplinary role, and does the threat of takeovers or the lack thereof affect the decision making by managers and the wealth of firm stakeholders? Second, when acquiring firms view M&As as major investments, what is the impact of various corporate governance mechanisms on the profitability of these transactions from the acquiring shareholders' perspective? Third, how are target shareholder gains from takeovers related to the incentives of target management? Fourth, is there any connection between the combined returns of acquiring and target shareholders and the corporate governance at the acquirer and target? This chapter is organized according to these four major themes.

Due to space constraints, this chapter is not meant to be exhaustive. Rather, it aims to discuss a representative set of relevant papers and to provide a clear and concise picture of the major issues and findings regarding the interplay of corporate governance and M&As. The papers referenced herein make important contributions to the literature, but they are not the only papers that do so. Those interested in delving into these topics in greater depth can easily find a wealth of additional interesting and relevant research.

M&As AS A MANAGERIAL DISCIPLINARY DEVICE

The diffuse ownership structure at large public corporations has the potential to generate agency conflicts between managers and shareholders, as the former do not bear the full costs of their actions while the latter face substantial coordination and free-rider problems in collectively exercising their control rights (Berle and Means, 1932; Jensen and Meckling, 1976). As a result, managers enjoy considerable discretion over corporate decision making, and they often operate firms in ways that benefit themselves at the expense of shareholders. Corporate governance is a collection of mechanisms that creates incentives for managers to make value-maximizing decisions and ensures that capital providers receive a fair return on their investments (Shleifer and Vishny, 1997). One such mechanism, as first argued by Maris (1963) and Manne (1965), is the market for corporate control. The idea is that managerial slack or poor decision making lowers a firm's value, presenting profit opportunities for other firms to acquire the ailing company and restore value by eliminating managerial inefficiencies.

A key prediction of this argument is that underperforming firms are more likely to become targets of M&As of a disciplinary nature. Various studies test this prediction by examining targets' premerger stock returns and operating perfor-mance, but the evidence has been mixed. Some researchers document significant underperformance by targets (e.g., Smiley, 1976; Asquith, 1983), while others re-port results that are either insignificant or contradictory (e.g., Dodd and Ruback, 1977; Malatesta, 1983; Martin and McConnell, 1991; Kini, Kracaw, and Mian, 1995; Agrawal and Jaffe, 2003). The prediction finds more consistent support in studies focusing on premerger target firm value. For example, Hasbrouck (1985), Palepu (1986), Morck, Shleifer, and Vishny (1988), and Barber, Palmer, and Wallace (1995) show that takeover targets are associated with significantly lower Tobin's q. Berger and Ofek (1996) and Graham, Lemmon, and Wolf (2002) find that firms suffer-ing greater value losses due to diversification are more likely to become takeover targets. Berger and Ofek also show that these firms are more likely to be targets of bust-up takeovers. Rather than focusing on aggregate performance measures, Mitchell and Lehn (1990) take a different approach by examining whether the mar-ket for corporate control disciplines managers engaging in activities that reduce shareholder value. They find that firms making shareholder value–destroying ac-quisitions are more likely to subsequently become takeover targets themselves, consistent with an ex post settling-up function performed by the market for cor-porate control.

Another implication of the market for corporate control as a managerial disci-plinary device is that firms that are more insulated from takeovers are subject to more agency conflicts between managers and shareholders. This occurs because managers do not have to worry as much about being displaced for their ques-tionable decision making and poor firm performance. The passage of second- and third-generation antitakeover legislation by various states in the 1980s provides re-searchers with a natural experiment to investigate the managerial incentive effects of takeover threats. Evidence shows that firms protected by these state antitakeover laws substantially reduce their leverage ratios (Garvey and Hanka, 1999); pay their chief executive officers (CEOs) significantly higher compensation, especially in the absence of an outside blockholder-director (Bertrand and Mullainathan, 1999); raise employee wages; slow down the pace of old plant closing and new plant opening; and experience declines in operating performance (Bertrand and Mullainathan, 2003). Collectively, these findings suggest that managers protected from takeover threats extract more private benefits and pursue a "quiet life." The findings also offer at least a partial explanation for why firms experience significantly negative stock price reactions when the states where they are incorporated pass antitakeover laws (Pound, 1987; Karpoff and Malatesta, 1989; Szewczyk and Tsetsekos, 1992).

Firm-level takeover defenses appear to have similar adverse effects on managerial incentives. The adoptions of antitakeover charter amendments by firms are followed by significant increases in CEO compensation (Borokhovich, Brunarski, and Parrino, 1997) and decreases in research and development (R&D) expenditures (Meulbroek, Mitchell, Mulherin, Netter, and Poulsen, 1990).

More recent research in this literature brings together firm-level and state-level takeover defenses. In their pioneering study, Gompers, Ishii, and Metrick (2003) construct a shareholder-rights index based on 24 antitakeover provisions (ATPs) using data provided by the Investor Responsibility Research Center (IRRC, now part of RiskMetrics). The value of the index is equal to the number of ATPs a firm has. In a sample of 1,500 large companies, they find that during the 1990s, an investment strategy that buys stocks of firms with an index value in the bottom 10 percent and sells stocks of firms with an index value in the top 10 percent generates an abnormal return of 8.5 percent per year. Gompers et al. also find that firms with fewer ATPs are associated with higher firm value, higher profits, higher sales growth, lower capital expenditures, and fewer corporate acquisitions made. The authors examine several alternative explanations for their evidence and do not find that either reverse causality or an omitted variable bias drives their results. Gompers et al. (p.131) conclude that their findings support the hypothesis that ATPs generate agency costs between manager and shareholders "through some combination of inefficient investment, reduced operational efficiency, or self-dealing."

Bebchuk, Cohen, and Ferrell (2009) refine the Gompers et al. (2003) index by focusing on six ATPs that they argue are the most effective in fending off unsolicited takeover attempts. This subset of ATPs includes staggered boards, limits to shareholder bylaw amendments, supermajority requirements for mergers, supermajority requirements for charter amendments, poison pills, and golden parachutes. Bebchuk et al. show that an index based on these six ATPs displays a stronger association with firm value and abnormal stock returns, while an index based on the other 18 ATPs is not significantly related to them. Bebchuk and Cohen (2005) also single out one important ATP, namely, staggered boards, and find that firms with staggered boards have lower firm value and poorer operating performance.

The long-run abnormal return evidence documented by these early investigations becomes the subject of several subsequent studies. Core, Guay, and Rusticus (2006) find that although firms with more ATPs have poorer operating performance, the market does not appear to be surprised as indicated by insignificant analyst earnings forecast errors and earnings announcement returns. This leads the authors to question whether the ATPs actually drive the long-run abnormal returns. Johnson, Moorman, and Sorescu (2009) find that high-index firms and low-index firms are concentrated in different industries. Once they take into account the industry clustering differences, the long-run stock return differential between high-index and low-index firms disappears. Giroud and Mueller (2008), on the other hand, show that high-index firms underperform low-index firms in noncompetitive industries, precisely where corporate governance is expected to play a meaningful role. They also find that analyst earnings forecasts exhibit significant errors for firms operating in non-competitive industries, suggesting that the market indeed is surprised by the poor performance of high-index firms in these industries. The within-industry nature of their evidence also suggests that different industry clustering patterns between high- and low-ATP firms are unlikely to be fully responsible for the long-run return differential.

The relation between ATPs and firm value is also a topic of much debate, though to a lesser extent than the long-run abnormal return evidence. Lehn, Patro, and Zhao (2007) argue that the causation runs from valuation to ATPs, as lower valued firms are more likely to adopt takeover defenses to preserve control. They find that the previously documented relationship between firm value and ATPs for firms during the 1990s disappears once they control for firms' valuation levels in the 1980s when many firms adopted ATPs. In contrast, Chi (2005) explores the relationship between within-firm time-series variations in firm value and ATPs and finds that changes in ATPs lead to changes in firm value, but not vice versa. The author also finds that the negative correlation between ATPs and firm value persists in firm fixed-effect regressions that control for time-invariant firm-specific factors unobservable to econometricians.

More fruitful research efforts focus on identifying channels through which ATPs cause lower firm value. Dittmar and Mahrt-Smith (2007) find that the stock market assigns a lower value to a firm's cash holdings if the firm has more ATPs. They interpret their evidence as suggesting that managers insulated from takeover threats tend to abuse corporate cash holdings in order to secure private benefits. Masulis, Wang, and Xie (2007) examine M&As, a specific type of major corporate investment decisions, and find that acquirers with more ATPs experience significantly lower announcement-period abnormal returns. Their results support the hypothesis that managers protected by more ATPs face weaker discipline from the market for corporate control and thus are more likely to indulge in empire-building acquisitions that destroy shareholder value. The authors also implement additional experimental designs to rule out the possibility that reverse causality or omitted variables drive their results.

Some researchers move away from the focus on shareholders and examine how ATPs affect the welfare of bondholders. Klock, Mansi, and Maxwell (2005) and Cremers, Nair, and Wei (2007) find that ATPs reduce a firm's cost of debt, suggesting that bondholders benefit from a lower probability of borrowing firms becoming takeover targets. This evidence, however, is somewhat surprising, considering that target bondholders, on average, experience significant wealth increases in M&As (Billett, King, and Mauer, 2004).

CORPORATE GOVERNANCE AND ACQUIRER WEALTH EFFECTS

Rather than being viewed as part of a comprehensive corporate governance system, M&As can also be considered as major corporate investments and are among the largest expenditures that corporations make. As such, they have the potential to heighten the conflicts of interest between managers and shareholders inherent in large public corporations. As the literature documents, managers do not always make shareholder value–maximizing acquisitions and they sometimes extract private benefits at the expense of shareholders. The free cash flow hypothesis in Jensen (1986) argues that managers realize large personal gains from empire building. The hypothesis predicts that firms with abundant cash flows, but few profitable investment opportunities, are more likely to make value-destroying acquisitions rather than returning the excess cash flow to shareholders. Lang, Stulz, and Walkling (1991) and Harford (1999) test this hypothesis and report supportive evidence, with the former focusing on firms' excess cash flows and the latter focusing on excess cash holdings. Morck, Shleifer, and Vishny (1990) identify several types of acquisitions (including diversifying acquisitions and acquisitions of high growth targets) that can yield substantial benefits to managers, while at the same time hurting shareholders. Recent studies by Bliss and Rosen (2001), Grinstein and Hribar (2004), and Harford and Li (2007) all document significant wealth increases for acquiring CEOs even when acquiring shareholders end up losing value.

Given the enormous potential for agency conflicts, a long line of research examines whether better corporate governance can improve managerial incentive and lead to improved decision making in M&As. These studies are organized into different categories based on the governance mechanism they investigate.

THE MARKET FOR CORPORATE CONTROL

As mentioned earlier, Masulis et al. (2007) show that acquirers protected by more ATPs experience significantly lower abnormal return around acquisition announcements, suggesting that managers more insulated from the discipline by the market for corporate control are more likely to engage in empire-building acquisitions that destroy shareholder value. In a separate study, Masulis, Wang, and Xie (2009) examine the dual-class ownership structure as another governance arrangement that disrupts the function of the market for corporate control. Since corporate insiders at dual-class companies typically own a majority of the voting rights, they are effectively shielded from takeover threats. As such, corporate insiders are apt to indulge in shareholder value–reducing activities without fearing punishment by the market for corporate control. Consistent with this conjecture, the authors find that acquisitions made by dual-class firms generate significantly lower shareholder value and that dual-class firms are less likely to withdraw from acquisitions to which the stock market reacts negatively.

PRODUCT MARKET COMPETITION

Leibenstein (1966) and Hart (1983) argue that product market competition has a disciplinary effect on managerial behavior. Shleifer and Vishny (1997) suggest that product market competition is perhaps the most effective mechanism to eliminate managerial inefficiency. Managers of firms operating in more competitive industries are less likely to shirk or put valuable corporate resources into inefficient uses. This is because the margin for error is thin in these industries and competitors can quickly exploit any missteps by managers, seriously jeopardizing firms' prospects for survival and managers' prospects for keeping their jobs. Building on this intuition, Masulis et al. (2007) hypothesize that firms in more competitive industries make better acquisitions. They measure an industry's product market competition by the industry's Herfindahl index and its median ratio of selling expenses to sales as a proxy for product uniqueness (Titman and Wessels, 1988). Industries with lower Herfindahl indexes and lower product uniqueness are more competitive. Consistent with their hypothesis, the authors find that indeed acquirers operating in more competitive industries experience higher announcement-period abnormal returns.

BOARD CHARACTERISTICS

Monitoring by the board of directors is an important internal control mechanism. Prior research identifies various board attributes that affect the monitoring effectiveness of boards including board independence (Weisbach, 1988), board size (Yermack, 1996), CEO/chairman duality (Core, Holthausen, and Larcker. 1999), busyness of independent directors (Fich and Shivdasani, 2006), and social ties between independent directors and CEOs (Hwang and Kim, 2009). Byrd and Hickman (1992) focus on board independence and find that acquirers with independent boards experience higher announcement-period abnormal returns. Masulis et al. (2007) examine the first three characteristics and find that the stock market reacts more favorably to acquisitions made by firms that separate the positions of CEO and chairman of the board. Schmidt (2009) argues that while social ties compromise director independence, they improve information flow between management and directors and enhance board advisory function. He finds that acquirers benefit from director-CEO social ties when board advisory service is more important and suffer from these social ties when board monitoring is more important.

MANAGERIAL EQUITY INCENTIVES

Equity ownership and well-designed executive compensation plans can help align the interests of managers with those of shareholders and discourage managers from making shareholder value–destroying acquisitions. Consistent with this argument, Lewellen, Loderer, and Rosenfeld (1985) find that acquirer returns are increasing in acquiring managers' stock ownership. Datta, Iskandar-Datta, and Raman (2001) find a significantly positive correlation between acquirer returns and the percentage of acquirer CEO annual compensation that is equity based. However, neither measure enters significantly in the acquirer return regressions reported by Masulis et al. (2007).

INSTITUTIONAL OWNERSHIP

Institutional investors have the potential to perform management oversight, as their large ownership stakes allow them to internalize the oversight costs and fill the monitoring void left by atomistic shareholders due to free-rider problems and coordination difficulties. As such, firms with significant institutional holdings will be less likely to make shareholder value–reducing acquisitions. However, institutional investors sometimes may not have the incentive to monitor corporate managers, either due to their short investment horizons or to their business ties with firms (Davis and Kim, 2007). This implies that not all institutional investors can be expected to rein in empire-building managers and improve the quality of firms' acquisition decisions. Consistent with these arguments, Chen, Harford, and Li (2007) show that only concentrated ownership by independent long-term institutions is associated with better postacquisition performance, and the presence of these institutional investors increases the probability that firms will withdraw takeover bids that the stock market judges harshly.

MONITORING BY INDIVIDUAL BLOCKHOLDERS

Shleifer and Vishny (1986) argue that the presence of large shareholders can mitigate the agency problems between managers and shareholders. This is because investors holding a large block of shares have the incentive to monitor the managers, overcoming the free-rider problem plaguing companies with a diffuse ownership structure. For example, Denis and Serrano (1996) find outside blockholders facilitate management turnover and restructurings at targets of unsuccessful control contests; Core et al. (1999) find that CEO compensation is lower at firms with outside blockholders; and Bertrand and Mullainathan (2001) discover that firms with large shareholders pay their CEOs less for luck. However, in their study of corporate governance and acquirer returns, Masulis et al. (2007) fail to find any significant effect of outside blockholder-directors, defined as nonofficer directors holding at least 5 percent of acquirer stock.

LEVERAGE AND CREDITOR CONTROL

Leverage is an important governance mechanism since higher debt levels help reduce future free cash flows and limit managerial discretion. Leverage also provides incentives for managers to improve firm performance. This occurs because managers have to cede significant control to creditors and often lose their jobs if their firms violate debt covenants or fall into financial distress (Roberts and Sufi, 2009; Gilson, 1989, 1990). These arguments predict that firms with higher leverage are less likely to make poor acquisition decisions. Some support exists for this conjecture, as Masulis et al. (2007), among others, find that leverage in general has a positive effect on acquirer returns, and the effect is statistically significant in some specifications.

CORPORATE GOVERNANCE AND TARGET WEALTH EFFECTS

In M&As, target shareholders, on average, receive a substantial premium for their shares. This stands in sharp contrast to acquiring shareholders who typically experience little or negative abnormal returns around acquisition announcements (Andrade et al., 2001). As a result, the effect of corporate governance on shareholder value at the target firm has not received as much academic interest as that on the acquirer's side. However, conflicts of interest arise between target managers and shareholders as target managers facing potential displacement from their positions may either resist shareholder value–enhancing takeover attempts or accept lower takeover premiums in exchange for personal benefits from acquirers. These possibilities leave room for corporate governance to play a meaningful role in protecting target shareholders from self-serving behaviors of managers.

Stulz, Walkling, and Song (1990) examine the effect of target ownership distribution on the division of acquisition gains between acquirers and targets. They find that in a sample of multiple-bidder takeover contests, target gains are positively correlated to target management ownership, consistent with the argument that managers with higher equity ownership are more likely to act in the best interest of shareholders. Cotter, Shivdasani, and Zenner (1997) focus on independent directors and find that target shareholder gains in tender offers are significantly higher when target boards comprise a majority of independent directors, suggesting that independent boards indeed look after the best interests of shareholders.

CORPORATE GOVERNANCE AND ACQUIRER-TARGET COMBINED RETURNS

Studies that fall under this category address the benefits of changes in control, which is one of the most important sources of synergistic gains from M&As. The question being investigated is whether acquisitions of poorly managed targets by well-managed bidders create more value than others. Early studies of this prediction such as Lang, Stulz, and Walkling (1989) and Servaes (1991) present supportive evidence—that the synergy of an acquisition is increasing in the bidder's Tobin's q and decreasing in the target's Tobin's q—with the premise that q can be interpreted as a measure of how well a firm is run. However, results from recent academic endeavors suggest otherwise. For example, Bhagat, Dong, Hirshleifer, and Noah (2005) find that the bidder's q has a negative effect, while the target's q has no impact on acquisition synergy. Moeller, Schlingemann, and Stulz (2004) and Dong, Hirshleifer, Richardson, and Teoh (2006) find that the bidder's q and its close surrogates, such as the market-to-book ratio, have negative effects on bidder returns.

In light of the conflicting evidence, the two studies take a different approach by employing a measure that is more fundamental than Tobin's q to capture how well a firm is managed. Wang and Xie (2009) use firm-level corporate governance metrics as a proxy for the strength of managerial incentives or the severity of agency problems. They argue that in a merger or acquisition that is accompanied by a change in control, the acquirer's corporate governance will apply to the combined company, in effect replacing the target's governance environment. Therefore, after the transaction, managers operating under the acquirer's governance scheme will control the target's assets. When the acquirer has stronger corporate governance than the target, the change in control will result in an improvement in corporate governance at the target. Such an acquisition leads to a better use of target assets and creates more value. The reverse is true when the acquirer has weaker governance than the target. Therefore, Wang and Xie posit that the synergy or the total value generated by an acquisition is an increasing function of the difference in the corporate governance quality between the acquirer and the target. They find strong support for their hypothesis in a sample of domestic acquisitions by U.S. firms using both announcement-period abnormal returns and operating performance change as measures of takeover gains.

Similarly, Bris and Carbolis (2008) link country-level corporate governance to the wealth effects of cross-border M&A transactions. They use the takeover premium as a measure of efficiency gains and find that it is increasing (decreasing) in the acquirer (target) country's investor protection and accounting standards; the pattern holds only when the target company's nationality changes. Eckbo and Thorburn (2000) and Moeller and Schlingemann (2005) find that acquirers perform significantly worse in cross-border deals than in domestic deals.

SUMMARY AND CONCLUSIONS

This chapter reviews the literature that falls at the intersection of corporate governance and M&As. When viewed as manifestations of the actions by the market for corporate control, M&As have powerful incentive effects on managers and valuation effects on shareholders and bondholders. In general, the extant evidence suggests that a lack of takeover threats exacerbates the agency problems between managers and shareholders, resulting in more managerial slack, poor decision making, and reduced shareholder value. Bondholders, however, appear to welcome a lower exposure to takeovers.

When viewed as either major corporate investments from the acquirers' perspective or important control events from the targets' perspective, M&As often pit managers' interests against those of shareholders. As such, various corporate governance mechanisms, including pressure from the takeover and product markets, board monitoring, institutional investors, managerial equity ownership, and debt, all could potentially impact shareholder gains from M&A transactions. The tenor of the evidence on this issue is that shareholders benefit more when their firms have better corporate governance in place (either internal or external) to protect them against self-serving managerial behavior.

On a macro level, M&As are also an important mechanism to allocate resources to their most efficient uses. Research shows that efficiency improvement or synergistic gains from these transactions are determined by, among other things, the corporate governance difference between acquirers and targets, as acquisitions of poorly governed firms by well-governed firms tend to generate the most value for target and acquirer shareholders combined.

DISCUSSION QUESTIONS

1. Most studies on corporate governance and M&As are based on domestic transactions involving U.S. companies. As a result, the investigations have been largely limited to the effects of firm-level corporate governance mechanisms on acquisition performance. Given the increasingly global nature of M&As, variations of country-level corporate governance will come into play. What are the potential interactions between firm-level and country-level corporate governance in M&As?

2. What are the likely impacts of corporate governance on cross-border acquisitions?

3. Why is there not stronger evidence on the effect of managerial equity incentives on acquisition performance?

4. What are the implications of the financial crisis of 2008 to 2009 for corporate governance and M&As?

REFERENCES

Agrawal, Anup, and Jeffery F. Jaffe. 2003. "Do Takeover Targets Under-perform? Evidence from Operating and Stock Returns." *Journal of Financial and Quantitative Analysis* 38:4, 721–746.

Andrade, Gregor, Mark Mitchell, and Erik Stafford. 2001. "New Evidence and Perspectives on Mergers." *Journal of Economic Perspectives* 15:2, 103–120.

Asquith, Paul. 1983. "Merger Bids, Uncertainty, and Stockholder Returns." *Journal of Financial Economics* 11:1–4, 51–83.

Barber, Brad M., Donald Palmer, and James Wallace. 1995. "Determinants of Conglomerate and Predatory Acquisitions: Evidence from the 1960s." *Journal of Corporate Finance* 1:3–4, 283–318.

Bebchuk, Lucian A., and Alma Cohen. 2005. "The Costs of Entrenched Boards." *Journal of Financial Economics* 78:2, 409–433.

Bebchuk, Lucian A., Alma Cohen, and Allen Ferrell. 2009. "What Matters in Corporate Governance?" *Review of Financial Studies* 22:2, 783–827.

Berger, Philip G., and Eli Ofek. 1996. "Bustup Takeovers of Value-Destroying Diversified Firms." *Journal of Finance* 51:4, 1175–1200.

Berle, Adolph A., and Gardiner C. Means. 1932. *The Modern Corporation and Private Property*. New York: Macmillian.

Bertrand, Marianne, and Sendhil Mullainathan. 1999. "Corporate Governance and Executive Pay: Evidence from Takeover Legislation." Working Paper, University of Chicago and Harvard University.

Bertrand, Marianne, and Sendhil Mullainathan. 2001. "Are CEOs Rewarded for Luck? The Ones Without Principals Are." *Quarterly Journal of Economics* 116:3, 901–932.

Bertrand, Marianne, and Sendhil Mullainathan. 2003. "Enjoying the Quiet Life? Corporate Governance and Managerial Preferences." *Journal of Political Economy* 111:5, 1043–1075.

Bhagat, Sanjay, Ming Dong, David A. Hirshleifer, and Robert B. Noah. 2005. "Do Tender Offers Create Value? New Methods and Evidence." *Journal of Financial Economics* 76:1, 3–60.

Billett, Matthew T., Dolly King, and David C. Mauer. 2004. "Bondholder Wealth Effects in Mergers and Acquisitions: New Evidence from the 1980s and 1990s." *Journal of Finance* 59:1, 107–135.

Bliss, Richard T., and Richard J. Rosen. 2001. "CEO Compensation and Bank Mergers." *Journal of Financial Economics* 61:1, 107–138.

Borokhovich, Kenneth A., Kelly R. Brunarski, and Robert Parrino. 1997. "CEO Contracting and Antitakeover Amendments." *Journal of Finance* 52:4, 1495–1517.

Bris, Arturo, and Christos Carbolis. 2008. "The Value of Investor Protection: Firm Evidence from Cross-Border Mergers." *Review of Financial Studies* 21:2, 605–648.

Byrd, John W., and Kent A. Hickman. 1992. "Do Outside Directors Monitor Managers? Evidence from Tender Offer Bids." *Journal of Financial Economics* 32:2, 195–221.

Chen, Xia, Jarrad Harford, and Kai Li. 2007. "Monitoring: Which Institutions Matter?" *Journal of Financial Economics* 86:2, 279–305.

Chi, Jianxin. 2005. "Understanding the Endogeneity between Firm Value and Shareholder Rights." *Financial Management* 34:4, 65–76.

Core, John E., Wayne R. Guay, and Tjomme O. Rusticus. 2006. "Does Weak Governance Cause Weak Stock Returns? An Examination of Firm Operating Performance and Investors' Expectations." *Journal of Finance* 61:2, 655–687.

Core, John E., Robert W. Holthausen, and David F. Larcker. 1999. "Corporate Governance, Chief Executive Officer Compensation, and Firm Performance." *Journal of Financial Economics* 51:3, 371–406.

Cotter, James F., Anil Shivdasani, and Marc Zenner. 1997. "Do Independent Directors Enhance Target Shareholder Wealth During Tender Offers?" *Journal of Financial Economics* 43:2, 195–218.

Cremers, Martijn K. J., Vinay B. Nair, and Chenyang Wei. 2007. "Governance Mechanisms and Bond Prices." *Review of Financial Studies* 20:5, 1359–1388.

Datta, Sudip, Mai Iskandar-Datta, and Kartik Raman. 2001. "Executive Compensation and Corporate Acquisition Decisions." *Journal of Finance* 56:6, 2299–2336.

Davis. Gerald F., E. Han Kim. 2007. "Business Ties and Proxy Voting by Mutual Funds." *Journal of Financial Economics* 85:2, 552–570.

Denis, David J., and Jan M. Serrano. 1996. "Active Investors and Management Turnover Following Unsuccessful Control Contests." *Journal of Financial Economics* 40:2, 239–266.

Dittmar, Amy, and Jan Mahrt-Smith. 2007. "Corporate Governance and the Value of Cash Holdings." *Journal of Financial Economics* 83:3, 599–634.

Dodd, Peter, and Richard Ruback. 1977. "Tender Offers and Stockholder Returns: An Empirical Analysis." *Journal of Financial Economics* 5:3, 351–374.

Dong, Ming, David A. Hirshleifer, Scott A. Richardson, and Siew Hong Teoh. 2006. "Does Investor Misvaluation Drive the Takeover Market?" *Journal of Finance* 61:2, 725–762.

Eckbo, B. Espen, and Karin S. Thorburn. 2000. "Gains to Bidder Firms Revisited: Domestic and Foreign Acquisitions in Canada." *Journal of Financial and Quantitative Analysis* 35:1, 1–25.

Fich, Eliezer M., and Anil Shivdasani. 2006. "Are Busy Boards Effective Monitors?" *Journal of Finance* 61:2, 689–724.

Garvey, Gerald T., and Gordon Hanka. 1999. "Capital Structure and Corporate Control: The Effect of State Antitakeover Laws on Firm Leverage." *Journal of Finance* 54:2, 519–546.

Gilson, Stuart C. 1989. "Management Turnover and Financial Distress." *Journal of Financial Economics* 25:2, 241–262.

Gilson, Stuart C. 1990. "Bankruptcy, Boards, Banks, and Blockholders: Evidence on Changes in Corporate Ownership and Control When Firms Default." *Journal of Financial Economics* 27:2, 355–387.

Giroud, Xavier, and Holger M. Mueller. 2008. "Corporate Governance, Product Market Competition, and Equity Prices." Working Paper, New York University.

Gompers, Paul A., Joy Ishii, and Andrew Metrick. 2003. "Corporate Governance and Equity Prices." *Quarterly Journal of Economics* 118:1, 107–155.

Graham, John R., Michael L. Lemmon, and Jack G. Wolf. 2002. "Does Corporate Diversification Destroy Value?" *Journal of Finance* 57:2, 695–720.

Grinstein, Yaniv, and Paul Hribar. 2004. "CEO Compensation and Incentives: Evidence from M&A Bonuses." *Journal of Financial Economics* 73:1, 119–143.

Harford, Jarrad. 1999. "Corporate Cash Reserves and Acquisitions." *Journal of Finance* 54:6, 1969–1997.

Harford, Jarrad, and Kai Li. 2007. "Decoupling CEO Wealth and Firm Performance: The Case of Acquiring CEOs." *Journal of Finance* 62:2, 917–949.

Hart, Oliver D. 1983. "The Market Mechanism as an Incentive Scheme." *Bell Journal of Economics* 14:2, 366–382.

Hasbrouck, Joel. 1985. "The Characteristics of Takeover Targets: Q and Other Measures." *Journal of Banking and Finance* 9:3, 351–362.

Hwang, Byoung-Hyoun, and Seoyoung Kim. 2009. "It Pays to Have Friends." *Journal of Financial Economics* 93:1, 138–158.

Jensen, Michael C. 1986. "Agency Costs of Free Cash Flow, Corporate Finance, and Takeovers." *American Economic Review* 76:2, 323–329.

Jensen, Michael C., and William H. Meckling. 1976. "Theory of the Firm: Managerial Behavior, Agency Costs, and Ownership Structure." *Journal of Financial Economics* 3:4, 305–360.

Jensen, Michael C., and Richard S. Ruback. 1983. "The Market for Corporate Control: The Scientific Evidence." *Journal of Financial Economics* 11:1–4, 5–50.

Johnson, Shane A., Theodore Moorman, and Sorin Sorescu. 2009. "A Reexamination of Corporate Governance and Equity Prices." *Review of Financial Studies* 22:11, 4753–4786.

Karpoff, Jonathan M., and Paul H. Malatesta. 1989. "The Wealth Effects of Second-Generation State Takeover Legislation." *Journal of Financial Economics* 25:2, 291–322.

Kini, Omesh, William Kracaw, and Shehzad Mian. 1995. "Corporate Takeovers, Firm Performance and Board Composition." *Journal of Corporate Finance* 1:3–4, 383–412.

Klock, Mark S., Sattar A. Mansi, and William F. Maxwell. 2005. "Does Corporate Governance Matter to Bondholders? *Journal of Financial and Quantitative Analysis* 40:4. 693–719.

Lang, Larry H. P., René M. Stulz, and Ralph A. Walkling. 1989. "Managerial Performance, Tobin's Q, and the Gains from Successful Tender Offers." *Journal of Financial Economics* 24:1, 137–154.

Lang, Larry H. P., René M. Stulz, and Ralph A. Walkling. 1991. "A Test of the Free Cash Flow Hypothesis: The Case of Bidder Returns." *Journal of Financial Economics* 29:2, 315–336.

Lehn, Kenneth, Sukesh Patro, and Mengxin Zhao. 2007. "Governance Indices and Valuation Multiples: Which Causes Which?" *Journal of Corporate Finance* 13:5, 907–928.

Leibenstein, Harvey. 1966. "Allocative Efficiency vs. 'X-efficiency'." *American Economic Review* 56:3, 392–415.

Lewellen, Wilbur, Claudio Loderer, and Ahron Rosenfeld. 1985. "Merger Decisions and Executive Stock Ownership in Acquiring Firms." *Journal of Accounting and Economics* 7:1–3, 209–231.

Malatesta, Paul H. 1983. "The Wealth Effect of Merger Activity and the Objective Functions of Merging Firms." *Journal of Financial Economics* 11:1–4, 155–182.

Manne, Henry G. 1965. "Mergers and the Market for Corporate Control." *Journal of Political Economy* 73:2, 110–120.

Maris, Robin. 1963. "A Model of the 'Managerial' Enterprise." *Quarterly Journal of Economics* 77:2, 185–209.

Martin, Kenneth J., and John J. McConnell. 1991. "Corporate Performance, Corporate Takeovers, and Management Turnover." *Journal of Finance* 46:2, 671–688.

Masulis, Ronald W., Cong Wang, and Fei Xie. 2007. "Corporate Governance and Acquirer Returns." *Journal of Finance* 62:4, 1851–1889.

Masulis, Ronald W., Cong Wang, and Fei Xie. 2009. "Agency Problems at Dual-class Companies." *Journal of Finance* 64:4, 1697–1727.

Meulbroek, Lisa K., Mark L. Mitchell, J. Harold Mulherin, Jeffry M. Netter, and Annette B. Poulsen. 1990. "Shark Repellents and Managerial Myopia: An Empirical Test." *Journal of Political Economy* 98:5, 1108–1117.

Mitchell, Mark L., and Kenneth Lehn. 1990. "Do Bad Bidders Make Good Targets?" *Journal of Political Economy* 98:2, 372–398.

Moeller, Sara B., and Frederik P. Schlingemann. 2005. "Global Diversification and Bidder Gains: A Comparison between Cross-Border and Domestic Acquisitions." *Journal of Banking and Finance* 29:3, 533–564.

Moeller, Sara B., Frederik P. Schlingemann, and René M. Stulz. 2004. "Firm Size and the Gains from Acquisitions." *Journal of Financial Economics* 73:2, 201–228.

Morck, Randall, Andrei Shleifer, and Robert W. Vishny. 1988. "Characteristics of Targets of Hostile and Friendly Takeovers." In Alan J. Auerbach (ed.), *Corporate Takeovers: Causes and Consequences*, 101–129. Chicago: University of Chicago Press.

Morck, Randall, Andrei Shleifer, and Robert W. Vishny. 1990. "Do Managerial Objectives Drive Bad Acquisitions?" *Journal of Finance* 45:1, 31–48.

Palepu, Krishna G. 1986. "Predicting Takeover Targets: A Methodological and Empirical Analysis." *Journal of Accounting and Economics* 8:1, 3–35.

Pound, John. 1987. "The Effects of Antitakeover Amendments on Takeover Activity: Some Direct Evidence." *Journal of Law and Economics* 30:2, 353–367.

Roberts, Michael R., and Amir Sufi. 2009. "Control Rights and Capital Structure: An Empirical Investigation." *Journal of Finance* 64:4, 1657–1695.

Schmidt, Breno. 2009. "Costs and Benefits of 'Friendly' Boards during Mergers and Acquisitions." Working Paper, Emory University.

Servaes, Henri. 1991. "Tobin's Q and the Gains from Takeovers." *Journal of Finance* 46:1, 409–419.

Shleifer, Andrei, and Robert W. Vishny. 1986. "Large Shareholders and Corporate Control." *Journal of Political Economy* 94:3, 461–488.

Shleifer, Andrei, and Robert W. Vishny. 1997. "A Survey of Corporate Governance." *Journal of Finance* 52:2, 737–783.

Smiley, Robert. 1976. "Tender Offers, Transaction Costs and the Theory of the Firm." *Review of Economics and Statistics* 58:1, 22–32.

Stulz, René M., Ralph A. Walkling, and Moon H. Song. 1990. "The Distribution of Target Ownership and the Division of Gains in Successful Takeovers." *Journal of Finance* 45:3, 817–834.

Szewczyk, Samuel H., and George P. Tsetsekos. 1992. "State Intervention in the Market for Corporate Control: The Case of Pennsylvania Senate Bill 1310." *Journal of Financial Economics* 31:1, 3–23.

Titman, Sheridan, and Roberto Wessels. 1988. "The Determinants of Capital Structure Choice." *Journal of Finance* 43:1, 1–19.

Wang, Cong, and Fei Xie. 2009. "Corporate Governance Transfer and Synergistic Gains from Mergers and Acquisitions." *Review of Financial Studies* 22:2, 829–858.

Weisbach, Michael S. 1988. "Outside Directors and CEO Turnover." *Journal of Financial Economics* 20:1–2, 431–460.

Yermack, David L. 1996. "Higher Market Valuation of Companies with a Small Board of Directors." *Journal of Financial Economics* 40:2, 185–212.

ABOUT THE AUTHOR

Fei Xie is an Assistant Professor of Finance at the School of Management, George Mason University. He received a B.S. in Finance from Tsinghua University in Beijing, China and a PhD in Finance from Vanderbilt University. Professor Xie's research interests are in the fields of corporate governance and M&As. He has published in such journals as the *Journal of Finance*, *Review of Financial Studies*, *Financial Management*, and *Journal of Banking and Finance*.

CHAPTER 5

Ethical and Social Issues in M&As

ROBERT W. McGEE
Director, Center for Accounting, Auditing and Tax Studies,
Florida International University

INTRODUCTION

Mergers and acquisitions (M&As) have drawn considerable negative press over the past few decades. People like Michael Milken (Bruck, 1988; Stewart, 1991; Kornbluth, 1992; Stein, 1992) made more than $500 million in a single year during the 1980s by financing them with non-investment-grade (junk) bonds. Milken, along with Ivan Boesky (Boesky, 1985; Bruck, 1988; Stewart, 1991), Martin Siegel (Stewart, 1991), Dennis Levine (Frantz, 1987; Bruck, 1988; Stewart, 1991; Hoffer and Levine, 1992), and several other Wall Street moguls went to prison as a result of some of their activities. Others were arrested and had their careers ruined as a result, although no charges were ever filed (Crovitz, 1990; McGee and Block, 1990). Yet, supporters of Milken (Fischel, 1995; Gilder, 2000) are quick to point out that his activities caused capital to become more productive, leading to much of the economic growth that has taken place since the 1980s.

The purpose of this chapter is to examine ethical and social issues in M&As. The remainder of the chapter has the following organization. The next section provides a discussion of ethical ground rules and focuses on utilitarian ethics and rights-based ethics. The discussion then turns to ethical issues that can be applied to M&As. Such topics as poison pills, greenmail, golden parachutes, and insider trading are examined. The final section provides a summary and conclusions.

APPLYING ETHICAL PRINCIPLES

Applying ethical principles to a particular set of facts is not always easy. One must first determine which set of ethical principles should be applied. Even ethicists cannot agree on this point. The crux of the problem is that there are several sets of ethical principles in the ethicist's toolbox and some principles conflict with others. While one may often reach the same conclusion regardless of which set of ethical principles is applied, that is not always the case. Applying one set of ethical principles may lead one to conclude that a certain act or policy is ethical, while the exact opposite conclusion may be reached if a different set of ethical principles is applied.

Several main options involve ethical principles. Utilitarian ethics are discussed because utilitarianism is one of the major approaches that philosophers, ethicists, economists, politicians, lawyers, and policy makers have used in the past. It remains a frequently used approach. Failure to discuss utilitarian perspectives would make the analysis incomplete, but utilitarianism is not the only ethical system being used today. Some would argue that it is not even the best system, so alternative systems such as rights-based ethics and Kantian ethics are discussed as well.

Utilitarian Ethics

The vast majority of economists tend to be utilitarians, but there are some exceptions (Rothbard, 1978, 1998; Hoppe, 1993). The subfield of welfare economics is based on utilitarian ethics (Little, 2002/2002; Arrow, 1951; Hare, 1951; Pigou, 1951, 1958; Scitovski, 1951; Quirk and Saposnik, 1968; Moon, 1977; Johansson, 1991; Van den Doel and van Velthoven, 1993), in spite of the many criticisms that have been made against this approach (Rowley and Peacock, 1975; Cordato, 1992; Köszegi and Rabin, 2007). Policy makers, politicians, and lawyers also apply utilitarian principles to most policy issues. Thus, any discussion of ethics would be incomplete without a discussion of utilitarian ethical principles.

However, utilitarian ethics is flawed, some would say fatally flawed due to structural deficiencies (McGee, 1994, 1997). But before discussing the structural deficiencies of utilitarian ethics, the main points of this popular ethical system should be examined. Utilitarian ethics can be summarized by the flowchart in Exhibit 5.1 (McGee, 2006, 2007).

Early utilitarians, such as Bentham (1988) and Mill (1993), say that an act or policy is good if it results in the greatest good for the greatest number. Economists say an act or policy is good if the result is a positive-sum game or if the winners exceed the losers.

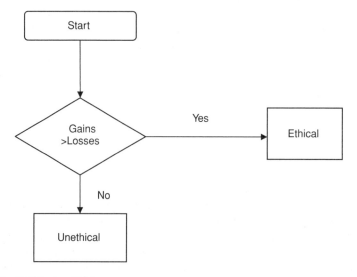

Exhibit 5.1   Utilitarian Ethics
Note: The flowchart illustrates the decision-making process using utilitarian ethical principles.

Although this approach seems reasonable at first, digging beneath the surface reveals problems. For example, maximizing more than one variable at the same time is mathematically impossible (von Neumann and Morgenstern, 1947). One may attempt to maximize total good or one may attempt to bestow good on the greatest number, but one may not do both at the same time.

Another problem involves measurement. While measuring the extent to which an individual prefers A to B is difficult, if not impossible, observing that one prefers A to B is feasible. Economics textbooks created the concept of utils to get around this problem and to make illustrating the point easier, but utils do not exist in the real world. Individuals rank their preferences; they do not attach numerical values to them (Viner, 1925; Rothbard, 1970).

One insurmountable problem of utilitarian ethics is that measuring or comparing interpersonal utilities is impossible (Kaldor, 1939; Rothbard, 1970). One way around this dilemma is to assume that all individuals derive the exact same pleasure or pain from identical acts or things. This is patently untrue, so some ethicists do not even make the assumption. They begin with the premise that rich people derive less utility from things than do poor people, a proposition that cannot be supported philosophically. For example, who is to say that a rich person derives less pleasure from a Hershey's chocolate almond bar than does a poor person?

Another inherent problem with attempting to apply utilitarian ethics is that identifying which individuals or groups gain or lose is not always easy. Bastiat (1964) pointed out this problem in the 1840s, and no one has been able to overcome it. In fact, Bastiat (p. 1) goes so far as to say that "There is only one difference between a bad economist and a good one: the bad economist confines himself to the visible effect; the good economist takes into account both the effect that can be seen and those effects that must be foreseen."

Determining in advance the effect an act or a policy will have on every potentially affected group is not always easy, or even possible. Who can predict with any degree of certainty what effect a merger or acquisition will have on various groups that are probably unidentifiable at the time the negotiations are taking place?

Furthermore, even if some individuals or groups are harmed by a merger, logic does not dictate that the merger should be stopped on that account. For example, the growth of the automobile industry destroyed the buggy whip industry as well as the buggy industry itself, yet no one other than the buggy and buggy whip unions would take the position that the automobile industry should be restrained or prevented from selling their products to willing consumers. According to rights theory, when consumers vote with their dollars or other monetary units to support one industry to the detriment of another industry, they should be allowed to do so, even if the industry they do not support goes out of business.

Another principle of utilitarian thought is that an act or policy is good if the result is increased efficiency. Posner (1979, 1983, 1998), the eminent American jurist and co-founder of the law and economics movement, espouses this view. For example, Posner (1983, p. 205) states: "The efficient society is wealthier than the inefficient—that is what efficiency means." Posner (1983, p. 115) also notes that "the criterion for judging whether acts and institutions are just or good is whether they maximize the wealth of society. This approach allows a reconciliation among utility, liberty, and even equality as competing ethical principles."

While something can be said for the efficiency approach, it has its limitations. For example, if the government finds a more efficient way to torture or kill people, this would not mean that the government is acting ethically. Thus, merely increasing efficiency is not enough. There must be something else as well.

So far this chapter has discussed various approaches to pure utilitarianism. An act or policy is successful if the result is a positive-sum game, meaning there are more winners than losers in the end, or if the result is greater efficiency, keeping in mind that precise measurement and comparing interpersonal utilities are impossible. But that is not the end of the story.

In the case of M&As, issues involving fiduciary duties are sometimes addressed. There is a fiduciary duty to do what is best for the employer or client even if this means foregoing personal profit opportunities. Corporate officers and directors have a duty to do what is best for their shareholders, even if it means they may be fired if a takeover is successful.

Including this topic complicates the ethical analysis because some utilitarian ethicists would automatically brand an act as unethical if a fiduciary duty is breached, whereas others would merely include breaches of fiduciary duty as a negative element in the utilitarian calculus. In other words, they would weigh the negative effects of fiduciary duty breaches against the positive effects. One might label this branch *eclectic* utilitarianism. This concept is illustrated by the flowchart depicted in Exhibit 5.2 (McGee, 2006, 2007).

Kantians (Sullivan, 1989, 1994; Baron, Pettit, and Slote, 1997; Kant, 1998, 2001) take the position that any breach of a duty is automatically unethical, whereas eclectic utilitarians may not reach this conclusion. Thus, if one can identify that a breach of fiduciary duty has occurred, one may immediately conclude that the act is unethical according to the Kantian view.

A final criticism can be made of utilitarian ethics. This flaw involves the total disregard of rights (McGee, 1994, 1997). To a utilitarian, violating rights is perfectly acceptable provided the result is a positive-sum game, or more end up winning than losing. Property rights, contract rights, association rights, and other rights may be violated, provided there is a net gain. This consequentialist approach to ethics states, as Shakespeare would say, "All's well that ends well."

This view can lead to some outrageous results. For example, if two wolves and one sheep vote on what to have for lunch, a vote of 2 to 1 to eat the sheep would be perfectly acceptable for a utilitarian because there are two winners and only one loser. Dostoevsky (1984) illustrates the flaw in the utilitarian approach when he asks whether torturing a small baby to death would be acceptable if the result would be eternal happiness for everyone else.

Rights-Based Ethics

Rights-based ethics overcome the structural deficiencies of utilitarian ethics. Rights-based ethics do not require calculating or estimating gains or losses. Attempting to identify all affected groups or individuals is also not necessary. All that is needed is to determine whether anyone's rights have been violated. If there are any rights violations, the act is automatically unethical. The right to life, whether it is a sheep or a baby, is superior to the wishes of the entire world. Exhibit 5.3 illustrates the rights-based ethical approach (McGee, 2006, 2007). If rights

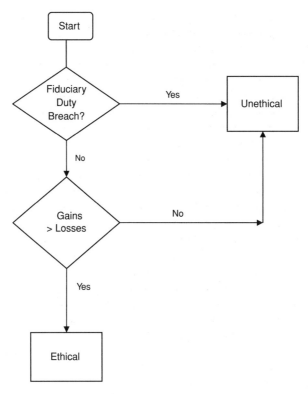

Exhibit 5.2   Eclectic Utilitarian Ethics
Note: The flowchart illustrates the decision-making process using utilitarian ethical principles using an eclectic approach.

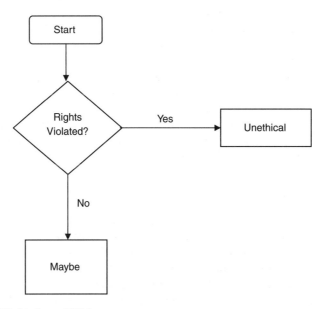

Exhibit 5.3   Rights-based Ethics
Note: The flowchart illustrates the decision-making process using a rights approach.

are violated, the act or policy is automatically unethical. If no rights are violated, the act or policy may or may not be ethical.

The flowchart indicates that the rights-based approach is an incomplete system. Although applying rights theory can enable one to determine whether certain acts are ethical, this ethical system cannot determine whether all acts are ethical or unethical. If someone's rights are violated, the act is clearly unethical, but rights theory does not provide ethical judgment for nonviolating acts. Victimless crimes (Rich, 1978; Feinberg, 1990; McWilliams, 1996) such as prostitution, drug taking, and certain sexual practices that may be illegal in some jurisdictions may or may not be ethical, but applying rights theory will not shed any light on the ethical nature of such acts. Some people see working on the Sabbath as a crime against God (or against the State, in cases where it is illegal), but rights theory cannot be applied to determine whether such acts are ethical. Rights theory is only applicable when acts violate rights, at which point, the theory labels the acts as unethical.

Although rights-based ethics is an incomplete system, it is still superior to utilitarian ethics because of the inherent flaws of utilitarian ethics. However, some ethicists would disagree with this conclusion. Jeremy Bentham, for example, believed that there is no such thing as natural rights. He even went so far as to state that such rights are "nonsense on stilts" (Waldron, 1987; Bentham, 1988). Whether Bentham might change his mind if he were stuck in the woods with two hungry wolves and a voting machine is a matter of speculation.

MERGERS AND ACQUISITIONS

Now that the ethical ground rules have been laid out, ethical principles can be applied to M&As. One argument in favor of M&As is the fact that they increase efficiency. This utilitarian argument is often used to justify them. There is some empirical evidence to support the view that M&As do in fact increase corporate or market efficiency (Scherer, 1988).

Based on his review of the literature on winners and losers and his own research, Jensen (1988) draws the following conclusions.

- Takeovers benefit shareholders of target companies by more than 30 percent on average and sometimes by more than 50 percent.
- Acquiring firm shareholders earn an average of about 4 percent in hostile takeovers and roughly zero in mergers.
- Takeovers do not waste credit or resources. They generate substantial gains, about 8 percent of the combined value of both companies.
- Actions by management that prevent offers or mergers are suspected to be harmful to shareholders.
- Golden parachutes generally do not harm shareholders.
- The activities of predators tend to benefit shareholders.
- M&A activity has not increased industrial concentration.
- Takeover gains do not come from the creation of monopoly power.

Of course, not all M&As turn out well. Sometimes M&As are not good ideas in terms of efficiency or profitability. The problem is that one does not arrive at this conclusion until after the fact. If the majority of M&As result in increased profitability or efficiency, the logical conclusion would be to allow them. Again, this argument is utilitarian based.

Some could argue that the government should undertake some preliminary investigation to determine whether the merger or acquisition would likely result in a net benefit to society. In fact, politicians and policy makers who want to regulate the activity have made this argument. They would require potential merger partners to obtain advance government approval before finalizing the proposed merger.

Such a position has several problems. For one, since government agencies often have different agendas, the companies themselves are better able to determine what is good for them. Those who take the government position would argue that both the merger parties and other members of the community such as workers, local residents, and businesses are affected. The effects a merger would have on these so-called stakeholders must also be considered, or so the argument goes.

This line of reasoning has several weaknesses. For one, the so-called stakeholders who might stand to lose if the merger goes forward have no stake in the business. They do not own shares in it. Their claim is based on the mere fact that they live in the community where one of the participating companies is located. Some members of this secondary stakeholder group might also be employees of one of the participants, and some of them may lose their jobs in the event that the merger negotiations are successful. Yet, they could possibly lose their jobs if the negotiations are unsuccessful. Failure to complete the negotiations successfully would make increased efficiency impossible, which might cause the target company to lay off workers or even go bankrupt. Sometimes a merger is needed to save a company in distress. One cannot merely assume that workers are threatened if a merger goes through and not threatened if it is stopped.

The problem with this line of reasoning is that it is utilitarian based. The real issue is one of property and contract rights. Those who own the shares in the corporation should be able to trade those shares without interference from the government or anyone else. Any interference with this transfer of property (shares) necessarily violates the rights of the shareholders. Any individual or group who does not own shares in one of the corporations has no rights to interfere with the transaction whatsoever. Any nonshareholder who attempts to use the government to prevent this nonviolating activity is acting unethically. This includes politicians and other government officials who have a duty to protect contract and property rights, not violate them. When a government stops protecting property and contract rights and starts violating them instead, it ceases to be legitimate. One of the reasons governments came into existence was to protect property rights. If a government ceases to perform that basic function, one could argue that it should be abolished or fired because of failure to do its job. Can the existence of an entity be justified if it fails to do its job?

Some individuals or groups might be harmed by a successful merger, but being harmed is not the same as violating one's rights. Someone who owns the paint store down the street from the factory that might be closed as a result of the merger might be harmed or might even go bankrupt if the factory was the paint store's main customer, but the paint store owner has no right to prevent the merger. There is no right to sell paint to a company that does not want to buy the paint just as there is no right to a job if an employer does not want to employ someone or if the public does not want to buy the product or service you are providing. To say otherwise would be to argue that the force of government should be used to compel individuals to enter into contracts that they would not otherwise enter into if they had a choice, a policy that necessarily violates property and contract rights.

A dynamic market economy has both winners and losers. Schumpeter (2008) calls it the process of creative destruction. In order for resources to be shifted to more productive uses, they must first be taken from less productive uses. When that happens, some people lose, but the increased efficiency benefits society in general. This argument is utilitarian, of course, but just because it is utilitarian does not mean that the argument is not true. As Bastiat (1964) would say, all individuals and groups who are affected must be considered, not just the obvious ones. Failure to do so constitutes being a bad economist. One must not think just about the paint store owner who stands to lose or go bankrupt. One must also think of the jobs and wealth that will be created if the merger is allowed to go forward. Further, one must consider the contract and property rights that would be violated if the government abused its power and came to the aid of the paint store owner.

One inherent problem in allowing governments to prevent mergers is the rent-seeking activity that inevitably results (Tullock, 1970, 1989, 1993; Buchanan, Tollison, and Tullock, 1980; Rowley, Tollison, and Tullock, 1988; Lockard and Tullock, 2001; Congleton, Hillman, and Konrad, 2008). Concentrated special interest groups that have much to gain or lose will use the government to benefit their own causes even at the expense of the unorganized general public. The politicians and government officials who have a fiduciary duty to protect the property and contract rights of everyone, including shareholders, breach that fiduciary duty by taking the side of the special interests and violating the very rights they were hired to protect.

The Organisation for Economic Cooperation and Development (OECD) agrees with this position. Its Principles of Corporate Governance (2004. p. 19) state: "Anti-takeover devices should not be used to shield management and the board from accountability."

Poison Pills

Although poison pills can take several forms, the main goal of poison pills is to make a target company less attractive to a predator by increasing the predator's takeover cost. One form is to issue preferred shares to the target's common shareholders, allowing them to redeem the shares at a premium after a takeover. Another way to make a company less attractive is to allow existing shareholders to purchase common shares at a deep discount, effectively watering down the predator's potential ownership percentage. Another method includes the target corporation taking on excessive debt or selling assets. From a utilitarian perspective, the obvious question to ask is who benefits and who loses from the use of a poison pill? The obvious winners are existing management of the target company since they get to keep their jobs, assuming the poison pill is successful in thwarting the takeover attempt.

The obvious loser from a poison pill is the predator. Poison pills make the target company less attractive and the hostile takeover attempt more costly. Even if the hostile takeover attempt is successful, the added cost strips value from the acquisition. Less obvious losers are the shareholders of the target company. A Securities and Exchange Commission (1986) study finds that the mere announcement of a poison pill plan by a target company causes the company's stock price to fall by 2.4 percent. Other studies also find that poison pills cause share prices to decline (Jensen, 1988; Ryngaert, 1988, 1989).

Poison pills apparently do not pass the utilitarian ethics test because they result in more losers than winners. Generally, shareholders and predators lose, while a small group of the target company's top management wins. Target company management seemingly breaches their fiduciary duty to the shareholders as well, causing them to fail the Kantian ethics test. They also misuse corporate assets to protect themselves at the expense of the shareholders, violating both the contract and property rights of the shareholders. Thus, poison pills appear to fail all ethical tests. Yet courts continue to permit them, mostly because of the false perception that they protect shareholders. Velasco (2002) discusses this irrational position at length.

Greenmail

Greenmail may be viewed as a bribe, a payment made by the target company's executives to a predator to make it go away and promise not to come back. Such a practice seems sinister, and perhaps it is. Yet, some studies find that greenmail payments cause the stock price to rise, which benefits shareholders (Holderness and Sheehan, 1985; Mikkelson and Ruback, 1985). Of course, shooing the predator away also removes the possibility of share premium benefits resulting from a takeover.

The ethical issue here is whether corporate officers are breaching their fiduciary duty to their shareholders by pursuing self-interest. It seems to be an agency problem because corporate officers apparently are acting in their own interest at the expense of the shareholders and are using shareholder funds to buy off the predator. Such an action would be like having someone knock on the door of an apartment building superintendent and offer to buy the apartment building, and having the superintendent use some of the landlord's rent money to bribe him to go away in order to protect his own job, which might be lost if the prospective buyer decides to replace the present superintendent with someone else.

Golden Parachutes

Golden parachutes are severance payments that certain corporate officers receive when they leave a company. About half of a target company's top management is no longer with the company three years after the takeover (Jensen, 1988), so the concern of top management that they might be fired in the event of a successful takeover is justified. However, not all of the individuals in that 50 percent were fired. Some took early retirement or left for other voluntary reasons.

Golden parachutes are neither ethical nor unethical per se but depend on several factors. Target company management may institute golden parachutes to protect itself in the event of a hostile takeover and may even give golden parachutes to hundreds of lesser managers as a kind of poison pill to make the target company look less attractive to the predator. When management takes such actions, they are clearly breaching their fiduciary duty to safeguard corporate assets for the shareholders.

However, golden parachutes can also have a beneficial effect on the company and its stock price if used properly. A well-structured golden parachute package can reduce the conflict of interest that would otherwise result when managers feel under attack during a hostile takeover. If managers feel protected by a golden parachute, they may be more likely to do what is in the shareholders' best interests rather than what is in their own interests. Some evidence suggests that stock prices rise by about 3 percent when a golden parachute package is publicly announced (Lambert and Larcher, 1985; Jensen, 1988).

Insider Trading

Similar to M&As, insider trading has received much bad press in the last few decades. Some politicians and pundits are upset that people can make substantial amounts of money with apparently little effort. Others perceive something shady about trading on information that is not equally available to the public at large. But when asked to apply ethical theory to the issue, Manne (1966, pp. 15 and 233) notes that one frequent response is to stomp on the floor or pound on the desk and merely assert "It's just not right."

Whether insider trading is ethical depends on a variety of factors. Merely profiting by trading on information in cases where the information is asymmetric is not inherently unethical, as has been pointed out (Manne, 1966; McGee and Block, 1990; McGee, 2008, 2010). When no one's rights are violated, a case can be made that there is nothing ethically improper about insider trading. Furthermore, some studies show that insider trading increases market efficiency, which would lead a utilitarian to conclude that the practice is ethical (McGee, 2008, 2010).

Ethical problems arise where there is a breach of fiduciary duty or where rights are violated. Part of the problem with the current state of insider trading is that property rights in information are not always clearly defined.

Other Ethical Issues

Some other ethical issues have been raised in the literature. For example, Serpa (1988) raises the issue of what to do with redundant employees. Some ethicists might question whether this is an ethical issue since nothing is inherently unethical about laying off unneeded employees (provided no contract terms are violated). If an employment contract exists, the firm has a moral duty to live up to the terms of the contract. However, when no contract exists, this represents an employment at will situation. Managers may provide some severance pay, provided that shareholders do not view such pay as a dissipation of corporate assets.

But offering a golden handshake in the form of an early retirement package might not be a good idea because some of the best employees may elect to take the retirement package, leaving the company with a shortage of experienced and highly qualified employees. The firm might rehire the best of these employees as consultants but usually at a higher cost (Serpa, 1988).

As Serpa (1988) suggests, a good performance evaluation system should be put in place to provide a better alternative than using seniority to determine who stays and who goes. Laying off employees on the basis of seniority is actually an inferior way to allocate human capital. Nothing is inherently fair about laying off better employees who happen to have less seniority than lesser qualified employees who have more seniority. In fact, a corporation usually serves its best interest by laying off the least meritorious employees first, regardless of seniority. Thus, the corporation benefits by keeping the best employees and getting rid of the worst ones. In fact, some may view laying off on the basis of seniority as a dissipation of corporate human capital. This practice is also unfair to the more productive employees, although choosing to lay off by seniority might be the safest option from a legal point of view.

Another issue is how to handle various stakeholder groups that might be adversely affected by the merger. Cooke and Young (1986) suggest that merger participants somehow have an ethical duty to see that stakeholders, such as stockholders, creditors, managers, employees, customers, suppliers, competitors, government, and communities are not harmed if possible, and that harm should be minimized where it is unavoidable. Unfortunately, they do not explain why there is such a duty.

The only group that is clearly owed is the shareholders. The evidence indicates that shareholders generally gain as a result of mergers (Jensen, 1988). What extra duties that are owed to other groups listed as stakeholders are unclear. Whatever duties that were owed before the merger are generally owed after the merger. Employees and managers who continue to work for the company should continue to be paid. Creditors should continue to be paid on time, as should suppliers, although the merger might result in changing some suppliers.

There does not seem to be any extra duty owed to the community, competitors, or government. The main duty a corporation owes to the community is to obey the laws and not pollute excessively. The only duties owed to government are to pay taxes on time and not break the laws, which are exactly the same duties that the company owed before the merger. The only duty owed to competitors is to play within the rules, a duty that does not change after the merger. Thus, what Cooke and Young (1986) have in mind when they assert that the merged corporation has some duty to these groups of stakeholders is unclear.

Commenting on Cooke and Young (1986), Lehman (1986) points out that stakeholder interests have to take second place to rights. Furthermore, whereas a moral duty exists to take rights into account, less clarity exists about whether a moral duty exists to take interests into account. In fact, most of the stakeholders that Cooke and Young mention have absolutely no moral claims as a result of the merger. The only stakeholders who have a moral claim on this act are the shareholders. All other groups are mere spectators.

Other studies also advocate taking the merger's effects on other stakeholders into account when making merger decisions (Chase, Burns, and Claypool, 1997). Unfortunately, those studies fail to adequately explain why a duty is owed to individuals and groups who have not invested in the corporation. Chase et al., for example, merely apply utilitarian ethics as though groups that are not a party to the transaction should somehow have a say in whether the merger goes through.

Werhane (1990) states that laid off employees somehow have a right to employer-paid retraining and job placement, although she does not state the source of this supposed right. She is an exponent of the view that the costs and benefits to everyone who might be affected should be taken into account, even if some of those groups do not care enough about the company to actually purchase its shares.

For example, a person does not take into account the costs and benefits to the local car wash when deciding to sell a car. Whether one decides to buy another car or take subways or taxis makes no difference. Subway employees and taxi drivers also have a stake in a person's decision. Yet, they have no right to be consulted, just as the teenager who works at the local car wash has no right to severance pay if a person stops using their services, unless the person agreed to pay severance in a preexisting contract. Werhane (1988) would assert that employees somehow have a right to participate in management decisions, although she does not present the source of this right.

Another ethical issue, which also relates to agency problems, is the motivation of managers to enter into the merger market. They should consider a merger if it is in the shareholders' best interests. On the contrary, studies show that they sometimes engage in M&As out of self-interest (Achampong and Zemedkun, 1995).

SUMMARY AND CONCLUSIONS

An examination of the literature shows the use of several conflicting ethical systems to analyze ethical issues in M&As. Utilitarian ethics suffer from some structural flaws, so analyses that take a utilitarian approach have some deficiencies from the start. The rights approach seems to provide better guidance because it avoids the structural deficiencies of utilitarianism. But rights theory does not always tell what acts are ethical. It only tells when certain acts are unethical. The best approach would seem to be to allow all M&A activity so long as no one's property or contract rights are violated. Nonparties to the transaction need not be considered, although their rights must not be violated.

Breaches of fiduciary duty are always a potential problem since managers often act in their best interest, to the detriment of shareholders. But such breaches can be handled under existing law. At first glance, there is no need for special legislation or regulation to handle such breaches. But a problem exists with relying on the legal system to protect shareholders given that numerous courts have approved poison pill maneuvers, which clearly allow management to act in their own self-interest to the detriment of the shareholders.

DISCUSSION QUESTIONS

1. What are the major ethical issues that have been raised regarding M&As?
2. What ethical principles have been applied to resolve the ethical issues regarding M&As? What are the strengths and deficiencies of each?
3. What is meant by a breach of fiduciary duty? Can such breaches be justified ethically if the merger benefits the shareholders?
4. Should M&As be regulated? Why or why not?

REFERENCES

Achampong, Francis K., and Wold Zemedkun. 1995. "An Empirical and Ethical Analysis of Factors Motivating Managers' Merger Decisions." *Journal of Business Ethics* 14:10, 855–865.

Arrow, Kenneth J. 1951. "Little's Critique of Welfare Economics." *American Economic Review* 41:5, 923–934.

Baron, Marcia W., Philip Pettit, and Michael Slote. 1997. *Three Methods of Ethics*. Malden, MA: Blackwell Publishers.

Bastiat, Frédéric. 1964. *Selected Essays on Political Economy*. Irvington-on-Hudson, NY: Foundation for Economic Education.

Bentham, Jeremy. 1988. *The Principles of Morals and Legislation*. Amherst, NY: Prometheus Books.

Boesky, Ivan F. 1985. *Merger Mania—Arbitrage: Wall Street's Best-Kept Money Making Secret*. New York: Holt Rinehart & Winston.

Bruck, Connie. 1988. *The Predators' Ball: The Junk-Bond Raiders and the Man Who Staked Them*. New York: Simon & Schuster.

Buchanan, James M., Robert Tollison, and Gordon Tullock (eds.). 1980. *Towards a Theory of a Rent-Seeking Society*. College Station, TX: Texas A&M University Press.

Chase, Daniel G., David J. Burns, and Gregory A. Claypool. 1997. "A Suggested Ethical Framework for Evaluating Corporate Mergers and Acquisitions." *Journal of Business Ethics* 16:16, 1753–1763.

Congleton, Roger D., Arye L. Hillman, and Kai A. Konrad (eds.). 2008. *40 Years of Research on Rent Seeking 2: Applications: Rent Seeking in Practice*. New York: Springer.

Cooke, Robert A., and Earl C. Young. 1986. "Mergers from an Ethical Perspective." *Business & Professional Ethics Journal* 5:3&4, 111–128.

Cordato, Roy E. 1992. *Welfare Economics and Externalities in an Open Ended Universe: A Modern Austrian Perspective*. Boston: Kluwer Academic Publishers.

Crovitz, L. Gordon. 1990. "How the RICO Monster Mauled Wall Street." *Notre Dame Law Review* 65, 1050–1072.

Dostoevsky, Fyodor. 1984. *The Brothers Karamazov*. New York: Bantam Classics.

Feinberg, Joel. 1990. *Harmless Wrongdoing: The Moral Limits of the Criminal Law*. New York: Oxford University Press.

Fischel, Daniel R. 1995. *Payback: The Conspiracy to Destroy Michael Milken and His Financial Revolution*. New York: HarperBusiness.

Frantz, Douglas. 1987. *Levine & Co.: Wall Street's Insider Trading Scandal*. New York: Henry Holt & Co.

Gilder, George. 2000. *Telecosm*. New York: Simon & Schuster.

Hare, A. E. C. 1951. "The Theory of Effort and Welfare Economics." *Economica* 18:69, 69–82.

Hoffer, Dennis, and William Levine. 1992. *Inside Out: An Insider's Account of Wall Street*. New York: Random House Business Books.

Holderness, Clifford G., and Dennis P. Sheehan. 1985. "Raiders or Saviors? The Evidence of Six Controversial Investors." *Journal of Financial Economics* 14:4, 555–579.

Hoppe, Hans-Hermann. 1993. *The Economics and Ethics of Private Property*. Auburn, AL: The Mises Institute.

Jensen, Michael C. 1988. "Takeovers: Their Causes and Consequences." *Journal of Economic Perspectives* 2:1, 21–48.

Johansson, Per-Olov. 1991. *An Introduction to Modern Welfare Economics*. New York: Cambridge University Press.

Kaldor, Nicholas. 1939. "Welfare Propositions in Economics and Interpersonal Comparisons of Utility." *The Economic Journal* 49:196, 549–552.

Kant, Immanuel. 1998. *Groundwork of the Metaphysics of Morals*. Cambridge: Cambridge University Press.

Kant, Immanuel. 2001. *Lectures on Ethics*. Cambridge: Cambridge University Press.

Kornbluth, Jesse. 1992. *Highly Confident: The Crime and Punishment of Michael Milken*. New York: William Morrow.

Köszegi, Botond, and Matthew Rabin. 2007. "Mistakes in Choice-Based Welfare Analysis." *American Economic Review* 97:2, 477–481.

Lambert, Richard A., and David F. Larcher. 1985. "Golden Parachutes, Executive Decision-Making and Shareholder Wealth." *Journal of Accounting and Economics* 7:1–3, 179–203.

Lehman, Craig K. 1986. "Comments on Cooke and Young's 'Mergers from an Ethical Perspective.'" *Business & Professional Ethics Journal* 5:3&4, 129–135.

Little, I. M. D. 1950/2002. *A Critique of Welfare Economics*. Oxford: Clarendon Press. Reissued by Oxford University Press in 2002.

Lockard, Alan, and Gordon Tullock (eds.). 2001. *Efficient Rent-Seeking: Chronicles of an Intellectual Quagmire*. New York: Springer.

Manne, Henry G. 1966. *Insider Trading and the Stock Market*. New York: Free Press.

McGee, Robert W. 1994. "The Fatal Flaw in NAFTA, GATT and All Other Trade Agreements." *Northwestern Journal of International Law & Business* 14:3, 549–565.

McGee, Robert W. 1997. "The Fatal Flaw in the Methodology of Law & Economics." *Commentaries on Law & Economics* 1, 209–223.

McGee, Robert W. 2006. "Why Is Insider Trading Unethical?" Andreas School of Business Working Paper, Barry University.

McGee, Robert W. 2007. "A Flow Chart Approach to Analyzing the Ethics of Insider Trading." Andreas School of Business Working Paper, Barry University.

McGee, Robert W. 2008. "Applying Ethics to Insider Trading." *Journal of Business Ethics* 77:2, 205–217.

McGee, Robert W. 2010. "Analyzing Insider Trading from the Perspectives of Utilitarian Ethics and Rights Theory." *Journal of Business Ethics* 91:1, 65–82.

McGee, Robert W., and Walter Block. 1990. "Information, Privilege, Opportunity and Insider Trading." *Northern Illinois University Law Review* 10:1, 1–35.

McWilliams, Peter. 1996. *Ain't Nobody's Business If You Do: The Absurdity of Consensual Crimes in Our Free Country*. Los Angeles: Prelude Press.

Mikkelson, Wayne H., and Richard S. Ruback. 1985. "An Empirical Analysis of the Interfirm Equity Investment Process." *Journal of Financial Economics* 14:4, 523–553.

Mill, John Stuart. 1993. *On Liberty and Utilitarianism*. New York: Bantam Books.

Moon, Marilyn. 1977. *The Measurement of Economic Welfare: Its Application to the Aged Poor*. New York: Academic Press.

Organisation for Economic Cooperation and Development. 2004. *OECD Principles of Corporate Governance*. Paris: OECD.

Pigou, Arthur Cecil. 1951. "Some Aspects of Welfare Economics." *American Economic Review* 41:3, 287–302.

Pigou, Arthur Cecil. 1958. *The Economics of Welfare*, 4th ed. London: Macmillan.

Posner, Richard A. 1979. "Utilitarianism, Economics, and Legal Theory." *The Journal of Legal Studies* 8:1, 103–140.

Posner, Richard A. 1983. *The Economics of Justice*. Cambridge, MA: Harvard University Press.

Posner, Richard A. 1998. *Economic Analysis of Law*, 5th ed. New York: Aspen Law & Business.

Quirk, James, and Rubin Saposnik. 1968. *Introduction to General Equilibrium Theory and Welfare Economics*. New York: McGraw-Hill.

Rich, Robert M. 1978. *Crimes without Victims: Deviance and the Criminal Law*. Lanham, NY: University Press of America.

Rothbard, Murray N. 1970. *Man, Economy and State*. Los Angeles: Nash Publishing.

Rothbard, Murray N. 1978. *For a New Liberty*. New York: Libertarian Review Foundation.

Rothbard, Murray N. 1998. *The Ethics of Liberty*. New York: New York University Press.

Rowley, Charles K., and Alan T. Peacock 1975. *Welfare Economics: A Liberal Restatement*. London: Martin Robertson.

Rowley, Charles K., Robert Tollison, and Gordon Tullock (eds.). 1988. *The Political Economy of Rent-Seeking*. Boston, Dordrecht & Lancaster: Kluwer Academic Publishers.

Ryngaert, Michael. 1988. "The Effect of Poison Pill Securities on Shareholder Wealth." *Journal of Financial Economics* 20:1/2, 377–417.

Ryngaert, Michael D. 1989. "Firm Valuation, Takeover Defenses, and the Delaware Supreme Court." *Financial Management* 18:3, 20–28.

Scherer, F. M. 1988. "Corporate Takeovers: The Efficiency Arguments." *Journal of Economic Perspectives* 2:1, 69–82.

Schumpeter, Joseph A. 2008. *Capitalism, Socialism and Democracy*. New York: Harper Perennial Modern Classics.

Scitovski, Tibor. 1951. "The State of Welfare Economics." *American Economic Review* 41:3, 303–315.

Securities and Exchange Commission. 1986. "The Economics of Poison Pills." Washington, D.C.: Office of the Chief Economist.

Serpa, Roy. 1988. "The Often Overlooked Ethical Aspect of Mergers." *Journal of Business Ethics* 7:5, 359–362.

Stein, Benjamin. 1992. *A License to Steal: The Untold Story of Michael Milken and the Conspiracy to Bilk the Nation*. New York: Simon & Schuster.

Stewart, James. 1991. *Den of Thieves*. New York: Simon & Schuster.

Sullivan, Roger J. 1989. *Immanuel Kant's Moral Theory*. Cambridge: Cambridge University Press.

Sullivan, Roger J. 1994. *An Introduction to Kant's Ethics*. Cambridge: Cambridge University Press.

Tullock, Gordon. 1970. *Private Wants, Public Means: An Economic Analysis of the Desirable Scope of Government*. New York: Basic Books.

Tullock, Gordon. 1989. *The Economics of Special Privilege and Rent Seeking*. London: Kluwer Academic Publishers.

Tullock, Gordon. 1993. *Rent Seeking*. Brookfield, VT: Edward Elgar.

Van den Doel, Hans, and Ben van Velthoven. 1993. *Democracy ad Welfare Economics*, 2nd ed. New York: Cambridge University Press.

Velasco, Julian. 2002. "The Enduring Illegitimacy of the Poison Pill." *Journal of Corporation Law* 27, 381–423.

Viner, Jacob. 1925. "The Utility Concept in Value Theory and Its Critics." *Journal of Political Economy* 33:6, 638–659.

von Neumann, John, and Oskar Morgenstern. 1947. *Theory of Games and Economic Behavior*. Princeton, NJ: Princeton University Press.

Waldron, Jeremy (ed.) 1987. *Nonsense upon Stilts: Bentham, Burke and Marx on the Rights of Man*. London: Methuen.

Werhane, Patricia H. 1988. "Two Ethical Issues in Mergers and Acquisitions." *Journal of Business Ethics* 7:1&2, 41–45.

Werhane, Patricia H. 1990. "Mergers, Acquisitions and the Market for Corporate Control." *Public Affairs Quarterly* 4:1, 81–96.

ABOUT THE AUTHOR

Robert W. McGee is Director of the Center for Accounting, Auditing and Tax Studies at Florida International University in Miami. He has published more than 50 books and more than 700 articles, book chapters, and conference papers in the fields of accounting, taxation, economics, law, philosophy, and business ethics. Several studies have ranked him first for business ethics scholarship or accounting ethics scholarship. He has lectured, worked or consulted in more than 30 countries. As a consultant for the United States Agency for International Development (USAID), he has assisted the Finance Ministries of Armenia and Bosnia and Herzegovina to convert those countries to International Financial Reporting Standards. He drafted the accounting law for Armenia and Bosnia and Herzegovina, and reviewed the accounting law for Mozambique and the securities law for Turkey. He has trained government ministry officials in Rwanda, Tanzania, and Bulgaria, economists in Ukraine, and accountants in Russia. He has been a visiting professor in Australia, China, Denmark, the Dominican Republic, India, Jamaica, Mexico, Panama, Romania, Russia, Thailand, and Ukraine.

CHAPTER 6

Theoretical Issues on Mergers, Acquisitions, and Divestitures

ABDUL H. RAHMAN
Professor in Finance and Economics, Telfer School of Management,
University of Ottawa

INTRODUCTION

This chapter considers mergers, acquisitions, and divestures (e.g., spin-offs, sell-offs, and equity carve-outs) as potential actions aimed at corporate restructuring and control. Mergers and acquisitions (M&As) represent management's choice to expand the boundaries of the firm, and this choice may be part of a broader strategic plan to achieve a long-term goal. Clearly, if the management of the acquiring firm can add economic value as a result of the acquisition, then the firm may pay a premium for the target firm and still benefit from the acquisition.

Various factors may motivate managers to optimize the value of the firm via corporate takeovers. One such motive involves synergy. For example, operational synergies may arise from achieving economies of scale and scope, improving resource allocation, reducing costs, and acquiring key technologies or competencies. Chatterjee (1986) distinguishes between operational synergies (i.e., efficiency gains) and allocative synergies, which are derived from increased market power and provide management with the ability to extract a consumer surplus. Recent evidence shows that efficiency gains are relatively more significant than gains arising from allocative synergies. Devos, Kadapakkam, and Krishnamurthy (2009) compare operational synergies, market power, and tax benefits as explanations of merger gains. They find evidence suggesting that mergers generate gains by improving resource allocation rather than by reducing tax payments or increasing the market power of the combined firm. Specifically, of the total 10.3 percent synergy gain, about 8.3 percent may be attributed to operational synergies. Further, the authors find that operational synergies are higher in more focused mergers.

Another justification for corporate takeovers involves the theory of corporate control (Weston, Mitchell, and Mulherin, 2004). Accordingly, managers of underperforming firms will be open for takeover by managers who optimize shareholder value. That is, inefficient managers supply the market with corporate control. The implication is that underperforming firms are likely to be the target of hostile takeovers by value-maximizing firms. Evidence, however, casts doubt that this is a primary reason for takeovers (Martin and McConnell, 1991; Schwert, 2000).

A third motive, set forth by Roll (1986), is hubris, in which overconfidence leads managers to overestimate their abilities to identify and to estimate potential synergies. Hubris may cause managers to overpay for the target firm and hence experience a winner's curse that increases the probability of failure (e.g., Dong, Hirshleifer, Richardson, and Teoh, 2006). Empirical studies provide evidence of hubris in takeover events (e.g., for the United States, Berkovitch and Narayanan, 1993; for European takeovers, Goergen and Renneboog, 2004). Bliss and Rosen (2001) find evidence that managers' compensation has a significant influence on merger decisions. New evidence of the role of managers' self-interest comes from behavioral finance, which finds that chief executive officer (CEO) overconfidence may influence investment decisions (e.g., Malmendier and Tate, 2005). Interestingly, Rau and Vermaelen (1998) find that hubris more likely exists among low book-to-market firms (i.e., glamour firms).

The agency motive, as embodied by Jensen's (1986) theory of managerial discretion, attributes the existence of excess free cash flow (i.e., liquidity) as the cause of unproductive takeovers. Martynova and Renneboog (2008) show that high levels of liquidity cause managers to choose negative net present value (NPV) acquisitions after they have exhausted value-increasing takeover targets. This motive is consistent with managers seeking takeover targets under the guise of minimizing the risk of replacement as discussed in the theory of managerial retrenchment proposed by Shleifer and Vishny (1989). Amihud and Lev (1981) present evidence that managers, as opposed to investors, engage in merger diversification to decrease their largely undiversifiable employment risk.

Corporate divestitures represent actions by management that contract the firm's existing boundaries. Further, these actions represent strategic motives that are similar to those associated with corporate takeovers (i.e., for the purpose of optimizing shareholder value). This view of corporate divestures is embodied in the study by Anslinger, Klepper, and Subramaniam (1999). Steiner (1997) and others note that firm characteristics such as financial performance and the level of diversification are key drivers of business divestitures. In particular, poor financial performance at the firm level may be the most important driver of business divestitures because the disposition of a business unit is unlikely when firms are experiencing average or superior performance in their primary businesses. Another driver of business divestitures is too much diversification, resulting in ineffective managerial monitoring and control (Kaiser and Stouraitis, 2001). Consequently, agency costs may increase and resources may be inefficiently allocated across business units (Goel, Nanda, and Narayanan, 2004).

This chapter also considers spin-offs, sell-offs, and equity carve-outs as examples of corporate divestitures. In a *spin-off*, a firm creates and distributes new shares to existing shareholders on a pro-rata basis; no cash is exchanged. In a *sell-off*, the parent firm completely sells off a subsidiary to another firm. In an *equity carve-out*, the parent firm sells a percentage of the newly created shares of the subsidiary in an initial public offering (IPO) and retains the rest of the new shares.

Sudarsanam (2003) provides a detailed discussion on managerial motives for corporate divestitures. However, some common factors motivating divestment include:

- *Strategic repositioning* in which the firm seeks a new strategy (Villalonga and McGahan, 2005). This is likely to occur when the firm faces unexpected discontinuities in its competitive environment.
- *Refocusing* in which a firm seeks to eliminate peripheral activities while maintaining the core strategy (Byerly, Lamont, and Keasler, 2003). Thus, the parent firm eliminates businesses unrelated to its core business. This may be accomplished by a sell-off where a subsidiary is sold because it does not fit into the core strategy of the parent company. The market may be undervaluing the combination because of a lack of synergy between the parent and the subsidiary. In this case, the primary goal of the divestiture is to eliminate negative synergies between the parent firm and the business unit. The implication is that diversified firms destroy value because they overinvest in some business units and underinvest in other others (Rajan, Servaes, and Zingales, 2000). For example, Nestle, a food and beverage company, was able to increase its combined value by $7 to $8 billion when it divested its Alcon division, which was evaluated as a pharmaceutical firm with higher multiples.
- *Reducing financial leverage* with an associated positive impact on the firm's equity beta (Lang, Poulsen, and Stultz, 1995; Lasfer, Sudarsanam, and Taffler, 1996). The main finding is that financially distressed firms benefit from the reduction in distress costs brought about by corporate disinvestments.
- *Reducing agency costs of conflict* associated with a firm whose size has surpassed what is deemed to be optimal. According to capital structure theory, divestitures that reduce agency costs have a positive valuation effect. Furthermore, several studies suggest that a firm focused in one specialized sector is more likely to outperform a more diversified firm (Berger and Ofek, 1995; Comment and Jarrell, 1995).

The remainder of this chapter consists of the following sections. The first section discusses the various theories and hypotheses that explain wave behavior for M&As. The chapter also presents the theories that explain the observed procyclical relationship between aggregate merger activity and stock market levels. The next section considers theoretical issues relevant for corporate divestitures. The final section summarizes and concludes.

THEORETICAL ISSUES FOR MERGERS, ACQUISITIONS, AND DIVESTITURES

M&As and divestitures may be viewed as strategic managerial actions under the umbrella of corporate restructuring. Hence, their strategic importance may be better understood when viewed in the context of the generalized theories of corporate restructuring.

Theories of Corporate Restructuring

Two generalized theories of corporate restructuring are behavioral and nonbehavioral. Behavioral or nonsynergistic theory includes motives involving empire building, hubris, and overindulgence in perquisites (e.g., Jensen, 1986; Shleifer and Vishny, 1989). This theory predicts that divestitures create wealth by eliminating agency costs arising from excess free cash flow or by permitting management to specialize on core competencies. On the contrary, M&As may lead to a reduction in firm value due to management's loss of focus in its pursuit of personal objectives. This asymmetric effect predicted by the behavioral theory favors corporate divestitures. In a sense, corporate divestitures may be seen as a strategic move to eliminate the agency costs of empire building.

According to the nonbehavioral or synergistic theory of corporate restructuring, management will restructure by either seeking to merge with or acquire another firm or to divest as a response to economic shocks arising from technological discontinuities and regulatory changes. Examples are the invention of the transistor and the repeal of the Glass-Stegall Act in the United States in 1999, respectively. This theory predicts that both M&As and divestitures can be wealth creating. An implication of this theory is that merit exists in considering the joint wealth effects of acquisitions and divestitures and in studying whether the wealth effects are symmetric (Mulherin and Boone, 2000).

Merger Waves and Their Attendant Pro-cyclical Behavior

Since the seminal work by Nelson (1959), considerable and consistent empirical evidence shows that M&As occur in wave-like patterns with clustering over time and across industries. Scherer and Ross (1990) provide evidence of pre-1980s merger waves while others present evidence for the 1980s and 1990s (e.g., Ravenscraft and Scherer, 1987; Golbe and White, 1988, 1993; Mitchell and Mulherin, 1996; Andrade, Mitchell, and Stafford, 2001; Harford, 2005). While little dispute exists about the wave-like behavior of M&As, the econometric identification of waves depends on the method used such as sine curve fitting and autoregressive modeling. Gartner and Halbheer (2009), who use a Markov regime switching technique with quarterly data from 1973 to 2003, are unable to identify the 1980s wave found by several U.S. studies. They attribute this finding to the more refined methods offered by the Gibbs sampling approach, which was introduced by Geman and Geman (1984). Similarly, Shughart and Tollison (1984) examine a sample of annual data on U.S. mergers during 1895 to 1979 and hypothesize that levels of mergers follow a random walk model or a stable autoregressive process. They conclude that the hypothesis could not be rejected. These findings raise doubts about the validity of the merger wave theory.

The wave behavior during the twentieth century in the United States suggests that M&A activity is subject to nonstationary regime shifts rather than just being a random process. Merger waves also seem to cluster by type. The first wave (1890 to 1905) involved mainly horizontal mergers and created monopolies, whereas the second wave (1924 to 1928) involved largely vertical mergers, leading to oligopolies. Conglomerate mergers characterized the third wave (1961 to 1969) (Beckenstein, 1979). The fourth wave (1981 to 1989) was associated with leveraged buyouts (LBOs) and hostile takeovers, with firms focusing on core competencies (Shleifer and Vishny, 1990; Jensen, 1993). The fifth wave, estimated to be the period 1993 to 2000, was conspicuous for global M&As (Harford, 2005). The post-2000 period has some similarity to the merger wave of the 1980s in that LBOs returned while private deals gained prominence.

Another empirical regularity is that merger waves are pro-cyclical. That is, relatively more M&A activity occurs during economic booms versus recessions. Numerous studies provide evidence of this co-movement (e.g., Nelson, 1959; Gort, 1969; Golbe and White, 1988; Maksimovic and Phillips, 2001; Jovanovic and Rousseau, 2002).

So why do M&As occur in waves? Andrade et al. (2001) contend that research on this issue is limited. In fact, Brealey, Myers, and Allen (2006) suggest that the question as to why merger waves occur is one of the 10 most important unresolved problems in finance. However, early studies offer several theories about merger waves. For example, Gort (1969) presents economic disturbance theory indicating that systematic valuation differences cause mergers. Hence, this theory is based on economic shocks only to the extent that they create information risk. More recently, Toxvaerd (2008) proposes an explanation based on a dynamic preemption game where an acquirer may delay taking action until more information is available. While the value of delay is positive, there is also a cost of undue delay, i.e., an increased probability of preemption by rivals. The model derived by Toxvaerd derives explanations that are mostly consistent with the empirical evidence presented by Mitchell and Mulherin (1996), who find that merger waves are industry specific.

Gorton, Kahl, and Rosen (2009) contend that firm size is an important determinant of merger activity in industries with economies of scale. Firms may want to merge or acquire in order to reduce the likelihood of being acquired. These takeover actions may not be value-maximizing because the main objective by management is to preserve their control of the firm. However, industries with a dominant firm may display waves of profitable acquisitions. This theory of firm size and merger waves offers an explanation of why mergers are concentrated in industries for which a regime shift (e.g., technology discontinuity) can be indentified, consistent with the empirical evidence presented by Mitchell and Mulherin (1996). An important prediction of the Gorton et al. model is that a negative correlation exists between the acquirer's announcement returns and its firm size, consistent with the empirical evidence presented by Moeller, Schlingemann, and Stulz (2004). The overall finding of the "size theory" is that the race for bigger firm size may be profitable but can otherwise be value decreasing if the objective is to enhance or preserve the private benefits of control.

Agency theory provides a common explanation for the merger wave. This theory proposes that managers prefer more assets under management and hence, if permitted, would likely expand the boundaries of the firm beyond its optimal scope (e.g., Jensen and Meckling, 1976; Morck, Shleifer, and Vishny, 1990). Clearly, such actions are value decreasing. Merger waves may easily hide such managerial empire building even if managers initiate mergers for value-increasing reasons. Duchin and Schmidt (2008) establish a link between agency theory and merger waves. They contend that merger waves created by strategic motives may be amplified by hidden value-destroying and self-serving actions of managers.

Goel and Thakor (2010) show that when CEO compensation increases with firm size and market value, CEO envy can cause merger waves even if the initial trigger for the wave is idiosyncratic. Several predictions emerge from their model.

For example, earlier acquisitions in a merger wave display higher synergies and involve smaller targets than later acquisitions. Importantly, the more envious CEOs are likely to engage in acquisitions and pay higher premiums. Finally, merger waves are more likely during periods of high market returns. CEO envy offers a convincing explanation for the puzzling fact that merger waves are not just a bull-market event but also a bear-market phenomenon. An implication of this envy-driven model is that bear-market mergers are not driven by envy and hence should exhibit greater synergies leading to better long-term performance. This view is consistent with the empirical finding by Bouwman, Fuller, and Nain (2009) that bear-market acquisitions exhibit better long-term performance compared to bull-market acquisitions. This prediction may also be inferred from Rhodes-Kropf and Viswanathan (2004).

An important point arising from Goel and Thakor (2010) is that the driving factor of merger waves is the dispersion of firm market values instead of a market trend, i.e., bull or bear markets. Indeed, after controlling for dispersion of market valuations, these authors show that the bull-bear effect is immaterial. This finding is consistent with the evidence presented by Dong et al. (2006) showing a positive correlation between the dispersion of market valuation of stocks and merger waves.

Market-driven explanations for merger waves date back to Nelson (1959), who asserts that merger expansion is not only a phenomenon of prosperity but also related to the state of the capital markets. Nelson indicates that mergers generally occur during periods of high stock market valuations and are typically equity financed. Andrade et al. (2001) support this observation and present evidence showing that stock-financed acquisitions are preponderant in high-valuation stock markets. One common explanation for merger waves is that a firm's cost of capital decreases during a market expansion, leading to higher stock market valuation. This explanation is consistent with Toxvaerd's (2008) dynamic game theory model.

Valuation-based acquisition theory assumes that the capital markets are inefficient and hence mispricing exists. According to the Shleifer and Vishny (2003) model, managers of the bidding firm have private information about the degree of misevaluation and seek arbitrage profits via M&As. This permits overvalued bidding firms to exchange expensive equity for relatively less expensive equity of target firms. This theory predicts that aggregate merger activity is higher during economic booms than during economic recessions, supporting previous findings by Nelson (1959) and Andrade et al. (2001). The bidding firm only has to find a less overvalued target and the former will obtain long-term value creation without having to earn any synergy. Another prediction is that takeover activity will be greater in industries with high valuations and equity financing will dominate other forms of financing.

Rhodes-Kropf and Viswanathan (2004) propose a second market-timing model, which is similar to that of Shleifer and Vishny (2003). In this model, the managers of the bidding firm have private information about the value of their firm as well as the potential value of the merged firm. Managers of the target firm cannot distinguish between systematic and idiosyncratic (i.e., firm specific) errors. Accordingly, market-wide overvaluation is likely to make bids more attractive to managers of the target firm. This is why target firms rationally accept offers from overvalued acquirers.

Lambrecht (2004) analyzes the case of mergers motivated by operational synergies, which in this case refers to economies of scale. The main feature of

Lambrecht's model is that any surplus gained by the firm from merging is stochastic and sold at a stochastic product price. Hence, the gain from a merger is positively correlated with an economic boom when product prices are expected to be higher due to higher product demand. This predicts pro-cyclical merger activity. Finally, in Lambrecht and Myers (2004), managers use takeovers as a mechanism to force disinvestment in declining industries or to reduce agency costs. Thus, incentives to merge during expansions are likely to be different than during downturns.

In summary, this section shows that existing theories are limited in explaining the two most important stylized facts about M&As: Mergers occur in waves and are pro-cyclical. The dynamic preemption game approach by Toxvaerd (2008) appears promising. Equally promising is the CEO envy model by Goel and Thakor (2010), where envy is the driving force behind merger waves and their attendant pro-cyclicality. The analysis presented therein leads to novel predictions of which several find strong empirical support.

THEORETICAL ISSUES MOTIVATING CORPORATE DIVESTITURES

From a theoretical perspective, determining whether financial performance or strategic positioning is a more important antecedent of corporate divestures is useful. This question is motivated by findings in the literature that favor both of these factors. For example, Steiner (1997) presents evidence that the probability of a divestiture is negatively related to financial performance and positively correlated with the firm's degree of diversification. This means that prior poor financial performance may motivate managerial action to divest, sell off, or spin off a subsidiary. On the other hand, the more diversified a company's assets, the more likely is the company to divest some of these assets. Markides (1992) indicates that reductions in the diversification level can lead to improved financial performance. Finally, a business divestiture can have a strategic benefit in creating a more optimal allocation of resources. Hence, a firm may seek both improved financial performance and strategic considerations when it chooses to reduce its asset portfolio. John and Ofek (1995) show that when firms divest, the probability of enhanced financial performance of the remaining assets over the subsequent three years is increased if there is a joint focus on strategic considerations.

Some studies examine corporate divestures jointly. For example, Mulherin and Boone (2000) study a joint estimation of acquisitions and divestitures. Their findings for U.S. data support the symmetric hypothesis in the 1990s implying that both types of restructuring are value increasing. These results are similar to those reported in Maksimovic and Phillips (2001), who find that both mergers and asset sell-offs improve total factor productivity. Finally, to emphasize the joint hypothesis, Linn and Rozeff (1984) as well as Afshar, Taffler, and Sudarsanam (1992) report a higher positive abnormal stock market reaction for sell-offs when the documentation accompanying the announcement contains both the price and motive for the sale of the asset. Both studies also report that the abnormal returns on the announcement date are positively correlated to the asset size of the divested business units.

Sell-Offs

Several motives are associated with sell-offs. Lang et al. (1995) propose that sell-offs may be motivated by a need for cash to reduce the firm's debt-to-equity ratio. They also find that stock prices react favorably when a firm announces a sell-off and uses the proceeds to repay debt. Yet, the stock price reaction is not statistically different from zero when the firm retains the proceeds. This evidence casts doubt on the synergy view of a sell-off because the synergy hypothesis does not rely on how the firm uses the proceeds from the sell-off. Since the stock market views the use of the proceeds to repay debt, there is implied support for Jensen's (1986) free cash flow argument that a firm may use debt to reduce agency costs and hence increase its value.

A second motive for a sell-off may be that the particular business unit has experienced chronic poor financial performance. Ravenscraft and Scherer (1987) examine previously acquired assets that a firm sells off. Using a logistic regression, they find a negative correlation between financial profitability and the sell-off decision. Dann and DeAngelo (1983) view sell-offs as a way to block hostile takeover attempts by firms interested in a particular division or business unit of the company. They present evidence to show that this type of action has negative but statistically insignificant wealth effects.

A third motive relates to the current level of diversification of the firm. The general hypothesis is that diversification reduces firm value. Findings by Lang and Stulz (1994), Berger and Ofek (1995), and Comment and Jarrell (1995) support this proposition. Hence, an overdiversified firm may have a higher propensity to sell off assets. Accordingly, the expectation is that a positive correlation exists between a firm selling off assets and its prior financial performance, financial leverage, or level of diversification.

Empirical studies support the hypothesis that both buyers and sellers of the divested asset experience positive wealth effects (e.g., Alexander, Benson, and Kampmeyer, 1984; Jain, 1985). Datta and Iskandar-Datta (1996) show that both stockholders and bondholders of the selling firm experience positive stock market announcement effects.

Spin-Offs

While spin-offs and sell-offs are quite similar, a key difference is that a sell-off does not result in the creation of separate new shares. Sell-offs may be seen as "reverse mergers" where the effective date is the date when the firm completes the sale. Spin-offs may be viewed as dividends-in-kind paid by the parent company to its shareholders. The motivation for spin-offs is similar to that of sell-offs. Yet, because spin-offs create two separate sets of shares, the announcement effect of a spin-off is expected to be greater than for a sell-off. This relatively higher announcement effect for spin-offs is likely due to the greater efficiency in the stock market (Ross, 1976) because in an imperfect market, the availability of two separate securities gives investors more choices. Indeed, the finance literature documents several examples where, for an imperfect market, the total value of two securities is worth more than the value of a single security that combines both securities (e.g., Jarrow and O'Hara, 1989).

The expectation of a higher announcement effect for spin-offs over sell-offs may also be explained by the clientele effect described by Vijh (1994). He posits that the shares of two different companies will attract different types of investors and analysts, and hence, a clientele demand would generate higher abnormal returns. This evidence of abnormal returns supports the clientele effect because there is no systematic arrival of new information on the effective date.

Khan and Mehta (1996) provide an answer as to whether a managerial preference exists for spin-offs over sell-offs. They show that a firm divests via a sell-off when the subsidiary is experiencing low growth and stable earnings but prefers a spin-off when the subsidiary has high growth prospects and uncertain earnings.

Apart from Vijh's (1994) clientele effect, some research deals with the hypothesis that the abnormal announcement effects of spin-offs are based on information asymmetry. Aron (1991) contends that spin-offs benefit the firm because after the spin-off event, stock prices provide a clearer signal of managerial productivity, as compared to when the spin-off unit was part of the combined firm. In particular, Aron's model predicts that stock-based compensation following a spin-off leads to improved managerial incentives and hence to higher equity market value.

Habib, Johnsen, and Naik (1997) derive a model in which a firm can increase its value by spinning off a subsidiary. They argue that the driving factor here is increased liquidity that arises after the spin-off. Furthermore, the resulting pricing mechanism experiences a decrease in information asymmetry, which leads to an increase in the total value of both the firm and its spin-off unit. This is especially true if the firm and its subsidiary currently operate in different industries, and so the degree of information asymmetry (and hence, mispricing) is expected to be high.

Comment and Jarrell (1995), Daley, Mehrotra, and Sivakumar (1997), and Desai and Jain (1999) show that spinning off a subsidiary in a different line of business from the parent increases firm value. According to Krishnaswami and Subramaniam (1999) as well as Nanda and Narayanan (1999), firm managers who believe that the degree of information asymmetry between insiders and outside investors is high are likely to engage in spin-offs. Further, the abnormal stock returns around the announcement date of spin-offs are positively correlated with the degree of information symmetry. A direct implication of the information effect is that the degree of information asymmetry is reduced after the spin-off.

Slovin, Sushka, and Ferraro (1995), Nanda and Narayanan (1999), and Habib et al. (1997) propose that spin-offs represent managerial actions signaling to the market that a firm's shares are undervalued. Managers take such actions because undervaluing a firm's shares can have harmful effects. These effects include difficulties in obtaining external financing and a higher likelihood of hostile takeover attempts. Spin-offs also have implications for compensation schemes tied to the share value (Nanda and Narayanan, 1999; Burch and Nanda, 2003; Chemmanur and Liu, 2005). This misevaluation hypothesis is similar to that proposed by Shleifer and Vishny (2003) for the pro-cyclical behavior of M&As. Thus, the announcement of a spin-off should have a positive effect on the parent firm's shares if the market views the announcement as a signal of undervaluation. The key premise is that undervaluation is the driving force of the positive wealth effect. Accordingly, the expectation is that parent firms are undervalued relative to the industry average value and that the size of the abnormal return upon announcement should be positively correlated with the degree of the parent's undervaluation.

A parent firm may experience positive wealth effects if it spins off an under-valued subsidiary, even if the parent itself is not undervalued. Managers may view this action as an attempt to unlock the hidden value of the subsidiary for the benefit of shareholders of the parent firm. Parent firms may also spin off overvalued divi-sions to take advantage of high market valuations, as reported by Sudarsanam and Qian (2006). Others such as Nanda and Narayanan (1999) combine the informa-tion and valuation theories. They contend that because of information asymmetry, investors may unknowingly be undervaluing a division with above-average per-formance and overvaluing another division with below-average performance. This could lead to an overall undervaluation of the parent company. Hence, managers of the company may be forced to spin off the overvalued division to correct for the overall undervaluation problem.

Sudarsanam and Qian (2006) propose a catering model of corporate spin-offs. This model assumes that when investors have excessive optimism regarding a par-ticular type of stock (e.g., glamour stocks), managers may rationally react to meet this demand by undertaking spin-offs or equity carve-outs. Hence, in such cases, corporate divestitures are not based on improving the resource allocation of the postdivestiture firms, but rather on catering to a short-term demand. Sudarsanam and Qian propose the following hypothesis: Parent firms of spin-offs, undertaken to cater to investor demand for glamour stocks, will have higher abnormal returns upon the announcement relative to other spin-offs. The authors provide evidence supporting this hypothesis.

Finally, Chemmanur and Yan (2004) develop another rationale for corporate spin-offs and for the subsequent stock market reaction based on corporate control considerations. They show that if an incumbent loses control to a more able rival, all shareholders, including the shareholders of the incumbent firm, benefit in terms of higher equity value, but the incumbent loses the private benefits of control. Thus, a disciplining effect exists in that the incumbent is forced to work harder at managing the firm in order to avoid loss of control.

The main prediction arising from Chemmanur and Yan (2004) is that the ob-served increase in equity market value upon the spin-off announcement arises from two simultaneous effects. That is, market participants incorporate into their equity valuations both the increased probability of a takeover by a rival with better ability in managing the firm and the expected increase in managerial efficiency arising from the disciplining effect of the spin-off on firm management. This pre-diction is supported by the empirical findings of Cusatis, Miles, and Woolridge (1993) demonstrating that both spin-offs and their parents experience significantly more takeovers than do control groups of similar firms. Further, those parents and corresponding spin-off units that do not experience any takeover activity within three years do not have positive long-term abnormal returns.

Equity Carve-Outs

An equity carve-out (ECO) occurs when a parent company divests a wholly owned subsidiary or division through an IPO. Empirical evidence suggests that ECOs are value-enhancing. For example, Schipper and Smith (1986), Allen and McConnell (1998), Mulherin and Boone (2000), and Vijh (2002) document significant positive abnormal returns after an ECO is announced. Two main hypotheses attempt to explain why ECOs are value creating. The first is the asymmetric information hypothesis, derived from a model developed by Nanda (1991). In this model, the parent company chooses an ECO when the assets of the subsidiary are overvalued and those of the parent are undervalued. Hence, the mere announcement of an ECO represents a signal that the parent is undervalued and its share value is revised upward. At the same time, a negative price revision occurs for the subsidiary. Empirical findings by Sloven, Sushka, and Ferraro (1995) support Nanda's prediction.

The second is the divestiture gains hypothesis, arising from operational and managerial efficiencies that are derived from divesting a subsidiary. Similar to spin-offs, this hypothesis states that ECO value creation arises from refocusing the firm's strategy by divesting a subsidiary in a different industry. This is a case of the parent attempting to eliminate negative synergies such as when assets unrelated to core operations prevent a firm from focusing on its core competencies. As Vijh (2002) shows, when the parent and subsidiary belong to different industries, the announcement effect of an ECO is higher than when they are from the same industry.

Finally, an even more significant announcement effect occurs if an ECO also includes a managerial commitment to use the proceeds to retire corporate debt. Corporate finance theory posits that managers value firm size and control. Thus, when asymmetric information or managerial discretion makes equity too expensive, managers will sell assets. Shareholders are likely to benefit from the resulting decrease in informational asymmetry when the firm announces the ECO. This would lead to a more optimal pricing mechanism. Further, the resulting decline in agency costs arising from the precommitment of the proceeds also has a positive equity valuation effect. Lang et al. (1995), Allen and McConnell (1998), and Vijh (1999) provide evidence supporting this precommitment of proceeds hypothesis.

ECOs seem to represent a temporary managerial action followed by a second stage event of a complete sell-off or reacquisition (e.g., Schipper and Smith, 1986; Klein, Rosenfeld, and Beranek, 1991; Hand and Skantz, 1998; Miles, Woolridge, and Tocchet, 1999). Apparently, the likelihood of a second-stage event is positively correlated with the percentage of the IPO retained by the parent. Further, the quicker the second stage occurs, the greater is the chance that the parent will choose to sell off its remaining shares of the subsidiary. However, the larger the parent's share of the equity carve-out, the more likely that the second stage event (if it occurs) will be a reacquisition.

SUMMARY AND CONCLUSIONS

This chapter considers the theoretical issues underlying corporate restructuring. In particular, M&As experience wave behavior with clustering over time and across industries. Among the proposed theoretical rationales for such behavior are Gort's (1969) economic disturbance theory and Toxvaerd's (2008) dynamic preemption game where an acquirer may delay taking action until more information is available. Explanations of wave behavior derived from Toxvaerd's model are largely consistent with the empirical evidence presented by Mitchell and Muherin (1996), who find that merger waves are industry specific.

As the model by Gorton et al. (2009) shows, managers who attempt to increase firm size may be a significant determinant of merger waves. Such takeover actions may be value decreasing if they are undertaken to preserve private benefits of control. M&As may also arise due to managerial discretion (Jensen, 1986) as well as hubris (Roll, 1986). Goel and Thakor (2010), whose assertion that CEO envy drives merger waves is compelling, show that envy-driven takeovers are likely to fail. Their model also leads to other predictions that are borne out by empirical findings. For example, bear-market mergers are not driven by CEO envy and hence should exhibit greater synergies compared to bull-market mergers as validated by Bouwman et al. (2009).

Evidence shows a positive correlation between merger activity and economic cycles, implying that merger activity is pro-cyclical. Shleifer and Vishny (2003) and Rhodes-Kropf and Viswanathan (2004) propose market-driven theories for this behavior. Goel and Thakor (2010) show that merger waves are more likely during periods of high-market versus low-market returns. However, the empirical findings by Dong et al. (2006) suggest that the dispersion of market valuation of stocks is positively correlated with merger waves.

While some view M&As as management actions to expand a firm's boundaries of the firm, corporate divestures (e.g., sell-offs, spin-offs, and equity carve-outs) are intended to contract its boundaries. Firms engage in expansionary and contractionary actions due to strategic considerations to maximize the value of the firm. The chapter shows that among the theoretical considerations proposed in the literature, management may pursue corporate divestments as strategic wealth-creating actions to signal undervaluation of the spin-off, a market-driven rationale similar to that proposed by Shleifer and Vishny (2003), or to remove agency costs associated with expansion arising from private motives such as empire building or hubris. If investors have excessive optimism for a particular type of stocks (e.g., glamour stocks), managers may rationally react to meet this demand by undertaking spin-offs or equity carve-outs. In this situation, as proposed by Sundarsanam and Qian (2006), firms engage in corporate divestures to cater to a short-term demand and not to improve their resource allocation after the divestiture.

DISCUSSION QUESTIONS

1. Evidence suggests that equity carve-outs are only a temporary managerial action and that a high likelihood exists that an equity carve-out will be followed by a sell-off or reacquisition. Under what conditions are there increased probabilities of a sell-off?

2. The Goel and Thakor (2010) model proposes that CEO envy is an important determinant of merger waves. How does this model differ from those that are based on Roll's (1986) hubris theory?

3. Both the Shleifer and Vishny (2003) model and the Rhodes-Kropf and Viswanathan (2004) model are based on market timing. What is the key difference between these models?

4. Andrade, Mitchell, and Stafford (2001) present evidence showing that stock-financed acquisitions are preponderant in high valuation stock markets. Explain this finding.

5. A dominant motive for divestitures is to increase the focus of the parent company. How does a focused divestment create corporate value?

6. Under what condition is a sell-off preferred to a spin-off?

REFERENCES

Afshar, Karim A., Richard. J. Taffler, and Puliyur S. Sudarsanam. 1992. "The Effect of Corporate Divestment on Shareholders' Wealth: The UK Experience." *Journal of Banking and Finance* 16:1, 115–135.

Alexander, Gordon J., George P. Benson, and Joan M. Kampmeyer. 1984. "Investigating the Effects of Announcements of Voluntary Selloffs." *Journal of Finance* 39:2, 503–517.

Allen, Jeffrey W., and John J. McConnell. 1998. "Equity Carve-Outs and Managerial Discretion." *Journal of Finance* 53:1, 163–186.

Amihud, Yakov, and Baruch Lev. 1981. "Risk Reduction as a Managerial Motive for Conglomerate Mergers." *RAND Journal of Economics* 12:2, 605–617.

Andrade, Gregor, Mark L. Mitchell, and Erik Stafford. 2001. "New Evidence and Perspectives on Mergers." *Journal of Economic Perspectives* 15:2, 103–120.

Anslinger, Patricia L., Steven J. Klepper, and Somu Subramaniam. 1999. "Breaking Up Is Good to Do: Restructuring through Spin Offs, Equity Carve-outs and Tracking Stocks Can Create Shareholder Value." *McKinsey Quarterly* 1, 16–27.

Aron, Debra J. 1991. "Using the Capital Market as a Monitor: Corporate Spin-Offs in an Agency Framework." *RAND Journal of Economics* 22:4, 505–518.

Beckenstein, Alan. 1979. "Merger Activity and Merger Theories: An Empirical Investigation." *Antitrust Bulletin* 24: Spring, 105–128.

Berger, Philip G., and Eli Ofek. 1995. "Diversification's Effect on Firm Value." *Journal of Financial Economics* 37:1, 39–65.

Berkovitch, Elazar, and M. P. Narayanan. 1993. "Motives for Takeovers: An Empirical Investigation." *Journal of Financial and Quantitative Analysis* 76:1, 347–362.

Bliss, Richard, and Richard J. Rosen. 2001. "CEO Compensation and Bank Mergers." *Journal of Financial Economics* 61:1, 107–138.

Bouwman, Christa H., Kathleen Fuller, and Amrita Nain. 2009. "Stock Market Valuations and Mergers." *Review of Financial Studies* 22:2, 633–679.

Brealey, Richard A., Stewart C. Myers, and Franklin Allen. 2006. *Principles of Corporate Finance*, 8th ed. New York: McGraw-Hill/Irwin.

Burch, Timothy R., and Vikram Nanda. 2003. "Divisional Diversity and the Conglomerate Discount: Evidence from Spinoffs." *Journal of Financial Economics* 70:1, 69–98.

Byerly, Robin T., Bruce T. Lamont, and Terrill Keasler. 2003. "Business Portfolio Restructuring, Prior Diversification Posture and Investor Reactions." *Managerial and Decisions Economics* 24:8, 535–548.

Chatterjee, Sayan. 1986. "Types of Synergy and Economic Value: The Impact of Acquisitions on Merging and Rival Firms." *Strategic Management Journal* 7:2, 119–139,

Chemmanur, Thomas, and Mark H. Liu. 2005. "Institutional Trading, Information Production, and the Choice between Spin-offs, Carve-Outs, and Tracking Stock Issues." Working Paper, Boston College.

Chemmanur, Thomas J., and An Yan. 2004. "A Theory of Corporate Spin-offs." *Journal of Financial Economics* 72:2, 259–290.

Comment, Robert, and Gregg Jarrell. 1995. "Corporate Focus and Stock Returns." *Journal of Financial Economics* 37:1, 65–89.

Cusatis, Patrick, James Miles, and Randall Woolridge. 1993. "Restructuring Through Spin-offs." *Journal of Financial Economics* 45:3, 257–281.

Daley, Lane, Vikas Mehrotra, and Ranjini Sivakumar. 1997. "Corporate Focus and Value Creation: Evidence from Spinoffs." *Journal of Financial Economics* 45:1, 257–281.

Dann, Larry Y., and Harry DeAngelo. 1983. "Standstill Agreements, Privately Negotiated Stock Repurchases, and the Market for Corporate Control." *Journal of Financial Economics* 11:1, 275–300.

Datta, Sudip, and Mai E. Iskandar-Datta. 1996. "Who Gains from Corporate Asset Sales?" *Journal of Financial Research* 19:1, 41–58.

Desai, Hemang, and Prem C. Jain. 1999. "Firm Performance and Focus: Long Run Stock Market Performance Following Spin-offs." *Journal of Financial Economics* 75:1, 75–101.

Devos, Erik, Palani-Rajan Kadapakkam, and Srinivasan Krishnamurthy. 2009. "How Do Mergers Create Value? A Comparison of Taxes, Market Power and Efficiency Improvements as Explanations for Synergies." *Review of Financial Studies* 22:3, 1179–1211

Dong, Ming, David A. Hirshleifer, Scott A. Richardson, and Siew Hong Teoh. 2006. "Does Investor Misvaluation Drive the Takeover Market?" *Journal of Finance* 61:2, 725–762.

Duchin, Ran, and Breno Schmidt. 2008. "Riding the Merger Wave." Working Paper, University of Michigan and University of Southern California. Available at http://ssrn.com/abstract=1102796.

Gartner, Dennis L., and Daniel Halbheer. 2009. "Are There Waves in Merger Activity After All?" *International Journal of Industrial Organization* 27:6, 708–718.

Geman, Stuart, and Donald Geman. 1984. "Stochastic Relaxation, Gibbs Distributions, and the Bayesian Restoration of Images." *IEEE Transactions on Pattern Analysis and Machine Intelligence* 6:6, 721–741.

Goel, Anand M., Vikram Nanda, and M. P. Narayanan. 2004. "Career Concerns and Resource Allocation in Conglomerates." *Review of Financial Studies* 17:1, 99–128.

Goel, Anand M., and Anjan V. Thakor. 2010. "Do Envious CEOs Cause Merger Waves?" *Review of Financial Studies* 23:2, 487–517.

Goergen, Marc, and Luc Renneboog. 2004. "Shareholder Wealth Effects of European Domestic and Cross-Border Takeover Bids." *European Financial Management* 10:1, 9–45.

Golbe, Devra L., and Lawrence J. White. 1988. "A Time-series Analysis of Mergers and Acquisitions in the U.S. Economy." In Alan J. Auerbach, (ed.), *Mergers and Acquisitions*, 265–310. Chicago: University of Chicago Press.

Golbe, Devra L., and Lawrence J. White. 1993. "Catch a Wave: The Time Series Behavior of Mergers." *Review of Economics and Statistics* 75:3, 493–499.

Gort, Michael. 1969. "An Economic Disturbance Theory of Mergers." *Quarterly Journal of Economics* 83:4, 624–642.

Gorton, Gary, Matthias Kahl, and Richard J. Rosen. 2009. "Eat or Be Eaten: A Theory of Mergers and Firm Size." *Journal of Finance* 64:3, 1291–1344.

Habib, Michel A., D. Bruce Johnsen, and Narayan Y. Naik. 1997. "Spinoffs and Information." *Journal of Financial Intermediation* 6:2, 153–176.

Hand, John R., and Terrence R. Skantz. 1998. "Market Timing through Equity Carve-outs?" Working Paper, University of North Carolina.

Harford, Jarrad. 2005. "What Drives Merger Waves?" *Journal of Financial Economics* 77:3, 529–560.

Jain, Prem C. 1985. "The Effect of Voluntary Sell-off Announcements on Shareholder Wealth." *Journal of Finance* 40:1, 209–224.

Jarrow, Robert A., and Maureen O'Hara. 1989. "Primes and Scores: An Essay on Market Imperfections." *Journal of Finance* 44:5, 1263–1287.

Jensen, Michael C. 1986. "Agency Costs of Free Cash Flow, Corporate Finance, and Takeovers." *American Economic Review* 76:2, 323–329.

Jensen, Michael C. 1993. "The Modern Industrial Revolution, Exit, and the Failure of Internal Control Systems." *Journal of Finance* 48:3, 831–880.

Jensen, Michael C., and William H. Meckling. 1976. "Theory of the Firm: Managerial Behavior, Agency Costs and Ownership Structure." *Journal of Financial Economics* 3:4, 305–360.

John, Kose, and Eli Ofek. 1995. "Asset Sales and Increase in Focus." *Journal of Financial Economics* 37:1, 105–126.

Jovanovic, Boyan, and Peter L. Rousseau. 2002. "The Q-theory of Mergers." *American Economic Review* 92:2, 198–204.

Kaiser, Kevin M., and Aris Stouraitis. 2001. "Reversing Corporate Diversification and the Use of Proceeds from Asset Sales: The Case of Thorn EMI." *Financial Management* 30:4, 63–102.

Khan, Qayyum A., and Dileep R. Mehta. 1996. "Voluntary Divestitures and the Choice between Selloffs and Spinoffs." *Financial Review* 31:2, 885–912.

Klein, April, James Rosenfeld, and William Beranek. 1991. "The Two Stages of an Equity Carveout and the Price Response of Parent and Subsidiary Stock." Managerial and Decision Economics 12:5, 449–460.

Krishnaswami, Sudha, and Venkat Subramaniam. 1999. "Information Asymmetry, Valuation, and the Corporate Spin-off Decision." *Journal of Financial Economics* 53:1, 73–112.

Lambrecht, Bart M. 2004. "The Timing and Terms of Mergers Motivated by Economies of Scale." *Journal of Financial Economics* 72:1, 41–62.

Lambrecht, Bart M., and Stewart C. Myers. 2004. "A Theory of Takeovers and Disinvestment." Working Paper, University of Lancaster.

Lang, Larry, Annette Poulsen and René M. Stulz. 1995. "Asset Sales, Firm Performance, and the Agency Costs of Managerial Discretion." *Journal of Financial Economics* 37:1, 3–37.

Lang, Larry, and René M. Stulz. 1994. "Tobin's Q, Corporate Diversification, and Firm Performance." *Journal of Political Economy* 102:6, 1248–1280.

Lasfer, Meziane, Puliyur S. Sundarsanam, and Richard J. Taffler. 1996. "Financial Distress, Asset Sales, and Lender Monitoring." *Financial Management* 25:3, 57–66.

Linn, Scott C., and Michael S. Rozeff. 1984. "The Corporate Sell-off." *Midland Corporate Finance Journal* 2:3, 428–436.

Maksimovic, Vojislav, and Gordon Phillips. 2001. "The Market for Corporate Assets: Who Engages in Mergers and Asset Sales and Are There Efficiency Gains?" *Journal of Finance* 56:6, 2019–2065.

Malmendier, Ulrike, and Geoffrey Tate. 2005. "CEO Overconfidence and Corporate Investment." *Journal of Finance* 60:6, 2261–2700.

Markides, Constantinos C. 1992. "The Economic Characteristics of De-diversifying Firms." *British Journal of Management* 3:2, 91–100.

Martin, Kenneth, and John McConnell. 1991. "Corporate Performance, Corporate Takeovers, and Management Turnover." *Journal of Finance* 46:2, 671–688.

Martynova, Marina, and Luc Renneboog. 2008. "A Century of Corporate Takeovers: What Have We Learned and Where Do We Stand?" *Journal of Banking and Finance* 32:10, 2148–2177.

Miles, James A., J. Randall Woolridge, and Mark Tocchet. 1999. *Spin-offs and Equity Carveouts. Achieving Faster Growth and Better Performance.* Morristown, NJ: Financial Executives Research Foundation.

Mitchell, Mark L., and Harold J. Mulherin. 1996. "The Impact of Industry Shocks on Takeover and Restructuring Activity." *Journal of Financial Economics* 41:2, 193–229.

Moeller, Sara B., Frederik P. Schlingemann, and René M. Stulz. 2004. "Firm Size and Gains from Acquisitions," *Journal of Financial Economics* 73:2, 201–228.

Morck, Randall, Andrei Shleifer, and Robert Vishny. 1990. "Do Managerial Objectives Drive Bad Acquisitions?" *Journal of Finance* 45:1, 31–48.

Mulherin, Harold J., and Audra L. Boone. 2000. "Comparing Acquisitions and Divestitures." *Journal of Corporate Finance* 6:2, 117–139.

Nanda, Vikram. 1991. "On the Good News in Equity Carve-outs." *Journal of Finance* 46:5, 1717–1737.

Nanda, Vikram, and M. P. Narayanan. 1999. "Disentangling Values: Financing Needs, Firm Scope and Divestitures." *Journal of Financial Intermediation* 8:3, 174–204.

Nelson, Ralph. L. 1959. *Merger Movement in American Industry, 1895-1956.* Princeton, NJ: Princeton University Press.

Rajan, Raghuram, Henri Servaes, and Luigi Zingales. 2000. "The Cost of Diversity: The Diversification Discount and Inefficient Investment." *Journal of Finance* 55:1, 35–80.

Rau, Rahgavendra P., and Theo Vermaelen. 1998. "Glamour, Value and Post-Acquisition Performance of Acquiring Firms." *Journal of Financial Economics* 49:2, 101–116.

Ravenscraft, David J., and Frederic M. Scherer. 1987. *Mergers, Selloffs and Economic Efficiency.* Washington DC: The Brookings Institution.

Rhodes-Kropf, Matthew, and S. Viswanathan. 2004. "Market Valuation and Merger Waves." *Journal of Finance* 59:6, 2685–2718.

Roll, Richard. 1986. "The Hubris Hypothesis of Corporate Takeovers." *Journal of Business* 59:2, 197–216.

Ross, Stephen A. 1976. "Options and Efficiency." *Quarterly Journal of Economics* 90:1, 75–89.

Scherer, Frederic M., and David Ross. 1990. *Industrial Market Structure and Economic Performance.* Boston: Houghton Mifflin.

Schipper, Katherine, and Abbie Smith. 1986. "A Comparison of Equity Carve-Outs and Seasoned Equity Offerings." *Journal of Financial Economics* 15:1/2, 153–186.

Schwert, William G. 2000. "Hostility in Takeovers: In the Eyes of the Beholder?" *Journal of Finance* 55:6, 2599–2640.

Shleifer, Andrei, and Robert W. Vishny. 1989. "Management Entrenchment: The Case of Manager-specific Investments." *Journal of Financial Economics* 25:1, 123–139.

Shleifer, Andrei, and Robert W. Vishny. 1990. "The Takeover Wave of the 1980s." *Science* 249: August 17, 745–749.

Shleifer, Andrei, and Robert W. Vishny. 2003. "Stock Market Driven Acquisitions." *Journal of Financial Economics* 70:3, 295–311.

Shughart, William F., and Robert D. Tollison. 1984. "The Random Character of Merger Activity." *RAND Journal of Economics* 15:4, 500–509.

Slovin, Myron B., Marie E. Sushka, and Steven R. Ferraro. 1995. "A Comparison of the Information Conveyed by Equity Carve-outs, Spin-offs, and Asset Sell-offs." *Journal of Financial Economics* 37:1, 89–104

Steiner, Thomas L. 1997. "The Corporate Sell-off Decision of Diversified Firms." *Journal of Financial Research* 20:2, 231–241.

Sudarsanam, Puliyur S. 2003. *Creating Value from Mergers and Acquisitions: The Challenges.* London: Prentice Hall International.

Sudarsanam, Puliyur S., and Binsheng Qian. 2006. "Catering Theory of Corporate Spinoffs: Evidence from Europe." Working Paper, Cranfield School of Management, United Kingdom.

Toxvaerd, Flavio. 2008. "Strategic Merger Waves: A Theory of Musical Chairs." *Journal of Economic Theory* 140:1, 1–26.

Vijh, Anand M. 1994. "The Spinoff and Merger Ex-date Effects." *Journal of Finance* 49:2, 581–609.

Vijh, Anand M. 1999. "Long-term Returns from Equity Carveouts." *Journal of Financial Economics* 51:2, 273–308.

Vijh, Anand M. 2002. "The Positive Announcement-period Returns of Equity Carveouts: Asymmetric Information or Divestiture Gains?" *Journal of Business* 75:1, 153–190.

Villalonga, Belen, and Anita M. McGahan. 2005. "Industrial Market Structure and Economic Performance." *Strategic Management Journal* 26:13, 1183–1208.

Weston, Fred J., Mark L. Mitchell, and Harold J. Mulherin. 2004. *Takeovers, Restructuring and Corporate Governance.* Upper Saddle River, NJ: Pearson Prentice Hall.

ABOUT THE AUTHOR

Abdul H. Rahman is a Professor of Economics and Finance and Telfer Teaching Fellow at the Telfer School of Management, the University of Ottawa. Previously, he was Associate Dean at the John Molson School of Business, Concordia University in Montreal. He has published in the *Journal of Banking and Finance, Journal of Financial and Quantitative Analysis, Review of Economics and Statistics*, and *Journal of Futures Markets*. He was named by the MBA Student Association as the best MBA teacher in the Telfer School of Management over the last 10 years. Professor Rahman's teaching interests are corporate finance, international finance, and international economics. He received a BSc in Mathematics and an MSc in Mathematics from McGill University, and both an MA in Economics and a PhD in Economics from Concordia University.

CHAPTER 7

The Short-Term and Long-Term Performance of M&As

SHANTANU DUTTA
Assistant Professor of Finance, University of Ontario Institute of Technology

SAMIR SAADI
PhD Candidate, Queen's School of Business

INTRODUCTION

Over the last three decades, much research has investigated the short-term and long-term gains and losses pertaining to takeover (or acquisition) activities. Although such activities involve many parties, empirical studies focus mainly on the gains and losses of the buyer and the seller of the target company. Regarding short-term performance, empirical evidence generally shows that the bidders' shareholders earn, on average, a zero abnormal return at the acquisition's announcement, but considerable variation exists in these results (Andrade, Mitchell and Stafford, 2001; Bruner, 2002; Fuller, Netter, and Stegemoller, 2002). Target shareholders generally earn significantly positive abnormal return. Long-term performance studies are more controversial because methodological choices can influence the results.

Despite having a rich literature, performance issues involving mergers and acquisitions (M&As) continue to draw substantial interest among academicians and practitioners. The reasons for this continuing interest are twofold. First, a lack of consensus still exists on various issues such as long-term performance, short-term gains to acquiring firms, the impact of governance issues, and the relationship between performance and the characteristics of targets and bidders. Second, major changes have occurred in the M&A market over the last two decades. Such changes include a shift in focus from unrelated to related targets and from hostile to friendly takeovers. Other changes involve modes of payment, deregulation in certain industries, increased levels of foreign competition, and renewed interest in corporate governance issues. These changes have resulted in analyses with a much broader focus.

This purpose of this chapter is to provide a synthesis of some of the more important M&A literature involving short-term and long-term performance issues. Given the vast literature, this synthesis is not intended to be exhaustive. The chapter has the following organization. The next section examines short-term performance of target and acquiring firms followed by a discussion of long-term stock return performance of acquiring firms. While discussing the long-term performance issues, this chapter separately examines long-term stock return performance and operating performance. The final section provides a summary and conclusions.

SHORT-TERM PERFORMANCE OF TARGET AND ACQUIRING FIRMS

The majority of the M&A performance studies focus on short-term gains or losses of the target and acquiring firms. Andrade et al. (2001) point out that the most statistically reliable evidence on whether mergers create value for shareholders comes from traditional short-window event studies around an announcement date. The main results of these studies and relevant issues are discussed below.

Short-Term Performance of Target Firms

Most of the short-term M&A studies show that mergers create value for shareholders on an aggregate basis (i.e., by combining the effects on target shareholders and bidder shareholders), and most of the gains accrue to the target shareholders (Andrade et al., 2001). Results from existing empirical studies confirm that the shareholders of target firms generally gain from takeover deals. These results are consistent across studies carried out for different time periods (e.g., Langetieg, 1978; Jensen and Ruback, 1983; Smith and Kim, 1994; Bradley, Desai, and Kim, 1988; Franks, Harris, and Titman, 1991; Eckbo and Thorburn, 2000; Mulherin 2000; Houston, James, and Ryngaert, 2001; Bruner, 2002). The finance literature contains the following reasons for the positive returns of target firm shareholders after the announcement of a merger or a takeover attempt.

Synergy Motive
The most commonly cited reason for acquisitions involves prospective synergies. The synergy motive assumes that the managers of both the targets and acquirers maximize shareholder wealth and engage in takeover activity only if it results in gains to both sets of shareholders. If this were true, then the measured gains to both the target and acquirer shareholders should be positive (Berkovitch and Naryanan, 1993).

Agency Problems
Agency theory predicts that shareholders should gain as a result of disciplinary actions taken against managers who perform poorly (Palepu, 1986). Therefore, if the target firms have agency problems, and if their management performance is expected to be poor in the future, the stock returns for the target company should increase after a merger announcement (Ghosh and Lee, 2000).

Multiple Bidders and Bargaining Power
If the target has some bargaining power due to its ability to resist the acquirer or competition exists among potential acquirers, then the target gain should increase (Berkovitch and Naryanan, 1993). This increase results from bidding firms having to pay a premium to acquire the target.

Short-Term Performance of Acquiring Firms

Unlike the short-term performance of target firms, much variation exists in the short-term performance results for acquiring firms (i.e., positive, negative or insignificant results). Most of the earlier studies using U.S. data report negative or insignificant abnormal returns for acquirers' shareholders. However, other studies using non-U.S. data consistently report significant and positive abnormal returns for acquirers' shareholders around the announcement date (Eckbo, 1986; Calvet and Lefoll, 1987; Masse, Hanrahan, and Kushner, 1990; Eckbo and Thorburn, 2000; Yuce and Ng, 2005). Such variation in short-term returns to bidding firms' shareholders is puzzling, and researchers have been unable to explain successfully much of this variation (Fuller et al., 2002). Prior studies have identified various difficulties in estimating bidders' returns (Eckbo, Giammarino, and Heinkel, 1990a; Fuller et al., 2002; Grinblatt and Titman, 2002; Hietala, Kaplan, and Robinson, 2003). First, if the target's relative size is small, it will not cause any significant impact on the bidder's returns. Second, abnormal returns present only the surprise component of the acquisition. If the market already knows the acquirer's motives from its past actions, the stock price reaction would only refer to the perceived deviation of the announced deal from the anticipated one. Third, when the takeover process takes a long time to conclude, the uncertainty of the event is increased. Thus, isolating the market's perception of the bid would be difficult. These factors could contribute to the inconsistent short-term abnormal returns reported in the past.

Firm-Specific and Deal-Specific Factors

The M&A literature also examines various firm-specific and deal-specific factors as well as their impact on abnormal returns. This subsection highlights the findings of these studies.

Type of Target Organization (Public, Private, and Subsidiaries)

Bidders acquire targets for a better price when they buy a nonpublic firm, as compared to a public firm, resulting in a better return for the acquiring firms' shareholders. Financial economists cite the following reasons for supporting this observation.

- *Liquidity impact and limited competition.* Private firms and subsidiaries cannot be bought and sold as easily as publicly traded firms. Because this lack of liquidity makes these investments less attractive, offers are generally less for private firms. This situation gives a better return to a bidding firm's shareholders (Fuller et al., 2002).
- *Monitoring hypothesis.* Firms acquiring privately held targets through common stock exchanges tend to create outside blockholders because a small group of shareholders owns the targets (Chang, 1998). The creation of outside blockholders can serve as an effective monitor of management, which in turn can increase bidder value (Shleifer and Vishny, 1986; Fuller et al., 2002).
- *Investors' portfolio preference.* Hansen and Lott (1996) hypothesize that because investors are diversified, the goal of the firm's managers is not to

maximize shareholder value, but to maximize the value of the shareholder's portfolio. Thus, when a public bidder acquires a public target, diversified shareholders will be indifferent to how the gains from the acquisitions are divided, assuming they own stock in both firms. Hence, there should not be any abnormal return for the bidding firm's shareholders if a public firm is acquired.

Further, Fuller et al. (2002) argue that a parent company would sell a subsidiary in order to have a better focus to its core business. As a result, the parent company might be willing to accept a lower offer for the subsidiary. Therefore, the market is likely to react positively if an acquiring firm makes an announcement to buy a subsidiary.

Studies, including Hansen and Lott (1996) and Moeller, Schlingemann, and Stulz (2003), report higher returns for private target acquisition. Chang (1998) examines bidder returns to firms acquiring 281 privately held targets (131 cash offers and 150 stock offers) and compares them to bidder returns for 255 public targets (101 cash offers and 154 stock offers). Chang finds no abnormal return for bidders in the case of cash offers. However, for stock offers, the author reports a 2.64 percent abnormal return for privately held targets and a –2.46 percent abnormal return for publicly held targets. Fuller et al. (2002) report positive abnormal returns for subsidiary acquisition, which is robust to different forms of payments.

Methods of Payment

Myers and Majluf (1984) argue that a bidder firm will use stock as the medium of exchange if the board believes that its own shares are overvalued. Alternatively, if the bidder firm is convinced that its shares are undervalued, it may offer cash in order to send a positive signal to the market. As a result, the market should view cash offers more favorably than stock offers (Travlos, 1987; Fishman, 1989; Eckbo, Maksimovic, and Williams, 1990b; Fuller et al., 2002). Also, if the bidder is uncertain about the target's value, the bidder may not want to offer cash, because the target will only accept a cash offer greater than its true value and the bidder will have overpaid (Fuller et al., 2002). An alternative tax-based hypothesis favors stock offers. If a target is acquired with cash, target shareholders are required to pay tax immediately. In the case of a stock offer, however, tax implications are deferred (Travlos, 1987; Fuller et al., 2002). Most empirical studies find support for the hypothesis that the shareholders of acquiring firms view cash offers more positively (Fishman, 1989; Martin, 1996; Fuller et al., 2002; Moeller et al., 2003). Eckbo and Thorburn (2000) do not find any significant difference for cash payments, while Ben-Amar and Andre (2006) find a significant, positive relationship between cash payments and acquirer's abnormal returns in a Canadian context.

Cash Reserves

Cash reserves can provide a valuable source of funds for investment opportunities. Firms often accumulate much more cash than they require. Jensen (1986) argues that a firm's agency problem can get compounded with the presence of large free cash flows. Excessive cash reserves insulate managers from being monitored by external market forces, and managers with an empire-building objective might use this extra cash in poor investment activities such as nonproductive acquisitions rather than distributing it to the shareholders (Harford, 1999). As a result, a higher level of cash reserves in an acquiring firm is likely to generate lower levels of abnormal returns. However, in a U.S. context, Moeller, Schlingemann, and Stulz (2004) do not find any support for this free cash flow hypothesis.

Relative Size

Acquiring a relatively large target is likely to be a more important economic event for the acquirer than acquiring a relatively small target (Eckbo et al., 1990a). Greater relative size could bring about more synergy (a positive effect). Alternatively, managing a larger target company could be more difficult (a negative effect). As the size of a target increases, the target should have greater bargaining power and the acquisition should become more expensive for the acquiring firm.

Various studies consider the issue of relative size. For example, Loderer and Martin (1992) exclude all acquisitions that are smaller than 10 percent of the acquirer's size, whereas Moeller et al. (2003) use a cut-off point of 1 percent. Other studies use an absolute value of the bid for an acquisition to be considered in the analysis. For example, Malatesta (1983) considers 10 million USD (or greater) deals, and Gregory (1997) considers 10 million £ (or greater) deals.

Agrawal, Jaffe, and Mandelker (1992) examine the issue more scientifically. They rank all the mergers by relative size and form quintile portfolios. Next, they calculate the long-run abnormal returns of each portfolio individually, but fail to detect any monotonic relationship. Moeller et al. (2003) report a positive effect, whereas Fuller et al. (2002) find that the effect of relative size is negative for public targets and positive for private targets. Overall, Moeller et al. report a positive relationship between the relative deal size and the acquiring firm's short-term abnormal returns.

Size of Acquiring Firms

Some studies show that small firms consistently experience significantly larger risk-adjusted returns than larger firms (Banz, 1981; Reinganum, 1983, 1992). More recently, Moeller et al. (2004) show that the acquiring firm's size has a negative effect on short-term abnormal returns. They report a 2 percent higher announcement return for smaller acquiring firms irrespective of the form of financing and whether the acquired firm is public or private. Possible reasons for such observations are the following: (1) Managers of larger firms may suffer from hubris and are likely to overpay; (2) larger firms tend to make acquisitions by stock, thus sending a negative signal to the market; and (3) smaller firms are more likely to acquire private firms, thus having a favorable reaction in the market.

Governance Characteristics of Acquiring Firms

In recent years, corporate governance issues have attracted considerable attention from both practitioners and academicians. Some argue that governance mechanisms can contribute to better firm performance, despite a lack of consensus based on empirical evidence. Commonly cited governance mechanisms that may influence abnormal returns of the bidding firms around the announcement period include board independence (more outsider directors and separation of chief executive officer [CEO] and board chairperson), managerial ownership, blockholder ownership, and CEO pay. The following provides a summary of the possible effects of corporate governance mechanisms on the returns of bidders.

Managerial Ownership

According to Berle and Means (1932) and Jensen and Meckling (1976), the level of managerial ownership is a potential source of agency problems. If the managerial ownership is too low, the interests of managers will not be aligned with that of other shareholders. As a result, management may make decisions that are not in the best interests of shareholders. On the other hand, if managers have considerable ownership in a firm, they may be more careful in making a decision that is more favorable for the existing shareholders because the increased level of managerial ownership would align managers' interests with those of the shareholders (Fama and Jensen, 1983; Subrahmanyam, Rangan, and Rosenstein, 1997). This should lead to better managerial decisions. However, some studies such as Morck, Shleifer, and Vishny (1988) show that such a relationship might not be monotonic.

Blockholder Ownership

Shleifer and Vishny (1986) predict that, with all else being equal, the presence of a large blockholder has a positive effect on the market value of the firm. The potential takeover threat that large blockholders can exert works as an effective device for monitoring management. Others contend that because of higher levels of ownership, blockholders are likely to take an active part in monitoring and hence make positive contributions to a firm's performance (Bhagat and Jefferis, 2002).

Faccio, McConnell, and Stolin (2006) examine announcement period abnormal returns to acquirers of listed and unlisted targets in 17 Western European countries over the period 1996 to 2001. Among other factors, the study examines the impact of ownership structure on abnormal returns, but does not report any significant results.

Ben-Amar and Andre (2006) investigate the relationship between ownership structure and acquiring firm performance with a sample of 327 Canadian transactions over the period from 1998 to 2002. They find that the presence of outside blockholders and family control firms has a positive influence on the acquiring firm performance. Further, this study also reports a negative relationship between ownership of a majority of the cash flow rights and the acquiring firm's abnormal returns.

A few studies examine the impact of a multiple voting share structure on abnormal returns. A multiple voting share structure leads to unequal voting and cash-flow rights to different groups of shareholders. For example, a particular group of shareholders may have the right of two votes for holding one share, whereas other shareholders may have one vote for holding one share. This structure creates opportunities for expropriation. Hanson and Song (1996) examine the effect of multiple voting shares on acquiring firms' abnormal returns using a sample of 69 M&As undertaken by 39 U.S. firms and report a negative relationship. However, using a Canadian sample that includes all completed Canadian M&As between

1993 and 2003, Jog, Zhu, and Dutta (2010) report no significant relationship between a multiple voting share structure and abnormal returns.

Bae, Kang, and Kim (2002) examine M&A deals undertaken by Korean business groups known as *chaebols*. Because chaebols involve a concentrate ownership, the distinction between ownership and management is unclear. Chaebol owners have substantial discretionary power, and minority shareholders do not enjoy strong legal protection in Korea. As the authors report, the market negatively views acquisitions by these firms in Korea.

Board Structure

Lipton and Lorsch (1992) as well as Jensen (1993) suggest that large boards can be less effective than small boards. When boards become too big, agency problems such as director free-riding increase, and the board becomes more symbolic and less a part of the management process (Jensen, 1993; Hermalin and Weisbach, 2003). Wu (2000) offers similar arguments as follows. First, small boards of directors facilitate better communication among directors and more effective coordination of the directors' expertise and speed up action when a problem occurs. Second, having a limited number of board members prevents a board from developing into a bureaucracy, dividing into cliques, and encouraging passivity at meetings. However, board independence, which is characterized by a majority of independent directors and an unrelated board chair, leads to greater monitoring of the bidding firm's management. This, in turn, is likely to result in better decisions from the shareholders' perspective. Similarly, an unrelated board chair may make more objective decisions that are in line with shareholders' interests.

Byrd and Hickman (1992) report that bidding firms with a majority of independent directors enjoy higher announcement-date abnormal returns than others. Cotter, Shivdasani, and Zenner (1997) report similar results for target firm shareholders. More recent studies use an acquiring firm's governance index based on adopted antitakeover provisions (ATPs) and firm performance (Gompers, Ishii, and Metrick, 2003). Managers in firms with more ATPs are more likely to make value-destroying investment decisions, which the market may view negatively. Evidence by Gompers et al. shows that firms with stronger shareholders rights (and fewer ATPs) outperform those with weaker shareholders rights (and more ATPs) by 8.5 percent abnormal returns per year. Using a similar governance index, Masulis, Wang, and Xie (2007) find that acquirers with more ATPs experience significantly lower announcement period stock returns than other acquirers.

LONG-TERM STOCK RETURN PERFORMANCE OF ACQUIRING FIRMS

M&A studies tend to investigate the short-term performance of target and acquiring firms. Although long-term performance studies are limited, the literature is growing. Agrawal and Jaffe (2000) present a detailed review of studies involving the long-term postacquisition performance of acquiring firms (based on 22 U.S. and U.K. studies) and critically analyze the results. Agrawal and Jaffe conclude that except for Franks et al. (1991), which shows strong evidence of abnormal underperformance after mergers, other studies show at least some evidence of underperformance. To provide deeper insight into the existing results, a summary of the relevant studies is presented below.

As Agrawal and Jaffe (2000) note, Mandelker (1974) is the first to treat the financial consequences of mergers in a systematic way by precisely determining the merger completion date and calculating abnormal returns (or residuals) relative to a benchmark. Mandelker analyzes 241 mergers that took place between 1941 and 1962. All the acquiring and acquired firms considered in the study were listed on the New York Stock Exchange (NYSE). The results show cumulative average abnormal returns (CAARs) of –1.4 percent over the 40 months following merger completion. Although the results reveal an economically significant drop in CAARs, this change is not statistically insignificant.

Langetieg (1978) examines 149 mergers among NYSE-listed firms during the period from 1929 to 1969. He employs two different approaches to performing the analyses. First, the author uses various measures of abnormal return including the capital asset pricing model (CAPM), the two-factor model, and two industry indexes. Regardless of the measures, Langetieg reports large, negative returns over three intervals following the mergers (+1 to +12 months, +13 to +24 months, and +25 to +70 months). Second, Langetieg uses a control firm approach and calculates abnormal performance as the difference between the acquiring firm's performance, using one of the four measures above, and the control firm's performance using the same measure. The author then compares these returns and finds that the "paired difference" results are still predominantly negative, but not statistically significant.

Asquith (1983) analyzes the abnormal stock price performance of 196 successful and 87 unsuccessful NYSE firms that engaged in merger bids over the period 1962 to 1976. Unlike the monthly return data used in the Mandelker (1974) and Langetieg (1978) studies, Asquith uses daily return data, which permits examining the entire merger process from 480 trading days before a merger bid until 240 trading days after a merger bid. Asquith reports a cumulative excess return of –7.2 percent over the 240 days after the outcome date for the "successful" bidders, and –9.6 percent for the "unsuccessful" bidders. However, the author mentions a valid methodological challenge by pointing out that merging two independent firms with different betas may cause a problem with calculating excess returns. That is, the excess returns for the merged firms are calculated for a time using the beta of only the bidding firms.

Malatesta (1983) examines 256 acquiring firms over the period 1969 to 1974 as reported in the United States Federal Trade Commission (FTC) Statistical Reports on M&As. These acquisitions include only target firms with an asset size greater than $10 million. The author uses the market model to calculate abnormal returns and pre-event data to estimate pre-event alphas and betas. He uses postevent data to estimate postevent alphas and betas. The study reports significant negative abnormal returns for acquiring firms over two periods (+1 to +6 months and +7 to +12 months) of –5.4 percent and –2.2 percent, respectively. However, in explaining such results, Malatesta (p. 180) indicates that this could result from "arbitrary details of experimental design," and thus, "drawing strong conclusions concerning returns of acquiring firms is inappropriate."

Magenheim and Muller (1988) examine 77 NYSE and American Stock Exchange (AMEX) firms that completed takeovers worth at least $15 million over the period 1976 to 1981. Like Malatesta (1983), they also use a market model but divide the sample into two subgroups: 51 of the acquisitions as mergers and 26 as tender offers. Their results show CAARs over the first three years after the announcement to be –24.37 percent and +6.3 percent, respectively, for the two groups as reported by Agrawal and Jaffe (2000).

Bradley and Jarrell (1988) examine the same 78 U.S. acquiring firms over the period 1976 to 1981 as used in the Magenheim and Muller (1988) study. They criticize the use of monthly data to estimate market model parameters, as used by Malatesta (1983) and Magenheim and Muller, by claiming that the estimates would be inefficient and nonstationary. Indeed, financial economists have long argued that if the true abnormal performance were nonzero during the estimation period, the measurement of abnormal performance in the forecast period would be biased (Agrawal and Jaffe, 2000). Using a similar methodology as Asquith (1983), Bradley and Jarrell find a statistically insignificant CAAR of –16 percent over the first three postacquisition years.

Limmack (1991) examines the postacquisition performance of acquirers in 448 completed bids and 81 abandoned bids from 1977 to 1986. The study reports CAARs for acquiring firms for the period from the bid month to 24 months after the outcome month separately for completed bids and abandoned bids. For completed bids, reported CAARs are –14.96 percent, –4.67 percent, and –7.43 percent for the market model, adjusted beta model, and index model, respectively. These CAARs are all statistically significant. Limmack also presents value-weighted returns, which are smaller in magnitude, but only the market model CAAR is statistically significant. For abandoned bids, reported CAARs are –24.2 percent, –26.25 percent, and –7.38 percent for the market model, adjusted beta model, and industry index model, respectively. These CAARs are all statistically significant. Value-weighted abnormal performance is similar in magnitude, but the CAAR for the adjusted beta model is statistically insignificant.

Franks et al. (1991) investigate 399 acquisitions and tender offers from 1975 to 1984 where both the acquirer and target were NYSE-listed or AMEX-listed firms. This landmark study is the first research study to focus on long-term postmerger returns, measuring abnormal returns relative to four benchmarks: the CRSP equally weighted index, the CRSP value-weighted index, a 10-factor model, and an eight-portfolio model. The authors prefer the last benchmark, which consists of four portfolios based on firm size, three based on dividend yields, and one based on past returns. Their results for a 36-month post–announcement date window indicate significant negative abnormal returns using the equally weighted benchmark, significant, positive abnormal returns using the value-weighted benchmark, and statistically insignificant results using the 10-factor or eight-portfolio approach. Franks et al. conclude that previous reports of significant, negative abnormal returns result from benchmark errors, rather than systematic mispricing by investors at the time of acquisitions.

Using a nearly exhaustive sample consisting of 937 mergers and 227 tender offers from 1955 to 1987 between NYSE acquirers and NYSE/AMEX targets, Agrawal et al. (1992) measure postacquisition performances after adjusting for both the firm size effect and beta risk. The authors use two methods to measure long-run abnormal returns that consider adjustments for the size effect and beta risk. They measure betas over +1 to +60 months relative to the month of the merger completion in order to account for changes in the firm's beta after acquisition.

Agrawal et al. find that stockholders of the acquiring firms suffer a statistically significant wealth loss of about 10 percent over the five years after the merger completion. However, they find that long-run abnormal returns after tender offers are insignificant under both methods. This conclusion is contrary to Franks et al.'s (1991) results, which, as Agrawal et al. show, are specific to the former study's sample time period and are also due to their mixing of tender offers with mergers.

Gregory (1997) presents a comprehensive work on long-run returns in which he considers 452 U.K. acquisitions over the period 1984 to 1992. In all cases, bid values are at least greater than 10 million pounds. The author calculates abnormal returns for acquiring firms using six different models (the CAPM, a Dimson and Marsh risk and size adjustment, a simple size control portfolio, a multi-index model, a value-weighted multi-index model, and the Fama-French three-factor model). Gregory reports that the CAARs for acquiring firms range between –11.8 percent and –18.0 percent over the two years after the month of the merger completion. All of these results are statistically significant.

Loughrun and Vijh (1997) measure the postacquisition performance of 947 firms that made acquisitions over the period 1970 to 1989, where both the target and the acquirer are traded on NYSE, AMEX, or NASDAQ. For the first time in this area of literature, the authors use the buy-and-hold abnormal return (BHAR) methodology. This methodology has become increasingly popular for investigating long-run abnormal returns after a corporate event. Under this methodology, Loughrun and Vijh calculate a five-year abnormal return as the difference between the buy-and-hold return of the acquirer and the buy-and-hold return of a control firm based on size and the book-to-market ratio. Like Agrawal et al. (1992), they also separate mergers (788 cases) from tender offers (135 cases) and find that postacquisition abnormal returns are significantly negative (–15.9 percent) after mergers but marginally significantly positive after tender offers. Loughrun and Vijh also report similar results after removing cases where the postacquisition periods overlap for acquisitions of the same acquirer.

Rau and Vermaelen (1998) examine a sample of 2,823 mergers and 316 tender offers, with the buyer listed on both the Center for Research in Security Prices (CRSP) NYSE/AMEX/NASDAQ tapes and Compustat. Their sample period covers transactions from January 1980 to December 1991. Adjusting for both firm size and book-to-market ratios, they report that acquirers underperform equally weighted control portfolios with similar sizes and book-to-market ratios by 4 percent over three years from the completion date. Regardless of statistical issues, Agrawal and Jaffe (2000) note that a –4 percent result over a three-year span is not economically significant. Rau and Vermaelen also find that acquirers in tender offers earn a significant and positive abnormal return of 8.56 percent. This is inconsistent with previous statistically insignificant findings and may reflect differences in sample composition (including a higher proportion of smaller firms) and the noted methodological bias.

Mitchell and Stafford (2000) examine long-run performance following three corporate events: takeovers, equity issues, and equity repurchases. Their sample of takeovers consists of 2,767 acquisitions (including both mergers and tender offers) of CRSP-listed firms from 1961 to 1993. They use three different methods to calculate abnormal return. First, they calculate BHAR for three years using appropriate size and book-to-market value portfolios. Second, they perform Fama-French regression analysis after forming calendar time portfolios (discussed in the next section). Third, they form portfolios each month using the sample of all acquirers with an acquisition within the last three years. The authors calculate abnormal return in each calendar month as the difference between the realized return on the event portfolio and an estimate of its expected return. They estimate the latter from either the Fama-French three-factor model or the appropriate size and book-to-market value portfolio. For all the three approaches, Mitchell and Stafford use equally weighted and value-weighted portfolios. Once considering the cross-sectional dependence, the BHAR approach does not give any significant abnormal returns. For the other two methods, the authors also report similar insignificant abnormal returns once considering value-weighted portfolios. Based on these results, Mitchell and Stafford contend that all of the earlier results on long-run abnormal returns need to be considered carefully and that earlier findings of long-run underperformance are most likely due to the misspecification of different methods.

Moeller et al. (2003) examine a sample of 12,023 acquisitions by public firms from 1980 to 2001 that are listed in the Securities Data Company's (SDC) U.S. Mergers and Acquisitions Database. Almost half of the sample involves acquisitions of private firms (5,583). The authors employ both "calendar time portfolio" and "event time" approaches to evaluate long-term performance. They also examine long-term returns for subsamples selected according to firm size, target organizational form, and form of payment. In the case of the calendar time portfolio approach, they report a monthly abnormal return of –0.04 percent for acquiring companies, which is statistically and economically insignificant. Moeller et al. also find that private firm acquisitions by large firms have positive, long-term abnormal returns, while private firm acquisitions by small firms have negative, long-term abnormal returns. In the case of the event time approach, they calculate the three-year BHARs, following the approach of Barber and Lyon (1997). By using an equally weighted BHAR technique, Moeller et al. find that acquiring firms have a negative abnormal return (–16.02 percent) over a three-year period, which is economically significant. However, they do not make corrections for possible cross-sectional dependence among the various events taking place within a short period of time (Mitchell and Stafford, 2000). This may lead to a significant abnormal return in the case of event time analysis.

Andre, Kooli, and L'Her (2004) examine a sample of 267 acquisitions by Canadian acquirers over the period 1980 to 2000, using different calendar-time approaches. They report a significant negative abnormal return for Canadian acquirers over the three-year postevent period considering the nonoverlapping cases (143 cases). However, the authors do not observe any significant abnormal returns when considering all cases together (overlapping and nonoverlapping cases). Further, Andre et al. report that glamour acquirers, equity financed deals, cross-border acquisitions, and related acquisitions exhibit long-run underperformance.

Dube and Glascock (2006) examine a sample of 255 U.S. acquisitions over the period 1975 to 1996. They use a calendar time portfolio approach, using Fama-French regression factors (three and four factors). Their results show no risk-adjusted abnormal performance in the stock returns of acquiring firms after acquisitions (36 months).

Most of these long-term studies conclude that acquiring firms experience significant negative abnormal returns over one to three years after the merger. These studies bring into question the notion of market efficiency. Such findings should be viewed critically for the following compelling reasons. First, neoclassical economic theory assumes that corporate management acts to maximize the shareholders' wealth. Thus, shareholders should not suffer wealth loss as a result of their company acquiring other companies (Limmack, 1991). Second, most research on mergers examines returns around announcement dates and over a very short period of time, assuming that the announcement-period stock price reaction fully impounds the information effects of merger. This approach implicitly assumes that markets are efficient in immediately digesting the full impact of the acquisition in a very short time period (Agrawal et al., 1992; Andrade et al., 2001).

Both of the reasons stated above reinforce the argument that acquiring firms should not show any systematic underperformance in the long run. Therefore, long-run underperformance by acquiring firms as reported in most of the relevant studies presents a puzzling situation. Further, results reported in the earlier studies differ with respect to methodological choices such as event time vs. calendar time approach and various factors such as payment methods and merger or tender offers that may affect the performance outcome.

However, two issues are worth mentioning about these studies. First, the introduction of BHAR methodology contributed considerably to the controversy involving reported results. Loughrun and Vijh (1997) used BHAR technique for the first time in this area but report a significant, negative long-run abnormal return after M&As. Other studies report similar negative results using BHAR methodology. As Mitchell and Stafford (2000) report, however, once researchers corrected for the biases in BHAR methodology, evidence shows that the long-term abnormal returns are not statistically significant. Second, studies using a comprehensive set of benchmarks and methodologies generally offer inconclusive evidence or no abnormal returns. That is, these studies do not support the view of long-term underperformance of acquiring firms. For example, Franks et al. (1991), who use four benchmarks in their study, find different results with different benchmarks and conclude that the observation of long-term underperformance is likely due to benchmarking errors.

In a similar spirit, Fama (1998) investigates a set of past studies that examines the long-term abnormal performance after a corporate event such as initial public offerings, mergers, and stock-splits. He dismisses any systematic claim of long-term abnormal returns. Fama (p. 304) concludes that "consistent with the market efficiency hypothesis that the anomalies are chance results, apparent overreaction of stock prices to information is about as common as under-reaction. And post-event continuation of pre-event abnormal returns is about as frequent as post-event reversal."

Some recent studies also show support for such arguments. Dutta and Jog (2009) empirically examine the long-term abnormal returns and operating performance of Canadian acquiring firms by using a comprehensive sample of 1,300 M&A events during the period 1993 to 2002. They use both event-time and calendar-time methodologies and improved benchmarks to detect long-term abnormal returns. Consistent with the viewpoint of Fama (1998) and Mitchell and Stafford (2000) and somewhat contrary to what is typically reported in the U.S. studies, Dutta and Jog do not find any significant, negative long-term abnormal returns for Canadian acquirers after controlling for methodological discrepancies. However, notwithstanding such arguments and findings, evidence of long-term underperformance as presented in Rau and Vermaelen (1998) remains a puzzle and keeps the issue controversial.

LONG-TERM OPERATING PERFORMANCE OF ACQUIRING FIRMS

Given a lack of consensus on market-based studies and counterintuitive results, Healy, Palepu, and Ruback (1992) suggest investigating accounting-based measures, such as operating performance, to explain the puzzle. Conjectures for long-term operating performance of acquiring firms generally concern synergy motives. A synergy motive of M&As envisages an improvement in the operating performance of the acquiring or the merged firm in the postacquisition period. Goold and Campbell (1998) find that synergy initiatives often fall short of management expectations. According to Goold and Campbell (p. 132), synergy programs may "actually backfire, eroding customer relationships, damaging brands, or undermining employee morale." Thus, synergy efforts ironically may lead to shareholder value destruction.

Cullinan, Le Roux, and Weddigen (2004) provide more insightful reasons leading to the overestimation of synergy gain and the failure of synergy efforts. They categorize various potential synergies as a series of concentric circles. The closest one to the center is the cost-saving synergy, emerging from shared operating activities. Others, in the order of distance from the center, are "facilities shared," "existing products sold through new channels," and "new products sold through new channels." The farther out the synergy component (saving or revenue) lies, the more difficult achieving synergy becomes and the longer it takes to realize. Cullinan et al. contend that managers of acquiring firms frequently overestimate their capabilities in realizing various categories of synergy, leading to failure in synergy efforts. As Goold and Campbell (1998) note, an unrealistic pursuit of synergy also represents an opportunity cost, as it distracts a manager's attention from core business priorities and pushes away other initiatives that have real potential. Failure in synergy efforts is likely to result in a lower level of operating performance during the postacquisition period.

A growing body of literature investigates the long-term operating performance of acquiring firms. Yet, previous empirical studies in this area report inconsistent results (Martynova, Oosting, and Renneboog, 2006). Most recent U.S.-based studies either report an improvement in operating performance (Linn and Switzer, 2001; Heron and Lie, 2002) or unchanged performance (Moeller and Schlingemann, 2005). Results from the studies on other markets are also inconsistent. For example, using U.K. data, Powell and Stark (2005) report modest improvements in operating performance for acquiring firms. For continental Europe, Gugler, Mueller, Yurtoglu, and Zulehner (2003) find an insignificant increase in postacquisition profit and Martynova et al. report an insignificant decrease in operating performance. In similar fashion, Asian studies also present inconsistent results (Sharma and Ho, 2002; Rahman and Limmack, 2004). Sharma and Ho find insignificant changes in acquirers' postacquisition operating performance for Australian firms, whereas Rahman and Limmack show that operating performance improves significantly for Malaysian acquirers.

SUMMARY AND CONCLUSIONS

A substantial body of literature examines the performance of M&A deals both for the acquiring firms and target firms. The literature examining the performance of M&As generally follows three approaches. The most common approach is to investigate gains and losses to shareholders around the deal announcement date. Evidence shows that target shareholders generally earn significantly positive abnormal returns but the acquirers' shareholders earn, on average, a zero abnormal return at the acquisition's announcement. Considerable variation exists in these results (Andrade et al., 2001; Fuller et al., 2002; Bruner, 2002). However, studies with non-U.S. data consistently report significant and positive abnormal returns for acquirers' shareholders around the announcement date (Eckbo and Thorburn, 2000; Yuce and Ng, 2005).

Other studies investigate the long-term stock return performance of acquiring firms. Most of these long-term studies conclude that acquiring firms experience significantly negative abnormal returns over one to three years after the merger (Agrawal et al., 1992; Gregory, 1997; Agrawal and Jaffe, 2000; Andrade et al., 2001). Such findings are puzzling for the following reasons. First, neoclassical economic theory assumes that corporate management acts to maximize the shareholders wealth (Limmack, 1991). Second, if markets are efficient, the full impact of the acquisition should be digested in a very short period of time (Agrawal et al., 1992; Andrade et al., 2001). Responding to such anomalies, Franks et al. (1991) and Fama (1998) argue that such negative abnormal returns could have resulted from benchmark errors rather than systematic mispricing by investors. In support of this argument, Mitchell and Stafford (2000) show that after correcting for methodological errors and considering cross-sectional dependence, no significant abnormal returns are observed using different methodologies.

Still, debate continues on this issue. Given a lack of consensus on market-based studies and counterintuitive results, Healy et al. (1992) suggest investigating accounting-based measures such as operating performance in explaining the puzzle. In this spirit, a smaller but growing body of literature investigates the long-term operating performance of acquiring firms. However, previous empirical studies in this area report inconsistent results (Martynova et al. 2006).

One of the most important questions in finance is whether managerial actions create shareholders' wealth. M&A performance studies directly examine this issue and, hence, are of substantial importance to shareholders, managers, regulators, and other stakeholders. M&As also serve as external corporate control mechanisms. In the recent past, increased attention has focused on corporate governance and control issues including managerial actions. Thus, both academicians and practitioners show continued interest in this field. As the market dynamics continue to change, a reasonable assumption is that new studies will emerge that may help to provide further insight into these and other issues.

DISCUSSION QUESTIONS

1. What are the main reasons cited in the literature for the positive returns of target firm shareholders?

2. Discuss some important firm-specific and deal-specific factors that may affect M&A performance for acquiring firms.

3. Discuss the challenges and controversies in long-term performance studies involving M&As.   *See Part 551*

REFERENCES

Agrawal, Anup, and Jeffrey F. Jaffe. 2000. "The Post-Merger Performance Puzzle." In Cary Cooper and Alan Gregory, (eds.), *Advances in Mergers and Acquisitions*, Volume 1, 7–41. New York: Elsevier Science.

Agrawal, Anup, Jeffrey F. Jaffe, and Gershon N. Mandelker. 1992. "The Post-merger Performance of Acquiring Firms: A Re-examination of an Anomaly." *Journal of Finance* 47:4, 1605–1621.

Andrade, Gregor, Mark Mitchell, and Erik Stafford. 2001. "New Evidence and Perspectives on Mergers." *Journal of Economic Perspectives* 15:2, 103–120.

Andre, Paul, Maher Kooli, and Jean-Francois L'Her. 2004. "The Long-run Performance of Mergers and Acquisitions: Evidence from the Canadian Stock Market." *Financial Management* 33:4, 27–43.

Asquith, Paul. 1983. "Merger Bids, Uncertainty and Stockholder Returns." *Journal of Financial Economics* 11:1, 51–83.

Bae, Kee-Hong, Jun-Koo Kang, and Jin-Mo Kim. 2002. "Tunneling or Value Added? Evidence from Mergers by Korean Business Groups." *Journal of Finance* 57:6, 2695–2740.

Banz, Rolf W. 1981. "The Relation between Return and Market Value of Common Stocks." *Journal of Financial Economics* 9:1, 3–18.

Barber, Brad M., and John D. Lyon. 1997. "Detecting Long-run Abnormal Stock Returns: The Empirical Power and Specification of Test Statistics." *Journal of Financial Economics* 43:3, 341–372.

Ben-Amar, Walid, and Paul Andre. 2006. "Separation of Ownership from Control and Acquiring Firm Performance: The Case of Family Ownership in Canada." *Journal of Business, Finance and Accounting* 33:3/4, 517–543.

Berle, Adolf A., and Gardiner C. Means. 1932. *The Modern Corporation and Private Property.* New York: Macmillan.

Berkovitch, Elazar, and M. P. Narayanan. 1993. "Motives for Takeovers: An Empirical Investigation." *Journal of Financial and Quantitative Analysis* 28:3, 347–362.

Bhagat, Sanjai, and Richard H. Jefferis. 2002. *The Econometrics of Corporate Governance Studies.* Cambridge, MA: MIT Press.

Bradley, Michael, Anand Desai, and E. H. Kim. 1988. "Synergistic Gains from Corporate Acquisitions and Their Division between the Stockholders of Target and Acquiring Firms." *Journal of Financial Economics* 21:1, 3–40.

Bradley, Michael, and Gregg A. Jarrell. 1988. "Comment on Are Acquiring-firm Shareholders Better Off after an Acquisition?" In John C. Coffee Jr., Louis Lowenstein, and Susan Rose-Ackerman, (eds.), *Knights, Raiders and Targets: The Impact of the Hostile Takeover*, 253–259, New York: Oxford University Press.

Bruner, Robert. 2002. "Does M&A Pay? A Survey of Evidence for the Decision-Maker." *Journal of Applied Finance* 12:1, 48–68.

Byrd, John W., and Kent A. Hickman. 1992. "Do Outside Directors Monitor Managers? Evidence from Tender Offer Bids." *Journal of Financial Economics* 32:2, 195–207.

Calvet, A. Louis, and Jean Lefoll. 1987. "Information Asymmetry and Wealth Effect of Canadian Corporate Acquisitions." *Financial Review* 22:4, 415–431.

Chang, Saeyoung. 1998. "Takeovers of Privately Held Targets, Methods of Payment, and Bidder Returns." *Journal of Finance* 53:2, 773–784.

Cotter, James F., Anil Shivdasani, and Marc Zenner. 1997. "Do Independent Directors Enhance Target Shareholder Wealth During Tender Offers?" *Journal of Financial Economics* 43:2, 195–218.

Cullinan, Geoffrey, Jean-Marc Le Roux, and Rolf-Magnus Weddigen. 2004. "When to Walk Away from a Deal." *Harvard Business Review* 82:4, 96–104.

Dube, Seema, and John L. Glascock. 2006. "Effects of the Method of Payment and the Mode of Acquisition on Performance and Risk Metrics." *International Journal of Managerial Finance* 2:3, 176–195.

Dutta, Shantanu, and Vijay Jog. 2009. "The Long-term Performance of Acquiring Firms: A Re-examination of an Anomaly." *Journal of Banking and Finance* 33:8, 1400–1412.

Eckbo, B. Espen. 1986. "Mergers and the Market for Corporate Control: The Canadian Evidence." *Canadian Journal of Economics* 19:2, 236–260.

Eckbo, B. Espen, Ronald M. Giammarino, and Robert L. Heinkel. 1990a. "Asymmetric Information and the Medium of Exchange in Takeovers: Theory and Tests." *Review of Financial Studies* 3:4, 651–676.

Eckbo, B. Espen, Vojislav Maksimovic, and Joseph Williams, 1990b. "Consistent Estimation of Cross-sectional Models in Event Studies." *Review of Financial Studies* 3:3, 343–365.

Eckbo, B. Espen, and Karin S. Thorburn. 2000. "Gains to Bidder Firms Revisited: Domestic and Foreign Acquisitions in Canada." *Journal of Financial and Quantitative Analysis* 35:1, 1–25.

Faccio, Mara, John J. McConnell, and David Stolin. 2006. "Returns to Acquirers of Listed and Unlisted Targets." *Journal of Financial and Quantitative Analysis* 41:1, 197–219.

Fama, Eugene F. 1998. "Market Efficiency, Long-Term Returns, and Behavioral Finance." *Journal of Financial Economics* 49:3, 283–306.

Fama, Eugene F., and Michael C. Jensen. 1983. "Separation of Ownership and Control." *Journal of Law and Economics* 26:2, 301–326.

Fishman, Michael J. 1989. "Preemptive Bidding and the Role of the Medium of Exchange in Acquisitions." *Journal of Finance* 44:1, 41–57.

Franks, Julian, Robert Harris, and Sheridan Titman. 1991. "The Postmerger Share-Price Performance of Acquiring Firms." *Journal of Financial Economics* 29:1, 81–96.

Fuller, Kathleen, Jeffry Netter, and Mike Stegemoller. 2002. "What Do Returns to Acquiring Firms Tell Us? Evidence from Firms That Make Many Acquisitions." *Journal of Finance* 57:4, 1763–1793.

Ghosh, Aloke, and Chi-Wen J. Lee. 2000. "Abnormal Returns and Expected Managerial Performance of Target Firms." *Financial Management* 29:1, 40–52.

Gompers, Paul, Joy Ishii, and Andrew Metrick. 2003. "Corporate Governance and Equity Prices." *Quarterly Journal of Economics* 118:1, 107–155.

Goold, Michael, and Andrew Campbell. 1998. "Desperately Seeking Synergy." *Harvard Business Review* 76:5, 130–143.

Gregory, Alan. 1997. "An Examination of the Long Run Performance of UK Acquiring Firms." *Journal of Business Finance and Accounting* 24:7/8, 971–1002.

Grinblatt, Mark, and Sheridan Titman. 2002. *Financial Markets and Corporate Strategy*. New York: McGraw Hill Irwin.

Gugler, Klaus, Dennis C. Mueller, Burcin B. Yurtoglu, and Christine Zulehner. 2003. "The Effects of Mergers: An International Comparison." *International Journal of Industrial Organization* 21:5, 625–653.

Hansen, Robert G., and John R. Lott Jr. 1996. "Externalities and Corporate Objectives in a World with Diversified Shareholders/Consumers." *Journal of Financial and Quantitative Analysis* 31:1, 43–68.

Hanson, Robert C., and Moon H. Song. 1996. "Ownership Structure and Managerial Incentives: The Evidence from Acquisitions by Dual Class Firms." *Journal of Business, Finance & Accounting* 23:5/6, 831–49.

Harford, Jarrad. 1999. "Corporate Cash Reserves and Acquisitions." *Journal of Finance* 54:6, 1969–1997.

Healy, Paul M., Krishna G. Palepu, and Richard S. Ruback. 1992. "Does Corporate Performance Improve After Mergers?" *Journal of Financial Economics* 31:2, 135–175.

Hermalin, Benjamin E., and Michael S. Weisbach. 2003. "Boards of Directors as an Endogenously Determined Institution: A Survey of the Economic Literature." *FRBNY Economic Policy Review* 9:1, 7–26.

Heron, Randall, and Erik Lie. 2002. "Operating Performance and the Method of Payment in Takeovers." *Journal of Financial and Quantitative Analysis* 37:1, 137–155.

Hietala, Pekka, Steven N. Kaplan, and David T. Robinson. 2003. "What Is the Price of Hubris? Using Takeover Battles to Infer Overpayments and Synergies." *Financial Management* 32:3, 5–31.

Houston, Joel F., Christopher M. James, and Michael D. Ryngaert. 2001. "Where Do Merger Gains Come From? Bank Mergers from the Perspective of Insiders and Outsiders." *Journal of Financial Economics* 60:2/3, 285–331.

Jensen, Michael C. 1986. "Agency Costs of Free Cash Flow, Corporate Finance and Takeovers." *American Economic Review* 76:2, 323–329.

Jensen, Michael C. 1993. "The Modern Industrial Revolution, Exit, and the Failure of Internal Control Systems." *Journal of Finance* 48:3, 831–880.

Jensen, Michael C., and William H. Meckling. 1976. "Theory of the Firm: Managerial Behavior, Agency Cost, and Ownership Structure." *Journal of Financial Economics* 3:4, 305–360.

Jensen, Michael C., and Richard S. Ruback. 1983. "The Market for Corporate Control: The Scientific Evidence." *Journal of Financial Economics* 11:1–4, 5–50.

Jog, Vijay, PengCheng Zhu, and Shantanu Dutta. 2010. "Impact of Restricted Voting Share Structure on Firm Value and Performance." *Corporate Governance: An International Review.* Forthcoming.

Langetieg, Terence C. 1978. "An Application of a Three-Factor Performance Index to Measure Stockholders Gains from Merger." *Journal of Financial Economics* 6:4, 365–384.

Limmack, Robin J. 1991. "Corporate Mergers and Shareholder Wealth Effects: 1977–1986." *Accounting and Business Research* 21:83, 239–251.

Linn, Scott C., and Jeannette A. Switzer. 2001. "Are Cash Acquisitions Associated with Better Postacquisition Operating Performance Than Stock Acquisitions?" *Journal of Banking and Finance* 25:6, 1113–1138.

Lipton, Martin, and Jay W. Lorsch. 1992. "A Modest Proposal for Improved Corporate Governance." *Business Lawyer* 48:1, 59–77.

Loderer, Claudio, and Kenneth Martin. 1992. "Postacquisition Performance of Acquiring Firm." *Financial Management* 21:3, 69–79.

Loughran, Tim, and Anand M. Vijh. 1997, "Do Long-Term Shareholders Benefit From Corporate Acquisitions?" *Journal of Finance* 52:5, 1765–1790.

Magenheim, Ellen B., and Dennis C. Mueller. 1988. "Are Acquiring-Firm Shareholders Better Off after an Acquisition?" In John C. Coffee Jr., Louis Lowenstein, and Susan Rose-Ackerman, (eds.), *Knights, Raiders and Targets: The Impact of the Hostile Takeover*, 171–193, New York: Oxford University Press.

Malatesta, Paul H. 1983. "The Wealth Effect of Merger Activity and the Objective Functions of Merging Firms." *Journal of Financial Economics* 11:1, 155–181.

Mandelker, Gershon. 1974. "Risk and Return: The Case of Merging Firms." *Journal of Financial Economics* 1:4, 303–335.

Martin, Kenneth J. 1996. "The Method of Payment in Corporate Acquisitions, Investment Opportunities, and Managerial Ownership." *Journal of Finance* 51:4, 1227–1246.

Martynova, Marina, Sjoerd Oosting, and Luc Renneboog. 2006. "The Long-term Operating Performance of European Mergers and Acquisitions." Working Paper No. 137/2006, European Corporate Governance Institute.

Masse, Isidore, Robert Hanrahan, and Joseph Kushner. 1990. "The Effect of the Method of Payment on Stock Returns in Canadian Tender Offers and Merger Proposals for Both Target and Bidding Firms." *Quarterly Journal of Business and Economics* 29:4, 102–112.

Masulis, Ronald, Cong Wang, and Fei Xie. 2007. "Corporate Governance and Acquirer Returns." *Journal of Finance* 62:4, 1851–1889.

Mitchell, Mark L., and Erik Stafford. 2000. "Managerial Decisions and Long-Term Stock Price Performance." *Journal of Business* 73:3, 287–329.

Moeller, Sara B., and Frederik P. Schlingemann. 2005. "Global Diversification and Bidder Gains: A Comparison between Cross-Border and Domestic Acquisitions." *Journal of Banking and Finance* 29:3, 533–564.

Moeller, Sara B., Frederik P. Schlingemann, and René M. Stulz. 2003. "Do Shareholders of Acquiring Firms Gain from Acquisitions?" Working Paper W-9523, National Bureau of Economic Research.

Moeller, Sara B., Frederik P. Schlingemann, and René M. Stulz. 2004. "Firm Size and the Gains from Acquisitions." *Journal of Financial Economics* 73:2, 201–228.

Morck, Randall, Andrei Shleifer, and Robert W. Vishny. 1988. "Management Ownership and Market Valuation: An Empirical Analysis." *Journal of Financial Economics* 20:1/2, 293–316.

Mulherin, J. Harold. 2000. "Incomplete Acquisitions and Organizational Efficiency." Working Paper, Pennsylvania State College.

Myers, Stewart C., and Nicholas S. Majluf. 1984. "Corporate Financing and Investment Decisions When Firms Have Information That Investors Do Not Have." *Journal of Financial Economics* 13:2, 187–221.

Palepu, Krishna. G. 1986. "Predicting Takeover Targets: A Methodological and Empirical Analysis." *Journal of Accounting and Economics* 8:1, 3–37.

Powell, Ronan G., and Andrew W. Stark. 2005. "Does Operating Performance Increase Post-Takeover for UK Takeovers? A Comparison of Performance Measures and Benchmarks." *Journal of Corporate Finance* 11:1/2, 293–317.

Rahman, Rashidah A., and Robin J. Limmack. 2004. "Corporate Acquisitions and the Operating Performance of Malaysian Companies." *Journal of Business, Finance and Accounting* 31:3/4, 359–400.

Rau, P. Raghavendra, and Theo Vermaelen. 1998. "Glamour, Value and the Post-Acquisition Performance of Acquiring Firms." *Journal of Financial Economics* 49:2, 223–253.

Reinganum, Marc R. 1983. "Portfolio Strategies Based on Market Capitalization." *Journal of Portfolio Management* 9:2, 18–28.

Reinganum, Marc R. 1992. "A Revival of the Small-Firm Effect." *Journal of Portfolio Management* 18:3, 55–62.

Sharma, Divesh S., and Jonathan Ho. 2002. "The Impact of Acquisitions on Operating Performance: Some Australian Evidence." *Journal of Business, Finance and Accounting* 29:1/2, 155–200.

Shleifer, Andrei, and Robert W. Vishny. 1986. "Large Shareholders and Corporate Control." *Journal of Political Economy* 94:3, 461–488.

Smith, Richard, and Joo-Hyun Kim. 1994. "The Combined Effects of Free Cash Flow and Financial Slack on Bidder and Target Stock Returns." *Journal of Business* 67:2, 281–310.

Subrahmanyam, Vijaya, Nanda Rangan, and Stuart Rosenstein. 1997. "The Role of Outside Directors in Bank Acquisitions." *Financial Management* 26:3, 23–36.

Travlos, Nickolaos G. 1987. "Corporate Takeover Bids, Methods of Payment, and Bidding Firms' Stock Returns." *Journal of Finance* 42:4, 943–963.

Wu, Yilin. 2000. "Honey, CalPERS Shrunk the Board." Working Paper, University of Chicago.

Yuce, Ayse, and Alex Ng. 2005. "Effects of Private and Public Canadian Mergers." *Canadian Journal of Administrative Sciences* 22:2, 111–124.

ABOUT THE AUTHORS

Shantanu Dutta is an Assistant Professor of Finance at University of Ontario Institute of Technology. Previously, he taught at St. Francis Xavier University, Nova Scotia, as a full-time faculty member. Professor Dutta's research focuses on corporate governance, M&As, market efficiency, dividend policy, and technology management. He has published in *Journal of Banking and Finance, Quarterly Journal of Finance and Accounting, Journal of Applied Finance, Global Finance Journal, Canadian Investment Review, Corporate Governance—An International Review (CGIR), International Journal of Theoretical and Applied Finance,* and *International Journal of Managerial Finance.* Professor Dutta has also participated and presented papers in many scholarly conferences. He is a recipient of the Senate Award for his outstanding achievements in the PhD program (2006) and Barclays Global Investors Canada Research Award (2006) for the best paper on the Canadian security market. Recently he has also received the Highly Commended Award at the Literati Network Awards for Excellence 2009 (Emerald Publishing House) for his published article in the *International Journal of Managerial Finance.*

Samir Saadi is a research associate and part-time instructor of Finance at Telfer School of Management, University of Ottawa. He is currently a finance PhD candidate at Queen's School of Business. His research interests include dividend policy, executive compensation, M&As, and international finance. He has published in finance and applied economics journals including the *Journal of Multinational Financial Management, Journal of Applied Finance, Journal of International Financial Markets, Institutions and Money, Journal of Theoretical and Applied Finance, Review of Financial Economics,* and *International Journal of Managerial Finance.* He also participated in several finance conferences such as the Financial Management Association, Eastern Finance Association, European Finance Association, and Southern Finance Association. Mr. Saadi is the recipient of several prestigious awards and scholarships from Social Sciences and Humanities Research Council of Canada, Europlace Institute of Finance, and American Finance Association. He was awarded the Joseph-Armand Bombardier Canada Graduate Scholarships, which is one of the most prestigious and lucrative scholarships in Canada. He also won the Canada Graduate Scholarships–Michael Smith Foreign Study Supplement to finance his research work at INSEAD (France) as a visiting scholar in 2010.

PART II

Valuation

CHAPTER 8

Standard Valuation Methods for M&As

PABLO FERNANDEZ
Professor of Finance, IESE Business School, University of Navarra

INTRODUCTION

Understanding the mechanisms of company valuation is indispensable for anyone involved in corporate finance, especially those dealing with capital restructuring. Generally speaking, a company's value differs among buyers and it may also differ for the buyer and the seller. Value should not be confused with price, which is the amount agreed between a buyer and a seller. Differing values for a specific company may occur for many reasons. For example, a large, technologically advanced foreign company wants to buy a well-known national company to gain entry into the local market, using the reputation of the local brand. In this case, the foreign buyer may only value the brand but not the physical assets (e.g., plant and machinery) because the buyer already has more advanced assets. However, the seller may give a high value to its material resources because such resources enable the firm to continue producing. From the buyer's viewpoint, the basic aim is to determine the maximum value it is willing to pay for the company. From the seller's viewpoint, the aim is to ascertain the minimum value it is willing to accept. The buyer and seller take these figures into a negotiation and often agree on a price somewhere between the two extremes. Potential bidders may assign different values to a company due to economies of scale, economies of scope, or different perceptions about the industry and the company.

In a corporate setting, valuation may have a wide range of purposes:

1. In a company's buying and selling operations
    - For the buyer, the valuation indicates the highest price that the firm should be prepared to pay.
    - For the seller, the valuation indicates the lowest price at which the firm should be prepared to sell.
2. Valuations of listed companies
    - An investor compares the value obtained with the share's price on the stock market to decide whether to buy, sell, or hold the shares.

- An investor examines the value associated with several companies to decide which securities to include in a portfolio, i.e., those that seem undervalued by the market.
- An investor uses the valuation of several companies to make comparisons between companies. For example, if an investor thinks that the future course of General Electric's (GE) share price will be better than that of Amazon, the investor may buy GE shares and sell Amazon shares short. With this position, the investor will gain provided that GE's share price does better (rises more or falls less) than that of Amazon.

3. Public offerings
   - The seller or its investment banker uses the valuation to justify the price at which the shares are offered to the public.
4. Compensation schemes based on value creation
   - The valuation of a company or business unit is fundamental for quantifying the value creation attributable to the executives being assessed.
5. Identification of value drivers
   - The valuation of a company or business unit is fundamental for identifying and stratifying the main value drivers.
6. Strategic decisions on the company's continued existence
   - The valuation of a company or business unit is a prior step in the decision to continue in the business, sell, merge, grow, or buy other companies.
7. Strategic planning
   - The valuation of the company and the different business units is fundamental for deciding what products, business lines, countries, and customers to maintain, grow, or abandon.
   - The valuation provides a means for measuring the impact of the company's possible policies and strategies on value creation and destruction.

This chapter describes four main groups comprising the most widely used company valuation methods: (1) balance sheet–based methods, (2) income statement–based methods or multiples, (3) discounted cash flow (DCF) methods, and (4) value creation methods using economic value added and economic profit. Each group is discussed in a separate section. The DCF methods are becoming increasingly popular and are conceptually "correct." These methods view the company as a cash flow generator and, therefore, assessable as a financial asset. Exhibit 8.1 lists valuation methods for each of the four main categories that are discussed in this chapter.

BALANCE SHEET–BASED METHODS

Balance sheet–based methods seek to determine the company's value by estimating the value of its assets. These traditional methods consider that a company's value lies basically in its balance sheet. Because they determine the value from a static viewpoint, balance sheet–based methods do not take into account the company's possible future evolution and ignore the time value of money. These methods also do not account for other factors that may affect the value such as the industry's current situation, human resources or organizational problems, and contracts that do not appear in the accounting statements. Some of the more common balance

Exhibit 8.1 Main Valuation Methods for M&As

Balance Sheet	Multiples	Discounted Cash Flow	Value Creation
Book value	Price-earnings (PE) ratio	Free cash flow	EVA
Adjusted book value	Price-to-book value	Equity cash flow	Economic profit
Liquidation value	Price-to-sales	Dividends	
	Price-to-cash flow	Adjusted Present Value	

Note: This exhibit shows the main valuation methods for each of the four main categories that are discussed in this chapter.

sheet–based methods are book value, adjusted book value, and liquidation value. Each of these methods is briefly discussed below.

Book Value

A company's book value or net worth is the value of the shareholders' equity stated in the balance sheet (capital and reserves). This quantity is also the difference between total assets and liabilities, that is, the surplus of the company's total goods and rights over its total debts with third parties. This value suffers from the shortcoming of its own definition criterion: Accounting criteria are subject to a certain degree of subjectivity and differ from market criteria, with the result that the book value rarely matches the market value. This can be seen in Exhibit 8.2, which shows the price/book value (P/BV) ratio of several international stock markets in 1999 and 2009.

Exhibit 8.2 Market Value/Book Value (P/BV), Price Earnings Ratio (PE), and Dividend Yield (Div/P) of Different National Stock Markets

	December 1999			December 2009		
	P/BV	PE	Div/P(%)	P/BV	PE	Div/P(%)
Canada	2.2	23.8	1.3	1.9	21.7	2.6
France	3.6	24.6	1.8	1.4	21.0	3.7
Germany	3.1	26.0	1.3	1.5	26.8	3.1
Hong Kong	2.2	26.8	2.0	2.0	18.4	2.4
Ireland	2.6	19.0	1.7	0.7	14.9	1.6
Italy	2.6	29.3	1.5	1.1	18.9	5.0
Japan	2.7	83.1	0.6	1.2	34.2	1.8
Spain	3.4	24.1	1.7	1.9	12.2	4.4
Switzerland	3.2	21.0	1.2	2.2	17.7	2.2
United Kingdom	3.7	26.7	2.4	1.8	12.4	3.3
United States	4.4	30.8	1.1	1.9	21.8	1.9

Note: This exhibit shows that P/BV as the share's price (P) divided by its book value (BV). PE ratio is the share's price divided by the earnings per share. Div/P(%) is the dividend per share divided by the price. Data come from Datastream.

Adjusted Book Value

Adjusted book value seeks to overcome the shortcomings that appear when applying purely accounting criteria in the valuation. When the values of assets and liabilities match their market value, the adjusted net worth is obtained.

Liquidation Value

Liquidation value represents a company's value after selling (liquidating) its assets and paying off its debts. This value is calculated by deducting the business's liquidation expenses (redundancy payments to employees, tax expenses, and other typical liquidation expenses) from the adjusted net worth. This method's usefulness is limited to a highly specific situation, namely, when the company is bought with the purpose of liquidating it at a later date. Liquidation value represents the company's minimum value. Assuming the company continues to operate, the firm's value is greater than its liquidation value.

INCOME STATEMENT–BASED METHODS

Income statement–based methods focus on a company's income statement. They seek to determine the company's value through the size of its earnings, sales or other indicators. For example, a common practice is to perform quick valuations of cement companies by multiplying their annual production capacity (or sales) in metric tons by a ratio (multiple); to value parking lots by multiplying the number of parking spaces by a multiple; and to value insurance companies by multiplying annual premiums by a multiple. The use of multiples is often called relative valuation because the multiples used are chosen among comparable companies. This category includes the methods such as the price-earnings (PE) ratio, price-to-book value, price-to-sales, and price-to-cash flow.

Value of Earnings

According to this method, the equity's value is obtained by multiplying the annual net income by a ratio called the PE ratio, that is: Equity value = PE x Net income. The PE of a share of stock indicates the multiple of the earnings per share (EPS) that investors are willing to pay in the stock market. Thus, if the EPS in the last year was $3 and the share's price is $26, its PE would be 8.67 ($26/$3). Sometimes, the PE ratio takes the forecasted EPS for the next year or the mean EPS for the last few years. On other occasions, investors use the relative PE, which is simply the company's PE divided by the industry's PE. The PE is the benchmark used predominantly by investors and is a parameter that relates a market item (share price) with a purely accounting item (earnings).

Value of the Dividends

Dividends represent that part of a company's earnings effectively paid out to the shareholder. In most cases, dividends are the only regular flow that shareholders receive. According to this method, a share's value is the net present value (NPV) of the dividends that investors expect to obtain from the firm. Various models make differing assumptions about dividend growth (e.g., no growth, constant growth, and supernormal growth). In the perpetuity case in which a firm is expected to pay the same dividend each year forever, this value can be expressed as follows:

$$\text{Equity value} = D_0/K_e \qquad (8.1)$$

where

$D_0 =$ dividends per share distributed by the company in the last year; and K_e
= required return to equity.

If the dividend is expected to grow indefinitely at a constant annual rate g, the result is the following constant growth rate formula:

$$\text{Equity value} = D_1/(K_e - g) \qquad (8.2)$$

where
D_1 is the dividends per share for the next year; and $g =$ the sustainable (constant) growth rate.

Companies paying a higher dividend payout often do not obtain growth in their share price as a result. When a company distributes more dividends, normally it reduces its growth because it distributes the money to its shareholders instead of plowing the funds back into new investments or projects.

Sales Multiples

This valuation method consists of calculating a company's value by multiplying its sales per share by a multiple. For example, in valuing a pharmacy, analysts may multiply the firm's annual sales (in dollars) by 2 or another number, depending on the market situation. Others value a soft drink bottling plant by multiplying its annual sales in liters by 500 or another number, depending on the market situation. The price/sales ratio consists of two ratios: Price/sales = PE (earnings/sales). The first ratio is the PE and the second (earnings/sales) is commonly called return on sales.

OTHER MULTIPLES

In addition to the PE and the price/sales ratio, some other frequently used multiples are:

- Value of the company/earnings before interest and taxes (EBIT).
- Value of the company/earnings before interest, taxes, depreciation, and amortization (EBITDA).
- Value of the company/operating cash flow.
- Value of the equity/book value.

DISCOUNTED CASH FLOW METHODS

DCF methods seek to determine the company's value by estimating its future cash flows and then discounting them at a discount rate matched to the riskiness of the flows. DCF methods are often based on the detailed forecasts for each period of each of the financial items related with the generation of the cash flows corresponding to the company's operations. In DCF-based valuations, a suitable discount rate is determined for each type of cash flow. Determining the discount rate is an important task and often takes into account the risk as measured by historic volatilities. In practice, interested parties often set the minimum discount rate so that the buyers or sellers are not prepared to invest or sell for less than a certain return.

General DCF Method

The different DCF methods start with the following expression:

$$V = \frac{CF_1}{(1+k)} + \frac{CF_2}{(1+k)^2} + \frac{CF_3}{(1+k)^3} + \cdots + \frac{CF_n + RV_n}{(1+k)^n} \qquad (8.3)$$

where

CF_i = cash flow generated by the company in the period I; RV_n = residual value of the company in the year n; and k = appropriate discount rate for the cash flows' risk.

Although the above formula may appear to consider the temporary duration of the flows, this is not necessarily so because the company's residual value in the year n (RV_n) can be calculated by discounting the future flows after that period. A simplified procedure for considering an indefinite duration of future flows after the year n is to assume a constant growth rate (g) of flows after that period. Then the residual value in year n is $RV_n = CF_n (1 + g)/(k - g)$. Although the flows may have an indefinite duration, ignoring their value after a certain period may be acceptable because their present value continues to decrease with longer time horizons. Furthermore, the competitive advantage of many businesses tends to disappear after a few years.

Determining the Appropriate Cash Flow for Discounting

Before looking in more detail at different DCF methods, the different types of cash flow that can be used in a valuation must be defined. To understand the basic cash flows that can be considered in a valuation, Exhibit 8.3 shows the different cash streams generated by a company and the appropriate discount rates for each flow.

There are three basic cash flows: (1) free cash flow (FCF), (2) equity cash flow, and (3) debt cash flow. The FCF provides the basis for calculating a firm's total value. The company's value is usually considered to be the sum of the value of the equity plus the value of the financial debt. The equity cash flow enables an analyst to obtain the value of the equity, which, combined with the value of the

Exhibit 8.3 Different Cash Streams Generated by a Company and the Appropriate Discount Rates for Each Flow

Cash Flows	Appropriate Discount Rate
Free cash flow	**WACC** = Weighted average cost of capital
Equity cash flow	K_e = Required return to equity
Debt cash flow	K_d = Required return to debt

Note: This exhibit indicates the appropriate discount rate to use when discounting various cash flows. Calculating a company's total value (equity plus debt) involves obtaining the present value of the free cash flow using a firm's WACC. The present value of the equity cash flow (using K_e) enables an analyst to obtain the value of the equity. To determine the present market value of the existing debt requires discounting the debt cash flow by the required rate of return to debt (K_d).

debt, provides a means of determining a company's total value. The debt cash flow is the sum of the interest to be paid on the debt plus principal repayments. To determine the present market value of the existing debt, this flow must be discounted at the required rate of return to debt (cost of the debt). In some cases, the debt's market value may be equivalent to its book value, which is why analysts often view book value as a sufficient approximation to the firm's market value. This is only valid if the required return to debt is equal to the debt's cost.

A company's (financial) assets refer to total assets less spontaneous financing provided by suppliers, creditors, and the like. That is, the company's (financial) assets consist of the net fixed assets plus the working capital requirements (WCR = cash + accounts receivable + inventories - accounts payable). Faus (1996) provides a discussion of working capital requirements. The company's (financial) liabilities consist of the shareholders' equity (the shares) and its debt (short-term and long-term debt). The shareholders' equity or capital can include, among others, common stock, preferred stock, and convertible preferred stock. The different types of debt can include, among others, senior debt, subordinated debt, convertible debt, fixed or variable interest debt, zero or regular coupon debt, and short-term or long-term debt. When discussing a company's value, this usually refers to the value of the debt plus the value of the shareholders' equity (shares).

Free Cash Flow

Free cash flow is the firm's operating cash flow, that is, the cash flow generated by operations, without taking into account borrowing (debt), after tax. FCF is the money that would be available in the company after covering fixed asset investment and working capital requirements, assuming no debt and, therefore, no financial expenses. Calculating future FCF requires forecasting the cash the company will receive and pay in each period. This is similar to the approach used to draw up a cash budget. However, in company valuation, this task requires forecasting cash flows further ahead in time than is normally done in a cash budget.

Accounting cannot directly provide this information because it uses the accrual approach but allocates its revenues, costs, and expenses using basically arbitrary mechanisms. These two features of accounting distort the perception of the

Exhibit 8.4 Income Statement for a Hypothetical Company

	2008	2009	2010
Sales	1,000.00	1,100.00	1,210.00
Cost of goods sold	−650.00	−715.00	−786.50
General expenses	−189.00	−207.90	−228.70
Depreciation	−20.00	−20.00	−20.00
Earnings before interest and taxes (EBIT)	141.00	157.10	174.80
Interest expense	−10.00	−10.00	−10.00
Profit before tax (PBT)	131.00	147.10	164.80
Tax	−45.85	−51.49	−57.68
Net income or profit after tax (PAT)	85.15	95.62	107.10
Dividends	−34.06	−38.25	−42.85
Retained earnings	51.09	57.37	64.28

Note: This exhibit shows that information given in the accounting statements must be adjusted to obtain the cash flows for each period, i.e., the sums of money actually received (cash inflows) minus the sums of money actually paid in each period (cash outflows).

appropriate approach when calculating cash flows. The "cash" approach refers to cash actually received or paid (collections and payments).

Using a hypothetical example of a company illustrates the basic components of FCF. The information given in the accounting statements (shown in Exhibit 8.4) must be adjusted to derive the cash flows for each period, that is, the sums of money actually received and paid in each period. Using these data enable determining the company's FCF, which must not include any payments to fund providers. Therefore, FCF excludes dividends and interest expenses.

Exhibit 8.5 shows how the FCF is obtained from earnings before interest and taxes (EBIT). The tax payable on the EBIT must be calculated directly. This gives net income without subtracting interest payments. Next, the depreciation for the period must be added because it is not a payment (cash outflow) but merely an accounting entry. The sums of money to be allocated to new investments in

Exhibit 8.5 Free Cash Flow for a Hypothetical Company

	2008	2009	2010
Earnings before interest and taxes (EBIT)	141.00	157.10	174.80
Tax paid on EBIT	−49.40	−55.00	−61.20
Net income without debt	91.65	102.10	113.60
Depreciation	20.00	20.00	20.00
Increase in fixed assets	−61.00	−67.10	−73.80
Increase in WCR	−11.00	−12.10	−13.30
Free cash flow	39.65	42.92	46.51

Note: Using the information given in the accounting statements and adjusting it enable determining a company's free cash flow. FCF excludes any payments to fund providers such as dividends and interest expense.

fixed assets and new working capital requirements (WCR) must be deducted in order to calculate the FCF. Calculating the FCF requires ignoring the financing of a company's operations and concentrating on the financial return on the company's assets after tax. FCF takes into account the investments required in each period for the firm's continued existence. If the company had no debt, the FCF would be identical to the equity cash flow, which is another cash flow variant used in valuations and which is discussed below.

Equity Cash Flow

Equity cash flow (ECF) is calculated by subtracting from FCF the interest and principal payments (after tax) made in each period to the debt holders and adding the new debt provided. In short, ECF is the cash flow remaining available after covering fixed asset investments and working capital requirements and after paying the financial charges and repaying the corresponding part of the debt's principal (in the event of debt). This can be represented in the following expression:

$$ECF = FCF - [\text{Interest payments} \times (1 - T)] - \text{Principal repayments} + \text{New debt}$$
(8.4)

When making projections, the dividends and other expected payments to shareholders must match the equity cash flows. This cash flow assumes the existence of a certain financing structure in each period, in which the firm pays the interest on existing debt, pays the installments of the principal at the corresponding maturity dates, and receives funds from new debt. What remains is the cash available to the shareholders, which is allocated to paying dividends or buying back shares.

When the equity cash flow is restated, this amounts to valuing the company's equity (E), and, therefore, the appropriate discount rate will be the required return to equity (K_e). To find the company's total value (D + E) requires adding the value of the existing debt (D) to the value of the equity (E).

CALCULATING THE VALUE OF A COMPANY USING FCF

To calculate the value of the company using this method, the FCFs are discounted (restated) using the weighted average cost of debt and equity or weighted average cost of capital (WACC) as follows:

$$E + D = \text{present value}[FCF; WACC] \quad \text{where} \quad WACC = \frac{E(K_e) + D(K_d)(1 - T)}{E + D}$$
(8.5)

where E = value of the equity; K_e = required return to equity, which reflects the equity's risk; D = value of the debt; K_d = cost of the debt before tax = required return to debt; and T = tax rate.

The WACC is calculated by weighting the cost of equity (K_e) and the cost of debt (K_d) with respect to the company's financial structure. This is the appropriate rate for this case because the company as a whole (debt plus equity) is being valued.

Thus, considering the required return to equity and debt in the proportion to the firm's capital structure is appropriate.

CALCULATING THE UNLEVERED VALUE OF THE COMPANY

The company's value may also be calculated by adding two values: (1) the value of the company assuming that it has no debt and (2) the value of the tax shield resulting from the use of debt. This method is called the adjusted present value (APV).

The value of the company without debt is obtained by discounting FCF using the required rate of return to equity that would be applicable to the company if it were to be considered as having no debt. This rate (K_u) is known as the unlevered rate or required return to assets. The required return to assets is smaller than the required return to equity if the company has debt in its capital structure. In this case, the shareholders would bear the financial risk implied by the existence of debt and would demand a higher equity risk premium. In those cases where a firm has no debt, the required rate of return to equity ($K_e = K_u$) is equivalent to the firm's WACC, because the only source of financing being used is capital.

The present value of the tax shield arises from the fact that the company is being financed with debt. It is the specific consequence of the lower tax paid by the company as a consequence of the interest paid on the debt in each period. Finding the present value of the tax shield requires calculating the saving obtained by this means for each year, multiplying the interest payable on the debt by the tax rate. Once these flows are obtained, they are discounted at the appropriate rate. Consequently, the APV condenses into the following formula:

$$E + D = NPV(FCF; K_u) + \text{value of the debt's tax shield} \qquad (8.6)$$

Controversy surrounds the discount rate to be used in this case. Some authors (e.g., Modigliani and Miller, 1963; Luehrman, 1997) suggest using the debt's market cost, which need not necessarily be the interest rate at which the company has contracted its debt. Others (e.g., Miles and Ezzell, 1985; Lewellen and Emery, 1986; Arzac and Glosten, 2005) assume that the firm's debt policy is determined by a market-value ratio. Thus, the amount of debt is proportional to the market-value of equity, and the appropriate discount rates are the cost of debt for the first year and K_u for the following years. Assuming that the amount of debt is proportional to the market-value of equity is unrealistic because it implies that a company has only two possible states of nature in the following period. Under the worst state (low share price), the company will have to raise new equity and repay debt. Under the good state, the company will have to issue debt and pay large dividends. This is not a good description of the debt policy of most companies.

Still other authors (Harris and Pringle, 1985; Ruback, 2002; Cooper and Nyborg, 2006) discount the tax shield of every year using K_u. This approach is correct only in continuous time and assuming that the amount of debt is proportional to the market-value of equity. Fernandez (2007), however, assumes that the amount of debt is proportional to the book-value of equity. He shows that debt is more correlated to the book-value of a firm's assets than to its market-value. He arrives at a different valuation formula that provides a value of the debt's tax shield between that of Modigliani and Miller (1963) and Miles and Ezzell (1985).

Calculating the Value of a Firm's Equity by Discounting the Equity Cash Flow

The market value of a firm's equity is obtained by discounting the equity cash flow at the rate of required return to equity for the company (K_e). Adding this value to the market value of debt results in a firm's total value. The required return to equity can be estimated using the following method:

$$K_e = R_F + \beta(MRP) \tag{8.7}$$

where R_F = rate of return for risk-free investments (e.g., Treasury bonds); β = share's beta; and MRP = required market risk premium.

Basic Stages in the Performance of a Valuation Using DCF

The five basic stages in performing an accurate valuation by cash flow discounting are as follows:

1. Historic and strategic analysis of the company and the industry
   A. Financial analysis
      - Evolution of income statements and balance sheets, cash flows generated by the company, company's investments, and company's financing.
      - Analysis of the financial health and risk of the business.
   B. Strategic and competitive analysis
      - Evolution of the industry and company's competitive position.
      - Identification of the value chain.
      - Competitive position of the main competitors.
      - Identification of the value drivers.
2. Projections of future flows
   A. Financial forecasts
      - Income statements and balance sheets.
      - Cash flows generated by the company.
      - Investments.
      - Financing.
      - Terminal value.
      - Forecast of various scenarios.
   B. Strategic and competitive forecasts
      - Forecast of the industry's evolution and the company's competitive position.
      - Competitive position of the main competitors.
   C. Consistency of the cash flow forecasts
      - Financial consistency between forecasts.

- Comparison of forecasts with historic figures.
- Consistency of cash flows with the strategic analysis.
3. Determination of the cost (required return) of capital
   - For each business unit and for the company as a whole.
   - Cost of the debt, required return to equity, and weighted cost of capital.
4. Net present value of future flows
   - NPV of the flows at their corresponding rate.
   - Present value of the terminal value.
   - Value of the equity.
5. Interpretation of the results
   - Benchmarking of the value obtained: comparison with similar companies.
   - Identification of the value creation and its sustainability (time horizon).
   - Analysis of the value's sensitivity to changes in the fundamental parameters.
   - Strategic and competitive justification of the value creation.

VALUE CREATION METHODS USING ECONOMIC VALUE ADDED AND ECONOMIC PROFIT

Another approach used to value the shares of a company is economic value added (EVA) and economic profit (EP). EVA is a registered trademark of Stern Stewart & Co. Steward (1991) and Baker, Deo, and Mukherjee (2009) provide a detailed discussion of EVA. Some consultants use economic profit as synonymous with EVA, but these two measures differ. Ehrhardt and Brigham (2011) define EVA as follows:

$$EVA = \text{Net Operating profit after taxes(NOPAT)} - \text{After-tax dollar cost of capital}$$

$$\text{used to support operations}$$

$$= EBIT(1 - T) - (\text{Total net operating capital})(WACC) \qquad (8.8)$$

Economic profit (EP), also called residual income, is the book profit less the equity's book value multiplied by the required return to equity (McTaggart, Kontes, and Mankins, 1994). EP is profit after tax (PAT) less equity book value (Ebv_{t-1}) multiplied by required return to equity (K_e). Note that the equity book value used is the one at the end of the previous period.

$$EP_t = PAT_t - K_e\,Ebv_{t-1} \qquad (8.9)$$

The concept of economic profit has been around since Marshall (2010) used the term in 1890. Economic profit mixes accounting parameters (profit and the equity's book value) with a market parameter (K_e, the required return to equity).

Another term is market value added (MVA), which is the difference between the market value of the firm's equity (or market value of the new investment) and the equity's book value (or initial investment). Equation 8.8 shows MVA as

$$MVA_0 = E_0 - Ebv_0 \qquad (8.10)$$

where E_0 = the market value of equity (stock) at $t = 0$ and Ebv_0 = the equity's book value (equity capital supplied by shareholders). As Equation 8.11 shows, the present value of economic profits discounted at the rate K_e is MVA.

$$MVA_0 = E_0 - Ebv_0 = NPV(K_e; EP) \qquad (8.11)$$

The difference ([$E_0 + D_0$] – [$Ebv_0 + D_0$]) is also called MVA and is identical (if the debt's market value is equal to its book value) to the difference ($E_0 - Ebv_0$). EVA is the term used to define:

$$EVA_t = NOPAT_t - (D_t - 1 + Ebv_t - 1)WACC \qquad (8.12)$$

where

NOPAT (net operating profit after taxes) = the profit of an unlevered (debt-free) firm. Sometimes, NOPAT is called EBIAT (earnings before interest and after tax). The present value of EVA discounted at WACC is MVA. NOPAT is also called NOPLAT (net operating profit less adjusted taxes).

$$MVA_0 = [E_0 + D_0] - [Ebv_0 + D_0] = NPV(WACC; EVA) \qquad (8.13)$$

Although Copeland, Koller, and Murrin (2000) note that economic profit is a synonym of EVA, this is obviously not true.

A Example of Valuation with EVA, EP, and MVA

The firm in Exhibit 8.6 is partly financed with $4 billion of debt. The firm's FCF is –$12 billion in year zero, $2.838 billion in years 1 to 4, and $4.838 billion in year 5. Therefore, this firm's internal rate of return (IRR) is 10 percent.

As the debt ratio increases over time, K_e (the required return to equity) grows from 10.62 percent to 20.12 percent (line 21), and the WACC decreases from 8.91 percent to 6.99 percent (line 26). The shares' baseline value (lines 22 and 24) is $8.516 billion, which is $516 million more than its book value.

The EP's present value discounted at K_e (line 27) is identical to the EVA's present value discounted at the WACC (line 29) and both agree with MVA = E – Ebv (line 25). This does not mean that EP or EVA indicate "value creation" in each period: The value ($516 million) "is created" when an investment with an expected return (10 percent) is greater than the cost of capital employed (WACC).

THE DISPERSION OF THE DISCOUNT RATE

Survey evidence shows that the discount rate used in the valuations differs substantially among professors and analysts. Fernandez and Campo (2010a) present a survey about the market risk premium (MRP) used by professors to calculate the required return to equity in 2010. Panel A of Exhibit 8.7 shows responses from 1,511 finance professors, while Panel B indicates 902 responses from finance professors who provide a figure for the MRP used in 2010.

Exhibit 8.6   Valuation with EVA, EP, and MVA (in $ million)

	Balance Sheet	0	1	2	3	4	5
1	WCR (Working Capital Requirements)	2,000	2,000	2,000	2,000	2,000	0
2	Gross fixed assets	10,000	10,000	10,000	10,000	10,000	10,000
3	− accumulated depreciation	0	2,000	4,000	6,000	8,000	10,000
4	Net Assets	12,000	10,000	8,000	6,000	4,000	0
5	Debt	4,000	4,000	4,000	4,000	4,000	0
6	Equity (book value)	8,000	6,000	4,000	2,000	0	0
7	Total Liabilities and Equity	12,000	10,000	8,000	6,000	4,000	0
	Income Statement						
8	Sales		10,000	10,000	10,000	10,000	10,000
9	Cost of sales		4,000	4,000	4,000	4,000	4,000
10	General and administrative expenses		2,730	2,730	2,730	2,730	2,730
11	Depreciation		2,000	2,000	2,000	2,000	2,000
12	Interest		320	320	320	320	320
13	Taxes		323	323	323	323	323
14	Profit after taxes		627	627	627	627	627
15	+ Depreciation		2,000	2,000	2,000	2,000	2,000
16	+ Δ Debt		0	0	0	0	−4,000
17	− Δ WCR		0	0	0	0	2,000
18	− Investment in fixed assets		0	0	0	0	0
19	ECF = Dividends		2,627	2,627	2,627	2,627	627
20	Free cash flow (FCF)		2,838	2,838	2,838	2,838	4,838
21	Return on Equity (ROE)		7.83%	10.45%	15.67%	31.34%	N.A.
22	Return on Assets (ROA)		6.98%	8.38%	10.47%	13.97%	20.95%
23	Write out (ROGI)		6.98%	6.98%	6.98%	6.98%	6.98%
24	Ke	10.62%	10.78%	11.08%	11.88%	20.12%	10.00%
25	E = NPV(Ke; ECF)	8,516	6,793	4,898	2,814	522	0
26	WACC	8.91%	8.74%	8.47%	8.00%	6.99%	10.00%
27	E = NPV(WACC; FCF) − D	8,516	6,793	4,898	2,814	522	0
28	MVA = E − Ebv	516	793	898	814	522	0
29	EP = PAT − Ke x Ebv		−223	−20	184	389	627
30	MVA = NPV(Ke; EP)	516	793	898	814	522	0
31	EVA		−232	−36	160	358	558
32	MVA = NPV(WACC; EVA)	516	793	898	814	522	0
33	EP − EVA		9	16	23	32	68

Note: This exhibit shows the calculation of EVA, EP, and MVA assuming a constant debt level of $4 billion. The IRR of the investment is 10 percent.

Exhibit 8.7 Market Risk Premium (MRP) Used by Professors in 2010

Panel A. Responses of 1,511 Finance Professors about the MRP in 2010.

With a number for MRP 2010	US	Europe	UK	Canada	Australia	Other	Total
Reported	462	194	49	23	29	145	902
Outliers	6	4	1	1	1		13
Different countries	1	17	1	1	2	33	55
Different universities/Business schools	271	132	34	17	21	105	580
Without a number for MRP 2010							
"I do not use MRP, I think about premiums for particular stocks."	41	12	9	7	2	23	94
"I would tend to use whatever MRP is specified in the textbook."	6	11		1		13	31
"I find that the CAPM is not very useful nor is the concept of MRP."	51	36	5	11	2	16	121
"I did not have to use an estimate of the MRP in 2010."	38	12	9	3		18	80
"I don't think about these things. I am an academic, not a practitioner."	3	8			2		13
"I teach derivatives: I did not have to use a MRP."	26	15	2	2			45
"The MRP changes every day."	37	21	9	3	8	15	93
Other reasons	46	19	9	7	6	32	119
Total	716	332	93	58	50	262	1,511

Europe: Austria, Belgium, Croatia, Denmark, Finland, France, Germany, Greece, Ireland, Italy, Netherlands, Norway, Portugal, Slovenia, Spain, Sweden and Switzerland. Australia: Australia and New Zealand. Other: Argentina, Brazil, Chile, China, Colombia, Czech Republic, Dubai, Egypt, Estonia, Hong Kong, Hungary, India, Indonesia, Iran, Israel, Japan, Malaysia, Mauritius, Mexico, Pakistan, Peru, Poland, Romania, Russia, Saudi Arabia, Singapore, South Africa, South Korea, Sri Lanka, Taiwan, Thailand, Tunis, Turkey, UA Emirates, Venezuela and Vietnam.

(Continued)

Exhibit 8.7 *(Continued)*

Panel B. Market Risk Premium Used by 902 Finance Professors in 2010

		US	Euro	UK	Canada	Australia	Other	Total
MRP used in 2010	Average	6.0	5.3	5.0	5.9	6.2	7.8	
	Standard deviation	1.7	1.7	1.6	1.1	1.7	4.2	
	Maximum	12.0	12.0	10.3	8.0	10.0	30.0	
	Q3	7.0	6.0	5.8	6.2	7.0	9.0	
	Median	6.0	5.0	5.0	6.0	6.0	7.0	
	Q1	5.0	4.3	4.0	5.5	5.0	5.5	
	Minimum	2.0	2.0	2.5	3.5	4.0	0.7	
	Number	462	194	49	23	29	145	902
Justify the number*								
I do not justify the number/do not answer		151	56	14	4	8	40	273
Reference to books or articles		191	110	29	12	18	77	437
Historic data		116	20	5	7	2	20	170
Own research/calculations		4	8	1	0	1	8	22

Note: This exhibit presents a survey by Fernandez and Campo (2010a) about the market risk premium (MRP) used by professors to calculate the required return to equity in 2010. Panel A reports the responses from 1,511 professors; Panel B reports the responses of 902 finance professors who provide a figure for the MRP used in 2010.

Exhibit 8.7 provides the mail results of this survey. As Panel B shows, the average MRP used by professors in the United States (6.0 percent) is higher than that used by their colleagues in Europe (5.3 percent), Canada (5.9 percent), and the United Kingdom (5.0 percent). However, great dispersion exists in the MRP used by the professors: The standard deviation of the MRP used by the professors in the United States, Europe, and Australia is 1.7 percent.

Fernandez and Campo (2010b) report the answers of 711 analysts, of which 601 provided a figure for the MRP used in 2010. Exhibit 8.8 provides the mail results of this survey. As Panel B shows, the average MRP used by analysts in the United States and Canada (5.1 percent) is similar to that used by their colleagues in Europe (5.0 percent). The dispersion of the MRP used is lower for analysts than for professors as reported in Fernandez and Campo (2010a).

Fernandez (2009) reviews 150 textbooks on corporate finance and valuation published between 1979 and 2009 and finds that their recommendations about the equity premium range from 3 percent to 10 percent. In fact, 51 books use different equity premiums. The 5-year moving average has declined from 8.4 percent in 1990 to 5.7 percent in 2008 and 2009.

THE EQUITY PREMIUM

The equity premium (also called market risk premium, equity risk premium, market premium, and risk premium) is one of the most important and discussed, but elusive parameters in finance. Part of the confusion arises from the fact that the term equity premium is used to designate four different concepts:

1. *Historical equity premium* (HEP) is the historical differential return of the stock market over treasuries.
2. *Expected equity premium* (EEP) is the expected differential return of the stock market over treasuries.
3. *Required equity premium* (REP) is the incremental return of a diversified portfolio (the market) over the risk-free rate required by an investor. It is used for calculating the required return to equity.
4. *Implied equity premium* (IEP) is the required equity premium that arises from assuming that the market price is correct.

The four concepts (HEP, EEP, REP, and IEP) designate different realities. Bostock (2004) notes that understanding the equity premium is largely a matter of using clear terms. The HEP is easy to calculate and is equal for all investors, provided that they use the same time frame, market index, risk-free instrument, and average (arithmetic or geometric). But the EEP, REP, and IEP may be different for different investors and are not observable magnitudes. As Brealey, Myers, and Allen (2005, p. 154) note about the expected equity premium, "Out of this debate only one firm conclusion emerges: Do not trust anyone who claims to know what returns investors expect."

In his investigation of 150 textbooks, Fernandez (2009) notes that some confusion arises from not distinguishing among the four concepts that the phrase equity

Exhibit 8.8 Market Risk Premium Used by Analysts in 2010

This exhibit present a survey by Fernandez and Campo (2010b) about the market risk premium (MRP) used by analysts to calculate the required return to equity in 2010. Panel A reports the responses from 711 analysts; Panel B reports the responses of 601 analysts who provide a figure for the MRP used in 2010.

Panel A. Responses of 711 Analysts about the MRP in 2010

	US and Canada	Europe	UK	Other	Total
Answers reported	107	197	31	266	601
Do not provide a figure:					
"My MRP changes weekly" or "monthly"	40	31	19	3	93
"It is confidential"	7	8	2		17

Europe: Austria, Belgium, Croatia, Denmark, Finland, France, Germany, Greece, Ireland, Italy, Netherlands, Norway, Portugal, Slovenia, Spain, Sweden and Switzerland. Other: Argentina, Australia, Brazil, Chile, China, Colombia, Czech Republic, Dubai, Egypt, Hong Kong, Hungary, India, Indonesia, Iran, Israel, Japan, Kazakhstan, Kuwait, Malaysia, Mexico, New Zealand, Pakistan, Peru, Poland, Qatar, R. Dominicana, Romania, Russia, Saudi Arabia, Singapore, South Africa, South Korea, Sri Lanka, Taiwan, Thailand, Turkey, UA Emirates, Ukraine, Uruguay, Venezuela, and Vietnam.

Panel B. Market Risk Premium Used by 601 Analysts in 2010

		US and Canada	Europe	UK	Other	Sum
MRP used in 2010	Average	5.1	5.0	5.2	6.3	
	St. dev.	1.1	1.3	1.4	2.2	
	MAX	10.0	11.9	10.0	25.0	
	Q3	5.5	5.5	5.7	7.0	
	Median	5.0	5.0	4.5	5.9	
	Q1	4.5	4.0	4.0	5.0	
	min	2.5	3.0	3.5	0.7	
	Number	104	197	31	269	601
Justify the number*						
Own research/calculations		24	70	5	96	195
I do not justify the number/do not answer		33	64	13	55	165
Reference to books or articles		33	40	8	69	150
Historic Data		12	19	3	49	83
Other analysts		2	2	0	3	7
Experience, subjective, own judgment		8	9	1	17	35

*Some respondents provided more than one answer.

145

premium designates: the historical, expected, required, and implied equity premium. For example, 129 books identify an expected and required equity premium whereas 82 identify an expected and historical equity premium. Fernandez concludes that finance textbooks should clarify the equity premium by incorporating distinguishing definitions of the four different concepts and conveying a clearer message about their sensible magnitudes.

The historical equity premium (HEP) is the historical average differential return of the market portfolio over the risk-free debt. The most widely cited sources are: Ibbotson Associates, whose U.S. database starts in 1926; Dimson, Marsh, and Staunton (2007), who calculate the HEP for 17 countries over 106 years (1900–2005); and the Center for Research in Security Prices (CRSP) at the University of Chicago.

Welch (2001) presents the results of a survey of 510 finance and economics professors performed in August 2001 and the consensus for the 30-year arithmetic EEP was 5.5 percent, much lower than just three years earlier (7 percent). In an updated study published in 2008, the mean is 5.69 percent, but the answers of about 400 finance professors range from 2 percent to 12 percent.

Miller (2000, p. 3) provides the following anecdote about the expected market return in the Nobel context:

> I still remember the teasing we financial economists, Harry Markowitz, William Sharpe, and I, had to put up with from the physicists and chemists in Stockholm when we conceded that the basic unit of our research, the expected rate of return, was not actually observable. I tried to tease back by reminding them of their neutrino—a particle with no mass whose presence was inferred only as a missing residual from the interactions of other particles. But that was eight years ago. In the meantime, the neutrino has been detected.

The required equity premium (REP) answers the following question: What incremental return does an investor require for investing in a diversified portfolio of shares (a stock index, for example) over the risk-free rate? REP is a crucial parameter because it is the key to determining the company's required return to equity, WACC, and required return to any investment project.

The implied equity premium (IEP) is the implicit REP used in the valuation of a stock (or market index) that matches the current market value. The most widely used model to calculate the IEP is the dividend discount model: The current price per share (P_0) is the present value of expected dividends discounted at the required rate of return (K_e). If D_1 is the dividend (equity cash flow) per share expected to be received at time 1, and g the expected long-term growth rate in dividends per share,

$$P_0 = D_1/(K_e - g), \text{ which implies that } IEP = D_1/P_0 + g - R_F \qquad (8.14)$$

The estimates of the IEP depend on the particular assumption made about the expected growth. Even if market prices are correct for all investors, there is not an IEP common for all investors: There are many pairs (IEP, g) that accomplish Equation (8.14).

CRITICAL ASPECTS OF A VALUATION

The critical aspects in performing a company valuation are:

- *Dynamic: The valuation is a process.* The process for estimating expected risks and calibrating the risk of the different businesses and business units is crucial.
- *Involvement of the company.* The company's managers should be involved in the analysis of the company, industry, and cash flow projections.
- *Multifunctional.* The valuation is not a task to be performed solely by financial management. To obtain a good valuation, managers from other departments should take part in estimating future cash flows and their risk.
- *Strategic.* The cash flow restatement technique is similar in all valuations, but estimating the cash flows and calibrating the risk should take into account each business unit's strategy.
- *Compensation.* The valuation's quality is increased when it includes goals involving such areas as sales, growth, market share, profits, and investments on which the managers' future compensation depends.
- *Real options.* If the company has real options, these must be valued appropriately. Real options require a totally different risk treatment from the cash flow restatements.
- *Historic analysis.* Although the value depends on future expectations, a thorough historic analysis of the financial, strategic, and competitive evolution of the different business units helps assess forecast consistency.
- *Technical correctness.* Technical correctness refers to the following: (1) calculation of the cash flows; (2) adequate treatment of the risk, which translates into the discount rates; (3) consistency of the cash flows used with the rates applied; (4) treatment of the residual value; and (5) treatment of inflation.

SUMMARY AND CONCLUSIONS

Understanding the mechanisms of company valuation is indispensable for anyone involved in corporate finance, especially those dealing with capital restructuring. This chapter describes the four main groups comprising the most widely used company valuation methods: balance sheet–based methods, income statement–based methods, discounted cash flow methods, and value creation methods using economic value added and economic profit. The methods that are conceptually correct are those based on cash flow discounting. The chapter also addresses the lack of agreement about how to calculate the value of tax shields. Finally, it provides survey evidence about the great dispersion that exists among finance professor and financial analysts regarding the appropriate market risk premium to use.

DISCUSSION QUESTIONS

1. List and briefly explain three common methods used to evaluate a firm.
2. Which valuation method is "conceptually" correct? Why?

3. Is there a single "correct" number for the market risk premium (MRP)? What methods are available for calculating the MRP?

4. What are the different meanings of the term "equity premium"?

REFERENCES

Arzac, Enrique, and Larry Glosten. 2005. "A Reconsideration of Tax Shield Valuation." *European Financial Management* 11:4, 453–461.

Baker, H. Kent, Prakash Deo, and Tarun Mukherjee. 2009. "EVA Revisited." *Journal of Financial Education* 35:Fall, 1–22.

Bostock, Paul. 2004. "The Equity Premium." *Journal of Portfolio Management* 30:2, 104–111.

Brealey, Richard A., Stewart C. Myers, and Franklin Allen. 2005. *Principles of Corporate Finance*, 8th ed. New York: McGraw-Hill/Irwin.

Cooper, Ian, and Kjell G. Nyborg. 2006. "The Value of Tax Shields Is Equal to the Present Value of Tax Shields." *Journal of Financial Economics* 81:1, 215–225.

Copeland, Tom E., Tim Koller, and Jack Murrin. 2000. *Valuation: Measuring and Managing the Value of Companies*, 3rd ed. New York: John Wiley & Sons, Inc.

Dimson, Elroy, Paul Marsh, and Mike Staunton. 2007. "The Worldwide Equity Premium: A Smaller Puzzle." In Rajnish Mehra, ed., *Handbook of Investments: Equity Risk Premium*, 467–514. Amsterdam: Elsevier Science.

Ehrhardt, Michael C., and Eugene F. Brigham. 2011. *Corporate Finance—A Focused Approach*, 4th ed. South-Western.

Faus, Josep. 1996. "Operational Finance: Analysis and Diagnosis." Technical Note No. 00803000, IESE Business School.

Fernandez, Pablo. 2007. "A More Realistic Valuation: APV and WACC with Constant Book Leverage Ratio." *Journal of Applied Finance* 17:2, 13–20.

Fernandez, Pablo. 2009. "The Equity Premium in 150 Textbooks." Available at http://ssrn.com/abstract=1473225.

Fernandez, Pablo, and Javier del Campo. 2010a. "Market Risk Premium Used in 2010 by Professors: A Survey with 1,500 Answers." Available at http://ssrn.com/abstract=1606563.

Fernandez, Pablo, and Javier del Campo. 2010b. "Market Risk Premium Used in 2010 by Analysts and Companies: A Survey with 2,400 Answers." Available at http://ssrn.com/abstract=1609563.

Harris, Robert S., and John J. Pringle. 1985. "Risk–adjusted Discount Rates Extensions from the Average-risk Case." *Journal of Financial Research* 8:3, 237–244.

Lewellen, Wilbur, and Douglas Emery. 1986, "Corporate Debt Management and the Value of the Firm." *Journal of Financial and Quantitative Analysis* 21:4, 415–426.

Luehrman, Timothy A. 1997, "Using APV: A Better Tool for Valuing Operations." *Harvard Business Review* 75:3, 145–154.

Marshall, Alfred. 2010. *Principles of Economics—Abridged Edition*. New York: Cosimo Classics.

McTaggart, James M., Peter W. Kontes, and Michael C. Mankins. 1994. *Value Imperative: Managing for Superior Shareholder Returns*. New York: The Free Press.

Miles, James A., and John R. Ezzell. 1985. "Reformulating Tax Shield Valuation: A Note." *Journal of Finance* 40:5, 1485–1492.

Miller, Merton. 2000. "The History of Finance: An Eyewitness Account." *Journal of Applied Corporate Finance* 13:2, 8–14.

Modigliani, Franco, and Merton Miller. 1963. "Corporate Income Taxes and the Cost of Capital: A Correction." *American Economic Review* 53:3, 433–443.

Ruback, Richard. 2002. "Capital Cash Flows: A Simple Approach to Valuing Risky Cash Flows." *Financial Management* 31:2, 85–103.

Stewart, III, G. Bennett. 1991. *The Quest for Value*. New York: Harper Business.
Welch, Ivo. 2001. "The Equity Premium Consensus Forecast Revisited." Cowles Foundation Discussion Paper No. 1325.

ABOUT THE AUTHOR

Pablo Fernandez started his career at IESE Business School (Spain) in 1985. Today he is a professor in the department of financial management and holder of the IESE's PricewaterhouseCoopers Corporate Finance Chair. He carries out extensive consultancy work for numerous firms and banks. Professor Fernandez was awarded his PhD in Business Economics from Harvard University. Before embarking on a career in academia, he was the financial analyst and financial coordinator of Pepsi Cola for the South of Europe. In 2004, he received the IESE award for outstanding research. Earlier in his career, he received the BARRA award for a project he undertook under the aegis of the Institute for Quantitative Investment Research (INQUIRE) titled "Convertible Bonds in Spain: A Different Security." Professor Fernandez is a widely published author. He has published four books about valuation and various articles appearing in the *Journal of Financial Economics, Journal of Applied Finance, International Journal of Finance Education, Quarterly Review of Economics and Finance, International Journal of Business*, and *Managerial Finance*. His work has also appeared in *The Financial Times* and *The Economist*.

CHAPTER 9

Real Options and Their Impact on M&As

HEMANTHA HERATH
Associate Professor, Brock University

JOHN S. JAHERA JR.
Colonial Bank Professor, Auburn University

INTRODUCTION

The increasing volume of merger and acquisition (M&A) activity both domestically and cross-border has brought increased attention to the valuation process, particularly with regard to existing embedded options. The overall complexity of M&A activity has also increased in recent years as financial systems have become more open with firms expanding not only domestically but also globally. Cross-border mergers in particular tend to be much more complex, and the valuation of such M&As are more involved with additional elements of risk exposure. The analysis of any merger or acquisition goes far beyond the simple stand-alone value of the target firm, given that the acquirer now has many decision points that can be modeled in the framework of real options.

Traditionally, M&A valuation closely followed capital budgeting methodology, predominantly the discounted cash flow (DCF) method with the focus on free cash flow. That is, cash flows are developed for a forecast period for the target firm, and then a terminal or horizon value is calculated at whatever is deemed a reasonable time period. This process involves the following: determining the appropriate time horizon, estimating free cash flows, considering growth opportunities, and specifying an appropriate risk-adjusted rate of discount. All of these parameters represent points of uncertainty. Of course, many other factors influence the parameters such as the timing of the M&A, competitor action, and the flexibility of exploiting a target firm's resources (marketing channels and production processes). The leverage factor can also be important as with a leveraged buyout (LBO). That is, many targets become attractive if they have strong debt capacity. The LBO type of transaction is a method whereby bidders may actually acquire controlling interest in a target firm with only minimal equity investment. The debt capacity of the target itself becomes the funding mechanism as the bidder uses a bridge loan to acquire the firm and then issues new debt using target firm assets as collateral.

Block (2009) elaborates on the application of traditional capital budgeting techniques to M&A analysis. As many studies note, traditional capital budgeting techniques, such as net present value (NPV), fail to adequately consider uncertainties in future time periods with regard to decisions that management may undertake (e.g., Dixit and Pindyck, 1994; Smith and Triantis, 1995; Trigeorgis, 1996). That is, firms typically have many opportunities to make other decisions based on the original merger or acquisition such as expanding into (or abandoning) new product or geographic markets. Also, the embedded options in an acquisition can have different risk levels. For instance, an option to abandon at some point in time may have different risk characteristics and hence would require a different rate of discount. Theory suggests that the greater the number of adjustment opportunities in terms of management decisions, the more value can be added (Dixit and Pindyck, 1994). Through real option analysis, managers can more explicitly consider any added value a result of these future decision opportunities. Such knowledge can enable both the bidder and the target firm management to negotiate and capture more value in the transaction.

The objective of this chapter is to provide a discussion of the various applications of real options within the context of M&As. Real option analysis allows for the explicit consideration of a number of value-enhancing factors. Clearly, the ability to identify and evaluate options associated with M&As can be of great value to corporate decision makers. Decision makers have many options including timing of the acquisition, entry and exit options, growth options, options on managerial flexibility, and options involving the merger terms. Managers value the opportunity to alter decisions further into the future and actively seek such opportunities. The literature as well as current financial practice has seen much attention focused on the inclusion of real option analysis in the M&A framework. This chapter discusses various M&A situations where real option analysis may be applicable.

The remainder of the chapter has the following organization. The chapter first discusses the origin, the conceptual idea, and different modeling techniques in real option analysis. Second, a detailed literature review of the state-of-the-art real option M&A is presented from three angles: (1) a standard valuation framework, (2) a game theoretic decision framework, and (3) a collaborative decision framework. Third, the chapter discusses the practice of real options and implementation challenges. Finally, a summary and conclusion argues for greater application of the state-of-the-art real option valuation models to M&A practice.

REAL OPTIONS ANALYSIS FOR M&As

Real option techniques for evaluating uncertain investments are now a part of mainstream financial economics literature (Merton, 1998; Grenadier, 2000, 2002; Hull, 2006). Myers (1977) introduces the idea of real options as the value above the market value of assets-in-place that contribute to the market value of equity. The market value of equity therefore is comprised of two value components: the assets-in-place and growth opportunities. Since a firm's management has the discretion to undertake future investment opportunities, growth opportunities can be structured as options or simply rights on nontrade assets, and hence, the term real options applies.

The basic insight underlying this valuation approach is that any investment opportunity can be conceptually compared to a financial option. In simple terms any investment opportunity with managerial flexibility to alter the course of action and exploit its upside potential has added value. Hull (2006) provides a complete primer on options and derivatives and their valuation. The application of option valuation to firm investment decision and firm valuation is presented through various sound examples. As Hull and others note, managers often simply ignore embedded options, resulting in a potential loss of value during an M&A.

Since the seminal work of Myers (1977), there has been extensive growth in real options research in the standard financial option framework, as well as in Bayesian and game theoretic (competitive and cooperative) valuation frameworks. The earliest models include direct applications of standard financial options, such as the Black-Scholes (B-S) model, but since then, models have evolved into more complex options, such as compound real options and other complex exotic options. These also include Bayesian learning models and game theoretic models with incentives and agency features. Real options applications are seen in various industries and business circumstances including forestry, oil and gas, M&As, pharmaceutical research and development (R&D) valuation, information technology, and manufacturing, among others (e.g., Dixit and Pindyck, 1994; Sick, 1995; Trigeorgis, 1996; Birge and Zhang, 1999; Herath and Park, 1999; Smit and Trigeorgis, 1999; Benaroch and Kauffman, 1999; Park and Herath, 2000; Lambrecht, 2004; Savva and Scholtes, 2005; Herath and Herath, 2004, 2009). More recent articles have investigated the deviation from all equity-financed firms and projects to those that have both debt and equity (Lambrecht and Myers, 2007, 2008).

Theoretically, real options have proven to be a powerful technique for analyzing investments under uncertainty. In the traditional DCF approach to valuation, an asset is valued at the present value of future cash flows or benefits. Future certain cash flows can be discounted at the risk-free rate, but stochastic cash flows introduce considerable complexity and require the valuation of an added dimension (i.e., value of active risk management). Researchers find the expected net present value (ENPV) criterion is inadequate in capturing the managerial flexibility to delay, grow, scale down, or abandon projects, exchange resource inputs, and incorporate learning or uncertainty resolution (when underlying asset values are uncertain). Thus, real options that combine strategy with valuation have increasingly attracted attention in the corporate finance literature. The application of the real options concept is counterintuitive to traditional risk mitigation in the sense that more uncertainty is beneficial from an option valuation point of view. In other words, option values are based in part upon uncertainty and volatility.

Financial economists use various real option modeling techniques depending upon the problem structure. These techniques include continuous time models, multinomial (lattice) and finite difference techniques, and simulation. Multinomial or lattice models provide more modeling latitude in capturing option complexities. Multiple correlated underlying assets, uncertain exercise prices, optimal timing, and varying asset volatilities can more easily be incorporated than continuous time models. Simulation is a promising alternative to multinomial and finite difference techniques but requires more rigorous validation testing.

LITERATURE REVIEW OF REAL OPTIONS IN THE M&A PROCESS

The real option approach to valuing managerial flexibility in M&A transactions is considered an integral part of an M&A valuation. The M&A real options literature consists of three broad areas. Typical M&A investments are embedded real options, which may include additional investment or growth (expansion) options, abandonment options, and wait-and-see (timing) options. Models can be categorized into the following: (1) a standard M&A real option framework where the exercise decision does not directly depend on the actions of competitors or collaborators; (2) strategic M&A interactions in a real option setting or game theoretic M&A real options framework, which deals with competition between parties; and (3) the collaborative or joint action M&A real option framework, which deals with cooperative options. The pertinent role of real options in each of these categories is discussed below.

Standard M&A Real Option Framework

In one of the earliest studies, Kogut (1991) presents the perspective that joint ventures are created as real options to expand in response to future technological and market developments. The exercise of the real option to expand accompanies the acquisition of the venture. Using joint venture data for the period from 1975 to 1983, Kogut offers empirical evidence that the timing of an acquisition depends on the unexpected growth in the product market. The unexpected shortfall in product shipments has no effect on the dissolution of the venture. The real option to dissolve remains unexercised. Kogut provides counter evidence to the prevailing assumption in organizational theories that firms engage in cooperative ventures as buffers against uncertainty. He provides a real option perspective that joint ventures are designed to exploit the upside and not simply to buffer uncertainty.

In the standard valuation framework, several researchers have developed models that investigate real option features in stock-for-stock exchanges. Stock-for-stock M&A transactions generally take more time to complete than transactions that are cash based (Gaughan, 1999). If a buying firm's and a selling firm's stock volatilities are high, the value of respective shares may fluctuate widely between the time a fixed exchange ratio is determined and the actual acquisition date. When a fixed exchange ratio is applied to determine a target's compensation, an acquiring firm would overpay when its stock price is higher on the merger date than on the agreement date or when a target's stock price is lower on the merger date than on the agreement date. Alternatively, a target would lose if an acquiring firm's stock price is lower on the merger date than on the agreement date or when a target's stock price has risen on the merger date.

Various authors have investigated how to exploit the fluctuations in the exchange ratios to increase the M&A deal value (e.g., Giacomello, 2008; Herath and Jahera, 2001, 2002, 2003, 2004). These real option models provide more elaborate methods for structuring an M&A deal than the naïve approach suggested by Gaughan (1999), which is to negotiate a provision to adjust the exchange ratio if stock prices go above or below a certain threshold. In other words, both parties to the transaction have the opportunity to structure the deal to exploit the upside potential due to stock price volatility.

Herath and Jahera (2001) argue that explicit valuation of managerial flexibility in setting the final terms of an acquisition may enhance the M&A deal value in the process. Accordingly, the deal may be optimally structured to benefit an acquiring firm if the stock prices are highly volatile between the announcement date and the closing date. In a deal where the stock exchange ratio is fixed, the shareholders of an acquiring firm may have to pay a premium for the net assets of the target firm. This will happen if the acquirer's stock appreciates in value over this period because the deal value would increase. As a result, Herath and Jahera model the right of an acquiring firm to optimally switch between alternate purchase considerations: either swap stock or pay the target's fair market value (of the net assets) as a switching option. The premium is a hidden loss to the shareholders of the acquiring firm. Using the BB&T Corporation's acquisition of BankFirst Corporation, the authors show that the deal value, including the cost of managerial flexibility to switch payment modes, is still $25.7 million lower than the actual closing value of the deal if the exchange ratio had been fixed. They show that the value of managerial flexibility in deal optimization, which is traditionally ignored, can be significant and, in this case, would have increased the deal value to both parties.

Herath and Jahera (2002) develop an extension of the above model in a subsequent paper. The authors demonstrate how an M&A deal may be optimally structured as a real options swap. They argue that consideration of both buyer and seller expectations often results in fairer deals. Herath and Jahera use real option analysis to model a stock-for-stock transaction as an exchange ratio swap when both the buyer's and the seller's stock prices are volatile. Hence, they show how to structure an acquisition to minimize the purchase price paid by a bidding firm and to maximize the deal value to a target. The theoretical value of an acquisition is defined as the deal value based on a fixed exchange ratio but dependent on the acquiring firm's stock price at consummation. Accordingly, in order to minimize the value of a deal, the authors suggest that an acquiring firm buy a call option or hold a cap, which guarantees a minimum deal value. On the other hand, a target should consider a put option or a floor, which ensures that the holder will receive the maximum deal value. Consequently, when stock prices are volatile, the flexibility available to management of both parties can be valued as an exchange ratio swap—holding a cap and selling a floor with an identical strike price. Herath and Jahera illustrate the model using the BB&T Corporation's acquisition of BankFirst Corporation. Additionally, the authors compare the valuation effects of alternate deal structures—an exchange ratio swap model and the switching real option model in Herath and Jahera (2001). The swap avoids earnings per share (EPS) dilution to both parties.

Herath and Jahera (2004) investigate how to provide price protection to both acquiring and target firm shareholders by setting conditions for active risk management by managers. The authors investigate the contingency effects of managerial flexibility to renegotiate the deal and hedge the market price risk by specifying a range within which the deal is allowed to fluctuate as in a collar-type arrangement. To minimize the value of a deal, an acquiring firm could buy a call option or a cap, which guarantees a minimum deal value. On the other hand, a target could consider a put option or a floor, which ensures that the holder would receive the maximum deal value. Since the cap and the floor have different strike prices, the managerial flexibility to both parties can be structured as a collar arrangement, in essence going long on a cap and shorting a floor. Herath and Jahera argue that in addition to the valuation effects, the contingency effects also enforce favorable managerial behaviors.

More recently, Giacomello (2008) analyzes how M&A exchange ratios can be assessed when a firm's economic capital valuation is carried out within a stochastic framework. He develops a quantitative model for exchange ratio accounting. Assets and liabilities with stochastic cash flows represent embedded real options such as minimum guarantees that have incremental value over traditional deterministic balance sheet values. Hence, Giacomello introduces important differences in exchange ratios. When stochastic cash flows are assumed to be contingent claims on underlying traded securities, the author shows that the no-arbitrage conditions hold. In the absence of liabilities, stochastic capital reserves are shown to be equivalent to a portfolio of European call options with a guaranteed and call component. In multi-period settings, the options embedded in the merger contracts have multiple options such as ratchet or cliquet options. A ratchet or cliquet option includes a series of consecutive forward start options. The first option is active immediately and then the second becomes active after the expiration of the first option. The above stream of literature primarily focuses on the exchange ratios in M&A transactions.

Subramanian (2004) develops an arbitrage-free framework to price stock options of firms involved in M&As when the deals are pending and where a possibility that the deal may be terminated exists. The B-S model for pricing options is inadequate to price options on M&A firms due to discontinuities that affect the underlying stock price process when deals are pending or may be terminated. The author's model is applicable for deals with stock-for-stock type considerations where a deal is announced but pending. Subramanian tests the model using options data and compares it to the B-S model. The results indicate that this model performs better than the B-S framework in explaining the observed option prices on stocks involved in merger deals. Although this model does not directly deal with real options, these findings are useful in extending real option methodology to M&A situations where such discontinuities exist.

In a conceptual article that includes numerical examples, Smith and Triantis (1995) consider three types of real options that arise in strategic acquisitions and influence overall value. The first refers to growth options. Through acquisitions, firms can exploit strategic synergies, which, in the long term, may affect the combined growth options of the acquiring and target firms by lowering exercise prices, thus increasing upside potential and improving exercise timing. More specifically, a firm, through a series of strategic acquisitions over time, can change the acquirer's competitive position through development of growth options, which traditional DCF cash flow analysis tends to overlook in restructuring deals.

Second, firms that have substantial flexibility in organization, marketing, manufacturing, and financing can benefit from acquisitions. For instance, a firm with a flexible distribution channel may acquire a target whose product demand is negatively correlated with that of the acquirer. Such a firm may then adopt the existing marketing and distribution channels to increase revenues.

The third type of real options is the divestiture (abandonment) option, which conventional acquisition analysis ignores. These divesture options limit the downside losses to the acquiring firm. Although there may be an opportunity to divest assets soon after an acquisition, firms may decide to hold these divesture options in hopes of a more optimal time. Smith and Triantis (1999) examine the valuations of such strategic options, which are necessary as they affect valuation of M&As and also determine the success of an M&A program.

Arzac (2008) discusses the application of real options to the entry and exit issue as well as to the foothold issue. That is, the timing of when to undertake a venture can be modeled in the context of real options. Delaying entry until a more favorable time can at first appear to be valuable, but this may increase risk exposure by allowing competitors time to enter the market. Likewise, the optimal time to exit a venture or project can be modeled as a real option. The foothold issue refers to the entry with subsequent opportunities to expand, including both geographically and in terms of production. As previously discussed, the traditional DCF method fails to account for any value associated with the options regarding the time to enter into an acquisition or to exit via divestiture. Arzac demonstrates the application of real options in these situations using discrete time option pricing and then continuous time option pricing through a series of real-world examples.

Baldi and Trigeorgis (2009) discuss another application of real options that focuses on accounting aspects of goodwill impairment tests. Specifically, they consider goodwill impairment that may have occurred subsequent to a merger. Goodwill represents the excess value paid over the market value of the target firm's assets. Under Financial Accounting Standards Board (FASB) statements, goodwill is not considered depreciable but rather is subject to periodic tests of impairment, which should reflect changes in the value of the recorded goodwill. Essentially, Baldi and Trigeorgis demonstrate how real options can be applied to consider those upside gains from the firm's growth alternatives and, hence, develop a more accurate assessment of goodwill at a particular point in time. They take the real options approach to growth opportunities and apply that to the accounting side while considering goodwill impairment. Baldi and Trigeorgis also demonstrate the advantages of using real option analysis.

Warner and Fairbank (2008) develop an integrated framework by combining real option concepts and dynamic capability theories to explain why information and communication technology (ICT) firms might acquire early, as well as which ICT firms are likely to do so. They provide a nonquantitative descriptive model of the relationship between factors affecting entry timing. Although real option analysis explains why firms invest in new technology through acquisitions, the authors argue that the dynamic capability theory is necessary to explain which firms can best incorporate new resources through alliance, political, and integration skills.

Game Theoretic M&A Real Options Framework

Smit and Trigeorgis (1999, 2001, 2009), Ferreira, Kar, and Trigeorgis (2009), and Grenadier (1996, 1999, 2000) discuss how combining real options analysis and game theory can help resolve valuation problems that involve strategic interaction among firms. Smit and Trigeorgis (1999) also emphasize that high takeover premiums have been a motivational factor for the embracing of real options approach by corporate strategists. The integration of competition into the real option valuation process has resulted in more articles that investigate (1) the strategic interaction in R&D, (2) the early preemptive investment by giving up the option premium to wait (of a wait-and-see approach), and (3) the competitive interaction in real option valuation of M&As.

Smit and Trigeorgis (2001) use a game theoretic framework to model strategic real option interactions in R&D as a two-person game in which the growth option value depends on exogenous competitive reactions. Accordingly, a firm invests in R&D to develop a more cost-efficient production process and then commercializes the product. This idea can be used in M&A valuation if the target and acquiring firms can combine resources to mitigate exogenous competitive reactions.

As Lambrecht and Myers (2007) note, formal models of takeover incentives and decisions are scarce. Lambrecht (2004) develops a real options model of mergers that is motivated by economies of scale in the absence of agency costs and rising product markets. Lambrecht's model and findings are discussed in more detail under collaborative models. Extending Lambrecht's work, Lambrecht and Myers consider takeovers in declining markets. M&As fall into two categories: One exploits synergies and growth opportunities while the other seeks greater efficiency through layoffs, consolidation, and divestment. Lambrecht and Myers develop a real option–based theory of takeovers and divestment for the second category. Thus, a firm can abandon a business voluntarily or be forced to do so by a takeover when product demand falls to a low threshold level.

Lambrecht and Myers (2007) also extend the line of research that uses real options to analyze the financing and investment decisions of firms vis-à-vis valuation of individual projects. The authors develop a dynamic infinite horizon model that incorporates the option to abandon the firm and release the assets to investors. In this model, the managers decide when to exercise the real abandonment options either voluntarily or when forced by a takeover. The authors provide new theoretical results and testable predictions on the optimal payout policy, the role of golden parachutes, and the link between debt and takeovers. Lambrecht and Myers show that debt service can reduce managerial rents and force managers to close the firm early. Thus, they contend that debt financing plays an important role in hostile takeovers.

Morellec and Zhdanov (2005) develop a dynamic real option model that jointly determines the timing and terms of takeovers by solving option exercise games between bidding and target firm shareholders. They examine the role of multiple bidders in the presence of competition and imperfect information on takeover activity. The authors base their model on two key elements. The first recognizes the analogy between exchange options and takeover opportunities, in the sense that a takeover can be compared to an option to exchange one asset (shares of the initial firm) either for shares in the new firm or for cash. The second element is imperfect information. Firms have complete information but outside investors have incomplete information. The analytical results allow for the following main predictions: (1) returns to target shareholders are higher than bidding shareholders; (2) returns to bidding shareholders are negative if competition exists for the acquisition; and (3) competition affects returns on takeover deals and speeds up the acquisition process. Further, any delay in consummating a merger affords competitors greater opportunity to enter the process. These predictions are consistent with the empirical evidence. This model departs from Lambrecht (2004) in the sense that it examines the impact of competition on timing and in terms of takeovers. The findings of Morellec and Zhdanov extend and complement the results derived in Lambrecht.

Toxvaerd (2008) develops a theory to explain the merger waves based on interaction between competitive pressure, irreversibility of mergers, and uncertainty when targets are scarce. The real options game model is based on three elements. First, there is a relative scarcity of desirable targets. Second, mergers can be viewed as irreversible investments containing considerable uncertainty. Specifically, there is an embedded delay option or an option value of waiting to acquire a target. Thus, irreversibility creates an option value, and a merger can be viewed as a problem of optimally exercising a real option since waiting is valuable in resolving uncertainty. The model's third element is imperfect competition for the target. Toxvaerd derives a complete information model, showing that waiting versus the preemption trade-off leads to a continuum of subgame perfect equilibrium. Next, he introduces noisy private information about merger profitability leading to a dynamic global model in a Bayesian setting.

Magsiri, Mello, and Rukes (2008) develop a model in which the acquisition price is endogenously determined as the outcome of a bargaining game between the acquirer and the seller. The authors analyze the fundamental trade-off between internal growth and growth via acquisition. The opportunity to grow internally affects the price of an acquisition because it is a fallback option in the event negotiations fail due to lower price and other factors. If the negotiations fail, the acquirer has the opportunity to grow internally through investments, which is a real option to expand. The above assumes the acquirer has the flexibility to decide if and when to undertake the investment. Assuming that an acquisition investment and an internal investment represent mutually exclusive strategies, the option's value to grow internally at the time of negotiations becomes a bargaining game option. This model complements the findings of Morellec and Zhdanov (2005) and shows that competition is unnecessary to generate negative earnings announcements. Inclusion of the internal growth opportunity is shown to force early acquisitions (rather than at a socially optimal time), which contrasts the finding in Morellec and Zhdanov and Lambrecht (2004).

Collaborative M&A Real Option Framework

Smit and Trigeorgis (1999) discuss how competing firms may cooperate and share opportunities in order to increase the total industry value. A cited example is the standardization of high-density compact discs (CDs), which resulted from cooperative R&D among competing firms. In a similar vein, Savva and Scholtes (2005) distinguish between cooperative and competitive options. Cooperative options are exercised jointly to maximize the total deal value, while competitive options are exercised unilaterally to increase the payoff for individual parties. These collaborative real options fall within the boundaries of risk-sharing contracts. Savva and Scholtes consider cooperative options, which are partnership deals such as joint ventures with future flexibility. Cooperative options allow better understanding of real options in partnership deals with regard to fair splits of risks and return of a partnership. In partnership deals, the idea is to develop synergies by combining core competencies to form unique offerings that neither party alone can provide. Thus, the exercise decisions are taken jointly with a view to maximizing the total value of the deal. The authors model the mathematical conditions for the real option effects on the core of a bilateral deal.

Lambrecht (2004) models the timing and terms of mergers that are motivated by economies of scale. The author positions the M&A problem as a real option. The argument is that mergers not only generate stochastic benefits but also have associated costs. Thus, since both firms have the right, but not the obligation to merge, each firm's payoff resembles an option. The decision to merge, in effect, is similar to the exercise of an option. Lambrecht uses a continuous time real option technique and game theoretic concepts. He develops a model based on the assumption that firms are price-takers and shows that firms have an incentive to merge in periods of economic expansion, resulting in pro-cyclical merger activity. Upon relaxing the assumption that firms are price-takers, Lambrecht shows that market power strengthens a firm's incentive to merge, thus speeding up merger activity. He also provides a closed-form solution for merger timing. Lambrecht shows that there is a unique Pareto optimal solution in execution of the merger option by the two friendly firms, such as in a cooperative framework. Compared to mergers, he shows that in hostile takeovers the target demands a larger share of ownership and there is a delay in the restructuring or low probability of takeover happening.

Thijssen (2008) adds to the discussion by considering a situation in which both parties in a transaction can make bids for each other. Assuming some agreement is reached, the firms then merge. Thijssen considers a takeover to be different from a merger, with the role of both parties being endogenous in a merger. He concludes that any value associated with options in the merger is eliminated if the actions of each party are endogenous. Thijssen further develops a theoretical model to support this finding.

Additionally, the presence of specific antitakeover defenses can create new option points. That is, many antitakeover measures are triggered by certain events with the intent of deterring a hostile takeover. In reality, defensive measures may not actually prevent a takeover, but they do have the effect of increasing the cost of a takeover. Hence, an acquirer could use the real option framework to incorporate the activation of various antitakeover measures a target would invoke if the attempt is hostile, that is, without board approval. A target could also apply real options to the valuation from its point of view in the context of activation of antitakeover provisions. Such an analysis may serve to facilitate negotiations and result in a friendly rather than hostile takeover. The reality is that most takeovers are the result of negotiation between the boards of the acquirer and the target firm, even if the initial offer was a hostile offer.

THE PRACTICE OF REAL OPTIONS

The actual implementation of real option analysis into the corporate decision-making framework has been somewhat difficult. Triantis and Borison (2001) employ a survey approach to gauge the actual use of real option methodology. They categorize the use of real options into three broad groups. The first is the qualitative use of options methodology as a thought process. Managers have long recognized that options or future decision points exist in almost any long-term investment opportunity. The second category is the analytical use of real options. The third is the use of real options in the context of much broader company-wide planning. Based on their survey, Triantis and Borison note that some respondents view the use of real options primarily as an endeavor of academic researchers. However, other responses indicate that the use of real options is evolving as managers seek to make better decisions. Overall, the acceptance of real option analysis in corporate decision making in general will depend upon its perceived value in terms of better financial outcomes.

Damodaran (2005) provides an overview of the actual implementation of real option analysis in corporate decision making. According to Damodaran, many managers believe that accurately placing a value on the many potential embedded options involved in a corporation is impossible. He notes, however, that others perceive that it is indeed possible to determine a quantitative value. Damodaran attempts to examine various options that arise in business decisions and then to develop a methodology to use the appropriate inputs and develop a true value. With regards to investment considerations (that would include M&A activity), he focuses on the timing option, expansion option, and termination option. The parameters for determining the option value include the cost, the variance, the exercise price, and the expiration period. While these seem straightforward, Damodaran points out that, in practice, developing these parameters is more difficult. For instance, the investment may or may not be traded, meaning that obtaining a true variance may be difficult. The same issues can apply to expansion decisions. Often the option to expand further, subsequent to an acquisition, has no time specification. Regarding the third issue of abandonment, Damodaran holds that applying option models is complicated because abandonment value can change over time. Regardless of the difficulties, the inclusion of option values may transform a negative NPV acquisition into a value additive acquisition.

Barnett and Dunbar (2007) offer a different perspective by examining what they call real options reasoning (ROR). They discuss how ROR can lead firms to undertake many investments because each has some option involved for future decisions. Accordingly, firms may be motivated to assume many investments, given multiple options associated with each. They discuss how ROR can lead firms to undertake many investments because each has some option involved for future decision. This would result in abandoning many such investments.

Illustration: Option Value to Delay an M&A Transaction

This section provides an example of the application of real option analysis to the situation where the acquirer has the opportunity to delay an M&A transaction. Consider Firm A that is planning to acquire a target Firm B. Assume considerable uncertainty exists surrounding the transaction since Firm B has just entered into an international market. The uncertainty in demand for its product in the international market is described by an analyst using the following two states of nature—a good state (θ_1) and a bad state (θ_2). Assume that the outcome can be either θ_1 or θ_2 in all future years. The discount rate is assumed to be 8 percent per year. The target's value derived from the present value of annual cash flows over a 10-year period,

Exhibit 9.1 Target Firm Data

State	Present Value of Annual Cash Flows ($ million)	Present Value of Residual Value ($ million)	Value of Target (Firm B) ($ million)	Probability
θ_1	150	130	280	0.5
θ_2	65	50	105	0.5

Note: This exhibit shows the present value of annual cash flows and residual values in each of the two random states of nature and their respective probabilities.

the present value of the residual value, and the probability of each state are shown in Exhibit 9.1.

The expected value of the target is $192.5 million (0.5 × $280) + (0.5 × $105). Suppose Firm A has the option to acquire Firm B today or defer the acquisition decision to a year later so that it can obtain more information regarding the true state. By delaying the M&A decision, a further assumption is that the following two signals are obtained from an information source (regarding the reliability of the information). The following set of conditional probabilities exists regarding whether similar M&As in the industry are profitable or not. That is, signal (δ_1) if the true state is good (θ_1), there is still a 10 percent chance that the proposed M&A may not be profitable; and signal (δ_2) if the true state is bad (θ_2), there is a 20 percent chance that the proposed M&A may not be profitable. Exhibit 9.2 shows the conditional probabilities available after one year.

In order to evaluate whether to go ahead with the M&A decision after one year, an analyst would need to compute the posterior probabilities. The reliability probabilities and the analyst's own prior probabilities determine, via Bayes's Theorem, the posterior probabilities. Bayes's Theorem revises the prior information:

$$P(\theta_i \,|\delta_k) = \frac{P(\theta_i)P(\delta_k \,|\theta_i)}{\sum_{j=1}^{2} P(\theta_j)P(\delta_k \,|\theta_j)} \tag{9.1}$$

Exhibit 9.2 Additional Information Regarding the True State of Nature

State	Signal $P(\delta_i \,|\theta_i)$	
	δ_1	δ_2
	Similar M&As Are Profitable	Similar M&As Are Not Profitable
θ_1	0.90	0.10
θ_2	0.20	0.80

Note: This exhibit provides the conditional probabilities indicating the reliability of additional information regarding the profitability of similar M&A decisions.

Exhibit 9.3   Computed Posterior Probabilities

State	$P(\theta_i)$	$P(\delta_i\mid\theta_i)$		Posterior $P(\theta_i\mid\delta_i)$	
		δ_1	δ_2	δ_1	δ_2
θ_1	0.5	0.9	0.1	0.8182	0.1111
θ_2	0.5	0.2	0.8	0.1818	0.8889

Note: This exhibit shows the prior probabilities, reliability probabilities, and the computed posterior probabilities.

Using the above formula, the prior and the reliability probabilities yield the following posterior probabilities as shown in Exhibit 9.3. The computational details are as follows:

$$P(\theta_1\mid\delta_1) = \frac{P(\theta_1)P(\delta_1\mid\theta_1)}{P(\theta_1)P(\delta_1\mid\theta_1)+P(\theta_2)P(\delta_1\mid\theta_2)} = \frac{0.5\times0.9}{0.5\times0.9+0.5\times0.2} = 0.8182;$$

$$P(\theta_2\mid\delta_1) = 1 - 0.8182 = 0.1818;$$

$$P(\theta_2\mid\delta_2) = \frac{P(\theta_2)P(\delta_2\mid\theta_2)}{P(\theta_1)P(\delta_2\mid\theta_1)+P(\theta_2)P(\delta_2\mid\theta_2)} = \frac{0.5\times0.8}{0.5\times0.8+0.5\times0.1} = 0.8889; \text{ and}$$

$$P(\theta_1\mid\delta_2) = 1 - 0.8889 = 0.1111.$$

The expected value of the target if the analysis includes more information as given by signal δ_1 is \$248.19 million (0.8182 × \$280 + 0.1818 × \$105). The present value of the expected value of the target is \$229.80 million ($\frac{\$248.19}{1.08}$). Similarly, the expected value of the target if the analysis obtains more information as given by signal δ_2 is \$124.44 million (0.1111 × \$280 + 0.8889 x \$105). The present value of the expected value of the target is \$115.23 million ($\frac{\$124.44}{1.08}$).

If Firm A acquires Firm B at \$192.5 million immediately, there is a 50 percent chance that the acquiring firm will lose \$87.5 million (\$105 – \$192.5) since the international market expansion may be unsuccessful. On the other hand, if Firm A can delay the M&A and obtain additional information, it will acquire Firm B only if similar M&As are found to be profitable (i.e., signal δ_1). Thus the value of the target is \$229.8 million. The additional amount Firm A may have to pay the target Firm B is \$37.3 million (\$229.8 – \$192.5). Firm A will forego the acquisition of Firm B if similar M&As are not found to be profitable (i.e., signal δ_2). Notice, however, that the extra amount Firm A will have to pay, \$37.3 million, is still smaller than the loss of \$87.5 million. Therefore, the value of the M&A option to defer is equal to the net saving \$50.5 million (\$87.5 – \$37.3). Both firms are likely to benefit if the M&A takes place a year later since the target firm can get a higher value and the acquiring firm will avoid a significant loss. This example demonstrates the real option value of delaying an M&A transaction. The analysis would be similar for other circumstances that may arise in the course of an M&A transaction.

SUMMARY AND CONCLUSIONS

Real option analysis represents a mechanism for managers to consider the additional value of a potential M&A due to managerial flexibility. That is, managers can include the value of various options such as expansion (products and geographical), optimal timing, resource flexibility, and abandonment. Further, boards of directors and managers may use real option analysis as they prepare the terms of an offer. In other words, implicit consideration of the bidding firm's managerial flexibility should enhance value for the firm. Likewise, the target firm's decision makers can consider managerial flexibility in merger terms to increase a target's value. Thus, all parties to a transaction can potentially benefit from the identification and valuation of any embedded options, which may differ between the acquirer and the target firm. Overall, the literature has a large body of research that is relatively recent in terms of financial modeling. The research to date is largely theoretical and the actual application for firm use is still somewhat limited due to the complexity of identifying the relevant inputs for valuation of the option. Much of the extant literature appears in the engineering economics literature and industry-specific applied research.

The literature emphasizes that managers, boards of directors, and other interested parties should consider the available options and incorporate them to determine the more accurate value of a deal. More precise valuation can result in M&A terms that more nearly reach an equilibrium point. Future research should focus on bridging the gap between the research and actual practice and make real options analysis less daunting for boards of directors and senior managers. The evidence to date suggests that the use of real options will continue to develop in all aspects of corporate decision making. The impact of real options on the M&A process has been to guide decision makers to more explicitly value all aspects of the potential M&A, ranging from the terms of the potential M&A to the timing of the transaction, divestiture, or spin-off entities. Many managers have long considered such issues, but the relatively recent ability to quantify the value has resulted in a greater understanding of any value that may be created.

Clearly, additional research is warranted to guide managers as they work to identify any options they may have and then to value such options. One hindrance in the use of real options lies in their perceived complexity. Future research should focus on providing a clear methodology for managerial use in the valuation of such real options.

DISCUSSION QUESTIONS

1. What are some limitations of using traditional capital budgeting methodology to value M&A transactions?
2. What are real options? How can an acquiring firm exploit uncertainty to add value in an M&A transaction?
3. Identify and briefly explain three different types of real options that may be embedded in an irreversible M&A deal.
4. Discuss the different ways in which a stock-for-stock M&A transaction can be structured from a real options perspective when stock prices are highly volatile.

5. What are the fundamental differences between competitive real options and cooperative real options? Why are these types of complex real options important to better understand M&A dynamics?

REFERENCES

Arzac, Enrique R. 2008. *Valuation for Mergers, Buyouts, and Restructuring.* Hoboken, NJ: John Wiley & Sons, Inc.

Baldi, Francesco, and Lenos Trigeorgis. 2009. "Assessing the Value of Growth Option Synergies from Business Combinations and Testing for Goodwill Impairment: A Real Options Perspective." *Journal of Applied Corporate Finance* 21:4, 115–124.

Barnett, Michael L., and Roger L. M. Dunbar. 2007. "Making Sense of Real Options Reasoning: An Engine of Choice That Backfires." In Gerard P. Hodgkinson and William H. Starbuck (eds.), *Oxford Handbook of Organizational Decision Making*, 383–398. Oxford, United Kingdom: Oxford University Press.

Benaroch, Michel, and Robert J. Kauffman. 1999. "A Case for Using Real Options Analysis to Evaluate Information Technology Project Investments." *Information Systems Research* 10:1, 70–86.

Birge, John R., and Rachel Q. Zhang. 1999. "Risk Neutral Option Pricing Methods for Adjusting Constrained Cash Flows." *Engineering Economist* 44:1, 36–49.

Block, Stanley. 2009. "Applying Capital Budgeting Techniques to Mergers." *Engineering Economist* 54: 4, 317–328.

Dixit, Avinash K., and Robert S. Pindyck. 1994. *Investment under Uncertainty.* Princeton, NJ: Princeton University Press.

Damodaran, Aswath. 2005. "The Promise and Peril of Real Options." New York University Working Paper No. S-DRP-05-02. Available at http://ssrn.com/abstract=1295849.

Ferreira, Nelson, Jayanti Kar, and Lenos Trigeorgis. 2009. "Option Games—The Key to Competing in Capital-Intensive Industries." *Harvard Business Review* 87:3, 101–107.

Gaughan, Patrick A. 1999. *Mergers, Acquisitions and Corporate Restructuring.* Hoboken, NJ: John Wiley & Sons.

Giacomello, Bruno. 2008. "Exchange Ratios in a Merger with Stochastic Capital Reserves: Fair Valuation and Embedded Options." *Managerial Finance* 34:4, 239–251.

Grenadier, Steven R. 1996. "The Strategic Exercise of Options: Development Cascades and Overbuilding in Real Estate Markets." *Journal of Finance* 51:5, 1653–1679.

Grenadier, Steven R. 1999. "Information Revelation through Option Exercise." *Review of Financial Studies* 12:1, 95–130.

Grenadier, Steven R. (ed.) 2000. *Game Choices: The Intersection of Real Options and Game Theory.* Haymarket House, London: Risk Books.

Grenadier, Steven R. 2002. "Option Exercise Games: An Application to the Equilibrium Investment Strategies of Firms." *Review of Financial Studies* 15:3, 691–721.

Herath, Hemantha S. B., and Tejaswini C. Herath. 2009. "Investments in Information Security: A Real Options Perspective with Bayesian Post-Audit." *Journal of Management Information System* 25:3, 337–375.

Herath, Hemantha S. B., and John S. Jahera, Jr. 2001. "Operational Risk in Bank Acquisitions: A Real Options Approach to Valuing Managerial Flexibility." *Advances in Operational Risk*, 53–65. London: Incisive RWG Ltd.

Herath, Hemantha S. B., and John S. Jahera, Jr. 2002. "Real Options: Valuing Flexibility in Strategic Mergers and Acquisitions as an Exchange Ratio Swap." *Managerial Finance* 28:12, 44–62.

Herath, Hemantha S. B., and John S. Jahera, Jr. 2003. "Operational Risk in Bank Acquisitions: A Real Options Approach to Valuing Managerial Flexibility." *Advances in Operational Risk*, 59–71. London: Incisive RWG Ltd.

Herath, Hemantha S. B., and John S. Jahera, Jr. 2004. "Measuring and Accounting for Market Price Risk as Real Options in Stock for Stock Exchanges." *Advances in Management Accounting* 12, 191–218.

Herath, Hemantha S. B., and Chan S. Park. 1999. "Economic Analysis of R&D Projects: An Options Approach." *Engineering Economist* 44:1, 1–35.

Hull, John C. 2006. *Options, Futures and Other Derivatives*, 6th ed. Upper Saddle River, NJ: Prentice Hall.

Kogut, Bruce. 1991. "Joint Ventures and the Option to Expand and Acquire." *Management Science* 37:1, 19–33.

Lambrecht, Bart M. 2004. "The Timing and Terms of Mergers Motivated by Economies of Scale." *Journal of Financial Economics* 72:1, 41–62.

Lambrecht, Bart M., and Stewart C. Myers. 2007. "A Theory of Takeovers and Disinvestment." *Journal of Finance* 62:2, 809-845.

Lambrecht, Bart M., and Stewart C. Myers. 2008. "Debt and Managerial Rents in a Real-Options Model of the Firm." *Journal of Financial Economics* 89:2, 209–231.

Margsiri, Worawat, Antonio S. Mello, and Martin E. Ruckes. 2008. "A Dynamic Analysis of Growth via Acquisitions." *Review of Finance* 12:4, 635–671.

Merton, Robert C. 1998. "Application of Option Pricing Theory: Twenty-Five Years Later." *American Economic Review* 88:3, 35–40.

Morellec, Erwan, and Alexei Zhdanov. 2005. "The Dynamics of Mergers and Acquisitions." *Journal of Financial Economics* 77:3, 649–672.

Myers, Stewart C. 1977. "Determinants of Corporate Borrowing." *Journal of Financial Economics* 5:2, 147–176.

Park, Chan S., and Hemantha S. B. Herath. 2000. "Exploiting Uncertainty—Investment Opportunities as Real Options: A New Way of Thinking in Engineering Economics." *Engineering Economist* 45:1, 1–36.

Savva, Nicos D., and Stefan Scholtes. 2005. "Real Options in Partnership Deals: The Perspective of Cooperative Game Theory." 9th Annual Real Option Conference, Paris, France, June 22–25.

Sick, Gordon 1995. "Real Options." In Robert Jarrow, Vojislav Maksimovic, and William T. Ziemba, eds. *Finance*, 631–690. North Holland: Elsevier.

Smit, Han T. J., and Lenos Trigeorgis. 1999. "Growth Options, Competition and Strategy: An Answer to the Market Valuation Puzzle?" In Lenos Trigeorgis, ed. *Real Options and Business Strategy: Applications to Decision Making*, 21–38. London: Risk Books.

Smit, Han T. J., and Lenos Trigeorgis. 2001. "R&D Option Strategies." *5th Annual Real Options Conference*. Los Angeles, July 13–16.

Smit, Han T. J., and Lenos Trigeorgis. 2009. "Valuing Infrastructure Investment: An Option Games Approach." *California Management Review* 51:2, 79–100.

Smith, Kenneth W., and Alexander J. Triantis. 1995. "The Value of Options in Strategic Acquisitions." In Lenos Trigeorgis, ed. *Real Options in Capital Investment-Models, Strategies and Applications*, 135–149. Westport, CT: Praeger.

Subramanian, Ajay. 2004. "Option Pricing on Stocks in Mergers and Acquisitions." *Journal of Finance* 59:2, 795–829.

Thijssen, Jacco J. J. 2008. "Optimal and Strategic Timing of Mergers and Acquisitions Motivated by Synergies and Risk Diversification." *Journal of Economic Dynamics and Control* 32:5, 1701–1720.

Toxvaerd, Flavio. 2008. "Strategic Merger Waves: A Theory of Musical Chairs." *Journal of Economic Theory* 140:1, 1–26.

Trigeorgis, Lenos. 1996. *Real Options*. Cambridge, MA: MIT Press.

Triantis, Alex, and Adam Borison. 2001. "Real Options: State of the Practice." *Journal of Applied Corporate Finance* 14:2, 8–24.

Warner, Alfred G., and James F. Fairbank. 2008. "Integrating Real Option and Dynamic Capability Theories of Firm Boundaries: The Logic of Early Acquisition in the ICT Industry." *International Journal of IT Standards and Standardization Research* 6:1, 39–54.

ABOUT THE AUTHORS

Hemantha Herath earned his PhD in Industrial and Systems Engineering from Auburn University. He is an Associate Professor of Accounting at Brock University, Canada. Previously he worked in the Oil and Gas Division of The World Bank, Washington D.C. He is a recipient of a Fulbright Scholarship. His research interests include real option analysis, economics of information security, and managerial accounting. Professor Herath has published in various journals including the *Journal of Accounting and Public Policy, Journal of Management Information Systems, Advances in Quantitative Analysis of Finance and Accounting, Advances in Investment Analysis and Portfolio Management, Advances in Management Accounting,* and *The Engineering Economist.* He received the Eugene L. Grant Best Paper Award from the American Society of Engineering Education (ASEE) in 2001 and 2008. He currently serves as an area editor of *The Engineering Economist.*

John S. Jahera Jr. is the Colonial Bank Professor of Finance in the College of Business at Auburn University. He has been a member of the Auburn University faculty since 1980 serving as a faculty member and also as Head of the Department of Finance since 1988. Professor Jahera has taught at both the graduate and undergraduate levels as well as in a number of executive education programs. He is the author of more than 70 articles in such journals as the *Journal of Financial Research, Journal of Law, Economics & Organization, Research in Finance, Journal of Real Estate Finance and Economics,* and *Journal of Banking & Finance.* The primary focus of his research has been in the area of corporate governance, the merger and acquisition process, and antitakeover strategies. Professor Jahera holds a B.S., MBA, and PhD from the University of Georgia.

CHAPTER 10

The Law and Finance of Control Premiums and Minority Discounts

HELEN BOWERS
Associate Professor of Finance, University of Delaware

INTRODUCTION

An unfortunate and unintended consequence of corporate control transactions, such as mergers, tender offers, and minority squeeze-outs, is that such transactions often result in expensive litigation concerning the relative economic rights of minority and majority shareholders. According to the Delaware Division of Corporations (2010), more than 850,000 businesses, including more than 50 percent of all U.S. publicly traded companies and 63 percent of the Fortune 500, are incorporated in Delaware. Delaware corporate law and decisions made by the Delaware Supreme and Chancery courts have substantial impact and sustained influence on how the economic benefits of control rights are distributed between minority and majority shareholders. This is particularly true when the majority seeks to eliminate the minority by acquiring the minority's shares in a cash transaction. Transactions of this kind are often referred to as minority "squeeze-out," "freeze-out," or "cash-out" mergers.

The law takes extra care to protect minority shareholder interests in squeeze-out mergers because the pricing of minority shares in such transactions does not emerge from a third-party arm's-length negotiation. Because the squeeze-outs create opportunities for the controlling majority to take advantage of the minority, such transactions are held to the "entire fairness" standard where the burden to prove the offer is fair lies entirely with the controlling shareholder(s). In such cases, minority shareholders can also exercise appraisal rights, whereby they are entitled to the "fair value" of their shares. Delaware General Corporation Law and Delaware court decisions such as *Weinberger v. UOP, Inc.* (1983) have held that, in minority squeeze-out transactions, the value of dissenting minority shares should be determined on a "going-concern" basis by methods "generally accepted by the finance community."

Although their stated intention is to use methods generally accepted by the finance community, Delaware courts have generally required that the value of minority shares be adjusted upward to offset an "implicit minority discount." The justification for the adjustment is that the implicit minority discount causes the shares of all publicly traded firms to trade at prices that are less than the pro rata share of the firm's intrinsic value (*Borruso v. Communications Telesystems Int'l* (1999, p. 21)). By correcting for a discount that in any plausibly efficient market does not exist, the effect of the implicit minority discount adjustment is the unintended reallocation of wealth from the controlling shareholders to the minority. This misallocation of wealth raises the cost of restructuring to controlling shareholders. Therefore, a firm will not undertake some restructurings that would have created value.

The finance, legal, and valuation literatures are replete with articles dealing with whether there are benefits and value to control and, if so, how these are distributed. Numerous studies attempt to provide empirical evidence on the value of control. Also, many authors offer explanations of how Delaware courts implement the valuation of minority shares and proffer arguments as to how minority shares should be valued. This chapter presents these arguments and the accompanying empirical evidence in an attempt to clarify the issues surrounding the control premium/minority discount issue as it affects the valuation of minority shares in appraisal actions in squeeze-out mergers.

The following section presents the literature that defines the concepts of the control premium and the minority discount. The next section summarizes the relevant sections of Delaware General Corporate Law and Delaware Supreme and Chancery court decisions that govern the valuation of minority shares in appraisal actions. The fourth section includes a discussion of the possible sources of value of control, followed by a section summarizing the empirical evidence on the value of control. Comments as to how practice can be reconciled with contemporary theory and empirical evidence are followed by a summary and conclusions.

DEFINITION OF CONTROL PREMIUM/MINORITY DISCOUNT

Hitchner (2006, p. 19) defines a control premium as "an amount or percentage by which the pro-rata value of a controlling interest exceeds the pro-rata value of a non-controlling interest in a business enterprise to reflect the power of control." Although the financial economics literature uses the term "control premium" most often, the legal and valuation literatures refer to the same concept as both control premium and minority discount. For example, if minority shares trade at $50 per share and shares that reflect the power of control trade at $55 per share, in percentage terms the minority discount would be 10 percent ($5/$50) and the control premium would be 9.09 percent ($5/$55).

Increasingly a distinction is being drawn between the pure benefits of control and any synergies that can be expected as a result from an acquisition (Hamermesh and Wachter, 2007; Mercer and Harms, 2008). In a contest for corporate control, the price paid for each target firm share can be expressed as:

$$\text{Acquisition price} = \text{Minority price} + \text{Control premium} + \alpha \, \text{Expected synergies}$$

$$(10.1)$$

where

> Acquisition price = Price per share paid by the acquiring firm for each share
> of the target firm;
> Minority price = Price per share of a minority interest in the target firm;
> Control premium = Economic value of control on a per share basis;
> Expected synergies = Value of any expected synergies expected to result from
> the acquisition per share of the target firm; and
> α = Portion of the expected synergies captured by the target
> firms' shareholders.

Debate concerns the extent to which future takeover attempts affect the pre-takeover announcement prices of potential target firms (Nath, 1990). For the basis of this discussion, however, the minority price is assumed to be the value on a per share basis of a minority interest in the target firm in the absence of the effects of the contemplated acquisition. If so, what is the difference between the control premium and expected synergies? Can a clear distinction be made between the control premium and expected synergies, which constitute the acquisition premium? The total acquisition premium offered to the target firms' shareholders consists of both the benefits of control and the portion of the expected synergies awarded to those shareholders by market forces. The synergies are expected to arise from any economies of scale or scope, elimination of inefficiencies and redundancies, or other economic benefits that result from combining operations of the acquiring and target firms. The portion of those expected synergies that is represented in the acquisition premium is determined by the relative positions of the acquiring and target firms in the market for corporate control. The control premium is the economic benefit of control in the absence of any operating synergies. The next section provides a discussion of the extent to which the acquisition premium can be divided into the control premium and expected synergies.

DELAWARE LAW, DELAWARE COURTS, VALUES, AND DISCOUNTS

Delaware General Corporate Law determines the general framework for the standards of value to be applied in various corporate restructuring situations. As Delaware law has also been described as relatively responsive and flexible, the Delaware courts exhibit considerable expertise in administering that law (Romano, 2006). This section contains a discussion of the salient portions of Delaware law and the most important court decisions on the subject of the use and valuation of control premiums and minority discounts.

Appraisal Value

Litigation in which the applicability of a control premium is at issue arises when dissenting minority shareholders exercise their appraisal rights in a squeeze-out acquisition where the controlling shareholders, who hold at least 90 percent of the voting stock, seek to acquire the remaining minority equity stake. In such cases, under Delaware law, the value of the dissenting shares is appraised within

an "entire fairness" framework. Specifically, Delaware General Corporate Law §
262(h) states: "the Court shall determine the fair value of the shares exclusive
of any element of value arising from the accomplishment or expectation of the
merger." In compliance with this statute, Delaware courts award the dissenting
shareholders a proportional share of the "going-concern value"—the present value
of the expected cash flows assuming the firm continued without the merger and the
minority retained their ownership rights. The desired outcome is that the minority
shareholders are not harmed and the majority receives the entire economic benefit
expected to result from the acquisition.

Appraisal value is determined in the absence of a third-party arm's-length
transaction, often in situations where, before the merger, the firms' equity shares
were not traded in a liquid market. Therefore, valuation methodologies are employed to determine appraisal value. Since *Weinberger v. UOP, Inc.* (1983), Delaware
courts have held that the appraisal value should be determined using valuation
methodologies that are generally accepted by the financial community. Discounted
cash flow (DCF) analysis and comparable company analysis are the most commonly employed valuation methodologies. If reliable data are available to satisfy
its assumptions, DCF is the favored approach. For example, consider the following
from the opinion in *Pinson v. Campbell-Taggart, Inc.* (1989, p. 26, footnote 11):

> *The Petitioners also attack the validity of the discounted cash flow approach as a valuation
> methodology, but that contention lacks merit. Today the discounted cash flow method is
> widely accepted in the financial community as a legitimate valuation technique. While
> the particular assumptions underlying its application may always be challenged in any
> particular case, the validity of that technique qua valuation methodology is no longer open
> to question.*

In DCF analysis, the value of the equity is the present value of the expected
free cash flows to which the equity holders have a claim. The value of the equity
can be found directly by estimating the free cash flows to equity and discounting
those cash flows using the required rate of return for equity. In practice, however,
the value of the equity is often found by discounting the expected cash flows for the
entire enterprise at the firm's weighted average cost of capital and subtracting the
value of the other claims, such as debt and preferred stock. The residual is then
the value of the equity. Because firms do not often produce reliable cash flow
forecasts within the normal course of business, and as cash-flow forecasts developed within the context of the acquisition can be biased and self-serving, Delaware
courts still rely on comparable company analysis to determine value in appraisal
proceedings.

The economic rationale for valuation using comparable company analysis is
the *law of one price*: In an efficient market, identical securities or goods should
have the same value and therefore, the same price. Using the known values of
comparable publicly held companies or premiums from comparable public transactions, multiples can be constructed that express value relative to some measure
of earnings or revenue. For example, one of the most commonly used multiples
is referred to as the EBITDA multiple, which stands for "earnings before interest,
taxes, depreciation, and amortization." The EBITDA multiple is constructed by
finding the enterprise values of the public comparable companies and dividing

those values by each firm's EBITDA. The resulting multiple represents how many dollars of enterprise value are represented by one dollar of EBITDA. The mean or median EBITDA multiple computed from the sample of comparable firms is multiplied by the EBITDA of the firm being valued. That product is an estimate of the enterprise value of the firm under consideration. After the market value of the other claims against the firm is subtracted from the estimate of the enterprise value, the computed value of the equity is the residual.

With this method, analysts can use the market values of public companies to infer the value of a company for which no market information is available. Although analysts often use multiples from comparable public companies to compute the terminal value in DCF analysis, the adjustment for the implicit minority discount used in Delaware courts is only applied to equity values derived entirely from comparable public company analysis.

Implicit Minority Discount

The adjustment for the implicit minority discount used by the Delaware judiciary is one of the most debated topics in valuation. The implicit minority discount arises from the court's view that the shares of public companies trade at values below their pro rata share of going-concern value because these share values reflect minority ownership. Specifically, in the Delaware court's view, this minority discount, which is inherent in all equity prices, causes the multiples derived from comparable company analysis to be biased downward and for values computed using these multiples to be less than fair values. Therefore, determining a going-concern value requires adjusting the value derived from comparable company analysis upward to correct for the implicit minority discount.

The opinion in *Borruso v. Communications Telesystems Int'l* (1999, p. 21) clearly states the court's definition of the implicit minority discount and the rationale as to why a correction for the discount is justified:

> . . .the comparable company method of analysis produces an equity valuation that inherently reflects a minority discount, as the data used for purposes of comparison is all derived from minority trading values of the comparable companies. Because that value is not fully reflective of the intrinsic worth of the corporation on a going concern basis, this court has applied an explicit control premium in calculating the fair value of the equity in an appraisal proceeding.

The economic implication of the court's reasoning is that regardless of the level of liquidity and disclosure in the securities market on which the shares trade, the market value of all publicly traded shares of equity is constantly and significantly less than the intrinsic value of their pro-rata share of the equity of the firm. As a result, value estimates resulting from comparable company analysis must be adjusted to offset this minority discount that is presumed to arise because equity markets are perennially inefficient and equity is always undervalued in these markets.

As would be expected, the Delaware courts are often criticized for using the implicit minority discount. Hamermesh and Wachter (2007, p. 5) describe the implicit minority discount as "a doctrinal weed sprung up in the late 1990s in what was otherwise a largely harmonious, well-tended garden of finance and law."

Matthews (2008, p. 108) laments that "the regrettable result is that the Court ends up adjusting guideline company valuations based on its questionable concept that market prices of publicly traded companies . . . are inherently 'undervalued.'"

The Delaware courts' use of an implicit minority discount adjustment for perceived market inefficiency is often confused with the application of a premium that confers to the minority shareholders some of the economic benefits of control. An oft-cited decision regarding the implicit minority discount, *Agranoff v. Miller* (2001, p. 23) seems to allude to the implicit minority discount as a method to redistribute control benefits to minority shareholders:

> As a practical matter, correction of a minority discount requires the court to add back a control premium to the value of the enterprise, and to spread that premium equally across all the enterprise's shares. The resulting value for a minority share is thus not what would be considered "fair market value" in valuation terms, but an artificial value that reflects policy values unique to the appraisal remedy. In simple terms, those values may be said to consist in this proposition: if a majority stockholder wishes to involuntarily squeeze-out the minority, it must share the value of the enterprise with the minority on a pro rata basis.

However, later in the *Agranoff v. Miller* (2001, p. 36) decision, the Vice Chancellor retreats from this position and affirms the view of inefficient capital markets that undervalue equity:

> The comparable companies analysis generates an equity value that includes an inherent minority trading discount, because the method depends on comparisons to market multiples derived from trading information for minority blocks of the comparable companies. In a § 262 appraisal, the court must correct this minority trading discount by adding back a premium designed to offset it.

Recognizing that the adjustment for the minority discount is economically significant is also important. Consider the following excerpt from the court's opinion in *Doft & Co. v. Travelocity.com* (2004, p. 46):

> . . . if the court is to accept the theory that "some minority discount from going concern value" is appropriate in a comparable company analysis, then the correct valuation would be above his stated value. Salomon conducted a review of precedent minority squeeze-out transactions and found that the average premium paid for a control block when compared to the stock price was approximately 50%. Travelocity, however, is not directly comparable to the companies in Salomon's data survey. In fact, the online travel industry, as already discussed in great detail, is unique when compared generally to publicly traded companies. Moreover, the recent appraisal cases that correct the valuation for a minority discount by adding back a premium "that spreads the value of control over all shares equally" consistently use a 30% adjustment.

According to Hamermesh and Wachter (2007), the probable genesis of the need for an adjustment for an implicit minority discount evolved from a misunderstanding of a claim frequently asserted in the academic finance community that equity securities typically trade on a minority basis. The minority basis is meant to imply that, if a buyer wants to achieve a controlling interest, he or she would have to pay a premium to do so. The minority status only implies that share prices do not reflect either the private benefits of control or the costs incurred by the minority if a controlling shareholder does not create enough value to offset the wealth that the controlling shareholder expropriates from the minority. If markets are reasonably efficient, then the market prices of comparable public companies' shares are efficiently priced. In such cases, the value of the equity that is computed using multiples derived from those comparable company prices will be the value of the equity as if there is no controlling shareholder. The value would reflect neither any economic benefits that could be generated by a controlling shareholder nor any costs imposed by a controlling shareholder. The value would represent the "intrinsic value" of the equity.

As discussed earlier, an acquisition premium is comprised of the control premium and the portion of the expected synergies allotted to the target firm's shareholders in the offer. Also, § 262(h) requires that the court determine the fair value of the shares on a going-concern basis without any benefits that would arise from the acquisition. Estimates of the adjustment for the implicit minority discount are usually based on acquisition premiums for transactions where there is a financial acquirer as opposed to a strategic acquirer. Acquisition premiums from transactions with financial acquirers are posited to be comprised solely of a control premium, whereas acquisition premiums when the acquirer is a strategic acquirer would be comprised of the value of expected synergies and the control premium.

For the time being, assume that expected synergies are totally absent from acquisition premiums with a financial acquirer even though they may in fact exist. A reconciliation of any premium paid to minority shareholders with § 262(h) that is not justified by severe and persistent market inefficiency would require that any economic value in the control premium should be shared on a pro rata basis with minority shareholders. If so, the question remains as to how to parse the control premium into the economic benefits of control that can only be realized through the acquisition and those economic benefits that are due to be shared with the minority shareholders as part of the going-concern value.

SOURCES OF THE ECONOMIC BENEFITS OF CONTROL

A controlling shareholder can affect value by creating value, reducing value, and affecting a transfer of value from the minority shareholders. The literature on shareholder activism contains many examples of how active, controlling shareholders can positively affect value (e.g., Holderness and Sheehan, 1985). For instance, a controlling shareholder can bring expertise that creates value, reduce agency costs, or bring more transparency to the firm's operations. However, controlling shareholders can also impose costs and expropriate wealth from the minority shareholders.

Hamermesh and Wachter (2007) use a list of five factors affecting the control premium from Pratt, Reilly, and Schweihs (2000) to explain why the majority is entitled to most, if not all, of the control premium. These five factors are: (1) the nature and magnitude of nonoperating assets; (2) the nature and magnitude of discretionary expenses; (3) the perceived quality of existing management; (4) the nature and magnitude of business opportunities that are not currently being exploited; and (5) the ability to integrate the acquiree into the acquirer's business or distribution channels.

The sources of premiums that do not belong either to the corporation or to the minority shareholders are those that reflect the economic benefits of control belonging solely to the controlling shareholders. The fifth factor—the ability to integrate the acquiree into the acquirer's business or distribution channels—should be classified as an expected synergy in equation 10.1 and is not relevant to the control premium discussion. Any economic benefits generated from the first three factors—the nature and magnitude of nonoperating assets, nature and magnitude of discretionary expense, and perceived quality of existing management—would result from the reduction in the agency costs associated with these factors. Hamermesh and Wachter (2007) argue that in corporations with widely dispersed ownership, the agency costs are reflected in the firm's going-concern value. Therefore, in a corporation with a controlling shareholder, the agency costs that are borne by the minority shareholders are reflected in the going-concern value of their shares. Because these agency costs are part of a firm's "operating reality" and would presumably continue at their current level in the absence of the acquisition, the minority is not entitled to any of the benefits from their reduction that result from the acquisition. Estimates of value derived from comparable company analysis would incorporate relevant agency costs because these costs would be reflected in the comparable company shares. However, because the comparable companies are valued as shares in a company with no controlling shareholder, agency costs should be at their minimum level where any additional expense on monitoring will be greater than the resulting reduction in agency costs.

Agency costs arise from the magnitude of the nonoperating assets because controlling shareholders have the incentive to invest in a higher level of current assets than would have otherwise been the case if the controlling shareholder could adequately diversify. These costs result from the lower rate of return earned on current assets relative to fixed assets. The overinvestment mitigates the unsystematic risk borne by the controlling shareholder, but the suboptimal rate of return on these assets is an agency cost borne by the minority. However, the level of this agency cost that is reflected in the comparable company valuation is the level that exists in the absence of a controlling shareholder and could be less than the cost borne by the minority in the presence of a controlling shareholder. In this sense, the comparable company estimate of value already includes an adjustment of any extra agency costs incurred because of the existence of a controlling shareholder. Because the minority will continue to bear this agency cost if the firm continues as a going concern, the minority is not entitled to any reduction in the cost that may result from the acquisition. Similar arguments regarding agency costs could be made for reductions in discretionary expenses and increases in the quality of management that occur as a result of the acquisition. In the absence of the acquisition, the minority value would continue to reflect these costs. Such costs are only represented in comparable company analysis value to the extent that they would exist in the absence of a controlling shareholder. In accordance with § 262(h), the minority is not entitled to any value that results from the reduction of these agency costs as a consequence of the acquisition.

The fourth item on the Pratt et al. (2000) list is the nature and magnitude of business opportunities that are not currently being exploited. If unexploited business opportunities exist that the firm could take advantage of as a going concern whether or not the acquisition occurs, then the benefits from these opportunities belong to the firm as a whole, and the minority has the right to benefit from them.

In describing *Levy v. Markal Sales Corp.* (1994), Bennedsen and Wolfenzon (2000) present a good example of how a controlling shareholder may try to expropriate the value of business opportunities to which the minority is entitled. Levy founded Markal Sales Corporation. At the time of the court action, Levy had been removed from the firm's day-to-day operations but still owned 40 percent of the corporation's stock. Gust and Bakal, two other shareholders active in the corporation's management, owned 40 percent and 20 percent of the firm's stock, respectively. Shortly after Levy left Markal's management, the firm had an opportunity to be a sales representative for Apple Computers. However, instead of contracting on behalf of Markal, Gust and Bakal formed their own corporation, G/B Marketing, to represent Apple. Levy argued (correctly, according to the court) that the Apple contract was the rightful property of Markal (as a firm) and that Gust and Bakal had expropriated wealth from Markal and its shareholders by transferring the contract to G/B Marketing.

Consider that if instead of forming G/B Marketing before finalizing the deal with Apple, Gust and Bakal decided to squeeze-out Levy. Because the Apple contract rightfully belonged to Markal as a firm and the contract could be executed without the acquisition, Levy would be entitled to his pro rata share of the expected benefits of the Apple contract. Hamermesh and Wachter (2005) concur with this view, arguing that the value of anticipated business opportunities belongs to the firm and therefore all of the firm's shareholders, whether or not the opportunity had been exploited at the time of the merger.

Levy v. Markal Corp. (1994) also serves as an example of other methods by which controlling shareholders can attempt to expropriate wealth from the minority. After establishing G/B Marketing, several G/B salespeople were put on the Markal payroll, expenses for business trips related to G/B were charged to Markal, and G/B rented office space from Markal at a below-market rate. These examples are particularly egregious and transparent. However, an analogous case is where the controlling shareholder is a private equity fund that has installed its own management team. The fund, as the controlling shareholder, has control of the board and has replaced existing lender agreements with financing from one of its affiliates at a higher rate. Another example would occur if the fund foresees a profitable business arrangement with another firm in which it has a majority interest and seeks to squeeze-out the minority shareholders to avoid having to share the benefits from a potential merger with the minority.

This type of wealth appropriation, which has been discussed in the finance literature since Jensen and Meckling (1976), is also well recognized in the valuation literature. For example, Pratt (2001, p. 18) offers the following:

> *Everyone recognizes that control owners have rights that minority owners do not and that the difference in those rights and, perhaps more importantly, how those rights are exercised and to what economic benefit, cause a differential in the per-share value of a control ownership block versus a minority ownership block.*

Numerous court cases contain evidence of controlling shareholders garnering wealth as a consequence of their control rights and, as discussed previously, many authors in the finance, legal, and valuation literature posit that control has value. However, the empirical evidence is inconclusive regarding whether there are any significant economic benefits to control.

EVIDENCE ON THE VALUE OF CONTROL

Shleifer and Vishny (1997) assert that large investors, by acting in their own best interest to maximize their own wealth, have both the incentive and the ability to expropriate wealth from other shareholders. Referring to large shareholders, Shleifer and Vishny (p. 758) state that "they have both the interest in getting their money back and the power to demand it." Shleifer and Vishny (p. 758) also argue that:

> *A more fundamental problem is that the large investors represent their own interests, which need not coincide with the interests of other investors in the firm or with the interests of employees and managers. In the process of using his control rights to maximize his own welfare, the large investor can therefore redistribute wealth in both efficient and inefficient ways from others.*

Noting the global prevalence of concentrated ownership, the authors reject the argument that the benefits of control enjoyed by large shareholders are offset by the significant costs that these shareholders incur because they may not be able to adequately diversity.

Pratt and Niculita (2008) present an extensive list of the rights with potential economic value that controlling shareholders have that minority shareholders do not. That list includes the right to choose managers and determine their compensation, set one's own compensation and the compensation of related-party employees, and declare and pay dividends. However, the value of these potential control rights is limited by legal constraints against self-dealing at the expense of minority shareholders. Thus, whether control rights carry benefits that are economically significant is an empirical question. Although the valuation literature generally recognizes control premiums, the empirical evidence in the finance literature on the value of control is mixed.

Shleifer and Vishny (1997) summarize the empirical evidence that control is valued, indicating that controlling shareholders received the benefits not enjoyed by minority shareholders. Examining blockholding transactions in the United States, Barclay and Holderness (1989, 1992) find that large equity blocks trade at a premium relative to the post-trade price of minority shares, indicating economic value is attached to blocks that may have a controlling influence. Studies of dual-class stock compare the prices of shares with identical dividend rights but differential voting rights. Basic finance theory implies that two classes of stock entitled to the identical dividend streams should have identical values, because the value of a share of stock is the present value of its expected cash flows. However, Lease, McConnell, and Mikkelson (1983), Levy (1983), DeAngelo and DeAngelo (1985), and Zingales (1995) all show that shares with superior voting rights trade at a premium in the United States. Although this premium is, on average, very small, Zingales finds that it rises sharply in cases where control over firms is contested, indicating that control has economic value. Because the only difference between the two classes of stock is voting rights, the additional premium for the shares with superior voting rights must be attributed to the additional control attached to those rights.

Atanasov, Boone, and Haushalter (2010) find evidence of "blockholder opportunism" in a study comparing majority-owned subsidiaries with minority-owned subsidiaries. The relationship they find is a nonlinear function of the parent's ownership stake: Parents with a large, nonmajority ownership stake in the subsidiary have the ability and the incentive to extract wealth from the minority, but, in general, majority owners maximize wealth by aligning their interest with the minority. In an examination of "freeze-out" transactions (acquisitions in which a controlling shareholder group seeks to acquire the remaining minority equity stake), Bates, Lemmon, and Linck (2006) conclude that minority shareholders in these transactions actually capture more than their pro-rata share of the firm.

Where the empirical evidence from the finance literature shows the existence of a positive economic value of control, that value is often not very large and does not approach the 30 percent level that is commonly used in Delaware courts to adjust for the supposed implicit minority discount. However, results of empirical studies of transactions that occur between relatively large publicly traded firms may not pertain to the highly illiquid and minimally transparent environment where many closely held corporations operate and where acquisitions occur in which minority shareholders are likely to exercise their appraisal rights.

Using a sample of closely held corporations gathered from the National Survey of Small Business Finances and a small sample of private property-casualty insurers that submit financial information to their state regulators, Nagar, Petroni, and Wolfenzon (2010) find evidence that wealth is appropriated from minority shareholders at levels that are economically significant. The authors acknowledge that although controlling shareholders can act to benefit themselves at the expense of the minority, these benefits are difficult to measure directly. Therefore, Nagar et al. look for evidence of wealth transfers in the form of lower revenues, higher costs, higher levels of unproductive assets, and general lower firm performance. They find that firms with a controlling shareholder and a dispersed set of minority shareholders significantly underperform those with no controlling shareholder and diverse ownership. This evidence implies that wealth appropriation is a major problem for minority shareholders in closely held corporations.

CAN PRACTICE BE RECONCILED WITH FINANCE THEORY AND EVIDENCE?

As discussed earlier, the implicit minority discount as defined by the Delaware courts results from the persistent undervaluation of firms in equity markets. This type of permanent market inefficiency is inconsistent with views commonly held by those in the financial community and is not supported by any empirical evidence. Hamermesh and Wachter (2007) posit that, because no evidence shows that public going-concern values contain a downward bias, Delaware courts may be using the adjustment for the implicit minority discount as a way to compensate the squeezed-out minority shareholders for the costs associated with the fiduciary misconduct by the controller shareholder. An anathema to most financial economists is that there is an implicit minority discount that results from permanent, observable market inefficiency. Consequently, there is the temptation to reinterpret the implicit minority discount as compensation to the minority for wealth expropriated from them by the majority.

The conflict concerning the implicit minority discount is not lost on the Delaware courts, and the conflict also puts those financial professionals who serve as experts in a peculiar position when advising the court. In *Highfields Capital, Ltd. v. AXA Fin., Inc.* (2007), both financial experts had impressive financial credentials. One was a professor of finance at a well-respected university and the other had a career in investment banking and an MBA from a highly ranked program. Both were probably aware that the adjustment for the implicit minority discount was not supported by extensive empirical evidence and would likely agree that markets would not allow a significant price inefficiency to persist. However, both were also probably familiar with the Delaware courts' relatively consistent use of the implicit minority discount adjustment. The opinion in the case stated that, even under questioning, both experts "stood by their decisions to remove an implicit minority discount in MONY's stock when conducting their comparable company analyses." However, the opinion in *Highfields Capital, Ltd. v. AXA Fin., Inc.* (2007; p. 68, footnote 72) goes on to state that, "Although Delaware courts now seem to accept that the application of this valuation metric requires such an adjustment, the debate in the legal and financial community continues," and cites Coates (1999), Booth (2001), and Hamermesh and Wachter (2007).

Coates (1999, p. 1264) posits that courts may exercise discretion in applying discounts, even if those are reflected in market prices. He distinguishes between using the "term discount in a legal sense or in a financial sense" and argues that no mandate exists that the discount becomes a legal discount just because a financial discount exists. The author also makes the case that implementing legal discounts can affect prices in securities markets. Coates (p. 1264) proposes that, without legal adjustments for discounts, the market prices of minority shares would decrease because the shares would be "subject to freeze-outs at fair values reflecting a legal discount." However, he does not address whether the discount is justified from a financial point of view given the court's goal of measuring the value of the minority shares on a going-concern basis.

Remedy for the implied minority discount conundrum could come from the courts, the Delaware legislature, or a combination of the two. In *Weinberger v. UOP, Inc.* (1983, p. 713), the court justified moving away from the so-called "Delaware Block Method" of valuation:

> *However, to the extent it excludes other generally accepted techniques used in the financial community and the courts, it is now clearly outmoded. It is time we recognize this in appraisal and other stock valuation proceedings and bring our law current on the subject.*

The opinion in *Weinberger v. UOP, Inc.* shows that Delaware courts can recognize when a method has outlived its usefulness, which bodes well for a transformation of the current treatment of minority shares. The Delaware legislature could further clarify how the value expected to arise from the accomplishment or expectation of the merger could be separated into the value of control and the value of expected synergies. The Delaware courts and legislature are in the best position to protect the rights of minority shareholders while allowing a shareholder with a substantial controlling block an expedient and efficient method to buy the small remaining minority stake.

SUMMARY AND CONCLUSIONS

The Delaware courts practice adjusting for an implicit minority discount when valuing minority shares in appraisal actions pursuant to squeeze-out mergers. The courts perceive that shares of publicly traded firms are persistently undervalued and therefore adjust estimates of value that are based on those market values to arrive an intrinsic or going-concern value. The implicit minority discount adjustment, which cannot be justified by either finance theory or evidence, causes an unintended reallocation of wealth from the controlling shareholders to the minority.

The comparable company method of valuation is subject to the implicit minority discount adjustment because the multiples that are computed using comparable company methodology are based on the stock prices that are valued on a minority basis. From a financial point of view, the minority status does not denote an implicit discount but rather that the shares are valued in the absence of a controlling shareholder. These share prices do not contain any costs that would be associated with the existence of a majority shareholder and, therefore, render the adjustment for the implicit minority discount even more punitive to the controlling shareholders.

The finance, legal, and valuation literature all acknowledge that controlling shareholders have the incentive to expropriate wealth from the minority but also acknowledge legal protections for the minority. The extra care given by the courts to the valuation of minority shares in appraisal actions is justified because, in squeeze-out mergers, the minority shareholders are forced to sell their shares without the benefits of a third-party arm's-length transaction. However, the broader empirical evidence on the economic benefits of control from the finance literature does not conclusively show that on a wide-scale basis, controlling shareholders expropriate wealth from the minority. Most of the evidence is based on transactions involving large, publicly traded companies in very liquid markets. New evidence from samples of firms that operate in illiquid, less-transparent markets, where appraisal rights are more likely to be exercised, shows some indirect evidence that benefits of control may come at the expense of minority shareholders.

Delaware courts have previously abandoned obsolete methodologies in favor of methods that are more consistent with contemporary theory and evidence. Also, the Delaware legislature can refine the specific attributes of minority and majority shareholder rights. Future court decisions are likely to be less reliant on implicit minority discount adjustments and allow the facts of the case to guide the valuation.

DISCUSSION QUESTIONS

1. When determining fair value, should a control premium be applied to find the value of the controlling equity interest? Explain why or why not.
2. The empirical evidence on whether control has substantial economic value in the financial economics literature is inconclusive. Explain whether there are still any valid reasons to try to value the control premium.

3. How is the application of the adjustment for the implicit minority discount inconsistent with the view that equity markets are reasonably efficient?

4. According to Delaware General Corporate Law § 262(h), how are the minority shares to be valued in an appraisal action?

5. Why are courts so involved with protecting the interests of the minority in squeeze-out mergers?

REFERENCES

Agranoff v. Miller, 791 Del. A.2d 880 (Del. Ch. 2001).

Atanasov, Vladimir, Audra Boone, and David Haushalter. 2010. "Is There Shareholder Expropriation in the United States? An Analysis of Publicly Traded Subsidiaries." *Journal of Financial and Quantitative Analysis* 45:1, 1–26.

Barclay, Michael J., and Clifford G. Holderness. 1989. "Private Benefits from Control of Public Corporations." *Journal of Financial Economics* 25:2 371–395.

Barclay, Michael J., and Clifford G. Holderness. 1992. "The Law and Large-block Trades." *Journal of Law and Economics* 35:2, 265–294.

Bates, Thomas W., Michael L. Lemmon, and James S. Linck. 2006. "Shareholder Wealth Effects and Bid Negotiation in Freeze-Out Deals: Are Minority Shareholders Left Out in the Cold?" *Journal of Financial Economics* 81:3, 681–708.

Bennedsen, Morten, and Daniel Wolfenzon. 2000. "The Balance of Power in Closely Held Corporations." *Journal of Financial Economics* 58:1–2, 113–139.

Booth, Richard A. 2001. "Minority Discounts and Control Premiums in Appraisal Proceedings." *Business Lawyer* 127:57, 148–151.

Borruso v. Communications Telesystems Int'l, 753 A.2d 451 (Del. Ch. 1999).

Coates, John C., IV. 1999. "Fair Value as an Avoidable Rule of Corporate Law; Minority Discounts in Conflict Transactions." *University of Pennsylvania Law Review* 147:6, 1251–1359.

DeAngelo, Harry, and Linda DeAngelo. 1985. "Managerial Ownership of Voting Rights: A Study of Public Corporations with Dual Classes of Common Stock." *Journal of Financial Economics* 14:1, 33–69.

Delaware Division of Corporations. 2010. Available at http://corp.delaware.gov.

Delaware General Corporation Law (8 Del. § 262).

Doft & Co. v. Travelocity.com Inc., Del.ch. LEXIS 75 (Del. Ch., May 21, 2004).

Hamermesh, Lawrence A., and Michael L. Wachter. 2005. "The Fair Value of Cornfields in Delaware Appraisal Law." *Journal of Corporation Law* 31:1, 119–166.

Hamermesh, Lawrence A., and Michael L. Wachter. 2007. "The Short and Puzzling Life of the Implicit Minority Discount in Delaware Appraisal Law." *University of Pennsylvania Law Review* 156:1, 1–61.

Highfields Capital, Ltd. v. AXA Fin., Inc. 939 A.2d 34; 2007 Del. Ch. LEXIS 126 (August 17, 2007).

Hitchner, James R. 2006. *Financial Valuation: Applications and Models*, 2nd ed. Hoboken, NJ: John Wiley & Sons.

Holderness, Clifford G., and Dennis P. Sheehan. 1985. "Raiders or Saviors? The Evidence on Six Controversial Investors." *Journal of Financial Economics* 14:4, 555–579.

Jensen, Michael C., and William H. Meckling. 1976. "Theory of the Firm: Managerial Behavior, Agency Costs and Ownership Structure." *Journal of Financial Economics* 3:4, 305–360.

Lease, Ronald C., John J. McConnell, and Wayne H. Mikkelson. 1983. "The Market Value of Control in Publicly Traded Corporations." *Journal of Financial Economics* 11:1–4, 439–471.

Levy, Haim. 1983. "Economic Evaluation of Voting Power of Common Stock." *Journal of Finance* 38:1, 79–93.

Levy v. Markal Sales Corporation, 268 Il.App.3d 455, 643 N.E.2d 1206, 205 Il Dec. 599 (September 16, 1994).

Matthews, Gilbert E. 2008. "Misuse of Control Premiums in Delaware Appraisals." *Business Valuation Review* 27:2, 107–118.

Mercer, Christopher Z., and Travis W. Harms. 2008. *Business Valuation: An Integrated Theory*, 2nd ed. Hoboken, NJ: John Wiley & Sons.

Nagar, Venky, Kathy Petroni, and Daniel Wolfenzon. 2010. "Governance Problems in Close Corporations." *Journal of Financial and Quantitative Analysis*. Forthcoming.

Nath, Eric W. 1990. "Control Premiums and Minority Interest Discounts in Private Companies." *Business Valuation Review* 9:2, 39–46.

Pinson v. Campbell-Taggart, Inc., 1989 Del.ch. LEXIS 50 (Del. Ch., November 8, 1989).

Pratt, Shannon. 2001. *Business Valuation: Discounts and Premiums*. Hoboken, NJ: John Wiley & Sons.

Pratt, Shannon P., and Alina V. Niculita. 2008. *Valuing a Business: The Analysis and Appraisal of Closely Held Companies*, 5th ed. New York: McGraw-Hill.

Pratt, Shannon P., Robert F. Reilly, and Robert P. Schweihs. 2000. *Valuing a Business: The Analysis and Appraisal of Closely Held Companies*, 4th ed. New York: McGraw-Hill.

Romano, Roberta. 2006. "The States as a Laboratory: Legal Innovation and State Competition for Corporate Charters." *Yale Journal on Regulation* 23:2, 209–247.

Shleifer, Andrei, and Robert W. Vishny. 1997. "A Survey of Corporate Governance." *Journal of Finance* 52: 2, 737–783.

Weinberger v. UOP, Inc., 457 A.2d 701 (Del. Ch. 1983).

Zingales, Luigi. 1995. "What Determines the Value of Corporate Votes?" *Quarterly Journal of Economics* 110:4, 1075–1110.

ABOUT THE AUTHOR

Helen M. Bowers is an Associate Professor of Finance at the Lerner College of Business and Economics at the University of Delaware. Before joining the faculty at the University of Delaware in 1997, she served on the faculties of Wake Forest University and the University of Notre Dame. Professor Bowers' research and teaching interests are in corporate finance, valuation, corporate governance, and M&As. She has published articles in corporate governance, Delaware corporate law, and valuing employee stock options. Professor Bowers' international assignments include teaching valuation at Université de Paris 1 Panthéon-Sorbonne and Université Lumière (Lyon 2), in Lyon, France, and corporate governance at the Hanken Swedish School of Economics and Business Administration, in Helsinki, Finland. Since 2002, she has been a Senior Advisor for the Woodward Group, a merchant bank and consulting practice. Professor Bowers earned her PhD in Finance from the University of South Carolina in 1987.

CHAPTER 11

Cross-Border Valuation Effects in Developed and Emerging Markets

WENJIE CHEN
Assistant Professor in International Business, George Washington University

INTRODUCTION

In early 2010, after four months of persistent wooing, American Kraft Foods finally succeeded in its bid to buy British candy maker giant Cadbury. The final price of $19.5 billion, 14 percent over the initial bid, certainly sweetened the deal for the British firm. The stock market reacted favorably to the announcement, and Kraft shares rose by 1.6 percent while Cadbury closed up 1 percent. The combined companies would be the world leader in chocolate and sweets. For Kraft, the deal would help boost overall sales and profit growth rate and greatly bolster its presence in international markets.

This marriage of sorts is just one of many examples of a cross-border acquisition transaction between two firms located in different nations. Cross-border mergers and acquisitions (M&As) generally attract interest in the business community and often arouse national sentiments. When Belgian brewing company Inbev acquired Anheuser-Busch, a prominent American beer company, even President Barack Obama commented. An article entitled "Love Me, Love Me Not" (2008, pp. 36–38) quotes him as saying that "no law barred shareholders from selling Anheuser-Busch to a foreign firm, but that such a deal would be 'a shame."' The more recent trend of emerging market firm acquisitions in developed countries has drawn even greater attention. In particular, the recent spate of cross-border acquisitions by Indian and Chinese companies is the subject of heated debate in policy circles. Chinese Lenovo's acquisition of IBM's Thinkpad and Tata Motors' acquisition of Jaguar and Land Rover have been much publicized. Coupled with national sentiments and security concerns, Congress met the acquisition bid by CNOOC, the Chinese state-owned oil company, to take over Unocal with considerable resistance and ultimately thwarted the deal.

Cross-border M&As play an integral part in a firm's capital restructuring. In particular, cross-border deals extend the boundaries of a firm across national borders. While the finance and economics literature have looked extensively at the wealth effects of M&A deals between same-country acquiring and target firms

185

(particularly for U.S. domestic transactions), the effects of cross-border M&As have not been well studied. Why do firms acquire assets outside their own country? How does a firm in one country undertake a valuation of a firm in a different country? National sentiments aside, what are the pros and cons of cross-border M&As? How can managers create shareholder value in engaging in cross-border deals?

This chapter tries to answer some of these questions while addressing their implications for researchers and practitioners by describing the current state of research on cross-border M&As and by highlighting differences between acquisitions in developed and emerging markets. The chapter has the following organization. The next section provides an overview of the current state in cross-border M&As and discusses the motivations and challenges of conducting cross-border M&As. The second part of this chapter contrasts cross-border M&As in developed and emerging markets. In particular, the chapter highlights the differences in wealth gains from cross-border M&As in developed countries versus emerging markets followed by various explanations from the literature on why these wealth differences persist. Next, the future direction of cross-border M&As and its effect on the academic literature are discussed. The chapter concludes with a summary of the main points on cross-border M&As.

CROSS-BORDER M&A DEALS: AN OVERVIEW

Cross-border M&As occur when companies from two different nations combine their assets to create a new corporate entity. This chapter includes a discussion of both cross-border M&As with minority acquisitions and majority acquisitions. The former refers to buying a minority stake in an existing company, and the latter refers to buying an entire company in which the target firm loses its identity and becomes part of the acquiring firm. Deals can be financed via stock options, cash, debt, or other assets.

As countries have opened their capital markets to foreign investors, cross-border M&A deals have become extremely prevalent. In 2007, the value of M&A transactions amounted to $1,637 billion, representing an increase of 12 percent from the previous record set in 2000 (UNCTAD, 2008). Broadly speaking, cross-border M&As make up the majority of foreign direct investments (FDIs). The global financial crisis in 2008 changed the overall landscape in FDIs, and therefore in cross-border M&As. Developed countries experienced a major decline in FDI inflows, while flows to developing countries and transition economies rose during the first half of 2008. This pattern reflects a delay as the economic downturn slowly worked its way through the economies of developing countries. Preliminary data show that global FDI inflows dropped by 54 percent and M&As by an even more astounding 77 percent during the first quarter of 2009 as compared to the same period a year earlier (UNCTAD, 2009). This time, all three groups of economies—developed countries, developing countries, and transition economies—were affected.

Exhibit 11.1 depicts the value of cross-border M&As from 1987 to the first half of 2009. Apart from the total value, the exhibit also separates the value by sales from developed and developing economies. Several patterns emerge. For example, the two peaks in the data that occur in 2000 and 2007 stand out from the rest of the yearly aggregate M&A activity measures. These peaks are signs of merger waves generally triggered by economic and technological shocks as well

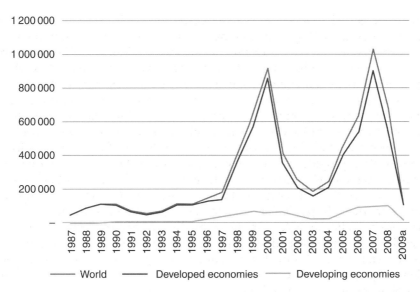

Exhibit 11.1   The Value of Net Cross-Border M&A Sales from 1987 to the First Half of 2009
Note: This exhibit depicts the value (in $ millions) of net cross-border M&A sales from 1987 to the first half of 2009. The exhibit breaks down the value by developed vs. developing economies. Data are from the UNCTAD cross-border M&A database.

as the availability of cheap capital. For instance, the 1990s wave, with its peak in 2000, could reflect the development of the Internet that led to an economic boom (Robin, 2011), representing a technology shock. The second peak around 2007 was accompanied by an extremely weak U.S. dollar compared to the euro. Because the United States is one of the largest acquirers as well as a target destination of cross-border M&As, this fluctuation in exchange rate has an effect on overall cross-border M&A values. Froot and Stein (1991) and Harris and Ravenscraft (1991) document this fact in their respective academic studies.

Exhibit 11.1 also shows that acquiring firms located in developed economies initiate most cross-border M&A deals. In fact, the majority of all deals happen between firms located in developed economies. In recent years, however, acquiring firms from developing countries conducted some of the most prominent deals. Exhibit 11.2 lists details of the "mega" deals in 2008 that were each worth more than $3 billion. As Exhibit 11.2 shows, developing country firms initiated a few of the largest deals, but European and U.S. firms conducted the majority of the deals.

Basic Facts about Cross-Border M&As

Brakman, Garretsen, and van Marrewijk (2006) provide a detailed set of facts on cross-border M&A deals worldwide using Thomson's Global Mergers and Acquisitions Database. Based on a sample of 27,541 cross-border M&A deals completed between 1986 and 2005, the authors establish the following facts:

- Payment for the deal usually involves cash (93.2 percent).
- Cross-border M&As come in waves.

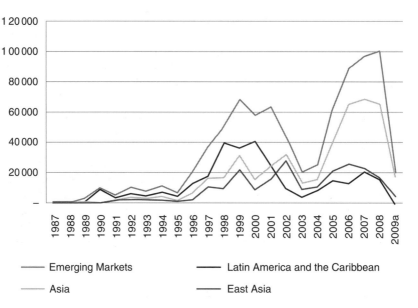

Exhibit 11.2   The Value of Net Cross-Border M&A Sales by Emerging Market Sellers from 1987 to the First Half of 2009
Source: This exhibit depicts the value (in $ millions) of net cross-border M&A sales by emerging market sellers from 1987 to the first half of 2009. The exhibit breaks down the value by emerging countries in Asia, East Asia, and Latin America. Data from UNCTAD cross-border M&A database.

- About half (49.4 percent) of the cross-border M&A deals are horizontal, that is, the acquirer and target are active in the same 2-digit SIC sector.
- Cross-border M&As take place mostly between high-income countries.
- The size of cross-border M&As grows over time.

These stylized facts are important when discussing the factors that drive cross-border M&As and the differences in cross-border M&As in developed and emerging markets.

Motivations for Cross-Border M&As

Caves (1996) provides a review of the motivations for engaging in FDI. Through a cross-border M&A, which is a form of FDI, firms can take advantage of economies of scale and scope as well as synergy effects, and use foreign market conditions such as lower labor costs. Once firms set up a multinational network, they should be able to reap additional benefits from positive network externalities, such as increased operational flexibility among various markets, by taking advantage of diverse conditions.

In many ways, motivations for cross-border M&As are similar to those of domestic M&As. One of the most prominent reasons for undertaking cross-border M&As is to gain new market penetration. Entering a market in a foreign country can be difficult because of the need to conform to the foreign government regulations and laws, assess a new customer base, deal with new suppliers and employees, and set up new distribution networks. Therefore, acquiring an already established firm with existing infrastructure and knowledge can make the transition into a new market much smoother. The importance of this new market-seeking strategy in a firm's decision to acquire a firm abroad is reflected in one of the facts established by Brakman et al. (2006), namely, that acquiring firms seek targets in the same industry.

Another reason for cross-border M&As is to obtain new technology that is unavailable in a firm's own country. For instance, some U.S. firms are much sought after as acquisition targets because of their unique research and development (R&D). Since many technological innovations are patented, the only way to obtain them is through buying the patent holding firm. Other motivations for cross-border M&As might stem from regulatory restrictions such as high tariff barriers for imports or legal barriers in entering certain sensitive industries, including defense, banking, and telecommunications, among others. By engaging in an M&A with a firm in the country with these regulations, the acquiring firm can sidestep adverse regulations.

Costs and Challenges of Cross-Border M&As

Cross-border M&A deals do not come cheaply. One of the costliest deals in recent history is that between Daimler, a German automobile company, and Chrysler, one of the largest U.S. automakers. Before a merger, firms already incur transaction costs due to legal expenses, banker fees, accounting fees, and advisor fees that are all necessary to conduct the merger. The other portion of the cost lies in restructuring and integration after the merger is effective. Those costs may involve stock option adjustments, implementing payroll, accounting, and information systems (Robin, 2011).

Apart from the financial costs, numerous other costs apply. Unlike joint ventures, M&As are permanent and involve a long-term commitment of a firm's strategy and resources. Abandoning the deal is generally not an option. Sometimes, however, deals go bad and firms usually part after incurring substantial financial losses and the resulting negative reputation. The Daimler-Chrysler deal represents a case in point.

Cross-country M&As involve additional challenges and complications. Due to differing political systems in the target and acquirer nations, adverse political developments can affect the success rate of the merger. Corporate governance and cultural differences are some other factors that can complicate M&A deals. A later section details how corporate governance structures might affect the valuation of cross-border M&As. Countries also have different sets of regulatory barriers preventing foreigners from owning domestic firms. These barriers often stem from nationalistic sentiments that add to the complexity of the transaction process and result in extra cost and time.

Valuation of Target Firm in Cross-Border M&As

A substantial challenge in the M&A process is assessing the worth of a potential target firm. The valuation of a target firm serves several functions in the M&A process. First, it serves as a mechanism to identify which target firm is the best fit for the acquiring firm. For instance, an acquiring firm often asks whether there will be synergy gains from the M&A. Second, valuation determines how much the acquiring firm is willing to pay for the M&A. The two decisions are intertwined because a better fit presumably leads to more gains from the M&A and therefore a higher bidding price.

One of the most common ways to assess a target's value is to evaluate its discounted future cash flows. This becomes challenging, however, when identifying the components that make up cash flows as well as the appropriate discount factor. Access to information about particular firms is critical to a successful valuation process. The transparency and disclosure of such information in the form of financial statements and information dissemination among financial analysts varies greatly from firm to firm and from country to country. Accounting practices, for instance, can differ substantially across countries. Legal environment also plays a role in the accessibility of information. Although management might be required by law to report financial information to its shareholders, the degree to which information is disseminated depends on the level of enforcement. Compared to developed countries, emerging markets often face much more challenging legal environments. Not only can accessing information be challenging, but also the accuracy of the information can be questionable.

Another important issue involves determining the appropriate discount factor. Should the discount factor of the acquiring or the target firm be used? The international setting further complicates the problem because of the multitude of issues that might affect risk, which goes into calculating the appropriate discount factor. To introduce further complications, consider acquisitions in emerging markets. Unlike financial markets in developed countries, financial markets in emerging countries are still on the cusp of development and often face uncertain political risks. In those situations, how should the appropriate discount factor be derived? Bodnar, Dumas, and Marston (2002) discuss this issue in an international asset pricing setting. Their paper provides an overview of methods by which various dimensions of risk can be incorporated into the discount factor.

These costs and challenges contribute to the success and failure of cross-border M&A deals and ultimately shareholder wealth gains. These factors are revisited when explaining wealth gains or the lack thereof as well as when examining the driving forces behind cross-border M&A deals.

CROSS-BORDER M&A DEALS IN DEVELOPED AND EMERGING MARKETS

As the stylized facts show in a previous section, the majority of cross-border M&A transactions take places between firms in developed markets. This is further supported by Exhibit 11.1, which depicts the value of net cross-border M&A sales by developed and emerging country targets. Evidence suggests, however, that cross-border M&As have been increasingly used as a means to invest from developed to emerging markets, although the changes are modest (Brakman et al., 2006). In their data sample, Brakman et al. find that the five largest net target (target minus acquiring) countries are the United States, Brazil, Germany, China, and Argentina. While Brazil and Argentina are consistently net target countries throughout the period from 1986 to 2005, China and Germany only became significant net target countries in the last 10 years.

Using data provided by UNCTAD, Exhibit 11.2 depicts the value of net cross-border M&A sales by emerging markets and several of its regions. The value of total cross-border M&A sales in emerging markets starts to pick up in 1995, reaching peaks around 1999 and 2001, while dipping drastically between 2003 and 2004, and peaking again at its current highest level in 2008 before dramatically falling in the first part of 2009. A surprising fact when comparing Exhibits 11.1 and 11.2 is that although the levels in cross-border M&A sales between developed and emerging market countries are vastly different, the trend and particularly the peaks are almost identical.

There are several explanations for the similarity in cross-border M&A movements between developed and emerging markets. One such reason is due to the fact that mergers move in waves caused by economic or technology shocks. Due to increased globalization, countries are now more likely to be affected by economic shocks that are triggered in a different part of the world. Another reason might be that the same group of acquirers does the purchasing in both developed and emerging markets. The basic facts indicate that not only are most targets in developed countries, but also firms in developed countries are the ones conducting the most acquisitions. Therefore, if acquirers are hit by a recession, for instance, they are likely to reduce cross-border M&A purchases in both developed and emerging markets.

These simple observations of developed and emerging market cross-border M&A deals show both differences and similarities. The following sections detail the valuation effects of cross-border M&As in developed and emerging markets. Because emerging market M&As are a more recent phenomenon, most research studies focus on developed markets. Several different ways are available to assess cross-border M&A valuations in developed and emerging markets. One is to evaluate the gains for acquirers in cross-border deals while differentiating between targets in developed and emerging markets. Another way is to analyze the target firm's gain by differentiating between acquirers in developed and emerging markets. The majority of the extant literature has not made a distinction between developed and emerging market target and acquirer firms. However, due to the rise of emerging market acquirers and targets, increased interest exists in the second group. The next few sections present the results from various approaches.

Wealth Gains in Cross-Border M&As

In one of the earliest studies on cross-border M&As, Doukas and Travlos (1988) study the impact of cross-border acquisitions on the stock return of U.S. acquiring firms. They find that the stock market shows positive abnormal returns when the U.S. acquirer ventures into new industries and geographic markets through a cross-border M&A. Yet, this result does not hold if the U.S. acquirer was already present in the target firm's country.

In their seminal work on acquisition FDI, Harris and Ravenscraft (1991) examine the shareholder wealth gains of U.S. target firms acquired by foreign firms between 1970 and 1987. Studying a sample of 1,273 U.S. target firms, they find that foreign acquiring firms prefer buying firms in R&D-intensive industries compared to domestic acquirers. Foreign firms are also willing to pay more than domestic firms in noncash bids. Target and acquirers tend to be in related industries in a majority of cross-border M&A deals. Moreover, using share price data, the authors find that U.S. targets of foreign acquisitions experience significantly higher wealth gains than targets of domestic acquisitions.

The importance of intangible assets on shareholder wealth gains is a reoccurring theme in cross-border M&A research. Morck and Yeung (1992) study the effect of cross-border acquisitions on the shareholder value of the U.S. acquiring firm. They find that U.S. acquirers with information-based intangible assets, such as R&D capabilities, experience positive stock market return in the event of a cross-border acquisition. This finding supports their earlier work (Morck and Yeung, 1991) in which they establish that the multinational nature per se does not lead to increases in the firm's value, but only in conjunction with the firm's intangible assets.

In another study of major acquisitions involving U.S. target firms acquiring foreign firms, Eun, Kolodny, and Scheraga (1996) directly measure the magnitude of shareholders' gains from cross-border acquisitions. They show that U.S. target shareholders realize significant wealth gains, $103 million on average, regardless of the nationality of acquirers. Furthermore, they also analyze the wealth gains in foreign acquiring shareholders. Unlike target shareholders, acquiring shareholder wealth gains vary greatly across acquiring countries. When acquiring a U.S. firm, shareholders of British acquirers experience, on average, a reduction of $123 million. Japanese shareholders, on the other hand, gain an average of $228 million. The authors also examine joint average wealth gains and find that cross-border M&As generate generally positive synergies. The joint wealth gain of U.S. target and acquiring firms from various countries averages $68 million but is varied across acquiring countries. Japanese acquisitions yield the highest combined gains of $398 million, whereas British acquisitions result in a loss of $28 million, suggesting a substantial wealth transfer from the British acquiring firm onto the U.S. target firm. Eun et al. argue that the discrepancy in wealth gains between Japanese and British acquirers is due to the fact that Japanese acquirers, who are also highly R&D intensive, are particularly successful in integrating the highly R&D intensive capabilities of their targets.

These early studies concentrate mostly on cross-border M&As involving U.S. firms either as targets or acquirers. Because few acquisitions occurred in emerging markets during those early years, the data are mainly limited to cross-border acquisitions between firms in developed markets. Nonetheless, the evidence is indicative of several overall trends. First, shareholders of target firms in cross-border M&As tend to gain from a foreign acquisition. In the case of acquisitions into the United States, U.S. target firms tend to be in industries with intangible assets. The acquiring firm's wealth gains, on the other hand, are not always positive and depend largely on the nationality of the acquiring firm. This result is similar to the findings in the domestic M&A literature. In a survey of U.S. domestic M&A literature, Andrade, Mitchell, and Stafford (2001) find that target firms generally experience the majority of the gains from an M&A, while acquiring firms often underperform.

With the increased participation of emerging markets firms in cross-border M&As, the academic literature has slowly developed an interest as well. Chari,

Ouimet, and Tesar (2010) explore the value of control in emerging market firm acquisitions compared to acquisitions in developed markets. Their paper is one of the most comprehensive in terms of cross-border M&A deal coverage and assessment. In their paper, the authors study acquiring firm gains from acquisitions in emerging markets and contrast them with acquisitions in developed countries. They construct a sample of cross-border M&A deals between the following groups: (1) developed market firm acquirers and emerging market firm targets; (2) developed market firm acquirers and targets; and (3) emerging market firm targets and acquirers. Returns are measured as cumulative abnormal returns (CARs) that are estimated over a 3-day event window centered on the deal announcement day. The median CAR for acquirer firms in group (1) is 0.26 percent, for group (2) –0.20 percent, and 0.12 percent for group (3). A particularly important finding relates to acquisitions with majority control. When developed-market acquirers gain control of emerging-market targets, that is, they own more than 50 percent of the target firm after the acquisition, they experience significantly higher positive stock abnormal returns (0.72 percent). Majority control does not play a role in the acquirer firm return in groups (2) and (3). Majority control plays an even stronger role for acquirer industries with high asset intangibility, especially when the contracting environment in the emerging market is weak.

Understanding the magnitude of shareholder wealth gains becomes difficult when looking only at returns. Therefore, Chari et al. (2010) translate CARs into dollar value gains. In their sample for shareholders of developed market acquiring firms buying controlling stakes in emerging market targets, these announcement returns translate into an aggregate dollar value gain of $10.5 billion. Furthermore, the authors analyze the median "net synergy return," which is the acquirer's dollar value gain divided by the transaction value. Again, for developed market acquirers, they find that the stock market anticipates a net present value (NPV) gain of 11 cents for every dollar the acquirers spend on obtaining an emerging-market target firm with majority control. In contrast, the net synergy return for developed-market acquirers into emerging markets without majority control only translates into a NPV gain of 2 cents per dollar spent on the acquisition.

These findings are in stark contrast with the domestic U.S. M&A literature that documents underperformance in acquiring firms (Andrade et al. 2001; Moeller, Schlingeman, and Stulz, 2005). Moreover, the findings are also different from the prior literature on cross-border M&As focusing mostly on acquisitions within developed markets. Chari et al. (2010) identify the importance of majority control in acquisitions of emerging market target firms. More specifically, their research shows that emerging markets need to be treated differently from developed markets in cross-border M&A valuation. Their research has led to further questions of why majority control in emerging markets plays such an important role in increasing wealth gains and what other factors apart from majority control might explain such discrepancies in wealth gains between acquisitions in developed and emerging markets. The next section addresses some of these questions.

Explaining Gains in Cross-Border M&As

Several distinctive patterns emerge from the wealth gain discussion in the previous section. Target firm shareholders generally emerge as winners of cross-border M&A

deals. On the acquirer side, however, value creation varies greatly, depending upon the acquirer country of origin as well as the type of acquisition. The joint return, however, seems to be positive, suggesting overall value creation in cross-border M&A deals. These results are similar to those in the domestic M&A literature. In their survey, Andrade et al. (2001) point out that the acquirer and joint returns often depend on the financing method of the M&A transaction.

Unlike in the domestic M&A literature, Chari et al. (2010) find that emerging market acquisitions involving majority control on the part of developed market acquirers create positive valuation effects for the buyer. They argue that acquirers from developed markets going into emerging markets are particularly keen on protecting their intangible assets such as brand and knowledge, which can only be accomplished with majority control. With control, acquirers from developed markets can improve corporate governance practices such as legal and accounting standards in the emerging-market target firm. Thus, the transfer of intangible assets plays a prominent role in shareholder value creation in cross-border M&As. Intangible asset–intensive industries have proprietary technologies that parent companies are unwilling to share unless they own the majority of the target and have better contract enforcing mechanisms. Because acquirer and target firms are situated in different countries in a cross-border M&A transaction, they often work under different legal institutions and corporate governance. Having majority control is a way to enable the acquirer company to transfer its corporate governance onto the target firm and therefore protect the intangible assets that change hands during the transaction.

In particular, acquisitions in emerging markets often raise questions of whether the emerging market target firm can enforce financial contract as well as protect the investor. For instance, Antras, Desai, and Foley (2009) find that when multinational firms want to exploit technologies abroad, where monitoring is costly and financial contracting is difficult, such firms deploy technology through ownership FDI, as opposed to arm's length licensing. This finding is consistent with the findings of Morck and Yeung (1992), who contend that internalizing multinational firm operations may be more important in R&D-intensive industries where the transfer of proprietary assets is an issue.

Cross-Border M&A Profitability and Restructuring

Apart from stock market returns, other ways are available to measure gains in M&As that ultimately explain some of the stock market reaction. For instance, what about firms that are not publicly listed on the stock market? What if investors care more about what happens to the firm in the long run rather than the short run? Another set of studies analyzes changes in total factor efficiency, profitability, and restructuring processes within firms after the acquisition has taken place. The results from these studies vary greatly by the acquirer's origins and the target firm's location. Research evidence shows that emerging market targets that receive foreign investment improve in productivity. In the domestic M&A literature, ownership changes are found to be positively related to productivity improvements at the plant level, but the same cannot be found in firm-level data (Andrade et al., 2001).

Harris and Robinson (2003) and Benfratello and Sembenelli (2006), who investigate foreign acquisitions of British and Italian firms, respectively, find that foreign ownership does not generally lead to an improvement in target firm performance measured as total factor productivity. Conyon, Girma, Thompson, and Wright (2002), on the other hand, find that foreign acquisitions lead to labor productivity increases in target firms in the United Kingdom. For emerging markets, Djankov and Hoekman (2000) and Arnold and Javorcik (2009) find that foreign ownership leads to improved performance in the target firm.

Besides productivity measures, Lipsey and Sjöholm (2004) report that foreign-owned establishments in Indonesia pay higher wages than domestic establishments for a given educational level. Girma and Görg (2007) focus on the food and electronics sectors in the United Kingdom and find that acquisitions by U.S. multinationals have sizeable effects on wages. Almeida (2007), however, finds no such effects in foreign acquisitions of domestic firms in Portugal. Instead, foreign acquirers tend to "cherry pick" domestic firms that are already very similar to foreign firms before acquisitions.

What Drives Cross-Border M&As?

In light of positive valuation and performance effects particularly in emerging markets, most cross-border M&As only happen between developed countries. Until the 1990s, hardly any emerging market firms were targets, let alone acquirers. Why would firms in emerging markets forego such an opportunity that could help them generate incremental value? The reason must be that emerging markets are fundamentally different from developed markets so as to either hinder cross-border M&As or prohibit positive gains from cross-border M&As. Both factors are likely at play.

If there were a frictionless world with no barriers to capital flows, no asymmetric information, problems of incomplete contracting, or agency conflicts would exist. Therefore, cross-border M&As should essentially be the same as domestic M&As. Target and acquiring firms not only are in different geographic locations in cross-border M&A deals but also they have different nationalities that result in diverse corporate governance regimes. Cross-border M&A deals also face transaction costs, asymmetries of information, and agency conflicts. Because these frictions inhibit transfers of control, emerging markets might be especially affected by these problems due to less developed institutions, poorer investor protection, and legal enforcement. A large body of literature has emerged that attempts to quantify the degree of these frictions by using measures of the quality of the legal and regulatory environment within a country. La Porta, Lopez-de-Silanes, Shleifer, and Vishny (1997) show that differences in laws, regulation, and enforcement are correlated with the development of capital markets, ownership structure of firms, and cost of capital.

Given this important role of corporate governance, a more recent body of literature investigates its impact as a driver of cross-border M&As. As a result of cross-border M&As, firms often change corporate governance. For instance, when the acquirer finances an M&A with stock, the target firm's shareholders now own the acquirer's stock and are subject to the corporate governance practices of the merged firm. Unlike in domestic M&As, where the acquirer and target reside in the same country, the target in a cross-border M&A is located in a different country. Target and acquirer country differences in laws and institutions can affect the valuation of the shareholders' wealth. Imagine a scenario in which target firm shareholders reside in a country with well-defined investor protection and solid governance. An acquisition by an acquirer from a different country would result in the target shareholder owning a share in the acquirer's firm. In fact, if the acquirer finances the deal with stock, the target shareholder would have exchanged the original target shares for the acquirer's shares. If the acquirer were in a country with inferior investor protection and bad corporate governance, the target firm shareholders would naturally demand compensation.

This argument is the premise for a study by Starks and Wei (2004) who analyze target takeover premiums in U.S. target firms that are acquired by foreign firms. In cross-border M&A deals that are financed by stock options, Starks and Wei find that the takeover premium decreases the better the quality of the bidder firms' home country corporate governance regimes. Furthermore, in a stock financed merger, the evidence suggests that the abnormal return to the target shareholder also decreases the better the quality of the bidder firms' home country corporate governance. These findings are consistent with Starks and Wei's hypothesis that bidder firms must compensate target firm shareholders if the quality of the corporate governance regime is reduced. This result does not hold for mergers that are cash financed because target firm shareholders no longer hold shares and thus are not subject to the corporate governance regime of the acquiring firm. In a related study, Bris and Cabolis (2008) analyze the value of investor protection on a sample of more than 500 cross-border mergers between 1989 and 2002. Their findings are consistent with Starks and Wei; namely, that the premium increases with improved legal protection of the target shareholders.

Rossi and Volpin (2004) find that corporate regimes with stronger investor protection encourage a more active market for M&As. They also show that targets are typically from countries with poorer investor protection. Specifically, firms in countries with weaker investor protection are often sold to buyers from countries with stronger investor protection. Their results also indicate that domestic investor protection is an important determinant in the competitiveness and effectiveness of the market for M&As within a country.

Apart from corporate governance, macroeconomic and financial variables also play a key role in driving cross-border M&A activity. Di Giovanni (2005) uses a gravity model framework common in the trade literature to uncover the determinants of the size and direction of international M&A flows. The underlying hypothesis is whether deep financial markets in the acquisition countries are positively associated with cross-border M&As. He finds that the size of financial markets, measured by stock market capitalization to the gross domestic product (GDP) ratio, is associated with increases in firms investing abroad.

These findings partly explain the scarcity of emerging market acquisitions in the data. The obstacles for emerging market firms to purchase abroad are higher than those for developed market acquirers. Along the same line, the uncertainty of payoffs when buying emerging market firms might deter developed market acquirers to invest in emerging markets in the first place. These hindrances are likely to change, and the next section details what those changes might entail for the landscape of future cross-border M&As.

THE FUTURE OF CROSS-BORDER M&A MARKET

The future of cross-border M&As should be exciting to watch. As alluded to in the introduction, not only are acquisitions in emerging markets increasing, but also emerging market firms themselves are starting to participate in the cross-border M&A market as active buyers. Although the sample of emerging market firm-initiated cross-border M&A deals remains relatively small, they are expected to rise in the future. This increase is expected considering financial resources available to emerging-market multinational firms, their need to expand beyond their local market, and their desire to seek established brands and knowledge in developed markets. This section provides a discussion of some of the first research on this new phenomenon and its impacts on developed market acquirers and targets.

Aybar and Ficici (2009) examine the value implications of cross-border acquisitions by acquirers from emerging markets. They employ event study methodology to measure the impact of cross-border announcements on the value of the acquiring firm. On average, emerging market acquirers in their sample do not gain from cross-border M&As. In fact, in half of the transactions, the authors find evidence of value destruction.

Gubbi, Aulakh, Ray, Sarkar, and Chittoor (2010) focus on a sample of Indian acquiring firms. For international acquisitions, they find that shareholders of Indian acquirers experience larger wealth gain with better quality of resources in the target firms. In other words, when firms make acquisitions in advanced markets that are characterized by better quality resources and institutions, the acquiring firm's shareholders from an emerging economy seem to benefit more.

Another area of research involves examining targets acquired by emerging market firms. Chari, Chen, and Dominguez (2009) conduct the first systematic examination of the recent phenomenon of U.S. firms being acquired by companies in emerging economies. Specifically, they ask what happens to an American firm's performance after a corporation in an emerging economy acquires it. The authors find that the stock market's response to the acquired firm is positive and significant around the time of the acquisition announcement. Average CARs on the target stock price within a three-day window around the announcement date increase by 8 percent. Yet, the magnitude of the gain is much smaller than the gain in targets of U.S. domestic acquisitions, which, on average, experience a gain of 16 percent (Andrade et al., 2001). The evidence suggests that U.S. target firms undergo significant restructuring after acquisition by emerging-market firms. Both employment and the capital stock decrease, suggesting that unprofitable divisions may be sold off or closed. This conjecture is supported by the fact that sales also decline after acquisition.

Instead of studying the effects of emerging market firm acquirers on their own, the question arises as to how such effects compare to acquisitions made by developed market firms. Chen (2010) studies the performance of U.S. firms that have been acquired by buyers from different countries. Acquiring firms from different parts of the world vary in endowments and productivity. Chen tests whether these heterogeneities have different impacts on the target firm's postacquisition performance. The author categorizes acquiring firms into three groups: industrial countries, developing countries, and U.S. companies. Regarding the acquired firm's postacquisition performance, the evidence indicates that the acquirer's country matters. More specifically, buyers from industrial countries lead to the highest postacquisition profits followed by acquisitions from emerging markets. U.S. domestic firm acquisitions result in the lowest profits out of the three groups of acquirers. Furthermore, the postacquisition restructuring process also differs depending on the acquirer country. U.S. firms acquired by buyers originating from developing countries tend to show significant decreases in employment. On the other hand, firms acquired by firms in industrial countries show increases in sales and employment.

Emerging market firms are expected to take on even more aggressive roles as international acquirers in the future. While companies and countries in the West are burdened with debt and are only slowly recovering from the global economic recession, the purchasing power of individuals and corporations within emerging markets is steadily growing, possibly resulting in acquisitions sprees. At the same time, with the economies in the West stuck in sluggish growth for years to come, the growing markets in emerging countries are as attractive as ever for acquirers from developed countries. In fact, one reason behind Kraft's bid for Cadbury might be due to the target's dominant presence in emerging countries like India.

Neither direction of cross-border M&As is without challenges and complications. Developed market firm managers often complain about the risks involved in investing in emerging markets. Transactions are frequently accompanied by political, social, and financial surprises that can turn a deal sour. The Asian financial crisis, for instance, had foreign investors fleeing out of many emerging countries in that area, resulting in tremendous losses for the investors as well as the target country. Emerging market acquirers often face large obstacles on their way to gaining a multinational presence. For instance, the 2005 bid for Unocal, a California oil firm, was met with intense American national security concerns that ultimately resulted in Congress thwarting the deal. Even the attempted bid of Chinese Haier on Maytag stirred up American national sentiments, and Congress intervened again, with the result of a takeover by American Whirlpool. These examples show the needs of emerging market firms for natural resources and established name brands. They also highlight the suspicions of the West that these emerging market firms face. Whether these interactions play out in the future will be interesting to observe.

SUMMARY AND CONCLUSIONS

The geographic composition of cross-border M&A transactions has shifted over time. Historically, the majority of M&A deals have taken place between industrialized countries. In recent years, however, emerging markets have started engaging in cross-border M&A activity. This shift in cross-border M&A composition has changed the business landscape and its effect will become clearer in the future.

Evidence suggests that the effects of cross-border M&As differ among the various participants in the transaction. Target firms are the main beneficiaries when measuring gains as abnormal returns on the stock market. Evidence also indicates that target firms might benefit from foreign acquisitions through improvements in productivity, and especially targets in emerging markets that gain from increases in wages and productivity. On the other hand, the evidence on acquiring firm gains is less clear. For acquisitions in developed markets, several factors affect acquirer firm outcomes such as the country of origin and industry sector. For acquisitions in emerging markets, however, an important ingredient in developed market acquirer gains is obtaining majority control of the emerging market target firm.

Corporate governance and financial institutions play important roles in realizing acquirer and target gains, as well as in facilitating cross-border M&A activities. Greater levels of financial and economic development, coupled with better investor protection, provide more attractive investments for potential acquirers. Because legal and financial environments are less developed in emerging markets than they are in developed markets, most cross-border M&A flows still occur between firms in developed markets. Therefore, one of the ways for governments in emerging markets to attract cross-border M&As into their countries is to improve conditions and to provide better assurances to investors that they will be able to reap the fruits of investment.

The role of emerging market firms is unlikely to be limited to participating on the cross-border M&A stage as target firms. The recent upsurge of outward acquisitions by firms in emerging countries, such as China's Lenovo's purchase of IBM's Thinkpad and India's Tata Motor's acquisition of Ford's Jaguar and Land Rover, has raised great attention in policy circles. Yet, little is known about how these emerging market acquisitions are different from acquisitions by acquirers from developed markets. The first academic studies on emerging market cross-border M&As into developed markets indicate that the restructuring process in the target firms differs significantly from those M&A transactions conducted by developed market acquirers. Furthermore, the global economic crisis has leveled the playing field for firms, allowing them to participate in the global M&A market. With many cash-strapped and debt-ridden firms in the developed market either on the brink of bankruptcy or on the way to a sluggish recovery, emerging market firms that have been left almost unharmed by the crisis are on the prowl for acquisitions that might not have been possible before the crisis. More time is likely to pass before researchers can analyze the long-term effects of these emerging market firms engaging in cross-border M&As.

DISCUSSION QUESTIONS

1. Discuss the motivations to engage in cross-border M&A activities.
2. Discuss the reasons cross-border M&As are successful or unsuccessful.
3. Chari, Ouimet, and Tesar (2010) find that majority control plays an important role in acquirer firm wealth gains when conducting M&As in emerging markets. The authors find that majority control does not matter when acquiring a firm in developed markets. What might explain the importance of majority control in emerging market acquisitions?
4. How is the recent trend of emerging market firms acquiring firms abroad different from or similar to those of developed market firms acquiring abroad?

REFERENCES

Almeida, Rita. 2007. "The Labor Market Effects of Foreign Owned Firms." *Journal of International Economics* 72:1, 75–96.

Andrade, Gregor, Mark Mitchell, and Erik Stafford. 2001. "New Evidence and Perspectives on Mergers." *Journal of Economic Perspectives* 15:2, 103–120.

Antras, Pol, Mihir A. Desai, and C. Fritz Foley. 2009. "Multinational Firms, FDI Flows and Imperfect Capital Markets." *Quarterly Journal of Economics* 124:3, 1171–1219.

Arnold, Jens M., and Beata S. Javorcik. 2009. "Gifted Kids or Pushy Parents? Foreign Direct Investment and Plant Productivity in Indonesia." *Journal of International Economics* 79:1, 42–53.

Aybar, Bülent, and Aysun Ficici. 2009. "Cross-border Acquisitions and Firm Value: An Analysis of Emerging-Market Multinationals." *Journal of International Business Studies* 40:8, 1317–1338.

Benfratello, Luigi, and Alessandro Sembenelli. 2006. "Foreign Ownership and Productivity: Is the Direction of Causality So Obvious?" *International Journal of Industrial Organization* 24:4, 733–751.

Bodnar, Gordon, Bernard Dumas, and Richard Marston. 2002. "Cross-Border Valuation: The International Cost of Equity Capital." Working Paper, Johns Hopkins University.

Brakman, Steven, Harry Garretsen, and Charles van Marrewijk. 2006. "Cross-Border Mergers & Acquisitions: The Facts as a Guide for International Economics." *CESifo Working Paper* 1823.

Bris, Arturo, and Christos Cabolis. 2008. "The Value of Investor Protection: Evidence from Cross-Border Mergers." *Review of Financial Studies* 21:2, 605–48.

Caves, Richard E. 1996. *Multinational Enterprise and Economic Analysis.* New York: Cambridge University Press.

Chari, Anusha, Wenjie Chen, and Kathryn M. Dominguez. 2009. "Foreign Ownership and Corporate Restructuring: Direct Investment by Emerging-Market Firms in the United States." Working Paper, University of Michigan.

Chari, Anusha, Paige P. Ouimet, and Linda L. Tesar. 2010. "The Value of Control in Emerging Markets." *Review of Financial Studies* 23:4, 1741–1770.

Chen, Wenjie. 2010. "The Effect of Investor Origin on Firm Performance: Domestic and Foreign Direct Investment in the United States." *Journal of International Economics.*

Conyon, Martin J., Sourafel Girma, Steve Thompson, and Peter Wright. 2002. "The Productivity and Wage Effects of Foreign Acquisition in the United Kingdom." *Journal of Industrial Economics* 50:1, 85–102.

DiGiovanni, Julian. 2005. "What Drives Capital Flows? The Case of Cross-Border M&A Activity and Financial Deepening." *Journal of International Economics* 65:1, 127–149.

Djankov, Simeon, and Bernard Hoekman. 2000. "Foreign Investment and Productivity Growth in Czech Enterprises." *World Bank Economic Review* 14:1, 49–64.

Doukas, John, and Nicholas Travlos. 1988. "The Effect of Corporate Multinationalism on Shareholders' Wealth: Evidence from International Acquisitions." *Journal of Finance* 43:5, 1161–1175.

Eun, Cheol S., Richard Kolodny, and Carl Scheraga. 1996. "Cross-Border Acquisitions and Shareholder Wealth: Tests of Synergy and Internalization Hypotheses." *Journal of Banking and Finance* 20:9, 1559–1582.

Froot, Kenneth A., and Jeremy C. Stein. 1991. "Exchange Rates and Foreign Direct Investment: An Imperfect Capital Markets Approach." *Quarterly Journal of Economics* 106:4, 1191–1217.

Girma, Sourafel, and Holger Görg. 2007. "Evaluating the Foreign Ownership Wage Premium Using a Difference-in-Difference Matching Approach." *Journal of International Economics* 72:1, 97–112.

Gubbi, Sathyajit R., Preet S Aulakh, Sougata Ray, M. B. Sarkar, and Raveendra Chittoor. 2010. "Do International Acquisitions by Emerging-economy Firms Create Shareholder Value? The Case of Indian Firms." *Journal of International Business Studies* 41:3, 397–418.

Harris, Richard, and Catherine Robinson. 2003. "Foreign Ownership and Productivity in the United Kingdom Estimates for U.K. Manufacturing Using the ARD." *Review of Industrial Organization* 22:3, 207–223.

Harris, Robert S., and David Ravenscraft. 1991. "The Role of Acquisitions in Foreign Direct Investment: Evidence from the U.S. Stock Market." *Journal of Finance* 46:3, 1022–1035.

La Porta, Rafael, Florencio Lopez-de-Silanes, Andrei Shleifer, and Robert W. Vishny. 1997. "Legal Determinants of External Finance." *Journal of Finance* 52:3, 1131–1150.

Lipsey, Robert E., and Fredrik Sjöholm. 2004. "Foreign Direct Investment, Education and Wages in Indonesian Manufacturing." *Journal of Development Economics* 73:1, 415–422.

"Love Me, Love Me Not." 2008. *The Economist* July 12, 388:8588, 36–38.

Moeller, Sara B., Frederik P. Schlingemann, and René M. Stulz. 2005. "Firm Size and the Gains from Acquisitions." *Journal of Financial Economics* 73:2, 201–28.

Morck, Randall, and Bernard Yeung. 1991. "Why Investors Value Multinationality." *Journal of Business* 64:2, 165–187.

Morck, Randall, and Bernard Yeung. 1992. "Internalization: An Event Study Test." *Journal of International Economics* 33:1-2, 41–56.

Robin, Ashok J. 2011. *International Corporate Finance*. New York: McGraw-Hill/Irwin.

Rossi, Stefano, and Paolo F. Volpin. 2004. "Cross Country Determinants of Cross-Border Mergers and Acquisitions." *Journal of Financial Economics* 74:2, 277–304.

Starks, Laura, and Kelsey D. Wei. 2004. "Cross-Border Mergers and Differences in Corporate Governance." Working Paper, University of Texas.

UNCTAD. 2008. *World Investment Report*. New York: United Nations.

UNCTAD. 2009. *World Investment Report*. New York: United Nations.

ABOUT THE AUTHOR

Wenjie Chen is an Assistant Professor of International Business at the George Washington University's School of Business in Washington, D.C. Her fields of concentration are international finance and applied econometrics with a special focus on M&As and their impacts on firm performance. Recent projects include outward direct investment strategies of emerging market firms, foreign direct investment and its impacts on domestic firms and their wages, M&As during financial crises, and the relationship between M&As and exchange rates. Professor Chen's teaching interests are in international finance, international economics, and M&As. She obtained a BA in Economics and Mathematics from Lawrence University in 2004, and a PhD in Economics from the University of Michigan in 2009.

PART III

The M&A Deal Process

CHAPTER 12

Sources of Financing and Means of Payment in M&As

MARINA MARTYNOVA
Associate, Cornerstone Research and Research Fellow, Tilburg University

LUC RENNEBOOG
Professor of Corporate Finance, Tilburg University

INTRODUCTION

Two of the major considerations in any takeover transaction are the choice of takeover financing sources and the means of payment. Although frequently considered as synonymous, these two considerations are driven by distinct determinants, and investors take into account the information signaled by the choice of both the payment method and financing sources.

The sources of takeover financing comprise the way an acquiring firm raises capital to fund an acquisition of another company. Financing sources can be classified into three general categories: (1) internally generated funds, (2) equity issues (including public and private equity placement), and (3) debt issues including issues of bonds or loan notes and borrowing from a bank. Many acquiring companies use more than one source to finance their takeovers. The means of payment is what the acquiring firm is actually offering to the target's shareholders in exchange for their shares. This can be equity of the acquiring (or combined) firm, cash, loan notes, or a combination thereof. Despite being closely related, the takeover financing sources and payment means do not always coincide. Financing the takeover with internally generated funds or with debt implies that the acquisition is entirely paid with cash. Debt-financed acquisitions may also involve payment with loan notes. In contrast, equity financing may be used in acquisitions that are fully paid with equity, with cash and equity, or entirely with cash. An acquiring firm may directly exchange the shares from a seasoned equity offering (SEO) for the shares of the target firm (in all-equity and cash-and-equity offers) or sell its new shares and use the proceeds to pay for the acquisition (all-cash payment). When the acquirer issues debt and equity, it may pay for the target firm's shares with a combination of cash (and loan notes) and equity or with cash (and loan notes) only.

Exhibit 12.1 summarizes the relationship between the financing sources and means of payment. It also shows that the choice of financing sources is typically conditioned by the acquirer's preference for a specific payment method. When the

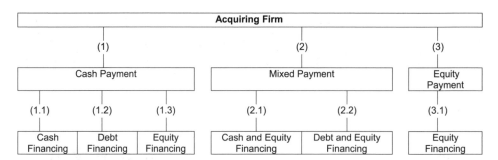

Exhibit 12.1   Relationship between the Means of Payment and Financing Decisions
Note: This exhibit shows the various financing methods of takeovers conditional on the required means of payment.

acquiring firm makes a financing choice, it first considers which means of payment the acquirer should offer in the takeover bid. Only subsequently does the acquiring firm decide on the sources of financing. Therefore, due to their implicit relation, the acquirer should never make the financing and means of payment choices in isolation because they are outcomes of a single decision-making process.

The optimal financing and payment structure of a takeover deal is the one that maximizes value for the acquiring firm. This optimal structure also minimizes the cost of capital, maximizes the wealth of the acquirer's shareholders, and diversifies the risks associated with the takeover transactions. Identifying the optimal financing and payment structure of a takeover deal is a complex process involving numerous factors. For example, factors outside the firm, such as changing economic conditions, regulatory environment, information asymmetry, and tax exposure heavily influence the choice of the optimal financing mix. On the other hand, the specifics of the takeover transaction and the acquirer's needs to diversify the risk of the takeover's failure and the risk of overpayment for the target firm have some bearing on the choice of the means of payment. However, both the financing sources and means of payment should be consistent with the profitability, growth, and corporate governance goals of the acquiring firm.

This chapter is organized as follows. First, it provides a brief historical overview of the financing choices in corporate takeovers. The chapter then shows how the choices, with respect to the sources of financing and means of payment, impact the wealth of the acquirers' shareholders. The remainder of the chapter focuses on the motives underlying the acquirer's decision as to how to finance a takeover and what to offer to the target's shareholders.

HISTORICAL OVERVIEW

Corporate growth via takeovers, often taking the form of mega-deals, requires considerable financial resources. Cash-constrained companies cannot grow by takeovers because they have no access to external capital. As the stock and credit markets have rapidly developed and have made equity and debt capital more accessible, the corporate world has experienced an unprecedented growth in merger and acquisition (M&A) activity over the past decades (Martynova and Renneboog,

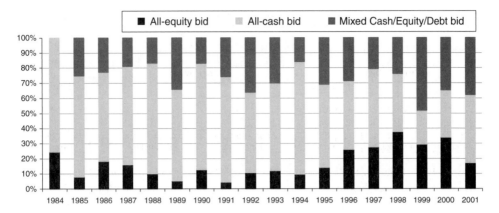

Exhibit 12.2 Composition of Form of Payments (Based on Total Value)
Note: This exhibit shows the percentage of takeovers paid entirely with cash, entirely with equity, and with a combination of cash, equity, and debt based on the total value of M&As during the period 1984 to 2001. Data from Thomson Financial Securities Data.

2008). Evidence shows a switch from all-cash deals toward takeover transactions with more equity and debt in the financial composition.

Exhibit 12.2 shows that the proportion of the total value of acquisitions paid with internal funds averaged about 67 percent in the 1980s but declined to 40 percent during the 1990s. A similar pattern can be observed when looking at the percentage of cash paid takeovers based on the total number of deals, which fell by half in the 1990s, as compared to the 1980s (see Exhibit 12.3). Whereas the proportion of common equity used in acquisitions augmented to a high 39 percent of the total value of all acquisitions (in 1998), the relative number of all-equity takeovers in the 1990s was still rather small. As Exhibit 12.3 shows, the combination of equity, debt, and cash became the most popular method of payment in M&A transactions during the 1990s, accounting for about 75 percent of all deals.

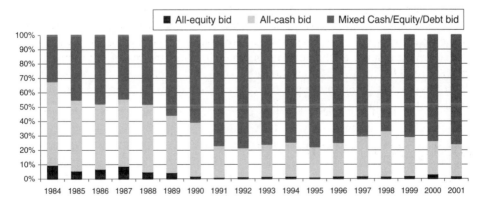

Exhibit 12.3 Composition of Form of Payments (Based on Total Number of M&As)
Note: This exhibit shows the percentage of takeovers paid entirely with cash, entirely with equity, and with a combination of cash, equity, and debt based on the total number of M&As during the period 1984 to 2001. Data from Thomson Financial Securities Data.

The empirical literature gives notable attention in recent years to the choice of the financing sources and the means of payment in corporate takeovers. Different theories emerge explaining the varying preferences of the acquiring firms for a particular financing and payment deal structure. However, before reviewing this literature, the most important question is: Does how the acquiring firm finance and pay for the takeover really matter? The next section addresses this question.

VALUATION EFFECT OF TAKEOVER FINANCING AND PAYMENT DECISIONS

An M&A announcement brings new and usually unexpected information to the market, enabling investors to update their expectations about the firm's prospects and adjust the share prices accordingly. Value-relevant takeover information comprises various takeover characteristics such as the form of the takeover bid, the attitude of the target's board towards the bid, cross-border expansion, and industry-relatedness as well as the sources of financing and the means of payment. The market combines these pieces of information into a signal about the quality of the takeover deal and the potential value creation. Empirical research shows that decisions about takeover financing and means of payment are associated with large differences in the market reaction to takeover announcements (Martynova and Renneboog, 2009). This section presents empirical evidence of the valuation effects of the announcements of takeovers financed and paid with different types of capital. It also reviews the theoretical explanations for the observed differences.

Exhibits 12.4 and 12.5 show the valuation effects of the payment and financing choices in corporate takeovers. These exhibits show the evolution of the cumulative average abnormal returns (CAARs) for acquiring firms over a six-month period starting 60 days before and ending 60 days after the initial takeover announcement day. Exhibit 12.4 presents the differences in valuation effects by the means of payment. It reveals that over the six-month window centered around the takeover announcement day, the returns to the acquirer's shareholders are significantly negative in deals involving equity payments (all-equity and mixed offers). The evidence is consistent with prior empirical findings (Andrade, Mitchell, and Stafford, 2001; Franks, Mayer, and Renneboog, 2001; Moeller, Schlingemann, and Stulz, 2004). However, as Exhibit 12.4 reveals, the poor share price performance of takeover bids is largely due to the postannouncement share price correction. Before the takeover announcement, all-equity offers experience a significant share price run-up exceeding that of all-cash offers.

The dominant explanation of this phenomenon is that investors consider an SEO as a signal that the acquirer's shares are overpriced and hence adjust the share price downward when equity financing is announced (Myers and Majluf, 1984). Managers attempt to time equity issues to coincide with surging stock markets or even with the peak of the stock market cycle (Baker, Ruback, and Wurgler, 2004). Shleifer and Vishny (2003) and Rhodes-Kropf and Vishwanathan (2004) argue that overvalued acquirers use equity to buy real assets of undervalued (or less overvalued) targets to take advantage of the mispricing premium before the overvaluation gets corrected. An equity payment may also be interpreted by the market as a negative signal reflecting uncertainty about the target firm's quality

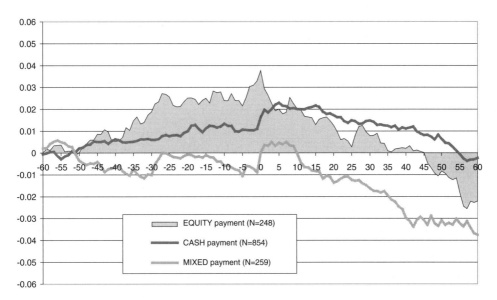

Exhibit 12.4   Acquirer CAARs by Means of Payment

Note: This exhibit shows the daily evolution of the acquirer's cumulative average abnormal returns (CAARs) starting from 60 trading days before the takeover announcement up to 60 days after the announcement. The day of the takeover announcement is denoted as day 0. The CAARs are shown for three subsamples of takeovers classified by the means of payment. The number of observations in each subsample is reported in brackets. Abnormal returns are computed as the difference between the realized and market model benchmark returns. For each firm, daily benchmark returns are calculated using MSCI index returns and the market model parameters are estimated over 240 days ending 60 days before the acquisition announcement.

and potential takeover synergies. If the quality of the acquired assets is more uncertain, the acquirer is likely to pay with equity in order to share with the target's shareholders the risks of being unable to realize the expected synergies.

Exhibit 12.5 presents the takeover valuation effects by sources of transaction financing. It reveals a negative price revision following the announcement of any corporate takeover that involves equity financing. This is also consistent with the view that an equity issue conveys a signal that the firm's shares may be overvalued, which in turn triggers an adverse revaluation effect (Andrade et al., 2001; Moeller et al., 2004). In addition to the significant share price decline (–5.73 percent) over the 3-month period after the deal announcement, all-equity-financed M&As are associated with substantially lower announcement returns (0.49 percent) when compared to deals financed with cash and debt (0.79 percent and 1.32 percent, respectively).

Remarkably, the only type of M&A that does not have a negative postannouncement price correction is a debt-financed acquisition. Over the [–60, +60] event window, debt-financed acquisitions are expected to create substantial value (of about 3 percent) to the acquiring firms. Such an increase in value significantly exceeds the negative returns of M&As financed by equity and cash (–3.4 percent and –0.1percent, respectively). Bharadwaj and Shivdasani (2003) document a similar positive market reaction to debt-financed M&As.

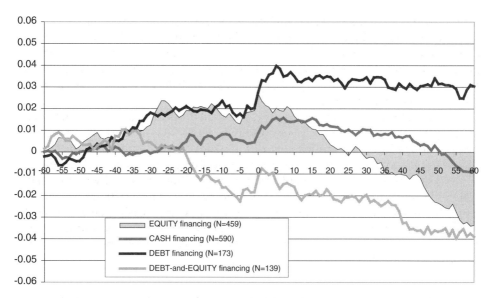

Exhibit 12.5   Acquirer CAARs by Sources of Financing
Note: This exhibit shows the daily evolution of the acquirer's cumulative average abnormal returns (CAARs) starting from 60 trading days before the takeover announcement up to 60 days after the announcement. The day of the takeover announcement is denoted as day 0. The CAARs are shown for three subsamples of takeovers classified by the financing sources. The number of observations in each subsample is reported in brackets. Abnormal returns are computed as the difference between the realized and market model benchmark returns. For each firm, daily benchmark returns are calculated using MSCI index returns and the market model parameters are estimated over 240 days ending 60 days before the acquisition announcement.

This evidence confirms the theoretical predictions that, in contrast to equity financing, the announcement of debt financing is expected to trigger a positive market reaction. First, the preference of debt over equity financing may signal that the acquirer's shares are not overvalued. When the internal sources of financing are insufficient and if the shares of the firm are undervalued or if there is a high risk that an equity issue will trigger a substantial share price decline, the managers opt for debt financing. Second, as debt capital is typically raised via borrowing from a bank, the bank's decision to provide funding may convey a positive signal about the takeover's profitability to the market. Banks are typically regarded as financial intermediaries with superior information and evaluation capabilities (Leland and Pyle, 1977; Diamond, 1984) that allows them to identify bad acquisitions and fund only deals with a positive net present value. Therefore, the market may interpret the news about debt financing as a certification that a takeover will be profitable. Third, the choice of debt financing may also signal that the cash flows of the merged firm will be sufficient to sustain an additional tax shield.

Exhibit 12.5 also shows that acquisitions financed with internally generated funds underperform debt-financed deals on the announcement day (0.79 percent versus 1.32 percent, respectively) and the former trigger significant negative share price revisions of –1.35 percent over the 3-month postannouncement period. This may be due to investor concerns that managerial empire-building motives may drive cash-financed deals. High cash flow reserves may encourage management to undertake acquisitions for empire-building reasons, which frequently leads to a reduction in shareholder value (Jensen, 1986). Consistent with these predictions, Lang, Stulz, and Walkling (1991) and Schlingemann (2004) find a significant negative correlation between internally generated cash flow reserves and acquirer returns in cash-paid M&As.

In sum, the acquirer's financing and payment decisions have a large impact on the market reaction to the takeover announcement. A significantly negative price revision following the announcement of a takeover frequently arises in cases of M&As fully paid with equity but also in takeovers that involve equity financing (including cash-paid and mixed-paid M&As). Acquisitions financed with internally generated funds underperform debt-financed deals, suggesting that investors are wary that managerial empire-building motives may drive cash-financed deals. In contrast, debt financing conveys a positive signal to the market that the firm's shares may not be overvalued and that the takeover is profitable, generating a tax shield.

THE DETERMINANTS OF TAKEOVER FINANCING AND PAYMENT DECISIONS

As the previous section shows, the acquirer's share price reductions arise when the acquirer uses equity as a funding source or a means of payment in M&As. Despite the negative price reactions, financing takeovers with equity issues has been a common phenomenon over the past two decades. Moreover, recent research documents a tendency towards a switch from cash to equity in the financial composition of takeover deals. Andrade et al. (2001) show that all-equity acquisitions represented 32.9 percent of all U.S. M&As in the 1980s versus 57.8 percent in the 1990s. Similarly, Martynova and Renneboog (2006) confirm that equity has become a popular source of financing in European M&As; the proportion of all-cash acquisitions fell by half in the 1990s compared to the 1980s. This section reviews existing theoretical and empirical literature about the factors that motivate acquirers to opt for equity financing/payment despite its negative impact on the takeover value.

Takeover Financing Decision

The Modigliani and Miller (1958) irrelevance proposition implies that in the world of perfect capital markets, companies should be indifferent between equity and debt financing. However, the irrelevance proposition no longer holds in a world with market imperfections or institutional rigidities, such as information asymmetries, agency costs, transaction costs, and taxes. The vast body of theoretical and empirical literature documents that market imperfections induce systematic corporate preferences for specific sources of financing. These imperfections can be partitioned into two dominant categories that explain financing preferences: cost of capital factors and agency-related issues. The former explanation upholds that market imperfections or institutional rigidities, such as information asymmetries, legal protection of shareholders and creditors, or taxes, may disproportionally affect the costs of debt and equity capital. The latter explanation endorses that a firm issues specific securities to mitigate agency problems among its management, shareholders, and creditors.

Pecking Order and Market Timing
Myers and Majluf (1984) show that, if information asymmetries exist between new investors and the management that acts in the interest of incumbent shareholders, firms prefer to finance investments by using internally generated funds or by debt rather than by issuing new equity. In their model, management has incentives to issue equity when shares of the firm are temporarily overvalued, as this would increase the wealth of the incumbent shareholders. Knowing this, outside investors consider the issue of new equity as a negative signal about the true value of the firm and adjust the share price accordingly. This adverse price effect of an equity issue increases its costs and forces firms to issue equity only when alternative sources of financing are unavailable or too costly.

However, the pecking order preferences may be weakened when financial markets are buoyant. Not only do buoyant equity markets overvalue shares in the short run (hence, making equity a relatively cheap source of financing), but they also induce investors to underreact to negative signals about the firms' fundamental values (Baker et al., 2004). Therefore, the value reduction induced by equity issues may be less severe in periods of stock market booms. When contracting debt is no longer advantageous as compared to issuing equity, firms are more likely to raise money for takeovers by performing SEOs (Choe, Masulis, and Nanda, 1993).

Empirical results support the pecking order and market timing predictions. Martynova and Renneboog (2009) find that cash-rich acquirers finance their M&As entirely with cash, whereas firms with insufficient internally generated funds opt for external sources of financing. Debt financing has priority over equity financing and is more likely when acquirers are cash-constrained but still have sufficient debt capacity. Equity financing takes place when a company has insufficient cash funds and limited debt capacity. However, firms also opt to raise capital via the stock market rather than employ internal funds or a debt issue when they experience substantial share price increases before the takeover announcement.

Regulatory Environment
A growing body of literature advocates that regulation is another important determinant of corporate financing decisions. La Porta, Lopez-de-Silanes, Shleifer, and Vishny (1998), Levine (1999), and Djankov, McLiesh, and Shleifer (2007) argue that regulation affects the terms at which financiers are willing to provide firms with funds. When a regulatory environment protects the providers of funds against expropriation by corporate management, external finance may be available at lower costs. Specifically, strong creditor protection assumes that lenders can more easily force repayment, take possession of collateral, or even gain control over the firm. This results in lower creditor risks and hence lower costs of borrowing. Similarly, strong shareholder protection increases the relative attractiveness of equity financing. Better legal investor protection facilitates using external sources of financing.

Empirical data support the importance of a regulatory environment in takeover financing decisions. Martynova and Renneboog (2009) show that acquisitions financed by equity (relative to those financed by cash) are more likely in countries having stronger protection of shareholder rights. This is in line with the prediction that strong shareholder protection reduces the cost of equity capital and hence increases the attractiveness of equity as a source of financing. Also, when creditor rights protection is high, acquirers prefer debt over equity financing. These results suggest that the legal protection of shareholders and creditors affects the costs of debt and equity capital, thereby inducing systematic corporate preferences for the most appropriate (less expensive) source of financing.

Debt Tax Shield

Tax-deductible interest payments may encourage the issuance of debt (Modigliani and Miller, 1963). Leveraged financing may provide substantial tax benefits to the firm in the form of an increased tax shield and a reduced cost of capital. This may encourage acquirers with higher tax liabilities to use debt to finance their takeovers.

Nonetheless, whether the potential tax benefits constitute a true motive for the debt financing choice is still up for debate. The increasing costs (with leverage bankruptcy) may offset the tax benefits of debt financing (Modigliani and Miller, 1963). The benefits of increased debt tax-shields also decrease when the nondebt tax deductions are present (DeAngelo and Masulis, 1980). Furthermore, Miller (1977) argues that tax advantages of debt become less certain when capital gains and personal income taxes are different.

Agency Costs of Equity and Takeover Threats

According to Jensen and Meckling (1976), the conflicts of interest between management and shareholders are an important determinant of the corporate preferences for specific financing instruments. For managers who pursue a personal agenda at the expense of shareholders' wealth, a debt issue may be regarded as the least preferred source of financing as it restricts the availability of corporate funds at their disposal. In contrast, an equity issue increases the funds under managerial discretion and hence may be strictly preferred by the entrenched manager. This agency conflict between the management and shareholders is most pronounced in widely-held corporations where shareholder activism and efficient monitoring of the management may be deficient. Therefore, acquiring firms with a dispersed ownership structure and weak corporate governance may be more likely to issue equity to finance takeovers.

However, Zwiebel (1996) claims that entrenched managers may voluntarily opt for debt financing because of the takeover threat from the market for corporate control. In his dynamic model, hostile acquirers target poorly performing firms and replace poorly performing management. The threat of losing their jobs and perquisites provides managers with an incentive to focus on the shareholder value maximization, and a debt issue allows them to credibly constrain their discretion over corporate funds. Therefore, acquiring firm managers anticipating a takeover threat are more likely to finance their investments with debt.

Empirical evidence confirms that managerial self-interest, as predicted by Jensen and Meckling (1976), drives the choice of equity financing in some acquisitions. Martynova and Renneboog (2009) find that widely held corporations tend to finance acquisitions more frequently with equity. In contrast, companies with a large blockholder (owning 20 percent or more of the firm's shares) prefer to finance their acquisitions with internal funds or debt. For a large sample of M&As, Martynova and Renneboog show that firms that are controlled by a blockholder make 67 percent of the cash-financed takeovers while widely held firms (i.e., firms without a blockholder and owning at least 20 percent of the shares) make 53 percent of equity-financed M&As. The data, however, provide no support for Zwiebel's (1996) prediction that entrenched managers of widely held firms voluntarily signal their commitment to shareholder value creation by adopting debt financing. In this way, they can constrain their discretion over corporate funds and reduce the likelihood that their company will be subject to a disciplinary takeover. In contrast to these predictions, the data show that for acquiring firms issuing debt, the estimated likelihood of being taken over is significantly lower than for firms financing their M&As with internal funds and for acquirers issuing equity.

Debt Overhang

Myers (1977) argues that the conflicting interests of shareholders and creditors encourage firms to issue equity rather than debt to raise external funds. In his view, the wealth-maximizing preferences of shareholders dictate that managers undertake a project only if its expected benefits exceed the payments to debtholders. This may lead to underinvestment because managers may forego positive net present value (NPV) investment projects if the expected benefits from the projects are sufficient to repay debt only, while leaving shareholders' pockets empty. To minimize the scope of underinvestment, firms with high quality projects may limit leverage and hence avoid further borrowing. As such, firms with high growth potential are more likely to issue equity to finance acquisitions.

The debt overhang argument in favor of equity financing is also consistent with the empirical evidence (Martynova and Renneboog, 2009). The probability of equity financing (versus cash and debt financing) increases with the growth potential of the acquiring firm, as measured by its Tobin's q ratio. When accounting-based measures of growth opportunities are considered, the evidence is even more pronounced: equity issuers have the highest average growth rate in capital expenditures, sales, and total assets over the three years before the year of the acquisition. Overall, acquiring firms with strong growth opportunities prefer financing M&As with equity.

Agency Cost of Debt and Financial Flexibility

Conflicts of interest between shareholders and creditors may also lead to another agency problem, namely, excessive risk-taking by the management. The equity of a leveraged firm is a call option on the firm's assets, whose value increases with the volatility of future cash flows. This implies that management can maximize shareholder wealth by increasing the risk of the projects in which it invests and hence can redistribute wealth from bondholders to shareholders (Jensen and Meckling, 1976). Higher earnings volatility increases the expected bankruptcy costs that creditors may anticipate by demanding better terms in the debt covenants. Consequently, the cost of borrowing increases, making debt financing less attractive or even prohibitively expensive for leveraged and risky firms. Therefore, highly leveraged and risky firms are less likely to use debt financing.

Bolton and Freixas (2000) formulate an alternative theory. In their capital market equilibrium, risky firms prefer bank loans to equity financing because banks are good at helping firms through times of financial distress. That is, firms that face high risk of bankruptcy are more likely to build their relationship with banks, which would provide them access to the cheapest form of flexible financing. However, Bolton and Freixas note that the riskiest firms (which are often start-up firms and risky ventures) either cannot obtain funding or are forced to issue equity, as they are considered too risky to be able to obtain a bank loan. Safer firms prefer to issue equity and thus avoid paying the intermediation cost associated with banks.

The data weakly support the agency costs of debt explanation (Martynova and Renneboog, 2009). Debt financing is more likely when the acquiring firm has a lower beta (less exposure to systematic risk) and when the acquiring firm is more mature. In contrast, equity financing prevails in M&As performed by relatively young (more risky) firms with higher betas.

The Means of Payment Decision

The acquirer's decision regarding the sources of takeover financing often coincides with or depends on the choice of the payment method in the takeover deal. The acquirer's decision on the payment method is typically driven by strategic considerations, such as the need to diversify the risk of overpayment for the target, the risk of a change in the firm's control structure, and the risk of the takeover's failure. This section draws on arguments from the extant literature to explain why acquirers prefer specific means of payment in corporate takeovers.

Risk Sharing

Information asymmetries between acquirer and target are an important determinant of the means of payment in corporate takeovers (Hansen, 1987). In particular, high uncertainty about the true value of the target firm induces the acquirer to pay with its own equity rather than cash. Capital participation in the combined firm makes the target shareholders share the risk of potential downward revaluations after the takeover's completion.

Hansen (1987) predicts that the probability of the stock offer increases with the size of the target firm and decreases with the size of the acquirer, as the revaluation adverse effect is more harmful when the target's assets constitute a sizeable addition to the acquirer. Consistent with this prediction, Martynova and Renneboog (2009) document that among M&As financed with equity, the average transaction value of equity-paid deals ($2.3 billion) is more than 16 times the average value of cash-paid M&As ($139 million). The difference is also important when considering the relative size of the takeover deal. That is, when a sizeable firm acquires a smaller firm, there is less need to share the risk of the transaction with the target's shareholders by means of an equity offer.

The Threat of Control Change

Acquirers prefer using cash over equity payment when they are vulnerable to the threat of control change. Faccio and Masulis (2005) document that the threat of a change in the corporate control structure (e.g., by means of voting power dilution or the emergence of an outside blockholder) may discourage acquirers from paying for the acquisition with equity. These findings support theories of Stulz (1988) and Jung, Kim, and Stulz (1996) showing that equity exchange is less likely to be used when stock issuance may dilute voting power of a blockholder or a manager of the acquiring firm.

The control structure of the acquiring and target firms largely determines the effect of the threat of control change on the likelihood of stock payment in a corporate takeover. In particular, a cash payment is strictly preferred to an equity payment when the target's share ownership is concentrated and an acquirer's largest blockholder only holds an intermediate level of voting power. This preference is greatly weakened if the target company is widely owned or if the acquirer's dominant shareholder has supermajority voting rights. Nonetheless, the acquirer's management may have incentives to avoid equity exchange if the target's share ownership is concentrated, and hence equity-paid acquisition would create an outside blockholder in the company. In sum, an acquirer is unlikely to offer an equity payment if this may significantly change the degree of control of the firm's shareholders.

Indeed, empirical data confirm that the threat of a change in the firm's control structure makes the acquiring firm averse to all-equity payments (Martynova and Renneboog, 2009). Acquirers are more likely to use cash versus equity payments if their largest shareholders control an intermediate voting stake (i.e., owning between 20 percent and 60 percent of the equity), which could be eroded by an equity payment to the shareholders of a closelyheld target firm. Further, the likelihood of cash versus equity payments increases with the percentage of shares that the target's largest blockholder would receive in the combined firm (if the M&A would be entirely paid with equity). However, the emergence of a new controlling shareholder appears to be of little concern to the acquiring firms' shareholders that either have no large controlling blockholders (owning 20 percent of the equity or more) or are controlled by blockholders holding a supermajority-voting stake (i.e., 60 percent of the equity or more). In those cases, the emergence of a new blockholder hardly challenges the control positions of the acquiring firms' shareholders. These companies frequently opt for equity payment.

Stock Misvaluation
Asymmetric information between the acquirer's management and outside investors regarding the true value of the acquiring firm may also have a bearing on the choice between cash or equity payments in an offer. If managers of the acquiring firm know that the firm's shares are worth more than their current market price, they will prefer to pay for the acquisition with cash. Conversely, if the acquirer's management believes that the shares are overvalued, they will prefer to pay for the acquisition with equity. These predictions are in the spirit of the Shleifer and Vishny (2003) and Rhodes-Kropf and Vishwanathan (2004) models, which show that overvalued acquirers use their equity to buy real assets of undervalued (or less overvalued) targets and take advantage of the mispricing premium over the long term, when the overvaluation will be corrected.

Empirical studies find support for the view that the mispricing premium is an important motive for choosing equity as a means of payment. In particular, studies show that equity-paying acquirers are, on average, more overvalued than their targets, and the probability of an equity offer increases with the degree of the acquirer's overvaluation (Dong, Hirshleifer, Richardson, and Teoh, 2003; Rhodes-Kropf, Robinson, and Vishwanathan, 2005). Martynova and Renneboog (2009) also document that takeovers paid with equity are preceded by a significant increase in the share price of the acquiring firm.

Characteristics of the Takeover Bid

The relative size of the target firm and the potential control change are not the only takeover characteristics that affect the acquirer's choice of the payment method. The choice of payment method also depends on characteristics of the takeover offer. First, the acquiring firm is less likely to offer an equity payment in cross-border takeovers. If the latter's shares are not traded in the target's country, target shareholders may be reluctant to accept an equity offer from a foreign acquirer. Also, regulation in the target's country may impose restrictions on foreign equity investments. In line with this prediction, Martynova and Renneboog (2009) document that the percentage of cross-border deals is highest when cash payment is offered and lowest when all-equity payment is offered.

Second, the choice between cash and equity payment depends on how the target receives the takeover bid. If the acquisition is opposed by the target's board and, rather than negotiate with the target's board, the acquirer makes a direct offer to the target's shareholders, a cash payment may play a catalytic role in encouraging the sale of their shares. Therefore, a cash payment increases the probability of the hostile takeover's success. Martynova and Renneboog (2009) document empirically a positive relationship between the takeover bid hostility and the choice of a cash payment.

Third, the incumbent owners of an unlisted target are more likely to accept a cash payment, as their primary incentive to sell the firm is frequently to cash out. The acquirer may also prefer to pay with cash for unlisted targets because of the control loss concerns discussed earlier. Therefore, equity payment is least likely when the target firm is unlisted or closely held. This pattern is also confirmed by data; acquisitions of listed targets are more common among all-equity takeovers than among all-cash takeovers (Martynova and Renneboog, 2009).

SUMMARY AND CONCLUSIONS

This chapter reviews the academic literature regarding an acquiring firm's choices of the sources of financing and the means of payment in corporate takeovers. The financing and payment decisions have a significant impact on the value of the acquiring firm. Investors take into account the information signaled by the choices of both the payment method and the sources of takeover financing when estimating the possible synergistic takeover value at the announcement. A significantly negative price revision following the announcement of a takeover is common for equity-paid takeovers and is also observed in any other takeover deals that involve equity financing (including cash-paid and mixed-paid M&As). The evidence confirms that investors consider equity issues to be a signal that the firm's shares are overvalued. Acquisitions financed with internally generated funds underperform debt-financed deals, suggesting that investors are wary that cash-financed deals may be driven by managerial empire-building motives.

Despite the negative price reactions, financing takeovers with equity issues has been a common trend over the past two decades. To further understand this phenomenon, the chapter reviews theoretical and empirical literature about the determinants of the financing and payment decisions by acquiring firms.

The acquirer's concerns about the cost of capital influences the financing decision. In particular, in line with the pecking order hypothesis, cash-rich acquirers opt for the least expensive source of financing—internally generated funds. Acquirers with insufficient internal funds raise external capital to finance M&As; they employ borrowing when their debt capacity is high (leverage is low and the collateral value of their assets is high). They opt for an equity issue when investor sentiment is positive regarding the firm's fundamental value (price run-up is high). However, the need for flexibility in managing corporate funds prevents firms with strong growth opportunities from financing the takeover with debt (which could create a debt overhang problem), forcing them to use equity capital instead even when they still have a high debt capacity.

Acquirers operating in a better corporate governance environment benefit from lower costs of external capital: Debt financing is more likely when creditor rights are well protected by law and courts, and the use of equity financing increases when shareholder rights protection is high. The financing decision may also be related to agency problems that may be induced by conflicts of interest between the management and shareholders. Firms with dispersed ownership structure may selectively prefer cash and equity financing over borrowing because this is the least preferred source of financing by entrenched managers.

The takeover financing decision is closely related to the acquirer's strategic preferences for specific types of means of payment. As equity financing of M&As enables the acquirer to make a direct equity offer to the target's shareholders, the acquirer may benefit from sharing the takeover's risk with the target's incumbent shareholders. The risk-sharing benefits of an equity offer increase with the relative size of the transaction. However, equity payment is less likely when the acquiring firm is vulnerable to the threat of a control change. Large shareholders of acquiring firms prefer financing with internal funds or debt (hence, a cash payment) if an all-equity takeover could threaten their control position. This would occur if the acquirer's large shareholders hold an intermediate level of control and the target has a concentrated control structure. The choice of the means of payment also depends on characteristics of the takeover deal such as its geographical scope (domestic versus cross-border), deal attitude (friendly versus hostile), and the legal status of the target company (public versus privately owned).

DISCUSSION QUESTIONS

1. What is the difference between the sources of financing and the means of payment?
2. What are the main determinants of the takeover financing choice?
3. What determines the means of payment choice in corporate takeovers?
4. Why does the market negatively react to the announcement of a takeover involving equity financing and payment?
5. Does regulatory environment affect the takeover financing decision? Why or why not?
6. What is the debt overhang problem and how does it affect the financing decision in M&As?

REFERENCES

Andrade, Gregor, Mark L. Mitchell, and Erik Stafford. 2001. "New Evidence and Perspectives on Mergers." *Journal of Economic Perspectives* 15:2, 103–120.

Baker, Malcolm, Richard S. Ruback, and Jeffrey Wurgler. 2004. "Behavioral Corporate Finance: A Survey." NBER Working Paper No. 10863.

Bharadwaj, Anu, and Anil Shivdasani. 2003. "Valuation Effects of Bank Financing in Acquisitions." *Journal of Financial Economics* 67:1, 113–148.

Bolton, Patrick, and Xavier Freixas. 2000. "Equity, Bonds, and Bank Debt: Capital Structure and Financial Market Equilibrium under Asymmetric Information." *Journal of Political Economy* 108:2, 324–351.

Choe, Hyuk, Ronald W. Masulis, and Vikram K. Nanda. 1993. "Common Stock Offerings across the Business Cycle." *Journal of Empirical Finance* 1:1, 3–31.

DeAngelo, Harry, and Ron Masulis. 1980. "Optimal Capital Structure under Corporate and Personal Taxation." *Journal of Financial Economics* 8:1, 3–29.

Diamond, Douglas. 1984. "Financial Intermediation and Delegated Monitoring." *Review of Economic Studies* 51:3, 393–414.

Djankov, Simeon, Caralee McLiesh, and Andrei Shleifer. 2007. "Private Credit in 129 Countries." *Journal of Financial Economics* 84:2, 299–329.

Dong, Ming, David Hirshleifer, Scott Richardson, and Siew H. Teoh. 2003. "Does Investor Misvaluation Drive the Takeover Market?" Working Paper, The Ohio State University.

Faccio, Mara, and Ronald W. Masulis. 2005. "The Choice of Payment Method in European Mergers and Acquisitions." *Journal of Finance* 60:3, 1345–1388.

Franks, Julian, Colin Mayer, and Luc Renneboog. 2001. "Who Disciplines Managers in Poorly Performing Companies?" *Journal of Financial Intermediation* 10:3–4, 209–248.

Hansen, Robert G. 1987. "A Theory for the Choice of Exchange Medium in Mergers and Acquisitions." *Journal of Business* 60:1, 75–95.

Jensen, Michael C. 1986. "Agency Costs of Free Cash Flow, Corporate Finance, and Takeovers." *American Economic Review* 76:2, 323–329.

Jensen, Michael C., and William H. Meckling. 1976. "Theory of the Firm: Managerial Behaviour, Agency Costs and Ownership Structure." *Journal of Financial Economics* 3:4, 305–360.

Jung, Kooyul, Yong-Cheol Kim, and René Stulz. 1996. "Timing, Investment Opportunities, Managerial Discretion, and the Security Issue Decision." *Journal of Financial Economics* 42:2, 159–185.

La Porta, Rafael, Forencio Lopez-de-Silanes, Andrei Shleifer, and Robert W. Vishny. 1998. "Law and Finance." *Journal of Political Economy* 106:6, 1113–1155.

Lang, Larry, René Stulz, and Ralph Walkling. 1991. "A Test of the Free Cash Flow Hypothesis: The Case of Bidder Returns." *Journal of Financial Economics* 29:2, 315–335.

Leland, Hayne, and David Pyle. 1977. "Informational Asymmetries, Financial Structure, and Financial Intermediation." *Journal of Finance* 32:2, 371–387.

Levine, Ross. 1999. "Law, Finance, and Economic Growth." *Journal of Financial Intermediation* 8:1–2, 36–67.

Martynova, Marina, and Luc Renneboog. 2006. "Mergers and Acquisitions in Europe: The Fifth Takeover Wave." In Luc Renneboog, (ed.), *Advances in Corporate Finance and Asset Pricing*, 15–75. Amsterdam: Elsevier.

Martynova, Marina, and Luc Renneboog. 2008. "A Century of Corporate Takeovers: What Have We Learned and Where Do We Stand?" *Journal of Banking and Finance* 32:10, 2148–2177.

Martynova, Marina, and Luc Renneboog. 2009. "What Determines the Financing Decision in Corporate Takeovers: Cost of Capital, Agency Problems, or the Means of Payment?" Journal of Corporate Finance 15:3, 290–315.

Miller, Merton, 1977. "Debt and Taxes." *Journal of Finance* 32:2, 261–275.

Modigliani, Franco, and Merton Miller. 1958. "The Cost of Capital, Corporation Finance and the Theory of Investment." *American Economic Review* 48:3, 261–297.

Modigliani, Franco, and Merton Miller. 1963. "Corporate Income Taxes and the Cost of Capital: A Correction." *American Economic Review* 53:3, 433–443.

Moeller, Sara B., Frederik P. Schlingemann, and René M. Stulz. 2004. "Firm Size and the Gains from Acquisitions." *Journal of Financial Economics* 73:2, 201–228.

Myers, Stewart C. 1977. "Determinants of Corporate Borrowing." *Journal of Financial Economics* 5:2, 147–175.

Myers, Stewart C., and Nicholas S. Majluf. 1984. "Corporate Financing and Investment Decisions When Firms Have Information That Investors Do Not Have." *Journal of Financial Economics* 13:2, 187–221.

Rhodes-Kropf, Matthew, David Robinson, and S. Viswanathan. 2005. "Valuation Waves and Merger Activity: The Empirical Evidence." *Journal of Financial Economics* 77:3, 561–603.

Rhodes-Kropf, Matthew, and S. Vishwanathan. 2004. "Market Valuation and Merger Waves", *Journal of Finance* 59:1, 2685–2718.

Schlingemann, Frederik. 2004. "Financing Decisions and Bidder Gains." *Journal of Corporate Finance* 10:5, 683–701.

Shleifer, Andrei, and Robert Vishny. 2003. "Stock Market Driven Acquisitions." *Journal of Financial Economics* 70:3, 295–311.

Stulz, René 1988. "Managerial Control of Voting Rights: Financing Policies and the Market for Corporate Control." *Journal of Financial Economics* 20:1–2, 25–54.

Zwiebel, Jeffrey. 1996. "Dynamic Capital Structure under Managerial Entrenchment." *American Economic Review* 86:5, 1197–1215.

ABOUT THE AUTHORS

Marina Martynova is an Associate at Cornerstone Research, the leading consulting company in economic and financial litigation in the United States. Before moving to the United States, Dr. Martynova held posts as an Assistant Professor of Finance at Sheffield University (United Kingdom) and a Research Fellow at Tilburg University (The Netherlands). She also participated in the European Commission research project "New Forms of Governance." Dr. Martynova's expertise is in corporate finance and corporate governance. She specializes in M&As, leveraged financing, equity issues, financial and accounting reporting, corporate governance regulation, and applied econometrics. Her research has been published in highly ranked academic journals such as *Journal of Corporate Finance, Journal of Banking and Finance*, and *Oxford Review of Economic Policy*. Dr. Martynova has been invited to give presentations at numerous conferences and seminars including annual meetings of American and European Finance Associations. She also acts as a referee for major journals in the field of finance. She holds a PhD in Financial Economics from Tilburg University.

Luc Renneboog is Professor of Corporate Finance at Tilburg University and a research fellow at CentER and the European Corporate Governance Institute (ECGI, Brussels). He graduated from the Catholic University of Leuven with degrees in management engineering (MSc) and philosophy (BA), the University of Chicago with an MBA, and the London Business School with a PhD in financial economics. He held appointments at the University of Leuven and Oxford University, and visiting appointments at London Business School, University Paris-Dauphine, University of Venice, University of Cardiff, and HEC (Paris). He has published in the *Journal of Finance, Journal of Financial Intermediation, Journal of Law and Economics,*

Journal of Corporate Finance, Journal of Banking and Finance, Oxford Review of Economic Policy, Cambridge Journal of Economics, and others. He has co-authored and edited several books on corporate governance, dividend policy, and venture capital with Oxford University Press and Elsevier. His research interests are corporate finance, corporate governance, takeovers, dividend policy, insider trading, law and economics, and the economics of art.

CHAPTER 13

Cultural Due Diligence

RONALD F. PICCOLO
Associate Professor of Management, Rollins College

MARY BARDES
Assistant Professor of Management, Drexel University

INTRODUCTION

According to Robbins and Judge (2010, p. 231), organizational culture refers to a "system of shared meaning held by members that distinguishes the organization" from others. In many diverse organizations across numerous industries, culture influences employee behavior, the decision-making process, the way members interact, and how particular behaviors are nurtured, rewarded, or discouraged. Values serve as guiding principles for individuals; likewise, values act as guiding principles in organizations. An organization's culture, which is deeply informed by both expressed and implicit expectations for interactions among stakeholders, is the foundation upon which members rely when making decisions about how to deal with clients, products, competitors, and services. Culture can be a strategic competitive advantage for firms (Barney, 1986) and ultimately affects an organization's performance over time (Latham, 2007).

Although culture reveals itself in a firm's regular day-to-day operations, the impact of culture is particularly salient in times of uncertainty and change. That is, when ambiguity and uncertainty characterize the operating environment surrounding a particular firm, the stability of an organization's culture is challenged and culture's impact on operations, employee motivation, and organizational success might be particularly salient (Miller, 2000). Thus, when two or more firms are engaged in an extended partnership, a situation commonly fraught with uncertainty, anxiety, and challenges, the respective cultures in the individual firms are critical to the merger's ultimate success. As Cartwright and Cooper (1993) report, research consistently finds that the most common explanation for the failure of a merger or acquisition is an inability to accurately assess the nature and compatibility of a new company's culture, along with the failure to foster adequate integration.

In that vein, the purpose of this chapter is to describe the importance of organizational culture in the successful integration of two or more independent organizations. The chapter describes and defines organizational culture including an explanation of how culture differs from climate. It also describes the impact of organizational culture in general and on firm integration in particular, including examples of how culture facilitates or undermines postmerger success. Additionally, the chapter describes how organization research typically measures culture, including the assumptions embedded in this measurement. Finally, the chapter includes recommendations for how organizational leaders can assess culture during the due diligence process.

Mergers and acquisitions (M&As) and extended partnerships are pervasive phenomena in modern business life. Despite arguments to the contrary, true mergers of equal companies rarely occur because one firm typically has the economic, market, or political "upper hand" (Schein, 2004). This dynamic fosters power struggles among employees in partner firms at nearly every structural level, especially the senior managers. Too often, senior managers in the buyer firm fail to consider the nature, strength, and stability of the partnering organization's culture, or if they do consider culture, they often discount its likely impact on a merger's ultimate success. This chapter offers guidance for enhancing the cultural due diligence process when firms embark on an M&A, partnership, or any major organizational change.

ORGANIZATIONAL CULTURE AND ITS IMPACT ON FIRMS

Organizational culture captures how members make sense of their organizations (Schneider, 2000) and is essential for describing and analyzing phenomena that occur in common organizational settings (Schein, 2000). The concept of organizational culture is built on an assumption of shared meaning in organizations, such that members possess a common understanding of critical aspects of the context in which an organization operates (Ostroff, Kinicki, and Tamkins, 2003). In particular, culture is a phenomenon that typically runs deep in organizations and is often based on symbolic interpretations of organizational events (Hatch, 1993) that reflect employees' core values and underlying assumptions and ideologies (Schein, 1992; Trice and Beyer, 1993). Comprehensive definitions such as that of Schein (1992) suggest that culture represents shared basic assumptions that are learned through solving problems of external adaptation and internal integration. *External adaptation* refers to responses by employees to external constituencies and environmental concerns, while *internal integration* refers to developing a vision and set of values that are shared among employees, encouraging strong identification with the organization (Tsui, Wang, and Xin, 2006). The shared assumptions at the heart of an organization's culture shape employees' perceptions and subsequent attitudes and behaviors (Ostroff et al., 2003). Culture is maintained through communication and socialization processes that transmit these basic assumptions from current to new organizational members (Schein, 1992).

Many scholars have proposed that organizational culture manifests itself in three fundamental layers: (1) observable artifacts, (2) espoused values, and (3) basic underlying assumptions (e.g., Rousseau, 1990; Schein, 1992, 2004). Artifacts, which represent the primary layer, are manifestations of an organization's culture that employees can easily observe (e.g., corporate logos, jargon, anecdotes, myths, and rituals). These observable symbols provide employees with information regarding which attitudes and behaviors are considered appropriate, and represent essential means for transmission of an organization's culture to its workforce (Trice and Beyer, 1993). Artifacts are expressions of an organization's culture that are salient and easily visible. Espoused values, the second layer of an organization's culture, include the beliefs, philosophies, and norms that both leaders and members of an organization explicitly outline. These values are also readily visible in published documents, such as mission and vision statements, and typically emerge in regular conversations between managers and employees. At Southwest Airlines, for example, the company's central interest in customer service is explicitly expressed in its mission statement: "The mission of Southwest Airlines is dedication to the highest quality of Customer Service delivered with a sense of warmth, friendliness, individual pride, and Company Spirit." Also explicit in this statement is the company's expectation for its employees' dispositions and behaviors in general and its customer service representatives in particular (e.g., warmth, friendliness, pride, and spirit). Thus, with a tangible expression of core values in the mission statement, employees, customers, vendors, and other key stakeholders are each made aware of expectations for interactions with members of the Southwest Airlines organization.

At United Parcel Service (UPS), managers rely on a set of 37 values that capture the company's vision for managing its broad and diverse workforce. These values are described in UPS's "policy book," which is required reading for all members of the company's management team (Colquitt, LePine, and Wesson, 2008). The following is a sample of UPS's core values statements:

- We build our organization around people.
- We treat our people fairly and without favoritism.
- We place great value on diversity.
- We promote an open-door for managing people.
- We respect each employee's point of view.

These statements serve as explicit expressions of the values at UPS, making clear to employees and managers how they are expected to interact with each other. Further, these value statements indicate the company's recognition of how important employees are to the day-to-day functioning of a large multinational corporation.

Last, the least observable level of organization culture is embedded in underlying, often unstated assumptions about how to conduct regular activities and transactions. These assumptions are often philosophies that are "taken for granted" and are so ingrained in an employee's mental heuristic that he or she simply acts on instinct, rather than critically examining the validity or relevance of behavior in a given situation. Structural engineers, for example, are expected to exercise extraordinary prudence and care by designing structures that are safe for all users; writers, too, are expected to properly cite all previously published material (i.e., avoid plagiarism) when crafting original work (Schein, 1990). Safety and honesty in exposition, as such, are norms that are deeply embedded in the functions of engineers and writers, as well as the organizations that employ them. These are pervasive aspects of an organization's culture that are so obvious that they rarely need to be explicitly stated. Safety and honesty are just two examples of underlying assumptions that exert powerful influences on the behaviors and expectations of an organization's members.

In sum, culture is social knowledge that is common and shared among members of an organization. Culture can be revealed in various ways ranging from explicit, observable artifacts (e.g., corporate slogans) to implicit assumptions about how employees should interact and the standards brought to bear in regular work. Nearly all organizations—business, social, or philanthropic—develop a system of controls that address the importance of the individual in the organization. This system typically specifies the behaviors and achievements used to determine rewards and promotion, the nature of interpersonal relations among members, the styles of leadership and ways in which power is managed, orientations towards customers, vendors, and other stakeholders, and how to deal with conflict, crisis, and change. Organizations facilitate the development of culture by establishing the rules, norms, and values that shape and reinforce attitudes and behaviors to align with an organization's mission.

Organizational Culture versus Organizational Climate

Most organizations, just like most individuals, have enduring and stable characteristics that predict behaviors distinguishing them from other organizations. As culture tends to be stable over time, it is distinct from organizational climate, which is usually more fluid and indicative of what organizational members are experiencing in their immediate work settings (James and Jones, 1974; James, Joyce, and Slocum, 1988; Schneider, 2000). These descriptions include employees' perceptions of policies, practices, procedures, and routines (e.g., Jones and James, 1979; Schneider, 1990). Thus, the concept of climate focuses on the link between the situation and employees' perceptions, feelings, and behaviors. In other words, Schneider, Bowen, Ehrhart, and Holcombe (2000, p. 21) note that climate is "a gestalt that is based on patterns of experiences and behaviors that people perceive in the situation." In contrast to culture, climate is temporal, subjective, and subject to change (Dennison, 1996).

Culture, on the other hand, is stable and has strong roots in the organization's history and founding (Rowlinson and Proctor, 1999). Climate is also more immediate than culture (Ostroff et al., 2003). Upon entering the organization, individuals get a sense of its climate by observing visible features such as the physical appearance of buildings, the decorations in the work environment, and the dispositions of employees. In contrast, an organization's culture, though informed by symbols and reinforced by rituals, stories, and ceremonies, is usually not as easily observable. As Ostroff et al. note, culture tends to influence an organization's structure, practices, policies, and routines, and, therefore provides the context for climate perceptions. Thus, climate is a by-product of culture.

Although the distinction between culture and climate might, at first glance, seem semantic, the implications for merging firms could be important. Managers involved in the due diligence process, for example, might easily recognize observable attributes of a merging partner (e.g., artwork, architecture, building locations, and spaces) and interpret these physical symbols as an indication of the organization's underlying culture. The modern furniture of an organization in a large, open, and welcoming space might lead casual observers to assert that the policies and procedures of the organization are flexible, that they encourage diversity and innovation, and that employees are empowered to be creative in their work. The same organization's underlying values, however, including the systems for rewards, incentives, and controls, might in fact be very rigid, reflective of an enduring management style that fosters a specific process for making organizational decisions. Although the easily observable climate would suggest flexibility and innovation, the enduring and influential cultural conditions embedded in policy might in fact reflect completely different values. As such, managers in the due diligence process should be conscientious in distinguishing between culture and climate.

Maintaining Organizational Culture

Senior managers in merging firms often expect that a "new" culture will form reflecting some combination of those cultures that existed in the independent firms. Given the challenge in the development, maintenance, and modification of culture, knowing how culture is typically fostered and maintained by organizations, as well as how culture components can be altered, is important.

Over the course of many years, organizations maintain their existing cultures through four related processes: attraction, selection, socialization, and attrition. The attraction-selection-attrition framework is a common way to understand and explain why people move in and out of organizations. In general, potential employees will be attracted to organizations whose cultures reveal values that are similar to their own. Similarly, organizations are likely to select employees who naturally fit with the organization's personality and represent a good "fit" between new hires and existing employees. Finally, those employees whose personalities, values, and work style preferences are not aligned with those of the organization are likely to be less engaged, happy, or committed to work and more likely to seek employment elsewhere.

Organizations often attempt to socialize new hires to shape the way these employees come to know the policies, norms, values, and expectations embedded in the existing culture. According to Colquitt et al. (2008, p. 569), "Socialization is the process by which employees learn the social knowledge that enables them to understand and adapt to the organization's culture." By carefully introducing essential aspects of culture to new members, organizations attempt to reinforce the core values and expectations for work. Some common methods in the socialization process offer new employees a realistic job preview, an orientation program, role models in the organization, and several specific requirements that must be met before one becomes part of the group.

Outcomes of Organizational Culture

Given the two primary functions of organizational culture (internal integration and external adaptation), firms emphasizing values related to both external adaptation and internal integration could possibly enjoy positive employee and organizational outcomes (Tsui et al., 2006). In terms of employee attitudes and behaviors, developing strong identification with the organization through internal integration may provoke high levels of commitment among the employees, which in turn may encourage greater individual productivity and improved firm performance. O'Reilly and Chatman (1986) support this idea, arguing that organizational culture can influence firm performance by positively affecting the commitment of employees. Additionally, Sheridan (1992) finds that organizational cultures, characterized as "people-oriented" and "supportive of families," are associated with positive employee attitudes such as job satisfaction and organizational commitment.

In addition to positively influencing employee-level outcomes, some view culture as a primary driver of organizational effectiveness and performance (e.g., Deal and Kennedy, 1982; Peters and Waterman, 1982) and sustained competitive advantage (e.g., Barney, 1986). For example, organizations with corporate cultures that emphasize flexibility perform better than those without that cultural orientation (e.g., Gordon and DiTomaso, 1992). Furthermore, Barney contends that organizational culture can provide a firm with a sustainable competitive advantage by generating valuable, intangible resources (e.g., reputation, experience, and tacit knowledge) that competitors cannot imitate.

Although research shows that culture is associated with employee-level and organizational-level outcomes, much remains unknown as to the impact of culture on organizations. In the last two decades, four summary reviews of literature have examined the relationship between culture and organizational effectiveness (i.e., performance) (Seihl and Martin, 1990; Lim, 1995; Wilderom, Glunk, and Maslowski, 2000; Ostroff et al., 2003). All four reviews reach similar conclusions: (1) There is a lack of testable theory that links culture to employee behavior; (2) the methods commonly used to measure both culture and performance are problematic; (3) the empirical evidence linking culture and firm performance is inconsistent; and (4) the literature lacks sound longitudinal research depicting the formation and effect of culture over time. Thus, while the impact of culture on organizations is undeniable, additional theoretical and empirical research is needed to fully understand its effects.

Nevertheless, while the summary of cultural effects on organization-level performance in the academic literature is still evolving, direct evidence about numerous high profile cases yields a strikingly similar pattern. The effects of cultural compatibility on the success of a merger or acquisition are on par with measures of financial, economic, or strategic compatibility (Cartwright and Cooper, 1993; The Conference Board, 2001). Most mergers fail to meet expectations for financial success. A persistent explanation for this observation is the failure of senior managers to adequately integrate the cultures of two otherwise distinct firms.

ASSESSING ORGANIZATIONAL CULTURE

Organizational culture is one factor that provides a strategic competitive advantage for firms (Barney, 1986), but validly assessing organizational culture is a daunting task. Attempts to objectively quantify characteristics of culture have been described as "controversial" (Rousseau, 1990) and unhelpful when facilitating actual change (Carleton, 1997). Although survey measures capture an empirically sound assessment of member judgments of organizational culture, the measures and processes for doing so are not without fault. While some trusted and well-established models estimate the financial health and operational efficiency of a potential acquisition partner, similar models for estimating culture are often vague and applied without consistency (Cartwright and Cooper, 1993). Indeed, the inability to objectively capture a number of critical aspects of culture may account for the confusion that persists in the management sciences and may also justify using more tangible measures of organizational fit during a merger (e.g., financial and market metrics), rather than some subjective assessment of an intangible phenomenon. As Cartwright and Cooper note, the due diligence process that is so treasured during partnership evaluations focuses almost exclusively on financial matters. Despite the fact that cultural issues are equal to financial issues when making a merger or acquisition succeed (The Conference Board, 2001), most senior managers discount the value of gathering cultural due diligence.

The process of measuring culture in the academic literature provides worthy guidance for practicing executives who are considering a merger, acquisition, or extended partnership. In particular, the process by which culture is typically measured can serve as a platform for assessments of the nature, complexity, and stability of a merging partner's organization culture, thus providing valuable information beyond the "hard" metrics associated with a firm's financial efficiency and health. Although skeptics dismiss the validity and utility of measuring an organization's culture (Trice and Beyer, 1993; Ashkanasy, Broadfoot, and Falkus, 2000; Schein, 2000), worthwhile information can be gained in the process.

A common method to assess organizational culture is to administer empirical surveys and then conduct quantitative analyses that capture members' perceptions of cultural trends (e.g., Buenger, Daft, Conlon, and Austin, 1996; Hofstede, 1998; Christensen and Gordon, 1999; Cooke and Szumal, 2000). These assessments often integrate viewpoints from a broad sample of the organization's population and indicate the extent to which members regard a diverse set of characteristics (e.g., innovation, risk-taking, team orientation, and attention to detail) as representative of their organization's culture. These assessments also serve as a means to distinguish one organization's culture from another and indicate a culture's strength by estimating the correspondence among an organization's members, avoiding the common situation in which cultural artifacts are considered exclusively in private meetings among executive leaders in the merging firms.

Although numerous methods are available to characterize culture, the management literature most often uses four surveys, each of which has been drawn from empirically validated models: (1) the Organizational Culture Inventory (OCI) (Cooke and Lafferty, 1987); (2) the Competing Values Framework (CVF) (Quinn and Rohrbaugh, 1983); (3) the Organizational Culture Profile (OCP) (O'Reilly, Chatman, and Caldwell, 1991); and (4) the work practices survey (Hofstede, Neuijen, Ohayv, and Sanders, 1990). Organization research commonly uses these surveys when attempting to capture the underlying values that drive employee behavior, and perhaps more importantly, the extent to which meaning about work is shared among diverse employees across otherwise distinct work units.

MULTIPLE CULTURES WITHIN THE SAME FIRM

To this point, this introduction of culture suggests that each organization maintains a singular, dominant culture that unifies members around shared values and expectations. According to this framework, a strong and distinct culture reflective of an organization's core values would influence the attitudes and behaviors of members throughout the firm. However, in many complex organizations with multiple functions, diverse product lines, dispersed locations, and numerous levels of formal hierarchy, several different subcultures are likely to exist (Greenberg, 2010). These subcultures may emerge within functional units or locations, such that the expectations and demands for employees in the sales department are different from those in accounting (as the expectations for employees in New York City might differ from those in Topeka, Kansas). Accounting professionals, for example, may be expected to work from a central office while adhering to strict and standard hours for service, whereas those same demands may not be enforced for sales professionals who are expected to work remotely while visiting customers. As such, there are likely multiple types of cultures that separate distinct organizations, as well as several different cultures that exist within the same organization.

One way to capture these differences is offered by an approach called the "competing values framework" (CVF) (Cameron and Quinn, 1999), which suggests that most cultures can be characterized by the extent to which procedures and norms differ along two complementary value sets: (1) the extent to which an organization values innovation, flexibility, and personal autonomy as opposed to stability, control, standards, and order; and (2) the relative focus that employees and managers pay to internal issues versus the external environment (Greenberg, 2010). Firms that rely on stable procedures, formal rules, and strict controls, while at the same time measuring success by how efficiently resources are deployed (an internal focus), are characterized by the CVF as "hierarchical." This example is evident in high-production manufacturing plants that focus on efficiency while closely monitoring standards and quality. Alternatively, "adhocracy" organizations emphasize innovation, flexibility, and autonomy in the way that jobs are crafted and decisions are made, while at the same time measuring success based on market share or new product introductions (an external focus). The implications of these differences are relevant in terms of how culture is developed, maintained, and evolves in the case of a merger or acquisition.

CULTURAL DUE DILIGENCE

This section offers recommendations for assessing organizational culture, recognizing that culture is generally a pervasive and important determinant of employee behavior and the most common reason otherwise attractive mergers fail to meet even modest expectations for sustainable financial performance (Cartwright and Cooper, 1993). The utility of snapshot assessments that are provided by simplistic analyses of culture may be minimal for managers seeking to estimate impact and induce change. Indeed, researchers have been criticized for using narrow surveys to measure culture (Trice and Beyer, 1993; Ashkanasy et al., 2000; Schein, 2000). However, the recommendations are organized around four considerations that go beyond first order (mean) snapshot assessments of an organization's culture. In particular, for managers attempting to estimate the impact of an organization's culture on employee decision making and behavioral patterns, cultural due diligence should consider the following: (1) a multidimensional view of organizational culture; (2) the stability of culture over time; (3) the strength of the culture in terms of member agreement; and (4) the tangible organizational features that make culture salient.

Measure Multiple Dimensions of Organizational Culture

The management literature offers several multidimensional characterizations of organizational culture of which the most common and extensively examined are presented here. While a single best culture is unlikely for the success of a merger or an individual company's performance, differences in the nature of an organization's culture foster variability in decisions among members over time (Cartwright and Cooper, 1993). As Robbins and Judge (2010, p. 231) note, culture refers to a "system of shared meaning held by members." One way to define this system involves highlighting seven primary aspects that, in the aggregate, define an organization's culture (O'Reilly et al., 1991). Appraising a potential partner on these seven characteristics provides a summary of an organization's cultural profile.

Robbins and Judge (2010) summarize the seven primary cultural characteristics and their respective definitions as follows:

1. *Innovation and risk taking*: The degree to which employees are encouraged to be innovative and take risks.
2. *Attention to detail*: The degree to which employees are expected to exhibit precision, analysis, and attention to detail.
3. *Outcome orientation*: The degree to which management focuses on results or outcomes, rather than on the techniques and processes used to achieve these outcomes.
4. *People orientation*: The degree to which management decisions take into consideration the effect of outcomes on people within the organization.
5. *Team orientation*: The degree to which work activities are organized around teams, rather than individuals.
6. *Aggressiveness*: The degree to which people are aggressive and competitive, rather than easygoing.
7. *Stability*: The degree to which organizational activities emphasize maintaining the status quo in contrast to growth.

These categories reflect O'Reilly et al.'s (1991) Organizational Culture Profile. The authors initially constructed the profile by asking survey respondents to indicate the extent to which these particular values are revealed in the form of shared expectations about what is important in the organization. They also asked respondents to indicate whether their organizations deemed these behaviors and attitudes appropriate and to sort the values most characteristic of the organization's culture from those least characteristic.

Companies interested in assessing culture along these dimensions can have employees across multiple levels indicate the extent to which this set of diverse practices characterizes the nature of their organizations. Organizations that identify themselves as team oriented, for example, are likely to have deeply held norms and expectations for how employees cooperate, defer individual recognition to the group, distribute resources in ways that are best for team functioning, set goals that are team/group oriented, and reward collective effort rather than individual success. Further, cultures that are strong in a team orientation are likely to marginalize those members who act in ways that conflict with group functioning. An employee who fails to share information that is needed for team success may be marginalized as one who does not adhere to "the way things are done" in a particular organization (Carleton, 1997). A firm merging with one that has a strong team orientation would be wise to structure work assignments, design incentive systems, and utilize communication patterns that foster cooperation rather than competition.

Estimate the Stability of Culture over Time

At the heart of most common considerations of culture is the notion that the values and norms that characterize an organization are persistent over time, often steeped in the organization's founding and history, or influenced by the disposition and values of the organization's chief executive officer (CEO) (Berson, Oreg, and Dvir, 2008). Batelle (2005) and others have highlighted the culture at Google, for example, for its strength and its encouragement of innovation and creativity. This culture is service-oriented with low formalization and low tolerance for extended meetings. Google's founders, Sergey Brin and Larry Page, fostered this culture and the policies that it has produced (e.g., preferring casual dress over the formality of business suits). Culture is so important at Google that its founders designated the company's director of human resources as "Chief Culture Officer" in 2006, responding to widespread concern that the company's culture would be compromised after an initial public offering on the New York Stock Exchange. The purpose of creating this position was to develop and maintain the culture and employee engagement at Google in ways that remain true to the core values on which the company was founded.

To estimate the stability of an organization's culture, managers gathering due diligence should assess culture at multiple stages throughout the information gathering process. Each assessment should be separated by some meaningful amount of time such as three months. By considering the correspondence of assessments taken across several time intervals, managers might be able to determine the extent to which an organization's culture endures over time. If employee descriptions of the outcome-oriented nature of an organization's culture as measured in January are highly correlated with similar assessments measured in June, managers can take comfort in the stability of that aspect of culture. Such estimates would inform managers of the commitment level of their employees to values that shape day-to-day behavior. On the one hand, strong organizational cultures are by their very nature not only stable and enduring but also strongly influenced by deeply held traditions. On the other hand, employees who do not identify a consistent set of core values that characterizes their organizations are potentially open to changes associated with an extended partnership in any form. If an organization's employees do not reveal consistency in their descriptions of cultural norms and expectations, potential partners may be less concerned with how existing cultural traditions affect the inevitable uncertainty associated with a merger or acquisition.

Consider the Strength of the Culture

Related to the above discussion of a culture's stability over time is the idea of cultural strength. Although most organizations strive for a culture that fosters consensus regarding the attitudinal and behavioral norms for its members (i.e., a strong culture), most organizations operate at varying levels of strength. A strong culture exists when employees have high levels of agreement about the way things are supposed to happen within an organization and when their behaviors are in line with expectations about norms and values (O'Reilly, 1989). In organizations that maintain strong cultures, there is clarity among members regarding the organization's mission and operating philosophy, traditions are regularly celebrated, and members have a strong sense of personal identity with the organization. As such, strong organizational cultures typically take a very long time to develop and are reinforced during an intense socialization process for new members.

By contrast, weak cultures exist when employees disagree (or are unaware) about organizational norms, an organization's core values, essential elements of mission and strategy, and behavioral expectations. Rarely are new employees screened for their fit with existing values, as little time is spent discussing core values and beliefs. In these organizations, culture has little effect on how employees come to identify with the organization or how expectations are formed for unwritten rules for behavior.

A strong culture is often considered beneficial because it serves to unite and direct employees by differentiating them from those external to the organization, allowing employees to identify with the organization, facilitating desired behaviors and attitudes among employees, and creating stability within the organization (Colquitt et al., 2008). For these reasons, many organizations work to create and maintain strong cultures. Regardless of these positive outcomes, however, research suggests that strong cultures are not always "good" (O'Reilly, 1989). That is, strong cultures also have a dark side. Strong cultures tend to guide and influence employees' attitudes and behaviors, but that does not necessarily mean the culture is aligned with desired outcomes. Also, given that strong cultures are often very resistant to change, a high level of cultural strength usually creates an inability to adapt to the environment in which the organization operates and can make merging with or acquiring another organization more difficult.

Further, strong cultures tend to compromise the success of partnerships, mergers, or acquisitions. Merging two companies with distinct cultures can be extremely difficult. Indeed, some view cultural compatibility as critical to the success of a merger as economic, financial, market, or strategic compatibility (The Conference Board, 2001). Ideally, mergers facilitate the development of a new organizational culture that represents the best characteristics of each of the merging firms. However, despite careful and extensive efforts and the best intentions of senior managers who are aware of culture's impact, new cultures do not usually emerge. In fact, most merger stories involving companies with very different cultures, such as AOL–Time Warner, Exxon–Mobil, and HP–Compaq, do not conclude happily (Colquitt et al., 2008).

An example of the difficulties associated with merging two cultures occurred when eBay, the Internet company that manages eBay.com (an online auction and shopping website), purchased PayPal, the e-commerce business that facilitates payments and money transfers to be made over the Internet. The acquisition was a logical step for eBay because of the intertwined nature of the companies' operations. The two companies appeared to enjoy strategic compatibility and had a symbiotic relationship in which both seemed to need each other to survive. During the late 1990s and early 2000s, PayPal became the de facto bank for almost all

transactions between parties buying and selling items on eBay. In 2002, eBay purchased PayPal for $1.5 billion. Although the companies' core products were com-
plementary and their technologies matched for seamless integration, the merger
of the two companies did not fare well. In fact, shortly after the two companies
began operating as one, many PayPal employees decided to quit the new entity.
Others departed shortly thereafter. Thus, despite good intentions and a reasonable
fit, eBay lost much of PayPal's key, talented employee base, resulting in a merger
that fell far short of its expectations (O'Brien, 2007).

   Although the merger of these two established companies seemed like a perfect
fit, it was doomed from the start because of the clash between their respective
organizational cultures. Throughout its history, PayPal hired extremely talented,
entrepreneurial, math-savvy individuals but would absolutely not hire "MBAs,
consultants, frat boys, or . . . jocks" (O'Brien, 2007, p. 98). PayPal was the epitome
of an organization that employed an antiestablishment mentality without strict
or rigid hierarchies (Colquitt et al., 2008). In contrast, eBay primarily employed
the types of people PayPal was adamant about not hiring. For example, Meg
Whitman, eBay's CEO at the time of the merger, had an MBA from Harvard
Business School, worked at prestigious marketing organizations including Disney
and Procter & Gamble, and was a management consultant for Bain, one of the
world's leading business and strategy consulting firms. Thus, Whitman was the
epitome of everything PayPal employees were not. Although eBay appeared to
be the traditional dotcom organization, the company was (and is) much more
traditional and mechanistic than most dotcom companies, with strict chains of
command and a persistent focus on common metrics for profitability and efficiency
(Brown, 2002).

   Overall, the two companies seemed similar from a business standpoint, but
their cultures were polar opposites, especially in terms of attracting, selecting, and
rewarding employees. Further, not only were the two cultures extremely different,
but they were also very strong in their own right, with each company believing
strongly in its own way of conducting business. Thus, the clash of these two cultures
created major issues, the most important being the postmerger mass exodus of most
of the talented PayPal employees.

   Unfortunately, M&As rarely result in the strong cultures that senior managers
hope will appear after decisions are made to merge. Instead, most merging organizations operate under a differentiated culture, which exists when a company has
separate subcultures that unite smaller subsets of the organization's employees
(Colquitt et al., 2008). If the values of the subcultures do not match, the subcultures
can often work in contrast to one another, as was the case with the eBay–PayPal
merger. These counter-subcultures can split the organization, resulting in a differentiated culture that reveals itself in varied norms, expectations, and operational
values sprinkled throughout a single firm. In the best possible situation, a differentiated culture lasts for only a short period of time. Eventually, a united company
takes on a culture that represents a healthy combination of the independent organizations. However, this rarely happens. Thus, differentiated cultures are usually one
of the reasons M&As fail to meet expectations for longevity or economic success.
As Colquitt et al. note, when deciding to merge, senior managers and executives
must consider the match and, more importantly, the strength of the existing companies' organizational culture. Taking these factors into account may help limit the

major issues that arise when attempting to integrate two strong cultures. These issues are the persistent resistance to change, the inability to adapt to the environment, and the lack of diversity in terms of work styles, thought patterns, and work preferences.

Identify Tangible Indicators of Culture

An organization's culture can be revealed in many ways. Too often during the due diligence process, attempts to assess culture are limited to brief discussions among upper-level managers (Cartwright and Cooper, 1993). These assessments are not only made in isolation but also may be vastly disconnected from the norms and standards that direct the interactions among an organization's key stakeholders such as employees, vendors, customers, and investors. Executive leaders in a potential partnering firm may offer vivid descriptions of an organization's traditions and espoused values, but these leaders may suffer from grandiose illusions of culture that conflict with what is actually happening during customer contact.

In nearly every organization, tangible features serve as expressions of culture and its underlying value set. Carefully examining these features can provide valuable insights into the nature and concentration of the norms that guide employee behavior (Miller, 2000). One important element on which to focus when evaluating a partner's culture is the employee performance appraisal system, including the specific criteria used to determine incentives, rewards, and promotions. Humans tend to gravitate towards those behaviors that are rewarded while drifting away from those that are not (Kerr, 1995). Thus, performance appraisal systems that include incentives for individual performance are likely to encourage competitive behavior among employees, who will often then limit cooperation with other organizational members. Further, if a performance appraisal system punishes failure to meet specific objectives or to reduce waste in the use of resources, a conservative culture focused on careful compliance with existing policy is likely to form such that employees minimize risk and avoid difficult and challenging assignments. In his important review of organizational culture in mergers, Miller suggests that additional indicators include operational long-range and short-range budgeting policies, training and development programs, informal organizational structures, and company publications.

In sum, beyond casual conversations with top executives, managers in the due diligence process would be wise to carefully examine aspects of the work environment that are visible indicators of the organization's values. Companies offering support for training and development outside of an employee's area of functional responsibility are likely to have a culture that values diversity, flexibility, and innovation. Alternatively, companies operating with strict job descriptions and clear guidelines regarding authority and responsibility are likely to value compliance and consistency while discouraging autonomous decision making. These and other tangible work characteristics reveal the policies that encourage and control employee behavior and serve as critical drivers in the success of a merger or acquisition.

Beyond the tangible indicators listed above, one can identify the source and strength of an organization's culture by considering the nature and composition of a firm's business. The precipitous decline and fall of Arthur

Andersen as an international accounting powerhouse serves as an example. Like many other prominent founders of successful corporations, Arthur Andersen, himself, built a strong culture that was marked by strict ethical standards for business practice and employee conduct. As Treviño and Brown (2004, p. 74) note, Andersen led the way in the establishment of universal accounting principles such that, "No matter where they were in the world, if customers were dealing with Andersen employees, they knew that they could count on the same high-quality work and the same integrity." Andersen's reputation for direct honesty was the foundation of the company's long-term growth and success.

For most of the firm's existence, Arthur Andersen's primary business was in accounting and auditing service, ensuring that their clients kept records accurately, paid taxes properly, and communicated financial information with clarity and integrity. To be successful over the long term in accounting and auditing, a firm must be trustworthy, direct, transparent, and honest in all business dealings. The public in general and financial markets in particular have come to depend on the integrity of financial reports issued by publicly traded companies. Accounting firms such as Arthur Andersen are entrusted with the responsibility for ensuring that clients adhere to the highest levels of accuracy and honesty when managing resources. The employees who thrive in such a firm tend to be oriented to serve in this manner, and for many years, the culture within Andersen was one that reflected the public's trust. The focus of managers as well as the firm's training, selection, and reward programs reflected the essential elements of success in an accounting firm—patience, accuracy, integrity, and steady adherence to public standards.

By the mid-1990s, however, the composition of Arthur Andersen's business portfolio began to shift (Treviño and Brown, 2004) with substantially higher revenues being generated by the management consulting arm of the business (originally "Andersen Consulting" but changed to "Accenture" in 2001). Whereas the company had long been committed to ethical principles and an obligation to the public good, management at the firm began to focus more extensively on revenue generation, attracted by high-margin management consulting contracts. Indeed, the consulting and auditing businesses are quite different, each with its own expectations for how employees should interact with clients and each with its own indicators of success. Whereas the best accountants serve clients through their willingness to be direct and critical of a client's operations, the best consultants simply try to keep their clients happy in the hopes of earning additional business. A troublesome inconsistency began to emerge within the firm driven by the demands and expectations of two otherwise distinct businesses. Similar examples can be found in financial services firms that simultaneously serve as financial analysts for a company and underwriters of the same company's debt and/or equity.

Eventually, employees began to receive mixed signals about the expected norms of behavior while the model for service in consulting became the expectation for service in the accounting and auditing business (Treviño and Brown, 2004). This is one explanation for Andersen's central role in the Enron accounting scandal, leading Cornford (2004, p. 9) to conclude, "Andersen did not fulfill its professional responsibilities in connection with its audits of Enron's financial statements, or its obligation to bring to the attention of Enron's Board concerns about Enron's internal contracts over the related-party transactions." According to many observers, Andersen's decline was due in large part to the emergence of an organizational culture that was vastly inconsistent with its tradition and with the essential fundamentals for success in its core business, namely accounting and auditing.

This is not to suggest that management consulting firms do not adhere to ethical principles or to imply that consulting is incompatible with honesty, integrity, transparency, or the public good. Instead, the Arthur Andersen example reveals how the nature of a firm's business and the demands on employees for success in a particular market are likely to shape the dominant culture that emerges within a firm. In Andersen's case, the company found itself in two very different markets—one steeped in the conservative traditions and standards associated with accounting and auditing service and another engaged in a consulting business that demanded flexibility and rewarded risk-taking behavior that was attractive to new clients. The consequences for Andersen for ignoring this issue were fatal.

INTEGRATING DIVERSE CULTURES

Once a valid assessment of cultures has been made, the next steps are to plan for a successful integration of cultures of the partnering firms. Beyond the aforementioned challenges associated with assessing and estimating culture's impact, there are additional considerations for the time immediately after the merger processes begin. Walker (1998) as well as Schraeder and Self (2003) provide suggestions for addressing task, political, strategic, and personal challenges. These authors offer succinct and powerful guidelines for integrating distinct cultures.

Walker (1998), for example, recommends that senior managers (1) celebrate small and incremental victories during the integration process and (2) acknowledge value in past practices. Doing so provides a foundation for the development of trust among the merging partners. Further, Walker recommends that senior managers (3) involve employees in managing the integration process; (4) identify ingrained behaviors that might become obstacles; (5) communicate details about the integration process; and (6) provide a clear rationale for the merger. Similarly, Schraeder and Self (2003, p. 522) offer a checklist of strategies that are likely to enhance M&A success: "(1) assess cultural compatibility; (2) anticipate employee reactions; (3) plan for possible task challenges; (4) develop a flexible and comprehensive integration plan; (5) share information and encourage communication; (6) encourage employee participation and involvement; (7) enhance commitment by establishing relationships and trust; (8) manage the transition through training, support, and socialization; and (9) be sensitive to individual and timing considerations."

SUMMARY AND CONCLUSIONS

Although highly conscientious managers carefully approach M&As with a comprehensive review of the financial, economic, and strategic analyses, most mergers fail to meet expectations for success. The due diligence process typically includes detailed analyses of economic conditions, strategic fit, financial statements and projections, and other "hard" data points, while ignoring or underestimating the "soft" issues related to culture, norms, and the human instinct. Whereas most merger situations are fraught with complexity, uncertainty, and change, human nature prefers simplicity, structure, and stability. Thus, despite the best intentions, most mergers fail. These failures are attributed to the difficulties in integrating organizations that adhere to diverse yet powerful cultural traditions. Researchers, practitioners, and investors are each becoming increasingly sensitive to cultural implications with regard to M&As.

In this chapter, an overview of the organization culture concept was presented, along with a brief summary of the academic research that has attempted to describe the manner in which culture shapes employee behavior. The chapter also described the most common ways of measuring culture along with suggestions for how managers involved in the due diligence process can more accurately estimate the nature, concentration, and impact of culture.

DISCUSSION QUESTIONS

1. How do organizations maintain their cultures? How do they change them?
2. What are some ways in which an organization reveals its culture?
3. How does fitting within an organization's culture affect job performance and organizational commitment?
4. What steps can organizations take to make sure that newcomers will fit in with their culture?
5. When two companies with distinct cultures merge, how can the integration process offer the greatest chance for success?

REFERENCES

Ashkanasy, Neal M., Lyndelle E. Broadfoot, and Sarah A. Falkus. 2000. "Questionnaire Measures of Organizational Culture." In Neal M. Ashkanasy, Celeste P. M. Wilderom, and Mark F. Peterson, eds. *Handbook of Organizational Culture and Climate*, 131–146. Thousand Oaks, CA: Sage.

Barney, Jay B. 1986. "Organizational Culture: Can It Be a Source of Sustained Competitive Advantage?" *Academy of Management Review* 11:3, 656–665.

Battelle, John. 2005. *The Search: How Google and Its Rivals Rewrote the Rules of Business and Transformed Our Culture*. New York: Penguin.

Berson, Yair, Shaul Oreg, and Taly Dvir. 2008. "CEO Values, Organizational Culture and Firm Outcomes." *Journal of Organizational Behavior* 29:5, 615–633.

Brown, Eryn. 2002. "How Can a Dot-Com Be This Hot?" *Fortune*, January 21, 78–83.

Buenger, Victoria, Richard L. Daft, Edward J. Conlon, and Jeffrey Austin. 1996. "Competing Values in Organizations: Contextual Influences and Structural Consequences." *Organizational Science* 7:5, 557–576.

Cameron, Kim S., and Robert E. Quinn. 1999. *Diagnosing and Changing Organizational Culture Based on the Competing Values Framework* Upper Saddle River, NJ: Prentice Hall.

Carleton, J. Robert. 1997. "Cultural Due Diligence." *Training*, 34:11, 67–75.

Cartwright, Susan, and Cary L. Cooper. 1993. "The Role of Culture Compatibility in Successful Organizational Marriage." *Academy of Management Executive* 7:2, 57–70.

Christensen, Edward W., and George G. Gordon. 1999. "An Exploration of Industry, Culture, and Revenue Growth." *Organizational Studies* 20:3, 185–198.

Colquitt, Jason. A., Jeffrey A. LePine, and Michael J. Wesson. 2008. *Organizational Behavior: Improving Performance and Commitment in the Workplace*. New York: McGraw-Hill Irwin.

Cooke, Robert A., and J. Clayton Lafferty. 1987. *Organizational Culture Inventory*. Plymouth, MI: Human Synergistics.

Cooke, Robert A., and Janet L. Szumal. 2000. "Using the Organizational Culture Inventory to Understand the Operating Cultures of Organizations." In Neal M. Ashkanasy, Celeste P. M. Wilderom, and Mark F. Peterson, eds. *Handbook of Organizational Culture and Climate* 147–162. Thousand Oaks, CA: Sage.

Cornford, Andrew. 2004. *Internationally Agreed Principles for Corporate Governance and the Enron Case*, UNCTAD, G-24 Discussion Paper Series No. 30, New York.

Deal, Terrence E., and Allan A. Kennedy. 1982. *Corporate Cultures: The Rites and Rituals of Corporate Life*. Reading, MA: Addison-Wesley.

Denison, Daniel R. 1996. "What Is the Difference Between Organizational Culture and Climate? A Native's Point of View on a Decade of Paradigm Wars." *Academy of Management Review* 21:3, 619–654.

Gordon, George, and Nancy DiTomaso. 1992. "Predicting Corporate Performance from Organizational Culture." *Journal of Management Studies* 29:6, 783–798.

Greenberg, Jerald. 2010. *Managing Behavior in Organizations*. Upper Saddle River, NJ: Prentice Hall.

Hatch, Mary Jo. 1993. "The Dynamics of Organizational Culture." *Academy of Management Review* 18:4, 657–693.

Hofstede, Geert. 1998. "Attitudes, Values and Organizational Culture: Disentangling the Concepts." *Organizational Studies* 19:3, 477–492.

Hofstede, Geert, Bram Neuijen, Denise D. Ohayv, and Geert Sanders. 1990. "Measuring Organizational Cultures: A Qualitative and Quantitative Study across Twenty Cases." *Administrative Science Quarterly* 35:2, 286–316.

James, Lawrence R., and Allan P. Jones. 1974. "Organizational Climate: A Review of Theory and Research." *Psychological Bulletin* 81:12, 1096–1112.

James, Lawrence R., William F. Joyce, and John W. Slocum, Jr. 1988. "Comment: Organizations Do Not Cognize." *Academy of Management Review* 13:1, 129–132.

Jones, Allan P., and Lawrence R. James. 1979. "Psychological Climate: Dimensions and Relationships of Individual and Aggregated Work Environment Perceptions." *Organizational Behavior and Human Performance* 23:2, 201–250.

Kerr, Steven. 1995. "On the Folly of Rewarding A, While Hoping for B." *Academy of Management Executive* 9:1, 7–14.

Latham, Gary P. 2007. *Work Motivation: History, Theory, Research and Practice*. Thousand Oaks, CA: Sage.

Lim, Bernard. 1995. "Examining the Organizational Culture and Organizational Performance Link." *Leadership and Organization Development Journal* 10:5, 271–299.

Miller, Roger. 2000. "How Culture Affects Mergers and Acquisitions." *Industrial Management* 42:5, 22–26.

O'Brien, Jeffrey. M. 2007. "The PayPal Mafia." *Fortune*. November 14, 96–106.

O'Reilly III, Charles. A. 1989. "Corporations, Culture, and Commitment: Motivation and Social Control in Organizations. *California Management Review* 31:4, 9–25.

O'Reilly III, Charles A., and Jennifer A. Chatman. 1986. "Organizational Commitment and Psychological Attachment: The Effects of Compliance, Identification, and Internalization on Prosocial Behavior." *Journal of Applied Psychology* 71:3, 492–499.

O'Reilly III, Charles A., Jennifer A. Chatman, and David F. Caldwell. 1991. "People and Organizational Culture: A Profile Comparison Approach to Assessing Person-Organization Fit." *Academy of Management Journal* 34:3, 487–516.

Ostroff, Cheri, Angelo J. Kinicki, and Melinda M. Tamkins. 2003. "Organizational Culture and Climate." In Walter C. Borman, Daniel R. Ilgen, and Richard J. Klimoski, eds. *Handbook of Psychology: Industrial and Organizational Psychology* 12, 565–593. Hoboken, NJ: John Wiley & Sons, Inc.

Peters, Tom J., and Robert Waterman. 1982. *In Search of Excellence*. New York: Harper and Row.

Quinn, Robert E., and John Rohrbaugh. 1983. "A Spatial Model of Effectiveness Criteria: Toward a Competing Values Approach to Organizational Analysis." *Management Science* 29:3, 363–377.

Robbins, Stephen R., and Timothy A. Judge. 2010. *Essentials of Organizational Behavior.* Upper Saddle River, NJ: Pearson Education.

Rousseau, Denise. 1990. "Assessing Organizational Culture: The Case for Multiple Methods." In Benjamin Schneider, (ed.), *Organizational Climate and Culture*, 153–192. San Francisco: Jossey-Bass.

Rowlinson, Michael, and Stephen Procter. 1999. "Organizational Culture and Business History." *Organizational Studies* 20:3, 369–396.

Schein, Edgar H. 1990. "Organizational Culture." *American Psychologist* 45:2, 109–119.

Schein, Edgar H. 1992. *Organizational Culture and Leadership: A Dynamic View*. San Francisco: Jossey-Bass.

Schein, Edgar H. 2000. "Sense and Nonsense about Culture and Climate." In Neal M. Ashkanasy, Celeste P. M. Wilderom, and Mark F. Peterson, eds. *Handbook of Organizational Culture and Climate*, xxiii–xxx. Thousand Oaks, CA: Sage.

Schein, Edgar H. 2004. *Organizational Culture and Leadership*. San Francisco: Jossey-Bass.

Schneider, Benjamin. 1990. "The Climate for Service: An Application of the Climate Construct." In Benjamin Schneider, ed. *Organizational Climate and Culture*, 383–412. San Francisco: Jossey-Bass.

Schneider, Benjamin. 2000. "The Psychological Life of Organizations." In Neal M. Ashkanasy, Celeste P. M. Wilderom, and Mark F. Peterson, eds. *Handbook of Organizational Culture and Climate*, xvii–xxi. Thousand Oaks, CA: Sage.

Schneider, Benjamin, David E. Bowen, Mark G. Ehrhart, and Karen M. Holcombe. 2000. "The Climate for Service: Evolution of a Construct." In Neal M. Ashkanasy, Celeste P. M. Wilderom, and Mark F. Peterson, eds. *Handbook of Organizational Culture and Climate*, 21-36. Thousand Oaks, CA: Sage.

Schraeder, Mike, and Dennis, R. Self. 2003. "Enhancing the Success of Mergers and Acquisitions: An Organizational Perspective." *Management Decision* 41:5/6, 511–522.

Seihl, Caren, and Joanne Martin. 1990. "Organizational Culture: A Key to Financial Performance?" In Benjamin Schneider, ed. *Organizational Climate and Culture*, 241–281. San Francisco: Jossey-Bass.

Sheridan, John E. 1992. "Organizational Culture and Employee Retention." *Academy of Management Journal* 35:5, 1036–1056.

The Conference Board, Inc. 2001. *Managing Culture in Mergers and Acquisitions*. New York: Lawrence Schein.

Treviño, Linda K., and Michael E. Brown. 2004. "Managing to Be Ethical: Debunking Five Business Ethics Myths." *Academy of Management Executive* 18:2, 69–81.

Trice, Harrison M., and Janice M. Beyer. 1993. *The Cultures of Work Organizations*. Englewood Cliffs, NJ: Prentice Hall.

Tsui, Anne S., Hui Wang, and Katherine R. Xin. 2006. "Organizational Culture in China: An Analysis of Cultural Dimensions and Culture Types." *Management and Organization Review* 2:3, 345–376.

Walker, Kevin. 1998. "Meshing Cultures in a Consolidation." *Training and Development*, 52:5, 83–88.

Wilderom, Celeste P. M., Ursula Glunk, and Ralf Maslowski. 2000. "Organizational Culture as a Predictor of Organizational Performance." In Neal M. Ashkanasy, Celeste P. M. Wilderom, and Mark F. Peterson, eds. *Handbook of Organizational Culture and Climate*, 193–210. Thousand Oaks, CA: Sage.

ABOUT THE AUTHORS

Ronald F. Piccolo is an Associate Professor of Management and Academic Director of the Center for Leadership Development in the Crummer Graduate School of Business at Rollins College. His primary research interests include leadership, motivation, and job design. Professor Piccolo has published in the *Academy of Management Journal*, *Journal of Applied Psychology*, *Personnel Psychology*, and *Journal of Organizational Behavior*. He teaches graduate courses in leadership, policy, and organizational behavior and serves on the editorial boards for the *Academy of Management Journal* and *Organizational Behavior and Human Decision Processes*. Professor Piccolo holds a PhD in Management from the University of Florida.

Mary Bardes is an Assistant Professor of Management at Drexel University. Her primary research interests include workplace deviance and destructive leader behaviors. Professor Bardes teaches undergraduate and graduate courses in organizational behavior and leadership. She has published in the *Journal of Applied Psychology*, *Organizational Behavior and Human Decision Processes*, and the *European Journal of Work and Organizational Psychology*. She has a PhD in Business Administration with a concentration in Management from the University of Central Florida.

CHAPTER 14

Negotiation Process, Bargaining Area, and Contingent Payments

WILLIAM A. GRIMM
Visiting Professor of Practice in Entrepreneurship and Negotiation, Rollins College

INTRODUCTION

This chapter examines the negotiation process that typically takes place in connection with mergers and acquisitions (M&As). For the purposes of this chapter, the acquiring party will be identified as the buyer and the selling, or merging party, as the seller. The negotiation process is conducted by many different players such as the executive officers in charge of the deal, investment bankers, corporate counsel, and boards of directors for both the buyer and seller.

To set the context of the first hypothetical transaction, assume the buyer is a large publicly held company and the seller is a small, publicly held company. Other assumptions include the following:

- Both companies are incorporated under Delaware law with headquarters in the United States and have substantial international operations.
- Both companies are listed on the Nasdaq Global Select Market.
- Both companies are widely owned with no shareholder owning more than 20 percent of the outstanding voting shares in each of them.
- The seller has not been seeking to be acquired before being approached by the buyer.
- The seller is not financially troubled or under pressure to be acquired.
- Both the buyer and the seller must obtain shareholder approval for this transaction if the buyer issues shares of common stock as the primary consideration for the deal. Buyer's shareholder approval is not required if the buyer acquires the seller for cash.
- Neither the buyer nor the seller is under investigation by the Securities and Exchange Commission (SEC) for its accounting practices, and no lawsuits are outstanding for either company other than lawsuits in the ordinary course of business.
- The seller has a standing relationship with an investment banking firm but has not engaged this firm to represent it in connection with a potential acquisition before receiving an expression of interest from the buyer.

- The buyer has engaged an investment banking firm to seek out meaningful acquisitions and the investment banker has identified the seller as an attractive candidate.
- The buyer has made an internal decision not to engage in a hostile takeover to acquire the seller.
- The chief executive officer (CEO) and other officers of the buyer are experienced in acquisitions.
- The CEO and chief financial officer (CFO) of the seller have modest experience in acquiring small, privately held companies.
- Both companies have experienced corporate counsel.
- The size of the proposed transaction and the size of the buyer will trigger the requirement for a premerger notification with the Federal Trade Commission (FTC) in the United States and similar filings in other countries.

COMMENCEMENT OF THE PROCESS

The process usually commences with a meeting or phone call between the CEOs of the buyer and the seller. Sometimes the process begins with lower-level discussions or even by the buyer's corporate counsel contacting the seller's corporate counsel. Or, the process may start with the buyer's investment banker contacting the seller's CFO or CEO. Whichever way the process begins, both the buyer and seller are highly concerned with confidentiality. Only those who have a need to know have knowledge of these preliminary discussions and have been warned of the need for confidentiality.

If the seller has any interest in further discussing the potential acquisition, the seller usually engages its investment banker. The investment banker responds quickly with an analysis of the potential valuation of the seller and an assessment of the buyer's acquisition execution capability. Discussing the fee arrangement that is likely to be made between the seller and its investment banker is beyond the scope of this chapter. However, experienced sellers understand that investment bankers have an enormous incentive to see that a transaction takes place since a large portion of their fee is usually contingent upon a successful transaction.

After the seller engages its investment banker, the investment banker usually contacts the buyer's investment banker and further discussions take place concerning the potential parameters of an acquisition. The buyer and the seller then execute a mutual nondisclosure agreement, agreeing that the existence of the discussions, among other things, is confidential. The seller usually demands that the nondisclosure agreement contains a provision that, in consideration of disclosing confidential information to the buyer, the buyer agrees not to initiate a hostile takeover attempt for a certain period of time, such as one year.

The Buyer Has a Negotiating Advantage at This Stage

Preparation is the key to successful negotiations (Mintzberg and Quinn, 1991; Watkins, 2002). The buyer has an advantage over the seller at the beginning of the process because the buyer has had time to study the seller through the seller's SEC filings and other public documents. Often, the buyer has conducted an extensive investigation into the seller's markets and selling practices and obtained information about the seller from trade shows and former employees (who are not under a duty of confidentiality). The buyer already has prepared a negotiating strategy, probably with a team of executives acting as the seller and trying to predict how the seller will behave in the negotiating process (Brodt, 1994).

Although the CEO of the seller may be the primary decision maker in this process, the buyer needs to predict the behavior not only of the seller's CEO but also of all others who have an input into the negotiation. If enough information is known about the players on the seller's side, the buyer may be able to predict how the group will behave on behalf of the seller.

On the other hand, the seller has probably been caught off-guard or surprised by the approach of the buyer. This means the seller is probably unprepared for the negotiating process and can be unprepared for a possible transaction. This is especially true if the acquisition takes the form of exchanging the buyer's stock for the seller's stock (through a merger mechanism or direct exchange), since the seller will not have had an opportunity to thoroughly study the buyer beforehand. When the deal is a stock-for-stock deal, the seller's board will essentially be recommending that the seller's shareholders "buy" a substantial amount of stock in the buyer. Therefore, the seller should approach this decision as carefully as an institutional investor would approach making a large investment in the buyer.

The seller suddenly has to "catch up" if it wants to level the playing field in the negotiating process. Of course, one of the roles of the seller's investment banker is to quickly educate the seller on all issues confronting the seller, not just valuing the seller in the transaction.

The Seller's Leverage Is the Ability to Say "No"

Although the buyer has a negotiating advantage compared to the seller at this stage, the seller has a strategic advantage because the seller can simply say "no" to the buyer at any time. This assumes that the buyer has agreed not to engage in a hostile takeover or that the seller knows the buyer will not try to bypass the seller's management and board in these negotiations by launching a hostile takeover. If the seller knows a hostile takeover will not occur, the buyer will have to satisfy many requirements imposed by the seller other than price in order to execute the deal.

A PROPOSAL IN PRINCIPLE BY THE BUYER

Usually, the buyer makes a proposal containing only the major terms of the acquisition. This is likely to be oral in order to avoid a paper trail of these early discussions. Unless the buyer and the seller can reach a preliminary understanding of an acquisition's major terms, the process usually stops. At this stage in the process, the seller must make a difficult decision. Should the seller lay out all of the issues that must be considered to get the issues on the table, or should it proceed by stating that the seller has a preliminary interest provided that many other issues can be agreed upon (Lewiki, Hiam, and Oleander, 1996)? The lawyers for the buyer and the seller will advise their clients to avoid reaching an understanding on all of the important issues, because once the transaction becomes probable, both the buyer and the seller, as publicly held companies, must disclose that negotiations are taking place. Such a disclosure can be premature since the parties have not yet entered into a definitive agreement. For this reason, most buyers and sellers prefer to go from the oral discussions to a definitive agreement before making an announcement of the potential transaction. Often there is more than one agreement in a transaction like this, but, taken together, they are referred to in this chapter as a *definitive agreement*.

OUTSIDE FACTORS AFFECTING THE NEGOTIATIONS

The buyer and seller must assess many factors before or at the onset of negotiations. The buyer has the advantage of knowing that it will make a proposal to the seller so that it can analyze the outside factors without being under time pressure. On the other hand, the seller will be under intense time pressure once negotiations have commenced and will have little time to evaluate the outside factors that should be considered. Among the outside factors that both the buyer and the seller should consider are:

- Will an announcement of the potential transaction attract another buyer? The seller will have a fiduciary obligation to "shop the deal" in any event.
- Will the potential transaction be reviewed by the Federal Trade Commission (FTC)? If so, what position is the FTC likely to take?
- If the buyer must obtain financing to effectuate the acquisition, how confident is the buyer of obtaining the financing?
- For both the buyer and the seller, how will the seller's largest suppliers and customers react to news of the potential transaction?
- Are any regulatory agencies in the United States or elsewhere likely to become involved in the transaction?
- Is there any legislation, state or federal, being proposed that could affect this transaction?

HOW SHOULD THE BUYER PREPARE FOR THE NEGOTIATION?

Since the buyer controls the timing of when it will commence the process, the buyer has the opportunity to plan for and simulate the negotiation that will take place. The following are matters for the buyer to consider in preparing for the negotiation:

- The buyer should develop the framework of the initial proposal, including the price to be paid with room for negotiation.
- The buyer should identify all issues that the seller is likely to raise, anticipate what the seller will propose, and develop a series of responses to these proposals.
- The buyer should establish its limits on the price and all issues within the framework of the proposal the buyer and seller will ultimately consider.

The buyer should develop trade-offs within the framework of the proposal. Because these trade-offs are difficult, the more time the buyer has to consider all of the potential trade-offs the better.

- How will the buyer insure against insider trading by persons affiliated with the buyer?
- The buyer's negotiating team should meet several times to rehearse the negotiation strategy and identify the roles of each team member.
- The buyer's team should participate in a mock negotiation with an experienced negotiator playing the role of the seller to reveal weaknesses in the buyer's strategy and possible tactics the seller may use (Carroll, Bazerman, and Maury, 1988; Thompson, 1998). The mock negotiation gives the team an opportunity to rehearse specific responses to issues to be negotiated.

HOW SHOULD THE SELLER PREPARE FOR NEGOTIATIONS?

Assuming the seller has initial interest, the preliminary discussions can accelerate rapidly because the buyer has thoroughly prepared for the discussions. The seller is clearly at a disadvantage if it has not prepared for the discussion.

What can the seller do to increase negotiating leverage in the short period of time after receiving the initial proposal? The most leverage the seller has is to simply take the position that it is not interested in being acquired, but this would ordinarily be a last resort. The next most effective way to gain leverage is to have a competing offer, but since the seller is surprised by the interest of the buyer, this will usually be infeasible at this stage (Docherty, 2006). Hopefully, the seller's investment banker is familiar with the seller's industry. The buyer will know that this investment banker can generate interest among other buyers very quickly. With this knowledge, the buyer will be forced to make an offer that will discourage other potential buyers.

As soon as preliminary discussions take place between the buyer and the seller, the seller should form its negotiating team, which usually mirrors the negotiating team of the buyer. This team should develop a negotiating strategy and execution plan, attempting to predict what the buyer will do. A useful approach is to have an experienced negotiator play the role of the buyer in a mock negotiation to prepare the team for the various issues that will arise, giving the team time to consider the alternatives to these issues before actually confronting them at the negotiating table (Koehn, 1997).

Some key questions that should be addressed include the following. Should the seller put golden parachutes in place for executive officers and key employees? Will the seller accelerate the vesting of outstanding stock options if an acceleration requirement is not already in the stock incentive plan? Will "stay" bonuses be offered to key employees? How will the seller control the confidentiality of the process to prevent insider trading and leaks to the public? How will the seller control the due diligence process imposed by the buyer so as not to alarm employees, large customers, and suppliers or lenders? If the deal involves the buyer's stock, what kind of due diligence should the seller do on the buyer given that the seller's stockholders will become stockholders in the buyer?

At the earliest possible moment when discussions are likely to take place, the CEO should convene a meeting of the board of directors to keep it fully advised of the potential discussions. The CEO should go into the negotiations with a high degree of confidence that the board will support the acquisition on acceptable terms. The CEO also needs to have an early sense that the seller's shareholders will approve the potential acquisition. Usually, the seller's investment banker can assess how the seller's shareholders are likely to react to the potential acquisition. All of this takes place within a few days or perhaps a few weeks.

In the hypothetical situation, the seller "is not for sale, but can be bought." The seller has not been seeking to be acquired and has no compelling reason to be acquired. The seller may have no choice but to enter into preliminary negotiations if the price proposed by the buyer is substantially above the current market price of the seller's stock, since the board of directors will have a fiduciary obligation to shareholders to consider the proposal. There is no clear test for when a board of directors must consider a proposal in order to meet its fiduciary obligation.

One of the major roles of the seller's investment banker is to provide advice about the intrinsic value of the seller. This is different from a fairness opinion. Of course, the seller will engage its investment banker to provide a fairness opinion as a protective measure for the board of directors, but a fairness opinion simply states that the transaction is fair to the shareholders from a financial viewpoint. The fairness opinion does not mean that a higher price could not have been obtained by the seller. If the buyer is unwilling to pay the "intrinsic value" of the seller, the seller's board can safely decline to negotiate with the buyer.

If an agreement is reached, under Delaware law, the seller's board is obligated to seek other acquirers in order to meet its fiduciary obligation to the shareholders. However, the buyer will likely offer a price that will be difficult for other potential acquirers to match. The buyer will attempt to impose a break-up fee if the seller is acquired by another company to discourage other buyers since, as a practical matter, another acquirer of the seller ends up bearing the economic burden of the break-up fee.

THE NEGOTIATING TEAM FOR THE BUYER AND THE SELLER

Because of the many people involved in each negotiating team, having the negotiations take place in as short a period of time as possible to avoid leaks to the public is extremely important. A spike in the price of the seller's stock during the negotiations almost always indicates that a leak has occurred. In the event that a leak is suspected, the best policy is usually to make a truthful announcement that the seller is in early discussions to be acquired. The announcement typically does not identify the potential buyer and states that an agreement may not be reached. The buyer and seller need to anticipate that a leak will occur and deal with that potential event in the nondisclosure agreement they have executed.

The dynamics of negotiating when many players are involved in the negotiations on each side are substantially different from the negotiation that takes place when two individuals are negotiating. For instance, those negotiating the deal inevitably do not have ultimate authority to make decisions. Only the board of directors and, if shareholder approval is required, the shareholders have that authority. But experienced negotiators can tell when the negotiating team on the other side has a high degree of confidence that the decision-making authority will approve the preliminary understandings reached during the negotiations.

One of the missions of each team is to find out the limits on each issue within which the other side is trying to work. Often the limits are unclear and change depending on the trade-offs that may be achieved. Each team must accept that they will work with imperfect information about the other side's "bottom line" throughout the negotiation process.

TYPICAL MATTERS TO BE NEGOTIATED

Unlike a hostile takeover where there are no negotiations, many matters must be negotiated in a friendly acquisition. Among the matters that usually have to be resolved are:

- What price will the seller or its shareholders receive and how will the buyer pay this price? If the deal is an all-cash deal, reaching an understanding on price is fairly easy. If, however, the price is to be paid in the form of the buyer's common stock or a combination of cash and stock, the negotiation becomes much more complicated.
- Will there be a break-up fee (and how much) if the seller, in the exercise of its fiduciary duty to its shareholders, agrees to be acquired by another company at a higher price after a definitive agreement has been executed?
- If the seller's shareholders do not approve the deal, will there be a break-up fee and, if so, how much?
- If the buyer's shareholders must approve the deal, will the buyer pay a break-up fee to the seller if the buyer's shareholders do not approve?
- Will the buyer have a certain period of time to continue to conduct due diligence with the right to terminate the agreement if it is not satisfied with the results of the due diligence? When will the buyer's due diligence period terminate?
- What process will the buyer and seller use in order for the buyer to conduct preliminary due diligence (before the definitive agreement is executed) so as not to alert employees (other than the executive officers) of the seller and to prevent insider trading? What limitations will be placed on the buyer, such as contacting key suppliers and key customers, at this stage?
- Will the seller have golden parachutes in place for executive officers and key employees? Will the buyer demand that the golden parachute agreements be renegotiated or eliminated?
- What consents may be required from lenders and others as a condition to closing? How far in advance of closing must these consents be obtained?
- Must the buyer either have the cash on hand to finance the purchase price or have a commitment from lenders to fund the purchase price before the seller signs the definitive agreement? How firm must this commitment be?
- If the FTC objects to the transaction, will the buyer, seller, or both have the right to terminate the definitive agreement?

- Will the buyer require that the seller's board of directors unanimously approve the deal and recommend it to the seller's shareholders? What will happen if only a majority of the seller's directors approve the deal?
- Will the buyer offer the seller's executive officers employment agreements? Will these employment agreements be made sufficiently attractive as to induce the key executives to support the transaction? Will these employment agreements contain unusually high compensation levels so as to induce the executive officers to support the transaction and create a conflict of interest for the executive officers?
- Will the seller offer "stay bonuses" to key executive officers and employees to assure the buyer and seller that they will stay with the seller for a certain period of time up to and after the closing?
- How confident are the parties that the seller will be able to obtain a fairness opinion from the seller's investment banker?
- If the deal involves shares of the buyer as part or all of the consideration, the seller will want to conduct due diligence on the buyer for a reasonable period of time following the execution of the definitive agreement. Will the seller have the right to terminate the agreement if it is not satisfied with the results of its due diligence?

Many more issues are likely to require negotiation besides those described above. A challenge for the buyer is figuring out how to get these issues discussed at the beginning of the negotiations.

ESTABLISHING A FRAMEWORK FOR THE NEGOTIATIONS

The buyer attempts to create an overall framework for the acquisition including all issues that the buyer contemplates must be resolved to reach an agreement. By establishing an overall framework, the buyer is attempting to limit the negotiations to trade-offs within the framework once the price has been established, so that the seller does not keep coming back with adjustments to the price depending on how other issues are resolved (Neale and Bazerman, 1985). The buyer will attempt to resolve all other issues without going back to price.

On the other hand, the seller wants to preserve the ability to keep the price open until all major issues have been resolved. Thus, the seller attempts to keep a framework open so as to not be forced to trade off provisions in the proposal against other provisions without going back to price. Experienced negotiators for both buyers and sellers know that these parties typically behave in this manner.

But most buyers and sellers reach a quick understanding on price while other major issues remain unresolved. In this hypothetical, reaching a price quickly tends to benefit the seller because the seller is in a good position to negotiate a high price and stand firm on that price while other issues are resolved. The buyer wants to have a soft understanding on price until the other issues are resolved so that the buyer can lower the price to reflect the economic impact of the other issues.

When acquiring a publicly held company, there is often no controlling shareholder and, therefore, no individual or entity to indemnify the buyer after the deal has closed if the seller's representations and warranties are false. As a result, the buyer takes the risk that, after closing, it discovers that the seller's financial statements or other matters are not true and correct (White, 1980). Who does the buyer sue? The buyer most likely is without a remedy after closing if there has been a misrepresentation by the seller. Therefore, the buyer must conduct thorough due diligence before closing.

NEGOTIATION STRATEGY FOR THE BUYER

Various books on negotiation, most of which apply to face-to-face negotiations, describe many negotiation tactics. Practice suggests that the value of thorough preparation exceeds the value of the various negotiation tactics by several fold. Thorough preparation sets the stage for the negotiation and allows the buyer to predict the seller's likely behavior in the upcoming negotiation regardless of the negotiation tactics used by the seller (Freund, 1975; Lewiki et al., 1996; Docherty, 2006).

Should the buyer's initial proposal contain most of the buyer's concerns or simply be a broad proposal focusing primarily on price and deal structure? If the initial proposal does not cover all of the likely issues on which the buyer and seller must agree, how can the buyer raise issues later? This is a dilemma, but experienced investment bankers and lawyers usually know how to get these issues on the table early in the discussions.

The buyer knows that the initial offering price elicits a counteroffer and therefore the buyer must leave room for further price negotiation. However, if the initially proposed price is too low, the seller may elect not to respond. The upper limit and lower limit of the price that is being considered may be called the "zone of reasonableness." When the price proposed by the buyer is below the zone of reasonableness or the counter made by the seller is above the zone of reasonableness, the other side is likely not to negotiate further. Determining the zone of reasonableness is an art. Investment bankers are ordinarily the most qualified persons to advise the buyer and the seller on the deal's zone of reasonableness (Shell, 1999). Keep in mind that this hypothetical transaction is assumed to be friendly and not hostile.

Usually, an all-cash deal allows the buyer to obtain the lowest price. Any other method of paying causes the seller to demand a higher price to take into consideration the risk of the noncash consideration for its shareholders. So the greatest risk for the seller is to agree to an all-stock transaction where the seller's shareholders receive shares of the buyer's stock for shares of the seller's stock. While the hypothetical deal does not involve the seller's shareholders receiving the buyer's notes as part of the consideration, a structure like this has a risk profile somewhere between an all-cash deal and an all-stock deal. Issuing notes to the seller's shareholders would involve registering the notes with the SEC, similar to registering stock, and complying with the Trust Indenture Act of 1939, as amended.

Even with e-mail, videoconferencing, and other collaboration tools, conducting face-to-face negotiations is still most effective. Much information is lost when the buyer cannot observe the body language of the representatives of the seller. Conducting face-to-face negotiations at a neutral location is also desirable to avoid speculation as to why representatives of both companies may be meeting. At the face-to-face negotiations, one of the senior members of the negotiating team should be a "strategic observer" and not involved in the details of the negotiation. The strategic observer can make sure the strategic goals are being achieved without getting bogged down on minor issues, while also keeping a clear mind during the negotiations that often become intense.

Negotiation by whining often occurs at some stage in the process where the seller's negotiator whines about something the buyer is demanding. Whining never works. In the context of this deal, the seller does not need to whine because the seller can threaten to "walk away." Likewise, simple persuasion or attempting to use logic to get agreement on a point seldom works in such negotiations, although lawyers attempt persuasion for the benefit of their clients. Only "quid pro quo" (this for that) produces agreements. In this case, the seller or the buyer may use the "nuclear option" by threatening to terminate the discussions if agreement is not reached on certain points—the quid is "we will continue negotiating" while the quo is "if you will agree with us on these points." Negotiators should use the nuclear option sparingly. Negotiations are always more productive if the parties stay with the quid pro quo attitude rather than using the many negotiating techniques described in popular how-to books (Lewiki et al., 1996; Shell, 1999).

Since most companies prefer to go straight from an oral understanding to a definitive agreement rather than a term sheet or preliminary memorandum of understanding, the buyer should have a draft of the proposed definitive agreement already prepared before the negotiation begins. Although modifications to this draft are likely, much of this draft will become part of the definitive agreement. If a buyer starts with a draft that is highly one-sided, the negotiators will focus on many issues that are insignificant in the overall scheme of a deal, wasting precious time that should be spent on the big issues. Extended negotiations over the terms of the definitive agreement increase the risk of leaks of the impending transaction.

A good practice is to announce at the beginning of every negotiating session that no points will be agreed upon until agreement exists on all points. Experienced negotiators know that backing off from an issue can be difficult once a preliminary agreement exists on the issue but before an overall agreement is reached.

REACHING A PRELIMINARY UNDERSTANDING

As previously discussed, the parties are likely to "creep up" to the definitive agreement to avoid having an agreement in principle until they sign the definitive agreement. This means that a point exists in the negotiations where the parties are sufficiently confident that they will make a deal so that the lawyers begin negotiating the definitive agreement. The seller's lawyers will have little time within which to review and propose changes to the initial draft of the definitive agreement. But highly experienced legal counsel for the seller can quickly review the draft of the definitive agreement to deal with major issues that are presented. Because of the urgency to enter into the definitive agreement, the seller's counsel can seldom "nit pick" the definitive agreement. Counsel can only counter on the major points of disagreement.

If the members of the seller's management team are not experienced in acquisitions, they often insist that various elements in the proposal be negotiated when, by custom, some of these elements are non-negotiable. Examples of items that are usually non-negotiable are the time period between reaching a definitive agreement and closing when the transaction must be approved by the buyer's shareholders due to time periods required by SEC rules; a requirement by the buyer that it have at least a few days to interview employees, customers, and suppliers of the seller before the definitive agreement becomes final; noncompetition agreements for key officers and employees of the seller; and the buyer's right to conduct a second stage of due diligence (for a limited period of time) after the definitive agreement has been signed with the commensurate right to terminate the agreement if this due diligence reveals a material misrepresentation by the seller. Experienced counsel and the investment banker for the seller can save the seller much time and agony by advising the seller's management team to focus on those points that are negotiable and accept those points that are ordinarily not negotiable (Naquin, 2002).

KEEPING THE DEAL TOGETHER

Once the parties execute the definitive agreement, the challenge is to keep the deal together if unexpected events take place. Both the buyer and the seller must anticipate such things as a substantial decline in the general stock market, a public relations disaster that hits either the buyer or the seller, or a disgruntled shareholder who initiates a lawsuit to prevent the transaction. The buyer and the seller should have contingency plans for each of these types of events. The buyer most likely wants to have automatic adjustment mechanisms in place if certain negative events take place so that the transaction will still occur, but with an adjustment in the price. Likewise, if the seller's shareholders will receive stock in the buyer, the seller typically wants to have the right to renegotiate or to terminate the transaction if certain negative things happen to the buyer.

HOW WOULD THIS PROCESS DIFFER IF THE SELLER IS A PRIVATELY HELD COMPANY?

The first hypothetical involves a large, publicly held company as the buyer and a small, publicly held company as the seller. If the seller is a small, privately held company, the context will be different. To set the context, assume:

- The seller is privately held by three founders, who make up the management team of the seller.
- The seller's financial statements are publicly unavailable and are treated as confidential by the seller.
- The seller's financial statements have been audited for the last five years, but the seller has made no attempt to implement the type of internal controls that the Sarbanes-Oxley Act of 2002 (SOX) requires of publicly held companies (the SOX requirement for internal controls does not apply to privately held companies). The auditing firm is a local accounting firm and is not a registered accounting firm under SOX.
- Each founder has an employment agreement with a five-year term that is triggered upon a change in control. The compensation under each

employment agreement substantially exceeds the level of compensation paid to executives of the buyer with similar responsibilities at divisions of the buyer comparable in size to the seller.

- None of the founders is willing to sell his stock to the buyer unless all founders sell their stock to the buyer.
- Several large companies have approached the seller during the past six months expressing an interest in acquiring the seller, but the seller is not in active negotiations to be acquired by any of these companies.
- The seller has not yet engaged an investment banker to represent it in the acquisition process, but several highly qualified investment bankers have courted the seller to serve as its investment banker.
- No transactions have occurred in the seller's stock, and the seller has never engaged a business valuation expert to appraise the seller's value.
- The founders have formed an opinion of the seller's value based on acquisitions that have been publicly reported for similar companies (although much larger than the seller).
- The seller has long- and short-term bank debt that is a normal amount for a company of the size and capitalization of the seller. The founders have personally guaranteed the bank debt.
- The buyer has set a target of $40 million as the highest price it will pay for the seller's stock. The founders of the seller are asking $60 million for their stock.
- The buyer will not be required to obtain the approval of its shareholders to acquire the seller.
- Before being approached by the buyer, the seller has not been seeking to be acquired.
- The seller is not financially troubled and is not under pressure to be acquired.
- The size of the proposed transaction is immaterial to the buyer.
- The buyer views the acquisition of the seller as a strategic acquisition.
- The buyer will pay cash for the seller.
- The size of the acquisition will not require a premerger notification to the FTC.
- The buyer desires to have the founders as consultants after the acquisition and will replace them as the management team with the buyer's executives.
- The buyer has concerns that an audit of the internal controls of the seller will reveal accounting issues that could adversely affect the historical earnings of the seller.
- The seller has provided to the buyer financial projections that appear overly optimistic. The founders cite the financial projections as justification for the asking price of $60 million.
- The buyer wants exclusivity for 90 days to negotiate a deal, but the seller is only willing to grant exclusivity for 45 days and will require a right to terminate the exclusivity if the seller determines in good faith that the parties will not reach an agreement.

The acquisition process usually commences with initial discussions between an executive of the buyer and the CEO of the seller. If the seller's CEO believes the buyer is sincerely interested and may be willing to pay a price acceptable to the founders, the seller requires the buyer to enter into a nondisclosure agreement, and the buyer reciprocates by requiring an exclusivity agreement. Since the founders will only sell if all founders sell, the buyer cannot attempt a hostile takeover.

Often, the seller will provide only summary financial information at this stage to allow the buyer to make a tentative proposal consisting of at least the price to be paid and possibly other significant terms, subject to further due diligence by the buyer. If the price is within range of the price that is acceptable to the founders, the negotiations continue. At this point, the seller ordinarily engages an investment banker to help with the process going forward. Sellers are usually advised to engage an investment banker if the transaction will exceed $20 million. The seller's investment banker contacts the buyer or the buyer's investment banker to invite further discussion.

Because the potential transaction will not be material to the buyer (the size of the buyer is such that the transaction is small in comparison to the financial condition of the buyer) and the seller is not publicly held, neither the buyer nor the seller has a duty to disclose the transaction to the public. This will allow the buyer and seller to reach an informal, nonbinding understanding without being concerned with making a premature announcement about the transaction before the parties have entered into a definitive agreement. The practical effect of this is to allow the buyer and seller to exchange drafts of term sheets in the negotiating process, summarizing the proposed terms of the transaction, instead of relying on oral discussions to "creep up" to a definitive agreement.

Based on the assumptions concerning this potential transaction, several important issues must be negotiated. As in the previous hypothetical, preparation for the negotiation is important for both the buyer and the seller. Unlike the first hypothetical where the seller is publicly held, the buyer will not have access to financial statements for the seller or disclosures required for a publicly held company before initiating discussions with the seller. The buyer has to rely on its own due diligence to collect information about the seller. Usually, the seller is unwilling to provide sufficient information until the seller believes the buyer will agree on terms acceptable to the seller's founders. Thus, the buyer will be in the position of making a preliminary proposal covering the price and perhaps other important terms before the buyer has conducted thorough due diligence.

The buyer clearly indicates that the initial proposal by the buyer assumes no problems will be revealed in due diligence that would materially reduce the historical or future financial results of the seller. On the other hand, the seller should disclose any negative information that may affect the buyer's offer at the onset of the discussions to head off any reason for the buyer to renegotiate the price if the buyer discovers this information after making its initial proposal (Langevoort, 1999).

In this hypothetical, the price the founders are willing to accept may be higher than the buyer is willing to pay up front. If so, the buyer could propose an "earn-out" as a means of hedging against overpaying. A proposed earn-out with future payments that is contingent upon the seller meeting the financial projections it has provided to the buyer is a way to test the seller's confidence level.

In this hypothetical, other companies have approached the seller expressing interest in acquiring the seller. Potential acquirers regularly approach almost all companies of the seller's size. Often, these inquiries give the seller a false sense of its potential value, which causes the seller to ask for and expect a "strategic price" rather than a "financial price" for the company. A "strategic price" is presumed to be higher than a "financial price" because it includes the "hoped for" synergies between the seller and the buyer, whereas a "financial price" is not based on any synergies the buyer may bring to the deal. The seller usually tells the buyer that it is being courted by other potential acquirers, and the buyer must assess whether this is true or merely a ruse (Shell, 1991). Most strategic buyers will not participate in a process that looks like an auction and will usually terminate further discussions if the seller will not grant the buyer exclusivity for a reasonable period. In this case, the seller grants the buyer exclusivity for 45 days, and the buyer agrees that the seller can terminate the exclusivity if the seller determines in good faith that the parties will not reach agreement. In addition to the exclusivity period, most definitive agreements for a transaction like this will have a 30- to 60-day period after signing for a closing, during which the seller may not engage in any efforts to sell the company to another buyer.

One of the first tasks for the seller's investment banker is to help the seller determine a realistic value for the company based on comparable deals or metrics that exist for valuing a company in the seller's industry. Rules of thumb are available for valuing a business in almost every industry, and many buyers use these rules of thumb for valuing a privately held business. In practice, the buyer will generally never disclose this information. In this hypothetical, the seller's investment banker would most likely have to dampen the expectations of the seller if any potential problems must be disclosed to the buyer, such as the five-year employment agreements for the founders and the potential for accounting treatment errors in the audited financial statements (since the auditing firm is not registered under SOX).

Once the buyer knows about the five-year employment agreements for the founders that will be triggered by a change in control, the buyer will usually require that the founders and the seller eliminate these agreements. The buyer will want employment agreements that it can terminate at will, but usually settles for a one- or two-year employment agreement with reasonable (not extraordinary) compensation and the ability to terminate the employment agreement if the founder is not performing his duties adequately. The buyer wants to minimize the expense caused by the employment agreements in the future, since the buyer wants to maximize the future earnings of the seller. The buyer will also want noncompetition agreements from the founders, which are customary in an acquisition of this type.

In this hypothetical, the buyer will pay cash for the seller, but often, the buyer will desire to acquire the seller for an exchange of stock or a combination of stock and cash. Unlike when the buyer acquires a publicly held company for stock and where the stock is freely tradable by necessity, the stock used in an acquisition of a privately held company is not freely tradable stock (unregistered stock) unless the buyer agrees to issue registered stock. The negotiation around the rights to have the stock registered and other aspects of the unregistered stock often take more negotiating time and effort than all other aspects of the transaction. Such registration rights and other aspects of unregistered stock are beyond the scope of this chapter.

In a transaction such as this hypothetical where there are only a few shareholders and each of whom will enter into the definitive agreement, the board of directors need not seek out other buyers in order for the board to comply with its fiduciary duty to shareholders who are not parties to the definitive agreement. In order to increase its negotiating power, the seller will probably attempt to obtain a competitive proposal from another potential buyer before the seller and the founders sign the exclusivity agreement with the buyer, even if the proposal from another potential buyer is very informal. The seller wants to create the perception that competition exists for the acquisition of the company. Of course, in this hypothetical, the primary negotiating power for the seller is to just say "no" to the buyer.

However, when the major shareholders in a privately held company start down the path to be acquired, they often convince themselves that this is the time to be acquired either by the buyer or another potential buyer. The realization of the liquid wealth that will result when they sell the company often becomes too tempting to "just say no" without knowing with certainty there is another buyer who will pay as much as this buyer is willing to pay.

Unlike an acquisition of a publicly held company where often no shareholder holds more than 5 percent of the outstanding shares, an acquisition of a privately held company almost always involves a limited number of shareholders holding all or a large portion of the outstanding shares. Thus, requiring the seller's shareholders to personally sign the acquisition agreement, which will contain customary representations and warranties as well as other terms pertaining to the deal, is feasible. A battle between the buyer and the seller will develop over the limits of liability (if any exist) for the founders in the event a breach of the agreement occurs. Usually the founders can negotiate a limit not to exceed the amount the individual shareholder receives in the deal, but sometimes, the shareholders are successful at negotiating a lower limit.

Requiring the seller's shareholders to agree to a "holdback" of part of the proceeds to serve as a source of payment if the shareholders breach the agreement may also be feasible. For example, a breach can occur if one or more of the representations and warranties turns out to be untrue. Often, the holdback is 20 to 30 percent of the purchase price and is held for two or more years, depending on the confidence level of the buyer that the buyer will know about claims to be asserted within that time frame. When a holdback is required, the shareholders will usually try to minimize the amount and to release portions of the holdback in phases, provided no claims have been made against the holdback.

One issue in this hypothetical that needs to be handled is the personal guarantee of the bank debt by each of the founders. This is common for a privately held company, but the bank will not simply grant a release to the founders because the company has been acquired. The bank usually requires the buyer to guarantee the debt in order to release the founders from their guarantees. Often, the buyer does not want to deal with this bank and will elect to pay off the bank debt instead of obtaining a release for the founders. A time delay often occurs in paying off the debt. In this case, the founders will negotiate an indemnification by the buyer to indemnify them against loss if the buyer does not pay off the bank debt.

Acquiring a privately held company usually involves many more issues than acquiring a publicly held company. Although the price to be paid is the most important issue, other issues may be of great value to the buyer or the seller and these issues interact with the price (Ertel, 2004). As a result, setting rigid limits on price is difficult for both the buyer and seller because an agreement on one issue affects the range of possible outcomes on other issues including price.

SUMMARY AND CONCLUSIONS

The negotiation process in an acquisition is complex. Preparation for the negotiation is the most important tactic for both the buyer and seller. As with all negotiations, the parties are testing each other to determine the limits each has set on the different issues involved. Since the issues interact, the negotiator or the negotiation team must be prepared for the trade-offs that are possible between the issues. If the negotiator has not already anticipated and analyzed the possible trade-offs, the negotiator probably has not given enough thought to the full range of consequences as trade-offs occur in the course of the negotiation.

Although the issues involved in an acquisition of a publicly held company versus a privately held company differ in some respects, the greatest difference lies in the availability of information about the seller before the acquisition process begins. For example, in the United States, a publicly held company makes comprehensive disclosures about its business in filings with the SEC. The buyer can study the financial information about the seller well before making a proposal to the seller. When approaching a privately held company, the buyer will base the initial proposal to the seller on little reliable information because a seller is usually unwilling to fully disclose its financial and other information to the buyer until the seller believes a reasonable probability exists to make a deal.

DISCUSSION QUESTIONS

1. Assume that a CFO of a publicly held company had not previously been part of a negotiation process. How could the CFO prepare himself and his management team for the negotiation process if a potential buyer were to express interest in acquiring the company?

2. How could the CFO of a buyer in negotiations for an acquisition prevent information leaks?

3. How should a buyer's management handle a situation in which the press reports a rumor, which is true, that acquisition negotiations are taking place?

4. Why should a seller's negotiating team predict the issues that will be negotiated and identify potential trade-offs on these issues?

REFERENCES

Brodt, Susan E. 1994. "Inside Information and Negotiator Decision Behavior." *Organizational Behavior and Human Decision Processes* 58:2, 172–202.

Carroll, John S., Max H. Bazerman, and Robin Maury. 1988. "Negotiator Cognitions: A Descriptive Approach to Negotiators' Understanding of Their Opponents." *Organizational Behavior and Human Decision Processes* 41:3, 352–370.

Docherty, Jayne S. 2006. "One Tool among Many." In Andrea K. Schneider and Christopher Honeyman, eds. *The Negotiator's Fieldbook*, 565–572. Chicago: American Bar Association.

Ertel, 2004. "'Getting Past Yes': Negotiation as if Implementation Mattered." *Harvard Business Review*, November 1, 1–10.

Freund, James C. 1975. *Anatomy of a Merger: Strategies and Techniques for Negotiating Corporate Acquisitions*. New York: Law Journal Seminars–Press.

Koehn, Dayrl. 1997. "Business and Game Playing: The False Analogy." *Journal of Business Ethics* 16:12–13, 1447–1452.

Langevoort, Donald C. 1999. "Half-Truths: Protecting Mistaken Inferences by Investors and Others." *Stanford Law Review* 52, 87–125.

Lewiki, Roy J., Alexander Hiam, and Karen W. Olander. 1996. *Think Before You Speak: The Complete Guide to Strategic Negotiation*. New York: John Wiley & Sons.

Mintzberg, Henry, and James B. Quinn. 1991. *The Strategy Process: Concepts, Contexts, Cases*. Englewood Cliffs, NJ: Prentice Hall.

Naquin, Charles E. 2002. "The Agony of Opportunity in Negotiation: Number of Negotiable Issues, Counterfactual Thinking, and Feelings of Satisfaction." *Organizational Behavior and Human Decision Processes* 91:1, 97–107.

Neale, Margaret A., and Max H. Bazerman. 1985. "The Effects of Framing and Negotiator Overconfidence on Bargaining Behaviors and Outcomes." *Academy of Management Journal* 28:1, 34–49.

Shell, Richard G. 1991. "When Is It Legal to Lie in Negotiations?" *Sloan Management Review* 32:3, 93–101.

Shell, Richard G. 1999. *Bargaining for Advantage: Negotiation Strategies for Reasonable People*. New York: Penguin Books.

Thompson, Leigh. 1998. *The Mind and the Heart of the Negotiator*. Englewood Cliffs, NJ: Prentice Hall.

Watkins, Michael. 2002. *Breakthrough Business Negotiations*. San Francisco: Jossey-Bass.

White, James J. 1980. "Machiavelli and the Bar: Ethical Limitations on Lying in Negotiation." *American Bar Foundation Research Journal* 5:4, 926–938.

ABOUT THE AUTHOR

William A. Grimm is a Visiting Professor of Practice in Entrepreneurship and Negotiation at the Crummer Graduate School of Business, Rollins College. Before joining academia, Professor Grimm practiced law as a securities lawyer for 35 years. His law practice focused on technology companies and the unique problems they face. He has handled numerous M&As as well as venture capital transactions for high technology and other companies. Professor Grimm is a well-known speaker in Central Florida at seminars on venture capital financing and initial public offerings. Additionally, he has served on the boards of directors of several high technology companies. He is the author of *What Entrepreneurs Need to Know: Avoiding Big Mistakes That Can Prevent Success*, published by Trafford Publishing in 2006. Professor Grimm holds a BS degree in Mechanical Engineering from Penn State, an MBA from the University of Florida, and a law degree from Stetson University College of Law.

CHAPTER 15

Merger Negotiations: Takeover Process, Selling Procedure, and Deal Initiation

NIHAT AKTAS
Professor of Finance, EMLYON Business School

ERIC DE BODT
Professor of Finance, Université Lille Nord de France

INTRODUCTION

Takeover processes include both private and public components. The private component starts with the initiation of contacts between the merging parties or parties interested in combining their activities and continues until the public announcement of the merger or takeover. The second part of the process corresponds with what is known as the public takeover process, which begins with the public announcement of the deal and ends with its consummation.

Before the publication of Boone and Mulherin (2007), finance researchers knew little about the private part of the takeover process. With its focus on the public component, the prior literature documents few public takeover auctions during the 1980s and 1990s. Most of the deals appeared ex post to be friendly negotiations between the target and the acquirer. For example, Betton, Eckbo, and Thorburn (2008) consider 35,727 takeover contest bids and report that 95 percent of their sample involves single-bid contests or "friendly" transactions with only one bidder. Only 3.4 percent of the deals in their sample entail multiple bid contests with rival bidders (i.e., public takeover auctions), and 1.6 percent generate multiple bids from a single bidder. Similar evidence appears in other research such as Schwert (2000), Andrade, Mitchell, and Stafford (2001), and Moeller, Schlingemann, and Stulz (2007).

Two main explanations have been proposed to explain the occurrence of few public auctions. First, both Schwert (2000) and Betton et al. (2008) argue that the diffusion of poison pills and other antitakeover defenses at the beginning of the 1990s virtually eliminated hostile takeovers or public auctions. Second, according to Hartzell, Ofek, and Yermack (2004), some target managers prefer negotiations because they enable managers to attain beneficial deals for themselves even at the expense of their shareholders (e.g., trading power or perks against a premium).

Using information from the merger background section of the U.S. Securities and Exchange Commission (SEC) 14A and S-4 filings for mergers and 14D filings for tender offers, Boone and Mulherin (2007) determine the chosen selling procedure during the private component of the takeover process. They document that half of the deals involve private auctions with multiple bidders, and the remaining half use direct negotiations with only one bidder. Their result therefore suggests that the merger and acquisition (M&A) market is much more competitive when the prepublic component of the takeover process is included in an analysis.

The finding that half the targets do not choose a competitive selling procedure seems puzzling at first. This is because according to general guidelines in auction theory (e.g., Bulow and Klemperer, 1996), competitive procedures always increase the seller's expected revenue as compared with direct negotiations with a single bidder. However, Subramanian (2009) indicates that after 15 bidders, the value of an extra bidder becomes negligible. Moreover, in some circumstances (e.g., high heterogeneity in potential buyers' valuations), auctions may even lead to disappointing results. This discussion explains why, instead of organizing full-scale auctions, some sellers prefer controlled sales procedures in which they voluntarily limit the number of potential bidders to a few companies (e.g., Hansen, 2001; Boone and Mulherin, 2009).

Two classical arguments may explain the existence of negotiations, namely, agency costs and information costs. According to the agency-based explanation, negotiations are better suited for self-interested managers to extract their own private benefits (Hartzell et al., 2004). The information costs argument further suggests that targets prefer negotiations when the dissemination of private information is costly (e.g., Boone and Mulherin, 2007; Aktas, de Bodt, and Roll, 2010). Hansen (2001) posits that competitive information is a determinant of selling procedure choice such that targets limit the number of bidders when sensitive competitive information can be revealed during the selling process (Bulow and Klemperer, 1996). Aktas et al. argue that another source of costs contributes to the choice of the selling procedure, that is, the target's eagerness to sell.

Using a sample of 400 large U.S. transactions, Boone and Mulherin (2007) report that the wealth effect for target shareholders does not depend on the choice of the selling procedure. Both one-on-one negotiations and auctions generate a takeover premium of about 40 percent (computed relative to the stock price of the target four weeks before the deal announcement). Without a difference in the wealth effect for target shareholders between negotiations and auctions, Boone and Mulherin conclude that this choice in a given takeover reflects a trade-off between competition and information costs.

This chapter describes the takeover process for a large sample of U.S. takeovers. The chapter focuses on two dimensions: the choice of the selling procedure (auction versus negotiation) by the parties and the deal initiator (target-initiated versus acquirer-initiated), because the acquirer does not initiate all transactions (Simsir, 2009). The chapter also investigates the relationship between the choice of the selling procedure and deal initiation. Aktas et al. (2010) report that targets more often initiate competitive auctions, but acquirers more often initiate negotiations. This evidence is consistent with the notion that initiating bidders attempt to avoid competition, whereas initiating targets seek to stimulate it.

The sample includes 1,774 deals by U.S. firms involving deal sizes greater than $100 million that were announced during the 1994 to 2007 period. To identify the selling procedure, the authors use the merger background section of SEC filings (14A and S-4 filings for mergers; 14D filings for tender offers), similar to Boone and Mulherin (2007). Among the 1,774 deals, the authors identify 847 negotiations without explicit competition (48 percent) and 927 auctions with multiple bidders (52 percent). Using the same SEC filings, they determine whether the initiator of the deal is the target or the winning bidder. Of the 1,774 transactions, 721 (41 percent) are target-initiated deals, whereas the remaining 1,053 deals (59 percent) are initiated by the acquirer.

The main results are consistent with prior research. Specifically, whether the target adopts a competitive selling procedure or private negotiations does not matter for target shareholders because the average bid premiums (roughly 40 percent) are virtually identical for both the negotiation and auction subsamples. However, in contrast with Boone and Mulherin (2008), the evidence shows that the wealth effects granted to acquirer shareholders differ statistically between auctions and negotiations. The average acquirer abnormal returns reach –3.11 percent and –1.91 percent for the negotiation and auction subsamples, respectively. In terms of firm size, there is, on average, no difference between acquirers that participate in auctions versus negotiations, but targets are (relative to the acquirer) much smaller in auctions than in negotiations. This (relative) size effect probably explains the difference in acquirer abnormal returns between auctions and negotiations in our sample. That is, large transactions undertaken by large firms are more value-destroying as shown in Moeller, Schlingemann, and Stulz (2004). Regarding the determinants of the selling method, the findings reveal that less diversified targets resort more often to auctions, and targets generally prefer auctions when the potential depth of the bidder pool is larger. Finally, the results indicate a relationship between the choice of the selling procedure and deal initiation. Unsurprisingly, target initiators prefer competitive sales processes over negotiation with a single bidder.

The remainder of this chapter is organized as follows. The next section presents the takeover process in more detail. This is followed by a section that describes the sample and the selling procedure as well as identifying the party initiating the deal. After discussing the determinants of the selling procedure choice and the interaction between the deal initiation and the selling procedure, the chapter ends with a summary and conclusions.

THE TAKEOVER PROCESS

This section describes the takeover process based on Betton, Eckbo, and Thorburn's (2009) two-stage negotiation framework and Boone and Mulherin's (2009) 11-step takeover model. As an illustration, the section ends with presenting two merger processes. The first example is the merger between Vicuron Pharmaceuticals (target) and Pfizer (acquirer) in which Vicuron Pharmaceuticals solicited the help of its investment bank to initiate the deal and organized a formal auction with 17 potential bidders. The second example refers to a one-on-one negotiation between Kulicke & Soffa (acquirer) and Cerprobe (target).

Betton, Eckbo, and Thorburn's Two-Stage Approach

According to Betton et al. (2009), takeovers can be modeled as a two-stage process that generally begins with a one-on-one merger negotiation (stage 1) between the initial bidder and the target, followed by a private or public auction (stage 2). The auction process initiates after either a negotiation failure between the initial acquirer and the target (private auction) or when rival companies are attracted by a public announcement of a merger between the initial bidder and the target (public auction). Therefore, negotiations explicitly take place under the shadow of an open auction. Aktas et al. (2010) consider a similar two-stage process in which the initial bidder negotiates with the target under the threat of an auction because the target always has the option to leave the negotiation and start a competitive selling procedure. These authors argue that the threat of an auction during negotiations may explain why the bid premiums in negotiated deals, on average, are identical to the bid premiums in auctions.

This two-stage takeover setup reflects an important fiduciary requirement under Delaware merger law. That is, target boards of directors must consider any additional bids received by rival bidders between the time of the public announcement of merger negotiations and the final approval date by target shareholders of the merger agreement. In addition to approval from target shareholders, some specific cases require approval from bidder shareholders and regulatory (e.g., antitrust) agencies. Based on their sample, Betton et al. (2009) document that an approval process takes an average of five months for successful initial bidders. This long delay gives potential rival bidders enough time to enter the takeover process and compete in a public auction.

Boone and Mulherin's 11-Step Model

Building on the theoretical analysis provided by Hansen (2001), Boone and Mulherin (2009) propose a practical framework for analyzing the takeover process. They divide the M&A process into 11 steps, starting with the initiation of the transaction and ending with the completion of the deal between the target and the winning bidder. According to their analysis, much of the M&A process takes place privately before the public announcement of the deal. Thus, the private part of the process includes seven steps, whereas the public part comprises only four steps, as shown in Exhibit 15.1.

Private Takeover Process
The private takeover process involves the following seven steps.

1. *Deal initiation.* The first step of the M&A process is deal initiation, whether by the target (i.e., its management, including the sale of the company or other forms of restructuring) or by the acquiring company.
2. *Selection of advisors.* After this initiation, the parties hire financial advisors and law firms to provide financial and legal advice about the deal.
3. *Selling process.* With the help of these advisors, the target company chooses the sales procedure, which may be anything from a formal auction among multiple bidders to a negotiation with a single bidder. To avoid divulging

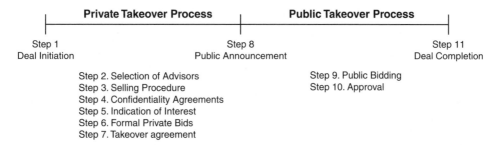

Exhibit 15.1 Timing of Takeover Process

Note: This exhibit provides a time line of the takeover process based on Boone and Mulherin's (2009) 11-step model. The private takeover process corresponds to the period from the initiation of the transaction to the public announcement of the merger agreement. The public takeover process is the period from the public announcement to the completion of the transaction.

sensitive information, the target might limit the auction process to a select number of bidders (Hansen, 2001). Moreover, some acquirers are reluctant to participate in competitive auctions and may impose a one-on-one negotiation by adopting preemptive bidding (Fishman, 1988, 1989).

4. *Confidentiality and standstill agreements.* The next step of the process is the signing of confidentiality and standstill agreements by the potential bidders and the start of due diligence. Confidentiality agreements allow bidders access to private information about the target. In exchange, standstill agreements prohibit bidders from making unsolicited offers for the target shares.

5. *Indications of interest.* This step leads to indications of interest by bidders and a subset of these bidders makes initial, nonbinding offers. The bidders often propose a range of possible prices for the target; the bidders with the best possible prices receive invitations to conduct additional due diligence.

6. *Formal private bids.* After the due diligence, the remaining bidders submit binding private bids. In some cases, the target and its investment bank may ask for best and final offers from the bidders.

7. *Takeover agreement.* The private takeover process results in a merger agreement between the winning bidder and the target. The agreement includes the offer price (or premium above a given market price), the method of payment (i.e., proportion of cash and stock payments), and various protection devices for the acquirer such as termination fees.

Public Takeover Process

The public takeover process involves four additional steps.

8. *Takeover announcement.* The public takeover process starts with announcing the merger agreement with the winning bidder.

9. *Public bidding.* The public announcement of the deal may attract rival bidders, prompting a public takeover battle, usually modeled as an auction, for control of the target. In practice, less than four percent of deals are subject to public competition (e.g., Moeller et al., 2007). Betton et al. (2009) show

that the initial bidder usually wins the public auction. For a sample of 7,076 public takeover contests during the period 1990 to 2002, they report that the initial bidder won the contest in 70.7 percent of the cases, a rival bidder won in only 3 percent, and a no winner outcome occurred for 26.4 percent of their sample.

10. *Approval of the deal.* After shareholders and regulatory agencies approve the deal, the acquirer completes the deal.

11. *Deal completion.* After approval, the deal is completed.

Regarding the duration of the process, Boone and Mulherin (2007, 2009) show that a full takeover process, from private initiation to deal completion, takes an average of almost one calendar year, and the private process is roughly as long as the public one.

Illustrations of Auctions versus Negotiations

To illustrate the two sales processes (auctions versus negotiations), two real M&A deals are described in Exhibit 15.2. SEC filings, downloaded from the Electronic Data Gathering and Retrieval (EDGAR) database of the SEC (www.sec.gov), provide the source for much of the information used to describe these takeover processes.

Formal Auction

The $1.91 billion cash merger between Pfizer (acquirer) and Vicuron Pharmaceuticals (target) was completed in September 2005, three months after the public announcement of the merger agreement and six months after the deal initiation. In March 2005, Vicuron's board decided to consider different strategic alternatives, including entering into a business alliance with a pharmaceutical company that had established sales and marketing capabilities. On March 10, the company retained Morgan Stanley as its financial advisor to launch a search for suitable acquirers through a formal auction process.

Morgan Stanley contacted 17 potential bidders between March 15 and 17. Of them, eight signed confidentiality/standstill agreements and received preliminary due diligence information. Between March 18 and May 2, five showed further interest in a potential transaction with Vicuron. Between May 2 and May 20, Vicuron's board of directors examined these indications with the help of their financial advisor and continued the due diligence process for three firms chosen by Vicuron's board of directors. On June 7, two interested firms made formal acquisition proposals, which the board of directors reviewed on June 9. Vicuron's board of directors then authorized legal and financial counsel, as well as management, to continue negotiating with the two parties to obtain a better final price. George Horner, Vicuron's chief executive officer (CEO), disclosed the final bids to the board on June 15 and Pfizer emerged as the winning bidder with an offer price of $29.10 per share. That offer price represented a bid premium of 68 percent relative to Vicuron's share price four weeks before the deal announcement.

In the public part of the takeover process, the execution of the merger agreement was announced on June 16. This occurred before the opening of the European markets and through a joint press release issued by the two parties. No other

Exhibit 15.2   Examples of M&A Processes

This exhibit presents examples of takeover processes. The first example is the acquisition of Vicuron by Pfizer through an auction process with multiple bidders. The second example is the one-on-one negotiation merger process between Kulicke & Soffa and Cerprobe.

	Deal 1 Pfizer–Vicuron	Deal 2 Kulicke & Soffa–Cerprobe
A. Deal Characteristics		
Acquirer	Pfizer	Kulicke & Soffa Industries
Target	Vicuron Pharmaceuticals	Cerprobe
Deal value[1]	$1.91 billion	$201.37 million
Relative size[2]	1%	25%
Form	Merger	Merger
Payment method	100% cash	100% cash
Termination fees	$58 million	$5.63 million
Bid premium[3]	68%	33%
B. Investment Banks		
Acquirer	Lazard	N/A
Target	Morgan Stanley	Bank of America Securities
C. Takeover Process		
Selling procedure	Auction	Negotiation
Date of initiation	March 10, 2005	March 16, 2000
Initiating party	Target	Acquirer
Number of		
Contacted bidder(s)	17	1
Confidentiality	8	1
Indications of interest	5	1
Private bids	2	1
Public bids	1	1
Announcement date	June 16, 2005	October 12, 2000
Completion date	September 14, 2005	November 28, 2000
D. Market Reactions[4]		
Acquirer abnormal returns	4.99%	6.70%
Target abnormal returns	73.88%	45.72%
Deal abnormal returns	5.32%	12.54%

[1] *Deal value* is the total value of consideration paid by the acquirer, excluding fees and expenses.

[2] *Relative size* is the ratio of deal value to acquirer size. Acquirer size corresponds to the market value of equity (number of shares outstanding multiplied by the stock price) 40 days before the announcement date.

[3] *Bid premium* corresponds to the premium (in percentage) of the offer price compared with the target closing stock price, four weeks before the announcement date.

[4] *Abnormal returns* derive from the beta-one model (net of market returns), which subtracts the daily market portfolio return from the daily return of each company. The market portfolio is the Center for Research in Security Prices (CRSP) value-weighted index. For each firm, the abnormal returns are cumulated between day −5 to day +5, relative to the announcement date. The abnormal returns for the deal equal the average of the acquirer abnormal returns and the target abnormal returns, weighted by their respective market value. Market values are estimated 40 days before the announcement date.

companies intervened in the public part of the takeover process to make additional bid offers. Following the approval of Vicuron's shareholders, the deal was completed on September 14, 2005.

One-on-One Negotiations
In the second deal, the $201.37 million cash merger between Kulicke & Soffa Industries (acquirer) and Cerprobe (target), the acquirer initiated the deal in March 2000. The deal was announced in October 2000 and completed near the end of November 2000. The selling procedure involved one-on-one negotiations because there was no explicit competition during either the private or the public parts of the takeover process.

In early March, Zane Close, CEO of Cerprobe, received a telephone call from James P. Spooner, vice president of corporate development for Kulicke & Soffa Industries. On April 13, the parties executed a confidentiality agreement. On May 9, Cerprobe engaged Bank of America Securities to advise it in connection with a possible transaction with Kulicke & Soffa. Between May and October, intense negotiations ensued. From an initial offer of $19 per stock, half in cash and half in stock, the negotiations ended with a final all-cash offer of $20 per stock, which represented a 33 percent premium relative to Cerprobe's stock price four weeks before the announcement date. The merger agreement appeared in a press release on October 12 and was completed on November 28 following the approval of shareholders. Exhibit 15.2 provides specifics on each of these deals.

In addition to the characteristics of the deals, Exhibit 15.2 documents the market reactions around the deal announcement dates. A classical event study method is used to compute the firms' abnormal returns. Financial markets reacted positively to the announcement of both deals. At the deal level, the 11-day abnormal returns around the announcement date are 5.32 percent (Pfizer–Vicuron) and 12.54 percent (Kulicke & Soffa–Cerprobe), which suggests both deals were synergistic according to investor anticipations. Because the acquirers' abnormal returns are substantially positive (4.99 percent for Pfizer and 6.70 percent for Kulicke & Soffa), neither acquirer appears to have overbid during the acquisition process.

SAMPLE SELECTION

The sample of transactions is constructed as follows (Aktas et al., 2010). A total of 2,006 completed corporate takeovers are extracted from the Securities Data Corporation (SDC) M&A database that satisfy the following criteria: (1) The deal announcements occurred between January 1, 1994, and December 31, 2007 (SEC filings are only available from 1994 in EDGAR); (2) both the targets and the bidders are listed U.S. firms; (3) each of the deal sizes is greater than $100 million; (4) the percentages held by the acquirers are less than 50 percent, before the deal announcements and more than 50 percent after completion; (5) the four-week bid premiums in percentage (i.e., ratio of offer price to target closing stock price four weeks before the original announcement date) are available in the SDC database; and (6) the targets' and acquirers' CUSIPs can be matched with the Center for Research in Securities Prices (CRSP) permanent number (PERMNO).

Following Boone and Mulherin (2007), the current study uses the deal background section of the SEC filings 14A and S-4 for mergers and 14D for tender offers to classify a selling procedure as a negotiation or auction. For an auction classification, multiple potential bidders should be mentioned; to be classified as a negotiation, there should be only a single bidder involved in the entire takeover process. From the initial sample of 2,006 SDC deals, the selling procedure for 1,774 deals using SEC filings is identified. Of these 1,774 transactions, 927 involved auctions (52 percent), and 847 deals are one-on-one negotiations (48 percent).

The deal background section of the SEC filings is also used to ascertain whether the initiator was the target or the winning bidder. If identifying the initiating party (less than 1 percent of cases) was impossible, the winning bidder is considered as the initiating party. In the sample of 1,774 transactions, 721 (41 percent) represent target-initiated deals and the remaining 1,053 (59 percent) are acquirer-initiated deals. Exhibit 15.3 shows the sample distribution by announcement year.

The first column reports all deals with an identifiable selling procedure in the SEC deal background sections; *Auction* is the subsample with multiple bidders (the remaining deals are negotiations with a single bidder). *Target-Initiated* is the subsample of deals for which the target firm initiated the transaction (the remaining deals are initiated by the winning bidder). The *All Deals* column reveals the peak in the number of transactions between 1997 and 2000. This is consistent with the well-documented "friendly" M&A wave at the end of the 1990s (Betton et al., 2008). The *Auction* and *Target-Initiated* subsamples display patterns similar to that of the *All Deals* sample year to year.

Exhibit 15.3 Sample Distribution by Announcement Year

This exhibit reports the distribution of takeovers by announcement year. *N* denotes the number of acquisitions, and % is the percentage of the sample in each year. The *All Deals* sample includes 1,774 acquisitions with selling procedures identified from SEC filings. The *Auction* subsample includes transactions with multiple bidders; the *Target-initiated* subsample includes deals for which the target is the initiator.

Year	All Deals		Auction		Target-Initiated	
	N	%	N	%	N	%
1994	32	1.80	20	2.16	16	2.22
1995	99	5.58	47	5.07	36	4.99
1996	130	7.33	55	5.93	43	5.96
1997	223	12.57	120	12.94	100	13.87
1998	221	12.46	104	11.22	94	13.04
1999	233	13.13	112	12.08	93	12.90
2000	175	9.86	84	9.06	71	9.85
2001	104	5.86	51	5.50	47	6.52
2002	62	3.49	38	4.10	22	3.05
2003	92	5.19	50	5.39	35	4.85
2004	107	6.03	58	6.26	45	6.24
2005	103	5.81	66	7.12	39	5.41
2006	108	6.09	67	7.23	45	6.24
2007	85	4.79	55	5.93	35	4.85
Total	1,774	100.00	927	100.00	721	100.00

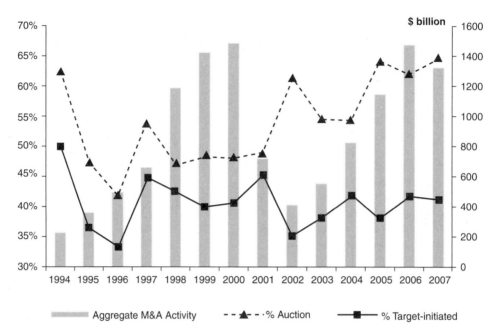

Exhibit 15.4 Proportion of Auctions and Target-initiated Deals over Time
Note: This exhibit plots the proportion of auctions and target-initiated transactions as well as the aggregate M&A activity over time.

To assess whether the selling procedure and deal initiation choices are related to aggregate activity in the M&A market, Exhibit 15.4 plots the proportion of auctions and target-initiated deals in the sample over time. Also reported in this exhibit is the aggregate value (billions USD) of the U.S. M&A market according to Thomson Financial. The proportion of auctions displays a decreasing pattern during the first half of the sample period and then increases during the 2000s to reach 65 percent by 2007. The proportion of target-initiated deals seems more stable over time. No clear-cut pattern emerges when comparing the proportions of auctions and target-initiated deals with aggregate M&A activity over time.

CHOICE OF SELLING METHOD AND DEAL INITIATION

Exhibit 15.5 reports summary statistics of firms and deals in the samples, conditional on the selling procedure they chose. The final column offers the *p*-value for the difference in means between the *Negotiation* and *Auction* subsamples. This exhibit also provides variable definitions at the bottom of the table. All financial ratios are Winsorized at 1 percent and 99 percent to limit the influence of outliers. Industry-related variables reflect the Fama-French 49-industry classification scheme. Specifically, the CRSP database serves as the source of the historical standard industrial classification codes, which are converted using the table provided by Kenneth French on his Web site:

(http://mba.tuck.dartmouth.edu/pages/faculty/ken.french/data_library.html).

Exhibit 15.5 Negotiations versus Auctions: Summary Statistics

This exhibit reports summary statistics about firms and deals in the negotiation and auction subsamples, as well as market reactions around the announcement date. *Negotiation* includes deals with a single buyer. *Auction* includes transactions with multiple bidders. *N* denotes the number of observations. For dummy variables, the mean gives the proportion of deals. The final column displays the *p*-value from a test of mean (or proportion) differences between the *Auction* and *Negotiation* subsamples.

	Negotiation		Auction		
	Mean	**N**	**Mean**	**N**	**p-value**
Panel A. Deal Characteristics					
Deal value ($ billions)	3.14	847	1.35	927	0.00
Relative size	49.90%	844	39.00%	920	0.00
Cash payment (dummy)	14.40%	847	27.08%	927	0.00
Stock payment (dummy)	52.77%	847	34.84%	927	0.00
Toehold	0.41%	847	0.20%	927	0.10
Bid premium	40.41%	847	40.91%	927	0.77
Target-initiated (dummy)	19.01%	847	60.41%	927	0.00
Duration in number of days					
Private process	179	840	238	915	0.00
Public process	132	840	131	915	0.82
Panel B. Firm Characteristics					
Acquirer size ($ billions)	17.73	844	15.49	920	0.25
Target size ($ billions)	2.16	847	0.84	927	0.00
Acquirer idiosyncratic risk	2.36%	791	2.04%	862	0.00
R&D intensive industry (dummy)	32.11%	847	28.46%	924	0.09
Target sales concentration	58.76%	844	63.12%	926	0.00
Target debt ratio	21.44%	803	20.95%	895	0.62
Target management ownership	6.61%	847	16.37%	927	0.10
Target institutional ownership	32.71%	666	29.82%	714	0.01

Exhibit 15.5 *(Continued)*

Panel C. Market reactions

Acquirer abnormal returns	−3.11%	791	−1.91%	856	0.01
Target abnormal returns	22.18%	736	21.92%	856	0.82
Deal abnormal returns	0.65%	703	0.89%	794	0.60

Note: Variable definitions are as follows:

Deal value is the total value of consideration paid by the acquirer, excluding fees and expenses.

Relative size is the ratio of deal value to acquirer size.

Cash payment (Stock payment) is a dummy variable that takes a value of 1 for purely cash-financed (stock-financed) deals and 0 otherwise.

Toehold is the percentage of target stocks held by the acquirer before the announcement date.

Bid premium corresponds to the premium (percentage) of the offer price to the target closing stock price four weeks before the announcement date.

Target-initiated is a dummy variable that takes a value of 1 if the deal is initiated by the target and a value of 0 otherwise.

Duration private process is the length in days of the private process from private initiation to public announcement.

Duration public process is the length in days of the public process from the public announcement to deal completion.

Target size (Acquirer size) is measured using the market value of equity (number of shares outstanding multiplied by the stock price) at day −40 relative to the announcement date.

R&D intensive industry is a dummy variable that takes a value of 1 if the target belongs to the top seven most R&D-intensive industries among the 49 Fama-French industries and 0 otherwise.

Sales concentration is the Herfindahl-Hirschman concentration index of the target's sales (sum of squares of sale shares by business and geographic segments, which were obtained from the Compustat Segment database).

Target debt ratio corresponds to long-term debt plus current liabilities divided by total assets.

Management ownership is the percentage of a firm's equity owned by the top management, as reported in the Compustat ExecuComp database.

Institutional ownership corresponds to the percentage of the target firm's equity owned by institutional investors.

Idiosyncratic risk is the standard deviation of abnormal returns from day −241 to day −42, relative to the announcement date (percentage per day).

To obtain the *Abnormal returns* required using the beta-one model (net of market returns), which subtracts the daily market portfolio return from the daily return of each company. The market portfolio is the Center for Research in Security Prices (CRSP) value-weighted index. For each firm, the abnormal returns are cumulated between day −5 and day +5, relative to the announcement date. The abnormal returns for the deal equal the average of the acquirer abnormal returns and the target abnormal returns, weighted by their respective market value. Market values are estimated 40 days before the announcement date.

According to Panel A in Exhibit 15.5, deal characteristics differ statistically in the comparison of auctioned to negotiated deals. Consistent with Boone and Mulherin (2007), the results show that negotiated deals are significantly larger than auctioned deals and that all-stock (all-cash) deals are more frequent for negotiations (auctions). A significant difference also exists in the relative size of auctions and negotiations. Relative to their buyers, targets involved in negotiations are much bigger than auctioned targets. However, no difference in relative size between auctions and negotiations appears in Boone and Mulherin's sample. Toehold acquisitions seem slightly more important for negotiations. Consistent with Boone and Mulherin, the average bid premium is 40.41 percent in the *Negotiation* subsample, which is not statistically different from 40.91 percent in the *Auction* subsample. This is consistent with the idea that competition plays a role in both negotiated and auctioned deals (Aktas et al., 2010). Betton et al. (2008) also find an average bid premium of the same magnitude.

Panel A of Exhibit 15.5 further indicates that targets initiate 60.41 percent of the deals that involve auctions but only 19.01 percent of negotiated deals. This suggests that bidders dodge competition whenever possible whereas targets do the opposite. An inference from these results is that acquirers "cherry-pick" good targets (for which latent competition is high). Yet, targets that decide to initiate a sale may be less attractive, so they need to stimulate competition to obtain the best offer. Regarding the duration of the takeover process, the duration of the private process (i.e., from private initiation to public announcement) is much longer for auctions (238 days) than for negotiations (179 days). This difference is statistically significant at normal levels. The duration of the public takeover process (i.e., from public announcement to deal completion) is roughly the same for the two selling procedures.

The information about the acquirers and targets in Panel B of Exhibit 15.5 reveals that acquirer size is not statistically different for auctions and negotiations, but acquirers that participate in negotiations have greater idiosyncratic risk than do acquirers in auctions. Consistent with Boone and Mulherin (2007), auctioned targets are significantly smaller than negotiated targets. The proportion of targets from R&D-intensive industries in the *Negotiation* subsample is marginally higher than in the *Auction* subsample, consistent with Hansen's (2001) argument that competitive information is a determinant of the selling procedure (i.e., targets are more willing to limit the number of bidders when sensitive competitive information could be disclosed).

Betton et al. (2008) emphasize that the selling procedure might depend on the complexity of the target because auctions are better suited to simple, standardized goods (Subramanian, 2009). The firm sales–based concentration index is used, according to business and geographic segments, as a proxy for the complexity of the target activities. The apportionment of sales by business and geographic segments comes from the Compustat Segment database. The concentration index declines with the degree of diversification of firm activities and thus is an inverse proxy for complexity. The difference in sales-based concentration is highly significant between auctions and negotiations. To some extent, auctioned targets are more focused than negotiated targets.

Management ownership is more important for an auctioned target, and the difference is marginally significant. Perhaps understandably, manager/owners favor competitive selling procedures. The average target debt ratio indicates that about 21 percent of targets' total assets are financed by debt. This proportion is stable across auctions and negotiations.

McConnell and Servaes (1990) report a positive relationship between institutional equity ownership and firm performance. Therefore, the expectation is that targets with large institutional shareholders are more likely to be approached by strategic buyers in the context of one-on-one negotiations, rather than through a competitive selling procedure. Moreover, Ferreira, Massa, and Matos (2010) argue that institutional investors act as deal facilitators in (international) M&A transactions. To assess whether the presence of institutional investors in the target shareholding structure favors one selling procedure over another, their position in the target firm is used, measured as a percentage of the target's total market value. Institutional investors own an average of 32.71 percent of target equity in negotiated deals and 29.82 percent in auctioned deals; this difference is significant. In comparison, Gaspar, Massa, and Matos (2005) report a 33 percent average institutional ownership for a sample of 3,746 target firms between 1980 and 1999.

Finally, Panel C of Exhibit 15.5 summarizes the market reactions around the announcement date using the classical event study method. To measure abnormal returns, the beta-one model (net of market returns) is used for the (–5, +5) event window, for which day 0 is the initial announcement date. The results in Exhibit 15.5 indicate that the average acquirer cumulative abnormal returns (CARs) differ statistically between auctions and negotiations, with values of –1.91 percent (p-value = 0.00) and –3.11 percent (p-value = 0.00), respectively. Boone and Mulherin (2008) do not uncover statistically different acquirer abnormal returns between auctions and negotiations. This perhaps occurs because their sample size (308 deals) is much smaller and they compute abnormal returns over a shorter event window (three days, centered on the initial announcement date). The average magnitude of the impact of the M&A announcement on target stock prices is the same for auctions and negotiations in the current sample, with an average 11-day abnormal return of approximately 22 percent. These results are consistent with Boone and Mulherin's (2007) findings. The wealth effects at the deal level are significantly positive in the current sample and roughly the same for both negotiations (abnormal returns = 0.65 percent, p-value = 0.07) and auctions (abnormal returns = 0.89 percent, p-value = 0.00).

Exhibit 15.6 presents a multivariate analysis of the determinants of the selling procedure. Specifically, a probit regression is used to model the probability of adopting one-on-one negotiations instead of organizing an auction. The dependent variable is therefore a dummy variable that takes a value of 1 for negotiated deals, and 0 otherwise. The analysis uses the following explanatory variables as determinants of the sales procedure:

- *A dummy variable that identifies targets in the top seven R&D-intensive industries among the 49 Fama-French industries* (measured as the average value of the R&D ratio for firms in that industry). Following Hansen's (2001) argument that targets are more willing to limit the number of bidders when they risk disclosing sensitive competitive information, targets in R&D-intensive industries are expected to resort more to negotiations.

Exhibit 15.6 Determinants of the Selling Procedure

This exhibit reports the results of two probit models in order to analyze the determinants of the selling procedure. In each model, the dependent variable is a dummy that takes a value of 1 for a negotiated deal and 0 otherwise. The selling procedure (negotiations versus auctions) is identified from the merger background section of corresponding SEC filings. The goodness of fit is measured by the likelihood ratio statistic. *% Correct prediction* denotes the percentage of transactions correctly classified by the corresponding probit model.

Variable	(1) Coefficient	*p*-value	(2) Coefficient	*p*-value
R&D intensive industry	−0.005	0.96	−0.091	0.32
Relative size	0.225***	0.01	0.166**	0.05
Acquirer size	0.000	0.45	0.000	0.45
Stock payment	0.511***	0.00	0.539***	0.00
Industry count	−0.141***	0.00	−0.105***	0.00
Target sales concentration	−0.413***	0.01	−0.312**	0.04
Target-initiated			−1.046***	0.00
Likelihood ratio statistic	92.29	0.00	262.14	0.00
% Correct prediction	62.51%		69.13%	
Number of observations	1,179		1,179	

Notes: Variable definitions are as follows:

R&D intensive industry is a dummy variable that takes a value of 1 if the target belongs to the top seven most R&D-intensive industries among the 49 Fama-French industries and 0 otherwise.

Relative size is the ratio of deal value to acquirer size.

Acquirer size corresponds to the market value of equity (number of shares outstanding multiplied by the stock price).

Stock payment is a dummy variable that takes a value of 1 for purely stock-financed deals and 0 otherwise.

Industry count corresponds to the number of firms in the same industry as the target with a market value greater than the target's in the year before the merger.

Target sales concentration is the Herfindahl-Hirschman concentration index of the target's sales (the sum of squares of sales shares by business and geographic segments, which come from the Compustat Segment database).

Target-initiated is a dummy variable that takes a value of 1 if the deal is initiated by the target and 0 otherwise.

- *Relative size or the ratio of deal value to acquirer size.* The expectation is that auctions are better suited to relatively small targets and negotiations align better with relatively large, strategic transactions with great value-creation potential (Boone and Mulherin, 2009; Subramanian, 2009).
- *Acquirer size.* Large, well-known firms might be reluctant to participate in competitive auctions, according to M&A professionals who advise companies (Aktas et al., 2010).
- *A dummy variable identifying the means of payment.* To facilitate their comparison of bids, targets are more likely to prefer a less sophisticated means of payment in auctions (e.g., all-cash payments) than they do in negotiations. Moreover, Houston and Ryngaert (1997) and Officer (2004) provide empirical evidence that the use of stock is inversely related to takeover competition.

- *Industry count or the number of firms in the target's industry with a market value greater than the market value of the target.* Prior research suggests that the likelihood of an auction relates to the potential depth of the bidder pool (e.g., Klemperer, 2002; Subramanian, 2009). Because acquirers tend to be relatively larger than targets (e.g., the median target-to-acquirer size ratio is between 12 and 18 percent in large sample studies such as Andrade et al. (2001) and Moeller et al. (2007)). Industry count is used as a proxy for potential buyers and is expected to be positively associated with auctions.
- *Target sales concentration, which provides an inverse proxy for the target's asset complexity.* Auctions should be the preferred choice when the exchanged asset can be specified precisely (Subramanian, 2009) or is less complex (Betton et al., 2008).

The parameters of the probit model are estimated with a sample of 1,179 M&A deals and the results are reported in column 1 of Exhibit 15.6. Negotiations display a positive association with stock payments and relative size significantly increases the probability of negotiations. The industry count coefficient is negative and significant, which supports the idea that auctions are more appropriate when the number of potential buyers is greater. The coefficient of target sales concentration is negative and statistically significant; negotiations are less (and auctions are more) likely when the target is a more focused company, as noted by Betton et al. (2008) or Subramanian (2009).

In column 2 of Exhibit 15.6, the target-initiated dummy is added as a control variable and used to re-estimate the probit model. The target-initiated dummy takes a value of 1 if the deal is initiated by the target and a value of 0 otherwise. The previously significant control variables retain their signs and significance. Consistent with the univariate evidence in Exhibit 15.5, the target-initiated coefficient is negative and significant. That is, target initiators prefer auctions to negotiations.

The explanatory power of the probit model increases substantially when the target-initiated dummy is included in the specification. This is indicated by the likelihood ratio statistic and the classification ratio of the two probit regressions.

Boone and Mulherin (2008) also provide results regarding the determinant of the selling procedure choice with their sample of 308 large U.S. transactions. Consistent with Comment and Schwert (1995), Boone and Mulherin document that targets in strong antitakeover states resort less to competitive selling procedures. Their evidence also reveals that a bidder and target engaged in an ongoing relationship are more likely to conduct a negotiated transaction. The quality of financial advisers used in a merger deal also affects the choice of the selling procedure, such that acquirers hiring a high-quality investment bank tend to engage more in negotiations than in auctions.

SUMMARY AND CONCLUSIONS

From the seller's point of view, the conventional wisdom indicates that the best way to get a good price is to resort to a competitive selling procedure. However, not all M&A transactions are auctions with multiple bidders. For large transactions, the proportion of negotiations is comparable to the proportion of auctions and the gains for target shareholders similarly are comparable between the two sales procedures. This prior evidence suggests that sellers in a takeover market tend to adopt an optimal selling procedure for their own situation and aim to maximize shareholder wealth.

Using a large sample of M&A deals between U.S. companies, this chapter has proposed a framework to describe the private part of the takeover process and an empirical analysis of the determinants of the selling procedure. Several factors affect the choice of an auction versus a negotiation including the number of potential buyers, the nature of the assets, and the target's eagerness to sell. The results indicate that the relative size of the deal and the complexity of the asset being sold increase the probability of negotiations. The evidence also shows that the likelihood of an auction is positively associated with the number of potential bidders. Finally, the results confirm that target initiators in the sample prefer a competitive sales procedure.

DISCUSSION QUESTIONS

1. Prior literature documents that the average bid premium and abnormal returns obtained by target shareholders are roughly the same for auctioned and negotiated deals. Therefore, the wealth effects of the transaction do not seem to depend on the selling procedure or the level of competition. What factors might drive the bid premium for negotiations and auctions to approximately the same level?

2. According to Boone and Mulherin's (2009) framework, what are the different steps in the private component of the takeover process?

3. List and discuss five factors that help explain the choice of selling method (negotiation versus auction).

4. Describe the private component of the takeover process of the $4.57 billion merger between McClatchy (acquirer) and Knight Ridder (target), announced on June 13, 2006. (Note: As a starting point, download the S-4 filing associated with the merger agreement from the SEC Web site [www.sec.gov]. Then, use the merger background section of that filing to describe the procedure. The date of the filing is April 14, 2006.)

REFERENCES

Aktas, Nihat, Eric de Bodt, and Richard Roll. 2010. "Negotiations under the Threat of an Auction." *Journal of Financial Economics* 98:2, 241–255.

Andrade, Gregor, Mark Mitchell, and Erik Stafford. 2001. "New Evidence and Perspectives on Mergers." *Journal of Economic Perspectives* 15:2, 103–210.

Betton, Sandra, B. Espen Eckbo, and Karin S. Thorburn. 2008. "Corporate Takeovers." In B. Espen Eckbo, ed. *Handbook of Corporate Finance, Empirical Corporate Finance*, Vol. 2, 291–429. North-Holland: Elsevier.

Betton, Sandra, B. Espen Eckbo, and Karin S. Thorburn. 2009. "Merger Negotiations and the Toehold Puzzle." *Journal of Financial Economics* 91:2, 158–178.

Boone, Audra L., and J. Harold Mulherin. 2007. "How Are Firms Sold?" *Journal of Finance* 62:2, 847–875.

Boone, Audra L., and J. Harold Mulherin. 2008. "Do Auctions Induce a Winner's Curse? New Evidence from the Corporate Takeover Market." *Journal of Financial Economics* 89:1, 1–19.

Boone, Audra L., and J. Harold Mulherin. 2009. "Is There One Best Way to Sell a Company? Auctions Versus Negotiations and Controlled Sales." *Journal of Applied Corporate Finance* 21:3, 28–37.

Bulow, Jeremy, and Paul Klemperer. 1996. "Auctions Versus Negotiations." *American Economic Review* 86:1, 180–194.

Comment, Robert, and William G. Schwert. 1995. "Poison or Placebo? Evidence on the Deterrence and Wealth Effects of Modern Anti-takeover Measures." *Journal of Financial Economics* 39:1, 3–43.

Ferreira, Miguel A., Massimo Massa, and Pedro Matos. 2010. "Shareholders at the Gate? Institutional Investors and Cross-border Mergers and Acquisitions." *Review of Financial Studies* 23:2, 601–644.

Fishman, Michael J. 1988. "A Theory of Preemptive Takeover Bidding." *RAND Journal of Economics* 19:1, 88–101.

Fishman, Michael J. 1989. "Pre-emptive Bidding and the Role of the Medium of Exchange in Acquisitions." *Journal of Finance* 44:1, 41–57.

Gaspar, José-Miguel, Massimo Massa, and Pedro Matos. 2005. "Shareholder Investment Horizons and the Market for Corporate Control." *Journal of Financial Economics* 76:1, 135–165.

Hansen, Robert G. 2001. "Auctions of Companies." *Economic Inquiry* 39:1, 30–43.

Hartzell, Jay C., Eli Ofek, and David Yermack. 2004. "What's in It for Me? CEOs Whose Firms Are Acquired." *Review of Financial Studies* 17:1, 37–61.

Houston, Joel, and Michael Ryngaert. 1997. "Equity Issuance and Adverse Selection: A Direct Test Using Conditional Stock Offers." *Journal of Finance* 52:1, 197–219.

Klemperer, Paul. 2002. "What Really Matters in Auction Design?" *Journal of Economic Perspectives* 16:1, 169–189.

McConnell, John J., and Henri Servaes. 1990. "Additional Evidence on Equity Ownership and Corporate Value." *Journal of Financial Economics* 27:2, 595–612.

Moeller, Sarah B., Frederik P. Schlingemann, and René M. Stulz. 2004. "Firm Size and the Gains from Acquisitions." *Journal of Financial Economics* 73:2, 201–228.

Moeller, Sarah B., Frederik P. Schlingemann, and René M. Stulz. 2007. "How Do Diversity of Opinion and Information Asymmetry Affect Acquirer Returns?" *Review of Financial Studies* 20:5, 2047–2078.

Officer, Micah. 2004. "Collars and Renegotiations in Mergers and Acquisitions." *Journal of Finance* 59:6, 2719–2743.

Schwert, William G. 2000. "Hostility in Takeovers: In the Eyes of the Beholder?" *Journal of Finance* 55:6, 2599–2640.

Simsir, Aziz S. 2009. "The Information Content of Deal Initiation in Mergers and Acquisitions." Working Paper, Sabanci University.

Subramanian, Guhan. 2009. "Negotiation? Auction? A Deal Maker's Guide." *Harvard Business Review* 87:12, 101–107.

ABOUT THE AUTHORS

Nihat Aktas joined EMLYON Business School in 2008, following five years on the faculty at Louvain School of Management. Being interested in empirical corporate finance in general, Professor Aktas is the coauthor of several research articles published in peer-reviewed international journals including the *Journal of Financial Economics, Journal of Financial and Quantitative Analysis, Economic Journal, Journal of Corporate Finance,* and *Journal of Banking & Finance.* His research has been featured on the programs of various international conferences, such as the American Finance Association and European Finance Association, and quoted in widely read international media, such as the *Financial Times* and *The New York Times*. He was a visiting researcher at the Anderson School of Management (UCLA, Los Angeles) in 2001–2002. Professor Aktas is a founding member of the European Center for Corporate Control Studies (ECCCS), which is dedicated to promoting top-level research on and best practices in corporate control in the European context (www.ecccs.eu).

Eric de Bodt is Professor of Finance at Université Lille Nord de France. With his ongoing interest in corporate finance and auction theory, he devotes his current research efforts mainly to M&A decisions. He is the coauthor of several articles published in various peer-reviewed international journals including the *Journal of Financial Economics, Journal of Financial and Quantitative Analysis, Journal of Corporate Finance, Economic Journal, Journal of Financial Markets,* and *Journal of Banking & Finance.* His research has been featured on the programs of various international conferences, such as the American Finance Association and European Finance Association, and quoted in widely read international media, such as *Financial Times, The New York Times,* and *USA Today.* Eric de Bodt is a founding member of the ECCCS and the current director of the Université Lille 2–Skema research center.

CHAPTER 16

Postacquisition Planning and Integration

OLIMPIA MEGLIO
Assistant Professor of Management, University of Sannio

ARTURO CAPASSO
Professor of Management and Corporate Finance, University of Sannio

INTRODUCTION

This chapter analyzes the postacquisition process. It focuses on the planning and implementation of the integration process, highlights their contribution to value creation, and identifies potential pitfalls. Jemison and Sitkin (1986) propose that an acquisition should be seen as a process. Describing the acquisition as a process means that it does not end with the closing of the deal but that it can last several years. Recognizing a process view of mergers and acquisitions (M&As) implies that the integration should start during the negotiation phase of the deal. A careful analysis of the time and costs of integrating the merging companies may modify how parties evaluate the deal.

The integration process is the process through which the acquiring company organizes the interaction with the target company and implements changes to exploit the expected synergies and forecasted cash flows. Haspeslagh and Jemison (1991, p.106) define the integration as an "interactive and gradual process in which individuals from two organizations learn to work together and cooperate in the transfer of strategic capabilities." Such a process is necessary, as the existence of a strategic, organizational, or cultural fit does not in itself assure that management will successfully exploit the expected benefits such as synergies.

The potential sources of synergy can be categorized into operating, managerial, and financial synergies.

1. Operating synergies affect the operations of the combined firm and include economies of scale and scope, increased market power, skills and technology transfer, and resources and capabilities sharing.
2. Managerial synergies result from substituting the acquired company's existing management with a more effective one.
3. Financial synergies include tax benefits, diversification, higher debt capacity, and appropriate use for excess cash.

Although financial synergies are generally easier to exploit, operating and managerial synergies may have a greater impact on the probability of success for the acquiring firm. Because financial synergies are less buyer specific and can be easily exploited, their value is typically included in the acquisition price and allocated to the seller in an active market for corporate control. In contrast, operating and managerial synergies largely depend on the characteristics of the acquirer. Therefore, the bidding and target firm's shareholders often share the value of these synergies based on the competition in the market for corporate control, the respective bargaining power of the players involved, and the evaluation of expected synergies from the acquiring firm's point of view. A fair sharing of synergies should leave the acquiring firm's stockholders with at least some of the incremental value created by the deal. From the acquiring firm's perspective, if those synergies are unspecific and likely to be attained by the seller, the potential synergies that actually count are those to be achieved through the integration process. Their potential value depends on the integration planning and implementation. Therefore, the basic choices regarding the integration process could influence the valuation procedure. The more intense the integration of the combining firms, the more valuable is the potential synergy. However, a strong integration between two firms usually requires direct and indirect costs that could affect the expected value of integration benefits. In deciding on the degree of postmerger integration, the acquiring firm's management should solve the crucial trade-off between potential synergies and integration costs, determine an optimal balance, and translate this into an effective integration plan. Thus, the integration process should start during the negotiation phase.

The integration process represents the sum of multiple, concurrent, and sometimes conflicting processes. Therefore, the integration process should be understood as a bundle of integration processes, each of which is intended to attain one or more acquisition goals. Having acknowledged that the integration process is not unitary, two distinct grand processes can be identified: (1) task integration, which deals with asset rationalization, and (2) human integration, which deals with employees' acculturation (Birkinshaw, 1999).

Task integration refers to how the value-adding activities that result from joining two companies generate synergies. It involves capabilities transfer from one company to the other and resource sharing between the two companies. Task integration often includes rationalization of activities through downsizing and asset sales. This usually occurs in the case of an "overcapacity" M&A in terms of Bower's (2001) typologies.

Human integration is the process of building a shared identity among the employees of the merging companies. In the period immediately after closing the deal, the human integration process has to alleviate the negative attitudes that change and uncertainty may bring. Afterwards, its objective switches toward building a unifying organizational culture. Such processes can be conflicting, depending on the priorities and the speed of integration. Evidence by Homburg and Bucerius (2006) shows that the speed of integration can substantially affect integration success. Yet, speed can also be troubling. If the integration team starts with rationalization (such as closing duplicate facilities and reducing overhead), the team will make rapid progress on reducing costs but may face the prospect of an unenthusiastic and scared workforce. If the team starts with acculturation (building relationships between employees from the two firms and fostering a common culture), the firm may have content employees but little cost savings. Doing both simultaneously may not be the ideal answer because of the apparent hypocrisy of telling employees that their involvement in the integration process is vital to the success of the enterprise while also announcing staff reductions.

Many managers involved in acquisitions face this basic dilemma because task integration and human integration are often at cross purposes. For example, in the days after an acquisition announcement, managers should meet with every employee to allay understandable concerns. The demand for rapid action and cost control could make such a move prohibitive. In contrast, closing one of the acquired firm's plants should help the task integration process but will almost certainly hinder the human integration process unless carefully handled. While the ultimate goal of full task and human integration is clear, the route chosen and the implied trade-offs are a source of continuous conflict for the individuals responsible for the integration process. This stresses the importance of effectively balancing these opposing needs according to the level of integration (Birkinshaw, 1999).

A widespread belief is that M&As result in a failure for the acquiring companies in more than half of the cases. A highly important factor producing such high failure rates is cultural clash. The existing literature deals with measuring the impact of cultural and organizational distance between the merging parties on postacquisition performance but has not yet provided consistent findings. Some scholars claim that cultural distance is detrimental and increases the likelihood of failure, while others claim that it depends on how the process is handled. Because the chapter shares this latter view, it provides a close look at what happens during the integration process and how to foster effective change within the merging companies.

The remainder of the chapter has the following organization. First, it analyzes what the integration process is, who leads this process, and needed integrating mechanisms. Then the chapter focuses on communication tools. The theoretical analysis is augmented with two examples of how to communicate an M&A to employees and financial markets. The next to last section provides an analysis of M&A performance measurement, and the final section offers a summary and conclusions.

THE INTEGRATION PROCESS: A CLOSER LOOK

Conventional wisdom depicts the integration planning process as made up of a basic option, generally referred to as the integration approach or integration level. The literature often depicts such a decision-making process as the choice among different integration typologies linked to the multiplicity of goals M&As intend to pursue (Napier, 1989; Haspeslagh and Jemison, 1991).

The integration typologies developed by Haspeslagh and Jemison (1991) are prominent among M&A scholars. They suggest four integration modes that describe how the acquiring company should integrate the target after the deal is signed. These modes are based on two factors: strategic interdependence and organizational autonomy. The identified typologies—absorption, symbiosis, preservation, and holding—represent different integrative strategies, which differ in terms of pervasiveness of the integration process and the goals of the M&A.

According to Haspeslagh and Jemison (1991, p.147), the absorption approach takes place when "the strategic task requires a high degree of interdependence to create the value expected but has a low need of organizational autonomy to achieve that interdependence: integration in this case implies a full consolidation." The preservation approach is adopted in the case of a low degree of interdependence and a high degree of autonomy. The symbiotic approach is probably the most difficult to implement and takes place in cases of high strategic interdependence and organizational autonomy. The ultimate goal of this approach is to find the right balance between integration and autonomy. In this case, integration generally starts with the two entities coexisting and then gradually becoming increasingly interdependent.

Although such typologies are useful tools to make sense of how to balance strategic and organizational factors, they reflect the acquiring firm's perspective and overlook the target firm's preferences. Nahavandi and Malekzadeh (1988) offer a nuanced view of acculturation modes and take this perspective into account. To describe the implementation strategy, they use the notion of acculturation. The authors claim that the degree of acculturation is dependent upon the type of acquisition, the acquiring company's degree of multiculturalism, the acquired company's attractiveness to the acquirer, as well as the acquired company's willingness to preserve its own culture.

The suggested typologies are: assimilation, integration, separation, and deculturation. These typologies are very similar to those provided by Haspleslagh and Jemison (1991). Yet, Nahavandi and Malekzadeh (1988) shift their focus from the combination of strategic and organizational factors to cultural factors, thus outlining the primacy of cultural aspects in shaping the overall success of a merger.

These typologies were popular among M&A scholars during the 1980s and 1990s. Despite their popularity, they are ineffective tools to guide executives in leading an acquisition process because they cannot deal with the complex, multistage, and multilevel nature of the integration process (Javidan, Pablo, Singh, Hitt, and Jemison, 2004). In most cases, acquiring companies need to apply a hybrid postacquisition integration approach with simultaneous short-term and long-term motives or orientations and segmentation at a different pace across different value chain components (Schweizer, 2005). Moreover, during the integration, the acquiring company needs to adapt action plans to new events or human reactions. Thus, integration is a dynamic process of adjustment in a context of uncertainty and incomplete information.

The decision-making process in the postintegration context consists of several interrelated decisions. The starting point can be understood as the choice between integration and autonomy. This choice depends on the specific goals and the time interval within which the acquiring company intends to reap benefits from the acquisitive strategy. A focus on a short time interval will probably emphasize a quick integration of the newly merged companies, while a focus on a long time interval could imply a slower integration process. The concurrent consideration of goals and timing will affect the choice about what, how, and when the merging companies should be integrated. What seems to be a linear decision-making process is actually not because each choice influences and is, in turn, influenced by previous ones (Capasso and Meglio, 2005).

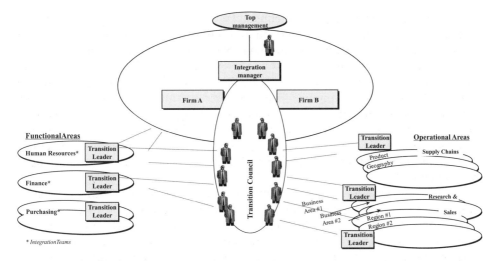

Exhibit 16.1 The Integration Structure for M&As

Note: The exhibit depicts the basic architecture of the integration structure that is made up of top management, integration manager, and transition team leaders. Responsibilities are classified in terms of functional as well as operational areas.

Leading the Integration Process

To fully depict the interrelationships among actors, levels of integration, and time horizons, this section analyzes the actors involved at different organizational levels and the associated integration mechanisms. Postmerger integration requires leadership. The days immediately after closing a deal are generally surrounded by great uncertainty and leadership vacuum. Thus, quickly deciding on who runs the process at different organizational levels and articulating tasks and responsibilities is essential. Given the complexity of such a process, several people often lead the process.

Exhibit 16.1 identifies three levels of managers or leaders: top management, the integration manager, and transition team leaders.

1. Top management is responsible for defining the integration model, appointing the integration manager, and approving its choices, such as the transition team leaders' appointments.
2. The integration manager is responsible for running the integration process. The role resembles that of any other process-leadership position that a company might create to drive any change-process implementation it undertakes. It involves project management. That is, the integration manager helps to create integration teams, consolidate operations, and transfer critical skills between companies. Yet, an effective integration manager does much more by not only reporting to top management but also by helping to set the company's agenda. The integration manager must have a strong decision-making instinct and distinctive skills to work cross functionally. A strong trust relationship with the key executives is critical because the integration manager often acts as their proxy and confidant.

3. Transition team leaders are responsible for undertaking specific integration tasks under the integration manager's supervision. All transition team leaders belong to a transition council, which is an ad hoc body aimed at fostering coordinative integration efforts.

Exhibit 16.1 depicts the architecture of the integration process. In this architecture, the integration manager performs a key role as the link between top management, who is responsible for setting the overall goal of the integration process, and the transition team leaders, who are concerned with achieving the integration within both functional and operational areas.

The integration manager's distinctive features are identified as:

• Leadership or the ability to lead people toward an intended change.
• The ability to gain commitment within the integration team.
• A networking capability to ease the permeability of the merging companies' boundaries.
• Communication and relational skills to facilitate interaction among people.
• The legitimacy to serve as the integration leader.

These different features are essential for the integration leader to perform different roles during the integration process. The first role that the integration leader performs, often called "organizational maverick," is to promote a cooperative atmosphere between integration teams. To achieve this end, leadership and communication skills are essential. Closely related to this role is the role of "transformational leader." Again, leadership and the ability to obtain commitment play key roles in acting as transformational leader. As the integration process unfolds, the integration leader performs a third role as "organizational buffer" to allay concerns, pressures, and political factors that can harm the effectiveness of the integration teams. To perform this role, legitimacy, networking capability, and communication skills are essential. The fourth role is the one of "network facilitator." Performing such a role means that the integration leader promotes cooperation among team members and fosters the creativity within teams (Dagnino and Pisano, 2008).

This integration leader's perspective reflects a top-down view of the integration process, according to which middle management would limit itself to implementing top management's plans. However, middle management may also play a more active role because it needs to operationalize the strategic content (Meyer, 2006). Middle management, for instance, can influence the strategic process upward, that is, during strategy formulation (Schilit, 1987). Still, middle managers can play either destructive or productive roles during the postmerger phase. Implementation problems are often the results of poor middle management understanding and inadequate commitment to strategy. However, recent studies, such as Meyer (2006) and Risberg (1999), challenge this idea, suggesting a more nuanced view in which middle managers may play an active and influential role promoting and facilitating change. Middle managers are uniquely suited to communicate change across the organization and can address employees' emotional distress during change. This, of course, depends on the middle managers' commitment to strategy, which, in turn, is linked to how the strategic intent fits with what managers perceive as the interests of the organization and with the personal interests of the managers. While Dagnino and Pisano (2008) depict the distinctive features of the integration leader and the different roles he or she performs, they do not discuss the most suitable tools necessary for achieving the single integration goals. These tools represent several integration mechanisms that are discussed in the following section.

Integration Mechanisms and Communication Plans

Larsson (1990) notes that attaining integration goals occurs as a result of integration mechanisms, which are the tools available to the acquirer to foster the interaction between the joining firms, the coordination of this interaction, and the collective, interpersonal, and individual levels of the human side of the combination. He identifies seven different integration mechanisms.

1. *Restructuring*: Targets asset rationalization through the accumulation or stabilization of similar activities and the combining or timing of flows of related activities.
2. *Formal planning*: Reduces ambiguity and uncertainty through the formal pre-adjustment of activities.
3. *Management information system*: Improves the communication process by budgeting and reporting system standardization.
4. *Transition teams*: Leverages the coordinative integration efforts and helps to facilitate communication of new information.
5. *Socialization*: Improves the coordination within merging companies and creates a common orientation. This mechanism reduces employee resistance and enhances the acculturation process.
6. *Mutual consideration*: Reduces resistance and possible sources of conflicts and creates a more favorable climate toward the intended changes.
7. *Human resources systems*: Reduces resistance from employees by dealing with job design, rewards systems, personnel policies, and career planning.

These tools require communication to be implemented. Communication is the vehicle to fostering integration and change. Open communication between the merging companies and within the acquired firm is needed to minimize ambiguity after a deal. M&As are often surrounded by uncertainty about the future. If nothing is communicated, employees seek their own answers, often leading to rumors that can increase anxiety. Managers should communicate to all relevant stakeholders as soon as possible. Arguably, the goals and the content of the message as well as the chosen medium depend on the target audience as illustrated in the synopsis below. Managing all communications during the postacquisition integration requires a comprehensive communication plan. Exhibit 16.2 provides an example of a communication plan. A comprehensive communication plan describes the audiences, what the goals are vis-à-vis the different audiences, and how they will be expressed in terms of content and media (Habeck, Kröger, and Träm, 2000).

By way of example, communicating the closure of a deal to employees requires a different medium and a different content, as compared with communicating the

Exhibit 16.2   A Communication Plan for M&As

Target Audience	Goals	Content	Medium
Top managers in both companies	Engage commitment	Merger goals Merger approach Golden parachutes plans	Cascade meetings Series of lunch meetings CEO confidential meetings
Transition leaders	Engage commitment Ensure understand their role	Merger goals Merger approach Individual team goals Team member selection criteria	Long meetings led by CEO
Employees	Ensure employees know the basic merger goals Start constructive discussions	Merger goals Merger approach Future potential Personnel policies	Cascade meetings E-mail Face-to-face communications
Investors	Secure investors' support	Merger goals Merger approach Future potential	Press news Company reports Analysts reports

Note: Adapted from Habeck et al. (2000, p. 110).
Exhibit 16.2 describes a comprehensive communication plan. The choice of the medium and the content of the message should be tied to the target audience and the goal to attain.

deal to financial markets. Moreover, if the goal is to let all employees know the basic facts about a deal, e-mail is a suitable tool. If the goal is to start a constructive discussion, then face-to-face communication along with cascade meetings are more suitable choices. Therefore, even if the audience is the same, the content of the message determines the most suitable communication tool to achieve the intended aim.

Communication can be analyzed from a process perspective, which implies recognizing the need for different communication strategies for different acquisition phases (Sinetar, 1981). This emphasizes the need to break down the communication plan into different time periods. In the premerger phase, steady communication that reassures employees is suitable, while during the transition phase, communication should direct employees in the new organization. Sinetar suggests that communication, if properly used, not only preserves morale but also prevents top management turnover.

To exemplify the proper communication tools vis-à-vis different audiences, two cases of recent acquisitions are presented. These examples illustrate how firms can handle communication with employees and financial markets. The first case involves the Zappos-Amazon merger while the second concerns the Dada-Upoc deal. Both are examples of effective ways to communicate a deal but use different media for different audiences.

The Zappos-Amazon Experience

The first case describes how Tony Hsieh, the chief executive officer (CEO) of Zappos, announced to his employees the agreement with Amazon and what changes the acquisition would bring about within the company. Furthermore, the case describes how he explains the implication of the acquisition for the employees at Zappos in terms of their careers and the evolution of internal and external relationships. This example illustrates how good internal communications help to smooth the anxiety that an announcement creates.

Hsieh relies on a letter that he sent to all employees. This letter is organized around several key issues: the importance of the acquisition, changes that the acquisition would imply, and implications in terms of career and turnover. The letter starts by offering some details about the deal. For example, it clarifies that although Amazon will become one of Zappos' shareholders, Zappos' vision of satisfying customers, employees, and vendors will remain the same. The letter depicts Amazon as essential in helping Zappos pursue its long-term strategic goals by accelerating the growth of the Zappos brand and culture, yet leaving enough independence to preserve the uniqueness of Zappos' identity and culture. The most important part of this letter focuses on answering what Hsieh defines as the top three burning questions: "Will I still have a job?" "Will the Zappos' culture change?" and "Are my colleagues leaving?"

Hsieh answers these questions with clarity and conciseness to avoid any ambiguity. Regarding the first question, he claims that Zappos will be a wholly owned subsidiary of Amazon, adding that their jobs are as secure as they were previously. The second question concerns the uniqueness of Zappos' culture. Hsieh reassures all employees that Zappos has full control of how its culture evolves and that Amazon praises Zappos' culture. However, he also reinforces the role of Amazon in helping Zappos to strengthen its brand identity. The third question concerns possible overstaffing troubles. He claims that no one will be asked to leave the company. The reason is that the merging companies are expected to grow and be more efficient than standing alone. The letter ends by providing an analysis of the strategic and operational implications of the agreement. Hsieh focuses attention on the cultural similarities between Zappos and Amazon, as well as on complementarities in market strategies, and states that their mission remains unchanged.

The Dada Mobile Inc. and Upoc Networks Inc. Experience

The second example is based on a press release issued from Dada Mobile Inc. to announce its acquisition of Upoc Network. This example focuses on how to communicate an acquisition to financial markets. As Exhibit 16.2 shows, a proper communication medium for this audience is a press release, which should focus on explaining the rationale for the agreement and the long-term benefits from the deal.

Dada Mobile Inc., a subsidiary of Dada S.p.A. (MTAX of the Italian Stock Exchange: DA.MI) based in New York, operates in the U.S. Web, mobile entertainment, and community services markets. In 2006, Dada formalized an agreement to acquire Upoc Networks Inc., an experienced player in the American Internet and mobile added-value services markets. To announce the deal to financial markets, Dada issued a press release that provided details about the target company's consumers, turnover, growth rate, and other key information as well as Dada's international strategy and Upoc's contribution to implement such a strategy. The press release also discussed how acquiring Upoc would result in benefits involving sales and the customer base and provided details about the financial aspects and timing of the deal.

As the examples above show, one of the most frequently cited topics in communicating a deal is the benefits the deal is expected to bring to the parties involved. This leads to analyzing how to measure M&A performance.

MEASURING M&A PERFORMANCE

How do M&As perform? This is the key question in much of the current M&A literature. Despite the sheer amount of empirical research dealing with measuring postacquisition performance, no consensus exists among scholars about the effectiveness of this strategic option, at least from the acquiring company's point of view. The reason for the widespread skepticism toward M&As is the absence of conclusive and coherent findings relating to postacquisition performance. The evolution of the M&A empirical literature can be understood as a collective attempt to identify the variables (independent, moderating, or mediating) that explain or predict M&A performance. The absence of conclusive findings seems to suggest that the M&A literature has not yet identified the right variables (King, Dalton, Daily, and Covin, 2004). Other possible explanations for inconsistency in M&A performance research are that the field is fragmented with substantive gaps (Larsson and Finkelstein, 1999), that an integrative framework needs to be developed (Javidan et al., 2004), and that the performance construct measurement deserves further attention (Zollo and Meier, 2008).

A review of the empirical M&A performance literature suggests that scholars tend to conceptualize M&A performance in narrow or broad ways and to focus on financial or nonfinancial performance (Meglio and Risberg, 2009). As Exhibit 16.3 shows, M&A performance measures can be categorized as belonging to two different domains. First, the financial domain comprises market- and accounting-based measures of performance. Second, the nonfinancial domain comprises operational and survival measures of performance. For each type of performance measurement, Exhibit 16.3 identifies different dimensions along which M&A performance can be measured and provides indicators for each dimension.

Within the financial domain, M&A scholars tend to equate M&A performance as market returns. Market returns examine the stock price changes around a fairly short event window, generally five days before and after the acquisition announcement. Such a measure presumes that the market, at the time of the announcement, can evaluate whether the transaction is expected to create value during the integration process. Therefore, the suitability of such a measure depends on the efficiency of financial markets (Fama, 1970; McWilliams and Siegel, 1997). The lack of market efficiency makes the measurement of M&A performance after a short event window questionable. For example, Oler, Harrison, and Allen (2008) find no relationship between short- and long-run measures (over three years). This evidence suggests that the market response at the time of the announcement was inaccurate

Exhibit 16.3 A Classification of M&A Performance Measures

Type of Performance	Dimensions	Indicators (Examples)
Financial: Market	Risk	Jensen's alpha
	Shareholder value	Cumulative abnormal return
		Cumulative average abnormal return
		Returns to shareholders
Financial: Accounting	Profit	Return on assets
		Return on investment
	Growth	Net income
		Sales growth
Nonfinancial: Operational	Marketing	Market share
	Innovation	Number of patents
	Productivity	New product cost savings
		Sabotage episodes
Nonfinancial: Survival	Survival	Divestiture and retention

Exhibit 16.3 provides a classificatory scheme of performance measures. M&A performance measures are placed into two different domains (financial and nonfinancial) and classified in terms of types of measures and dimensions along which performance is measured. Examples of indicators are provided.

and incomplete and that the market is self-correcting as new information becomes available.

Also within the financial domain are accounting-based measures of performance. Such measures are supposedly backward looking and do not account for changes in risk. M&A scholars often use such measures when they cannot rely on market data. For instance, Zollo and Singh (2004) measure acquisition performance as the variation in the acquiring firm's return on assets (ROA). This choice is driven by the difficulty of valuing the postacquisition decisions, as well as the learning processes, from the financial market's standpoint. Accounting-based measures possess the typical drawbacks of single indicators (Boyd, Gove, and Hitt, 2005).

Operational and survival measures of M&A performance are outside the financial domain and are therefore placed within the nonfinancial domain. As a measure of survival, divestitures play a prominent role. The popularity of such a measure is probably due to Porter's (1987) claim that divestment is a proxy for failure. Yet, Montgomery, Thomas, and Kamath (1984) identify large and significant gains occurring for divestments within a strategic context.

Larsson and Finkelstein (1999) conceptualize acquisition performance as operational performance and measure it in terms of synergy realization. They define it as the actual net benefits (reduced cost per unit and increased outcome) created by the interaction of merging firms. The authors split synergy realization into eleven items belonging to three different dimensions (combination potential, organizational integration, and employee resistance), offering a multidimensional and subjective (as well as objective) measure of acquisition performance.

From the excursus above, it appears that M&A scholars generally favor objective measures of M&A performance. However, when objective data are unavailable, M&A scholars tend to use perceptual data. Executives' judgments offer a subjective, ex-post assessment of the success or failure of a transaction. Such measures can be inherently flawed by managerial (Risberg, 1999) and retrospective (Isabella, 1990) biases. Very, Lubatkin, Calori, and Veiga (1997) use three performance appraisal items (earnings, sales, and market shares) regarding acquired firms and justify their choice with the unavailability of secondary data about target firms. While Nayyar (1992) contends that self-reported performance measures are generally reliable, Schoenberg (2006) shows that ex-ante capital market reactions to an acquisition announcement exhibit little relation to corporate managers' ex-post judgment.

This brief comparison of alternative measures currently employed by M&A scholars seems to indicate that they attach different meanings to the label "M&A performance." Scholars sometimes conceptualize M&A performance as financial performance and sometimes as nonfinancial performance. Moreover, they may measure M&A performance a few days after the announcement of the deal and, in other cases, five or seven years after the merger, as in the case of divestitures. Which is the best way to measure M&A performance? This lack of consensus seems to be the current state of debate among M&A scholars, who are called upon to judge the different measures of success in terms of reliability and validity with the aim of finding the best measure (Zollo and Meier, 2008).

Meglio and Risberg (2010) provide a different understanding of this state of affairs. They claim that M&A scholars are overlooking that contradictory results arise from adopting different performance measures embedded in different research methods. In a literature review of M&A studies on performance published in top-tier management journals, Meglio and Risberg (2009) find patterns indicating that the definitions of M&A performance are almost as many as the studies in terms of operational definitions, indicators, temporal orientations, and units of analysis. Even within the narrower realm of technology-driven M&As, Meglio (2009) notes that M&A scholars sometimes measure performance in terms of such measures as inventors' postacquisition productivity, abnormal returns, or knowledge transfer. The answer is not, however, to look for the best and true measure of M&A performance. Rather, the answer is to be aware of a multiplicity of measures for M&A performance, each of which reflects the different stakeholders within M&As. Therefore, developing a set of different M&A performance indicators is essential.

Thus, M&A researchers should avoid focusing on one-size-fits-all measures. Instead, they should provide a clear and comprehensive answer to the following questions: What is M&A performance? How and when is M&A performance measured? What is the unit of analysis for such a measure?

The choice should be guided by the research question that the M&A scholar intends to answer and the setting under investigation. An example will help clarify this issue. Assume that a researcher is investigating a single merger or acquisition or a sample of M&As taking place within a high-technology industry or is interested in measuring the performance of a transaction, which could be labeled as a substitute for research and development (R&D). According to Bower's (2001) typologies, measuring the market reaction to the deal's announcement would not make sense. In such a case, the number of patents issued, say three or four years after the M&A, could better account for its capability to improve the innovative performance of the acquiring company. Although mergers may represent strategically heterogeneous events (Halpern, 1983; Lubatkin, 1987; Bower, 2001), empirical studies treat them as homogeneous. Performance measures should reflect different motives and typologies. Because a transaction could be strategic or financial, related or unrelated, this makes a difference in terms of both the depth and the length of the integration process. As for the unrelated transaction, the integration process will be quite fast with a low impact on human resources. If the acquisition is related, many contextual factors may affect the acquisition performance and the time lag, and the reciprocal relationships among all factors outlined above may require a multitemporal and multidimensional measure.

When Is M&A Performance Measured?

The temporal scale of performance measurement is an important boundary condition in measuring M&A performance. If the deal being investigated is a strategic one, then studying how the integration process unfolds over time is important. However, limiting the measurement of performance to the days immediately after the transaction can provide only an incomplete picture of M&A outcomes.

Researchers have generally underestimated the temporal scale of measurement and have not discussed the choice of different temporal scales for measurement. While M&As are conceived as a process, researchers often treat them as instantaneous events. They assume that identifying the starting point and each phase of the process is possible (Risberg, 1999). To date, many consider the announcement date as the starting point of the acquisition process, even if it represents the end of the negotiation process. When does an M&A end? In other words, when is it meaningful to assess the outcomes of an acquisition? Again, the answer leads back to the specific question that the researcher wants to answer and the kind of deal that is under investigation.

What Is the Unit and Level of Analysis for M&A Performance?

Several stakeholders take part in the acquisition process, so assessing who gains and who loses in M&As would be useful. Is the unit of analysis the acquiring firm, the target firm, the investment bank, or the business consulting firm? Clearly specifying the unit of analysis that the M&A performance wants to measure would help researchers understand the results of empirical research dealing with M&A performance.

Moreover, scholars should distinguish the organizational level from the individual level. Acquiring firms, target firms, the combination of the two, investment bankers, and business consulting firms represent the organizational level, while employees and customers represent the individual level. Because each takes part in the acquisition process with different motives and at different times, this distinction should be incorporated when measuring acquisition performance.

How Is M&A Performance Measured?

The operationalization of performance construct and the method employed in M&A studies can be considered different sides of the same coin. To date, M&A scholars have generally used cross-sectional data. Granted the process nature of

M&As (Jemison and Sitkin, 1986), longitudinal research could provide a proper approach to address questions of causality, produce a clearer understanding of the dynamic and ongoing nature of change processes, allow identifying contextual constraints, and aid in designing effective implementation plans (Van de Ven, 2007). Thus, process data and models can effectively cope with the multiple time scales that often occur in postmerger processes.

SUMMARY AND CONCLUSIONS

This chapter applies a process approach for analyzing M&As. Consistent with such an approach, the chapter examines what happens after a deal is signed, because M&As do not end with signing a deal. The potential benefits of M&As materialize during the integration process. Thus, the handling of this process can largely determine whether M&As are successful.

Integrating two companies into a single one is difficult. Because each M&A is unique, the route the acquiring firm chooses to implement changes depends on many contextual factors. Integrating mechanisms and a consistent communication plan are essential to attaining management's goals in an M&A. Both integrating tools and effective leadership are important to the success of M&As. Integration leaders play a key role in reaping benefits from the transaction.

Because M&As are often surrounded by an aura of failure, M&A scholars are often concerned with finding the true and best way to measure M&A performance. A universal measure does not exist, and any single measure can offer a different understanding of M&A performance. Researchers should clearly define what they are measuring as M&A performance and adopt measures that are consistent with the research question and the setting.

DISCUSSION QUESTIONS

1. Why are M&As depicted as a process, and what does that imply?
2. What is the integration process?
3. Who are the leading actors in the integration process?
4. What are the distinctive features of the integration manager?
5. What integrating mechanisms can the integration leader use during the integration process?
6. How should M&A performance be measured?

REFERENCES

Birkinshaw, Julian. 1999. "Acquiring Intellect: Managing the Integration of Knowledge Intensive Acquisitions." *Business Horizons* 42:3, 33–40.
Bower, Joseph L. 2001. "Not All M&As Are Alike and That Matters." *Harvard Business Review* 79:3, 93–101.
Boyd, Brian K., Steve Gove, and Michael A. Hitt. 2005. "Construct Measurement in Strategic Management Research: Illusion or Reality?" *Strategic Management Journal* 26:3, 239–257.
Capasso, Arturo, and Olimpia Meglio. 2005. "Knowledge Transfer in Mergers and Acquisitions: How Frequent Acquirers Learn to Manage the Integration Process." In Arturo

Capasso, Giovanni B. Dagnino, and Andrea Lanza, eds. *Strategic Capabilities and Knowledge Transfer within and between Organizations*, 199–225. Cheltenham: Edward Elgar.

Dagnino, Giovanni Battista, and Vincenzo Pisano. 2008. "Unpacking the Champion of Acquisition: The Key Figure in the Execution of the Post-acquisition Process." In Cary L. Cooper and Sidney Finkelstein, eds. *Advances in Mergers and Acquisitions*, Volume 7, 51–70. Bingley: Emerald.

Fama, Eugene F. 1970. "Efficient Capital Markets: A Review of Theory and Empirical Work." *Journal of Finance* 25:2, 383–417.

Habeck, Max M., Fritz Kröger, and Michael R. Träm. 2000. *After the Merger*. London: Pearson.

Halpern, Paul J. 1983. "Corporate Acquisition: A Theory of Special Cases?" *Journal of Finance* 38:2, 297–317.

Haspeslagh, Philippe, and David Jemison. 1991. *Managing Acquisitions. Creating Value Through Corporate Renewal*. New York: Free Press.

Homburg, Christian, and Matthias Bucerius. 2006. "Is Speed of Integration Really a Success Factor of Mergers and Acquisitions? An Analysis of the Role of Internal and External Relatedness." *Strategic Management Journal* 27:4, 347–367.

Isabella, Lynn A. 1990. "Evolving Interpretation as a Change Unfolds: How Managers Construe Key Organizational Events." *Academy of Management Journal* 33:1, 7–41.

Javidan, Mansour, Amy L. Pablo, Harbir Singh, Michael Hitt, and David Jemison. 2004. "Where We've Been and Where We're Going." In Amy L. Pablo and Mansour Javidan, eds. *Mergers and Acquisitions: Creating Integrative Knowledge*, 245–261. Oxford: Blackwell Publishing.

Jemison, David B., and Sim B. Sitkin. 1986. "Corporate Acquisitions: A Process Perspective." *Academy of Management Review* 11:1, 145–163.

King, David R., Dan R. Dalton, Catherin M. Daily, and Jeffrey Covin. 2004. "Meta-analysis of Post-acquisition Performance: Indications of Unidentified Moderators." *Strategic Management Journal* 25:2, 187–200.

Larsson, Rikard. 1990. *Coordination of Action in M&A. Interpretive and System Approach Toward Synergy. Lund Studies in Economics and Management 10*. Lund: Lund University Press.

Larsson, Rikard, and Sidney Finkelstein. 1999. "Integrating Strategic, Organizational, and Human Resource Perspectives on Merger and Acquisitions: A Case Survey of Synergies Realization." *Organization Science* 10:1, 1–26.

Lubatkin, Michael. 1987. "Merger Strategies and Stockholder Value." *Strategic Management Journal* 8:1, 39–53.

McWilliams, Abagail, and Donald Siegel. 1997. "Event Studies in Management Research: Theoretical and Empirical Issues." *Academy of Management Journal* 40:3, 626–657.

Meglio, Olimpia. 2009. "Measuring Performance in Technology-driven M&As: Insights from a Literature Review." In Cary L. Cooper and Sidney Finkelstein, eds. *Advances in Mergers and Acquisitions*, Volume 8, 103–118. Bingley: Emerald.

Meglio, Olimpia, and Annette Risberg. 2009. "The M&A Performance Construct: A Critical Analysis." *European Academy of Management Conference*, Liverpool.

Meglio, Olimpia, and Annette Risberg. 2010. "Mergers and Acquisitions: Time for a Methodological Rejuvenation of the Field?" *Scandinavian Journal of Management* 26:1, 87–95.

Meyer, Christine B. 2006. "Destructive Dynamics of Middle Management Intervention in Post-merger Processes." *Journal of Applied Behavioral Science* 42:4, 397–419.

Montgomery, Cynthia A., Ann R. Thomas, and Rajan Kamath. 1984. "Divestiture, Market Valuation and Strategy." *Academy of Management Journal* 27:4, 93–97.

Nahavandi, Afsaneh, and Ali R. Malekzadeh. 1988. "Acculturation in Mergers and Acquisitions." *Academy of Management Review* 13:1, 79–90.

Napier, Nancy K. 1989. "Mergers and Acquisitions, Human Resource Issues and Outcomes: A Review and a Suggested Typology." *Journal of Management Studies* 26:3, 271–289.

Nayyar, Praveen. 1992. "On the Measurement of Corporate Diversification Strategy: Evidence from Large U.S. Service Firms." *Strategic Management Journal* 13:3, 219–235.

Oler, Derek K., Jeffrey S. Harrison, and Matthew R. Allen. 2008. "The Danger of Misinterpreting Short-window Event Study Findings in Strategic Management Research: An Empirical Illustration Using Horizontal Acquisitions." *Strategic Organization* 6:2, 151–184.

Porter, Michael. 1987. "From Competitive Advantage to Corporate Strategy." *Harvard Business Review* 65:1, 43–59.

Risberg, Annette. 1999. *Ambiguities Thereafter: An Interpretive Approach to Acquisitions*. Lund Studies in Economics and Management 46. Lund: Lund University Press.

Schilit, Warren K. 1987. "An Examination of the Influence of Middle-level Managers in Formulating and Implementing Strategic Decisions." *Journal of Management Studies* 24:2, 271–293.

Schoenberg, Richard. 2006. "Measuring the Performance of Corporate Acquisitions: An Empirical Comparison of Alternative Metrics." *British Journal of Management* 17:4, 361–370.

Schweizer, Lars. 2005. "Organizational Integration of Acquired Biotechnology Companies: The Need for a Hybrid Approach" *Academy of Management Journal* 48:6, 1051–1074.

Sinetar, Marsha. 1981. "Mergers, Morale and Productivity." *Personnel Journal* 60:6, 863–867.

Van de Ven, Andrew H. 2007. *Engaged Scholarship: A Guide for Organizational and Social Research*. New York: Oxford University Press.

Very, Philippe, Michael Lubatkin, Roland Calori, and John Veiga. 1997. "Relative Standing and the Performance of Recently Acquired European Firms." *Strategic Management Journal* 18:8, 593–614.

Zollo, Maurizio, and Degenhard Meier 2008. "What Is M&A Performance?" *Academy of Management Perspectives* 22:3, 55–77.

Zollo, Maurizio, and Harbir Singh. 2004. "Deliberate Learning in Corporate Acquisitions: Post-acquisition Strategies and Integration Capability in US Bank Mergers." *Strategic Management Journal* 25:13, 1233–1256.

ABOUT THE AUTHORS

Olimpia Meglio earned a PhD in Management from the University of Naples Federico II. She is currently an Assistant Professor of Management at the University of Sannio where she teaches service management as well as tourism management. She has been a visiting scholar at ESADE and the Copenhagen Business School. She is member of AOM, EURAM, and EGOS. Her research interests involve postacquisition integration processes, M&A performance measurement, and process research methods. Professor Meglio has published in *Advances in Mergers and Acquisitions* and the *Scandinavian Journal of Management*.

Arturo Capasso teaches corporate finance at the University of Sannio, where he is the Director of the Graduate Program in Economics and Finance. He is also a Faculty Member of the Masters Program in Economics and Finance (MEF) at the University of Naples Federico II. His research areas are corporate governance and corporate finance, specifically involving M&As, private equity, and venture capital. He held visiting positions at Columbia University, New York University, and the Massachusetts Institute of Technology. As an academic member of ECGI, he serves on the editorial boards of *Journal of Management and Governance*. He has authored/edited 10 books and numerous articles in Italian refereed journals. Professor Capasso is the guest editor of a special issue on Corporate Governance and Strategic Management to be published in *Journal of Management and Governance*.

CHAPTER 17

Organizational and Human Resource Issues in M&As

SIDDHARTHA S. BRAHMA
Instructor, Corporate Training, Saudi Industrial Development Fund

INTRODUCTION

Mergers and acquisitions (M&As) worldwide have experienced remarkable growth as many companies, regardless of size, are using this strategy as an alternative way of expansion. In 2004, firms globally announced $1.95 trillion in deals and completed 30,000 acquisitions. Despite this mammoth growth, prior research reveals that nearly half of all acquisitions fail (Young, 1981; Porter, 1987; Hunt and Downing, 1990; Devine, 2003; Cartwright and Schoenberg, 2006). This high failure rate attracted the attention of scholars primarily from two disciplines—finance and strategy. The main interest of finance scholars is whether acquisitions create or destroy value for shareholders. Overall, the results show that target firm shareholders gain in the short term. In the long term, however, the benefits to the acquiring firm are doubtful (Bruner, 2004). Researchers from the strategy field focus on the roles of strategic fit and synergistic benefits as prime determinants of acquisition performance. Some argue that related acquisitions provide synergistic benefits that arise from economies of scale and, therefore, exhibit superior performance (Salter and Weinhold, 1979; Lubatkin, 1983). Based on this argument, researchers such as Chatterjee (1986), Lubatkin (1987), Singh and Montgomery (1987), Shelton (1988), and Seth (1990) test whether a positive relationship exists between strategic fit and value creation in acquisitions. Because the research evidence offers considerable diversity, little consensus has emerged from this line of work (King, Dalton, Daily, and Covin, 2004). Recently, a growing body of literature focuses on M&As from organizational and human resource perspectives (Cartwright and Cooper, 1992; Larsson and Finkelstein, 1999; Stahl and Voigt, 2008). This literature, with its diverse origins in organizational science, anthropology, sociology, and psychology, has sought to explain how the integration process and employees' psychological and behavioral reactions affect the M&A outcome. This literature suggests that financial and strategic factors may be insufficient in explaining why M&As fail so often. The key to value realization lies on the successful integration of operations and people. As a result, managers should not be myopic to financial and strategic factors because they may be blindsided by unexpected problems arising during the integration.

Although a wealth of knowledge has been accumulated, researchers criticize many of these studies because they are anecdotal, unrelated to theory, marginally informative, unsystematic, and fragmented (Napier, 1989; Larsson and Finkelstein, 1999; Schweiger and Goulet, 2000). Therefore, the primary purpose of this chapter is to review the literature that offers adequate theoretical underpinnings and important empirical findings in order to understand how organizational and human resource issues affect the outcomes of M&As. Given the vast literature, the bipartite classification of the perspectives adopted in this chapter may seem arbitrary because of overlap in the elements constituting the classification. Nonetheless, the remainder of the chapter has the following organization. The next section examines the organizational perspective, which covers two areas: organizational fit and the postacquisition integration process. This section is followed by one on the human resource perspective, which includes the broad topics of employee reaction, communication, postmerger identification, and organizational justice. The final section offers a summary and conclusions.

ORGANIZATIONAL PERSPECTIVE

The theoretical rationale behind M&As generally focuses on creating value through synergy. Yet, M&A deals do not automatically create synergy. Value creation may emerge in the form of market power, economies of scale or scope, financial gains of coinsurance, and diversification of risk (Seth, 1990). Thus, scholars from the strategic management field advocate that strategic fit (product–market compatibility) between the acquiring and target firms offers the potential for value creation in M&As. Whether the value is realized, however, depends on the successful integration of the merging firms because faulty and poor integration is often a cause of merger failure (Kitching, 1967; Shrivastava, 1986). Integration success depends on two factors: organizational fit and the postacquisition integration process (Payne, 1987).

Organizational Fit

Understanding the fact that strategic issues alone are insufficient in explaining M&A performance, organizational scholars emphasize organizational fit to explain how it affects acquisition outcomes. In this context, *organizational fit* is the extent to which acquiring and target firms have compatible organizational systems that influence the ease with which two different organizations are assimilated during the postacquisition integration. This literature argues that the greater the organizational fit, the higher is the probability of success during acquisition integration (Buono and Bowditch, 1989; Finkelstein and Haleblian, 2002). This is because organizational compatibility helps in integrating two firms' operations by facilitating resource sharing, increasing knowledge-transfer skills, and enhancing communication effectiveness (Hitt, Ireland, and Harrison, 2008). Organizational fit can be assessed in terms of the similarity in organizational culture, structure, and systems.

Organizational culture is the shared values of the employees' belief, values, and assumptions about the organization (Schein, 1985). When two dissimilar cultures are integrated or changed, employees may react negatively. The most cited reactions are a "we versus them" mentality and a loss of identity (Marks and Mirvis, 1998), as well as cultural ambiguity (Buono, Bowditch, and Lewis, 1985). Such reactions are likely to be detrimental and hinder the process of integration. Following this argument, researchers who advocate the "cultural-distance" hypothesis examine the cultural differences between the merging firms and its impact on postacquisition performance.

Chatterjee, Lubatkin, Schweiger, and Weber (1992) study related mergers and find a negative relationship between the perceived cultural differences of the top management teams and the acquiring firm's stock price performance. Datta (1991) also supports the hypothesis that differences in management styles are negatively associated with the acquiring firm's postacquisition performance. However, Weber (1996), who examines the role of cultural fit, autonomy removal, and managerial commitment on performance, concludes that the relationship is complex and varies across industries and measures of performance. Evidence by Krishnan, Miller, and Judge (1997) also favors an opposing view where top management team complementarily, in terms of different functional backgrounds, appears to have a positive impact on performance through fostering organizational learning and reducing the turnover rate. In a meta-analytic study, Stahl and Voigt (2003) conclude that cultural difference might have a positive or negative effect depending on the type of outcome variable. For instance, they find that cultural difference is negatively related to integration at a sociocultural level, unrelated to an accounting-based measure of postacquisition performance, but positively related to the abnormal return of the acquirer's shareholders.

Although organizational culture has received widespread attention in the literature, the link between cultural fit and performance is mixed. In an attempt to resolve the paradox, Teerikangas and Very (2006) speculate that cultural difference per se does not affect M&A performance. Instead, integration strategy, which delineates the interaction between firms and the acculturation modes, may mediate the culture–performance relationship.

Scholars argue that differences in structure can lead to problems in integration. For example, delays that may occur in resolving any change in reporting relationships may result in widespread anxiety and uncertainty among employees (Daniel and Metcalf, 2001). However, research in this area is scant and restricted to surveys and case studies (Kitching, 1967; Mehta, 2001). Researchers have examined a relationship closely associated with the fit concept, namely, the relationship between compatibility in the compensation and performance evaluation systems and M&A performance. When the acquiring firm tries to impose its system over the acquired firm, this can adversely affect the performance of merging firms (Jemison and Sitkin, 1986; Schweiger and Weber, 1989). Even an existing difference may lead to low morale and uncertainty among employees (Napier, 1989). However, Datta's (1991) study does not support this view as the author argues that this difference might be easily and quickly reconciled so as not to significantly affect the postacquisition performance. Although conceptually, organizational fit and M&A performance are positively related, empirical results are inconclusive and not fully supportive.

Postacquisition Integration Process

In a broad sense, the acquisition process can be divided into two phases: preacquisition and postacquisition. During the preacquisition phase, target screening and due diligence are critical. However, value can either be realized or destroyed during the postacquisition integration phase (Larsson and Finkelstein, 1999; Ranft and Lord, 2002). The literature of postacquisition integration is based on two theoretical foundations that are discussed below.

Decision-Making Process

In a separate stream of research, organizational scholars use decision science theory to better understand the integration process. The central argument of this procedural view is that the acquisition process itself, independent of strategic and organizational fit, may affect the acquisition outcome under some conditions (Jemison and Sitkin, 1986). In other words, the acquisition process is affected by individual, organizational, and situational characteristics, which in turn affects the acquisition outcome specifically when value creation requires some degree of integration between merging firms (Pablo, Sitkin, and Jemison, 1996). In essence, the theoretical proposition of the process school is built around the dominant paradigms of the strategic decision process of rationality and bounded rationality (Eisenhardt and Zbaracki, 1992). This paradigm acknowledges that decision makers are rational but boundedly so and are cognitively limited in the decision-making process (March and Simon, 1958). Although the rationalistic view examines the postacquisition impediments of the integration decision process, contemporary researchers are now looking at the problem from political, strategic, and knowledge-sharing points of view.

Jemison and Sitkin (1986) make an influential contribution in the process school by arguing that process-based variables are critical determinants of acquisition success or failure. They identify four impediments in integration: activity segmentation, escalating momentum, expectational ambiguity, and management system misapplication. First, M&A integration often requires task segmentation due to the technical complexity of the required analysis. This may result in disproportionate attention to strategic fit over organizational fit, thereby decreasing the effectiveness of integration. Second, management's desire to complete the integration process quickly may lead to a suboptimal decision. Jemison and Sitkin call it "escalating momentum." Third, expectational ambiguity, created over various issues during the negotiation phase, gets magnified in the integration phase. Disputes and conflicts surface, thereby creating a sense of distrust that negatively affects the acquisition outcome. Fourth, when the acquiring firm tries to impose its systems on the target firm, it may lead to defensiveness and arrogance. Defensiveness comes from unfamiliarity with the acquired firm's procedures, and arrogance stems from the belief that one system is superior to the other's system. This outcome is detrimental and adversely affects acquisition performance. Though the first three impediments arise from the preacquisition decision-making process, they also have a subsequent effect on the postacquisition integration process and final M&A outcome (Pablo et al., 1996). The fourth impediment of management system misapplication is related to the postacquisition integration process.

Based on United Kingdom–based samples, Hunt (1990) puts the acquisition process in a wider framework to suggest that contextual variables (e.g., buyer's strategy, industry relatedness, share ownership, health of the seller, relative size, experience of the acquirer, and access to an audit of the seller) are better predictors of acquisition success only when they are analyzed with the acquisition process–related variables (e.g., targeting, negotiating, implementing, and converting). That is, contextual variables affect process variables to determine the acquisition outcome. To understand the acquisition outcome, Hunt finds that success scenarios are composed of certain context and process variables. As far as the postacquisition integration is concerned, the author suggests that in friendly acquisitions of healthy firms, the acquirers should adopt hands-off approaches, whereas in contested acquisitions of fairly healthy firms or in hostile bids for healthy sellers, the acquirers should adopt hands-on approaches.

In the M&A process literature, the most prominent work is by Haspeslagh and Jemison (1991). They contend that if the process of resource or capability transfer is flawed, this will affect value creation. Furthermore, they note three types of problems in capability transfer: determinism, value destruction, and leadership vacuum. Determinism occurs when the management cannot adjust its integration strategy when new information arrives. In other words, integration flexibility is a necessity. Value destruction is the other side of value creation, as creating value for shareholders may destroy value for employees. Therefore, decision makers must strike a balance between people's needs and concerns and other value-creating activities. Last, a leadership vacuum hinders capability transfer by failing to create an atmosphere where capability transfer can take place.

In a separate group of studies (Napier, 1989; Haspeslagh and Jemison, 1991; Pablo, 1994), researchers portray integration decision making as a choice involving the particular types of integration approach or design (interdependence versus autonomy). Pablo examines how decision-making processes of key managers mediate the relationship between acquisition characteristics (task, cultural, and political) and the level or design of integration choices. Task characteristics consist of both strategic and organizational tasks, and inherent tension exists between the two task types. Strategic tasks require sharing critical resources and skills along two firms' value chains. On the other hand, organizational tasks require some differentiation between firms to protect capabilities that are embedded in specific organizational context. As hypothesized, strategic tasks appear to have a significantly positive effect and organizational tasks seems to have a significantly negative effect on the level of integration. In cultural characteristics, multiculturalism has an inverse effect on the level of integration. A highly multicultural acquirer might choose a modest level of integration because it tolerates and encourages cultural diversity to allow the target firm to retain its separate culture. A political characteristic, such as high compatibility of visions, leads to lower integration. Pablo does not find a relationship between the other political characteristics of power differentiation (in terms of relative sizes of firms) and the level of integration. However, he does find support for his hypothesis that service industries tend to weigh multiculturalism more heavily than manufacturing industries in decision criteria.

Napier (1989) suggests a typology of mergers, which he contends affects the integration level. In the case of an extension merger (a type of conglomerate merger), integration may be limited because such a merger is not value maximizing. Collaborative mergers require the blending of operations, assets, and cultures, exchanging technologies or other skills to create value. In a redesign merger, the policies and practices of one firm are adopted by the other. Therefore, collaborative and redesign mergers may require a wide-scale change by one or both of the merging firms and consequently require a high level of integration.

On the basis of a capability-based framework, Haspeslagh and Jemison (1991) propose three approaches to integration: preservation, absorption, and symbiosis. Preservation, as characterized by low interdependence and high autonomy, needs a modest degree of integration to preserve the acquired firm. In absorption, the degree of integration is high because the acquirer absorbs the acquired firm fully and assimilates it into its own culture. The symbiotic approach requires both high interdependence and high autonomy because both firms need to coexist and learn from each other during the initial period of preservation before making any gradual change to be united.

Schweiger (2005) argues that when two firms have complementary assets to share, a symbiotic approach, as suggested by Haspeslagh and Jemison (1991), may not work in value creation. Based on some acquisitions of biotechnology firms by pharmaceutical companies, he demonstrates that the best strategy to achieve integration success would be a hybrid approach, when an acquirer pursues two goals (improving market share in the short run and overall growth by acquisition of knowledge and technology in the long run) simultaneously. A hybrid approach requires rapid and high integration of all non–research and development (R&D) portions of the target. High autonomy needs to be granted to the target's R&D unit to protect the specific knowledge and biotech culture. Although this eclectic approach offers new insights into the process perspective, it lacks generalization because of the study's sample size and scope.

In the literature, speed of integration has also received considerable attention as one of the key integration variables. Studies in this area, however, yield conflicting results. Some, including Olie (1994) and Ranft and Lord (2002), suggest that slow integration is beneficial because this reduces conflict and enhances trust between merging firms. Others, such as Homburg and Bucerius (2005), find a weak, positive impact of speed on M&A performance. Moreover, Gerpott's (1995) study on R&D integration reveals that centralization of R&D and speed of integration have positive interactive effects on performance. Homberg and Bucerius (2006) conclude that the impact of integration speed on acquisition success depends on the fit of the two firms. When the product–market compatibility (external or strategic fit) between the two firms is low and management style similarity (internal or organizational fit) is high, speed is positively correlated to outcome.

Vaara's (2003) orientation is the opposite of the rationalistic view. He sees integration from a sense-making perspective that emphasizes the irrationality in decision making during postacquisition integration. Sense-making is a cognitive aspect of organizational decision making that includes politics. Politics, as a separate paradigm in strategic decision making, suggests that individuals are rational but not collectively so, because in any organization, groups of people with competing interests engage in politics to gain favorable decisions (Eisenhardt and Zbaracki, 1992). In a case study, Vaara concludes that inherent ambiguity, cultural confusion, organizational hypocrisy, and issue politicization are the main impediments to the organizational integration process. Internal divisions of people surrounding an acquisition create ambiguities in decision making as every group has contradictory frames of reference and sense-making logic. Vaara calls this the basic impediment. In the cross-national context, this ambiguity is often linked to cultural differences of communication and decision-making practices, posing another hindrance to postacquisition integration. Organizational hypocrisy exists when the intended integration plans and organizational changes cannot be implemented and are lost in the corporate management's decision-making process. In the situation of ambiguity and confusion, actors often engage in the politicization of integration issues to promote their own ideas. Business unit managers, due to their superior knowledge of business operations, are more powerful groups in this respect to create resistance during the postacquisition decision-making process.

More recently, researchers analyze the integration process from a strategic point of view. Birkinshaw, Bresman, and Hakanson's (2000) seminal work sheds light on how the two aspects of integration process—task integration and human integration—affect acquisition outcome. They define *task integration* as the identification and realization of operational synergies. *Human integration* means creating a positive attitude among people from both sides toward integration. The authors conclude that the relationship between task integration and acquisition outcome is mediated both by the operating units' current performance and by the level of human integration already in place. In practice, this finding suggests that achieving task integration for operational synergy would be cost effective if achieved through a high level of human integration.

Based on a resource-based view, Cording, Christmann, and King (2008) argue that, in horizontal acquisitions, integration decisions are characterized by a high degree of intrafirm linkage ambiguity. *Intrafirm linkage ambiguity* is the lack of understanding of the causal link between integration decisions and outcomes, leading to poor decision quality. Two reasons for this ambiguity in M&A integration decisions are complexity and interdependence of decisions and temporal distance between integration decisions and outcomes. The authors further argue that the integration decisions and acquisition performance link is influenced by the extent to which the firm can reduce ambiguity through achievement of some intermediate goals such as consolidating operations, coordinating knowledge and information, and leveraging coordinated marketing activities. By using a structural model, they find that the two intermediate goal achievements of internal reorganization and market expansion mediate the relationship between integration decisions and acquisition performance.

Given the fact that knowledge transfer between parties creates acquisition value through postacquisition integration (Shrivastava, 1986; Haspeslagh and Jemison, 1991), a study by Bresman, Birkinshaw, and Nobel (1999) examines a relatively unexplored area of factors and patterns of knowledge transfer in R&D acquisitions. This study reveals that tacit knowledge (technical expertise) can be transferred by communication, frequent visits, and meetings when the target is fully integrated. On the other hand, two other factors—articulation of knowledge and elapsed time since acquisition—can significantly affect a less tacit kind of knowledge (patent) transfer with a relatively low level of integration. Regarding the patterns of knowledge transfer, Bresman et al. show that transfer of knowledge increases over time. Initially, the flow of knowledge tends to be mostly from the acquiring firm to the target firm, whereas in later years, the flow becomes bi-directional.

Ranft and Lord (2002) conduct a case-based study and observe that knowledge transfer is a complex process that cannot be clearly understood by considering each variable in isolation. Tacit and socially complex knowledge are difficult to transfer. Here, the integration follows an initial period of autonomy. Thus, the acquirer has to adopt a slow integration strategy in order to have time to learn from the acquired firm. Moreover, talent retention and rich communication (face-to-face communication) along with greater autonomy help in knowledge sharing in M&As.

Integration of Organizational Cultures

Many view M&A integration as a process of merging two different organizational cultures. Consequently, their focus shifts toward acculturation. In anthropology, acculturation means the cultural change process as a result of contact and diffusion of cultural elements in both directions (Berry, 1980). According to anthropologists, modernization or voluntary migration produce less conflict and upheaval. But this may not be the case with M&As as diffusion of culture rarely occurs in both directions. One group usually dominates the other to force adoption of their culture, thereby creating conflict and resistance. Experts, therefore, frequently suggest that the merging of two different organizational cultures in M&As may have a significant effect on the outcome. A cultural clash during integration can lead to conflict, value leakage, failure to achieve synergies, and loss of shareholder value (Schuler and Jackson, 2001; Schweiger, 2002; Camara and Renjen, 2004). Admittedly, the outcome of the acculturation process in M&As depends on how the process evolves and is managed and how conflicts are resolved.

Scholars recommend that the mode of acculturation during the integration could affect the M&A outcome. In this respect, Nahavandi and Malekhzadeh (1988) elaborate on a model to explain the cultural dynamics from the perspectives of both acquirer and target firms. To the target firm, the acculturation process is a function of the degree to which it values and seeks to preserve its own culture as well as its perception of the acquirer's attractiveness. For the acquirer, acculturation is driven by the degree of multicultural tolerance, the desire to seek a unified culture, and the degree of relatedness between the merging firms. Based on these dimensions, the model unfolds the acculturation process in four different ways: assimilation, deculturation, separation, and integration. *Assimilation* means replacing one's culture with the new culture. *Deculturation* is giving up one's culture without adopting the new culture. *Separation* means maintaining one's own culture and rejecting the other culture. *Integration* is maintaining one's own cultural elements while moving toward the new. Cultural integration in this model is jointly determined by both firms. The authors contend that the congruence of the two firms' mode of acculturation influences the M&A outcome.

Researchers in this field also argue about how an acquirer's integration strategy affects the cultural dynamics by influencing the interaction between the participating firms (Teerikangas and Very, 2006). Napier (1989) expects greater cultural dynamics in redesign and collaborative mergers. Some large-scale studies, such as Cartwright (2005), confirm that when employee autonomy increases, the acculturation process tends to operate smoothly in firms adopting a redesign strategy. Employee behavior and organizational performance is problematic when autonomy is reduced. Larsson and Lubatkin (2001) offer a conflicting view. The authors test the impact of various variables on the degree of achieved acculturation and find that social control (and not autonomy removal) is significantly associated with acculturation. Moreover, they find that when the autonomy removal is high, both aspects of social control (coordinative effect and degree of socialization) correlate significantly with acculturation. In the condition of low autonomy removal, only socialization in terms of introduction programs, training, cross-visits, and joint celebration correlates positively with acculturation. Larsson and Lubatkin conclude that when both aspects of social control are present, autonomy removal does not hinder the process of acculturation.

As discussed earlier, the acculturation process may geminate conflict and hostility because of the dominating attitude of one culture over the other. In a study of a merger of two banks, Buono et al. (1985) find that cultural differences lead to a hostile rivalry between the two groups of workers. The former employees of the displaced culture are less satisfied and less committed than the group whose culture is retained by the newly merged organization. However, these employees have a more favorable attitude toward change than the other group before the merger.

Marks and Mirvis (1998) observe that cultural differences first manifest themselves in the form of a "we-versus-they" relationship among employees of the two companies. People start to ascribe their respective cultural values as superior and others as inferior and then begin attacking others to defend their own values. Finally, the winners' values are adopted. Researchers suggest that when two distinct cultures are forced into one or when one firm imposes its culture on the other, the employees whose culture is displaced often experience a substantial amount of acculturation stress and tension (Mirvis and Marks, 1992; Cartwright and Cooper, 1993).

A frequent suggestion is that the cultural conflict and resistance can be reduced when employees learn about the other company's culture through greater interaction and communication such as intercompany seminars, training sessions, and reflective cultural discussions (Elsass and Veiga, 1994; Schweiger and Goulet, 2005). Schweiger (2002) cites a large-scale study among 236 employees involved in a merger. He finds support for his "cultural mirroring" approach where groups of people clarify all differences between their own self-perceptions and the other group's perceptions of them. Later, actual cultural differences are isolated and these are further addressed. He opines that this procedure of integration reduces the chance of stereotyping and potential conflict, resulting in greater employee support toward integration, commitment, cooperation, trust in management, and performance.

HUMAN RESOURCE PERSPECTIVE

Some scholars study the human side of M&As, mainly from the standpoint of the acquired firm, because M&As are associated with a myriad of people-related problems (Jemison and Sitkin, 1986). The literature covers the following broad areas: employee responses, communication, social integration and creation of postmerger identity, and organizational justice. Each of these areas enhances understanding of the human resource dynamics and complements the others. Anecdotal references, case studies, laboratory experiments, and empirical studies document this line of work.

Employee Responses

Psychologists and behavioral researchers examine how people behave during M&As. This is because M&As are considered to be different from any other types of organizational change regarding the speed of change, extent of change, and amount of uncertainty created among people. In general, the employees of the acquired firm are affected the most as they become anxious, insecure, and uncertain about their future. People become insecure because they neither know what will be expected from them nor the acquirer's real intentions. Their uncertainty mostly revolves around their jobs. When people feel that they have lost control over the situation, they may even decide to leave the organization or resort to politicking or sabotaging the integration process (Marks and Mirvis, 1998). Past research on how employees respond during M&As is organized into three areas: sense of loss, stress, and executive turnover.

Sense of Loss

Given that M&As can be a major life change, considerable attention should focus on understanding how employees react in this situation (Napier, 1989; Marks and Mirvis, 1998). In general, several common and mostly negative reactions are typically attributed to the acquired firm's employees. One such reaction is the sense of loss of organizational identity (Levinson, 1970; Sineter, 1981; Napier, 1989), which is often compared with the feelings of bereavement from loss of a close friend or relative or a child separated from her mother (Mirvis, 1985; Schweiger, Ivancevich, and Power, 1987). To describe such feelings, Marks and Mirvis (1992, p. 21) write:

> ... employees mythologize their old jobs. They forget the nettlesome parts of their former work and remember only the present aspects. These are reactions to loss: the loss of old friendship, familiar stimuli and comfortable routines. Many employees of merged companies even seem to grieve the past.

Mirvis (1985) observes that in this situation, the employees' psychological responses can be better understood within the Kübler-Ross (1969) framework of personal bereavement: Stage one is disbelief and denial; stage two is anger through rage and resentment; stage three is emotional bargaining, beginning in anger and ending in depression; and stage four is acceptance. Initially, employees deny the situation and either underreact (nothing will happen) or overreact (everything will change). Employees become angry with their leaders (who sell out the company), as well as with the buyer. The next stage involves bargaining when some employees may leave, others may try to become indispensable, and still others guard information for survival. Finally, people accept the situation and move on. Fixation at stage one, two, or three results in preoccupation and unproductive behavior or causes employees to leave the organization. Although this model has not been tested empirically, Cartwright and Cooper (1992) comment that how strongly employees will respond depends on the length of their service and the degree of their attachment to the previous organization. Schweiger et al. (1987) further argue that this sense of loss of attachment may lead to loss of individual ego ideal as an individual's motivation for job advancement and career opportunities decline, causing frustration and confusion.

Stress

Researchers note that M&As are stressful, which is similar to other organizational changes. For instance, studies by Schweiger and Ivancevich (1985), Williams and Cooper (1996), and Marks (1997) report the presence of employee stress surrounding M&As. Cartwright and Cooper (1993) measure stress symptoms clinically and find that managers of both firms exhibit poorer mental health even when the cultures are similar and the merger is financially successful. They further note that the expectancy of change and fears of future survival trigger the merger stress instead of the actual change itself. Some prior studies identify the following as potential sources of individual stress in M&As: uncertainty, lack of participation in the decision-making process, role ambiguity, role conflict, role overload, unfair treatment of terminated employees, and the acculturation process.

According to Milliken (1987), uncertainty is an individual's perceived inability to predict something accurately. This inability may result from something ambiguous, a disparity of information, and a lack of information (Berger and Calabrese, 1975; Putnam and Sorenson, 1982). Bordia, Hobman, Jones, Gallois and Callan (2004) find that job-related uncertainty is paramount during an organizational change, yet, other types of uncertainty such as strategic (e.g., reasons for change) and structural (e.g., a future reporting relationship) uncertainty are also common. In M&As, even before the actual integration starts, employees may feel uncertain about a range of issues of possible changes such as job security, careers, future roles and responsibilities, future reporting relationship, and fear of diminished power, control, and the unknown (Bastien, 1987; Marks and Mirvis, 1992, 1998). Schweiger and DeNisi (1991) indicate that mergers produce much uncertainty among employees. Bastien also finds widespread existence of personal uncertainty in employees at all levels. Psychologists believe that stress is a function of perceived uncertainty (Schuler and Jackson, 1986; Pollard, 2001), and the intensity of stress depends on the degree and duration of the uncertainty (Ivancevich, Schweiger, and Power, 1987). According to Bordia et al. (2004), uncertainty causes stress because individuals feel a lack of control to affect a change in their desired direction.

A study by Fried, Tiegs, Naughton, and Ashforth (1996) shows that changes in job control and unfair treatment of terminated employees are two other sources of merger stress. Any change in the acquired company's structure threatens the jobs of the employees. This tends to centralize authority in the hands of senior managers to protect their own position. As a result, the middle-level managers' participation in the decision process decreases. Senior managers may also hold back necessary information to create job ambiguity. Both the lack of participation and increased role ambiguity are indicative of lower job control, which may be stressful because it hinders a manager's ability to fulfill formal job responsibilities.

Role ambiguity itself is also stressful because an individual may have concerns about how to do a job, leading again to frustration and ultimately to tension (Schaubroeck, Cotton, and Jennings, 1989). Expectational ambiguity in the negotiation phase, if carried on to the integration phase, may lead to role conflict between parent and subsidiary managers in an acquisition (Jemison and Sitkin, 1986). According to Schaubroeck et al., this lack of agreement reduces an individual's perceived effectiveness in the work unit, thereby producing an uncomfortable attitude toward the job and causing stress. Work pressure generally increases during M&As. This increases the difficulty faced by managers in handling the role agreement process, which also produces stress (Beehr and Newman, 1978; Marks and Mirvis, 1998).

As Fried et al. (1996) note, if the acquirer fails to treat terminated employees fairly and equitably, this can be a stressful experience for surviving employees. This argument is consistent with the procedural and equity distributive rule acknowledging that: (1) People are not just concerned with the outcome but also about the fairness of procedures used in eliminating jobs in M&As (Werhane, 1988; Meyer, 2001); and (2) people should receive rewards in accordance with the input they contribute (Serpa, 1988; Meyer, 2001). Finally, several scholars define acculturative stress as a disruptive tension felt by members of one culture when they are required to interact with a second culture and adopt its ways (Cartwright and Cooper, 1993; Elsass and Veiga, 1994; Very, Lubatkin, and Calori, 1996).

Although Fried et al. (1996) examine stress only among the middle-level managers, all acquired employees, irrespective of managers, supervisors, and lower-level workers, experience stress in acquisitions. This is mainly because boundaries shift from the organizational hierarchy to the common organizational identity of the acquired firm (a view of the acquirer as an enemy). Regardless of the sources of stress, behavioral researchers posit that stress impairs job performance and increases turnover tension among employees through various attitudinal outcomes such as job dissatisfaction and reduced organizational commitment (Parasuraman and Alutto, 1984; Hunter and Thatcher, 2007).

From the standpoint of social psychology, stress has also been examined at the group level. Ullrich and Van Dick (2007) argue that if the premerger identification is high, many of the stressors in M&As may pose a threat to a group of employees rather that an individual. So, individuals within a group can use the social support as a stress-coping mechanism. However, Ullrich and Van Dick contend that the causality between the postmerger identification and stressors is not clear. Stressors can affect the postmerger identification negatively. On the other hand, if the postmerger identification develops over time, it can help a group of employees cope with stress.

Executive Turnover

A common observable phenomenon is that M&As lead to higher levels of executive turnover, especially in the acquired firm. Based on previous studies, Krug (2003) concludes that a high percentage of acquired executives (on average, 23 percent) depart during the first year after the acquisition, which is three times higher than normal. Within two years after the acquisition, the turnover rate returns to normal. Researchers use several theories to explain the possible reasons for executive departure. From the lens of the agency theory (Fama, 1980), different management teams compete for the rights to manage their companies' resources. This market has a disciplinary effect that punishes underperformers. Accordingly, less successful companies become acquisition targets because the acquiring firm's management believes that it can do a better job of managing these targets. Soon after the acquisition, the acquirer replaces the old management team of the acquired firm with a better one. Thus, according to this theory, postacquisition retention of acquired executives is actually undesirable (Cannella and Hambrick, 1993). Empirical evidence supports this theory (Walsh, 1988, 1989; Walsh and Ellwood, 1991;

Hambrick and Cannella, 1993; Krug and Hegarty, 1997; Lubatkin, Schweiger, and Weber, 1999).

Researchers also explain this departure from the perspective of Becker's (1962) human capital theory. According to this theory, top executives are considered as human capital possessing value in terms of both firm-specific and industry-specific knowledge and skills. An acquired executive and the acquirer both conduct a cost-benefit analysis to determine the value of retaining the employment status quo. When considering whether to make the investment to retain and develop human capital, the acquirer compares the cost of retention and the future benefits. The acquired executive also compares the cost of time and effort of making adjustments to the new rules and expectations of the acquirer, as well as the future benefits. Based on this theory, Buchholtz, Ribbens, and Houle (2003) find that the "age" of the top executives and "relatedness" between the two firms serve as important factors in calculating the firm-specific and industry-specific human capital, respectively. Support favors a U–shaped relationship between chief executive officer (CEO) age and turnover, which signifies that the youngest and oldest CEOs experience the greatest departure rate.

Hambrick and Canella (1993) put forth another theoretical concept of "relative standing," originally proposed by Frank (1985), to understand the departure of acquired executives. They argue that when acquired executives feel inferior, the acquirer also perceives them as inferior, autonomy is removed, status is removed, and a climate of acrimony prevails. As these conditions increase, so does the higher rate of departure. Hambrick and Cannella hypothesize an inverse relationship between turnover and relative standing of acquired executives. Their study finds mixed support for the hypothesis in the sense that the relationship is strong only after the first year of acquisition, then weakens in the second and third year, only to reappear strongly but in the opposite direction in the fourth year. Lubatkin et al. (1999) find additional support for this theory with similar relationship patterns in year one. Krug and Hegarty (2001), however, find that executives' perceptions of the merger announcements, postmerger interaction with the acquiring firm managers, and the long-term effect of the mergers have a significant effect on departure.

Experts note that the departure of top executives is a major reason many mergers fail (Kay and Shelton, 2000; Schuler and Jackson, 2001). Others examine how these departures affect M&A performance. Canella and Hambrick's (1993) empirical work supports the hypothesis that executive departure and acquisition performance are negatively related. They further conclude that the departure of the seniormost executives has the greatest effect on subsequent performance. Bergh (2001) supports this view. On the basis of resource-based theory, he contends that long-tenured top executives are valuable firm resources and possess unique and nontransferable firm-specific knowledge to facilitate the integration process implementation. Bergh finds that the probability of an acquisition outcome is increased if the acquirer retains longer tenured top executives, as compared to shorter tenured ones.

Behavioral researchers also examine this issue, but the few available studies address turnover intention as a behavior. A field study by Van Dick, Ullrich, and Tissington (2006) finds that the socioemotional orientation, in terms of organizational support and postmerger identification, is positively related to turnover intention. Cartwright and Cooper (1992) contend that employees leave because of the prolonged directional uncertainty of the proposed change and the lack of control over the imposed situation. Fried et al. (1996) build a causal model to show that surviving mid-level managers' attitudes of intention to leave is influenced by their psychological withdrawal. In turn, this is influenced by the feeling of helplessness, the impact of the acquisition on their career development, and their ability to identify with poorly treated terminated employees. Surprisingly, a majority of the research on turnover focuses on top executives, and little is known about the reasons behind the turnover of other employees. Yet, unplanned turnover occurs at all levels (Cartwright and Cooper, 1992; Cartwright, 2005).

Communication with Employees

Communicating with employees is critical throughout the M&A process. In fact, Schuler and Jackson (2001) cite poor communication as a major reason that M&As fail. According to Devine (2003), a survey conducted in 1998 and 1999 by Watson Wyatt, a global consulting firm, reveals that respondents rate effective communication as the second most important factor contributing to successful merger integration. Why is communication so important in M&As? During any organizational change, people become uncertain about various aspects of change (Ashford, 1988; Schweiger and DeNisi, 1991). According to uncertainty reduction theory (Berger and Calabrese, 1975), when people experience uncertainty, they seek information through communication (DiFonzo and Bordia, 1998). Research indicates that during organizational change, communication can create openness that can lessen employee uncertainty, thereby enhancing employees' well-being, customer orientation, and job satisfaction (Bordia et al., 2004; Jimmieson, Terry, and Callan, 2004).

Past research on M&As mainly focuses on the quantity (how much to communicate) and quality (what to communicate) aspects of communication. Bastien (1987) observes that quantity, quality (formal or collegial communication), and congruence are the three most important areas of communication during M&As. He notes that formal communication is effective in situations of extreme uncertainty. Although collegiality is effective overall, vertical collegiality is more effective than horizontal collegiality. Bastien also notes that in the absence of adequate quantity and congruence of communication, rumor mills spread to fill the gap.

Based on a study of bank mergers, Napier, Simmons, and Stratton (1989) find that although information requirements vary from one group of employees to another, employees believe that communication is insufficient, with it being more prevalent with the acquired firm. They also find a need for continuous and repeated communication and contact in the form of honest information from top management, especially when people are confused and anxious and need reassurance. Finally, the authors report that staff employees need more information about job security than do other employees of the acquired firm.

In a longitudinal study, Schweiger and DeNisi (1991) compare two plants' communication programs (minimum information versus realistic merger preview). Their results show that realistic communication programs help employees cope with uncertainty better than when employees receive little information. A realistic merger preview provides employees with frequent, honest, and relevant information, handles employees fairly, and answers employees' queries to the fullest extent possible.

Nikandrou, Papalexandris, and Bourantas (2000) also find that frequency of communication, mainly after the acquisition, correlates positively with all factors contributing to creating good working conditions, such as developing trust, creating satisfaction, and meeting expectations. Yet, communication generally does not reduce uncertainty. The authors show that only frequent postacquisition communication about implementation changes helps to reduce economic uncertainty, but this relationship is weak. Recent studies identify that both communication climate and the amount of communication during the merger contribute positively to the postmerger identification (Bartels, Douwes, deJong, and Pruyn, 2006; Van Dick et al., 2006).

Social Integration and Creation of Postmerger Identity

Researchers use Tajfel and Turner's (1979) social identity theory to explain how people behave during the M&A integration in creating the postmerger identity of the new organization. The abstraction is mainly at the organization or group level and concerns the social perspective of the integration process. Social identity theory is based on three principles: categorization, identification, and comparison. People assign individuals to categories so that their perception of others becomes depersonalized and people are considered as group members rather than individuals. Through the identification process, personal identity is converted to the group (respective organization) identity, and people see their groups as positively distinct from others. While comparing one's own group with another, even if the other group is perceived to be more attractive, individuals continue to favor their own group unless they move into the other group. In the context of M&A integration, this theory suggests that, as a result of this social process, the emergence of the merged company's newly created identity is desirable. This is because a high level of postmerger identification leads to positive outcomes such as increased work efforts to achieve goals, higher performance, reduced turnover, and higher organizational citizenship behavior (Cartwright and Schoenberg, 2006; Van Dick et al., 2006). The underlying factors that contribute to postmerger organizational identification are premerger identification, a sense of continuity, and expected merger benefits.

Haunschild, Moreland, and Murrell (1994) find that people who share a common identity based on the prior interaction exhibit more merger resistance. However, several studies show a significant, positive relationship between premerger and postmerger identification (Van Knippenberg, Van Knippenberg, Monder, and de Lima, 2002; Van Dick, Wagner, and Lemmer, 2004; Bartels et al., 2006; Van Dick et al., 2006). This contrasting result can be due to the unbalanced merger groups in terms of the degree of changes and the level to which employees perceive their premerger identity. For instance, Van Leeuwen, Van Knippenberg, and Ellemers (2003) find that when employees expect minor changes, the relationship is positive; when employees expect major changes, the relationship is negative.

Bartels et al. (2006) hypothesize that at the work group level, premergers and postmergers have a negative relationship because a merger might represent a major threat at this level. At the organizational level, premerger and postmerger identification have a positive relationship because the social identification might

not be as strong as it is at the group level. However, the results do not show a
negative relationship at the group level but show support for a positive relationship
at the organizational level.

Researchers also find that a sense of continuity is another factor that can affect
postmerger organizational identification. In the literature, a sense of continuity
is conceptualized mainly in terms of uncertainty, threat, and trust. For example,
Jetten, O'Brien, and Trindall (2002) find that uncertainty in the premerger phase
produces negative feelings in the postmerger phase and hinders postmerger identification. Yet, Terry and O'Brien (2001) report an inverse relationship between
perceived threat and postmerger identification. A study by Bartels et al. (2006)
finds that trust is positively related to postmerger identification. Van Knippenberg
et al. (2002) find that postmerger identity depends on the sense of identity continuity, which, in turn, is contingent upon an individual's own perception of whether
the premerger organization is dominating or being dominated by the other. Thus,
if the employees feel that their organization will dominate and a sense of continuity is present, the organization will likely preserve its identity and this will be
reflected in the new organization's identity. In the qualitative study of an industrial
merger, Ullrich, Wieseke, and Van Dick (2005) state that in order to have a sense
of continuity, both elements of continuity—observable continuity and projected
continuity—have to be established. *Observable continuity* means the continuity of
identity and job contents from the past to the present, whereas *projected continuity*
refers to people's perception that the merged organization's future path, or goal
relationship, is clear and controllable. Finally, Jetten et al. (2002) find that future
expected merger benefits, such as team performance and better opportunities, are
positively correlated with postmerger identification.

Apart from the above dominant theme of research, several other studies provide a worthwhile contribution to the literature. Terry, McKimmie, and Doherty
(2003) focus on a merger between two airline companies. They examine how relative status, perceived permeability of boundaries, and the degree of intergroup
contact affect M&A social integration. The results show a possible interaction of
relative status between permeability of boundary and degree of contact. That is, the
high-status group exhibits low permeability (as expected with low commitment),
but the low-status group does not exhibit high permeability (though this group's
identification and commitment increase). Contact produces more unfavorable outcomes in high-status groups than in low-status groups. Other studies examine
cultural interaction and clash as a process of seeking social identity (Soderberg
and Vaara, 2003) and how smaller firms seek social identity in order to prosper by
merging with bigger and higher-status firms (Hogg and Terry, 2000; Panchel and
Cartwright, 2001).

Organizational Justice

Recent scholarly interest focuses on organizational justice in the context of M&As
about how employees are treated with pay, promotions, and allocations of new
roles and how termination decisions are made. Scholars indicate that two types of
justice—distributive and procedural—are particularly relevant in an M&A context.
Distributive justice has two rules: equity and equality. The equity rule says that an
individual should be rewarded in accordance with the input that is contributed,
as compared to a referent (Adams, 1965). Equality means that everyone is equal

with respect to reward allocation and regardless of performance (Gilliland, 1993). Procedural justice connotes that individuals are concerned not only with the outcome of decisions but also with the fairness of the procedures used in making such decisions (Serpa, 1988; Meyer, 2001).

The justice literature suggests that the equity rule enhances economic productivity. Based on this view, Serpa (1988) opines that mergers offer an ethical challenge to create a new organization where all employees are treated equitably. Without this, there is a little chance of success. Equality, on the other hand, enhances intergroup learning, and it fosters social integration process. But excessive application of equality undermines merit and may compromise economic productivity. Marks and Mirvis (1992), therefore, suggest that managers strike a balance between the two.

Evidence also suggests that distributive and procedural rules can interact (Brockner and Wiesenfeld, 1996), and the choice of either or both of the rules depends on several factors. In her study of two Norwegian companies, Meyer (2001) finds that a firm has two goals to achieve during integration: economic productivity and employee relationships. The firm can achieve these goals with distributive and procedural justice. However, power differential and stability can influence the relationship. She opines that when the power differs between parties and the environment is stable, the firm can simultaneously achieve the two goals by equity and procedural justice. When both parties are equally powerful and the environment is unstable, the firm can choose either economic goals through equity or employee satisfaction goals through the equality principal, but not both. Meyer notes that by applying equity, the firm achieves economic efficiency, but people might perceive this as a power play. Because this violates equality, procedural justice ends up being questioned. In contrast, by choosing equality, the firm can achieve employee relationship goals. Efficiency is compromised as equality leads to less efficient selection of people and delaying the integration process. There is no need to apply procedural rules because equality replaces the bias suppression and accuracy principle of procedural justice.

Meyer and Altenberg (2007) argue that if equality is applied in the postmerger process (as opposed to the premerger perceptions of the equality of parties), it can also have a negative effect on social integration. In the merger of two Scandinavian firms, the authors show that the operationalization of equality in the group or organizational level may lead to perceptual and structural fallacy to disintegrate the social integration process. This is because the equality criterion, in a merger of firms of unequal sizes and cross-national context, may be masked by the perceptual fallacy of subjective, egocentric, and nationalistic interpretation. The structural fallacy, resulting from equal size and the power balance of the respective members of the top management team, paralyzes the top management decision-making process. Lipponen, Olkkonen, and Moilanen (2004) find that perceived procedural justice in M&As is a strong predictor of postmerger organizational identification and common in-group identity.

SUMMARY AND CONCLUSIONS

Despite the preponderance of finance and strategic research, considerable performance variance among M&As remains unexplained (Stahl and Voigt, 2003). Research on organizational and human resource issues surrounding M&As has helped to explain some of this variance. During the past several decades, researchers have used different perspectives and theories to examine complex issues involving M&As. In response to the call of Larsson and Finkelstein (1999), researchers need to adopt an integrative approach in order to provide a deeper understanding of the complex dynamics of organizational and human resource issues in M&As. More research needs to be conducted under the process school. Some view that the process school has not addressed the complexity of the process and lacks adequate empirical research (Schweiger, 2005). Future research may also incorporate other theories such as institutional theory or impression management to further enrich the process perspective of M&As (Pablo et al., 1996). Similarly, behavioral researchers need to explain how M&As affect different stakeholders, especially customers and suppliers, as research in these areas is scant. Finally, researchers should address the relatively unexplored, yet important areas of leadership, trust, and motivation in M&As. The emerging trend of social integration and organizational justice views are encouraging, but viewing M&As from conflict and ethical points of view would be equally promising. To advance understanding of such an important area requires persistence rather than resignation and a synthetic rather than a fragmented research view. These suggestions are neither exhaustive nor absolute.

DISCUSSION QUESTIONS

1. A high level of organizational fit assures smooth integration without any problems. Comment on this statement.
2. How do researchers view the integration process in M&A literature?
3. What is the contribution of the social integration and organizational justice literature in M&As?

REFERENCES

Adams, John S. 1965. "Inequity in Social Exchange." In Leonard Berkowitz, ed. *Advances in Experimental Social Psychology*, Volume 2, 267–299. New York: Academic Press.

Ashford, Susan J. 1988. "Individual Strategies for Coping with Stress during Organizational Transitions." *Journal of Applied Behavioral Science* 24:1, 19–36.

Bartels, Jos, Rynke Douwes, Menno deJong, and Ad Pruyn. 2006. "Organizational Identification during a Merger: Determinants of Employees' Expected Identification with the New Organization." *British Journal of Management* 17:Special Issue, 49–67.

Bastien, David T. 1987. "Common Patterns of Behavior and Communication in Corporate Mergers and Acquisitions." *Human Resource Management* 26:1, 17–33.

Becker, Gary S. 1962. "Investment in Human Capital: A Theoretical Analysis." *Journal of Political Economy* 70:5, 9–49.

Beehr, Terry A., and John E Newman. 1978. "Job Stress, Employee Health, and Organizational Effectiveness." *Personnel Psychology* 31:4, 665–698.

Berger, Charles R., and Richard J. Calabrese. 1975. "Some Exploration in Initial Interaction and Beyond: Toward a Developmental Theory of Interpersonal Communication." *Human Communication Research* 1:2, 99–112.

Bergh, Donald D. 2001. "Executive Retention and Acquisition Outcomes: A Test of Opposing Views on the Influence of Organization Tenure." *Journal of Management* 27:5, 603–622.

Berry, John W. 1980. "Social and Cultural Change." In Harry C. Triandis and Richard W. Brislin, eds. *Handbook of Cross Cultural Psychology*, Volume 5, 211–299. Boston: Allyn and Bacon.

Birkinshaw, Julian, Henrik Bresman, and Lars Hakanson. 2000. "Managing the Post-acquisition Integration Process: How the Human Integration and Task Integration Processes Interact to Foster Value Creation." *Journal of Management Studies* 37:3, 395–425.

Bordia, Prashant, Elizabeth Hobman, Elizabeth Jones, Cindy Gallois, and Victor J. Callan. 2004. "Uncertainty during Organizational Change: Types, Consequences and Management Strategies." *Journal of Business and Psychology* 18:4, 507–532.

Bresman, Henrik, Julian Birkinshaw, and Robert Nobel. 1999. "Knowledge Transfer in International Acquisitions." *Journal of International Business Studies* 30:3, 439–462.

Brockner, Joel, and Batia M. Wiesenfeld. 1996. "An Integrative Framework for Explaining Reactions to Decisions: Integrative Effects of Outcomes and Procedures." *Psychological Bulletin* 120:2, 189–208.

Bruner, Robert F. 2004. *Applied Mergers and Acquisitions*. Hoboken, NJ: John Wiley & Sons.

Buchholtz, Ann K., Barbara A. Ribbens, and Irent T. Houle. 2003. "The Role of Human Capital in Post-acquisition CEO Departure." *Academy of Management Journal* 46:4, 506–514.

Buono, Antony F., and James L. Bowditch. 1989. *The Human Side of Mergers and Acquisitions*. San Francisco: Jossey-Bass.

Buono, Antony F., James L. Bowditch, and John W. Lewis. 1985. "When Cultures Collide: The Anatomy of a Merger." *Human Relations* 38:5, 477–500.

Camara, Don de, and Punit Renjen. 2004. "The Secrets of Successful Mergers: Dispatches from the Front Lines." *Journal of Business Strategy* 25:3, 10–14.

Cannella, Albert A., and Donald C. Hambrick. 1993. "Effects of Executive Departures on the Performance of Acquired Firms." *Strategic Management Journal* 14: Special Issue, 137–152.

Cartwright, Susan. 2005. "Mergers and Acquisitions: An Update and Appraisal." In Gerard P. Hodgkinson and J. Kevin Ford, (eds.), *International Review of Industrial and Organizational Psychology*, Volume 20, 1–38. Chichester: John Wiley.

Cartwright, Susan, and Cary L. Cooper. 1992. *Mergers and Acquisitions: The Human Factor*. Oxford: Butterworth-Heinemann.

Cartwright, Susan, and Cary L. Cooper. 1993. "The Psychological Impact of Merger and Acquisition on the Individual: A Study of Building Society Managers." *Human Relations* 46:3, 327–374.

Cartwright, Susan, and Richard Schoenberg. 2006. "Thirty Years of Mergers and Acquisitions Research: Recent Advances and Future Opportunities." *British Journal of Management* 17: Special Issue, 1–5.

Chatterjee, Sayan. 1986. "Types of Synergy and Economic Value: The Impact of Acquisitions on Merging and Rival Firms." *Strategic Management Journal* 7:2, 119–139.

Chatterjee, Sayan, Michale Lubatkin, David M. Schweiger, and Yaakov Weber. 1992. "Cultural Differences and Shareholder Value in Related Mergers: Linking Equity and Human Capital." *Strategic Management Journal* 13:5, 319–334.

Cording, Margaret, Petra Christmann, and David R. King. 2008. "Reducing Causal Ambiguity in Acquisition Integration: Intermediate Goals as Mediators of Integration Decisions and Acquisition Performance. " Academy of Management Journal 51:4, 744–767.

Daniel, Teresa A., and Gary S. Metcalf. 2001. *The Management of People in Mergers and Acquisitions*. Westport, CT: Quorum Books.

Datta, Deepak K. 1991. "Organizational Fit and Acquisition Performance: Effects of Post Acquisition Integration." *Strategic Management Journal* 12:4, 281–298.

Devine, Marion. 2003. *Successful Mergers—Getting The People Issues Right*. London: Profile Books Limited.

DiFonzo, Nicholas, and Prashant Bordia. 1998. "A Tale of Two Corporations: Managing Uncertainty during Organizational Change." *Human Resource Management* 37:3, 295–303.

Eisenhardt, Kathleen M., and Mark J. Zbaracki. 1992. "Strategic Decision Making." *Strategic Management Journal* 13:Special issue, 17–37.

Elsass, Priscilla M., and John F. Veiga. 1994. "Acculturation in Acquired Organizations: A Force-field Perspective." *Human Relations* 47:4, 431–453.

Fama, Eugene F. 1980. "Agency Problem and the Theory of the Firm." *Journal of Political Economy* 88:2, 288–307.

Finkelstein, Sydney, and Jerayr Haleblian. 2002. "Understanding Acquisition Performance: The Role of Transfer Effects." *Organization Science* 13:1, 36–47.

Frank, Robert H. 1985. *Choosing the Right Pond: Human Behavior and the Quest for Status.* New York: Oxford University Press.

Fried, Yitzhak, Robert B. Tiegs, Thomas J. Naughton, and Blake E. Ashforth. 1996. "Managers' Reactions to a Corporate Acquisition: A Test of an Integrative Model." *Journal of Organizational Behavior* 17:5, 401–427.

Gerpott, Torsten J. 1995. "Successful Integration of R&D Functions after Acquisition: An Exploratory Empirical Study." *R& D Management* 25:2, 161–178.

Gilliland, Stephan W. 1993. "The Perceived Fairness of Selection Systems: An Organizational Justice Perspective." *Academy of Management Review* 18:4, 694–734.

Hambrick, Donald C., and Albert A. Cannella. 1993. "Relative Standing: A Framework for Understanding Departure of Acquired Executives." *Academy of Management Journal* 36:4, 733–762.

Haspeslagh, Philippe C., and David B. Jemison. 1991. *Managing Acquisitions: Creating Value through Corporate Renewal.* New York: The Free Press.

Haunschild, Pamela R., Richard L. Moreland, and Audrey J. Murrell. 1994. "Sources of Resistance to Mergers between Groups." *Journal of Applied Social Psychology* 24:13, 1150–1178.

Hitt, Michael A., R. Duane Ireland, and Jeffery S. Harrison. 2008. "Mergers and Acquisitions: A Value Creating or Value Destroying Strategy?" In Michael A. Hitt, R. Edward Freeman, and Jeffrey S. Harrison, (eds.), *Handbook of Strategic Management*, 384–408. Oxford: Blackwell Publishing.

Hogg, Michael A., and Deborah J. Terry. 2000. "Social Identity and Self Categorization Processes in Organizational Contexts." *Academy of Management Review* 25:1, 121–140.

Homburg, Christian, and Matthias Bucerius. 2005. "A Marketing Perspective on Mergers and Acquisitions: How Marketing Integration Affects Post-merger Performance." *Journal of Marketing* 69:1, 95–113.

Homburg, Christian, and Matthias Bucerius. 2006. "Is Speed of Integration Really a Success Factor of Mergers and Acquisitions? An Analysis of the Role of Internal and External Relatedness." *Strategic Management Journal* 27:4, 347–367.

Hunt, John W. 1990. "Changing Patterns of Acquisition Behavior in Takeovers and the Consequences for Acquisition Process." *Strategic Management Journal* 11:1, 69–77.

Hunt, John W., and Stephen Downing. 1990. "Mergers, Acquisitions and Human Resource Management." *International Journal of Human Resource Management* 1:2, 195–209.

Hunter, Larry H., and Sherry M. B. Thatcher. 2007. "Feeling the Heat: Effects of Stress, Commitment, and Job Experience on Job Performance." *Academy of Management Journal* 50:4, 953–968.

Ivancevich, John M., David M. Schweiger, and Frank R. Power. 1987. "Strategies for Managing Human Resource Issues during Mergers and Acquisitions." *Human Resource Planning* 10:1, 19–35.

Jemison, David B., and Sim B. Sitkin. 1986. "Corporate Acquisitions: A Process Perspective." *Academy of Management Review* 11:1, 145–163.

Jetten, Joanda, Anne T. O'Brien, and Neil Trindall. 2002. "Changing Identity: Predicting Adjustment to Organizational Restructure as a Function of Subgroup and Superordinate Identification." *British Journal of Social Psychology* 41:2, 281–297.

Jimmieson, Nerina L., Deborah J. Terry, and Victor J. Callan. 2004. "A Longitudinal Study of Employee Adaptation to Organizational Change: The Role of Change Related Information and the Change Related Self-efficacy." *Journal of Occupational Health Psychology* 9:1, 11–27.

Kay, Ira T., and Mike Shelton. 2000. "The People Problems in Mergers." *McKinsey Quarterly* 4, 27–37.

King, David R., David R. Dalton, Catherin Daily, and Jeffery G. Covin. 2004. "Meta-analysis of Post-acquisition Performance: Indications of Unidentified Moderators." *Strategic Management Journal* 25:2, 187–200.

Kitching, John. 1967. "Why Do Mergers Miscarry?" *Harvard Business Review* 45:6, 84–107.

Krishnan, Hema, Alex Miller, and William Q. Judge. 1997. "Diversification and Top Management Team Complementarity: Is Performance Improved by Merging Similar or Dissimilar Teams?" *Strategic Management Journal* 18:5, 361–374.

Krug, Jeffery A. 2003. "Executive Turnover in Acquired Firms: An Analysis of Resource-based Theory and the Upper Echelons Perspective." *Journal of Management and Governance* 7:2, 117–143.

Krug, Jeffery A., and W Harvey Hegarty. 1997. "Post-acquisition Turnover among US Top Management Teams: An Analysis of Effects of Foreign vs. Domestic Acquisitions of US Targets." *Strategic Management Journal* 18:8, 667–675.

Krug, Jeffery A., and W Harvey Hegarty. 2001. "Predicting Who Stays and Leaves after an Acquisition: A Study of Top Managers in Multinational Firms." *Strategic Management Journal* 22:2, 185–196.

Kübler-Ross, Elisabeth. 1969. *On Death and Dying*. New York: Macmillan.

Larsson, Rikard, and Sydney Finkelstein. 1999. "Integrating Strategic, Organizational and Human Resource Perspectives on Mergers and Acquisitions: A Case Study of Synergy Realization." *Organization Science* 10:1, 1–26.

Larsson, Rikard, and Michael Lubatkin. 2001. "Achieving Acculturation in Mergers and Acquisitions: An International Case Survey." *Human Relations* 54:12, 1573–1607.

Levinson, Harry. 1970. "A Psychologist Diagnoses Merger Failures." *Harvard Business Review* 48:2, 139–147.

Lipponen, Jukka, Marina E. Olkkonen, and Minna Moilanen. 2004. "Perceived Procedural Justice and Employee Responses to an Organizational Merger." *European Journal of Work and Organizational Psychology* 13:3, 391–413.

Lubatkin, Michael. 1983. "Mergers and Performance of the Acquiring Firm." *Academy of Management Review* 8:2, 218–255.

Lubatkin, Michael. 1987. "Merger Strategies and Stakeholders Value." *Strategic Management Journal* 8:1, 39–53.

Lubatkin, Michael., David M. Schweiger, and Yaakov Weber. 1999. "Top Management Turnover in Related M&As: An Additional Test of the Theory of Relative Standing." *Journal of Management* 25:1, 55–73.

March, James G., and Herbert Simon. 1958. *Organizations*. New York: John Wiley & Sons, Inc.

Marks, Mitchell L. 1997. "Consulting in Mergers and Acquisitions: Interventions Spawned by Recent Trends." *Journal of Organizational Change Management* 10:3, 267–279.

Marks, Mitchell L., and Philip H. Mirvis. 1992. "Rebuilding After the Merger: Dealing with Survivor Sickness." *Organizational Dynamics* 21:2, 18–35.

Marks, Mitchell L., and Philip H. Mirvis. 1998. *Joining Forces: Making One Plus One Equal Three in Mergers, Acquisitions, and Alliances*. San Francisco: Jossey-Bass.

Mehta, Shuchi. 2001. "Human Resource Management in Mergers and Acquisitions." In Biju Varkkey, Pradnya Parasar, and Gautam Brahma, eds. *Human Resource Management—Changing Roles, Changing Goals*, 76–100. New Delhi: Excel Books.

Meyer, Christine B. 2001. "Allocation Processes in Mergers and Acquisitions: An Organizational Justice Perspective." *British Journal of Management* 12:1, 47–66.

Meyer, Christine B., and Ellen Altenberg. 2007. "The Disintegrating Effects of Equality: A Study of a Failed International Merger." *British Journal of Management* 18:3, 257–271.

Milliken, Frances J. 1987. "Three Types of Perceived Uncertainty about the Environment: State, Effect, and Response Uncertainty." *Academy of Management Review* 12:1, 133–143.

Mirvis, Philip H. 1985. "Negotiation after the Sale: The Roots and Ramifications of Conflict in an Acquisition." *Journal of Occupational Behavior* 6:1, 65–84.

Mirvis, Philip H., and Mitchell L. Marks. 1992. *Managing the Merger: Making It Work*. Englewood Cliffs, NJ: Prentice Hall.

Nahavandi, Afsaneh, and Ali R. Malekzadeh. 1988. "Acculturation in Mergers and Acquisitions." *Academy of Management Review* 13:1, 79–90.

Napier, Nancy K. 1989. "Mergers and Acquisitions, Human Resource Issues and Outcomes: A Review and Suggested Typology." *Journal of Management Studies* 26:3, 271–289.

Napier, Nancy K., Glen Simmons, and Kay Stratton. 1989. "Communication during a Merger: The Experience of Two Banks." *Human Resource Planning* 12:2, 105–122.

Nikandrou, Irene, Nancy Papalexandris, and Dimitris Bourantas. 2000. "Gaining Employee Trust after Acquisition: Implications for Managerial Action." *Employee Relations* 22:4, 334–355.

Olie, René. 1994. "Shades of Culture and Institutions in International Mergers." *Organizational Studies* 15:3, 381–405.

Pablo, Amy L. 1994. "Determinants of Acquisition Integration Level: A Decision Making Perspective." *Academy of Management Journal* 37:4, 803–836.

Pablo, Amy L., Sim B. Sitkin, and David B. Jemison. 1996. "Acquisition Decision-making Process: The Central Role of Risk." *Journal of Management* 22:5, 723–746.

Panchel, Sheila, and Susan Cartwright. 2001. "Group Differences and Post Merger Stress." *Journal of Managerial Psychology* 16:6, 424–434.

Parasuraman, Saroj, and Joseph A. Alutto. 1984. "Sources and Outcomes of Stress in Organizational Settings: Toward the Development of a Structural Model." *Academy of Management Journal* 27:2, 330–350.

Payne, Adrian F. 1987. "Approaching Acquisitions Strategically." *Journal of General Management* 13:2, 5–27.

Pollard, Tessa M. 2001. "Changes in Mental Well-being, Blood Pressure and Total Cholesterol Levels during Workplace Reorganization: The Impact of Uncertainty." *Work and Stress* 15:1, 14–28.

Porter, Michael E. 1987. "From Competitive Advantage to Corporate Strategy." *Harvard Business Review* 65:5, 43–59.

Putnam, Lindal L., and Ritch L. Sorenson. 1982. "Equivocal Messages in Organizations." *Human Communication Research* 8:2, 114–132.

Ranft, Annette L., and Michale D. Lord. 2002. "Acquiring New Technologies and Capabilities: A Grounded Model of Acquisitions Integrations." *Organization Science* 13:4, 420–441.

Salter, Malcolm S., and Wolf A. Weinhold. 1979. *Diversification through Acquisitions*: Strategies for Creating Economic Value. New York: Free Press.

Schaubroeck, John, John L. Cotton, and Kenneth R. Jennings. 1989. "Antecedents and Consequence of Role Stress: A Covariance Structure Analysis." *Journal of Organizational Behavior* 10:1, 35–58.

Schein, Edger H. 1985. *Organizational Culture and Leadership—A Dynamic View*. London: Jossey-Bass.

Schuler, Randall S., and Susan E. Jackson. 1986. "Managing Stress through PHRM Practices: An Uncertainty Interpretation." In Kendrith M. Rowland and Gerald R. Ferris, eds. *Research in Personnel and Human Resource Management*, Volume 4, 183–224. Greenwich CT: Jai Press.

Schuler, Randall S., and Susan E. Jackson. 2001. "HR Issues and Activities in Mergers and Acquisitions." *European Management Journal* 19:3, 239–253.

Schweiger, David M. 2002. *M&A Integration.* New York: McGraw-Hill.

Schweiger, David M., and Angelo S. DeNisi. 1991. "Communications with Employees following a Merger: A Longitudinal Field Experiment." *Academy of Management Journal,* 34:1, 110–135.

Schweiger, David M., and Philip K. Goulet. 2000. "Integrating Mergers and Acquisitions: An International Research Review." In Cary L. Cooper, and Sydney Finkelstein, eds. *Advances in Mergers and Acquisitions.* Volume 1, 61–91. New York: Jai Press.

Schweiger, David M., and Philip K. Goulet. 2005. "Facilitating Acquisition Integration through Deep-Level Cultural Learning Interventions: A Longitudinal Field Experiment." *Organization Studies* 26:10, 1477–1499.

Schweiger, David M., and John M. Ivancevich. 1985. "Human Resources: The Forgotten Factor in Mergers and Acquisitions." *Personnel Administrator* 30:11, 47–54, 58–61.

Schweiger, David M., John M. Ivancevich, and Frank R. Power. 1987. "Executive Actions for Managing Human Resources before and after Acquisition." *Academy of Management Executive* 1:2, 127–138.

Schweiger, David M., and Yaakov Weber. 1989. "Strategies for Managing Human Resources during Mergers and Acquisitions: An Empirical Investigation." *Human Resource Planning* 12:2, 69–86.

Schweiger, Lars. 2005. "Organizational Integration of Acquired Biotechnology Companies into Pharmaceutical Companies: The Need for a Hybrid Approach." *Academy of Management Journal* 48:6, 1051–1074.

Serpa, Roy. 1988. "The Often Overlooked Ethical Aspects of Mergers." *Journal of Business Ethics* 7:5, 359–362.

Seth, Anju. 1990. "Value Creation in Acquisitions: A Reexamination of Performance Issues." *Strategic Management Journal* 11:2, 99–115.

Shelton, Lois M. 1988. "Strategic Business Fits and Corporate Acquisition Strategies: Empirical Evidence." *Strategic Management Journal* 9:2, 279–287.

Shrivastava, Paul. 1986. "Post-merger Integration." *Journal of Business Strategy* 7:1, 65–76.

Sineter, Marsha. 1981. "Mergers: Morale and Productivity." *Personnel Journal* 1:8, 863–867.

Singh, Harbir, and Cynthia A. Montgomery. 1987. "Corporate Acquisition and Economic Performance." *Strategic Management Journal* 8:4, 377–386.

Soderberg, Anne-Marie, and Eero Vaara. 2003. *Merging Across Borders.* Copenhagen: Copenhagen Business School.

Stahl, Gunter, and Andreas Voigt. 2003. "Meta Analysis of Performance Implications of Cultural Differences in Mergers and Acquisitions: Integrating Strategic, Financial and Organizational Perspective." INSEAD Working Paper Series 2003/99/ABA.

Stahl, Gunter, and Andreas Voigt. 2008. "Do Cultural Differences Matter in Mergers and Acquisitions? A Tentative Model and Examination." *Organization Science* 19:1, 160–176.

Tajfel, Henri, and John C. Turner. 1979. "An Integrative Theory Intergroup Conflict." In William G. Austin and Stephen Worchel, (eds.), *The Social Psychology of Intergroup Relations,* 33–47. Monterey, CA: Brooks/Cole.

Teerikangas, Satu, and Philippe Very. 2006. "The Culture-Performance Relationship in M&A: From Yes/No to How." *British Journal of Management* 17:Special Issue, 31–48.

Terry, Deborah J., Blake McKimmie, and Nicole Doherty. 2003. "Responses to a Merger: The Effects of Premerger Group Status and Interaction Pattern." *Australian Journal of Psychology* 55:1, 55–64.

Terry, Deborah J., and Anne T. O'Brien. 2001. "Status, Legitimacy and Ingroup Bias in the Context of Organizational Merger." *Group Processes and Ingroup Relations* 4:3, 271–289.

Ullrich, Johannes and Rolf Van Dick. 2007. "The Group Psychology of Mergers and Acquisitions: Lessons from the Social Identity Approach." In Cary L. Cooper and Sydney

Finkelstein, eds. *Advances in Mergers and Acquisitions*, Volume 6, 1–15. Oxford: Elsevier Ltd.

Ullrich, Johannes, Jan Wieseke, and Rolf Van Dick. 2005. "Continuity and Change in Mergers and Acquisitions: A Social Identity Case Study of a German Industrial Merger." *Journal of Management Studies* 42:8, 1549–1569.

Vaara, Eero. 2003. "Post-acquisition Integration Sensemaking: Glimpses of Ambiguity, Confusion, Hypocrisy, and Politicization." *Journal of Management Studies* 40:3, 859–894.

Van Dick, Rolf, Johannes Ullrich, and Patrick A. Tissington. 2006. "Working under a Black Cloud: How to Sustain Organizational Identification after a Merger." *British Journal of Management* 17:Special Issue, 69–79.

Van Dick, Rolf, Ulrich Wagner, and Gunnar Lemmer. 2004. "Research Note: The Winds of Change-Multiple Identification in the Case of Organizational Mergers." *European Journal of Work and Organizational Psychology* 13:2, 121–138.

Van Knippenberg, Daan, Barbara Van Knippenberg, Laura Monden, and Fleur L. de Lima. 2002. "Organizational Identity after a Merger: A Social Identity Perspective." *British Journal of Social Psychology* 41:2, 233–252.

Van Leeuwen, Esther, Daan Van Krippenberg, and Naomi Ellemers. 2003. "Continuing and Changing Group Identities. The Effects of Merging on Social Identification and Ingroup Bias." *Personality and Social Psychology Bulletin* 29:6, 679–690.

Very, Philippe, Michael Lubatkin, and Roland Calori. 1996. "A Cross National Assessment of Acculturative Stress in Recent European Mergers." *International Studies of Management and Organization* 26:1, 59–86.

Walsh, James P. 1988. "Top Management Turnover Following Mergers and Acquisitions." *Strategic Management Journal* 9:2, 173–183.

Walsh, James P. 1989. "Doing a Deal: Merger and Acquisition Negotiations and Their Impact upon Target Company Top Management Turnover." *Strategic Management Journal* 10:4, 307–322.

Walsh, James P., and John W. Ellwood. 1991. "Mergers, Acquisitions and the Pruning of Managerial Dead-wood: An Examination of the Market for Corporate Control." *Strategic Management Journal* 12:3, 201–217.

Weber, Yakkov. 1996. "Corporate Cultural Fit and Performance in Mergers and Acquisitions." *Human Relations* 49:9, 1181–1202.

Werhane, Patricia H. 1988. "Two Ethical Issues in Mergers and Acquisitions." *Journal of Business Ethics* 7:1–2, 14–45.

Williams, Stephen, and Cary L. Cooper. 1996. *The Pressure Management Indicator*. Harrogate, United Kingdom: Resource System.

Young, James B. 1981. *Handbook of Mergers, Acquisitions and Buyouts*. Englewood Cliffs, NJ: Prentice Hall.

ABOUT THE AUTHOR

Siddhartha S. Brahma is a corporate trainer in Saudi Industrial Development Fund, Saudi Arabia. He was previously on the business faculty in an affiliated college under the University of Calcutta. He has extensive research experience in Indian M&As. His research interests include M&A integration issues and corporate strategy. His research has been published in several refereed journals, books, and case studies. He received an MBA from the Indian Institute of Social Welfare and Business Management and a PhD from the Indian Institute of Technology.

PART IV

Takeovers and Behavioral Effects

CHAPTER 18

Takeover Strategies

SHAILENDRA (SHAIL) PANDIT
Assistant Professor of Accounting, University of Illinois at Chicago

INTRODUCTION

Takeover strategies are a function of several factors including macroeconomic and capital market conditions, acquirer's motivations and strategic objectives, expected synergies from the deal, and acquirer's beliefs about potential competition and outcome of the takeover process. Many researchers view the takeover process as a game between two players—the acquirer and the target—with the potential for entry of other players such as rival bidders, regulators, and other market participants. Other scholars characterize takeovers in a specialized, two-party auction setting. In either event, the path adopted by acquirers in pursuing potential takeover targets is likely to be a function of many related factors.

The framework adopted here covers the three components of an acquirer's strategies that correspond to the sequence of events associated with takeovers: antecedents, characteristics, and consequences. Broadly, *antecedents* refer to forces in the external and internal environments of the two firms; *characteristics* are related to various attributes of the acquirer's approach; and *consequences* deal with the impact of the acquirer's chosen strategy. Scholars such as Wiedman (2000) and Hirst, Koonce, and Venkataraman (2008) use a similar framework to organize the management earnings forecasts literature.

In the context of takeover strategies, antecedents, characteristics, and consequences are not necessarily mutually exclusive categories but may overlap in many areas. For example, bidding managers may choose to embark on a hostile, all-cash offer if they expect resistance from target managers (e.g., Berkovitch and Narayanan, 1993). The probability of success for such an offer differs substantially from a friendly, all-stock offer. Cash offers are also known to lead to different postacquisition consequences when compared with stock offers (Mitchell and Stafford, 2000). Thus, factors affecting an acquirer's takeover strategy are interlinked with takeover success and post-takeover outcomes. Nonetheless, examining takeover strategies on dimensions related to ex-ante factors, actual strategy implementation, and ex-post realization provides a useful means of highlighting important aspects of the takeover process.

The chapter has the following organization. It first examines some external and internal factors affecting takeover strategies and then covers the implementation and outcomes of such strategies. Agency problems and free riding within the acquirer and target firms affect the incentives for undertaking takeovers and also create frictions in the takeover process once the acquirer decides to launch a bid for the target. In addition to the above internal factors, macroeconomic, technological, and regulatory forces outside the firm leave their imprint on the specific form of the acquirer's strategy. Finally, since the route undertaken by the acquirer can have a significant bearing on the outcome of the bid, takeover strategies also have long-term consequences for both the acquirer and the target.

ANTECEDENTS

Takeover strategies are shaped by the acquirer's objectives, the expected response from the target, and the external macroeconomic environment. Characteristics of the acquirer and the target, such as their capital structure and shareholding, affect the route that the acquirer takes. At the same time, external conditions, such as government regulation, taxes, and merger and acquisition (M&A) waves, also leave their mark on takeover strategies. Additionally, other stylized features of the takeover process have a bearing on the acquirer's strategies. These include agency problems in the acquiring and target firms, problems of the "winner's curse," and information and signaling issues. Takeovers are also often characterized as specialized auctions with one buyer (acquirer) and one seller (target), where the acquirer interacts with target shareholders or target management. To the extent that auction theory accurately models takeovers, it can provide useful insights into various aspects of the takeover process including acquisition strategies and their impact on shareholder and social welfare to firm insiders and regulators (Dasgupta and Hansen, 2007). On the whole, takeover strategies are intertwined with the broader theories of M&As as reviewed in more detail below.

Agency Problems, Free Riding, and Takeovers

The separation of ownership and control in large firms causes agency problems (Jensen and Meckling, 1976; Grossman and Hart, 1983). If managers (agents) do not own a majority share in the firm, they are likely to exert suboptimal effort and consume perquisites. This is presumably because managers can pass on the costs to the majority shareholders (principals). Such problems are exacerbated due to the principal's inability to write exhaustive and enforceable contracts that would force the agent to maximize shareholder value (Hart and Moore, 1988, 1999). Further, large firms are subject to the problem of free riding among shareholders. An individual owner who is willing to monitor agents has to bear the full cost of monitoring, but all owners share the rewards. This causes shirking on the part of shareholders (Holmstrom, 1979, 1982). Both acquirer and target firms are subject to efficiency losses due to agency and free-rider problems.

Firms can mitigate these problems in several ways. For example, compensation contracts and the managerial labor market can create incentives for managers to act in the best interest of shareholders (Fama, 1980). Also, external capital markets act as a monitoring mechanism by providing via stock prices a summary firm performance measure to various stakeholders who can then discipline managers (Fama and Jensen, 1983). Takeovers are another solution and possibly a last resort to mitigating inefficiencies in firms. When agency problems are so large that they cannot be reined in by other mechanisms, outsiders may attempt to gain control of the firm through a tender offer or proxy fight to improve firm performance (Manne, 1965).

Some scholars view M&As not as a solution to but rather as a result of firm-level inefficiencies. According to this view, managers have incentives to engage in empire building and to increase firm size because managerial compensation and private benefits tend to be positively correlated with these two actions (Shleifer and Vishny, 1989; Morck, Shleifer, and Vishny, 1990). This view corresponds with Jensen's (1986) "free cash flow hypothesis," according to which managers who are faced with declining investment opportunities and surplus cash have incentives to deploy the surplus in potentially value-destroying projects rather than returning it to shareholders. Thus, while takeovers act as an external disciplining device for inefficient target firms, they could also be a manifestation of agency problems in acquirer firms.

Rational acquirers can anticipate frictions in target firms and take measures to mitigate them. Such measures include post-takeover dilution (Grossman and Hart, 1980) and pretakeover toehold acquisition (Shleifer and Vishny, 1986). Post-takeover dilution is aimed at achieving wealth transfer from the remaining minority target shareholders to the acquirer, who then becomes the majority shareholder in the target. Valuation dilution may result from imposing transfer pricing on the subsidiary, disposing of acquired assets, and paying generous compensation to acquirer managers. As Betton, Eckbo, and Thorburn (2008, 2009) note, such dilution may enhance the efficiency of the takeover process but can be controversial and difficult to implement.

While acquirers can implement the above strategies after the acquisition, they can also try to mitigate free-rider problems before initiating a bid. For example, a potential acquirer can purchase shares and acquire a toehold in the target. In the case of toeholds, the acquirer also hopes to gain on its prebid purchase because the market is generally unaware of the acquirer's intentions of embarking on a takeover bid at that time. After the takeover offer becomes public knowledge the target's stock price likely rises, leading to a potential profit for the acquirer.

Technology, Regulation, and Macroeconomic Factors

The intensity of M&As in the economy follows systematic variations over time. Technological developments, changes in federal, state, and local regulation, investor sentiment, and other exogenous factors are linked to the emergence of merger waves (Martynova and Renneboog, 2008; Betton et al., 2009).

To explain the clustering of acquisition activity in time, Gort (1969) proposes an economic disturbance theory of mergers. He argues that forces generating discrepancies in valuation are decisive in determining variations in merger rates both among industries and over time. According to this view, economic disturbances randomly alter individual expectations and generate valuation discrepancies, leading to increased merger activity. Consistent with this view, Lambrecht (2004) finds evidence of a positive correlation between M&A intensity and product market demand in the broader economy, implying that product market cycles can lead to systematic temporal patterns in M&As. Empirical findings in other studies, such as Nelson (1966), Gort (1969), and Golbe and White (1987, 1993), also support the notion that exogenous macroeconomic factors, such as aggregate growth and changes in capital market prices, are related to the intensity of M&As.

Mitchell and Mulherin (1996) study the relationship between acquisition activity and industry shocks such as deregulation, changes in input costs, and technological or financial innovations that affect industry structure. Business combinations are often an efficient means for firms to respond to common exogenous shocks and to readjust industry structure. Along similar lines, Gorton, Kahl, and Rosen's (2009) theory of mergers combines managerial motives with an industry-level regime shift that leads to value-increasing merger opportunities. In their model, anticipation of merger opportunities leads to defensive acquisitions, where managers acquire other firms to avoid losing private benefits if their firms are acquired, or to positioning acquisitions, where firms position themselves as more attractive takeover targets to earn takeover premiums.

Aggregate stock market valuations can also affect M&A waves. Shleifer and Vishny (2003) present an analytical model based on stock market misvaluation of the merging firms. The model is driven by the relative valuations of the merging firms and the market's perception of deal synergies. Predictions from the model include why certain acquirers take over specific targets as well as particular takeover strategies, such as the choice of the payment method (e.g., stock versus cash) and merger waves. Along similar lines, Rhodes-Kropf and Viswanathan (2004) report that potential market value deviations from fundamental values for both firms can lead to a correlation between stock merger activity and market valuation. Thus, aggregate stock market misvaluation can drive merger waves and clustering of cash and stock purchases.

Corporate and Personal Taxation

Tax considerations can affect the specific form of takeover strategy as well as the basic decision to acquire another firm. The U.S. Internal Revenue Code (IRC) recognizes acquisitions (or "business combinations") fulfilling certain criteria under IRC Section 368 as tax-free reorganizations. For example, deals in which acquirer stock is given as compensation to target shareholders generally qualify for tax-free status. In such transactions, taxes on the capital gains of target shareholders are deferred until they actually sell the shares received. Further, unless the acquirer chooses to apply IRC Section 338, there is a carry-over of the target's tax basis to the acquirer. This implies that the acquiring firm has no tax liability for gains arising from the takeover of the target's net assets. If the acquirer chooses to apply Section 338, a step-up of the tax-basis of the target assets applies, potentially leading to a capital gains tax. However, the acquirer infrequently makes such choices, which generally apply to cases when the target has net operating losses due to expire or when the target is a subsidiary of the acquirer (Auerbach and Reishus, 1988; Gilson, Scholes, and Wolfson, 1988; Bruner, 2004). Given these implications for both acquirer and target firms, prior M&A literature recognizes tax effects as an important influence on takeover strategies (Hayn, 1989; Weston, Siu, and Johnson, 2001).

To summarize, several important antecedents to takeover strategies exist on account of the inherent firm characteristics of the acquirer and the target and factors in the external environment such as regulation, taxes, industry shocks, and systematic variations in stock market valuations. The following section examines some specific characteristics of takeover strategies.

CHARACTERISTICS

Characteristics of takeover strategies include the tone and terms of the offer, payment method, provision of termination fee and collar provisions, and pretakeover toehold purchases. Some of these characteristics are discussed below in more detail.

Friendliness vs. Hostility

A key characteristic of takeover strategies is the perceived aggressiveness of the acquirer. When an acquirer wants to take over an inefficiently run target to improve its performance, the target management may not react positively to the acquirer's advances and the takeover process is unlikely to be friendly (Schwert, 2000). Regulators, practitioners, and academics often view hostile takeovers and proxy bids as corporate control mechanisms that improve efficiency and social welfare (Manne, 1965; Jensen and Ruback, 1983; Jensen, 1988). Conversely, friendly bids are perceived to create synergy through the business combination. Studies, such as Shivdasani (1993), find that target management turnover increases following hostile takeovers. Therefore, the perceived hostility of the acquirer's offer is associated with not only the probability of the bid's success but also real postacquisition consequences. In hostile takeovers, resistance from the target management and board of directors is not always aimed at protecting their entrenched positions. Such resistance can actually improve target shareholder value by forcing the acquirer to revise the offer terms. Thus, target resistance in hostile takeovers can have strategic motives besides entrenchment (Stulz, 1988).

In practice, judging ex post whether offers were friendly or hostile ex ante is difficult. Schwert (2000) argues that hostility could be just a perceptual distinction based on different patterns of public disclosure about the takeover process. Since a majority of takeovers tend to be negotiated deals, transactions could be characterized as friendly when bargaining remains undisclosed and hostile when the public becomes aware of the ongoing negotiations. Thus, hostility could be simply an issue of perception. Schwert presents evidence that most deals labeled as hostile in the press are indistinguishable from friendly deals in economic terms. Thus, on the whole, while thinking of hostile takeovers as creating value through removing inefficiencies and friendly takeovers leading to synergistic gains seems rational in practice, distinguishing between the two kinds of takeover strategy is often difficult.

Form of Compensation

The method of payment employed by acquirers is a key element of takeover strategies since it is related not only to the probability of acquisition success and postacquisition performance but also to other characteristics such as tax treatment and the offer's "friendliness." Takeover compensation can range from an all-stock payment, debt securities, or combinations of securities and cash to an all-cash payment. Betton et al. (2009) report that from 1980 to 2005, 26 percent of the initial bids comprise all-cash offers, while all-stock and mixed offers each cover 37 percent of the bids. The authors also find a significant association between the form of compensation and the acquirer's approach. Specifically, merger bids are likely to contain a higher proportion of acquirer's stock, whereas tender offers are more likely to contain a substantial proportion of cash. Stock-for-stock deals are also more likely to qualify for the tax-free treatment (Brown and Ryngaert, 1991). Finally, before pooling-of-interests accounting was abolished in the United States, the accounting choice for business combinations was also linked with the method of takeover financing (Pandit, 2009). Thus, on the whole, 100 percent stock offers are more likely to be friendly, leading to tax savings for both acquirer and target shareholders and a greater chance of success.

The payment method choice is related to information asymmetries between the acquirer and the target. Consistent with Myers and Majluf (1984) and Myers's (1984) pecking order theory, when the bidder and target do not have symmetric information about the true value of their respective firms, the payment method can reveal the firm's private information and affect both the division of takeover gains and the probability of takeover success. The choice of payment also has implications for the investors' reaction to the takeover offer in the Myers and Majluf framework. That is, if the acquirer offers to issue its own stock to target shareholders and if investors infer from the offer that the acquirer's stock is overpriced, a negative market reaction may ensue. Studies, such as Hansen (1987), Fishman (1989), and Eckbo, Giammarino, and Heinkel (1990), provide explicit models of the acquirer's payment choice conditional on the adverse selection problem described above. As surveyed in Andrade, Mitchell, and Stafford (2001) and Betton et al. (2009), the empirical evidence behind the method of payment in acquisitions is consistent with stock offers being met with a significantly lower market reaction, as compared with cash offers.

Capital structure and control considerations on the part of the acquirer can also affect the payment choice. Issuance of new shares to target shareholders alters the acquirer's capital structure and dilutes ownership concentration of the existing shareholders. Consistent with this notion, Yook (2003) reports that bidder gains are greater in cash offers when the takeover causes downgrading of the merged firm's debt due to increased leverage. This evidence is also consistent with Jensen's (1986) free cash flow argument. Other studies examine whether the type of cash financing affects the market reaction to the payment method announcement. While investors know about preacquisition security issues, the takeover announcement could resolve uncertainty about the use of the issue proceeds. Thus, the source of financing for the cash portion of the bid can affect the market reaction (Schlingemann, 2004).

As discussed above, concerns over potential dilution of control rights can affect the choice of takeover exchange methods (Harris and Raviv, 1988; Stulz, 1988). A cash offer leaves the acquirer shareholders' existing control rights unchanged, whereas issuing more equity to target shareholders leads to a dilution of control. Consistent with this line of reasoning, Amihud, Lev, and Travlos (1990), Martin (1996), and Ghosh and Ruland (1998) find that acquirer management shareholding has a negative effect on the probability of using stock as the acquisition currency. Faccio and Masulis (2005) report that, in a European context, corporate control incentives to choose cash are particularly strong in acquirers with relatively concentrated share ownership structures.

Macroeconomic conditions can affect the method of payment in takeovers. As discussed under takeover strategy antecedents, exogenous shocks due to regulatory or technological changes affect the intensity of M&A activity in the economy. If such shocks affect equity valuations, they can also affect the method of payment choice. For example, Rhodes-Kropf and Viswanathan (2004) outline a scenario where potential targets rationally accept more bids from overvalued acquirers during peaks in market valuations because targets tend to overestimate synergies during such times. Betton et al. (2009) report that the proportion of mixed cash-stock offers is similar to that of all-stock offers even in periods of high market valuations and merger activity. They propose that offering part-cash compensation to targets allows undervalued acquirers to stand out from other (overvalued) acquirers who may offer all-stock deals.

Collars and Termination Fees

Takeover offers include several other features besides the form of compensation. For example, when acquirers use their own shares as the acquisition currency, they may incorporate floating exchange ratios or collars. The most common type of stock offer, known as a fixed stock offer, is characterized by the acquirer offering a fixed number of its shares for each target share. In contrast, a floating stock offer allows variation in the number of shares exchanged. The actual exchange ratio is determined as either a fixed dollar amount divided by the acquirer's stock price or the ratio of the target's and the acquirer's stock prices. A third type, termed a fixed collar offer, sets upper and lower bounds around the fixed exchange ratio within which the deal may be realized. Finally, floating collar offers have a floating exchange ratio that is set just before the deal's closing, if the acquirer's price is within a prespecified range. For either type of collar, if the acquirer's stock price moves outside the range, either firm has the option to cancel the deal.

Collar offers can be viewed as insurance against unanticipated variations in the acquirer's stock price. Since the compensation paid to the target is in the form of acquirer's shares, both parties should ensure that the final payment is within reasonable bounds of the initially agreed price. Thus, collars can protect both sets of shareholders against adverse selection and, at least until the deal is complete, moral hazard problems. For example, if the acquirer manager has more information about the acquirer firm's value, a fixed share offer is more attractive than other types of stock offers to an overvalued acquirer. In such deals, the value of the target's claim on the combined entity decreases as the acquirer's share price falls before deal completion. In a floating share offer, however, the target's share of the combined entity is largely unaffected by changes in the value of the acquirer. In return for offering this protection, the acquirer can negotiate better deal terms and expect a higher probability of success, resulting in value gains to both parties.

While the empirical evidence is generally consistent with the target firms benefiting from stock offers containing floating exchange rates and collars, there is mixed evidence about the acquirers gaining from such features. For example, Fuller (2003) reports that targets receiving floating collar offers experience higher abnormal returns than targets receiving cash or fixed or floating stock offers and experience returns similar to targets receiving fixed collar offers, potentially due to the associated cancellation option. She also finds that including a fixed or floating collar has a significantly negative effect on bidder returns.

Officer (2004) reports that collars are more likely to be offered when a large difference exists between stock return volatilities, consistent with collars offering protection for both acquirers and targets against adverse price movements. He further finds that including a collar in a stock-for-stock exchange offer significantly reduces the probability of renegotiation, consistent with collars offering an acquirer's advantage in terms of a higher probability of deal success. On the whole, collars can be an important part of takeover strategies, particularly for all-stock or mixed offers.

In addition to collars, acquirers often include termination or breakup fees in the takeover offer. A target termination fee clause requires that the target pay the bidder a fixed cash fee if the target does not complete the proposed merger. Termination fees can thus be viewed as a deterrent imposed by the acquirer that discourages the target from "shopping around" and inviting competing bids. In turn, termination fees create incentives for acquirers to make deal-specific investments and disclose more predeal information (Officer, 2004). Thus, on the whole, termination fees are designed to expedite decision making and to reduce contracting costs between the two firms.

Bates and Lemmon (2003) examine the provision of termination fee clauses in merger agreements between 1989 and 1998. They report that such fees are observed more frequently when bidding is costly and a high potential for information expropriation exists by third parties. Fee provisions appear to benefit target shareholders through higher deal completion rates and greater takeover premiums. This evidence is consistent with termination fees serving as an efficient contracting device. Bates and Lemmon find no evidence that termination fees act as a deterrent for competing bids, a finding that is corroborated by Officer (2004).

Toeholds

Acquirers sometimes obtain a preacquisition shareholding in the target firm to mitigate potential resistance during the takeover process. Such toehold ownership gives a dual advantage to the acquirer. Specifically, the toehold not only reduces the number of shares that must be purchased when the takeover bid is launched, but the toehold stake may also be sold at a premium if another acquirer enters the contest and takes over the target. Prior studies, such as Walkling (1985), Jennings and Mazzeo (1993), and Betton and Eckbo (2000), show that toehold bidding increases the probability of takeover success. Betton and Eckbo also report that toeholds are associated with lower offer premiums in successful bids, consistent with the deterrence effects of toeholds on rival acquirers.

Harrington and Prokop (1993) develop an analytical model to explore the dynamics of a takeover bid. In their model, if the initial takeover bid is unsuccessful, a raider is allowed to make a new tender offer for the remaining shares. The anticipation of a higher tender offer in the future makes target shareholders hold their shares and forces the raider to offer a higher premium. Burkart (1995) develops a model of private-value auctions in which the optimal strategy for a bidder with partial ownership is to bid more than its valuation. This strategy, however, can lead to the "winner's curse" and the bidder realizing a loss. The overbidding also implies that the presence of a large shareholder increases the bid premium in single-bidder takeovers at the expense of reducing the probability of the takeover actually occurring. Goldman and Qian (2005) offer an explanation for why raiders do not acquire the maximum possible toehold before announcing a bid. They show that a raider may optimally acquire a small toehold, even if the acquisition does not drive up the pretender target price. This occurs because although a larger toehold increases profits if the takeover succeeds, it also conveys a higher level of managerial entrenchment and hence a lower firm value if the takeover fails. Target firms may encourage toeholds to attract "white knights" when there is a threat of an unwanted takeover. Also, the impact of toeholds in private-value auctions is relatively small. Along these lines, results in Bulow, Huang, and Klemperer (1999) are consistent with toeholds helping buyers win the auction. A controlling minority shareholder may therefore be effectively immune to outside offers. A target may benefit by requiring sealed-bid offers or selling a cheap toehold or options to a white knight.

Burch (2001) examines the use of lockup options in mergers that are granted by target managers to discourage competition and to select a preferred acquirer, thus harming target shareholder wealth. His evidence suggests that lockup options inhibit competition, but on average, deals with lockup options have higher target announcement and overall returns and lower bidder announcement returns. An examination of merger proxy statements suggests lockup options are no more prevalent in privately negotiated, preemptive deals, and average target returns are higher when such deals include a lockup option. Thus, on the whole, Burch's evidence is more consistent with managers using lockup options to enhance bargaining power than with lockup options harming shareholder wealth.

To summarize, the characteristics of acquirers' takeover strategies include features such as the tone (friendliness) of the takeover offer, form of payment offered, additional terms such as collar or termination fees, and pretakeover moves such as acquiring a toehold share ownership in the target. Such strategies are designed to help the acquirer meet takeover objectives speedily and efficiently. To that end, the above characteristics of takeover strategies help the acquirer mitigate problems of information asymmetry and target resistance and improve both the chances of offer acceptance and post-takeover performance.

CONSEQUENCES

Since rational acquirers design their takeover strategies in the backdrop of internal (firm level) and external (macroeconomic and regulatory) factors and do so with the desired takeover objectives in view, the antecedents and characteristics of such strategies are inextricably linked to their consequences. For example, takeovers motivated by synergistic gains are likely to follow a different path and lead to different post-takeover consequences when compared with takeovers motivated by market power gains. This section reviews findings in the prior literature regarding the outcomes of the various routes acquirers take in pursuing target firms. While other chapters in the book discuss post-takeover performance of the combined firm, the focus here is on relating specific aspects of the acquirer's takeover strategy to the outcome.

A large body of research investigates the effect of industry structure and the relatedness of merging firms on takeover strategies and post-takeover performance. For example, some contend that firms emphasizing unrelated diversification through M&As are often located in unfavorable market positions in terms of the attractiveness of their industries and their competitive positions within these industries. However, whether such positions are also linked to firms using nonconglomerate acquisition strategies is unclear. Hopkins (1987) sheds light on this issue by examining acquisition strategy and the market position of acquirers. He uses three strategies—conglomerate, technology-related, and marketing-related—to motivate differences in the market position of acquirers. His results show that while acquisitive growth is generally associated with a decline in market position, marketing-related strategy is linked to a distinctly superior position. Firms using this strategy operate in more profitable industries and have higher market shares.

Singh and Montgomery (1987) investigate the argument that takeovers that are related in product/market or technological terms create higher value than unrelated acquisitions. Their results are consistent with related acquisitions having greater total gains when compared with unrelated acquisitions. Also, target firms in related acquisitions have substantially higher gains than targets in unrelated acquisitions. These results indicate that related target firms benefit more from acquisition than do unrelated target firms.

In a similar vein, Chatterjee (1992) studies the sources of value in takeovers alternatively derived from synergy or restructuring motives. A common view is that targets should accept takeover bids because unsuccessful targets tend to lose market value. Thus, consistent with takeovers acting as external disciplining devices, takeover bids for underperforming targets unlock firm value and benefit their shareholders. However, other scholars point to the poor postacquisition performance of the combined firm and recommend rejecting takeover bids by the target. Chatterjee argues that the influence of the source of takeover gains has an important bearing on the decision to reject or accept takeover bids. He proposes that the target firm should agree to be taken over only if the synergy component in the takeover is dominant. The author tests the dominance of the source of value in takeovers by examining takeovers that were unsuccessful. Chatterjee concludes that restructuring, not synergy, motivates the mergers in his sample and that target firms can create the same value independently. Further, even if restructuring is the motive behind a takeover, the target firm has to carry out the restructuring or else no value is created.

Turning to strategy characteristics, many studies examine the effects of the medium of exchange (stock, mixed, or cash) on takeover performance. Such studies largely rely on the framework developed by Myers and Majluf (1984). Fishman (1989) and Berkovitch and Narayanan (1990) extend the above framework to examine the role of the exchange medium in competition among bidders and its effect on shareholder returns. Their models show that stockholders of both acquiring and target firms get higher returns when a takeover is financed with cash rather than equity and that returns to target shareholders increase with competition. The models also predict that the fraction of synergy captured by the target decreases with the level of synergy. Finally, as competition increases, both the cash component of the offer and the proportion of cash offered tend to increase. These predictions are borne out by numerous empirical studies that link the method of payment in acquisitions to takeover success, abnormal returns at takeover announcement, and postacquisition performance.

For example, all-stock acquisition announcements tend to cause a statistically significant (approximately) 1 percent negative return for acquirers, at least in the case of offers made to public targets (Asquith, Bruner, and Mullins, 1983; Travlos, 1987; Servaes, 1991; Brown and Ryngaert, 1991; Martin, 1996; Heron and Lie, 2004; Schlingemann, 2004). This underperformance appears to persist even after the acquisition is completed. Loughran and Vijh (1997) report that postacquisition abnormal returns for stock acquisitions are lower when compared with all-cash deals. Linking postacquisition performance to takeover strategy antecedents, Rosen (2006) finds that deals taking place during merger waves have high preacquisition share prices followed by low postacquisition performance. Empirical evidence of long-run merger performance, especially when measured as an abnormal stock return, should be viewed skeptically due to methodological concerns (Barber and Lyon, 1997; Betton et al., 2009; also see surveys by Jensen and Ruback, 1983; Jarrell, Brickley, and Netter, 1988; Andrade et al., 2001).

Empirical studies of other features of takeover strategies, such as collars and termination fees, present evidence generally supportive of such measures helping acquirers achieve their takeover objectives. For example, Officer (2004) reports that including collars in stock-financed offers is associated with positive announcement returns for acquirers. Thus, by assuring targets of the eventual payment amount and thus reducing the elasticity of stock bids with respect to the acquirer's stock price, collars mitigate the problems of information asymmetry and adverse selection outlined in prior analytical studies such as Myers and Majluf (1984). Officer also finds evidence consistent with collars being associated with a reduced probability of renegotiation, thus expediting the takeover process and reducing the overall costs of acquisition.

In the context of termination fees, Bates and Lemmon (2003) find that target fee clauses are provided more often in deals involving a significant degree of information asymmetry between the bidder and the target and in more complex deals. Their evidence is consistent with termination fee provisions being used to secure target wealth gains in deals with higher costs associated with negotiation and bid failure. In another study of termination fees, Officer (2003) examines whether self-interested target managers use termination fees to deter competing bids and protect "sweetheart" deals with white knights, which could result in lower gains for target shareholders. As discussed above, an alternative hypothesis is that target managers use termination fees to encourage bidder participation by ensuring that the bidder is compensated for the revelation of valuable private information released during merger negotiations. Officer's empirical evidence indicates that deals with target termination fees involve significantly higher premiums and success rates than deals without such clauses. Furthermore, he finds only weak support for the contention that termination fees deter competing bids. Overall, his evidence suggests that termination fees are at least not harmful and are likely beneficial for target shareholders. Finally, results in empirical studies involving toeholds, such as Bulow et al. (1999) and Betton and Eckbo (2000), support the argument that purchasing stock ownership in targets before launching a takeover bid helps acquirers win the takeover contest.

SUMMARY AND CONCLUSIONS

Takeover strategies involve many dimensions of the takeover process and are influenced by factors such as market conditions, acquirer's strategic objectives, expected gains from the takeover, and potential competition. This chapter discusses three components of takeover strategies: antecedents, characteristics, and consequences. Antecedents refer to internal and external forces leading to the takeover. Characteristics involve various attributes of the acquirer's approach. Consequences deal with the impact of the acquirer's strategies in the takeover process. These categories are not mutually exclusive and often overlap.

While the acquirer's objectives and the expected target response are important determinants of takeover strategies, the external macroeconomic environment also plays a key role. Characteristics of the acquirer and the target, such as their capital structure and shareholding pattern, give rise to agency and free-rider problems and exacerbate information asymmetry. Rational acquirers need to adopt effective measures to mitigate these issues. At the same time, takeover strategies are also shaped by the intensity of M&A activity in the broader economy that follows systematic variations over time. Technological developments, regulatory changes, and investor sentiment often cause such merger waves.

Takeover strategies are aimed at minimizing frictions in the takeover process and increasing the probability of success. Specific characteristics of takeover strategies include the aggressiveness of the acquirer's approach, offer structure and payment method, provisions such as termination fees and collars, and pre-takeover toehold purchases. Various aspects of takeover strategies often overlap and separating purely semantic aspects from economically material ones is sometimes difficult. For example, while the "friendliness" of the offer may appear to affect the takeover process, judging ex post whether the offers were friendly or hostile ex ante is difficult. Nonetheless, the large body of prior analytical, empirical, and behavioral research on takeover strategy formation offers important insights into various routes undertaken by acquirers in pursuit of target firms.

Takeover strategies have a bearing not only on the success of the bid but also on long-term performance after the acquisition. For example, several empirical studies confirm the analytical prediction that both acquirer and target stockholders get higher returns at takeover announcement and in the postacquisition period when the takeover bid is made in a competitive environment and largely financed with cash. Similarly, evidence supports the claim that including termination fees and collars by acquirers in takeover offers improves the chances of success and reduces the acquisition costs. Thus, rational acquirers can achieve substantial economic gains by carefully crafting their takeover strategies.

DISCUSSION QUESTIONS

1. What is the nature of free-rider problems in potential target firms? How can acquirers mitigate such problems?
2. Do taxes affect acquirers' takeover strategies? If so, how?
3. What is the difference between friendly and hostile takeover offers?

4. What are the main determinants of the method of payment choice in takeovers? Does the form of compensation have any relationship with postacquisition performance?

5. What is the role of collars and termination fees in takeover offers?

6. What are toeholds and how do they benefit acquirers?

REFERENCES

Amihud, Yakov, Baruch Lev, and Nickolaos G. Travlos. 1990. "Corporate Control and the Choice of Investment Financing: The Case of Corporate Acquisitions." *Journal of Finance* 45:2, 603–616.

Andrade, Gregor, Mark Mitchell, and Erik Stafford. 2001. "New Evidence and Perspective on Mergers." *Journal of Economic Perspectives* 15:2, 103–120.

Asquith, Paul, Robert Bruner, and David Mullins. 1983. "The Gains to Bidding Firms from Merger." *Journal of Financial Economics* 11:1-4, 121–139.

Auerbach, Alan J., and David Reishus. 1988. "Taxes and the Merger Decision: An Empirical Analysis." In Alan J. Auerbach, ed. *Corporate Takeovers: Causes and Consequences*, 157–183. Chicago: National Bureau of Economic Research (NBER) and University of Chicago Press.

Barber, Brad M., and John D. Lyon. 1997. "Detecting Long-Run Abnormal Stock Returns: The Empirical Power and Specification of Test Statistics." *Journal of Financial Economics* 43:3, 341–372.

Bates, Thomas W., and Michael L. Lemmon. 2003. "Breaking Up Is Hard to Do? An Analysis of Termination Fee Provisions and Merger Outcomes." *Journal of Financial Economics* 69:3, 469–504.

Berkovitch, Elazar, and M. P. Narayanan. 1990. "Competition and the Medium of Exchange in Takeovers." *Review of Financial Studies* 3:2, 153–174.

Berkovitch, Elazar, and M. P. Narayanan. 1993. "Motives for Takeovers: An Empirical Investigation." *Journal of Financial and Quantitative Analysis* 28:3, 347–362.

Betton, Sandra, and B. Espen Eckbo. 2000. "Toeholds, Bid Jumps, and Expected Payoff in Takeovers." *Review of Financial Studies* 13:4, 841–882.

Betton, Sandra, B. Espen Eckbo, and Karin S. Thorburn. 2008. "Corporate Takeovers." In B. Espen Eckbo, ed. *Handbook of Corporate Finance: Empirical Corporate Finance*, Volume 2, 291–430. Amsterdam: Elsevier/North-Holland.

Betton, Sandra, B. Espen Eckbo, and Karin S. Thorburn. 2009. "Merger Negotiations and the Toehold Puzzle." *Journal of Financial Economics* 91:2, 158–178.

Brown, David T., and Michael D. Ryngaert. 1991. "The Mode of Acquisition in Takeovers: Taxes and Asymmetric Information." *Journal of Finance* 46:2, 653–669.

Bruner, Robert F. 2004. *Applied Mergers & Acquisitions*. Hoboken, NJ: John Wiley & Sons.

Bulow, Jeremy, Ming Huang, and Paul Klemperer. 1999. "Toeholds and Takeovers." *Journal of Political Economy* 107:3, 427–454.

Burch, Timothy R. 2001. "Locking Out Rival Bidders: The Use of Lockup Options in Corporate Mergers." *Journal of Financial Economics* 60:1, 103–141.

Burkart, Mike. 1995. "Initial Shareholdings and Overbidding in Takeover Contests." *Journal of Finance* 50:5, 1491–1515.

Chatterjee, Sayan. 1992. "Sources of Value in Takeovers: Synergy or Restructuring—Implications for Target and Bidder Firms." *Strategic Management Journal* 13:4, 267–286.

Dasgupta, Sudipto, and Robert G. Hansen. 2007. "Auctions in Corporate Finance." In B. Espen Eckbo, ed. *Handbook of Corporate Finance: Empirical Corporate Finance*, Volume 1, 87–143. Amsterdam: Elsevier/North-Holland.

Eckbo, B. Espen, Ronald M. Giammarino, and Robert L. Heinkel. 1990. "Asymmetric Information and the Medium of Exchange in Takeovers: Theory and Tests." *Review of Financial Studies* 3:4, 651–675.

Faccio, Mara, and Ronald W. Masulis. 2005. "The Choice of Payment Method in European Mergers and Acquisitions." *Journal of Finance* 60:3, 1345–1388.

Fama, Eugene, F. 1980. "Agency Problems and the Theory of the Firm." *Journal of Political Economy* 88:2, 288–307.

Fama, Eugene, F., and Michael C. Jensen. 1983. "Separation of Ownership and Control." *Journal of Law and Economics* 26:2, 301–325.

Fishman, Michael J. 1989. "Preemptive Bidding and the Role of the Medium of Exchange in Acquisitions." *Journal of Finance* 44:1, 41–57.

Fuller, Kathleen, P. 2003. "Why Some Firms Use Collar Offers in Mergers." *Financial Review* 38:1, 127–150.

Ghosh, Aloke, and William Ruland. 1998. "Managerial Ownership and the Method of Payment for Acquisitions, and Executive Job Retention." *Journal of Finance* 53:2, 785–797.

Gilson, Ronald J., Myron S. Scholes, and Mark A. Wolfson. 1988. "Taxation and the Dynamics of Corporate Control: The Uncertain Case for Tax Motivated Acquisitions." In John O. Coffee Jr., Louis Lowenstein, and Susan Rose-Ackerman, eds. *Knights, Raiders, and Targets: The Impact of the Hostile Takeover*, 271–299. New York: Oxford University Press.

Golbe, Devra L., and Lawrence J. White. 1987. "A Time Series Analysis of Mergers and Acquisitions in the US Economy." In Alan J. Auerbach, ed. *Corporate Takeovers*, 265–305 Chicago: University of Chicago Press.

Golbe, Devra L., and Lawrence J. White. 1993. "Catch a Wave: The Time Series Behavior of Mergers." *Review of Economics and Statistics* 75:3, 493–499.

Goldman, Eitan, and Jun Qian. 2005. "Optimal Toeholds in Takeover Contests." *Journal of Financial Economics* 77:2, 321–346.

Gort, Michael. 1969. "An Economic Disturbance Theory of Mergers." *Quarterly Journal of Economics* 83:4, 624–642.

Gorton, Gary, Matthias Kahl, and Richard J. Rosen. 2009. "Eat or Be Eaten: A Theory of Mergers and Firm Size." *Journal of Finance* 64:3, 1291–1344.

Grossman, Sanford J., and Oliver D. Hart. 1980. "Takeover Bids, the Free-Rider Problem and the Theory of the Corporation." *Bell Journal of Economics* 11:1, 42–64.

Grossman, Sanford J., and Oliver D. Hart. 1983. "An Analysis of the Principal-Agent Problem." *Econometrica* 51:1, 7–45.

Hansen, Robert G. 1987. "A Theory for the Choice of Exchange Medium in the Market for Corporate Control." *Journal of Business* 60:1, 75–95.

Harrington, Jr., Joseph E., and Jacek Prokop. 1993. "The Dynamics of the Free-Rider Problem in Takeovers." *Review of Financial Studies* 6:4, 851–882.

Harris, Milton, and Artur Raviv. 1988. "Corporate Control Contests and Capital Structure." *Journal of Financial Economics* 20:1, 55–86.

Hart, Oliver, and John Moore. 1988. "Incomplete Contracts and Renegotiation." *Econometrica* 56:4, 755–785.

Hart, Oliver, and John Moore. 1999. "Foundations of Incomplete Contracts." *Review of Financial Studies* 66:1, 115–138.

Hayn, Carla. 1989. "Tax Attributes as Determinants of Shareholder Gains in Corporate Acquisitions." *Journal of Financial Economics* 23:1, 121–153.

Heron, Randall A., and Erik Lie. 2004. "A Comparison of the Motivations for and the Information Content of Different Types of Equity Offerings." *Journal of Business* 77:3, 605–632.

Hirst, D. Eric, Lisa Koonce, and Shankar Venkataraman. 2008. "Management Earnings Forecasts: A Review and Framework." *Accounting Horizons* 22:3, 315–338.

Holmstrom, Bengt. 1979. "Moral Hazard and Observability." *Bell Journal of Economics* 10:1, 324–340.

Holmstrom, Bengt. 1982. "Moral Hazard in Teams." *Bell Journal of Economics* 13:2, 324–340.

Hopkins, H. Donald. 1987. "Acquisition Strategy and the Market Position of Acquiring Firms." *Strategic Management Journal* 8:6, 535–547.

Jarrell, Gregg A., James A. Brickley, and Jeffry M. Netter. 1988. "The Market for Corporate Control: The Empirical Evidence since 1980." *Journal of Economic Perspectives* 2:1, 49–68.

Jennings, Robert H., and Michael A. Mazzeo. 1993. "Competing Bids, Target Management Resistance, and the Structure of Takeover Bids." *Review of Financial Studies* 6:4, 883–909.

Jensen, Michael, C. 1986. "Agency Costs of Free Cash Flow, Corporate Finance and Takeovers." *American Economic Review* 76:2, 323–329.

Jensen, Michael C. 1988. "Takeovers: Their Causes and Consequences." *Journal of Economic Perspectives* 2:1, 21–48.

Jensen, Michael C., and William Meckling. 1976. "Theory of the Firm: Managerial Behavior, Agency Costs and Ownership Structure." *Journal of Financial Economics* 3:4, 305–360.

Jensen, Michael C., and Richard S. Ruback. 1983. "The Market for Corporate Control: The Scientific Evidence." *Journal of Financial Economics* 11:1-4, 5–50.

Lambrecht, Bart M. 2004. "The Timing and Terms of Mergers Motivated by Economies of Scale." *Journal of Financial Economics* 72:1, 41–62.

Loughran, Tim, and Anand M. Vijh. 1997. "Do Long-Term Shareholders Benefit from Corporate Acquisitions?" *Journal of Finance* 52:5, 1765–1790.

Manne, Henry G. 1965. "Mergers and the Market for Corporate Control." *Journal of Political Economy* 73:2, 110–120.

Martin, Kenneth, J., 1996. "The Method of Payment in Corporate Acquisitions, Investment Opportunities, and Management Ownership." *Journal of Finance* 51:4, 1227–1246.

Martynova, Marina, and Luc Renneboog. 2008. "A Century of Corporate Takeovers: What Have We Learned and Where Do We Stand?" *Journal of Banking and Finance* 32:10, 2148–2177.

Mitchell, Mark L., and J. Harold Mulherin. 1996. "The Impact of Industry Shocks on Takeover and Restructuring Activity." *Journal of Financial Economics* 41:2, 193–229.

Mitchell, Mark L., and Erik Stafford. 2000. "Managerial Decisions and Long-Term Stock Price Performance." *Journal of Business* 73:3, 287–329.

Morck, Randall, Andrei Shleifer, and Robert W. Vishny. 1990. "Do Managerial Objectives Drive Bad Acquisitions?" *Journal of Finance* 45:1, 31–48.

Myers, Stewart C. 1984. "The Capital Structure Puzzle." *Journal of Finance* 39:3, 575–592.

Myers, Stewart C., and Nicholas S. Majluf. 1984. "Corporate Financing and Investment Decisions When Firms Have Information That Investors Do Not Have." *Journal of Financial Economics* 13:2, 187–221.

Nelson, Ralph L. 1966. "Business Cycle Factors in the Choice between Internal and External Growth." In William W. Alberts and Joel E. Segall, eds. *The Corporate Mergers*, 52–70. Chicago: University of Chicago Press.

Officer, Micah S. 2003. "Termination Fees in Mergers and Acquisitions." *Journal of Financial Economics* 69:3, 431–467.

Officer, Micah S. 2004. "Collars and Renegotiation in Mergers and Acquisitions." *Journal of Finance* 59:6, 2719–2743.

Pandit, Shailendra. 2009. "Accounting Choice, Announcement Returns and Operating Performance in Stock-for-Stock Acquisitions." University of Illinois at Chicago (UC) College of Business Administration Research Paper No. 09–06.

Rhodes-Kropf, Matthew, and S. Viswanathan. 2004. "Market Valuation and Merger Waves." *Journal of Finance* 59:6, 2685–2718.

Rosen, Richard J. 2006. "Merger Momentum and Investor Sentiment: The Stock Market Reaction to Merger Announcements." *Journal of Business* 79:2, 987–1017.

Schlingemann, Frederik P. 2004. "Financing Decisions and Bidder Gains." *Journal of Corporate Finance* 10:5, 683–701.

Schwert, G. William. 2000. "Hostility in Takeovers: In the Eyes of the Beholder?" *Journal of Finance* 55:6, 2599–2640.

Servaes, Henri. 1991. "Tobin's Q and the Gains from Takeovers." *Journal of Finance* 46:1, 409–419.

Shivdasani, Anil. 1993. "Board Composition, Ownership Structure, and Hostile Takeovers." *Journal of Accounting and Economics* 16:1-3, 167–198.

Shleifer, Andrei, and Robert W. Vishny. 1986. "Large Shareholders and Corporate Control." *Journal of Political Economy* 94:3, 461–488.

Shleifer, Andrei, and Robert W. Vishny. 1989. "Management Entrenchment: The Case of Manager-Specific Investments." *Journal of Financial Economics* 25:1, 123–139.

Shleifer, Andrei, and Robert W. Vishny. 2003. "Stock Market Driven Acquisitions." *Journal of Financial Economics* 70:3, 295–311.

Stulz, René. 1988. "Managerial Control of Voting Rights: Financing Policies and the Market for Corporate Control." *Journal of Financial Economics* 20:1/2, 25–54.

Singh, Harbir, and Cynthia A. Montgomery. 1987. "Corporate Acquisition Strategies and Economic Performance." *Strategic Management Journal* 8:4, 377–386.

Travlos, Nickolaos G. 1987. "Corporate Takeover Bids, Method of Payment, and Bidding Firms' Stock Returns." *Journal of Finance* 42:4, 943–963.

Walkling, Ralph. 1985. "Predicting Tender Offer Success: A Logistic Analysis." *Journal of Financial and Quantitative Analysis* 20:4, 461–478.

Weston, J. Fred, Juan A. Siu, and Brian A. Johnson. 2001. *Takeovers, Restructuring & Corporate Governance.* Upper Saddle River, NJ: Prentice Hall.

Wiedman, Christine I. 2000. "Discussion of Voluntary Disclosure and Equity Offerings: Reducing Information Asymmetry or Hyping the Stock?" *Contemporary Accounting Research* 17:4, 663–669.

Yook, Ken C. 2003. "Larger Returns to Cash Acquisitions: Signaling Effect or Leverage Effect?" *Journal of Business* 76:3, 477–498.

ABOUT THE AUTHOR

Shail Pandit joined the University of Illinois at Chicago (UIC) in 2008. Previously, he taught at The Ohio State University and Tulane University. His research interests include M&As, corporate governance, and financial reporting. He has published in *Contemporary Accounting Research (CAR)* and the *Journal of Accounting, Auditing and Finance (JAAF)*. Professor Pandit's teaching interests include introductory and intermediate financial accounting and financial statement analysis. He received a BS in electronics engineering from Jiwaji University, India, an MBA in finance from the University of Indore, India, and a PhD in accounting with a minor concentration in finance from the University of Rochester.

CHAPTER 19

Defensive Strategies in Takeovers

CHRISTIAN RAUCH
Research Assistant, Goethe University Frankfurt

MARK WAHRENBURG
Professor, Chair of Banking and Finance, Goethe University Frankfurt

INTRODUCTION

Since the inception of the first large merger and acquisition (M&A) deals in the United States toward the end of the 19th century, the market for corporate control has been one of the central pillars of a modern financial system. As such, it serves many important roles and provides various tools for market participants directed at increasing firm value and allocating capital in efficient ways (e.g., Allen and Kraakman, 2004). The possibility of transferring assets from one owner to another imposes a system of checks and balances on management and shareholders. That is, if managers fail to use capital in a way that maximizes financial output, capital and assets can be transferred to different owners and/or managers who are better capable of maximizing the value of these assets (e.g., Deakin and Slinger, 1997). In order to gain efficiency and increase overall value, the owners of assets can pool separately owned/managed assets within a given market, thus exploiting potential synergies. In a Modigliani and Miller-free (1958) world, business transactions can also increase corporate value simply by changing the financing structures of acquired companies.

Despite the many economic benefits of the theoretically free transferability of assets in capital markets, a free transferability is often impossible. The process can be hampered if the interests of different market participants are not aligned. If two shareholder or management groups have differing views on how to efficiently use assets or believe that a different group of people should own or manage the assets, battles can ensue. An example for this misalignment of interests is a hostile takeover attempt in which the target company attempts to fend off the unwelcomed acquirer. In a hostile takeover, an acquiring company launches a bid to buy shares from the target company's shareholders at a premium over the stock price. The bidder makes this solicitation without the knowledge or consent of the target company's management. The hostile attempt results from a failure to successfully acquire the company in a friendly way (i.e., with the support of the target's management) or is initiated if the potential acquirer believes that the target management would reject a friendly offer.

The target company, however, can attempt to repel these hostile takeover attempts. Target management possesses several different tools and tactics to defend against a hostile takeover. These tools can make a hostile takeover attempt more difficult, more costly, or even impossible. As a hostile takeover may take various forms, target management has many ways to fend off the takeover attempt. With a growing number of deals, more experienced transaction parties, and increasingly sophisticated advisors, hostile transactions in today's corporate control markets have become versatile and highly complex. Since the boom of the leveraged buyout (LBO) wave in the 1980s, modern hostile takeover attempts involve much more than just offering to buy target shares at a premium or asking target shareholders for their proxy votes before the annual meeting of the target corporation (Bhagat, Shleifer, and Vishny, 1990).

Today, takeover attempts may involve shareholder activism by the acquiring company before initiating the bid, multiple offers to shareholders, different premiums for different offers, complex financing structures for paying the premiums, and other hostile and friendly ways of dealing with the target's management. As a reaction to this multitude of takeover possibilities, advisors and companies have jointly developed many different defense strategies to fend off hostile takeover attempts. These strategies can be clustered into two different groups: preventive and remedial defense strategies. A firm implements preventive defense strategies before it receives a bid from an acquiring company. Such strategies are aimed at preventing the bid altogether or organizing the target company's governance in the best way to defend against a hostile bid. Remedial strategies comprise different means of dealing with existing bids. The strategies mostly center on defense against proxy contests and tender offers. Some examples are subtle, such as staggered boards of directors, while others are blunt or aggressive, such as selling valuable assets or terminating important employees.

These aggressive and blunt actions have caused an intense academic, political, and public discussion about the economic nature of antitakeover provisions. The discussion focuses on two main issues: (1) determining how and when to successfully employ a particular strategy, and (2) determining who benefits economically from implementing different strategies (Shleifer and Vishny, 1986; Stout, 2002; Pearce and Robinson, 2004). Both questions are closely linked. Deciding on an antitakeover provision has implications for target and bidder shareholders including both their corporations and their managements (Parkinson, 1991; Hanly, 1992).

Some remedial strategies that aim to decrease the economic value of the target involve selling off valuable assets, buying another company without economic benefits (but only to increase the size of the corporation), and buying back their own shares from a potential acquirer at a premium. Most of these and other actions can trigger a decrease in shareholder value.

The second part of the discussion focuses on the target company's management. The target board of directors can decide whether to accept a takeover bid. It can recommend accepting or fighting the bid to the shareholders. If the target chooses to fight, the board can determine how it intends to fend off the hostile bid. Thus, the target's management must decide on the takeover strategy and how it wants to benefit from it (Easterbrook and Fischel, 1981). Although today's corporate governance tries to align the interests of a corporation's management with its shareholders, directors and officers of corporations still have much leeway on deciding who should own a corporation's assets and equity. Management can still try to place its own interests over the shareholders' interests when deciding on a corporation's ownership. Hostile takeover attempts are mostly launched on inefficiently operated companies, the cause of which can be the result of inefficient management. A hostile bidder will thus most likely replace the target's management following a successful takeover. Knowing this, target management might oppose a hostile bid not because it believes the bid is too low or the acquirer is an unlikely fit, but simply because management wants to stay in office and not be removed.

When looking at different antitakeover provisions, taking into account the implications each antitakeover provision has for target management and shareholders is crucial. Besides introducing the specifics of the most widely known and used antitakeover provisions and actions, this chapter focuses on the economic evaluation of each antitakeover provision and examines who benefits from such actions. The chapter also briefly explains each strategy and discusses its implementation and usage in actual cases. To account for more current developments, the chapter presents recent cases of hostile takeovers.

PREVENTIVE DEFENSE TACTICS

A preventive defense tactic has the goal of incorporating several procedures in a company's bylaws that can be made effective once a hostile takeover attempt is made. These procedures involve various actions aimed at preventing a bidding company from successfully taking over the target company. Most of these actions involve changing the capitalization of the company by issuing new shares or establishing rules regarding the voting of shareholders upon a takeover attempt (DePamphilis, 2005). Further corporate governance features can be enacted in a company's bylaws, such as a staggered board of directors. Preventive antitakeover provisions can also set forth rules regarding actions the company is not allowed to perform upon a takeover attempt. Usually, all of these tactics are not only aimed at successfully defending a hostile takeover attempt but also at retaining corporate value during the course of the takeover battle.

The Poison Pill in Its Many Variations

The poison pill is the most widely used and most popular preventive antitakeover strategy. Also known as "shareholder rights plans," poison pills allow a company to issue new shares to existing shareholders at a discount of the actual share price. This strategy increases the number of existing shares in the market. Thus, a potential acquirer would have to buy a greater amount of stock to gain a controlling share in the company. There are many different forms regarding how and when the new shares or the rights to acquire these shares are issued.

Different variations of the poison pill have developed historically over three different stages. The first-generation poison pill started in 1982 when a firm registered convertible preferred stock with the Securities and Exchange Commission (SEC). In this case, the firm issued shares to shareholders at a discount, granting the existing shareholders the right to convert the preferred stock into common stock upon successful completion of a hostile takeover. The second-generation pill included the so-called "flip-over" pill, allowing existing shareholders to buy at a discount the newly issued stock of the combined entity after a successful takeover. As shareholders are given a right to purchase these stocks, the second-generation pill is also known as the "shareholder rights plan." Finally, the third-generation pill, generally known as the "flip-in" pill, involves issuing rights to the target's existing shareholders to buy stock of the target company at a substantial discount before a takeover attempt.

The use of poison pills has been heavily disputed for many years (Datta and Iskandar-Datta, 1996; Kahan and Rock, 2002). Shareholder activist groups, as well as regulators and managers of stock listed corporations, argue about the benefits and challenges of the pill. Two major arguments support the view that a poison pill benefits shareholders (Coates, 2000). First, poison pills can protect target shareholders from coercive offers. Second, poison pills permit the company to offer the shareholders a superior alternative to the hostile bidder's initial offer. Tender offers can be highly coercive, forcing the shareholders into tendering their shares even if the offer is not high enough. In this case, shareholders might be pressured into accepting the offer in order to not be "left behind" or be bought at a lower price than the original offer. Some contend, however, that the mere existence of a poison pill prevents coercive bids from being initiated because the acquiring company knows that the odds of the offer being successful are substantially diminished (Oesterle, 1985). To account for that, bidders mostly use the all-cash, all-shares offer, including a commitment to pay off the remaining shareholders at the same price in order to allow the target shareholders to freely decide when to tender. Because this usually does not lead to the poison pill defense, the takeover is much more likely to succeed (Flom, 2000).

The second argument aims at the possibility of putting the company up for auction once it has become subject to a hostile takeover attempt (i.e., actively looking for other bidders offering a higher purchase price per share). This would benefit the company's shareholders because an auction usually leads to higher premiums. Using the poison pill in this way would clearly benefit the target's shareholders (Velasco, 2002).

However, empirical research questions the benefits of the poison pill. Often, it supports the fact that management uses this power to entrench itself. Different studies find a strong negative relationship between the presence of takeover defenses, especially poison pills and the value of the corporation and managers' level of ownership of the corporation (Chakraborty and Baum, 1998). Thus, public corporations in which managers do not hold any ownership are both undervalued and equipped with takeover defenses. If shareholders view poison pills as a means to reach optimal contracting with their managers, companies with these means are not undervalued. Studies conclude that the market views poison pills as a means for entrenchment rather than optimal contracting. This is supported by empirical evidence suggesting slight stock decreases upon the announcement of poison pill adoptions (Malatesta and Walkling, 1988; Ryngaert, 1988).

An Example: Oracle and PeopleSoft

In 2004, Oracle and PeopleSoft, U.S.-based software corporations, engaged in an aggressively fought takeover battle involving high media attention and publicly displayed dislike between the companies' boards. The starting point for Oracle's takeover attempt of PeopleSoft was the announcement of a friendly merger between PeopleSoft and J. D. Edwards, a fellow U.S.-based software developer. By acquiring PeopleSoft, Oracle saw a prime opportunity to attack its then main competitor and industry leader, the German company SAP.

Oracle launched the first hostile bid in 2003 and the acquisition culminated in 2004. From the beginning of the bidding process, PeopleSoft publicly announced that it would fight Oracle in order to remain an independent company. Consequently, PeopleSoft engaged in antitakeover actions, among which a poison pill played a major role. Before the deal, PeopleSoft had enacted a shareholder rights plan in its corporate bylaws. Oracle knew of this obstacle and tried to circumvent the triggering of the shareholder rights plan by suing PeopleSoft and demanding a removal of the poison pill. According to PeopleSoft's annual report in 2003, the PeopleSoft poison pill would trigger the issuance of common stock "ten days after a tender offer or acquisition of 20 percent or more of our common stock by a hostile bidder." Although the lawsuit had not finished before PeopleSoft's shareholders started to tender their shares to Oracle, judges and experts at the time believed Oracle would have lost the court battle. Both companies are incorporated in Delaware, a state in which courts had upheld numerous poison pill antitakeover contests in prior hostile mergers.

Another feature of the Oracle and PeopleSoft takeover battle was a different type of antitakeover provision, in which, if enacted, PeopleSoft guaranteed all customers between two to five times their licensing fees in the case of a successful hostile takeover. Oracle would ultimately have to pay for this provision. Although Oracle filed a lawsuit against PeopleSoft involving this provision, a verdict could not be reached before shareholders tendered their shares.

Golden, Silver, and Tin Parachutes

Having golden, silver, or tin parachutes are tactics that do not involve selling assets but rather "laying off" employees. Many corporations include employee severance agreements in their corporate charter or bylaws setting forth termination arrangements coupled with large lump-sum payments for top-level management or other important corporate employees. These agreements are triggered in the case of a forced change of control. Hence, whenever a corporation acquires a controlling share of stock of another corporation, the employees covered by the "golden parachute" agreement are free to terminate their contracts with the target company and receive a large monetary compensation for doing so. This can be an effective defense strategy if the value of a corporation is strongly dependent on the skills of specific employees or management.

The difference between the so-called "golden" and "silver" parachutes is that golden parachutes refer to severance agreements for top-level management and thus only cover a small number of people. In contrast, silver parachutes apply to a larger number of employees who are not necessarily part of top-level management. Tin parachutes contain provisions that grant monetary benefits to every employee following a change of control.

Although these provisions usually do not contain termination agreements, they can be costly for the joint entity following a merger, especially for large companies with many employees. However, their power to repel a potential bidder is limited. Only in cases in which a bidder intends to acquire "people" (e.g., managers or researchers) is a parachute hypothetically strong enough to fend off a bidder successfully. This is why empirical studies show that poison pills and golden parachutes are mostly used together as an antitakeover statue in corporate bylaws (Chakraborty, 2008). Consequently, empirical research shows that shareholders do not always see the adoption of golden parachutes positively. Studies such as Small, Smith, and Yildirim (2007) show that shareholders fear that golden parachutes might foster management entrenchment. Therefore, shareholder reactions to the adoptions of parachutes strongly depend on the number of outside directors in compensation committees (Davidson, Pilger, and Szakmary, 2005) or the board structure itself (Singh and Harianto, 2007).

Another Example: Microsoft and Yahoo!

Although short-lived and unsuccessful, a recent hostile takeover attempt in the United States involved the use of golden parachutes in which software developer Microsoft attempted to acquire the Internet service provider Yahoo!. Before the takeover attempt, Yahoo! had enacted a so-called "severance benefits plan," which set forth the payments made to Yahoo! employees who left the company in the case of a successful hostile takeover attempt. Microsoft planned the purchase to gain insight into Yahoo!'s search engine technique and its advertisement business. As both areas are mainly skill driven by the people who run them, losing key employees would have made the acquisition considerably less attractive to Microsoft. Additionally, paying large lump-sum benefits to Yahoo!'s board members and directors would have also made the acquisition much more costly to Microsoft. The "severance benefits plan" thus acted as a natural determent to potential hostile bidders. After abandoning the takeover attempt, Microsoft officials admitted that the golden parachutes as well as statements from Yahoo! directors threatening to make use of these parachutes made Microsoft more wary of the negative consequences a hostile takeover might have for both companies.

Staggered Boards of Directors

A widely used and very effective preventive strategy is staggering a company's board of directors, also known as "classifying" a board. The term "staggering" describes the way in which the board members are elected. An effective antitakeover provision can prohibit electing all board members (or at least the majority) in one setting (i.e., at one shareholder assembly). As previously explained, a firm can attempt a hostile takeover by obtaining enough voting rights to successfully replace the board members of the target company. If a staggered board is in place, a hostile investor cannot replace the board members in one shareholder assembly regardless of the amount of votes held. Today, this strategy is a common part of almost any corporation's bylaws.

Generally, staggering a board is regarded as one of the most effective anti-takeover provisions (Bebchuk and Cohen, 2005). Empirical results show that in the period from 1996 to 2000, not a single hostile takeover attempt succeeded against a staggered board (Bebchuk, Coates, and Subramanian, 2002). Although staggering a board was once an undisputed defense mechanism believed to cause no economic harm to a company, shareholder activist groups have recently put more pressure on corporations to destagger their boards (Guo, Kruse, and Nohel, 2008).

The main argument is that staggered boards serve as an entrenchment mechanism for inefficient managements, which denies shareholders the chance for a change in control after a hostile takeover (Faleye, 2007). An empirical study by Bebchuk et al. (2002) supports this argument. In the nine months following a hostile takeover bid, companies with staggered boards show a stock increase of 31.8 percent, whereas stocks of companies without staggered boards increase by 43.4 percent. Politicians have recently become aware of this issue and introduced a "shareholder bill of rights" banning staggered boards. Although many corporations followed suit and had their classified boards removed from the corporate bylaws, unified boards offer less protection. Thus, staggering a board involves trade-offs between management accountability as well as controllability and the possibility of defending the company successfully against economically insufficient hostile takeover bids.

A Third Example: InBev and Anheuser-Busch

A recent example is the hostile takeover of U.S. brewery Anheuser-Busch by Belgian beverage corporation InBev. Until 2006, Anheuser-Busch had a staggered board, which involved electing one-third of the directors each year. Although the company had been a potential takeover candidate for many years, a hostile attempt had never been initiated. Following shareholder pressure, Anheuser decided to unify its board and have all members elected each year. Just as Anheuser-Busch had completed the unification, InBev offered a hostile bid for Anheuser-Busch shares. InBev subsequently acquired the controlling majority in the company without much resistance from Anheuser.

Exhibit 19.1 presents a summary of all three cases and provides some key numbers and figures for the deals. The deals are among the most prominent high-profile transactions during the past decade using the respective preventive defense tactics. In summary, neither the poison pill nor the staggering of a board could successfully prevent a takeover from happening. Only golden parachutes, in the cases involving people-driven and knowledge-driven industries, could successfully deter a bidder from initiating an attempt.

REMEDIAL DEFENSE TACTICS

Once a hostile takeover attempt is under way, target management can use various strategies designed to fend off the attempt. Hostile takeovers are usually attempted if the bidder is interested in acquiring certain knowledge, production facilities, brands, products, or market share of the target, which the bidder can use to

Exhibit 19.1 Overview of Preventive Defense Tactics and Cases

Defense Tactic	Bidder	Target	Deal Volume ($US billion)	Duration of Takeover Process	Takeover Battle Won By
Poison pill	Oracle	PeopleSoft	10.3	January 6, 2003, to December 13, 2004	Oracle
Golden, silver, and tin parachutes	Microsoft	Yahoo!	50.0	April 28, 2008, to May 5, 2008	Yahoo!
Staggered boards of directors	InBev	Anheuser-Busch	52.0	May 23, 2008, to November 20, 2008	InBev

The exhibit provides an overview of preventive defense tactics and indicates prominent cases using these tactics. Each case reports the transaction parties, total volume of the takeover attempt, duration of the takeover battle, and outcome of the takeover.

create synergies that will increase the economic value of the combined postmerger corporation (DePamphilis, 2005). Therefore, some tactics involve destroying these potential synergies by eliminating the item of interest. Postbid defenses have the power to fend off hostile takeover attempts, but at a high cost for the target company and its shareholders. If the economic value of the target is decreased to make it less attractive for an acquirer, target shareholders will suffer accordingly due to the decrease in share value.

"Scorched-Earth" or "Jonestown" Strategies

"Scorched-earth" or "Jonestown" defenses focus on the economic destruction of the target company through its management. The ultimate goal is to strip the target company of its important assets, employees, and cash to make it as unattractive as possible to the bidder. The target company's management can use many different strategies to reach that goal, most notably the so-called "suicide pill" or the sale of "crown jewels." The term "Jonestown defense" refers to a 1987 mass suicide of the pseudoreligious organization People's Temple, in which 918 people died at an area located in northwestern Guyana, commonly known as "Jonestown."

Of all the tactics intended to quickly and drastically reduce the value of a company, the sale of "crown jewels" is the most widely used. It refers to the example given above in which a target company sells off its most important or profitable assets or the assets that the acquirer wants most to make the acquirer lose interest in the target. This strategy is radical and immediately destroys the economic value of the company. The only way in which this tactic can be useful in both fending off the takeover attempt and retaining shareholder value is if the asset of interest is neither very profitable nor part of the target's core business. The "suicide pill" strategy comprises the sale of "crown jewels," as well as several further means of destroying corporate value. If a "suicide pill" is triggered, the company is also stripped of cash and/or important employees such as top-level management. These tactics are the most economically questionable because the firm deliberately destroys corporate value at the sole cost to shareholders. Shareholders lose not only their anticipated takeover premium but also the initial value of their stock before the takeover bid.

An Example: Vodafone and Mannesmann

An example is the takeover of the German industrial corporation Mannesmann AG by U.K.-based telecommunications network provider Vodafone Group plc. In this 1999 transaction, Vodafone was primarily interested in acquiring the mobile telecommunications segment of Mannesmann, which at the time was only one of many different business units of Mannesmann's portfolio. The deal involved the strategies of "selling of crown jewels" and two "white knights." Mannesmann performed the first white-knight transaction before the initial takeover bid through Vodafone. As rumors spread that Vodafone might be interested in a merger between the two companies, Mannesmann acquired Orange Limited, a U.K.-based telecommunications network provider and direct competitor of Vodafone. The deal was meant to discourage potential acquirers because Mannesmann had grown substantially larger through the move. Antitrust issues also came into play since Orange's and Mannesmann's D2 mobile network were both leading mobile telecommunication providers in Europe.

After Mannesmann rejected Vodafone's first two offers for purchasing Mannesmann shares at a premium, Mannesmann attempted a second transaction. Mannesmann negotiated a deal agreement with Vivendi Universal, a French media company, in which either firm could purchase a major share block in the other company. However, for reasons unknown to the public, Mannesmann did not complete the second deal and Vodafone subsequently acquired Mannesmann.

When the Vodafone offers became more coercive and tempting to Mannesmann shareholders, shareholder groups and Mannesmann's management discussed whether Mannesmann should simply dispose of its mobile network segment in order to stave off Vodafone and its tender offer. At the time, Mannesmann was a major industrial conglomerate comprised of many different business segments such as steel, industrial machinery, and automotive parts. Although the mobile networks segment was the rising star of the company, it was only one of many business areas. A sale of this segment to another mobile telecommunications company could have saved Mannesmann from being taken over by Vodafone because the U.K.-based company was only interested in the telecommunications segment.

Although this kind of defense would have contested the takeover attempt successfully, this tactic would have also had negative economic implications for Mannesmann and its shareholders. Mobile telecommunications was the major growth sector at the end of the 1990s, and Mannesmann's "D2" and Deutsche Telekom's "D1" network were the two major mobile telecommunications networks at the time in Germany. Thus, the network contributed substantially to Mannesmann's profits and growth opportunities. A sale of this business segment would have resulted in a stark decrease of the company's value. Consequently, corporate insiders and the media assumed at the time that Mannesmann unsuccessfully wanted to sell the segment. Analysts and the media believed that strong shareholder pressure caused the failure to sell it.

"Pac-Man" Defense

The name of this strategy refers to the 1980s video game in which the main hero, Pac-Man, is chased by ghost-like enemies trying to eat him. Pac-Man completes the different game levels and "survives" the ghost-like enemies by eating little white dots and also by even eating the ghost-like enemies themselves. Consequently, the name describes a strategy in which the target itself makes a hostile bid for the acquirer in order to "eat it up" before it can be "eaten up" (DeMott, 1983). This strategy is highly disputed because targets tend to be smaller than their acquirers. Therefore, a bid for the acquirer often involves considerable debt financing for the target, which, in the case of a successful takeover, leaves the combined entity highly leveraged and in financial distress. Consequently, Pac-Man defenses are employed whenever the acquirer and target are of similar size and profitability. Disregarding the aforementioned financial difficulties, this strategy has the advantage that both companies can benefit from postacquisition potential synergies if a company interested in merger synergies makes the initial hostile bid.

An Example: BHP Billiton and Rio Tinto

In 2007, BHP Billiton and Rio Tinto, two mining and resources heavyweights, engaged in a takeover battle. The target ultimately won because BHP Billiton officially withdrew its offer to buy Rio Tinto shares almost one year after initiating the first bid. Although the reasons for the takeover failure were different, Rio Tinto considered using the Pac-Man defense tactic by bidding for BHP Billiton shares itself. Although Rio Tinto decided against using this defense, insiders, analysts, and the media widely believed that Rio Tinto could have succeeded with the strategy because both companies are of almost equal size and operate in similar industrial areas. Hypothetically, Rio Tinto could have financed the deal with its own shares and limited debt and benefited from synergies between the companies.

White Knights and Squires

A "white knight" or "white squire" refers to a company that rescues a potential hostile takeover target by acquiring a controlling share of stock in the target. Whenever target management believes that the initial hostile bidder should not be the new majority shareholder of the company for economic or other reasons, the target's board can ask a third company to act as white knight. The potential white knight then makes a bid for the target company's shares. Target management backs this bid, which is usually supported by lockup provisions or call option–like agreements on the target's stock. These agreements serve to protect the white knight in the case of a bidding war. They mostly include contractual obligations for the target to sell certain assets to the white knight or call options on yet-to-be issued stock. A white squire is similar to a white knight except that it only buys a large minority stake in the target company in exchange for special voting rights.

Economically, target shareholders might benefit from the white knight defense strategy, especially when compared to some of the "scorched-earth" defenses such as "selling of crown jewels" or "golden parachutes." A white knight launches a takeover bid involving a premium on the price of stock, thus not cheating the shareholders out of their profits from the initial hostile takeover bid. Further, white knights are typically direct competitors of the target. Due to the similarity between the companies, a high likelihood exists that the firms can exploit existing synergies, creating economic value and benefits for shareholders. Value can only be destroyed if an inefficiently working target management pursues an entrenchment strategy, which a hostile bidder wants to end. If the white knight denies a change of management following a takeover, the company will continue to be operated inefficiently. Although any buyer would hypothetically aim at increasing efficiency and profits at a target company, target management would usually prefer a friendly white knight, allowing the target company to continue its operations mostly unchanged. In this case, management entrenchment is possible and shareholders suffer a loss of value.

Although the term "white knight" mostly refers to M&A transactions, white knights can also be companies saving financially distressed companies from liquidation. Some examples include the acquisition of the insolvent U.S.-based brokerage house Bear Stearns by JP Morgan Chase in the wake of the subprime crisis, and the acquisition of Chrysler by Italian car manufacturer Fiat Group following Chrysler's Chapter 11 restructuring.

An Example: Sanofi-Synthélabo and Aventis

An example of the white knight strategy can be seen in the takeover battle between Sanofi-Synthélabo, a French pharmaceuticals company, and Aventis, a French-German pharmaceuticals company. Although both companies pronounced the transactions as a merger of equals, the "merger" had been preceded by a hostile takeover bid of Sanofi by Aventis. Aventis initially tried to defend against the hostile bid by using the white knight strategy.

As Sanofi's tender offer put more pressure on Aventis, its management board suggested the possibility of a merger of equals with Novartis, a Swiss pharmaceuticals company and direct competitor. Following the suggestion, Novartis evaluated a possible merger and publicly stated that it welcomed the opportunity to engage in a transaction, conditional upon the fulfillment of certain requirements. When Novartis's interests became public, the French government intervened and threatened not to support a deal between Aventis and Novartis. The background of this intervention was purely political. Because Sanofi was much smaller than Aventis and Novartis, Sanofi would have become a potential takeover candidate itself, in the case of a potential merger between Aventis and Novartis. In this case, France would have lost its last major pharmaceuticals company.

According to French Prime Minister Jean-Pierre Raffarin, a second official explanation from the French government was that Aventis's research and vaccine production were of strategic importance and should thus remain in France. The French government also tried to force Sanofi into increasing its bid for Aventis shares in order to complete the takeover successfully. Aventis's price was the decisive issue in the takeover battle. Novartis retreated from its merger offer following the French government intervention, and Sanofi raised its offer from 48.5 to 55 billion euros. After Sanofi agreed to a stronger representation of Aventis's management on the Sanofi-Aventis board, Aventis finally agreed to the takeover and the companies merged as equal partners.

Greenmail

"Greenmail" is a term derived from "blackmail" with "green" referring to money (U.S. dollars) green. It describes a defense strategy in which a hostile bidder acquires a large share of stock in the target and offers the resale of the stocks to the target company at a premium. Analysts view greenmail as a variation of blackmail because the acquirer threatens the target with a takeover, pressuring target management to reacquire the target's own shares at a large (and sometimes unjustifiably large) premium. In most cases, the potential acquirer buys shares in the market until reaching a mandatory ownership disclosure stake. At this point, a potential acquirer performs a "street sweep," i.e., buying large blocks of stock from single institutional owners to get close to a controlling share of stock.

The greenmailing can then happen actively through the potential acquirer or passively through the target. In the active case, the acquirer asks the target management to repurchase the shares, as described above. The passive case is a result of target management trying to defend against the threatening takeover. The target's management can offer the acquirer the opportunity to repurchase the stock at a premium in order to avoid the takeover. This strategy works especially well if the acquirer is a financial investor with a purely monetary interest in the company. If that monetary interest can be served by the offered premium of the target, the investor should forego a takeover of the company. If the acquirer is a strategic investor looking for specific assets, the repurchase premium might be insufficient to dissuade the acquirer from the takeover attempt. The history of hostile takeover attempts shows that this strategy was mainly employed in the 1980s by corporate raiders such as T. Boone Pickens, Carl Icahn, and Ronald Perelman. These investors had no strategic interest in the potential target companies.

The economic validity of this defense tactic is difficult to evaluate (Eckbo, 1990; Bhagat and Jefferis, 1994). Some argue that a company should not have to buy its own shares at a premium to avoid a hostile takeover because the company could invest the cash that it would have to use for the transaction in profitable projects from which the shareholders could benefit. Also, the company would most likely have to pay a premium for the shares, which might overstate the true value of the shares.

Yet, others contend that financial investors, especially the corporate raiders from the 1980s or private equity firms today, do not necessarily have the long-term development of a target company as a primary goal when acquiring it. Instead, earning short-term profits for their investors has the investors maximize the value of the target in a short period of time. This strategy involves highly leveraged acquisitions that cause financial stress for the targets due to vast amounts of debt. The debt payback is conducted using the company's free cash flow, which as a result cannot be invested in profitable projects. Towards the end of the investment period, which often does not exceed five or six years, the targets are broken up and the different entities are sold off separately. In light of this strategic focus, shareholders might favor a greenmail defense tactic to avoid financial investors as majority owners, that is, if they favor long-term development over short-term profits.

An Example: Sir James Goldsmith and St. Regis Paper Company

St. Regis Paper and Sir James Goldsmith provide a classic example of a hostile takeover battle in which a corporate raider tried to acquire an industrial company. Goldsmith was an infamous corporate raider who was mostly active in the 1980s and early 1990s. He acquired corporations, broke them up, and resold the parts at a premium. In this exemplary deal with St. Regis paper, he acquired a 9 percent stake in the paper company and expressed his interest in taking over control of the company. However, as he was a finance investor, he had no interest in the operating business of the company (paper manufacturing and recycling). Thus, he offered the company's management an opportunity to repurchase its own shares at a substantial premium over the shares' market value at the time. To remain independent, target management decided to accept the offer and repurchase the shares.

Exhibit 19.2 presents some key numbers and figures for these high-profile transactions involving remedial defense tactics. In summary, the use or attempted

Exhibit 19.2 Overview of Remedial Defense Tactics and Cases

Defense Tactic	Bidder	Target	Deal Volume ($US billion)	Duration of Takeover Process	Takeover Battle Won By
Jonestown strategy	Vodafone	Mannesmann	172.2	November 14, 1999, to February 3, 2000	Vodafone
Pac-Man defense	BHP Billiton	Rio Tinto	140.0	November 8, 2007, to November 25, 2009	Rio Tinto
White knights and acquirers	Sanofi-Synthélabo	Aventis	54.5	January 26, 2004, to April 26, 2004	Sanofi-Synthélabo
Greenmail	Sir James Goldsmith	St. Regis Paper Company	16.0	Throughout 1985	St. Regis Paper Company

The exhibit provides an overview of remedial defense tactics of prominent cases using these tactics. Each case reports the transaction parties, total volume of the takeover attempt, duration of the takeover battle, and outcome of the takeover.

use of the tactics cannot always successfully fend off a hostile bidder. Although Mannesmann did not use all the means the Jonestown mechanism offered, Vodafone did not feel pressured enough by a looming fire-sale of crown jewels to abolish the takeover attempt. The white knight attempts could also not prevent Sanofi-Synthélabo from acquiring Aventis. The Pac-Man defense worked well for Rio Tinto because both companies are of equivalent size. Thus, a takeover battle could have also ended in Rio Tinto buying BHP Billiton. The hostile bid was therefore retracted. Finally, evaluating who really "won" the greenmail takeover attempt is difficult. Although St. Regis could stay independent, Goldsmith reached his goal of selling St. Regis shares back to the company at a premium. In return, he would refrain from his attempt to acquire the company.

THE FINANCIAL CRISIS AND HOSTILE TAKEOVERS

The global financial crisis, started by the 2007 U.S. subprime meltdown, has so far had some unexpected implications for the hostile takeover market. After the boom and bust of the late 1990s and early 2000s (during the wake of the dot-com era), global M&A markets had been steadily increasing in volume and number of deals until the escalation of the subprime crisis brought everything to a sudden halt. Lower stock prices, limited credit availability, and insecurity about the economic growth slowed M&A activity substantially. Now that the initial panic of the crisis has begun to fade, hostile M&A activity has started to increase in international capital markets.

The reasons for the surge in hostile takeover attempts are rooted in the consequences of the financial crisis. First, many corporations went into survival mode at the beginning of the crisis by cutting costs, conserving cash, and strengthening their capital basis. Companies with excess cash, a strong capital basis, and efficient operations are in a superior position to those negatively affected by the crisis. Combining these factors with decreasing corporate valuations, low stock prices, and historically low interest rates, healthy companies can easily impose hostile takeovers on weakened target firms. The fact that many corporations have come close to the verge of distress since the beginning of the crisis might force them into acquiescing in a hostile takeover bid in order to survive.

Another factor contributing to hostile takeovers is the abandoning of anti-takeover provisions by many corporations. During the 2000s, corporate governance lobbyists and shareholder activists exerted tremendous pressure on corporations to erase poison pills or similar preventive and remedial defense tactics from their bylaws. A recent report shows that the success rate of the activists is astonishing. According to Stendevad, Shivdasani, and Kimyagarov (2009), 60 percent of all S&P 500 companies had some sort of poison pill provision or staggered board status included in their corporate bylaws in 2002. As of July 2009, these numbers had fallen to only 19 percent for poison pills and 30 percent for staggered boards. This lack of protection is now paying off for hostile acquirers, especially since financially distressed corporations do not possess sufficient economic means, such as war chests or high profitability to increase corporate value, to successfully fend off hostile takeover attempts. Consequently, many corporations have taken advantage of this market environment to buy competitors or to expand their business portfolios through acquisitions. Some high-profile deals include Kraft Foods and

Cadbury, Rio Tinto and BHP Billiton, Porsche and Volkswagen, and InBev and Anheuser-Busch.

But the current state of the economy is not the only influence on the developments in domestic and international takeover markets. Recently, political debates have started to deal with the regulations of hostile takeovers. For example, in the United States, Senator Charles E. Schumer, a Democrat from New York, proposed a bill in May 2009 asking for more shareholder rights. This "Shareholder Bill of Rights" contains an expansion of shareholders' voting rights and management accountability. The bill can be regarded as a clear sign that shareholder protection will be a priority in the United States following the financial crisis.

However, this is not necessarily the case in other economies. Korea provides a recent example of a capital market in which some believe that the poison pill will be introduced in the near future. Foreign investors own two of the country's largest and most prominent companies, electronics manufacturer Samsung and steel maker POSCO. Consequently, the Korean government seeks to protect its national champions by complicating hostile takeovers. Although analysts, shareholder activists, and economists condemn the move as antishareholder politics, the Korean government is seeking ways to enact the pill quickly and thoroughly.

Given the current state of the economy and the lively regulatory discussions, the future for hostile M&As appears intriguing. With rising stock prices worldwide and a resurging economy in the United States and Europe, companies will not only possess more financial firepower to acquire competitors, but potential targets will also be able to better defend themselves due to the same economic reasons. In the case that stricter regulation is enacted or as in the case of Korea, new and different takeover attempts and defense strategies circumventing the changes in regulation may arise.

SUMMARY AND CONCLUSIONS

Hostile M&As are among the most complex transactions of modern-day corporate finance. Such transactions involve not only money or economic value but also a changing of the corporate landscape, which attracts media attention and public interest. This chapter shows how target firms can defend themselves from a hostile transaction. Takeover defenses to counteract an initiated tender offer can be subtle and preemptive or sudden and reactionary. Antitakeover actions can be aimed at preventing or impeding the transaction itself or at altering the corporate value of the target to a degree where a transaction becomes infeasible for the bidder.

When looking at defense strategies and especially in evaluating the economic reasoning behind them, the issue of who benefits should be considered. The presented economic evaluation of remedial and preventive strategies shows that some antitakeover actions can be successful in fending off hostile takeover bids, while also simultaneously destroying corporate value. This ambiguity is both a risk and an opportunity. It is a risk for corporate advisors or the transaction parties to choose the wrong strategy and thereby disadvantageous for shareholders. This ambiguity can be an opportunity for researchers to further determine which strategy is most fitting for a particular kind of takeover attempt and what implications the respective strategy holds for the involved parties.

Finally, the chapter shows that the future will most likely see more hostile corporate transactions in many different shapes and forms. The reasons for this surge in hostile corporate activity is rooted both in the current economic crisis and its financial implications, such as low interest rates and stock price levels, and in recent and planned developments regarding the regulation of corporate transaction markets. Should the planned regulatory changes be implemented, markets might also experience different or previously unknown hostile takeover strategies and defenses as a reaction to these changes. Should the shareholder activists, who advocate abandoning staggered boards of directors, feel the need for stronger protection of "their" corporations, hostile takeover markets will adjust accordingly. The future of hostile takeovers will remain an exciting playing field for corporations and their advisors, as well as for researchers trying to understand the inner workings of hostile M&A transactions.

DISCUSSION QUESTIONS

1. After the financial crisis of 2007 to 2009, some U.S. politicians called for better shareholder protection in hostile takeovers. Which developments during the financial crisis caused this call for shareholder protection? What could the politicians expect to achieve with stronger shareholder protection in hostile takeovers?

2. Stockholder A's primary objective is short-term stock price appreciation whereas stockholder B wants long-term stock appreciation. What type of preventive measure and remedial takeover provisions would stockholders A and B prefer their corporation to take? Why?

3. Which antitakeover strategy is best for management entrenchment? Why?

4. Is an unregulated market for corporate control beneficial for shareholders? If yes, explain the circumstances in which this would be true.

REFERENCES

Allen, William T., and Reinier H. Kraakman. 2004. *Commentaries and Cases on the Law of Business Administration*. Aspen: Law & Business.

Bebchuk, Lucian A., John C. Coates, and Guhan Subramanian. 2002. "The Powerful Antitakeover Force of Staggered Boards: Theory, Evidence and Policy." *Stanford Law Review* 54:9, 887–951.

Bebchuk, Lucian A., and Alma Cohen. 2005. "The Cost of Entrenched Boards." *Journal of Financial Economics* 78:5, 409–433.

Bhagat, Sanjai, and Richard Jefferis. 1994. "The Causes and Consequences of Takeover Defense: Evidence from Greenmail." *Journal of Corporate Finance* 1:2, 201–231.

Bhagat, Sanjai, Andrei Shleifer, and Robert Vishny. 1990. "Hostile Takeovers in the 1980s: The Return to Corporate Specialization." *Brookings Papers on Economic Activity* 1:1990, 1–72.

Chakraborty, Atreya. 2008. "Golden Parachutes and Shark Repellents and Shareholders' Interests: Some New Evidence." *Global Finance Journal* 18:3, 373–384.

Chakraborty, Atreya, and Christopher F. Baum. 1998. "Poison Pills, Optimal Contracting and the Market for Corporate Control: Evidence from Fortune 500 Firms." *International Journal of Finance* 10:3, 1120–1138.

Coates, John C. 2000. "Takeover Defenses in the Shadow of the Poison Pill: A Critique of the Scientific Evidence." *Texas Law Review* 79:2, 271–287.

Datta, Sudip, and Mai Iskandar-Datta. 1996. "Takeover Defenses and Wealth Effects on Securityholders: The Case of Poison Pill Adoptions." *Journal of Banking and Finance* 20:7, 1231–1250.

Davidson III, Wallace N., Theodore Pilger, and Andrew Szakmary. 2005. "Golden Parachutes, Board and Committee Composition, and Shareholder Wealth." *Financial Review* 33:4, 17–32.

Deakin, Simon, and Giles Slinger. 1997. "Hostile Takeovers, Corporate Law and the Theory of the Firm." *Journal of Law and Society* 24:1, 124–151.

DeMott, Deborah A. 1983. "Pac-Man Tender Offers." *Duke Law Journal* 83:1, 116–132.

DePamphilis, Donald. 2005. *Mergers, Acquisitions, and Other Restructuring Activities*. New York: Academic Press.

Easterbrook, Frank H., and Daniel R. Fischel. 1981. "The Proper Role of a Target's Management in Responding to a Tender Offer." *Harvard Law Review* 94:6, 1161–1166.

Eckbo, B. Espen. 1990. "Valuation Effects of Greenmail Prohibitions." *Journal of Financial and Quantitative Analysis* 25:4, 491–505.

Faleye, Olubunmi. 2007. "Classified Boards and Long-term Value Creation." *Journal of Financial Economics* 83:2, 501–529.

Flom, Joseph H. 2000. "Mergers & Acquisitions: The Decade in Review." *University of Miami Law Review* 54:1, 753–767.

Guo, Re-Jin, Timothy A. Kruse, and Tom Nohel. 2008. "Undoing the Powerful Antitakeover Force of Staggered Boards." *Journal of Corporate Finance* 14:3, 274–288.

Hanly, Ken. 1992. "Hostile Takeovers and Methods of Defense." *Journal of Business Ethics* 11:12, 895–913.

Kahan, Marcel, and Edward B. Rock. 2002. "How I Learned to Stop Worrying and Love the Pill: Adaptive Responses to Takeover Law." *University of Chicago Law Review* 69:1, 871–915.

Malatesta, Paul H., and Ralph Walkling. 1988. "Poison Pill Securities—Stockholder Wealth, Profitability and Ownership Structure." *Journal of Financial Economics* 20:1, 347–376.

Modigliani, Franco, and Merton H. Miller. 1958. "The Cost of Capital, Corporation Finance and the Theory of Investment." *American Economic Review* 48:3, 261–279.

Oesterle, Dave A. 1985. "Target Managers as Negotiating Agents for Target Shareholders in Tender Offers: A Reply to the Passivity Thesis." *Cornell Law Review* 71:1, 60–62.

Parkinson, Chris. 1991. "Hostile Takeover Bids and Shareholder Wealth." *European Management Journal* 9:4, 454–459.

Pearce, John A., and Richard B. Robinson Jr. 2004. "Hostile Takeover Defenses That Maximize Shareholder Wealth." *Business Horizons* 47:5, 15–24.

Ryngaert, Michael. 1988. "The Effect of Poison Pill Securities on Shareholder Wealth." *Journal of Financial Economics* 20:1, 377–417.

Shleifer, Andrei, and Robert Vishny. 1986. "Greenmail, White Knights, and Shareholders' Interests." *Rand Journal of Economics* 17:3, 293–309.

Singh, Harbir, and Farid Harianto. 2007. "Top Management Tenure, Corporate Ownership Structure and the Magnitude of Golden Parachutes." *Strategic Management Journal* 10:1, 143–156.

Small, Kenneth, Jeff Smith, and H. Semih Yildirim. 2007. "Ownership Structure and Golden Parachutes: Evidence of Credible Commitment or Incentive Alignment?" *Journal of Economics and Finance* 31:3, 368–382.

Stendevad, Carsten, Anil Shivdasani, and Gavriel Kimyagarov. 2009. *M&A: Hostility on the Horizon*. New York: *Citigroup Research Report*.

Stout, Lynn. 2002. "Do Antitakeover Defenses Decrease Shareholder Wealth? The Ex Post/Ex Ante Valuation Problem." *Stanford Law Review* 55:1, 845–861.

Velasco, Julian. 2002. "The Enduring Illegitimacy of the Poison Pill." *Journal of Corporate Law* 27:3, 381–414.

ABOUT THE AUTHORS

Christian Rauch is a research and teaching assistant in the finance department of Goethe University, Frankfurt, Germany. He graduated in Business Administration and Corporate Law at European Business School and New York University. He has been with Goethe University since October 2007, researching and teaching in the fields of banking regulation and corporate finance, especially M&As. His work has been presented at international conferences, such as those of the Financial Management Association and the European Association for Research in Industrial Economics, and published in the international finance literature, such as the *European Journal of Finance* and the *International Finance Review*. He is also an associate researcher for Deutsche Bundesbank and the research institutes E-Finance Lab and Center for Private Equity Research (CEPRES).

Mark Wahrenburg is a tenured Professor of Finance at Goethe University in Frankfurt, Germany. Besides his extensive research and teaching at Goethe University, he serves as Associate Dean for Goethe University's Business School. Professor Wahrenburg is also President of the Goethe Finance Association and a founding member of the research institute E-Finance Lab. Before coming to Frankfurt in 1999, he was a tenured Professor at the University of Witten-Herdecke, Germany and worked as a consultant for McKinsey & Co. His research in the fields of banking, risk management, and M&As has been published in leading international journals such as the *Journal of Banking and Finance*, *European Financial Management*, and *Empirical Economics*. Professor Wahrenburg also serves as board member and external consultant to industrial and financial companies in Germany.

CHAPTER 20

The Impact of Restructuring on Bondholders[*]

LUC RENNEBOOG
Professor of Corporate Finance, Tilburg University and ECGI

PETER G. SZILAGYI
Lecturer in Finance, Judge Business School, University of Cambridge

INTRODUCTION

During the past two decades, a surge in corporate restructuring has occurred around the world, driven by technological shocks, market deregulation, and global competition for capital supply. Restructuring activity has been particularly pronounced in the United States, where consecutive merger waves have shown that sheer size is no longer a deterrent to takeover threat. As a result and also motivated by other sources of managerial discipline, restructuring activity has largely focused on increasing corporate efficiency through corporate refocusing and financial restructuring. In Europe, where market-based disciplinary mechanisms have historically been weaker, corporate restructuring has accelerated in response to the ongoing economic and financial integration in the European Union. In Japan, though, the restructuring process has been painful, as most firms have undergone some form of reorganization in response to the asset bubble burst of the 1980s and the following economic stagnation.

This chapter provides a comprehensive overview of the literature on the impact of corporate restructuring on bondholder wealth. Fixed creditor claims are affected not only by the firm's postrestructuring performance, but also by unexpected changes in its capital structure and cash flow volatility. The view that restructuring can lead to the expropriation of creditor wealth is generally accepted. The literature offers several examples of such expropriations including the 1985 leveraged buyout of Revlon, the 1988 establishment of Polaroid's executive stock option plan, and the 1997 spin-off of Marriott's management businesses.

Agency costs of the shareholder-creditor conflict are more pronounced in the market-oriented corporate governance systems of the common-law

---

[*]This chapter is based on Renneboog and Szilagyi (2008) and is reprinted with the publisher's permission.

Anglo-American countries. These regimes view creditors and other stakeholders as independent parties that maintain "arm's length" relationships with the firm (Jensen and Meckling, 1976). In the civil law–based stakeholder-oriented systems of continental Europe and Japan, the dynamics of the firm–creditor relationship are very different. Banks act as concentrated lenders and delegated monitors, playing a key role in mitigating informational asymmetries and agency problems (Stiglitz, 1985; Diamond, 1991) and reducing the marginal utility of external market mechanisms. Other stakeholders also develop long-term relationships with the firm, and closely held equity and pyramid-like group memberships are commonplace. The greater influence of banks and other risk-averse stakeholders dictates that creditors in these regimes could be less affected by corporate restructuring.

Existing studies on bondholder wealth preclude the impact of such institutional factors on bondholders' wealth as they mostly focus on restructuring activity in the United States only. Evidence on how restructuring affects bondholders is often inconclusive or conflicting. The empirical results can be summarized as follows. *Asset portfolio restructuring* transactions make disposals from or additions to a firm's businesses. Evidence shows the following:

- Spin-offs and asset sell-offs reduce bondholder wealth by expropriating collateral and increasing cash flow volatility, unless subsequent improvements in operating performance are large enough to compensate.
- M&As reduce or leave bondholder wealth unchanged except under specific conditions, even though they create larger, less risky firms *ceteris paribus*.

Financial restructuring transactions, on the other hand, change the firm's capital structure instead of its asset portfolio. Evidence suggests that:

- New debt issues do not reduce bondholder wealth unless motivated by cash flow shortfalls, but bondholders respond negatively to new bank loans.
- New equity issues tend to increase bondholder wealth, though negative signaling effects can dominate.
- The impact of security exchanges is unclear due to the strong signaling effects of these transactions.
- Executive stock options reduce bondholder wealth, reflecting the realignment of managerial and shareholder interests at the expense of creditors.
- Leveraged buyouts reduce bondholder wealth, but conflicting evidence exists regarding the impact of leveraged recapitalizations.
- The impact of dividend changes and share repurchases is ambiguous, reflecting the strong signaling implications of these transactions.

The analysis presented here identifies major gaps in the literature, emphasizes the potential differences in bondholder wealth changes between market and stakeholder-oriented governance systems and provides insights into the evolution of the methodologies used. The rest of this chapter consists of three sections. The first section provides a theoretical overview of the motivations and bondholder wealth effects of corporate restructuring. The second section contains a detailed analysis of the empirical evidence. The final section provides concluding remarks and raises questions for future research.

THEORETICAL BACKGROUND

Restructuring activity is generally associated with three motivations in the academic literature: (1) to address poor performance, (2) to exploit strategic opportunities, and (3) to correct valuation errors. The literature distinguishes three different types of transactions, encompassing multiple forms of change in firm organization (Stewart and Glassman, 1988; Bowman and Singh, 1993; Gibbs, 1993). *Portfolio restructuring* makes disposals from and additions to a firm's businesses, through asset sales, spin-offs, equity carve-outs, or M&As. *Financial restructuring* changes the firm's capital structure instead of its asset portfolio, some examples being leveraged buy-outs (LBOs), recapitalizations (LRs), share repurchases, or employee stock ownership plans (ESOPs). Finally, *organizational restructuring* represents a change from a functional to a business-unit design.

Value Creation

The classic motivation for corporate restructuring is to redeploy the firm's assets to higher valued uses. As long as the restructuring improves the firm's operating performance and increases its posttransaction cash flow and debt servicing ability, it should create value for both shareholders and creditors.

Agency Costs of Outside Equity

Corporate restructuring can also be motivated by management's incentive to extract private benefits from the firm, while transferring some or all of the costs incurred to the outside shareholders. Murphy (1985) and Jensen (1986) argue that managers are naturally risk-averse and seek to build large, diversified firms with low leverage to reduce the uncertainty of their human capital investment. To that end, the risk preferences of managers are closely aligned with those of creditors and are thus in direct conflict with those of shareholders.

The realignment of managerial and shareholder interests inevitably damages creditor interests. In market-oriented governance regimes in particular, management is typically made a residual claimant in the firm through equity-based compensation plans. Managerial discretion, with respect to risk taking, is also controlled by a variety of disciplinary mechanisms such as independent boards and the markets for corporate control (Manne, 1965) and managerial labor (Fama, 1980). Grossman and Hart (1983) and Jensen (1986) additionally describe the implicit incentive effect of increased leverage, which commits the firm's free cash flow to repaying debt. In stakeholder-oriented systems where ownership and credit supply are more concentrated, the active involvement of risk-averse stakeholders in the monitoring of management has historically provided a substitute for these devices.

Agency Costs of Risky Debt

Corporate decision making can be specifically motivated by the principal-agent conflict between creditors and shareholders. For example, Jensen and Meckling (1976) describe how shareholders may substitute high-risk assets for low-risk ones to expropriate creditor wealth. These problems are anticipated by creditors, who price their debt accordingly and transfer the ensuing costs to the firm. Creditors can also mitigate outright expropriation by keeping the debt maturity short and writing protective covenants into the debt contract, while private lenders may have the capacity to step up monitoring and force contract renegotiations.

The creditor-shareholder conflict is, of course, multidimensional and may have significant costs for shareholders, leading to investment distortions (Myers, 1977). Since shareholders ultimately bear the costs of inefficient investments through lower equity values, they have strong incentives to resolve or ameliorate the shareholder–creditor conflict by accepting restrictive debt covenants. John and Nachman (1985) show that shareholders may also want to mitigate these problems due to reputational concerns.

Signaling Effect of Restructuring Decisions

Several theoretical models show that under informational asymmetries, corporate restructuring has important signaling implications. As Leland and Pyle (1977), Ross (1977), and DeAngelo and Masulis (1980) show, leverage-increasing transactions that potentially exert discipline on management induce positive stock prices reactions. The response of bond prices then depends on the trade-off between the negative risk effect of increased leverage and the positive role of the same in controlling managerial discretion. Flannery (1986) argues that the choice of debt maturity also sends a signal about the firm's default probability. Other studies emphasize that new capital offerings inherently emit a negative signal. Additional security issues may suggest that the firm is overvalued (Myers and Majluf, 1984), or that its future cash flows are less than anticipated (Miller and Rock, 1985). Bhattacharya (1979), Kalay (1980), and Miller and Rock (1985) emphasize the signaling effects associated with corporate payout decisions.

Tax Benefit of Debt

Fama and Miller (1972) show that when a firm employs leverage in its capital structure, the firm's value increases by the market value of the tax subsidy on the interest payments. These gains accrue to the shareholders of the firm but may also indirectly benefit all stakeholders including creditors through improved cash flows. The tax benefit of debt may be highly important for firms that undergo leveraged restructuring. Nonetheless, financial economists still debate the question of whether this tax benefit constitutes a true motive for such corporate actions (Modigliani and Miller, 1963; Miller, 1977; DeAngelo and Masulis, 1980).

Expected Bankruptcy and Reorganization Costs

The theoretical literature shows that the expected costs of involuntary bankruptcy and reorganization have a significant effect on the value of levered firms. These costs include lawyer and accountant fees, legal costs, and the costs of managerial time involved in bankruptcy and reorganization proceedings. Warner (1977) estimates that the direct costs of bankruptcy are fairly small relative to firm value.

Masulis (1980) approximates capital structure changes by investigating exchange offers but does not detect any such bankruptcy cost effect.

EMPIRICAL EVIDENCE

This section discusses how the various forms of corporate restructuring should affect creditors and provides empirical evidence. Empirically, according to the literature, creditor wealth effects are approximated by bond price shocks. This is an imperfect measure because it does not account for other creditors such as banks and other intermediaries. However, quantifying the impact of restructuring in an event study framework is difficult.

Asset Portfolio Restructuring

Portfolio restructuring changes the contracting relationship that exists between shareholders and creditors by altering the firm's underlying collateral and liquidation value. Also, changes in the volatility (or *co-insurance*) of cash flow streams can lead to wealth redistributions between shareholders and creditors.

Asset Portfolio Expansion: M&As

The conventional objective of M&As is the realization of synergies that would raise the value of the combined firm. Operating synergies can be derived from economies of scale, greater market power, or the elimination of duplicate activities. There is also scope for financial synergies such as lower cost of capital, reduced tax liability, or better efficiency of the internal capital market. The latter prescribes that the cash flow streams of the merging firms be imperfectly correlated, which reduces bankruptcy risk through co-insurance (Levy and Sarnat, 1970; Lewellen, 1971; Higgins and Schall, 1975).

Modern theory proposes that synergistic gains are often insufficient to justify M&As. Roll (1986) argues that there may be no synergies in the first place, due to the susceptibility of managers to make mistakes. Another undesirable explanation is that M&As occur because they enhance the welfare of the acquirer's management. Under informational asymmetries and inadequate monitoring, managers are afforded sufficient discretion to pursue such strategies. Accordingly, Morck, Shleifer, and Vishny (1990) show that M&As, potentially motivated by managerial private benefits, induce a reduction in shareholder wealth.

The complexity of these issues makes predicting how bondholders are affected by M&As difficult. Creditors benefit from a reduction in default risk. Hence, if the deal induces a co-insurance of cash flows or is motivated by managerial agency problems, it should increase bondholder wealth. If the deal otherwise creates no value, this can occur through a wealth shift from shareholders to bondholders. Galai and Masulis (1976) make this point for conglomerate M&As, which are typically penalized with a "conglomerate discount" as there is no discernible economic relationship between the parties (Rajan, Servaes, and Zingales, 2000). In nonconglomerate M&As, operating synergies dominate, but bondholders can still share some of the ensuing wealth benefits. However, strong shareholders may try to reverse any reduction in default risk, for example, by financing the deal with leverage.

Empirically, the literature provides ambiguous results but suggests that the bondholders of U.S. acquiring firms do not gain from M&As (see Exhibit 20.1). Billett, King, and Mauer (2004) report significantly negative abnormal bond returns around M&A announcements regardless of the acquirer's bond rating, the payment method, or whether the deal is conglomerate or not. Earlier, Kim and Mc-Connell (1977), Asquith and Kim (1982), Walker (1994), and Dennis and McConnell (1986) find that bondholders neither gain nor lose around M&A announcements. Eger (1983) and Maquieira, Megginson, and Nail (1998) focus on stock-for-stock M&As exclusively, omitting any effect the payment method may have. Eger finds positive abnormal returns, but Maquieira et al. only confirm these for nonconglomerate deals.

Earlier studies investigating target firms report insignificant abnormal returns for target bondholders. Since target firms tend to be smaller and lower rated than acquiring firms, this seems to be contradicting the expectation that target bondholders should benefit more from co-insurance. Billett et al. (2004) nonetheless find positive abnormal returns, although these are not uniform across all specifications. The positive gains are driven by junk-grade targets, which profit relatively more from lower credit risk in the combined firm. Abnormal returns in investment-grade targets are significantly negative, showing that the benefits of co-insurance can be negligible in creditworthy firms.

Renneboog and Szilagyi (2007) investigate European M&As using a large sample of investment-grade Eurobonds, providing non-U.S. evidence on the bondholder wealth effects of corporate restructuring for the first time. The authors confirm that M&As involving European firms are generally more bondholder-friendly than U.S. domestic deals. First, bondholders benefit more from deals involving continental European firms, where banks and other risk-averse stakeholders actively support creditor interests. Second, acquirer bondholders earn lower returns from cross-border deals, but the negative cross-border effect is counterbalanced if creditor protection is better in the target country, and if a British acquirer approaches a target firm in continental Europe. Third, acquirer bondholders earn higher gains from acquisitions, a result previously documented for shareholder returns by Faccio, McConnell, and Stolin (2006).

Asset Portfolio Reduction: Corporate Refocusing

Increasing a firm's business focus has been a distinctive element of U.S. corporate activities since the 1980s. Firms may choose three main mechanisms to divest an operating unit: *equity carve-outs*, *spin-offs*, and *asset sell-offs*. Aside from the economic gains associated with asset restructuring, carve-outs and spin-offs may be particularly effective in reducing agency costs. These transactions take subsidiaries public. As a result, disclosure and external monitoring are improved, and managerial compensation can be tied closer to the subsidiary's market value. Carve-outs can also signal that the subsidiary is overvalued, while the parent firm is undervalued (Welch, 1989; Nanda, 1991). Spin-offs have no signaling effect, as the subsidiary's shares are distributed on a pro rata basis to the parent firm's existing shareholders. Spin-offs do not provide the parent with cash either, which mitigates agency problems related to free cash flow.

Sell-offs transactions are typically perceived less favorably than spin-offs and carve-outs. These transactions tend to be negotiated privately and therefore bypass

Exhibit 20.1 Bondholder Wealth Effects of Mergers and Acquisitions

Study	Sample Period/ Country	Deal Type	Transaction Party	Event Window	N	Abnormal Return (%)	Benchmark
Kim and McConnell (1977)	1960–1973 U.S.	Completed conglomerate	All	Month [0]	44	−1.48	Matching bonds
Asquith and Kim (1982)	1960–1978 U.S.	Completed conglomerate	All	Month [0]	62	1.07	Matching bonds
			Acquirer		38	1.08	
			Target		24	1.05	
Eger (1983)	1958–1980 U.S.	Completed stock-for-stock	Acquirer	Days [−30,0]	33	1.01***	Matching portfolios
Dennis and McConnell (1986)	1962-1980 U.S.	Completed	Acquirer	Days [−1,0]	67	−0.17	Dow Jones Industrial Bond Index
			BBB or below		31	−0.51*	
			Target		27	0.03	
			BBB or below		19	0.35	
Walker (1994)	1980–1988 U.S.	Completed	All	Month [0]	92	0.31	Treasury bonds
			Target		33	0.83	
		Cash-for-stock	All		35	−0.73	
		Stock-for-stock	All		12	1.39	
Maqueira, Megginson, and Nail (1998)	1963–1996 U.S.	Conglomerate, completed, stock-for-stock	All	Months [−2,2]	253	0.44	Treasury bonds
			Acquirer		222	0.33	
			Target		31	1.22	

(Continued)

Exhibit 20.1 (*Continued*)

Study	Sample Period/Country	Deal Type	Transaction Party	Event Window	N	Abnormal Return (%)	Benchmark
		Nonconglomerate, completed, stock-for-stock	All		282	1.44***	
Billett, King, and Mauer (2004)	1979–1997 U.S.	All	Acquirer	Months [-1,0]	189	1.90***	Lehman Brothers corporate bond indices
			Target		93	0.50	
			Acquirer		831	-0.17***	
			BBB– or above		680	0.09*	
			Below BBB–		151	-0.55*	
			Target		265	1.09**	
			BBB– or above		167	-0.80***	
			Below BBB–		98	4.30***	
Renneboog and Szilagyi (2007)	1995–2004 Europe	All	Acquirer	Months [-1,0]	225	0.56***	Corporate Eurobond indices
			A. Continental European		146	0.48***	
			U.K.		79	0.71***	
			B. Domestic target		79	0.84***	
			Cross-border target		146	0.41**	
			Worse creditor rights in target country		70	0.12	
			Better creditor rights in target country		37	0.88***	
			C. Unlisted target		149	0.65***	
			Listed target		76	0.39*	

Note: *, **, and *** indicate significance at the 0.10, 0.05, and 0.01 level, respectively.
This table summarizes univariate analyses of abnormal bond price changes around M&A announcements.

external monitoring, potentially generating free cash flow concerns. The reverse side of sell-offs, partial acquisitions, induce agency problems similar to those seen in M&As. However, partial acquisitions are usually smaller in size and typically friendly and synergistic.

All three forms of corporate refocusing can trigger wealth transfers between shareholders and creditors. Galai and Masulis (1976) describe how unexpected spin-offs expropriate collateral and liquidation value, with carve-outs and sell-offs having a similar impact. Corporate refocusing also leads to a loss of co-insurance, particularly in cross-industry transactions where the cash flows of the parent and subsidiary are not highly correlated (John, 1993).

The empirical literature on the wealth effects of corporate refocusing remains scarce (see Exhibit 20.2). No evidence is available on how equity carve-outs affect bondholders. Schipper and Smith (1983) examine the behavior of bond prices and bond ratings around spin-off announcements and find little evidence of bondholder expropriation. While Hite and Owers (1983) report significant positive gains for shareholders in corporate spin-offs, they find negative abnormal bond returns (which are insignificant due to small sample size). This suggests that in these transactions there is a wealth transfer from bondholders to shareholders. Veld and Veld-Merkoulova (2008) confirm this latter argument by reporting insignificant or significant gains, depending on the specification. These findings suggest that positive signaling effects can compensate for wealth redistributions.

Maxwell and Rao (2003) find that, on average, parent bondholders suffer significant losses, the size of which depends on the change in leverage and the underlying collateral, but not on the loss of co-insurance. Their results coincide with Dittmar (2004), who finds that spin-offs tend to leave parent firms with more leverage than their spun-off subsidiaries. Parrino (1997) shows how parents can deliberately undertake spin-offs to expropriate bondholders using the 1993 spin-off of Marriott's management businesses.

Datta and Iskandar-Datta (1996) and Datta, Iskandar-Datta, and Raman (2003) document the wealth effects of sell-offs. Both papers find that these transactions lead to bondholder losses, though the size of these depends on the underlying motive and the way the proceeds are distributed. Datta and Iskandar-Datta (1995) and Datta et al. (2003) find that bondholders in the acquirers of the disposed assets also suffer losses. This implies that the benefits of partial acquisitions in terms of co-insurance and increased collateral do not compensate for a simultaneous increase in leverage and the deterioration of performance expectations.

Easterwood (1998) examines divestments made by firms that underwent leveraged buyouts in the 1980s. He reports positive abnormal bond returns for firms that are not financially distressed, but negative returns for those that are. Furthermore, the bondholder losses in distressed firms are only significant when core assets are divested. These results, along with Easterwood's finding that abnormal returns are negatively related to the firm's postbuyout capital structure, lend some support to the intracreditor wealth transfer hypothesis of Rajan (1992) and Diamond (1993). This hypothesis postulates that when a firm is in distress, secured private lenders (banks) may press for the early liquidation of assets at the expense of less senior creditors such as bondholders. Early liquidation may be most detrimental when it involves core assets, whereas the disposal of noncore assets may be beneficial to the extent that firms use the proceeds to pay off existing debt.

Exhibit 20.2 Bondholder Wealth Effects of Corporate Refocusing

Study	Sample Period/ Country	Deal Type	Transaction Party	Event Window	N	Abnormal Return (%)	Benchmark
Panel A. Spin-offs							
Hite and Owers (1983)	1963–1981 U.S.	All	Parent	Days [–10,10]	15	–0.30	Treasury bonds
Maxwell and Rao (2003)	1974–1997 U.S.	All	Parent	Month [0]	80	–0.89***	Treasury bonds
			A. >20% of assets		41	–1.46***	
			<20% of assets		38	–0.24***	
			B. Cross-industry		64	–0.74***	
			Same-industry		16	–1.43***	
			C. Investment-grade		64	–0.47***	
			Junk-grade		16	–2.51***	
Veld and Veld-Merkoulova (2008)	1995–2002 U.S.	All	Parent	Days [–1,1]	77	0.80	Merrill Lynch corporate bond indices
Panel B. Asset Sales							
Datta and Iskandar-Datta (1995)	1982–1990 U.S.	All	Acquirer	Days [–1,0]	63	–0.66***	Treasury bonds

Study	Period/Country	Event	Subgroup	Window	N	Abnormal return	Benchmark
Easterwood (1998)	1982–1990 U.S	Post-LBO asset sales	Parent	Month [0]	134	−0.22	Blume and Keim (1988) corporate bond index and Merrill Lynch High Yield Index
			Nondistressed parent		81	0.75***	
			Distressed parent		53	−1.70*	
			Core asset sales		30	−2.34***	
			Non-core asset sales		23	−0.87	
			Onset of distress		31	−2.55**	
			Core asset sales		17	−2.48**	
			Non-core asset sales		14	−2.62	
Datta, Iskandar-Datta, and Raman (2003)	1982–1992 U.S.	All	Parent	Days [−1,0]	113	−0.54***	Treasury bonds
			Acquirer		96	−0.40**	

Note: *, **, and *** indicate significance at the 0.10, 0.05, and 0.01 level, respectively.
This table summarizes univariate analyses of abnormal bond price changes around corporate refocusing announcements.

Financial Restructuring

Transactions of financial restructuring are fundamentally different from portfolio restructuring because they alter the firm's capital structure rather than its underlying asset portfolio. Creditors can be heavily affected by such capital structure changes because they can entail a sizeable change in the firm's leverage and *ceteris paribus* can change the firm's default probability. Masulis (1980) takes account of three effects: a wealth redistribution effect (Jensen and Meckling, 1976), an expected bankruptcy cost effect (Robichek and Myers, 1966; Kraus and Litzenberger, 1973), and a corporate tax effect (Modigliani and Miller, 1963). The direction and size of creditor wealth changes should also be affected by signaling, reflecting expectations on managerial discipline, firm performance, and any ensuing investment effects.

Debt Issues and Bank Loans

The creditor wealth effects of capital structure changes can be best investigated through bondholder response to borrowing announcements. The empirical literature provides little and inconclusive evidence in this area (see Panel A of Exhibit 20.3). Kolodny and Suhler (1988) report that debt issue announcements have a positive effect on bond prices, and the price gains actually increase in the borrowing firm's initial leverage and the size of the debt issue. This implies that the positive signal conveyed by the new issue dominates the risk implications of increased leverage. To a large extent, this result is compatible with Akhigbe, Easterwood, and Pettit (1997), who find that bondholders respond negatively to new debt issues only when these are motivated by cash flow shortfalls. In a recent paper, however, Ongena, Roscovan, and Werker (2007) show that bank loan announcements are generally met with a negative bondholder response.

Seasoned Equity Offerings

Financial theory suggests that stock markets react negatively to new equity issues (Myers and Majluf, 1984; Asquith and Mullins, 1986; Masulis and Korwar, 1986). The perception that seasoned equity offerings (SEOs) convey a negative signal about the issuing firm's prospects is supported by evidence that operating performance declines after these transactions (Loughran and Ritter, 1997; Jegadeesh, 2000).

Creditors are also expected to respond negatively to adverse signals about the firm's prospects. However, they should benefit from the leverage-reducing effect of equity issuance. Kalay and Shimrat (1987) find that the former effect dominates as bond prices react negatively to SEO announcements (see Panel B of Exhibit 20.3). Elliott, Prevost, and Rao (2009) find stronger evidence for wealth redistributions from shareholders to bondholders, reporting considerable bondholder gains that increase with debt maturity and firm default risk. Eberhart and Siddique (2002) find similar results across event windows spanning from one month to five years.

Exchange Offers and Recapitalizations

Security exchange offers and recapitalizations come closest to approximating pure capital structure changes, as they do not involve simultaneous asset structure changes. However, while exchange offers are voluntary, recapitalizations

Exhibit 20.3 Bondholder Wealth Effects of Security Issues and Exchanges

Study	Sample Period/ Country	Deal Type	Event Window	N	Abnormal Return (%)	Benchmark
Panel A. Debt Issues and Bank Loans						
Kolodny and Suhler (1988)	1973–1981 U.S.	Debt issues	Month [0]	66	1.95**	Matching bonds
Akhigbe, Easterwood, and Pettit (1997)	1980–1992 U.S.	Debt issues	Week [0]	466	0.04	Treasury bonds
		Cash flow shortfall		125	−0.40**	
		Capital expenditure		141	0.19	
		Leverage change		117	0.29	
		Debt refinancing		155	0.29	
Ongena, Roscovan, and Werker (2007)	1997–2003 U.S.	Bank loans	Days [−1,1]	3589	0.17***[1]	Collin-Dufresne, Goldstein, and Martin (2001) credit spread model
Panel B. Equity Issues						
Kalay and Shimrat (1987)	1970–1982 U.S.	Seasoned equity issues	Days [−2,0] [−1,1] or [−1,0]	58	−2.13**	Matching bonds
Eberhart and Siddique (2002)	1980–1992 U.S.	Seasoned equity issues	Month [1]	140	0.90**	Matching portfolios
Elliott, Prevost, and Rao (2009)	1980–2000 U.S.	Seasoned equity issues	Days [0,1]	103	0.42***	Treasury bonds
		A. Effect on long-term debt		69	0.69***	

(Continued)

Exhibit 20.3 (Continued)

Study	Sample Period/Country	Deal Type	Event Window	N	Abnormal Return (%)	Benchmark
		Effect on short-term debt		49	−0.11	
		B. Moody's rating > median		57	0.43	
		Moody's rating < median		50	0.87***	
Panel C. Security Exchanges						
Masulis (1980)	1962–1976 U.S.	Debt-for-equity exchanges and recapitalizations	Days [−1,0]	49	−0.30***	Matching portfolios
		No covenant protection		18	−0.84***	
Mikkelson (1981)	1963–1978 U.S.	Forced conversion of convertible debt	Week [0]	19	0.52	Treasury bonds
Cornett and Travlos (1989)	1973–1983 U.S.	Debt-for-equity exchanges	Day [0]	10	0.11	Matching portfolios
		Equity-for-debt exchanges		40	−0.48***	
Panel D. Executive Stock Option Plans						
DeFusco, Johnson, and Zorn (1990)	1978–1982 U.S.	Executive stock option plans	Day [−1]	26	−0.40**	Dow Jones Industrial Bond Index

Note: *, **, and *** indicate significance at the 0.10, 0.05, and 0.01 level, respectively.
This table summarizes univariate analyses of abnormal bond price changes around announcements of security issues and exchanges.
[1]Ongena, Roscovan, and Werker (2007) analyze abnormal changes in credit spreads rather than bond prices.

generally require the participation of all security holders and consequently have a greater impact on capital structure. Masulis (1980) jointly examines debt-for-stock exchange offers and recapitalizations (see Panel C of Exhibit 20.3). The author reports bondholder losses and simultaneous shareholder gains, which are largest when bondholders are unprotected by covenants. Masulis (1983) later develops a linear model to estimate the firm valuation effects of these transactions, broadly finding the same results.

Cornett and Travlos (1989) report different results that are consistent with signaling. The authors show that bondholders do not lose from debt-for-equity exchanges due to better performance expectations. The importance of signaling considerations is reinforced by their finding that leverage-reducing equity-for-debt exchanges induce a negative bondholder response.

Mikkelson (1981) examines how the forced conversion of convertible bonds affects security holders in the firm. Debt conversion reduces leverage much in the same way that equity-for-debt exchanges do. There is no evidence that bondholders benefit from such transactions, which Mikkelson attributes to negative signaling effects.

Executive Stock Option Plans

ESOPs are an increasingly controversial device used to mitigate the manager-shareholder conflict. The issuance of stock options tends to have a relatively modest impact on capital structure and does not induce an immediate change because the options are out of the money and cannot be immediately exercised. However, ESOPs should induce bondholder losses by realigning managerial and shareholder interests. Accordingly, DeFusco, Johnson, and Zorn (1990) show that ESOP announcements lead to significant reductions in bondholder wealth (Panel D of Exhibit 20.3). Bruner and Brownlee (1990) report similar results using a case study of Polaroid's 1988 leveraged ESOP.

Public-to-Private Transactions

Public-to-private transactions are often referred to collectively as leveraged buyouts (LBOs), as they are almost exclusively financed with massive debt. The majority of LBOs are management-led, but firms can be taken private by a variety of entities: the incumbent management (management buyout, MBO), outside management (management buyin, MBI), employees (employee buyout, EBO), or institutional investors and private equity firms (institutional buyout, IBO).

Jensen (1986) notes that LBO firms typically provide strong incentives for management to maximize firm value. Accordingly, the literature observes that LBOs are often followed by disposals of noncore assets. LBOs contain managerial agency problems by introducing high leverage and concentrating equity ownership. The control function of debt is pronounced since the restructured firm's posttransaction leverage ratio often approaches unity. At the margin, this mostly requires management to borrow from banks, which are often given an equity interest through strip financing. To the extent that managers become shareholders themselves, LBOs can also directly realign managerial and shareholder interests (Renneboog, Simons, and Wright, 2007).

While LBOs tend to improve expectations of future firm performance, this does not compensate creditors for the huge risk effect of increased leverage. Marais,

Schipper, and Smith (1989) find that the credit rating agency Moody's Investor Service regularly downgrades firms undergoing LBOs, although they find that bondholder losses are not systematic in LBO firms (see Panel A of Exhibit 20.4). Asquith and Wizman (1990), Walker (1991), Cook, Easterwood, and Martin (1992) and Warga and Welch (1993) conversely report substantial bondholder losses around LBO announcements. The literature reports that the abnormal returns are sensitive to covenant protection, maturity, and the prior credit rating (Collin-Dufresne, Goldstein, and Martin, 2001).

Leveraged Recapitalizations

Firms often use leveraged recapitalizations (LRs) to fend off hostile takeover bids. Under this strategy, firms take out substantial debt to repurchase shares or distribute a special dividend to the current shareholders. Like LBOs, LRs entail huge increases in leverage, and as a consequence should induce significant wealth redistributions from bondholders to shareholders. In lieu of the cash payout, managers also tend to increase their own shareholdings (through stock options or retirement plans), which should instigate better performance but actually increases the realignment of managerial and shareholder interests.

While the massive leverage associated with LRs should induce considerable bondholder losses, the empirical literature offers limited evidence in this regard (see Panel B of Exhibit 20.4). Handa and Radhakrishnan (1991) find that bondholders incur insignificant negative abnormal returns around LR announcements, and significant gains immediately before the announcement date. Gupta and Rosenthal (1991) report insignificant negative returns for longer time periods. Nonetheless, the samples used in these studies are small. Moreover, many LR firms are under imminent takeover threat, which complicates the investigation of announcement returns. The regular downgrades of post-LR firms by Moody's and Standard and Poor's indicate longer-term bondholder losses.

Corporate Payout

Firms borrowing cash to pay dividends or repurchase shares are often cited as classic cases of deliberate creditor expropriation. The creditor wealth implications of these corporate actions can be driven by both wealth redistributions and signaling effects. The signaling hypothesis (Bhattacharya, 1979; Kalay, 1980) suggests that distributing cash to shareholders conveys positive information about the firm's prospects. This holds for dividend increases in particular because they indicate a permanent commitment to higher payouts. However, these payout mechanisms also increase leverage, and in the absence of adequate protection, creditors may suffer losses as a result.

Numerous studies examine the signaling versus wealth redistribution hypotheses. Evidence on the impact of dividends on bondholder wealth is mixed (see Panel A of Exhibit 20.5). Dhillon and Johnson (1994) find that bond prices fall around dividend increases, which supports the wealth redistribution hypothesis. However, Jayaraman and Shastri (1988) find that the announcement of special dividends does not affect bondholders, which implies a positive signaling effect. Woolridge (1983) and Handjinicolaou and Kalay (1984) provide evidence for signaling by showing that unexpected dividend reductions reduce bondholder wealth, while dividend increases have no impact.

Exhibit 20.4 Bondholder Wealth Effects of Leveraged Transactions

Study	Sample Period/ Country	Deal Type	Event Window	N	Abnormal Return (%)	Benchmark
Panel A. Public-to-Private Transactions						
Marais, Schipper, and Smith (1989)	1974–1985 U.S.	All	Days [–69,0]	33	–0.00	Two-index model using Dow Jones Bond Index and CRSP equal-weighted stock index
Asquith and Wizman (1990)	1980–1988 U.S.	All	Days [0, C] Month [0]	30 199	–0.00 –1.10***	Shearson-Lehman-Hutton corporate bond indices
		Strong covenants Weak covenants No covenants		29 60 70	–0.10 –0.30 –2.60***	
Walker (1991)	1982–1989 U.S.	All	Month [0]	24	–2.60**	Treasury bonds
Cook, Easterwood, and Martin (1992)	1981–1989 U.S.	MBOs	Month [0]	62	–2.56***	Shearson-Lehman-Hutton Treasury indices
		Completed		32	–3.35***	

(Continued)

Exhibit 20.4 (*Continued*)

Study	Sample Period/Country	Deal Type	Event Window	N	Abnormal Return (%)	Benchmark
Warga and Welch (1993)	1985–1989 U.S.	All	Months [−2,2]	36	−5.91***	Lehman Brothers corporate bond indices
Panel B. Leveraged Recapitalizations						
Handa and Radhakrishnan (1991)	1984–1989 U.S.	All	Days [−1,0]	19	3.00**	Mean-adjusted returns
Gupta and Rosenthal (1991)	1984–1988 U.S.	Firms in takeover play	Days [−15,15]	19	−6.15	Dow Jones Bond Index
			Days [TS−1,−2]	18	−3.56***	
		Firms not in takeover play	Days [−1,0]	18	0.17	
			Days [1, C−2]	18	2.51	
			Days [−1,0]	9	−0.26	
			Days [1, C−2]	8	−3.09	

Note: *, **, and *** indicate significance at the 10, 5, and 1% level, respectively.
This table summarizes univariate analyses of abnormal bond price changes around announcements of leveraged transactions. *C* indicates the date of the transaction's completion. *TS* indicates the date of a takeover attempt against the restructuring firm.

Exhibit 20.5 Bondholder Wealth Effects of Corporate Payout

Study	Sample Period/ Country	Deal Type	Event Window	N	Abnormal Return (%)	Benchmark
Panel A. Dividends						
Woolridge (1983)	1970–1977 U.S.	Dividend increases	Days [−10,10]	248	0.10	Matching portfolios
		Dividend cuts		45	−0.55**	
Handjinicolaou and Kalay (1984)	1975–1976 U.S.	Dividend increases	Days [−1,1]	143	0.01	Treasury bonds
		Dividend cuts		42	−0.48***	
Jayaraman and Shastri (1988)	1962–1982 U.S.	Special dividends	Days [−2,0], [−1,1] or [−1,0]	65	0.02	Treasury bonds
Dhillon and Johnson (1994)	1978–1987 U.S.	Dividend increases	Days [0,1]	61	−0.37*	Treasury bonds
		Dividend cuts		70	0.69***	
Panel B. Share Repurchases						
Dann (1981)	1962–1976 U.S.	All	Days [0,1]	20	−0.33	Raw returns
Maxwell and Stephens (2003)	1980–1997 U.S.	All	Month [0]	945	−0.19***	Treasury bonds
		Increase in firm value		526	0.29***	
		Decrease in firm value		397	−0.71***	

*,**, and *** indicate significance at the 0.10, 0.05, and 0.01 level, respectively.
This table summarizes univariate analyses of abnormal bond price changes around corporate payout announcements.

Dann (1981) investigates the wealth effects of share repurchases (see Panel B of Exhibit 20.5). The author finds insignificant negative abnormal bond returns and positive stock returns, which indicate both wealth redistributions and signaling effects. Maxwell and Stephens (2003) find much stronger evidence for both hypotheses, reporting significant bondholder losses on average but sizeable gains in firms where shareholders respond favorably to the transaction. The authors show that bondholder losses are greater when the repurchase program is large and when the firm's bond rating is junk-grade. This implies that repurchase programs are viewed as a positive signal, but this is often insufficient to offset the bondholder losses that arise from increased default risk. Maxwell and Stephens (2003) report that rating agencies are twice as likely to downgrade bond ratings after repurchase announcements.

SUMMARY AND CONCLUSIONS

This chapter provides an overview of the empirical literature on how corporate restructuring affects bondholder wealth. Evidence on restructuring and its consequences for creditors remains inconsistent. This is largely due to the fact that restructuring is a complex and multidimensional event whose impact on creditor wealth is the net effect of multiple factors.

The existing empirical literature has been criticized for issues relating to sample size, data quality, and the employed methodologies. Bessembinder, Kahle, Maxwell, and Xu (2009) find that the various methodologies used to examine bondholder wealth changes, such as mean-adjusted models, value-weighted portfolio approaches, and factor models, may be subject to serious misspecification. The authors propose that bonds should be priced using matched equal-weighted portfolios or individual bonds, and that these two methods are complements, not substitutes.

Another important gap in the literature is the lack of studies on the stakeholder-oriented governance systems of continental Europe and Japan. U.S. studies unambiguously show that restructuring can trigger significant wealth transfers between bondholders and shareholders. In stakeholder-oriented systems, the power of banks and other risk-averse stakeholders dictates that restructuring may be more creditor-friendly (Renneboog and Szilagyi, 2007). Ongoing developments in the international corporate environment demand greater attention to these countries. In Europe, market deregulation, increased competition, economic and financial integration, new tax and accounting regulations, and recent struggles with pension reform have not only encouraged restructuring, but also set off a gradual convergence of stakeholder-oriented governance regimes towards the market-oriented model. This comes at a time when market-oriented systems are being increasingly questioned in their ability to control agency problems.

DISCUSSION QUESTIONS

1. What are the agency costs of outside equity?
2. What are the agency costs of debt?
3. What are the key types of corporate restructuring?

4. What are public-to-private transactions and their relevance in corporate restructuring?

5. How does corporate restructuring affect bondholder wealth?

REFERENCES

Akhigbe, Aigbe, John C. Easterwood, and R. Richardson Pettit. 1997. "Wealth Effects of Corporate Debt Issues: The Impact of Issuer Motivations." *Financial Management* 26:1, 32–47.

Asquith, Paul, and E. Han Kim. 1982. "The Impact of Merger Bids on the Participating Firms' Security Holders." *Journal of Finance* 37:5, 1209–1228.

Asquith, Paul, and David W. Mullins. 1986. "Equity Issues and Offering Dilution." *Journal of Financial Economics* 15:1–2, 61–89.

Asquith, Paul, and Thierry A. Wizman. 1990. "Event Risk, Covenants, and Bondholder Returns in Leveraged Buyouts." *Journal of Financial Economics* 27:1, 195–213.

Bessembinder, Hendrik, Kathleen M. Kahle, William F. Maxwell, and Danielle Xu. 2009. "Measuring Abnormal Bond Performance." *Review of Financial Studies* 22:10, 4219–4258.

Bhattacharya, Sudipto. 1979. "Imperfect Information, Dividend Policy and the 'Bird in Hand' Fallacy." *Bell Journal of Economics* 10:1, 259–270.

Billett, Matthew T., Tao-Hsien Dolly King, and David C. Mauer. 2004. "Bondholder Wealth Effects in Mergers and Acquisitions: New Evidence from the 1980s and 1990s." *Journal of Finance* 59:1, 107–135.

Bowman, Edward H., and Harbir Singh. 1993. "Corporate Restructuring: Reconfiguring the Firm." *Strategic Management Journal* 14:4, 5–14.

Bruner, Robert F., and E. Richard Brownlee, II. 1990. "Leveraged ESOPs, Wealth Transfer, and "Shareholder Neutrality": The Case of Polaroid." *Financial Management* 19:1, 59–74.

Collin-Dufresne, Pierre, Robert S. Goldstein, and J. Spencer Martin. 2001. "The Determinants of Credit Spread Changes." *Journal of Finance* 56:6, 2177–2208.

Cook, Douglas O., John C. Easterwood, and John D. Martin. 1992. "Bondholder Wealth Effects of Management Buyouts." *Financial Management* 21:1, 102.

Cornett, Marcia Million, and Nickolaos G. Travlos. 1989. "Information Effects Associated with Debt-for-Equity and Equity-for-Debt Exchange Offers." *Journal of Finance* 44:2, 451–468.

Dann, Larry Y. 1981. "The Effects of Common Stock Repurchase on Security Holders' Returns." *Journal of Financial Economics* 9:2, 101–138.

Datta, Sudip, and Mai E. Iskandar-Datta. 1995. "Corporate Partial Acquisitions, Total Firm Valuation and the Effect of Financing Method." *Journal of Banking & Finance* 19:1, 97–115.

Datta, Sudip, and Mai E. Iskandar-Datta. 1996. "Who Gains from Corporate Asset Sales?" *Journal of Financial Research* 19:1, 41–58.

Datta, Sudip, Mai Iskandar-Datta, and Kartik Raman. 2003. "Value Creation in Corporate Asset Sales: The Role of Managerial Performance and Lender Monitoring." *Journal of Banking & Finance* 27:2, 351–375.

DeAngelo, Harry, and Ronald W. Masulis. 1980. "Optimal Capital Structure under Corporate and Personal Taxation." *Journal of Financial Economics* 8:1, 3–29.

DeFusco, Richard A., Robert R. Johnson, and Thomas S. Zorn. 1990. "The Effect of Executive Stock Option Plans on Stockholders and Bondholders." *Journal of Finance* 45:2, 617–627.

Dennis, Debra K., and John J. McConnell. 1986. "Corporate Mergers and Security Returns." *Journal of Financial Economics* 16:2, 143–187.

Dhillon, Upinder, and Herb Johnson. 1994. "The Effect of Dividend Changes on Stock and Bond Prices." *Journal of Finance* 49:1, 281–289.

Diamond, Douglas W. 1991. "Monitoring and Reputation: The Choice between Bank Loans and Directly Placed Debt." *Journal of Political Economy* 99:4, 689–722.

Diamond, Douglas W. 1993. "Seniority and Maturity of Debt Contracts." *Journal of Financial Economics* 33:3, 341–368.

Dittmar, Amy. 2004. "Capital Structure in Corporate Spin-offs." *Journal of Business* 77:1, 9–43.

Easterwood, John C. 1998. "Divestments and Financial Distress in Leveraged Buyouts." *Journal of Banking & Finance* 22:2, 129–159.

Eberhart, Allan C., and Akhtar Siddique. 2002. "The Long-term Performance of Corporate Bonds (and Stocks) Following Seasoned Equity Offerings." *Review of Financial Studies* 15:5, 1385–1406.

Eger, Carol E. 1983. "An Empirical Test of the Redistribution Effect in Pure Exchange Mergers." *Journal of Financial and Quantitative Analysis* 18:4, 547–572.

Elliott, William B., Andrew K. Prevost, and Ramesh P. Rao. 2009. "The Announcement Impact of Seasoned Equity Offerings on Bondholder Wealth." *Journal of Banking and Finance* 33:8, 1472–1480.

Faccio, Mara, John J. McConnell, and David Stolin. 2006. "Returns to Acquirers of Listed and Unlisted Targets." *Journal of Financial and Quantitative Analysis* 41:1, 197–220.

Fama, Eugene F. 1980. "Agency Problems and the Theory of the Firm." *Journal of Political Economy* 88:2, 288–307.

Fama, Eugene F., and Merton H. Miller. 1972. *The Theory of Finance.* New York: Holt, Rinehart and Winston.

Flannery, Mark J. 1986. "Asymmetric Information and Risky Debt Maturity Choice." *Journal of Finance* 41:1, 19–37.

Galai, Dan, and Ronald W. Masulis. 1976. "The Option Pricing Model and the Risk Factor of Stock." *Journal of Financial Economics* 3:1–2, 53–81.

Gibbs, Philip A. 1993. "Determinants of Corporate Restructuring: The Relative Importance of Corporate Governance, Takeover Threat, and Free Cash Flow." *Strategic Management Journal* 14:S1, 51–68.

Grossman, Sanford J., and Oliver D. Hart. 1983. "Corporate Financial Structure and Managerial Incentives." Working Paper No. R0398, National Bureau of Economic Research.

Gupta, Atul, and Leonard Rosenthal. 1991. "Ownership Structure, Leverage, and Firm Value: The Case of Leveraged Recapitalizations." *Financial Management* 20:3, 69–83.

Handa, Puneet, and A. R. Radhakrishnan. 1991. "An Empirical Investigation of Leveraged Recapitalizations with Cash Payout as Takeover Defense." *Financial Management* 20:3, 58–68.

Handjinicolaou, George, and Avner Kalay. 1984. "Wealth Redistributions or Changes in Firm Value: An Analysis of Returns to Bondholders and Stockholders around Dividend Announcements." *Journal of Financial Economics* 13:1, 35–63.

Higgins, Robert C., and Lawrence D. Schall. 1975. "Corporate Bankruptcy and Conglomerate Merger." *Journal of Finance* 30:1, 93–111.

Hite, Gailen L., and James E. Owers. 1983. "Security Price Reactions around Corporate Spin-off Announcements." *Journal of Financial Economics* 12:4, 409–436.

Jayaraman, Narayanan, and Kuldeep Shastri. 1988. "The Valuation of Specially Designated Dividends." *Journal of Financial and Quantitative Analysis* 23:3, 301–312.

Jegadeesh, Narasimhan. 2000. "Long-term Performance of Seasoned Equity Offerings: Benchmark Errors and Biases in Expectations." *Financial Management* 29:3, 5–30.

Jensen, Michael C. 1986. "Agency Costs of Free Cash Flow, Corporate Finance and Takeovers." *American Economic Review* 76:2, 323–329.

Jensen, Michael C., and William H. Meckling. 1976. "Theory of the Firm: Managerial Behavior, Agency Costs and Ownership Structure." *Journal of Financial Economics* 3:4, 305–360.

John, Kose, and David C. Nachman. 1985. "Risky Debt, Investment Incentives, and Reputation in a Sequential Equilibrium." *Journal of Finance* 40:3, 863–878.

John, Teresa A. 1993. "Optimality of Spin-offs and Allocation of Debt." *Journal of Financial and Quantitative Analysis* 28:1, 139–160.

Kalay, Avner. 1984. "Signalling, Information Content, and the Reluctance to Cut Dividends." *Journal of Financial and Quantitative Analysis* 15:4, 855–869.

Kalay, Avner, and Adam Shimrat. 1987. "Firm Value and Seasoned Equity Issues: Price Pressure, Wealth Redistribution, or Negative Information." *Journal of Financial Economics* 19:1, 109–126.

Kim, E. Han, and John J. McConnell. 1977. "Corporate Mergers and the Co-insurance of Corporate Debt." *Journal of Finance* 32:2, 349–365.

Kolodny, Richard, and Diane R. Suhler. 1988. "The Effects of New Debt Issues on Existing Security Holders." *Quarterly Journal of Business and Economics* 27:2, 51–72.

Kraus, Alan, and Robert H. Litzenberger. 1973. "A State-Preference Model of Optimal Financial Leverage." *Journal of Finance* 28:4, 911–922.

Leland, Hayne E., and David H. Pyle. 1977. "Informational Asymmetries, Financial Structure and Financial Intermediation." *Journal of Finance* 32:2, 371–381.

Levy, Haim, and Marshall Sarnat. 1970. "Diversification, Portfolio Analysis and the Uneasy Case for Conglomerate Mergers." *Journal of Finance* 25:4, 795–802.

Lewellen, Wilbur G. 1971. "A Pure Financial Rationale for the Conglomerate Merger." *Journal of Finance* 26:2, 521–537.

Loughran, Tim, and Jay R. Ritter. 1997. "The Operating Performance of Firms Conducting Seasoned Equity Offerings." *Journal of Finance* 52:5, 1823–1850.

Manne, Henry G. 1965. "Mergers and the Market for Corporate Control." *Journal of Political Economy* 73:2, 110–120.

Maquieira, Carlos P., William L. Megginson, and Lance Nail. 1998. "Wealth Creation versus Wealth Redistributions in Pure Stock-for-Stock Mergers." *Journal of Financial Economics* 48:1, 3–33.

Marais, Laurentius, Katherine Schipper, and Abbie Smith. 1989. "Wealth Effects of Going Private for Senior Securities." *Journal of Financial Economics* 23:1, 155–191.

Masulis, Ronald W. 1980. "The Effects of Capital Structure Change on Security Prices: A Study of Exchange Offers." *Journal of Financial Economics* 8:2, 139–178.

Masulis, Ronald W. 1983. "The Impact of Capital Structure Change on Firm Value: Some Estimates." *Journal of Finance* 38:1, 107–126.

Masulis, Ronald W., and Ashok N. Korwar. 1986. "Seasoned Equity Offerings: An Empirical Investigation." *Journal of Financial Economics* 15:1–2, 91–118.

Maxwell, William F., and Ramesh P. Rao. 2003. "Do Spin-offs Expropriate Wealth from Bondholders?" *Journal of Finance* 58:5, 2087–2108.

Maxwell, William F., and Clifford P. Stephens. 2003. "The Wealth Effects of Repurchases on Bondholders." *Journal of Finance* 58:3, 895–919.

Mikkelson, Wayne H. 1981. "Convertible Calls and Security Returns." *Journal of Financial Economics* 9:3, 237–264.

Miller, Merton H, and Kevin Rock. 1985. "Dividend Policy under Asymmetric Information." *Journal of Finance* 40:4, 1031–1051.

Miller, Merton H. 1977. "Debt and Taxes." *Journal of Finance* 32:2, 261–275.

Modigliani, Franco, and Merton H. Miller. 1963. "Corporate Income Taxes and the Cost of Capital: A Correction." *American Economic Review* 64:6, 433–443.

Morck, Randall, Andrei Shleifer, and Robert W. Vishny. 1990. "Do Managerial Objectives Drive Bad Acquisitions?" *Journal of Finance* 45:1, 31–48.

Murphy, Kevin J. 1985. "Corporate Performance and Managerial Remuneration: An Empirical Analysis." *Journal of Accounting and Economics* 7:1–3, 11–42.

Myers, Stewart C. 1977. "Determinants of Corporate Borrowing." *Journal of Financial Economics* 5:2, 147–175.

Myers, Stewart C., and Nicholas S. Majluf. 1984. "Corporate Financing and Investment Decisions When Firms Have Information That Investors Do Not Have." *Journal of Financial Economics* 13:2, 187–221.

Nanda, Vikram. 1991. "On the Good News in Equity Carve-outs." *Journal of Finance* 46:5, 1717–1737.

Ongena, Steven, Viorel Roscovan, and Bas J. M. Werker. 2007. "Banks and Bonds: The Impact of Bank Loan Announcements on Bond and Equity Prices." Working Paper, Tilburg University.

Parrino, Robert. 1997. "Spinoffs and Wealth Transfers: The Marriott Case." *Journal of Financial Economics* 43:2, 241–274.

Rajan, Raghuram G. 1992. "Insiders and Outsiders: The Choice between Informed and Arm's Length Debt." *Journal of Finance* 47:4, 1367–1400.

Rajan, Raghuram G., Henri Servaes, and Luigi Zingales. 2000. "The Cost of Diversity: The Diversification Discount and Inefficient Investment." *Journal of Finance* 55:1, 35–80.

Renneboog, Luc, Tomas Simons, and Mike Wright. 2007. "Why Do Public Firms Go Private in the UK? The Impact of Private Equity Investors, Incentive Realignment and Undervaluation." *Journal of Corporate Finance* 13:4, 591–628.

Renneboog, Luc, and Peter G. Szilagyi. 2007. "Bond Performance in Mergers and Acquisitions: The Impact and Spillover of Governance and Legal Standards." Working Paper No. 125, European Corporate Governance Institute.

Renneboog, Luc, and Peter G. Szilagyi. 2008. "Corporate Restructuring and Bondholder Wealth." *European Financial Management* 14:4, 792–819.

Robichek, Alexander A., and Stewart C. Myers. 1966. "Conceptual Problems in the Use of Risk-adjusted Discount Rates." *Journal of Finance* 21:4, 727–730.

Roll, Richard. 1986. "The Hubris Hypothesis of Corporate Takeovers." *Journal of Business* 59:2, 197–216.

Ross, Stephen A. 1977. "The Determination of Financial Structure: The Incentive-Signalling Approach." *Bell Journal of Economics* 8:1, 23–40.

Schipper, Katherine, and Abbie Smith. 1983. "Effects of Recontracting on Shareholder Wealth: The Case of Voluntary Spin-offs." *Journal of Financial Economics* 12:4, 437–467.

Stewart, G. Bennett, III, and David M. Glassman. 1988. "The Motives and Methods of Corporate Restructuring, Part II." *Journal of Applied Corporate Finance* 1:2, 79–88.

Stiglitz, Joseph E. 1985. "Credit Markets and the Control of Capital." *Journal of Money, Credit and Banking* 17:2, 133–152.

Veld, Chris, and Yulia V. Veld-Merkoulova. 2008. "An Empirical Analysis of the Stockholder-Bondholder Conflict in Corporate Spin-offs." *Financial Management* 37:1, 103–124.

Walker, M. Mark. 1991. "Leveraged Buyouts and Bondholder Wealth: The Role of Indenture Covenants." *Akron Business and Economic Review* 22:4, 121–131.

Walker, M. Mark. 1994. "Determinants of Bondholder Wealth Following Corporate Takeovers (1980-1988)." *Quarterly Journal of Business and Economics* 33:1, 12–29.

Warga, Arthur, and Ivo Welch. 1993. "Bondholder Losses in Leveraged Buyouts." *Review of Financial Studies* 6:4, 959–982.

Warner, Jerold B. 1977. "Bankruptcy Costs: Some Evidence." *Journal of Finance* 32:2, 337–347.

Welch, Ivo. 1989. "Seasoned Offerings, Imitation Costs and the Underpricing of Initial Public Offerings." *Journal of Finance* 44:2, 429–449.

Woolridge, J. Randall. 1983. "Dividend Changes and Security Prices." *Journal of Finance* 38:5, 1607–1615.

ABOUT THE AUTHORS

Luc Renneboog is Professor of Corporate Finance at Tilburg University and a research fellow at CentER and the European Corporate Governance Institute (ECGI,

Brussels). He graduated from the Catholic University of Leuven with degrees in management engineering (MSc) and philosophy (BA), the University of Chicago with an MBA, and the London Business School with a PhD in financial economics. He held appointments at the University of Leuven and Oxford University and visiting appointments at the London Business School and HEC (Paris). He has been published in the *Journal of Finance, American Economic Review, Journal of Financial Intermediation, Journal of Law and Economics, Strategic Management Journal, Journal of Corporate Finance*, and *Journal of Banking and Finance*, among others. He has co-authored and edited several books on corporate governance, dividend policy, and venture capital. His research interests are corporate finance, corporate governance, takeovers, dividend policy, insider trading, law and economics, and the economics of art.

Peter Szilagyi has been at the University of Cambridge since 2007, having completed his PhD at Tilburg University and worked as a research fellow at the University of Oxford as a member of the European Corporate Governance Training Network. His research interests include corporate finance, corporate governance, international finance, and financial market development. He has been published in finance, economics and statistics journals and co-edited a special issue of *European Financial Management* as well as volumes for Elsevier and John Wiley & Sons. Professor Szilagyi has previously worked for the BBC World Service and contributed to consulting projects for the Asian Development Bank.

CHAPTER 21

Behavioral Effects in M&As

JENS HAGENDORFF
Senior Lecturer, The University of Edinburgh

INTRODUCTION

Most studies included in this book analyze the motivation and implications of mergers and acquisitions (M&As) within a traditional finance paradigm. The critical assumption underlying this paradigm is that the behavior of economic agents is fully rational. This suggests that economic agents can impartially process complex information and that their choices are aimed at utility maximization. One consequence of this rationality assumption is that merger activity is motivated by economic reasons and should, therefore, lead to measurable postmerger performance improvements.

Some economic reasons for M&As include the acquirers' desire to realize synergetic gains, or alternatively, to increase profits via unique asset combinations or increases in market power. However, the effects of M&A performance are difficult to reconcile within this framework. Empirical evidence highlights that many mergers destroy shareholder value and fail to result in long-term performance gains in the post-M&A period (e.g., Fuller, Netter, and Stegemoller, 2002; Moeller, Schlingemann, and Stulz, 2005). This divide between the economic motivations of M&As and their realized performance effects has given rise to the so-called "merger performance puzzle." In essence, if mergers perform so poorly, why are they so popular? The neoclassical paradigm outlined above, with its strong emphasis on rational expectations and utility maximization, cannot explain why merger activity has continued to grow despite empirical evidence, which is critical of this activity, leading to benefits for shareholders and other stakeholders.

Parallel to the M&A literature, the last decade has seen increased interest in behavioral finance, which breaks with the assumptions of rationality and utility maximization. In a comprehensive survey of the behavioral finance literature, Barberis and Thaler (2003, p. 1055) argue that the standard finance framework "is appealingly simple, and it would be very satisfying if its predictions were confirmed in the data. Unfortunately, after years of effort, it has become clear that basic facts about the aggregate stock market, the cross-section of average returns and individual trading behavior are not easily understood in this framework."

Breaking with the neoclassical finance framework allows for decision-making biases of economic agents. Such biases could play an important part in explaining both the volume and the outcome of merger activity. This chapter reviews the literature bridging the divide between ex-ante merger motivations and the type of ex-post M&A results that are inconsistent with the rationality assumption. This review is by no means meant to be exhaustive. Instead, the main focus of this chapter is to highlight how behavioral assumptions behind M&A activity can explain the occurrence and performance results of M&As. The chapter distinguishes between two behavioral perspectives: the behavior of managers and the behavior of investors that are inconsistent with the rationality assumption.

First, the managerial perspective is mainly concerned with executives' personalities and how deviations from the M&A rationality assumption are likely to affect merger performance (Roll, 1986; Doukas and Petmezas, 2007; Malmendier and Tate, 2008). Essentially, this work contends that managers' overconfidence in their own abilities to bring about merger performance gains is to blame. Some could, therefore, argue that mergers can be viewed as a form of good-faith mismanagement (Paredes, 2005). Early work on cognitive managerial decision-making biases focuses on takeover pricing as an indicator of managerial hubris (Hayward and Hambrick, 1997). More recent work concentrates on the changing announcement returns along a sequence of serial acquisitions and provides support for managerial overconfidence and self-attribution bias. However, as indicated below, the results of this more recent work on managerial hubris can also be reconciled with the neoclassical paradigm and learning effects.

Second, the investor-focused perspective relaxes the assumption of investor rationality. If rational managers deal with irrational investors, mergers can be viewed as a form of arbitrage by managers in markets lacking information efficiency. For instance, temporary overvaluations of the acquiring firm's equity could prompt bidding firm managers to lock in excess value by purchasing undervalued target equity with their overvalued shares (Shleifer and Vishny, 2003). Unlike the irrational managers' perspective of M&A activity, the market timing approach to acquisitions offers a promising route to understanding merger waves in particular.

Further, agency theory has identified several frictions between managers and shareholders. These frictions could explain the underperformance of corporate control transactions, such as when executives seek pecuniary and nonpecuniary benefits from mergers, leaving shareholders exposed to underperforming M&As (Masulis, Wang, and Xie, 2007; Hagendorff, Collins, and Keasey, 2007). Executive compensation, in particular, offers routes to understanding what motivates merger activity. However, most research in the area of merger executive compensation is firmly rooted in agency theory. As such, this work is unsuitable for shedding further light on behavioral aspects in mergers. The agency-theoretic view assumes that managers may act selfishly and rationally. This perspective is in stark contrast to the utility maximizing, irrational behavior of executives who overestimate their value-extracting abilities. However, while finance has focused on agency cost explanations of executive compensation, management and sociology have advanced behavioral explanations based on wage dispersion. Therefore, existing theoretical concepts should be complemented. This will, in turn, allow for behavioral effects as seen in M&As driving executive compensation. For instance, the positive feedback from above-peer compensation could conceivably cause executive overconfidence, leading to underperforming M&As.

The intent of this chapter is not to suggest that behavioral explanations are the primary drivers behind merger activity. This would ignore the anecdotal and empirical evidence that merger gains do exist. Harford (2005), for instance, contrasts behavioral with neoclassical explanations behind M&A activity. He studies merger waves during the 1980s and 1990s, especially those responding to external shocks such as deregulation and changes in industry valuations. Similarly, Rhodes-Kropf, Robinson, and Viswanathan (2005) estimate that 15 percent of M&A activity is attributable to misevaluations. This finding highlights the continued importance of neoclassical motivations behind M&As. Overall, this chapter argues for a more balanced view of M&A explanations that also incorporates behavioral explanations to a greater extent than previously done.

The remainder of this chapter is organized as follows. The next section reviews the evidence regarding neoclassical M&A theories, which emphasizes purely economic reasons for merger activity. The following section allows for behavioral effects in M&As by relaxing the managerial rationality assumption and the investor rationality assumption. Corporate governance research is delineated from M&A behavioral explanations. The chapter notes that executive compensation offers a promising route to linking a governance mechanism to behavioral effects in the market for corporate control. The final section offers a summary and conclusions.

NEOCLASSICAL EXPLANATIONS FOR M&AS

Neoclassical theories emphasize that economic, technological, and regulatory shocks to an industry environment generate merger activity. In response to these shocks, firms both inside and outside a particular industry typically embark on an asset reallocation process through M&As. As firms simultaneously react to identical shocks and compete for the most suitable asset reallocations, merger activity clusters in time, leading to merger waves. Coase (1937) is one of the earliest to establish an economic rationale for merger activity by linking acquisitions to technological change. Shleifer and Vishny (1992) argue that merger activity is clustered in economic booms because economic growth increases firm cash flows and reduces asset buyers' financial constraints. This also increases asset prices close to their fair value. More recently, Harford (2005) analyzes the prewave industry characteristics and notes that merger waves tend to be preceded by external shocks. Such shocks primarily take the form of firm valuation changes and periods of industry deregulation.

Work in corporate law theory has a slightly different view of the reasons behind acquisitions. While this detours slightly from the purely economic arguments, a large body of law and economics literature exists that analyzes M&As within the institutional context in which this activity occurs. Corporate law theory posits that the degree to which capital market investors are legally protected determines the volume of merger activity. In their seminal work on law and finance, La Porta, Lopez-De-Silanes, Shleifer, and Vishny (2000) show that when insiders (i.e. managers) protect outside investors from expropriation, this is associated with various market-based institutions such as high-volume stock markets and active markets for corporate control.

However, some recent studies question the applicability of corporate law theory as a way of explaining differences in institutional development. For example, Rajan and Zingales (2003) show that stock market capitalizations at the beginning of the twentieth century were higher in Germany and France than in the

United States. This is surprising because the overall institutional framework has changed little compared with that of today. Consequently, the legal and regulatory framework in the United States would have favored a market-based system at the beginning of the twentieth century in the way that it favors such a system today. In the same vein, Dyck and Zingales (2004) show that the private benefits of control (a measure of contracting costs between managers and shareholders) vary across countries with very similar corporate disclosure and transparency regulations. Based on this work, Roe (2003) argues that the growth of institutions, such as an active market for corporate control, is not caused by laws and regulations but by social consensus and political will. Roe stresses, for example, that while many countries have in place legislation that prohibits insider trading surrounding merger announcements and other corporate events, few countries are willing to enforce this legislation. Consequently, the laws and regulations that protect and encourage both widespread equity ownership and active asset restructuring do not provide sufficient conditions for greater M&A activity.

Despite questions about the causes of M&A activity, strong correlations exist between the legal protection of minority investors and M&A activity. This leads to the widely accepted view that the overall institutional context is one reason that mergers occur. The work summarized at the beginning of this section clearly links merger activity to economic rationales. However, while the relevance of economic reasons for some mergers is undisputed, the underlying theoretical implications cannot always be reconciled with ex-post merger results. The widespread evidence of underperforming deals sits uneasily with the notion of managers as utility maximizers in efficient markets. The next section relaxes this assumption.

BEHAVIORAL EXPLANATIONS FOR M&AS

At the heart of M&A behavioral explanations is the determination to replace the view that stakeholders in the merger process act rationally in a frictionless environment with more realistic behavioral assumptions. Echoing the general behavioral finance literature (Baker, Ruback, and Wurgler, 2007), the possibility exists of differentiating between studies that focus on irrational managerial behavior and irrational investor behavior. The discussion below is grouped around these two approaches of irrational managers and irrational investors.

Irrational Managers

Warren Buffett (1981, p. 2) states his view on what motivates merger activity:

> [M]any managements apparently were overexposed in impressionable childhood years to the story in which the imprisoned handsome prince is released from a toad's body by a kiss from a beautiful princess. Consequently, they are certain their managerial kiss will do wonders for ... profitability .... We've observed many kisses but very few miracles. Nevertheless, many managerial princesses remain serenely confident about the future potency of their kisses—even after their corporate backyards are knee-deep in unresponsive toads.

Buffett's comments are consistent with what is known as the hubris hypothesis of takeover activity, which is perhaps the most widely known M&A behavioral explanation. Roll (1986), who developed the hubris hypothesis, proposes that executives overestimate their own ability to identify and realize potential gains from a merger. As a result, acquiring firm managers have a habit of overvaluing the equity of the target firm. Overconfident managers are likely to believe that their ability will enhance the value of either the target company or the current company and will, hence, overpay for targets (Malmendier and Tate, 2008). Consequently, disappointing firm performance in the postmerger period is the result of unrealistic expectations on the part of the bidding firm's executives.

The key assumption underlying M&A behavioral explanations is that executives do not deliberately jeopardize shareholder value through acquisition activities. Instead, overconfident executives, convinced of the positive effects of their actions, suffer from cognitive bias. Hence, executive hubris may lead to good-faith mismanagement in mergers, but this by no means rules out that all chief executive officers (CEOs) are well intentioned and work hard to achieve a positive merger outcome.

Empirical tests of the hubris hypothesis can be classified into two groups. The first group analyzes the main implication of Roll's (1986) work that overconfident managers overpay for acquisitions. A second and more recent stream of research looks at other testable and more indirect implications of managerial hubris in the market for corporate control. Both strands of the literature are discussed below.

First, in literature based directly on the hubris hypothesis, overconfidence is displayed by overbidding. Hayward and Hambrick (1997) study the acquisition premiums paid in large U.S. deals. The authors view premiums as a statement representing the gains that CEOs expect to extract from a deal and, thus, serving as indicators of managerial overconfidence or manager hubris. Hayward and Hambrick show that three indicators of hubris increase acquisition premiums: superior corporate performance, higher executive compensation (relative to the next highest paid executive), and praise for the CEO from the financial press. Regarding press coverage, the authors find that for every media article portraying the CEO in a positive light, the premiums paid in acquisitions increase by nearly 5 percent. To counter the argument that higher CEO pay and premiums are reflective of greater CEO talent and expected gains from acquisitions, Hayward and Hambrick also show that higher premiums lead to underperforming deals. Hence, the overall results show that hubris causes overinvestment in the market for corporate control and has negative consequences on performance.

Second, more recent work does not use takeover pricing to detect hubris but instead examines the implications of hubris on managerial behavior during the merger process. For instance, a commonly accepted fact in merger research is that the acquirer announcement returns are positive for the first deal and decline with subsequent deals (e.g., Fuller et al., 2002). The M&A behavioral literature views declining merger returns for serial acquirers as evidence of growing CEO hubris across the sequence of deals. Among others, Doukas and Petmezas (2007) argue that overconfidence in the market for corporate control can be self-sustaining over time. The authors demonstrate CEO overconfidence by using the number of acquisitions completed within a short time period. Doukas and Petmezas contend that multiple acquirers suffer from cognitive bias and inflated beliefs in their own skills. When initial acquisitions produce performance gains, managerial overconfidence turns into self-attribution bias because managers end up believing that their ability to identify superior targets and manage the post–M&A integration process are the main reasons for the initial success. Self-attribution bias, a by-product of initial success in the market for corporate control, then causes managers to engage in a string of subsequent deals with negative performance implications.

Consistent with the view that hubristic CEO mismanagement is conducted in good faith, Doukas and Petmezas (2007) show that overconfident managers (i.e., managers engaged in multiple acquisitions) double their ownership stake in the acquiring firm vis-à-vis managers engaged in a single acquisition. Hence, overconfident CEOs hurt their own financial interests, which is a salient indication of how trusting they are in their own abilities. Malmendier and Tate (2008) introduce a slightly different measure of overconfidence by examining acquiring managers who bet on their own positively biased perception. The authors proxy CEO overconfidence using CEO tolerance of voluntary exposure to firm-specific risk via their firm's option holdings. Specifically, Malmendier and Tate calculate the amount of exercisable in-the-money options that CEOs hold on their firm's equity. Similar to Doukas and Petmezas, Malmendier and Tate show that overconfident CEOs hurt their own acquisition-based financial interests as well as shareholder interests.

Aktas, de Bodt, and Roll (2009) argue that declining acquirer announcement returns across a sequence of mergers for serial acquirers is insufficient to back M&A behavioral explanations. The authors contend that rational and risk-averse CEOs who learn from previous investor reactions will also pay higher takeover premiums in an effort to complete deals quickly. As target shareholders' acquisition gains increase with subsequent deals, bidding firm announcement returns become increasingly negative for each subsequent deal. In other words, the further down a deal is situated along the merger wave, the lower the returns for bidding firm shareholders. This is a result of concessions made to target firm shareholders. Consequently, decreasing merger announcement returns do not necessarily point to behavioral explanations behind M&As but could equally be consistent with economic M&A motivations.

One reason more recent research proffers findings that are consistent with hubris as well as economic rationales for M&As is that studies have increasingly moved away from the core of the argument. Originally proposed by Roll (1986), this core revolves around target valuations. As such, future research should compare the bidding firm shareholders' realized losses with the target shareholders' value gains. If the synergetic gains from deals are low or nonexistent and hubris acts as a driver of the merger decisions, the target shareholders' gains should be more than offset by the bidders' losses on a value-weighted basis. This is because bidding firms tend to be larger than targets, so the relatively small losses that bidding firm shareholders realize are more likely to be larger than the smaller target firms' losses.

Irrational Investors

The discussion above provides some M&A behavioral explanations that can reconcile ex-ante motivations with their observable ex-post results. This is done by relaxing the neoclassical assumption of rational managers. As discussed above, when allowing managers to act irrationally, initially puzzling empirical relationships in the market for corporate control can be explained by managerial overconfidence.

Nonetheless, some empirical observations in the takeover market still cannot be reconciled with the biased manager's or rational investor's view of the world. There are two examples of this. First, overconfidence cannot explain merger waves. Assuming that a large number of executives do not simultaneously suffer from hubris, the overconfidence literature cannot explain why merger waves exist. Second, the mode of finance in acquisitions has measurable performance implications. For example, Loughran and Vijh (1997) show that bidding firms engaged in stock-financed acquisitions substantially underperform when compared to firms engaged in cash-financed acquisitions. The authors show that firms completing stock mergers earn 25 percent less returns over the five years following the merger, while firms completing cash acquisitions earn 60 percent excess returns. Rau and Vermaelen (1998) and Rhodes-Kropf et al. (2005) report similar results after controlling for firm size and market-to-book values. Since behavioral explanations cannot explain this, one has to relax the assumption of efficient markets (and consequently, the assumption that investor behavior is fully rational) and allow for the possibility that investors may be biased.

When investors are biased, this can thwart arbitrage in capital markets and cause security prices to deviate from their fundamental values over sustained periods. The biased investor approach in behavioral finance underpins various well-known stock market anomalies such as the January effect, the post–earnings announcement drift, and momentum trading (for an overview, see Baker et al., 2007). Regarding the application of this M&A approach, market timing has been one of the central theoretical advances. Nelson (1959) first advanced the notion that variations in company valuations over time could drive merger waves. Nelson (as cited in Shleifer and Vishny, 2003, p. 297) states, "[I]t appears that merger expansion was not only a phenomenon of prosperity, but that it was also closely related to the state of the capital market. Two reference cycle expansions, unaccompanied by a strong upswing in stock prices, were marked by the absence of a merger revival." Consistent with this notion, Jovanovic and Rousseau (2001) show that periods of high valuations since the 1980s are correlated with increased merger activity. Baker, Foley, and Wurgler (2004) find that the volume of cross-border acquisitions increases with the acquirer's stock market valuation.

Shleifer and Vishny (2003) present a model of market timing and M&As. They argue that management's perception of a company's valuation drives acquisitions. If managers believe their firm is overvalued, they will seek to preserve some of the excess value for shareholders by purchasing relatively undervalued equity with overvalued stock. Thus, Shleifer and Vishny's model advances a behavioral rationale for both the occurrence of M&As (i.e., to capitalize on temporary equity overvaluations or undervaluations), as well as the payment mode in acquisitions (i.e., equity for overvalued bidders). In essence, the model describes managers as acting rationally when they identify inefficiencies in asset prices and act to capitalize on these inefficiencies. As Shleifer and Vishny (p. 296) note, "[M]ergers are a form of arbitrage by rational managers acting in irrational markets."

Rhodes-Kropf et al. (2005) offer empirical support to many of the predictions made in Shleifer and Vishny's (2003) model. The authors show that high value-to-book firms purchase low-valuation firms. Also, they estimate fundamentally based sector-level and firm-level valuations and compare these against actual valuations to gauge the extent to which acquiring firms are incorrectly valued. The results show that 60 percent of the market-to-book value of bidder valuations is due to firm-specific error, while almost none of the target's valuation is due to firm-specific error. Thus, managers engaging in market timing help to explain why merger activity may occur in clusters as well as why cash-financed deals (which are not financed by the overvalued equity of the acquirer) outperform stock-financed deals.

Recently, Bouwman, Fuller, and Nain (2009) compared merger wave deals with deals that are not completed in booming acquisition markets. They find evidence showing that high-valuation markets produce higher announcement returns than deals announced in low-valuation markets. However, after a two-year period following the announcement, the higher performance finding reverses. Overall, when examined against long-term returns, mergers announced during high-valuation periods (i.e., boom periods) produce smaller long-term gains than those deals announced during low-valuation periods. The authors, therefore, contend that boom period deals produce lower synergies and are of lower quality. Interestingly, firms that enter into M&As toward the end of a merger wave drive the long-term underperformance of boom period deals. This implies management herding behavior resulting in late-movers performing particularly poorly.

While herding is indicative of irrational behavior, it can still be reconciled with the rationality assumption for management. For instance, Persons and Warther (1997) develop a model in which the value of an innovation is uncertain ex ante and can only be determined ex post once the impact on the profitability of the adopting firm has been established. The model, which can be applied to merger waves, suggests that the positive experience of early adopters encourages wider adoption. The merger wave ends when the ex-post experience of recent adopters is sufficiently poor, deterring remaining firms from adoption ex-ante. Thus, merger waves and the underperformance of late-movers into a wave are consistent with the rational behavior of management and not with late-movers making the wrong decision.

In sum, rational managers can be distinguished from irrational investors in order to arrive at behavioral explanations of M&A activity. Theoretical works differentiate between behavioral explanations that allow for irrational behavior on either the part of management or, alternatively, of investors but, critically, not on both. However, the reality is that once acknowledging the presence of irrationality in merger-related decision making, there is no reason to presume that such behavior will be restricted to a single party in the merger transaction.

CORPORATE GOVERNANCE AND BEHAVIORAL EFFECTS IN M&AS

The corporate governance literature attempts to explain persistent findings of underperformance in the merger literature with reference to agency theory. Mergers offer personal gains to managers. Mergers offer private benefits to bidding firm managers (Dyck and Zingales, 2004) as well as increases in CEO prestige and executive remuneration (Bliss and Rosen, 2001). For instance, Masulis et al. (2007), for a general industry sample, and Anderson, Becher, and Campbell (2004), for a sample of banking firms, show that when external CEO monitoring is weak, mergers are value destroying.

The two subsections below make a distinction between two explanations behind M&As: agency-theoretic and CEO compensation. The latter offers a promising route to examine the behavioral consequences of CEO pay in the market for corporate control.

Agency Theory and M&As

In his free cash flow hypothesis, Jensen (1986) puts forth one of the most widely accepted agency-theoretic explanations of M&A activity. He contends that managers accumulate excess cash in order to avoid the type of monitoring by external capital providers that would result if they had to raise funds externally. Therefore, managers who build up cash reserves engage in wasteful acquisitions strategies. Harford (1999) and others confirm the theoretical arguments originally advanced by Jensen and show that cash-rich acquirers engage in value-destroying acquisitions and are more prone to empire building.

While maintaining that corporate governance arrangements affect managerial behavior sounds plausible, the arguments put forward by agency-theoretic explanations of M&As are very different from the type of behavioral work discussed in the sections above. The main difference is that agency theory relies on the presence of managerial moral hazard (or opportunism). This is different from the assumption that inflated takeover valuations and underperforming deals are by-products of hubris. In other words, agency theory views managers as opportunistic, while the behavioral school believes that managers engage in good-faith mismanagement. Although the theoretical distinction between the two concepts is relatively straightforward, there are no attempts so far in the empirical literature to examine the implications of this distinction.

For instance, a worthwhile endeavor would be to examine if Jensen's (1986) free cash flow argument is part of a conscious strategy by managers (and thus, indicative of agency conflict) or not, in which case, behavioral or other explanations could be applied instead. A simple way to examine this question is to analyze if CEOs systematically build up cash reserves in the years before an acquisition. One way to achieve this is to examine the payout policy during the premerger years and relate this to the mode of acquisition finance chosen by the CEO. If CEOs withhold dividend payments and hoard premerger cash before engaging in value-destroying acquisitions financed by free cash flows, this is consistent with agency explanations of M&A activities. If not, then behavioral or other explanations may be linked to free cash flows in acquisitions. While most agency-theoretic perspectives on merger activity cannot be reconciled with M&A behavioral explanations, executive compensation could be an exception.

Executive Compensation and Behavioralism

The role of executive remuneration in the market for corporate control is somewhat ambivalent. On the one hand, firm size is the most reliable determinant of CEO compensation (for an extensive overview, see Murphy, 1999). If pay is sensitive to firm size but greatly insensitive to firm performance, managers are incentivized to engage more in growth-enhancing acquisitions than in value-enhancing ones. On the other hand, compensation could play an important role in curbing managerial opportunism and aligning managerial interests with those of the shareholders. Bliss and Rosen (2001) show that bank CEOs with performance-based compensation are less likely to engage in acquisitions. Datta, Iskandar-Datta, and Raman (2001) investigate whether CEOs should engage in acquisitions and find that larger shares of performance-based compensation lead to higher announcement returns.

However, some recent studies suggest that existing remuneration practices are ill-equipped to align the interests of shareholders with managers and may even motivate CEOs to engage in mergers. The rationale behind this argument is as follows. If executive pay is more sensitive to firm size than to firm performance, CEO wealth losses stemming from value-destroying M&A strategies will not deter CEOs from engaging in such activities. Since acquisitions are one of the most salient ways to increase firm size, CEO wealth losses from M&As may be outweighed by CEO compensation increases in the postmerger pay, resulting from merger-induced growth in the firm's assets (Harford and Li, 2007).

Some contend that executive compensation may be viewed as a corporate governance instrument. Such a view relies on the assumption that managers suffer from moral hazard. Also, compensation issues can be used to explain this type of good-faith mismanagement, which gives rise to behavioral explanations such as overconfidence. Essentially, the argument is that excessive compensation may breed managerial overconfidence. Stressing the behavioral consequences of CEO pay on overconfidence offers a behavioral approach, which can explain why managers overinvest in the market for corporate control.

Managers who rise to the top of an organizational hierarchy can be seen as the winners of a series of labor market tournaments (Lazear and Rosen, 1981). Tournament winners take the prize of higher compensation, which they receive irrespective of whether their advancement in the corporate hierarchy is due to skill, luck, or a combination of both. In fact, the proponents of tournament theory argue that the purpose of a rank order payment scheme is to avoid the difficulties associated with observing performance and linking performance with pay. Therefore, tournament prizes (i.e., pay raises) are fixed in advance and largely unrelated to job performance. The important point is that job candidates may not necessarily view pay raises as unrelated to performance. CEO candidates in particular, who have a history of winning tournaments, are likely to attribute this and the associated pay raises to their self-perceived superior decision-making skills. For instance, Paredes (2005, p. 717) quotes Tyco CEO Dennis Kozlowski as saying in 1997, "If it's a system that's truly gauged toward incentivization or success for shareholders, compensation is your scorecard. It's a way of keeping score at what you're doing."

If higher CEO pay packages provide positive feedback to CEOs and signal to them that they are successful, higher pay is likely to boost confidence. Another reasonable assumption is that the most highly paid CEOs in an industry suffer from the greatest inflation of self-worth. Next to absolute levels of pay, the dispersion of pay across the industry is likely to breed managerial overconfidence. Hayward and Hambrick (1997) find evidence backing the view that a greater pay gap between CEOs and the next highest paid officer increase acquisition premiums. Higher pay, therefore, equates to overinvestment in the market for corporate control.

Similarly, Bebchuk, Cremers, and Peyer (2007), who refer to the share of a firm's aggregate top-five executives' compensation attributable to the CEO as "CEO centrality," find that higher paid CEOs are more likely to engage in value-destroying acquisitions. The authors report that an increase of one standard deviation in CEO centrality leads to an average bidding firm value loss of $18 million during the announcement period. While Bebchuk et al. interpret their results in the context of agency theory (more powerful CEOs are less likely to be disciplined by the board), their findings could also be explained using behavioral explanations regarding the role of pay in M&As. Thus, more powerful CEOs could be seen as suffering from cognitive bias, which increases the likelihood of engaging in well-intentioned but value-destroying acquisition activity.

SUMMARY AND CONCLUSIONS

This chapter offers a survey of the main developments in the literature that analyze the motivations and performance effects of deals driven by economic agents whose behavior is not consistent with the rationality assumption that underlies the neoclassical view of M&As. Anecdotal and empirical evidence points to the continued relevance of neoclassical motivations behind M&As, for instance, when technological change or deregulation brings about merger waves. Yet, the literature's persistent findings, which report postmerger underperformance, point to explanations that are inconsistent with the rationality assumption.

Depending on which group of economic agents is acting irrationally, the possibility exists to distinguish between two types of studies in the behavioral literature. First, if managers act irrationally, executive hubris and self-attribution bias can motivate M&As. Under this assumption, overconfident managers engage in good-faith mismanagement. Cognitive biases, such as inflated self-belief, lead managers to overvalue the NPV of acquisition gains and, hence, to systematically overpay for acquisition targets. Second, if managers are rational but deal in inefficient markets, they may exploit temporary misevaluations in equity prices. If their firm's equity is overvalued, managers may opt to purchase undervalued firms and thus lock in excess value for shareholders.

Considerable scope for growth exists in the behavioral literature and its applications in the market for corporate control. As discussed, a common finding in the literature is that indicators of CEO hubris are positively correlated with takeover pricing. While this confirms the intuition behind Roll's (1986) hubris hypothesis, more recent work links managerial acquisition behavior to what these studies view as hubris implications (e.g., if managers engage in serial acquisitions or voluntarily seek risk exposure to their firm). However, the issue with this work is that much of it disengages with Roll's original argument, which refers to takeover valuation–based hubris. Therefore, many of the conclusions proffered by this more recent work can also be explained with reference to nonbehavioral work where rational managers act on economic motivations. Therefore, future research should do more to understand what motivates managerial behavior in the market for corporate control.

Further, future research in this area should try to understand the behavioral processes underlying the choices of executives. For instance, free cash flows are commonly associated with underperforming deals as managers seek to avoid the type of market scrutiny that is associated when executives have to raise external funds to finance takeovers. However, to date, researchers have not examined the issue of whether executives deliberately accumulate cash reserves over time. A worthwhile project is to examine if executives hoard cash through low dividend payout ratios in the years preceding a deal. Thus, more clearly delineating behavioral aspects about mergers from agency theory is particularly important.

Besides the two standard approaches to M&A behavioral effects (irrational managers–rational investors and rational managers–irrational investors), other sociological approaches link pay dispersion to acquisition activity behavioral effects. Issues relating to executive compensation are largely rooted in agency theory in which theoretic foundations are based on moral hazard caused by opportunistic, rational managers. However, compensation issues can also be interpreted in a behavioral context. Future research should try to better understand the ways in which executive compensation gives rise to irrational CEO behavior. Overly generous pay packages can breed executive hubris and increase the probability that CEOs, who are certain of their superior decision-making skills, engage in a series of value-destroying acquisitions.

In sum, behavioral effects can help explain why M&A activity occurs, along with some of its negative performance implications. This is not to say that mergers do not also occur for economic reasons. However, relaxing some of the rigid assumptions underlying the neoclassical view of mergers, specifically the rationality assumption, gives rise to other realistic assumptions about M&A activity. The existing behavioral literature can be used in many ways to complement neoclassical work on M&As as well as to lead to new theory development by combining behavioral aspects and agency theory.

DISCUSSION QUESTIONS

1. Describe the implications of neoclassical merger theory for the motivations and performance implications of M&As.
2. How do neoclassical and behavioral theories explain merger waves?
3. Why do cash-financed mergers typically outperform stock-financed deals?
4. How can agency theory be linked to behavioral aspects in M&As?

REFERENCES

Aktas, Nihat, Eric de Bodt, and Richard Roll. 2009. "Learning, Hubris and Corporate Serial Acquisitions." *Journal of Corporate Finance* 15:5, 543–561.

Anderson, Christopher W., David A. Becher, and Terry L. Campbell II. 2004. "Bank Mergers, the Market for Bank CEOs, and Managerial Incentives." *Journal of Financial Intermediation* 13:1, 6–27.

Baker, Malcolm, C, Fritz Foley, and Jeffrey Wurgler. 2004. "The Stock Market and Investment: Evidence from FDI Flows." NBER Working Paper No. 10559.

Baker, Malcolm P., Richard S. Ruback, and Jeffrey Wurgler. 2007. "Behavioral Corporate Finance: A Survey." In Espen Eckbo, ed. *Handbook of Corporate Finance: Empirical Corporate Finance*, 149–188. Amsterdam: Elsevier.

Barberis, Nicholas, and Richard H. Thaler. 2003. "A Survey of Behavioral Finance." In George Constantinides, Milton Harris and René Stulz, eds. *Handbook of the Economics of Finance*, 1053–1121. Amsterdam: Elsevier/North-Holland.

Bebchuk, Lucian A., Martijn Cremers, and Urs Peyer. 2007. "CEO Centrality." NBER Working Paper No. 13701.

Bliss, Richard T., and Richard J. Rosen. 2001. "CEO Compensation and Bank Mergers." *Journal of Financial Economics* 61:1, 107–138.

Bouwman, Christa H. S., Kathleen Fuller, and Amrita S. Nain. 2009. "Market Valuation and Acquisition Quality: Empirical Evidence." *Review of Financial Studies* 22:2, 633–679.

Buffett, Warren. 1981. "Letter to Shareholders of Berkshire Hathaway Inc." *Berkshire Hathaway Annual Report.*

Coase, Ronald. 1937. "The Nature of the Firm." *Economica* 4:16, 386–405.

Datta, Sudip, Mai Iskandar-Datta, and Kartik Raman. 2001. "Executive Compensation and Corporate Acquisition Decisions." *Journal of Finance* 56:6, 2299–2336.

Doukas, John A., and Dimitris Petmezas. 2007. "Acquisitions, Overconfident Managers and Self-Attribution Bias." *European Financial Management* 13:3, 531–577.

Dyck, Alexander, and Luigi Zingales. 2004. "Private Benefits of Control: An International Comparison." *Journal of Finance* 59:2, 537–600.

Fuller, Kathleen, Jeffry Netter, and Mike Stegemoller. 2002. "What Do Returns to Acquiring Firms Tell Us? Evidence from Firms That Make Many Acquisitions." *Journal of Finance,* 57:4, 1763–1793.

Hagendorff, Jens, Michael Collins, and Kevin Keasey. 2007. "Bank Governance and Acquisition Performance." *Corporate Governance: An International Review* 15:5, 957–968.

Harford, Jarrad. 1999. "Corporate Cash Reserves and Acquisitions." *Journal of Finance,* 54:6, 1969–1997.

Harford, Jarrad. 2005. "What Drives Merger Waves?" *Journal of Financial Economics* 77:3, 529–560.

Harford, Jarrad, and Kai Li. 2007. "Decoupling CEO Wealth and Firm Performance: The Case of Acquiring CEOs." *Journal of Finance* 62:2, 917–949.

Hayward, Mathew L. A., and Donald C. Hambrick. 1997. "Explaining the Premium Paid for Large Acquisitions: Evidence of CEO Hubris." *Administrative Science Quarterly* 42:1, 103–127.

Jensen, Michael C. 1986. "Agency Costs of Free Cash Flow, Corporate Finance, and Takeovers." *American Economic Review* 76:2, 323–329.

Jovanovic, Boyan, and Peter L. Rousseau. 2001. "Mergers and Technological Change: 1885-1998." Working Paper, Vanderbilt University.

La Porta, Rafael, Florencio Lopez-De-Silanes, Andrei Shleifer, and Robert Vishny. 2000. "Investor Protection and Corporate Governance." *Journal of Financial Economics* 58:1–2, 3–27.

Lazear, Edward P., and Sherwin Rosen. 1981. "Rank-Order Tournaments as Optimum Labor Contracts." *Journal of Political Economy* 89:5, 841–864.

Loughran, Tim, and Anand M. Vijh. 1997. "Do Long-Term Shareholders Benefit from Corporate Acquisitions?" *Journal of Finance* 52:5, 1765–1790.

Malmendier, Ulrike, and Geoffrey Tate. 2008. "Who Makes Acquisitions? CEO Overconfidence and the Market's Reaction." *Journal of Financial Economics* 89:1, 20–43.

Masulis, Ronald W., Cong Wang, and Fei Xie. 2007. "Corporate Governance and Acquirer Returns." *Journal of Finance* 62:4, 1851–1889.

Moeller, Sara B., Frederik P. Schlingemann, and René M. Stulz. 2005. "Wealth Destruction on a Massive Scale? A Study of Acquiring-Firm Returns in the Recent Merger Wave." *Journal of Finance* 60:2, 757–782.

Murphy, Kevin J. 1999. "Executive Compensation." In Orley Ashenfelder and David Card, eds. *Handbook of Labor Economics*, Volume 3, 2485–2563. Amsterdam: Elsevier.

Nelson, Ralph. 1959. *Merger Movements in American Industry, 1895–1956.* Washington, DC: National Bureau of Economic Research.

Paredes, Troy. 2005. "Too Much Pay, Too Much Deference: Behavioral Corporate Finance, CEOs, and Corporate Governance." *Florida State University Law Review* 32:2, 673–762.

Persons, John C., and Vincent A. Warther. 1997. "Boom and Bust Patterns in the Adoption of Financial Innovations." *Review of Financial Studies* 10:4, 939–967.

Rajan, Raghuram G., and Luigi Zingales. 2003. "The Great Reversals: The Politics of Financial Development in the Twentieth Century." *Journal of Financial Economics* 69:1, 5–50.

Rau, P. Raghavendra, and Theo Vermaelen. 1998. "Glamour, Value and the Post-Acquisition Performance of Acquiring Firms." *Journal of Financial Economics* 49:2, 223–253.

Rhodes-Kropf, Matthew, David T. Robinson, and S. Viswanathan. 2005. "Valuation Waves and Merger Activity: The Empirical Evidence." *Journal of Financial Economics* 77:3, 561–603.

Roe, Mark J. 2003. *Political Determinants of Corporate Governance: Political Context, Corporate Impact*. Oxford: Oxford University Press.

Roll, Richard. 1986. "The Hubris Hypothesis of Corporate Takeovers." *Journal of Business* 59:2, 197–216.

Shleifer, Andrei, and Robert W. Vishny. 1992. "Liquidation Values and Debt Capacity: A Market Equilibrium Approach." *Journal of Finance* 47:4, 1343–1366.

Shleifer, Andrei, and Robert W. Vishny. 2003. "Stock Market Driven Acquisitions." *Journal of Financial Economics* 70:3, 295–311.

ABOUT THE AUTHOR

Jens Hagendorff has been a senior lecturer in banking and finance at the University of Edinburgh since 2010. Before that, he was an economist at the Regulation Department of the Spanish central bank (Banco de España) and a lecturer in accounting and finance at the University of Leeds, United Kingdom. He teaches a range of subjects in finance, banking, and accounting including executive and MBA programs. His work concentrates on corporate governance and regulation in M&As, especially in the financial services industry. Professor Hagendorff's work examines the motivations behind M&As and the risk implications of merger strategies in Europe and the United States. His recent work on M&As has appeared in journals such as the *Journal of Banking & Finance* and *Corporate Governance: An International Review*.

PART V

Recapitalization and Restructuring

CHAPTER 22

Financial Restructuring

OTGONTSETSEG ERHEMJAMTS
Assistant Professor of Finance, Bentley University

KARTIK RAMAN
Associate Professor of Finance, Bentley University

INTRODUCTION

Beginning with the pioneering work of Modigliani and Miller (1958), capital structure theories emerged by relaxing the assumptions of efficient capital markets as well as perfect market assumptions, especially taxes, bankruptcy costs, asymmetric information, and transaction costs (e.g., Kraus and Litzenberger, 1973; DeAngelo and Masulis, 1980; Myers and Majluf, 1984; Fischer, Heinkel, and Zechner, 1989; Leland, 1994, 1998). Another set of capital structure theories developed by Jensen and Meckling (1976), Myers (1977), and Jensen (1986) emphasizes the contracting role of debt in influencing corporate policies through the effects on managerial incentives. Still another set of theories, influenced by the work of Ritter (1991), drops the assumption of market efficiency and advances hypotheses based on windows of opportunity and inertia. In particular, Baker and Wurgler (2002) and Welch (2004) argue that the costs of issuing debt and equity vary over time due to market inefficiencies and thus create potential opportunities for firms to benefit by timing external financing decisions.

Recognizing that various factors influence firms to dynamically rebalance their capital structures over time, recent empirical studies examine the speed at which firms adjust toward their target leverage, ultimately offering mixed evidence. For instance, while some studies note that firms' debt ratios adjust slowly toward their targets (e.g., Fama and French, 2002), others find that the equity issuance effect on leverage completely vanishes within two to four years, suggesting a relatively faster adjustment toward target leverage (e.g., Leary and Roberts, 2005; Alti, 2006; Flannery and Rangan, 2006).

Given that financial restructuring activities undoubtedly influence the speed and extent to which firms approach their target capital structures, this chapter discusses theory and evidence on important vehicles for financial restructuring. The chapter has the following organization. The next section begins with a discussion of share repurchases followed by separate sections on dual-class recapitalizations, exchange offers and swaps, and debt restructurings via private workouts and formal bankruptcy. The final section offers a summary and conclusions.

SHARE REPURCHASES

On average, the prices of firms that announce a share repurchase program increase significantly both in the short run (Dann, 1981; Vermaelen, 1981) and in the long run (Ikenberry, Lakonishok, and Vermaelen, 1995; Peyer and Vermaelen, 2009). Types of share repurchase programs include open-market share repurchases, fixed price tender offers, and Dutch auction tender offers.

In the open-market share repurchase program, a firm usually announces its intent to repurchase a specified number or percentage of its shares over an unspecified period of time in the open market. In a conventional fixed-price tender offer, a firm announces the number of shares it seeks, the conditions under which it may buy more or less, and the price it will pay. In a Dutch auction tender offer, investors set the tender price. The firm states the number of shares it will buy during a specified period and sets a price range between which the firm will accept shareholder bids. Upon expiration, the firm determines the lowest price enabling it to acquire the announced number of shares from stockholders' bids and pays all bids at and below that clearing price.

The relative popularity of the types of share repurchase programs has shifted over time. Before 1981, firms executed virtually all tender offer repurchases using a fixed-price tender offer. Although Dutch auction share repurchases were introduced in 1981, they surpassed the fixed-price tender offer in popularity by 1988 (Gay, Kale, and Noe, 1996). Currently, the most common share repurchase method in the United States is the open-market share repurchase program. According to Grullon and Michaely (2002), between 1984 and 2000, corporations spent approximately 26 percent of their total annual earnings on repurchases. Over 90 percent of these repurchases were open-market repurchase programs, compared to only 10 to 15 percent in the early 1980s. Stephens and Weisbach (1998) report that typical open-market repurchase programs target 5 percent of the share base, last two to three years, and result in a buyback of 74 percent of the targeted shares.

Motives for Share Repurchases

The literature offers multiple theories for share repurchases. These motives include signaling, distributing excess cash, substituting for cash dividends, defending against takeovers, altering capital structure, mimicking, and managing earnings.

Signaling Undervaluation
Signaling undervaluation theory, the most prevalent explanation for share repurchases, posits that firms undertake repurchases to explicitly signal management's belief that the firm's stock is undervalued (Dann, 1981; Vermaelen, 1981, 1984; Asquith and Mullins, 1986; Ofer and Thakor, 1987; Constantinides and Grundy, 1989). Based on survey evidence from top financial executives in the United States, Baker, Powell, and Veit (2003a) find that the most highly cited reasons for repurchasing shares are consistent with the signaling hypothesis, specifically the undervaluation version of this hypothesis. Survey evidence by Brav, Graham, Harvey, and Michaely (2005) indicates that more than 86 percent of responding managers agree that the motivation for repurchasing is that the stock is a "good deal."

Comment and Jarrell (1991) compare three forms of common stock repurchases. They find that tender offers tend to be for the largest number of shares and to have the largest stock price reaction. Open-market share repurchase programs tend to be the smallest, in terms of both the number of shares targeted and the stock-price reaction. The authors interpret their results by suggesting that fixed-price tender offers generally provide the most information to investors while open-market repurchases give the least. They also find that firms tend to announce open-market share repurchase plans following a decline in their share price, when their stock is more likely to be undervalued. Ikenberry et al. (1995) find that subsequent performance, especially for value firms, is sufficiently high so that even investors purchasing after the announcement earn abnormal returns. This abnormal performance strongly suggests that these firms were in fact undervalued at the repurchase announcement.

Most empirical studies of share repurchases assume that repurchase announcements are carried through and the firm actually repurchases its stock. However, Bhattacharya and Dittmar (2008) report that 46 percent of all firms that announce share repurchase programs do not purchase a single share within the announcement quarter or the quarter following. Of the firms that announce, 27 percent do not repurchase within four fiscal years of the announcement or before dropping out of Compustat. To explain why share repurchase announcements evoke stock price increases even though the announcing firms are not committed to actual repurchase, Oded (2005) develops a signaling model where an open-market share repurchase program is a costly signal for bad firms. Similarly, Bhattacharya and Dittmar develop a model, providing supporting evidence by showing that firms announcing share repurchases without actually carrying them out tend to be smaller with fewer analysts following them than those firms that do carry out their share repurchases.

Baker, Veit, and Powell (2003b) provide survey-based evidence about how top financial executives view repurchasing fewer shares than announced. Their evidence shows that while managers are uncertain about the legality of this activity, they believe that the intentional repurchase of fewer shares than announced is unethical, sends a false signal to the market, and damages the firm's credibility with its stockholders. Despite these beliefs, managers report that repurchasing fewer shares than announced is a common practice.

Distributing Excess Cash
According to the free cash flow hypothesis (Jensen, 1986), firms experiencing reductions in growth opportunities and asset returns are more likely to pay out cash through repurchases. Yet, as many repurchase programs go unfulfilled or, in some cases, even uninitiated, an important premise of this hypothesis is that firms actually buy back stock to disgorge cash.

Grullon and Michaely (2004) offer supporting evidence for this hypothesis by finding that repurchasing firms reduce their current levels of capital expenditures and research and development (R&D) expenses. Furthermore, the level of cash reserves on repurchasing firms' balance sheets significantly declines. They also find that the market reaction to share repurchase announcements is stronger among firms that are more likely to overinvest. These findings, combined with the evidence that repurchasing firms underperform when compared to their peers, indicate that firms increase their cash payouts in response to deterioration in their investment opportunity set. Nevertheless, Brav et al. (2005) provide survey-based evidence that 80 percent of the responding executives do not believe that the discipline imposed by repurchases is important.

Altering Capital Structure

Repurchases can be a tool for managing capital structure if firms perceive their current leverage to be below the target. One common reason for such a distortion is the use of stock options. Options, when exercised, have the effect of increasing equity financing in the firm. Kahle (2002) finds that firms tend to announce repurchases when executives have large numbers of options outstanding and when employees have large numbers of currently exercisable options. Once the decision to repurchase is made, the amount repurchased is positively correlated to the total options exercisable by all employees but independent of managerial options. These results are consistent with managers repurchasing both to maximize their own wealth and to fund employee stock option exercises. The market appears to recognize this motive, however, and reacts less positively to repurchases announced by firms with high levels of nonmanagerial options. Similarly, Weisbenner (2004) finds that employee stock options are generally associated with increased share repurchases and increased total payouts. The positive relationship between options and share repurchases is stronger for firms with high stock returns (high stock returns lead to greater dilution of earnings per share from options).

Substituting for Cash Dividends

According to the substitution hypothesis, repurchases substitute for dividends as a means to payout earnings. In fact, share repurchases have become more popular than dividends since 1999 (Grullon and Michaely, 2002; Skinner, 2008). Earlier studies that jointly examine dividends and repurchases focus either on their relative efficacy as predictors of future performance or on their relative efficiency for distributing cash. Ofer and Thakor (1987) demonstrate theoretically that firms should use repurchases to correct large misvaluations, while dividends are more efficient for smaller misvaluations. Choi and Chen (1997) also find empirical support for this prediction. Bagwell and Shoven (1988), as well as Talmor and Titman (1990), contrast the two methods on tax effects while Barclay and Smith (1988) highlight differing transaction costs. The tax incentive for substituting dividends with repurchases is important because capital gains, at that period, were taxed at more favorable rates than ordinary income. However, wider bid-ask spreads makes share repurchases costlier than dividends.

Based on the notion that dividend increases are implicitly permanent commitments, Guay and Harford (2000) hypothesize that repurchases disburse temporary cash-flow shocks while dividend changes disburse relatively more permanent shocks. Consistent with this hypothesis, the authors find that when compared to repurchasing firms, the postshock cash flows of dividend-increasing firms exhibit less reversion to preshock levels. Similarly, Jagannathan, Stephens, and Weisbach (2000) find that firms with higher "permanent" operating cash flows pay dividends while firms with higher "temporary" nonoperating cash flows use repurchases.

Fenn and Liang (2001) find a negative relationship between dividends and management stock options but a positive relationship for repurchases, suggesting that the growth in stock options may help explain the rise in repurchases relative to dividends. Grullon and Michaely (2002) note the importance of regulatory changes in the early 1980s in explaining the growth of share repurchases. Until the Securities Exchange Commission (SEC) adopted Rule 10b-18 in 1982, repurchasing firms were exposed to the risk of being charged with illegally manipulating stock prices during repurchase programs. Rule 10b-18 provides a safe harbor for repurchasing firms against the antimanipulative provisions of the Securities Exchange Act (SEA) of 1934. Grullon and Michaely find that even after controlling for other factors, the effect of Rule 10b-18 on share repurchase activity is highly significant.

Skinner (2008) shows that changes in the earnings cross-section help explain changes in payout policy over the last three decades. He also shows that repurchases increasingly substitute for dividends both for firms that have traditionally paid dividends (and continue to do so) and for firms that have only made repurchases. Of the several distinct payers emerging after 1980, the most important is the relatively small group of firms paying annual dividends and making regular repurchases. Skinner finds that these firms continue to pay dividends largely because of history. Because firms have paid dividends for many years, they are essentially obliged to continue the practice. However, managers of these firms increasingly use repurchases every other year while, in turn, repurchases increasingly absorb the variation in earnings.

Deterring Takeovers
Various studies show how firms use share repurchases to deter unwanted takeover attempts. Harris and Raviv (1988) and Stulz (1988) model how firms issue debt and use the proceeds to repurchase shares to deter takeovers. Bagnoli, Gordon, and Lipman (1989) show that stock repurchases serve as a defense against takeovers by signaling management's private information regarding firm value. According to Bagwell (1991a), when shareholders possess heterogeneous valuations, the shareholders who are willing to tender in a repurchase are systematically those with the lowest valuations. The repurchase skews the distribution of the remaining shareholders toward a more expensive pool, thereby raising the cost of takeover.

Empirical research provides evidence consistent with these theories regarding tender offers (Bagwell, 1991b, 1992; Persons, 1994) and open-market share repurchases (Dittmar, 2000; Billett and Xue, 2007). Between the types of tender offers, Dutch auction repurchases are more effective takeover deterrents while fixed price repurchases are more effective signals of undervaluation (Persons, 1994). Billett and Xue argue that open-market repurchases affect takeover process differently from tender offers. While tender offers are an effective defense in the midst of takeover battles, open-market repurchases may deter unwanted bids, preempting would-be acquirers from bidding in the first place. Billett and Xue find that firms' repurchase activity increases when faced with a high takeover probability.

Another extensively studied repurchase method is the privately negotiated share repurchase, also called a targeted repurchase. Compared to open-market repurchases, private repurchases, through public tender offers or Dutch auctions, have the following unique characteristics: The seller can initiate the share repurchase instead of the corporation, and the seller is typically a large investor. Earlier studies on private repurchases such as Dann and DeAngelo (1983), Bradley and

Wakeman (1983), Klein and Rosenfeld (1988), Denis (1990), and Mikkelson and Ruback (1991) report significant negative announcement returns, although companies pay large premiums to repurchase their own stock. The general interpretation of these results is that private repurchases are defensive measures used to fight takeovers, given the fact that the repurchase is often accompanied by a standstill agreement where the investor agrees to limit holdings.

Using a more recent and much larger sample, Peyer and Vermaelen (2005) find that private repurchases are associated with significantly positive announcement returns. Unlike the 1970s and early 1980s, companies no longer pay a substantial premium relative to the market price two days before the announcement. However, when Peyer and Vermaelen investigate the 60 greenmail events individually (about 8 percent of their sample), their results are similar to earlier research. The authors conclude that a firm repurchases shares from outsiders only when its stock is undervalued. The market does not seem to realize this, especially regarding greenmail transactions and discounted repurchases. Finally, in contrast to other forms of repurchases, the bargaining strengths of the firm and the seller primarily determine targeted repurchase premiums.

Recent Explanations for Share Repurchases

Recent studies offer additional explanations for share repurchases such as managing earnings and industry or economic factors. Consistent with Bens, Nagar, Skinner, and Wong (2003), who find that incentives to manage diluted earnings per share (EPS) drive repurchase decisions, Baker et al. (2003a) and Brav et al. (2005) report that CFOs frequently mention "improving EPS numbers" as a reason their firms repurchase shares. Hribar, Jenkins, and Johnson (2006) find a disproportionally large number of EPS-increasing repurchases among firms that would have missed analysts' forecasts without the repurchase. Chan, Ikenberry, Lee, and Wang (2009) also provide similar evidence.

Compared to tender offer repurchase methods, open-market repurchase programs are simply authorizations, not commitments. This leads to a concern that open-market authorizations pose few barriers to managers who might want to engage in mimicking behavior. Massa, Rehman, and Vermaelen (2007) show that, in concentrated industries, managers choose repurchases as a strategic reaction to other firms' repurchase decisions and are not motivated by the desire to take advantage of undervaluation. Specifically, in concentrated industries, a repurchase announcement lowers the stock price of the other competing firms in the industry. The other firms react by repurchasing shares to undo these negative effects. This mimicking effect is positively correlated to the degree of strategic interaction within the industry.

Dittmar and Dittmar (2008) examine the correlation in financing waves from 1971 to 2004 by studying the patterns of share repurchases, equity issuances, and mergers. They find a positive correlation between repurchases and equity issues or mergers, suggesting that market timing (e.g., repurchasing when the firm's equity is undervalued) is unlikely to drive patterns in corporate financing events. Their results also show that the growth in gross domestic product (GDP) has a positive and significant impact for predicting future repurchase activity (i.e., share repurchase activity increases during economic expansion). Dittmar and Dittmar conclude that changes in the business cycle rather than changes in relative market valuation drive patterns in corporate financing decisions.

DUAL-CLASS RECAPITALIZATIONS

The typical dual-class firm issues two classes of common stock: a publicly traded "inferior" class of stocks with one vote per share and a non–publicly traded "superior" class of stock with 10 votes per share. Almost without exception, the class of shares with superior voting rights sells at a premium over the class with inferior voting rights. The superior class is usually owned by the firm's insiders and causes a significant wedge between their voting and cash-flow rights. Because of this wedge, dual-class firms are virtually immune to hostile takeovers.

In their comprehensive analysis of dual-class firms in the United States between 1995 and 2002, Gompers, Ishii, and Metrick (2010) report that dual-class firms comprise about 6 percent of the number of public companies and 8 percent of the overall market capitalization. The most common voting structure is 10:1, in which the superior class has 10 votes per share, and the inferior class has one vote per share. On average, the insiders of dual-class firms own a majority of the voting rights (about 60 percent) and a large minority of the cash flow rights (about 40 percent). Both classes are publicly traded for 15 percent of dual-class firms.

Dual-class share structure is more prevalent outside the United States, particularly in countries whose economies are dominated by family-controlled firms. According to a recent survey of 16 European countries conducted by Institutional Shareholder Services (2007), dual-class firms represent 59 percent of sample firms in Sweden, 58 percent in France, and 41 percent in the Netherlands. Other studies report that the percentage of dual-class firms is 40 percent for the Milan Stock Exchange (Zingales, 1994), 13 percent for the Toronto Stock Exchange (Amoako-Adu and Smith, 2001), and 40 percent for the Tel Aviv Stock Exchange (Hauser and Lauterbach, 2004).

Adams and Ferreira (2008) and Burkart and Lee (2008) provide recent surveys of the theoretical and empirical literature that analyze why firms might deviate from a one share–one vote regime. In particular, in a symmetric information setting, Grossman and Hart (1988) and Harris and Raviv (1988, 1989) show that an inefficient team might end up managing the firm under a dual-class structure because it can extract more private benefits. The studies conclude that the one share–one vote structure is optimal in terms of shareholder wealth maximization. Chemmanur and Jiao (2007) offer a theoretical analysis in a setting with asymmetric information between the incumbent and outside shareholders about the incumbent's ability and later, regarding how effective the incumbent has been in implementing the firm's project. This asymmetric information interacts with the incentive problem faced by the incumbent, so dual-class structure is optimal in some situations and single-class share structure is optimal in others. Substantial empirical literature deals with firms' adoptions of dual-class share structures, either at initial public offering (IPO) (Taylor and Whittred, 1998; Field and Karpoff, 2002; Smart and Zutter, 2003; Arugaslan, Cook, and Kieschnick, 2009) or afterwards, stirring a debate on whether these corporate initiatives are value-enhancing or value-destroying.

The seminal work of DeAngelo and DeAngelo (1985) describes dual-class structure as an intermediate organizational structure that fits somewhere between dispersed-ownership public corporation and the closely held firm. DeAngelo and DeAngelo report that in almost every firm in their sample, management's common stock holdings are tilted toward the security with the superior voting rights, and in more than half of the firms, corporate officers and their families hold majority control.

Several studies examine the effects of dual-class recapitalization on shareholder wealth including work by Partch (1987), Jarrell and Poulsen (1988), and Cornett and Vetsuypens (1989). The event period's abnormal returns in these studies are small and not always significant or of the same sign, suggesting that the short window event period results are inconclusive. Further, Jarrell and Poulsen as well as Ruback (1988) discuss how firms can use dual-class recapitalization as a takeover deterrence device. Lehn, Netter, and Poulsen (1990) compare dual-class recapitalizations with leveraged buyouts and find that firms with higher growth opportunities are more likely to adopt a dual-class recapitalization and undertake secondary equity offerings to finance growth. Dimitrov and Jain (2006) show that, on average, stockholders earn significant positive abnormal returns of 23.11 percent during the period of four years following recapitalization announcements. Abnormal returns are even larger for dual-class firms that issue equity.

Recent literature documents a trend moving away from dual-class structures via share unifications in the United Kingdom (Ang and Megginson, 1989), Canada (Amoako-Adu and Smith, 2001), Israel (Hauser and Lauterbach, 2004), the United States (Smart, Thirumalai, and Zutter, 2007), and Germany (Dittmann and Ulbricht, 2007). Using monthly share prices, Ang and Megginson report no significant effect of share unification on the firm's market capitalization. In contrast, Dittmann and Ulbricht find a 10 percent significant positive abnormal return for nonvoting shares and a 3 percent marginally significant, positive abnormal return for voting shares, suggesting that for those firms that choose to unify, dual-class structures destroy value.

EXCHANGE OFFERS AND SWAPS

Exchange offers and swaps are noncash transactions that alter the capital structure of the firm without changing its asset structure. An exchange offer gives one or more security classes the right to exchange part or all of their holdings for a different class of firm securities. The terms of exchange offered to the tendering securityholders typically involve a new securities package of greater market value (at the time of the exchange offer announcement) than those being tendered, with the difference in values considered as an exchange offer premium. Types of exchange offers and swaps include leverage-increasing exchange offers (debt-for-common, debt-for-preferred, and preferred-for-common) and leverage-decreasing exchange offers (common-for-debt, preferred-for-debt, and common-for-preferred).

Although the capital structure consequences of both exchange offers and swaps are similar, Finnerty (1985) notes important differences: Swaps are made exclusively with the financial institution that purchased the bonds in the open market before the swap offer. In contrast, exchange offers are made to all holders of the affected class of security. Shah (1994, 1997) and Lie, Lie, and McConnell (2001) document that firms carrying out swaps are usually well established, with large market capitalization and investment grade ratings. However, firms that conduct exchange offers tend to be associated with financial distress.

The literature identifies three main explanations for exchange offers and swaps: signaling, tax savings, and wealth transfer. The signaling theory assumes that managers want to increase the wealth of long-term shareholders, and thus, the market will interpret swap transactions as signals of managers' private information (e.g., Ross, 1977; Leland and Pyle, 1977). Accordingly, managers of firms with undervalued equity will issue debt and repurchase equity while managers of firms with overvalued equity will issue more equity and retire debt. Empirical evidence tends to support the signaling hypothesis in that leverage-reducing (increasing) exchange offers are associated with negative (positive) stock price reactions (e.g., Masulis, 1980, 1983; Finnerty, 1985; Cornett and Travlos, 1989; Shah, 1994, 1997; and Lie et al., 2001). However, O'Brien, Klein, and Hilliard (2007) show that when a firm's debt and equity are both undervalued due to the market underestimating total firm value and overestimating volatility, issuing undervalued equity to exploit the relative mispricing of the firm's securities may be optimal.

The tax effects hypothesis of Modigliani and Miller (1963) posits that leverage-reducing exchange offers should be associated with negative stock returns due to the loss of tax benefits associated with debt. On the other hand, leverage-increasing exchange offers should be associated with positive stock returns due to the increasing tax credits. The empirical evidence appears to be mixed. Masulis (1980, 1983) documents results consistent with the tax effects hypothesis for debt-for-common exchange offers, preferred-for-common exchange offers, and debt-for-preferred exchange offers. However, later studies such as Cornett and Travlos (1989) and Copeland and Lee (1991) fail to find supporting evidence for the tax hypothesis. According to the wealth transfer hypothesis, an unexpected debt-for-equity exchange offer makes outstanding debt more risky, with the size of wealth transferred from bondholders to stockholders posited to be positively related to the increase in leverage. Consequently, stock prices are expected to increase following leverage-increasing exchange offers. On the other hand, an unexpected equity-for-debt exchange offer makes debt less risky and results in wealth transfer from stockholders to bondholders (Galai and Masulis, 1976). As a result, stock prices are expected to increase (decrease) following leverage-increasing (decreasing) exchange offers. The evidence on the wealth transfer hypothesis is mixed (e.g., Masulis, 1980, 1983; Finnerty, 1985; Cornett and Travlos, 1989, Copeland and Lee, 1991). According to Kitsabunnarat-Chatjuthamard, Lung, Nishikawa, and Rao (2010), results from previous studies may be confounded by the fact that they do not always distinguish between swaps and exchange offers. They argue that under financial distress, managers have an incentive to align with bondholders for self-preservation. Therefore, the authors hypothesize and find supporting empirical evidence that managers undertake leverage-decreasing exchange offers (not swaps) at the expense of stockholders when under financial distress.

DEBT RESTRUCTURINGS VIA PRIVATE WORKOUTS AND FORMAL BANKRUPTCY

A firm is financially distressed if it has insufficient cash flows to meet its debt payments. To remedy or avoid default, the firm can restructure the terms of its debt contracts through private workouts with its creditors or a bankruptcy filing. Many firms first attempt to resolve financial distress via private workouts due to the cost savings relative to the formal bankruptcy process. A common belief is that direct and indirect costs of workouts are lower than bankruptcy because of Chapter 11's procedural demands and legal complexity. Gilson, John, and Lang (1990), as well as Franks and Torous (1994), report that almost half of the companies in financial distress successfully restructure their debt through private renegotiation or exchange offers. However, Altman and Stonberg (2006) find that about 60 percent of defaults are restructured through bankruptcy filings, suggesting that private workouts are becoming less common.

Private Workouts

The Trust Indenture Act of 1939 prohibits altering interest or principal provisions on publicly traded debt without the consent of each affected bondholder. Since gaining unanimous consent from a diffuse set of bondholders is difficult, private restructuring of public debt generally takes the form of an exchange offer. Firms face at least two impediments to the success of the exchange offer. First, if some bondholders make concessions (i.e., reduce the face value of their claims) and the exchange offer is successful, the value of the claims of nontendering bondholders increases. As a result, if individual bondholders believe they are not pivotal to the offer's success, they will hold out and not participate in the exchange offer (e.g., Grossman and Hart, 1980; Gertner and Scharfstein, 1991). Second, even in the absence of holdout problems, information asymmetries may lead bondholders to prefer bankruptcy over private debt restructuring (Giammarino, 1989; Wruck, 1990; Mooradian, 1994).

Chapter 11 Reorganizations

The provisions of Chapter 11 of the Bankruptcy Code are intended to promote reorganization of economically viable firms as going concerns and thereby avoid inefficient liquidation of distressed firms. When a firm files for bankruptcy, all of its debt becomes due, but an *automatic stay* is invoked, stopping all principal and interest payments. Thus, secured creditors lose the right to take possession of their collateral. In Chapter 11, control of a firm, known as the *debtor in possession*, typically remains with current management and the board of directors. Creditors are paid in accordance with the absolute priority rule, so equity holders get nothing unless all creditors are paid in full. Chapter 11 bankruptcy is a complex, lengthy, and costly process (Franks and Torous, 1989).

Kalay, Singhal, and Tashjian (2007) examine a sample of 459 firms filing Chapter 11 during the period from 1991 to 1998 and find that firms experience significant improvements in their operating performance during the filings. Firms with higher debt ratios experience greater improvements in operating performance and the complexity of the reorganization process negatively affects the improvement. Heron, Lie, and Rodgers (2008) find that firms substantially reduce their debt burden in Chapter 11 reorganizations, yet emerge with higher debt ratios than what is typical in their respective industries. Also, prereorganization debt ratios affect postreorganization debt ratios. Thus, inefficiencies in the Chapter 11 process prevent firms from completely abandoning their old capital structure.

Debtor-in-possession (DIP) financing is a unique form of secured financing available to firms filing Chapter 11. Such financing is made possible by the "automatic stay" provision of bankruptcy law and the ability of the court to grant super-priority status to the DIP lender. The borrower has to pay off DIP loans completely before emerging from Chapter 11. According to Dhillon, Noe, and Ramirez (2007), about half the firms filing for Chapter 11 obtain DIP financing. Dahiya, John, Puri, and Ramirez (2003) find that the DIP financed firms, relative to non–DIP financed firms, are both more likely and are quicker to emerge from Chapter 11, have a shorter reorganization period, and are quicker to liquidate. Dhillon et al. develop a model in which DIP financing resolves informational asymmetries (between the creditors and management of the distressed firm) regarding the true economic value of the distressed firm. The authors find evidence of a positive stock price reaction to DIP announcements and that firms employing DIP financing have more successful reorganizations.

Choosing Between Private Workouts and Formal Bankruptcy

Gilson et al. (1990) examine the determinants of firms' choices between formal bankruptcy and private renegotiation. They find that the probability of completing a private renegotiation is higher if the firm has more intangible assets. As the value of intangible assets is more likely to erode in bankruptcy (e.g., through asset fire sales or perishing customer demand), firms with more intangible assets have greater incentives to preserve value via a private renegotiation. According to Asquith, Gertner, and Scharfstein (1994), firms with more secured private debt and complex public debt structures are more likely to enter Chapter 11 than private renegotiation. The larger fraction of secured debt may indicate a relatively low proportion of intangible assets and thus less costly bankruptcy proceedings.

So far, the focus has been on the choice between bankruptcy and private renegotiation. However, the Bankruptcy Code also permits firms to make "prepackaged" Chapter 11 filings in which the bankruptcy petition and reorganization plan are filed together. Therefore, prepackaged Chapter 11 filings incorporate both conventional bankruptcy and privation renegotiation. Prepackaged bankruptcies are similar to conventional Chapter 11 filings in that the reorganization occurs under court guidance and all claimholders must participate in any exchange of securities. They are similar to private renegotiations in that the creditors and the debtor have the opportunity to agree to the restructuring terms outside of court. Prepackaged bankruptcies eliminate the holdout problem associated with private renegotiations and avoid a prolonged stay in Chapter 11. Baird and Rasmussen (2003) estimate that 25 percent of 93 large firm Chapter 11 bankruptcies in 2002 were prepackaged bankruptcies.

Betker (1995) and Tashjian, Lease, and McConnell (1996) examine the characteristics of prepackaged bankruptcies. By most measures including time spent in reorganization, the direct fees as a percentage of predistress assets, recovery rates by creditors, and the incidence of violations of absolute priority rule, Tashjian et al. find that prepackaged bankruptcies lie between private renegotiations and Chapter 11 bankruptcies. Chatterjee, Dhillon, and Ramirez (1996) analyze all three choices for debt restructurings simultaneously and find that economically distressed firms file for Chapter 11, while economically viable firms prefer private renegotiations. Firms that are economically viable but face immediate liquidity problems use prepackaged bankruptcies.

SUMMARY AND CONCLUSIONS

Much theoretical and empirical research focuses on rationalizing and characterizing different financial restructuring activities that significantly change corporate capital structures. This rich and growing literature offers multiple explanations for leverage-increasing (e.g., share repurchases and debt-for-equity exchange offers) and leverage-decreasing transactions (e.g., equity-for-debt exchange offers). However, signaling theory appears to have received the most empirical support. Leverage-increasing transactions are associated with positive stock price reactions, signaling undervaluation, while leverage-decreasing transactions are associated with negative stock price reactions, signaling overvaluation.

Open-market share repurchases have become increasingly popular, compared to tender offers, representing more than 90 percent of all repurchases, mostly due to their flexibility. Such repurchases have also become the most dominant form of corporate payout, surpassing dividends. For this reason, a large part of the chapter examines share repurchases. Dual-class recapitalizations and exchange offers are relatively rare. Dual-class share structure is the most extreme case of takeover protection and is more popular in Europe than in the United States. Recently, there has been a trend toward share unifications.

To avoid default, financially distressed firms can restructure their debt through private workout or bankruptcy. Both processes are aimed at restoring the firm's financial health. Evidence suggests that restructuring firms experience significant improvements in their operating performance. Also, an increase in the use of DIP financing has increased the power of creditors in bankruptcy in recent years.

As previously mentioned, this chapter is not intended to provide a comprehensive examination of papers of financial restructuring that make important contributions to the literature. Instead, it provides a representative set of relevant articles that offer a concise summary of recent trends, underlying theories, and current empirical evidence on financial restructuring activities.

DISCUSSION QUESTIONS

1. If share repurchases and dividends appear to be substitute payout methods, why did corporations not repurchase more intensely before the mid-1980s when the tax benefits of capital gains were much higher?
2. How do share repurchases serve as a defense against takeovers? Does the type of repurchase program matter?
3. What is the most extreme example of antitakeover protection?
4. What is debtor-in-possession (DIP) financing? What explains the increasing prevalence of DIP financing in Chapter 11 reorganizations?

REFERENCES

Adams, Renée, and Daniel Ferreira. 2008. "One Share–One Vote: The Empirical Evidence." *Review of Finance* 12:1, 51–91.
Alti, Aydoğan. 2006. "How Persistent Is the Impact of Market Timing on Capital Structure?" *Journal of Finance* 61:4, 1681–1710.

Altman, Edward I., and William Stonberg. 2006. "The Market in Defaulted Bonds and Bank Loans." *Journal of Portfolio Management* 32:4, 93–106.

Amoako-Adu, Ben, and Brian F. Smith. 2001. "Dual Class Firms: Capitalization, Ownership Structure and Recapitalization Back into Single Class." *Journal of Banking and Finance* 25:6, 1083–1111.

Ang, James S., and William L. Megginson. 1989. "Restricted Voting Shares, Ownership Structure, and the Market Value of Dual-Class Firms." *Journal of Financial Research* 12:4, 301–318.

Arugaslan, Onur, Douglas O. Cook, and Robert Kieschnick. 2009. "On the Decision to Go Public with Dual Class Stock." *Journal of Corporate Finance* 16:2, 170–181.

Asquith, Paul, and David W. Mullins Jr. 1986. "Signalling with Dividends, Stock Repurchases and Equity Issues." *Financial Management* 15:3, 27–44.

Asquith, Paul, Robert Gertner, and David Scharfstein. 1994. "Anatomy of Financial Distress: An Examination of Junk Bond Issuers." *Quarterly Journal of Economics* 109:3, 625–658.

Bagnoli, Mark, Roger Gordon, and Barton L. Lipman. 1989. "Stock Repurchase as a Takeover Defense." *Review of Financial Studies* 2:3, 423–443.

Bagwell, Laurie S. 1991a. "Share Repurchase and Takeover Deterrence." *RAND Journal of Economics* 22:1, 72–88.

Bagwell, Laurie S. 1991b. "Shareholder Heterogeneity: Evidence and Implications." *American Economic Review* 81:2, 218–221.

Bagwell, Laurie S. 1992. "Dutch Auction Repurchases: An Analysis of Shareholder Heterogeneity." Journal of Finance 47:1, 71–105.

Bagwell, Laurie S., and John B. Shoven. 1988. "Cash Distributions to Shareholders." *Journal of Economic Perspectives* 3:3, 129–140.

Baird, Douglas G., and Robert K. Rasmussen. 2003. "Chapter 11 at Twilight." *Stanford Law Review* 56:3, 673–699.

Baker, H. Kent, Gary E. Powell, and E. Theodore Veit. 2003a. "Why Companies Use Open-Market Repurchases: A Managerial Perspective." *Quarterly Review of Economics and Finance*, 43:3, 483–504.

Baker, H. Kent, E. Theodore Veit, and Gary E. Powell. 2003b. "Stock Repurchases and False Signals." *Journal of Applied Business Research* 19:2, 33–46.

Baker, Malcolm, and Jeffrey Wurgler. 2002. "Market Timing and Capital Structure." *Journal of Finance* 57:1, 1–32.

Barclay, Michael J., and Clifford W. Smith Jr. 1988. "Corporate Payout Policy: Cash Dividends versus Open-Market Repurchases." Journal of Financial Economics 22:1, 61–82.

Bens, Daniel A., Venky Nagar, Douglas J. Skinner, and M. H. Franco Wong. 2003. "Employee Stock Options, EPS Dilution, and Stock Repurchases." Journal of Accounting and Economics 36:1-3, 51–90.

Betker, Brian L. 1995. "An Empirical Examination of Prepackaged Bankruptcy." *Financial Management* 24:1, 3–18.

Bhattacharya, Utpal, and Amy Dittmar. 2008. "Costless versus Costly Signaling: Theory and Evidence." Working Paper, Indiana University and University of Michigan.

Billett, Matthew T., and Hui Xue. 2007. "The Takeover Deterrent Effect of Open Market Share Repurchases." *Journal of Finance* 62:4, 1827–1850.

Bradley, Michael, and L. McDonald Wakeman. 1983. "The Wealth Effects of Targeted Share Repurchases." *Journal of Financial Economics* 11:1–4, 301–328.

Brav, Alon, John R. Graham, Campbell R. Harvey, and Roni Michaely. 2005. "Payout Policy in the 21st Century." *Journal of Financial Economics* 77:3, 483–528.

Burkart, Mike, and Samuel Lee. 2008. "One Share–One Vote: The Theory." *Review of Finance* 12:1, 1–49.

Chan, Konan, David L. Ikenberry, Inmoo Lee, and Yanzhi Wang. 2009. "Share Repurchases as a Potential Tool to Mislead Investors." *Journal of Corporate Finance* 16:2, 137–158.

Chatterjee, Sris, Upinder S. Dhillon, and Gabriel G. Ramirez. 1996. "Resolution of Financial Distress: Debt Restructurings via Chapter 11, Prepackaged Bankruptcies, and Workouts." *Financial Management* 25:1, 5–18.

Chemmanur, Thomas J., and Yawen Jiao. 2007. "Dual Class IPOs, Share Recapitalizations, and Unifications: A Theoretical Analysis." Available at http://papers.ssrn.com/sol3/papers.cfm?abstract_id=1108857.

Choi, Dosoung, and Sheng-Syan Chen. 1997. "The Differential Information Conveyed by Share Repurchase Tender Offers and Dividend Increases." *Journal of Financial Research* 20:4, 529–543.

Comment, Robert, and Gregg A. Jarrell. 1991. "The Relative Signaling Power of Dutch-Auction and Fixed-Price Self-Tender Offers and Open Market Share Repurchases." *Journal of Finance* 46:4, 1243–1271.

Constantinides, George M., and Bruce D. Grundy. 1989. "Optimal Investment with Stock Repurchase and Financing as Signals." *Review of Financial Studies* 2:4, 445–465.

Copeland, Thomas E., and Won Heum Lee. 1991. "Exchange Offers and Stock Swaps—New Evidence." *Financial Management* 20:3, 34–48.

Cornett, Marcia M., and Nickolaos G. Travlos. 1989. "Information Effects Associated with Debt-for-Equity and Equity-for-Debt Exchange Offers." *Journal of Finance* 44:2, 451–468.

Cornett, Marcia M., and Michael R. Vetsuypens. 1989. "Voting Rights and Shareholder Wealth: The Issuance of Limited Voting Common Stock." *Managerial and Decision Economics* 10:3, 175–188.

Dahiya, Sandeep, Kose John, Manju Puri, and Gabriel G. Ramirez. 2003. "Debtor-in-Possession Financing and Bankruptcy Resolution: Empirical Evidence." *Journal of Financial Economics* 69:1, 259–280.

Dann, Larry Y. 1981. "Common Stock Repurchases: An Analysis of Returns to Bondholders and Stockholders." *Journal of Financial Economics* 9:2, 113–138.

Dann, Larry Y., and Harry DeAngelo. 1983. "Standstill Agreements Privately Negotiated Stock Repurchases, and the Market for Corporate Control." *Journal of Financial Economics* 11:1–4, 275–300.

DeAngelo, Harry, and Linda DeAngelo. 1985. "Managerial Ownership of Voting Rights: A Study of Public Corporations with Dual Classes of Common Stock." *Journal of Financial Economics* 14:1, 33–69.

DeAngelo, Harry, and Ronald Masulis. 1980. "Optimal Capital Structure under Corporate and Personal Taxation." *Journal of Financial Economics* 8:1, 3–29.

Denis, David. 1990. "Defensive Changes in Corporate Payout Policy: Share Repurchases and Special Dividends." *Journal of Finance* 45:5, 1433–1456.

Dhillon, Upinder S., Thomas Noe, and Gabriel G. Ramirez. 2007. "Debtor-in-Possession Financing and the Resolution of Uncertainty in Chapter 11 Reorganizations." *Journal of Financial Stability* 3:3, 238–260.

Dimitrov, Valentin, and Prem C. Jain. 2006. "Recapitalization of One Class of Common Stock into Dual-Class: Growth and Long-Run Stock Returns." *Journal of Corporate Finance* 12:2, 342–366.

Dittmann, Ingolf, and Niels Ulbricht. 2007. "Timing and Wealth Effects of German Dual Class Stock Unifications." *European Financial Management* 14:1, 163–196.

Dittmar, Amy K. 2000. "Why Do Firms Repurchase Stock?" *Journal of Business* 73:3, 331–355.

Dittmar, Amy K., and Robert F. Dittmar. 2008. "The Timing of Financing Decisions: An Examination of the Correlation in Financing Waves." *Journal of Financial Economics* 90:1, 59–83.

Fama, Eugene, and Kenneth French. 2002. "Testing Trade-Off and Pecking Order Predictions about Dividends and Debt." *Review of Financial Studies* 15:1, 1–34.

Fenn, George W., and Nellie Liang. 2001. "Good News and Bad News about Share Repurchases." *Journal of Financial Economics* 60:1, 45–72.

Field, Laura, and Jonathan Karpoff. 2002. "Takeover Defenses of IPO Firms." *Journal of Finance* 57:5, 1857–1889.

Finnerty, John D. 1985. "Stock-for-Debt Swaps and Shareholder Returns." *Financial Management* 14:3, 5–17.

Fischer, Edwin O., Robert Heinkel, and Josef Zechner. 1989. "Dynamic Capital Structure Choice: Theory and Tests." *Journal of Finance* 44:1, 19–40.

Flannery Mark J., and Kasturi P. Rangan. 2006. "Partial Adjustment toward Target Capital Structures." *Journal of Financial Economics* 79:3, 469–506.

Franks, Julian R., and Walter N. Torous. 1989. "An Empirical Investigation of U.S. Firms in Reorganization." *Journal of Finance* 44:3, 747–769.

Franks, Julian R., and Walter N. Torous. 1994. "A Comparison of Financial Recontracting in Distressed Exchanges and Chapter 11 Reorganizations." *Journal of Financial Economics* 35:3, 349–370.

Galai Dan, and Ronald W. Masulis. 1976. "The Option Pricing Model and the Risk Factor of Stock." *Journal of Financial Economics* 3:1–2, 53–81.

Gay, Gerald D., Jayant R. Kale, and Thomas H. Noe. 1996. "(Dutch) Auction Share Repurchases." *Economica* 63:249, 57–80.

Gertner, Robert, and David Scharfstein. 1991. "A Theory of Workouts and the Effects of Reorganization Law." *Journal of Finance* 46:4, 1189–1222.

Giammarino, Ronald M. 1989. "The Resolution of Financial Distress." *Review of Financial Studies* 2:1, 25–47.

Gilson, Stuart C., Kose John, and Larry H. P. Lang. 1990. "Troubled Debt Restructurings: An Empirical Study of Private Reorganization of Firms in Default." *Journal of Financial Economics* 27:2, 315–353.

Gompers, Paul, Joy Ishii, and Andrew Metrick. 2010. "Extreme Governance: An Analysis of Dual-Class Firms in the United States." *Review of Financial Studies* 23:3, 1051–1088.

Grossman, Sanford J., and Oliver D. Hart. 1980. "Takeover Bids, the Free-Rider Problem and the Theory of the Corporation." *Bell Journal of Economics* 11:1, 42–64.

Grossman, Sanford J., and Oliver D. Hart. 1988. "One Share–One Vote and the Market for Corporate Control." *Journal of Financial Economics* 20:1–2, 175–202.

Grullon, Gustavo, and Roni Michaely. 2002. "Dividends, Share Repurchases, and the Substitution Hypothesis." *Journal of Finance* 57:4, 1649–1684.

Grullon, Gustavo, and Roni Michaely. 2004. "The Information Content of Share Repurchase Programs." *Journal of Finance* 59:2, 651–680.

Guay, Wayne, and Jarrad Harford. 2000. "The Cash-Flow Permanence and Information Content of Dividend Increases versus Repurchases." *Journal of Financial Economics* 57:3, 385–415.

Harris, Milton, and Arthur Raviv. 1988. "Corporate Control Contests and Capital Structure." *Journal of Financial Economics* 20:1–2, 55–86.

Harris, Milton, and Arthur Raviv. 1989. "The Design of Securities." *Journal of Financial Economics* 24:2, 255–287.

Hauser, Shmuel, and Beni Lauterbach. 2004. "The Value of the Voting Rights to Majority Shareholders: Evidence from Dual-Class Stock Unifications." *Review of Financial Studies* 17:4, 1167–1184.

Heron, Randall A., Erik Lie, and Kimberly J. Rodgers. 2008. "Financial Restructuring in Fresh Start Chapter 11 Reorganizations." *Financial Management* 38:4, 727–745.

Hribar, Paul, Nicole T. Jenkins, and W. Bruce Johnson. 2006. "Stock Repurchases as an Earnings Management Device." *Journal of Accounting and Economics* 41:1–2, 3–27.

Ikenberry, David, Josef Lakonishok, and Theo Vermaelen. 1995. "Market Underreaction to Open Market Share Repurchases." *Journal of Financial Economics* 39:2–3, 181–208.

Institutional Shareholder Services. 2007. "Proportionality between Ownership and Control in EU Listed Companies: External Study Commissioned by the European Commission." Available at http://www.ecgi.org/osov/documents/final_report_en.pdf.

Jagannathan, Murali, Clifford P. Stephens, and Michael S. Weisbach. 2000. "Financial Flexibility and the Choice between Dividends and Stock Repurchases." *Journal of Financial Economics* 57:3, 355–384.

Jarrell, Gregg A., and Annette B. Poulsen. 1988. "Dual-Class Recapitalizations as Antitakeover Mechanisms: The Recent Evidence." *Journal of Financial Economics* 20:1–2, 129–152.

Jensen, Michael C. 1986. "Agency Costs of Free Cash Flow, Corporate, Finance and Takeovers." *American Economic Review* 76:2, 323–329.

Jensen, Michael C., and William H. Meckling. 1976. "Theory of the Firm: Managerial Behavior, Agency Costs and Ownership Structure." *Journal of Financial Economics* 3:4, 305–360.

Kahle, Kathleen M. 2002. "When a Buyback Isn't a Buyback: Open Market Repurchases and Employee Stock Options." *Journal of Financial Economics* 63:2, 235–261.

Kalay, Avner, Rajeev Singhal, and Elizabeth Tashjian. 2007. "Is Chapter 11 Costly?" *Journal of Financial Economics* 84:3, 772–796.

Kitsabunnarat-Chatjuthamard, Pattanaporn, Peter Lung, Takeshi Nishikawa, and Ramesh Rao. 2010. "Leverage-Reducing Exchange Offers and Bondholder–Stockholder Wealth Transfers: A Re-evaluation." *International Review of Economics and Finance* 19:1, 81–94.

Klein, April, and James Rosenfeld. 1988. "The Impact of Targeted Share Repurchases on the Wealth of Non-Participating Shareholders." *Journal of Financial Research* 11:2, 89–97.

Kraus, Alan, and Robert H. Litzenberger. 1973. "A State-Preference Model of Optimal Financial Leverage." *Journal of Finance* 28:4, 911–922.

Leary, Mark T., and Michael R. Roberts. 2005. "Do Firms Rebalance Their Capital Structure?" *Journal of Finance* 60:6, 2575–2619.

Lehn, Kenneth, Jeffry Netter, and Annette Poulsen. 1990. "Consolidating Corporate Control: Dual-Class Recapitalizations versus Leveraged Buyouts." *Journal of Financial Economics* 27:2, 557–580.

Leland, Hayne E. 1994. "Corporate Debt Value, Bond Covenants, and Optimal Capital Structure." *Journal of Finance* 49:4, 1213–1252.

Leland, Hayne E. 1998. "Agency Costs, Risk Management, and Capital Structure." *Journal of Finance* 53:4, 1213–1243.

Leland, Hayne E., and David Pyle. 1977. "Information Asymmetries, Financial Structure and Financial Intermediaries." *Journal of Finance* 32:2, 371–387.

Lie, Erik, Heidi J. Lie, and John J. McConnell. 2001. "Debt-Reducing Exchange Offers." Journal of Corporate Finance 7:2, 179–207.

Massa, Massimo, Zahid Rehman, and Theo Vermaelen. 2007. "Mimicking Repurchases." *Journal of Financial Economics* 84:3, 624–666.

Masulis, Ronald W. 1980. "The Effects of Capital Structure Change on Security Prices: A Study of Exchange Offers." *Journal of Financial Economics* 8:2, 139–178.

Masulis, Ronald W. 1983. "The Impact of Capital Structure Change on Firm Value: Some Estimates." *Journal of Finance* 38:1, 107–126.

Mikkelson, Wayne H., and Richard S. Ruback. 1991. "Targeted Repurchases and Common Stock Returns." *RAND Journal of Economics* 22:4, 544–561.

Modigliani, Franco, and Merton H. Miller. 1958. "The Cost of Capital, Corporate Finance, and the Theory of Investment." *American Economic Review* 48:4, 261–297.

Modigliani, Franco, and Merton H. Miller. 1963. "Corporate Income Taxes and the Cost of Capital: A Correction." *American Economic Review* 53:3, 433–443.

Mooradian, Robert M. 1994. "The Effect of Bankruptcy Protection on Investment: Chapter 11 as a Screening Device." *Journal of Finance* 49:4, 1403–1430.

Myers, Stewart C. 1977. "Determinants of Corporate Borrowing." *Journal of Financial Economics* 5:2, 147–175.

Myers, Stewart C, and Nicholas S. Majluf. 1984. "Corporate Financing and Investment Decisions When Firms Have Information That Investors Do Not Have." *Journal of Financial Economics* 13:2, 187–221.

O'Brien, Thomas J., Linda S. Klein, and James I. Hilliard. 2007. "Capital Structure Swaps and Shareholder Wealth." *European Financial Management* 13:5, 979–997.

Oded, Jacob. 2005. "Why Do Firms Announce Open Market Repurchase Programs?" *Review of Financial Studies* 18:1, 271–300.

Ofer, Aharon R., and Anjan V. Thakor. 1987. "A Theory of Stock Price Response to Alternative Corporate Disbursement Methods: Stock Repurchases and Dividends." *Journal of Finance* 42:2, 365–394.

Partch, M. Megan. 1987. "The Creation of a Class of Limited Voting Common Stock and Shareholders' Wealth." *Journal of Financial Economics* 18:2, 313–339.

Persons, John C. 1994. "Signaling and Takeover Deterrence with Stock Repurchases: Dutch Auctions versus Fixed Price Tender Offers." *Journal of Finance* 49:4, 1373–1402.

Peyer, Urs C., and Theo Vermaelen. 2005. "The Many Facets of Privately Negotiated Stock Repurchases." *Journal of Financial Economics* 75:2, 361–395.

Peyer, Urs C., and Theo Vermaelen. 2009. "The Nature and Persistence of Buyback Anomalies." *Review of Financial Studies* 22:4, 1693–1745.

Ritter, Jay R. 1991. "The Long-Run Performance of Initial Public Offerings." *Journal of Finance* 46:1, 3–27.

Ross, Stephen A. 1977. "The Determination of Financial Structure: The Incentive Signaling Approach." *Bell Journal of Economics* 8:1, 23–40.

Ruback, Richard S. 1988. "Coercive Dual-Class Exchange Offers." *Journal of Financial Economics* 20:1–2, 153–173.

Shah, Kshitij. 1994. "The Nature of Information Conveyed by Pure Capital Structure Changes." *Journal of Financial Economics* 36:1, 89–126.

Shah, Kshitij. 1997. "Why Do Firms Undertake Intra-Firm Exchange Offers?" *Research in Finance* 15, 1–34.

Skinner, Douglas J. 2008. "The Evolving Relation Between Earnings, Dividends, and Stock Repurchases." *Journal of Financial Economics* 87:3, 582–609.

Smart, Scott B., and Chad J. Zutter. 2003. "Control as a Motivation for Underpricing: A Comparison of Dual and Single-Class IPOs." *Journal of Financial Economics* 69:1, 85–110.

Smart, Scott, Ramabhadran S. Thirumalai, and Chad J. Zutter. 2007. "What's in a Vote? The Short- and Long-Run Impact of Dual-Class Equity on IPO Firm Values." *Journal of Accounting and Economics* 45:1, 94–115.

Stephens, Clifford P., and Michael S. Weisbach. 1998. "Actual Share Reacquisitions in Open-Market Repurchase Programs." *Journal of Finance* 53:1, 313–334.

Stulz, René M. 1988. "Managerial Control of Voting Rights: Financing Policies and the Market for Corporate Control." *Journal of Financial Economics* 20:1, 25–54.

Talmor, Eli, and Sheridan Titman. 1990. "Taxes and Dividend Policy." *Financial Management* 19:2, 32–35.

Tashjian, Elizabeth, Ronald C. Lease, and John J. McConnell. 1996. "Prepacks: An Empirical Analysis of Prepackaged Bankruptcies." *Journal of Financial Economics* 40:1, 135–162.

Taylor, Stephen, and Greg Whittred. 1998. "Security Design and the Allocation of Voting Rights: Evidence from the Australian IPO Market." *Journal of Corporate Finance* 4:2, 107–131.

Vermaelen, Theo. 1981. "Common Stock Repurchases and Market Signaling: An Empirical Study." *Journal of Financial Economics* 9:2, 139–183.

Vermaelen, Theo. 1984. "Repurchase Tender Offers, Signaling, and Managerial Incentives." *Journal of Financial and Quantitative Analysis* 19:2, 163–181.

Weisbenner, Scott J. 2004. "Corporate Share Repurchases: What Role Do Stock Options Play?" Working Paper, University of Illinois.

Welch, Ivo. 2004. "Capital Structure and Stock Returns." *Journal of Political Economy* 112:1, 106–131.

Wruck, Karen H. 1990. "Financial Distress, Reorganization, and Organizational Efficiency." *Journal of Financial Economics* 27:2, 419–444.

Zingales, Luigi. 1994. "The Value of the Voting Right: A Study of the Milan Stock Exchange Experience." *Review of Financial Studies* 7:1, 125–148.

ABOUT THE AUTHORS

Otgontsetseg Erhemjamts is an Assistant Professor of Finance at Bentley University. Her primary research interests are corporate finance and corporate governance topics such as M&As, going-public and debt financing decisions, executive compensation, and risk management. Her work appears in academic journals including the *Journal of Money, Credit, and Banking* and *The Financial Review*. Prior academic experience includes teaching corporate finance and risk management courses at Georgia State University. Professor Erhemjamts earned a BSc (with Honors) in information technology from Mongolian Technical University and an MSc in economics from the University of Idaho. She received a PhD in finance from Georgia State University in 2005.

Kartik Raman is the George and Louis Kane Professor of Finance and Associate Professor at Bentley University. Professor Raman's research focuses on the roles of agency, product markets, and accounting decisions in corporate restructuring activities such as takeovers, divestitures, and equity and debt financing decisions. His research also examines how earnings management considerations are influenced by firms' relationships with suppliers and customers. Professor Raman has published in such journals as the *Journal of Finance, Journal of Business, The Accounting Review, Journal of Banking and Finance, Journal of Financial Intermediation, The Financial Review*, and the *Journal of Applied Corporate Finance*.

CHAPTER 23

Going Private and Leveraged Buyouts

ONUR BAYAR
Assistant Professor of Finance, University of Texas at San Antonio

INTRODUCTION

In a public-to-private or a going-private transaction, a public company is acquired and subsequently delisted. Almost all such transactions are financed by borrowing substantial amounts of debt. Hence, they are called leveraged buyouts (LBOs). In a leveraged buyout, a company is acquired by a specialized investment firm using a relatively small portion of equity and a relatively large portion of external debt financing. LBO investment firms are generally referred to as private equity firms. In a typical LBO transaction, the private equity firm buys a majority control of an existing or mature public firm. In reality, however, LBOs comprise not only public-to-private transactions but also private firms that are bought by private equity firms.

LBOs emerged as an important phenomenon in the 1980s. As LBO activity increased in that decade, Jensen (1989) predicted that the leveraged buyout organizations would eventually become the dominant corporate organizational form. Jensen argued that LBO organizations combined concentrated ownership stakes, performance-based managerial compensation, highly leveraged capital structures, and active governance by private equity firms investing in them. According to Jensen, these structures are superior to those of the typical public corporation with dispersed shareholders, low leverage, and weak corporate governance.

Renneboog, Simons, and Wright (2007) document that the United States going-private buyout market developed from less than $1 billion in 1979 to a peak of more than $60 billion in 1988. However, a few years after Jensen's (1989) prediction of the eclipse of the public corporation, the U.S. recession of the early 1990s, along with the junk bond market crash following the fall of the investment bank Drexel Burnham Lambert, ultimately brought the first LBO wave to an end, as many of the deals from later in that period defaulted. The number of LBOs of public companies (public-to-private transactions) had drastically declined by the early 1990s. LBO activity slowed abruptly to less than $4 billion in 1990 (Kaplan and Stein, 1993). In the 10-year time frame of the first LBO wave, $1.3 trillion in total asset value had changed hands (Shleifer and Vishny, 1991).

While LBOs of public companies were relatively scarce during the 1990s and early 2000s, LBO firms continued to purchase private companies and divisions. In the mid-2000s, public-to-private transactions reappeared. Fewer than 20 years after the previous crash, the world economy experienced a second LBO boom. In 2006 and 2007, investors committed a record amount of capital to private equity, both in nominal terms and as a fraction of the overall stock market. The extent of private equity commitments and activity overtook the first wave in the late 1980s that reached its peak with the buyout of RJR Nabisco. However, in 2008, with the turmoil in the debt markets and the ensuing global economic recession, private equity declined again.

This chapter reviews some recent trends and motives for public-to-private LBO transactions. The potential sources of value creation in such transactions include the following: improvements in managerial incentives and firm governance, improvements in operating performance and productivity, tax shield benefits of leverage, asymmetric information, and market timing. Value creation in these deals is also closely associated with the availability of debt financing in credit markets and general market conditions. The chapter then describes the actors in the private equity industry, the key properties of a typical LBO transaction, recent private equity waves in the United States and other countries, and exit opportunities, followed by a discussion of some of the existing theories and evidence of the value created in going-private transactions. Finally, some conclusions are drawn about the direction of future research.

PRIVATE EQUITY INDUSTRY AND PROPERTIES OF TYPICAL LBO TRANSACTIONS

Private equity firms are typically organized as a partnership or limited liability corporation (LLC). Blackstone, Carlyle, and Kohlberg Kravis Roberts (KKR) are three of the most prominent private equity firms. Jensen (1989) describes these organizations as lean, decentralized organizations with relatively few investment professionals and employees. In his survey of seven large LBO partnerships in the late 1980s, Jensen finds that these firms employ an average of 13 investment professionals, who tend to come from an investment banking background. Twenty years later, Kaplan and Strömberg (2009) report that private equity firms are substantially larger today and that at least five large private firms employ more than 100 investment professionals. Also, private equity firms now appear to employ professionals with a wider variety of skills and experience. Acharya, Hahn, and Kehoe (2010) distinguish between private equity firms whose general partners have predominantly an operational background (e.g., ex-consultants or ex–industry managers) and those firms whose general partners have a background in finance (e.g., ex-bankers or ex-accountants).

The private equity firm raises equity capital through a private equity fund. Investors commit to providing a certain amount of money to pay for investments in portfolio companies as well as management fees to the private equity firm. Private equity funds are organized as limited partnerships in which the general partners manage the fund and the limited partners provide most of the capital. The limited partners typically include institutional investors, such as corporate and public pension funds, endowments, and insurance companies, as well as wealthy individuals. The private equity firm serves as the fund's general partner. Kaplan and Strömberg (2009) document that the general partners typically provide a small fraction of the total capital (1 percent or more).

The private equity fund typically has a fixed life, usually 10 years, but can be extended for up to three additional years (Kaplan and Strömberg, 2009). The general partner (the private equity firm) typically has up to five years to invest the committed capital into companies and then has an additional five to eight years to return the capital to its limited partners. After committing their capital, the limited partners have little control over how the general partners use the investment funds, as long as the general partners follow the basic covenants in the fund agreement. Common fund covenants place restrictions on how much fund capital can be invested in a single company, the types of securities in which a fund can invest, and the levels of debt at the fund level (as opposed to borrowing at the portfolio company level). Axelson, Strömberg, and Weisbach (2009) discuss the economic rationale for these fund structures.

The private equity firm or general partner is compensated in three different ways. First, the general partner earns an annual management fee as a percentage of committed capital and, as investments are realized, a percentage of capital employed. Second, the general partner earns a share of the fund's profits, referred to as "carried interest," which is typically equal to 20 percent. Third, some general partners charge transaction fees and monitoring fees to the companies in which they invest. Metrick and Yasuda (2010) describe the structure of fees in detail and provide empirical evidence on those fees. Among their sample of 238 private equity funds raised between 1993 and 2006, they estimate that about two-thirds of expected revenue comes from fixed-revenue components that are not sensitive to performance. They also report significant differences between venture capital (VC) and buyout funds and find that buyout fund managers build on their prior experience by increasing the size of their funds faster than VC managers do. This leads to substantially higher revenue per partner and per professional in later buyout funds compared to later VC funds. Thus, these results suggest that buyout funds are more scalable than VC funds and that past success has a differential impact on the terms of their future funds. The scalability of their business allows buyout firms to sharply increase the size of their funds and the size of the capital managed per partner or professional while keeping the number of companies per partner and per professional fairly constant, which is not the case for VC firms. Metrick and Yasuda argue that the crucial difference between buyout firms and VC firms derives from the fact that a buyout firm's manager's skill can add value to extremely large companies, whereas a VC manager's skill can only add value to small companies.

In public-to-private LBO transactions, the private equity firm typically pays a large premium over the current stock price (Kaplan, 1989a; Bargeron, Schlingemann, Stulz, and Zutter, 2007). Guo, Hotchkiss, and Song (2010) report a median premium of 29.2 percent for their sample of public-to-private LBOs conducted from 1990 to 2006 compared to the median premium of 43 percent for the 1980s, reported by Kaplan and Stein (1993). Renneboog et al. (2007) examine U.K. public-to-private transactions from 1997 to 2003 and find that pretransaction shareholders, on average, receive a premium of 40 percent.

LBOs are typically financed with large amounts of debt financing raised at the portfolio company level. Guo et al. (2010) document a sample median of nearly 70 percent postbuyout debt-to-capital ratio (and a median percentage increase in leverage of 45.7 percent) for their sample of LBOs between 1990 and 2006. Similarly, debt as a multiple of earnings before interest, taxes, depreciation, and amortization (EBITDA) increases from 1.8 to 6.0 in their full sample. This leverage in the Guo et al. sample corresponds to an equity-to-capital ratio of about 30 percent compared to the sample average of 6.52 percent from Kaplan and Stein (1993) for their sample of LBOs in the 1980s. Although the deals in the second LBO wave are highly levered, they are more conservatively financed than the deals of the late 1980s, where leverage ratios approached 90 percent. Documentation shows that a potentially large source of value for firms that go private through an LBO is an increase in interest tax shields. For the first half of the 1980s, Kaplan (1989b) estimates the tax benefits of U.S. public-to-private transactions to be between 21 and 72 percent of the premium paid to shareholders to take the company private. The high level of postbuyout debt may also serve as a disciplining mechanism, as firms take on substantial default risk in these transactions. The requirement to generate cash for debt service may curb wasteful spending and force improvements in operating efficiency.

In most LBO transactions, debt includes a senior and secured loan portion that is arranged by a bank. According to Kaplan and Strömberg (2009), banks during the 1980s and 1990s were also the primary investors in these loans. However, more recent deals in the 2000s have involved institutional investors who purchased a large fraction of the senior and secured loans through securitizations. Those investors include hedge fund investors and collateralized loan obligation (CLO) managers, who combine a number of term loans into a pool and then carve the pool into different pieces (with different seniority) to sell to institutional investors. Guo et al. (2010, p. 27) comment on this recent trend as follows: "While growth in the junk bond market may have fueled the buyout boom of the 1980s, the impact of collateralized debt obligation (CDO) packaging of senior bank debt on credit spreads may have served that role more recently." The debt in LBOs also often includes a junior, unsecured portion that is financed by either high-yield (junk) bonds or "mezzanine debt" (that is, debt that is subordinated to the senior debt). Demiroglu and James (2010) give detailed descriptions of these structures. Public debt financing is used in about 45 percent of all deals in Guo et al. (2010), similar to what Kaplan and Stein (1993) report for deals in the late 1980s. Renneboog et al. (2007) claim that the nature and extent of debt financing in U.S. public-to-private transactions differ substantially from U.K. deals. Whereas U.S. LBOs are (and were especially in the 1980s) partially financed with junk bonds, privately placed mezzanine debt seems to be the standard in the United Kingdom (Toms and Wright, 2005). Also, the debt levels associated with U.K. transactions across the 1980s and 1990s are generally lower than the leverage ratios in U.S. deals.

Private equity firms invest funds from their investors as equity to cover the remaining portion of the purchase price. The new management team of the purchased company, which may or may not be identical to the prebuyout management team, typically contributes to the new equity, but this is usually a small fraction of the contributed equity dollars. To date, management-led transactions comprise the majority of public-to-private activity. When the incumbent management team takes over the firm (backed by private equity investors), the LBO is called a management buyout (MBO). Axelson, Jenkinson, Strömberg, and Weisbach (2010) provide further detailed descriptions of capital structures in leveraged buyouts. Kaplan and Strömberg (2009) document an exponential increase in capital committed each year to U.S. private equity funds since the early 1980s, from $0.2 billion in 1980 to more than $200 billion in 2007. They measure committed capital as a percentage of the total value of the U.S. stock market. Evidence provided by Kaplan and Strömberg (p. 125) suggests that private equity commitments are cyclical: "[Private equity commitments] increased in the 1980s, peaked in 1988, declined in the early 1990s, increased through the late 1990s, peaked in 1998, declined again in the early 2000s, and then began climbing in 2003. By 2006 and 2007, private equity commitments appeared extremely high by historical standards, exceeding 1 percent of the value of the U.S. stock market."

WAVES OF PRIVATE EQUITY TRANSACTIONS

Kaplan and Strömberg (2009) report the number and combined transaction value of worldwide leveraged buyout transactions backed by a private equity fund sponsor based on the data they collect from CapitalIQ (a large database covering public and private firms and investment firms). In total, they report that 17,171 private equity–sponsored buyout transactions occurred from January 1, 1970, to June 30, 2007. The patterns they document in private equity fundraising are also mirrored in overall buyout transaction activity, suggesting a similar cyclicality in fundraising and transactions. Kaplan and Strömberg (pp. 126–127) note the following:

> Transaction values peaked in 1988; dropped during the early 1990s, rose and peaked in the later 1990s, dropped in the early 2000s; and increased dramatically from 2004 to 2006. A huge fraction of historic buyout activity has taken place within the last few years. From 2005 through June 2007, CapitalIQ recorded a total of 5,188 buyout transactions at a combined estimated enterprise value of over $1.6 trillion (in 2007 dollars), with those 2 years accounting for 30 percent of the transactions from 1984 to 2007 and 43 percent of the total real value of these transactions, respectively.

Kaplan and Strömberg report that the number of announced LBOs continued to increase until June 2007 when a record number of 322 deals were announced. Since then, deal activity has decreased substantially following the turmoil in the credit markets. In January 2008, only 133 new buyouts were announced.

Kaplan and Strömberg (2009) also show how the characteristics of the transactions have evolved over time. The first buyout wave during the late 1980s was predominantly concentrated in the United States, Canada, and, to a smaller extent, the United Kingdom. From 1985 to 1989, the authors show that these three countries accounted for 89 percent of all global LBO transactions and 93 percent of the value of these transactions. They also report that acquisitions of relatively large companies in mature industries such as manufacturing and retail dominated this first LBO wave and that public-to-private deals accounted for 49 percent of the total value of private equity transactions. Early private equity research examines the first buyout wave, which mainly consisted of the going-private transactions of large firms in mature industries.

After the fall of the junk bond market in the late 1980s, Kaplan and Strömberg (2009) report that public-to-private activity declined dramatically, dropping to less than 10 percent of transaction value, while the average enterprise value of the companies acquired dropped from $401 million to $132 million (both in 2007 U.S. dollars). Instead, "middle-market" buyouts of non–publicly traded firms (either independent companies or divisions of larger corporations) grew substantially and accounted for the bulk of private equity activity. Manufacturing and retail firms became less dominant as buyout targets, and buyout activity spread to new industries such as information technology, media, and telecommunications as well as financial services and health care. Although the aggregate value of transactions fell, twice as many deals occurred from 1990 to 1994 compared to the 1985 to 1989 period.

Kaplan and Strömberg (2009) describe in detail how the market evolved as private equity activity experienced steady growth over the period from 1995 to 2004 (with the exception of the dip in 2000 to 2001). They note that buyouts of public companies increased, although buyouts of private companies still accounted for more than 80 percent of the value and 90 percent of the transactions during this time. An increasing share of buyout deal flow came from other private equity funds exiting their old investments. From early 2000 to 2004, these so-called secondary buyouts made up more than 20 percent of total transaction value. However, large corporations selling off their divisions represent the largest source of deals in this period.

Kaplan and Strömberg (2009) also document the rapid spread of the buyout phenomenon to continental Europe. In the 2000 to 2004 period, the Western European private equity market had 48.9 percent of the total value of worldwide LBO transactions, compared with 43.7 percent in the United States. The scope of the industry also continued to broaden during this time, with companies in the services and infrastructure industries becoming increasingly popular buyout targets. Finally, Kaplan and Strömberg note that, in the private equity boom from the start of 2005 to mid-2007, public-to-private deals and secondary buyouts grew rapidly both in number and size, together accounting for more than 60 percent of the $1.6 trillion in total LBO transaction value over this time. As large public-to-private transactions returned, average deal sizes almost tripled between 2001 and 2006.

EXIT EVENTS AND HOLDING PERIODS IN PRIVATE EQUITY INVESTMENTS

Investment exits and harvesting are important aspects of the private equity process because most private equity funds have a limited contractual lifetime. Kaplan and Strömberg (2009) analyze the exit behavior of private equity funds using their sample of buyouts. They report that 54 percent of the 17,171 transactions in their total sample (going back to 1970) had not yet exited as of November 2007. Thus, drawing conclusions about the long-run economic impact of LBOs is impossible without suffering from some selection bias.

Among all realized exits in that sample, the most common route is the sale of the company to a strategic (i.e., nonfinancial) buyer; this occurs in 38 percent of all exits. The second most common exit route is a sale to another private equity fund in a so-called "secondary leveraged buyout" (24 percent), the frequency of which has increased considerably over time. Initial public offerings (IPOs), where the company is listed on a public stock exchange (and the private equity firm can subsequently sell its shares in the public market), account for 14 percent of exits. According to Kaplan and Strömberg (2009), IPOs have decreased significantly in relative importance as an exit route for LBOs over time. Given the high debt levels involved in LBO transactions, the expected frequency of bankruptcy in these transactions can be relatively high. Consistent with this, Andrade and Kaplan (1998) find that 29 percent of public-to-private transactions of the 1980s default at some point. Guo et al. (2010) document that 23 firms entered Chapter 11 or a distressed restructuring, which is 12 percent of their full sample of 192 firms that went private between 1900 and 2006. Yet, only 53 percent of firms in their full sample reached a known exit outcome (16 percent sell to a strategic acquirer, 15 percent engage in IPOs, 12 percent enter Chapter 11 or a distressed restructuring, and 10 percent engage in a secondary LBO).

According to Kaplan and Strömberg (2009), the median holding period for individual LBO transactions is around six years in their full sample. Recently, private equity funds have been accused of short-termism and quickly flipping their investments rather than keeping their ownership of companies to fully realize their value potential. Kaplan and Strömberg find that only 12 percent of deals in their sample are exited within 24 months of the LBO acquisition date, which they define as a quick flip. Finally, because of the high fraction of secondary buyouts in recent years, the authors note that individual holding periods underestimate the total time period in which private equity funds hold LBO firms. Accounting for secondary buyouts, Strömberg (2008) finds that the median LBO is still in private equity ownership nine years after the original buyout transaction. Since Kaplan (1991) finds that the median LBO target remained in private ownership for around seven years, the most recent evidence suggests that privately owned holding periods have increased since the 1980s.

VALUE CREATION IN PUBLIC-TO-PRIVATE TRANSACTIONS

Several advantages accrue for a firm having a public status rather than remaining private. The extant literature on a private firm's decision to go public is extensive (e.g., Chemmanur and Fulghieri, 1999; Chemmanur, He, and Nandy, 2010; Bayar and Chemmanur, 2010). A stock exchange listing combined with the separation of ownership and control allows the firm access to capital markets, specialization in managerial skills, and a higher degree of analyst and media coverage. Going public also helps the firm's investors, founders, and entrepreneurs to diversify their portfolios since the firm's stock becomes more liquid. Other benefits include advantages in product market competition and the use of stock price–based remuneration packages. However, public corporations have a major drawback due to the separation of ownership and control: An unaccountable management could impose substantial agency costs to the shareholders, leading to corporate value destruction. The size of the inefficiencies induced by agency conflicts led Jensen (1989) to predict that the eclipse of the public corporation was near. In the 1980s, a first important wave of leveraged public-to-private transactions, with a value of about $250 billion, occurred in the United States (Opler and Titman, 1993).

Before the first wave of LBOs, the media criticized corporate America for a lack of focus on shareholder value. However, a wave of corporate restructurings tended to address the deficiencies in corporate governance regulation and the lack of managerial incentives to focus on corporate value. Renneboog et al. (2007) note that, in addition to an increased number of hostile corporate takeovers, LBOs and MBOs arose as powerful catalysts to reduce the excess capacity in what Jensen (1991) calls "complacent corporate America." In less than a decade, the U.S. going-private buyout market developed from less than $1 billion in 1979 to a peak of more than $60 billion in 1988. However, the culmination of this first LBO wave was associated with many bankruptcies and fierce public and political resistance (i.e., antitakeover legislation) such that transaction activity abruptly slowed to less than $4 billion in 1990 (Kaplan and Stein, 1993). In this first wave, a total of $1.3 trillion in asset value had changed hands (Shleifer and Vishny, 1991). Kaplan (1997) and Holmstrom and Kaplan (2001) argue that the 1980s-style deals are no longer necessary because the focus on shareholder value has since been institutionalized by public corporations. Nevertheless, from 1997 onwards, a rise in U.S. public-to-private transactions has been observed, culminating in the boom of the second LBO wave between 2005 and 2007.

In public-to-private LBO transactions, private equity firms buy public companies, fix them, and then exit (sell their equity holdings). What are the sources of value created by private equity firms during this process, and why were the companies unable to fix themselves without going private? Most papers in the existing literature studying LBOs in the 1980s contend that private equity firms mitigate managerial agency problems, thereby creating value by improving management and operating efficiency. These papers emphasize three mechanisms: (1) increased managerial incentives through concentrated equity ownership, (2) the disciplining effect of greater debt on managers, and (3) enhanced governance and monitoring by private equity firms.

Management Incentives

The separation of ownership and control in public corporations creates a divergence of interests between managers and stockholders, which in turn can create agency costs that lead to destroying firm value (Jensen and Meckling, 1976). The need to realign the incentives of managers with those of shareholders is frequently mentioned as an important factor in public-to-private transactions (Kaplan, 1989a). The reunification of ownership and control after public-to-private LBO transactions is expected to improve the incentive structure and increase managerial effort to maximize firm value.

The existing literature documents that private equity firms provide higher managerial incentives to the top management of their portfolio companies. They give the management team a large equity upside through stock and options, which was not a standard practice among public firms in the early 1980s (Jensen and Murphy, 1990). Kaplan (1989a) finds that management ownership percentages increase by a factor of four when going from public-to-private ownership. Private equity firms also require management to make a meaningful investment in the company so that management has both a substantial upside and downside. Because the portfolio companies are private, management cannot easily sell its equity or exercise its options until the value is provided by an exit transaction (Kaplan and Strömberg, 2009). This is due to the illiquidity of private equity, and it reduces management's incentive to myopically focus on short-term performance. Most of the public-to-private U.S. transactions in the 1980s were management buyouts (MBOs) where the incumbent management seeks institutional support from private equity firms to purchase a major stake in the firm and fund the transaction.

Using a sample of 43 LBOs in the United States from 1996 to 2004, Kaplan and Strömberg (2009) report that the management teams of LBO target firms still obtain substantial equity stakes in the portfolio companies. They find that the chief executive officer (CEO) gets 5.4 percent of the equity upside (stock and options) while the entire management team gets 16 percent. Leslie and Oyer (2009), who analyze a sample of reverse LBOs (private equity firms that undergo an IPO) from 1996 to 2006, report that CEOs of private equity–owned firms own about twice as large a share of the firm, earn about 10 percent less in base pay, and receive a substantially larger share of cash compensation through variable pay relative to their counterparts at publicly traded companies in the same industry with similar observable characteristics. The authors conclude that the difference in managerial incentives that existed in the 1980s between public companies and private equity–owned firms is still present during the period from 1996 to 2006. Acharya et al. (2010) find similar results in the United Kingdom for 59 large buyouts from 1997 to 2004. In their sample, the median CEO gets 3 percent of the equity, and the median management team gets 15 percent. These studies confirm that, even though similar equity-based compensation schemes have become more prevalent in public firms since the 1980s, management's ownership stakes are still greater in LBOs than in public companies.

Consistent with the potential for increased incentive realignment after going private, Renneboog et al. (2007) find that, in their sample of 177 public-to-private LBOs from 1997 to 2003, expected shareholder wealth gains (premiums and cumulative average annual returns) are higher for firms with lower levels of prebuyout managerial ownership.

The Disciplining Effect of Higher Debt

By exchanging debt for equity, managers credibly precommit to pay out future cash flows rather than retaining them to invest in negative net present value (NPV) projects because they are obligated to generate more cash for debt service. The increased risk of default resulting from the recapitalization of the LBOs can force the firm to curb wasteful investment spending and operate more efficiently (Jensen, 1986). While LBOs increase managerial share ownership, allowing managers to reap more of the benefits from their efforts, higher leverage forces the managers to run the company efficiently and avoid default (Cotter and Peck, 2001). In a study of MBOs in the 1980s, Singh (1990) shows that MBOs have substantially higher levels of cash flows than similar matched firms. Thus, high leverage associated with public-to-private LBO transactions can be expected to reduce the "free cash flow" problems described by Jensen by bonding the managers to pay out more cash flows to service the debt. However, higher leverage also increases the probability of incurring costs of financial distress. Axelson et al. (2010) also argue that leverage provides discipline to the acquiring LBO fund.

The Effects of Better Monitoring and Active Governance by Private Equity Firms

The boards of LBO companies tend to be dominated by their financial sponsors. These boards are more actively involved in governance than the boards of public companies. Empirical evidence shows that boards of private equity portfolio companies are smaller than comparable public companies and meet more frequently (Gertner and Kaplan, 1996; Cornelli and Karakas, 2008; Acharya et al., 2010). Acharya et al. report that portfolio companies have 12 formal meetings per year and many more informal meetings. Management turnover in these companies is relatively high. The authors also report that one-third of these firms' CEOs are replaced in the first 100 days and two-thirds are replaced at some point over a four-year period. Renneboog et al. (2007) find that, in firms with stronger outside blockholders (especially corporations), the expected shareholder wealth gains are smaller. This is consistent with the claim that these types of firms have less scope of operating performance improvements because they are already well monitored by strong outside shareholders.

Industry and Operating Expertise of Private Equity Executives

According to Kaplan and Strömberg (2009) most large private equity firms in recent decades have also contributed industry and operating expertise to the portfolio companies in which they invest. They note that most top private equity firms are now organized around industries and that private equity firms now often hire professionals and consultants with operating backgrounds and an industry focus. Many top private equity firms use their industry and operating expertise to select promising investments; develop strategic plans to identify cost-cutting opportunities, productivity improvements, and acquisition opportunities; and implement changes in management practices (Acharya et al., 2010).

Toms and Wright (2005) contend that U.K. venture capital and buyout markets have traditionally been more closely linked than those in the United States. Moreover, public-to-private activity in the United Kingdom has focused more on growth opportunities, whereas U.S. LBOs have occurred more frequently in mature, cash-rich industries. Acharya et al. (2010) show that general partners with an operational background (ex-consultants or ex–industry managers) generate significantly higher performance in "organic deals" with a focus on internal value creation through operating performance improvements. In contrast, they show that general partners with a background in finance (e.g., ex-bankers or ex-accountants) generate higher performance in deals with merger and acquisition (M&A) events. Acharya et al. suggest that deal partner background and human capital skills of private equity executives are important determinants of the persistent abnormal financial returns generated by large private equity firms for their investors (documented by Kaplan and Schoar, 2005).

Improvements in Operating Performance

Many empirical studies based on transactions from the 1980s document large improvements in operating performance and productivity following LBOs. For instance, Kaplan (1989a) reports large industry-adjusted increases in operating profit margins (10 to 20 percent) and cash flow to sales ratios (45.5 percent, 72.5 percent, and 28.3 percent for the first three years after the buyout, respectively). Lichtenberg and Siegel (1990), Smith (1990), and Cotter and Peck (2001) report similar operating gains. Kaplan also shows declines in the ratio of capital expenditures to sales, which is consistent with cost-cutting and productivity improvements. Other studies of the first LBO wave show that firm values increase from the time of the LBO to a subsequent exit event, producing large returns for the investors of portfolio companies, which is consistent with evidence on improvements in operating performance (e.g., Kaplan, 1989c, 1994; Andrade and Kaplan, 1998). Empirical studies on LBOs in Europe in the 1990s find that these LBOs are associated with significant operating and productivity improvements (e.g., Harris, Siegel, and Wright, 2005; Bergström, Grubb, and Jonsson, 2007; Boucly, Sraer, and Thesmar, 2009).

Empirical studies on more recent public-to-private LBO transactions report much smaller gains in operating performance after the transition to the private status (e.g., Leslie and Oyer, 2009; Guo et al., 2010). Nevertheless, the same studies document that the LBO firms in these more recent transactions experienced very large increases in value from the time of their buyout to their subsequent exit from a private equity firm's portfolio, producing large returns to invested debt and equity capital. Studying a sample of 192 buyouts of over $100 million completed between 1990 and 2006, Guo et al. find that gains in operating performance are either comparable to or slightly exceed those observed for benchmark firms matched on industry and prebuyout characteristics. The magnitudes of the gains in profitability that they report are substantially smaller than those reported by Kaplan (1989a) for deals completed in the 1980s, and these gains appear to be small relative to the high investor returns that Guo et al. document. For the 94 deals completed by 2005 with postbuyout data available, median market and risk-adjusted returns to prebuyout capital invested are 72.5 percent (40.9 percent for postbuyout capital). Nevertheless, consistent with the agency benefits of higher debt, Guo et al. find that cash flow gains are greater for firms with significant increases in leverage post-LBO. They also report that cash flow performance is greater when the private equity firm has replaced the CEO of the portfolio company. Leslie and Oyer also find some weak evidence suggesting that private equity–owned firms are more profitable and have higher sales per employee than comparable public firms in the United States between 1996 and 2004. Acharya et al. (2010) and Weir, Jones, and Wright (2008) find relatively small operating improvements for more recent public-to-private deals in the United Kingdom.

As Kaplan and Strömberg (2009) note, these more recent empirical results suggest that post-1980s public-to-private transactions may differ from those of the 1980s in how they create value for private equity investors and the portfolio companies in which they invest. Empirical studies of investor returns at the private equity fund level or the portfolio company level show that returns to private equity investors are high (e.g., Kaplan and Schoar, 2005; Acharya et al., 2010; Guo et al., 2010), but these high investor returns cannot be solely attributed to improvements in operating performance after going private. For instance, Guo et al. show that increases in industry and market valuation multiples and tax shield benefits of debt are each as important in explaining the realized returns to capital as changes in operating performance.

Several pieces of existing empirical evidence are inconsistent with the frequently cited claim that private equity firms have short-term incentives. Lerner, Sorensen, and Strömberg (2008) show that buyout transactions do not lead to declines in the long-term innovation of the portfolio firms that engage in patenting. They find that patents filed by these firms after the buyout receive more subsequent citations than those filed before the buyout, as firms tend to focus their innovation activities in selected core areas. Cao and Lerner (2009) report that LBO firms that exit through an IPO (reverse LBOs) have positive industry-adjusted long-term stock performance after going public.

Overall, existing empirical evidence is mostly consistent with the notion that LBOs lead to value creation through improvements in operating performance and productivity. However, more recent evidence regarding the going-private transactions of the second private equity wave (1995 to 2007) suggests that these operational gains are more modest, relative to those of the first private equity wave of the 1980s.

Some critics of LBOs argue that most of the operational benefits of private equity are obtained at the expense of large cuts in employment and wages. However, Kaplan and Strömberg (2009) note that, overall, the empirical evidence suggests that employment actually grows at firms experiencing LBOs but at a slower rate than at other similar firms. Thus, existing evidence dismisses claims over job destruction and is also consistent with the notion that LBO firms create economic value by operating more efficiently (see also Kaplan, 1989a; Lichtenberg and Siegel, 1990; Amess and Wright, 2007; Boucly et al., 2009; Davis, Haltiwanger, Jarmin, Lerner, and Miranda, 2009) for empirical evidence regarding private equity and employment).

Tax Shield Benefits of Higher Leverage

Higher leverage can increase firm value not only by disciplining the managers of the LBO firm (as explained above) but also by reducing the taxes the firm has to pay and thereby increasing the cash flows available to the capital providers. These valuable interest tax shields are created through the tax deductibility of interest expenses. The magnitude of the impact of increasing tax shields depends on the assumptions as to whether leverage will be maintained after the exit from the private equity firm's portfolio. Therefore, estimates of the value of increased interest tax shields after the LBO exhibit a large range of variation depending on the assumptions about the permanence of debt.

Kaplan (1989b) finds that, depending on the assumption, the reduced taxes from the higher interest deduction can explain from 4 percent to 40 percent of a firm's value. He estimates that the tax benefits of U.S. public-to-private transactions are between 21 percent and 72 percent of the premium paid to shareholders to take the company private for the first half of the 1980s. According to Kaplan and Strömberg (2009), a reasonable estimate of the value of lower taxes due to increased leverage for the 1980s might be 10 to 20 percent of firm value. They argue that these estimates would be lower for leveraged buyouts in the 1990s and 2000s because both the corporate tax rate and the extent of leverage used in these deals are lower compared to earlier deals. Guo et al. (2010) report that, for the full sample returns to prebuyout capital, they can attribute 33.8 percent of the return to capital to tax benefits from increasing leverage. However, they also note that the magnitude of the tax benefits is likely to be overstated for certain outcome groups, such as distressed restructurings, where the firm is unlikely to remain as highly levered after exiting the private equity firm's portfolio. Evidence by Renneboog et al. (2007) indicates that higher premiums are paid for public firms with low prebuyout levels of leverage because these firms have more unused debt capacity to create a large additional tax shield.

Overall, existing empirical evidence suggests that higher financial leverage after an LBO can create significant value for the firms going private by reducing their taxes. Yet, critics argue that a public company could obtain the same tax benefits without going private by simply restructuring its financial structure.

Asymmetric Information and Market Timing

High returns to private equity capital and positive operating performance improvements in LBOs can also be consistent with the notion that private equity investors can acquire undervalued public firms as a result of having private information about future company performance. A related hypothesis is that the incumbent management may supply valuable inside information to private equity sponsors and choose not to bargain for the best possible price in order to protect their jobs. Kaplan and Strömberg (2009) maintain that the empirical evidence does not support this hypothesis (Kaplan, 1989a; Ofek, 1994) and that management turnover after LBOs is high (Acharya et al., 2010). They also point out that private equity investors near the end of the boom and bust cycles of private equity (the end of the 1980s and possibly the first half of 2007) tend to overpay and experience losses as defaults of companies increase.

Guo et al. (2010) present strong evidence suggesting that private equity firms can buy firms and later exit at a higher valuation multiple, producing substantial returns to private equity investors. Acharya et al. (2010) also show that increases in valuation multiples are much higher for deals with an M&A focus. Bargeron et al. (2007) find that private equity firms pay lower premiums than public acquirers. Thus, recent evidence on the public-to-private LBO transactions in the second buyout wave suggests that private equity firms may have some market timing ability in buying undervalued public firms and then exiting them at higher prices. Guo et al. suggest that this ability of private equity firms may partially be explained by extremely favorable credit market conditions during their sample period. By taking on large amounts of cheaply priced debt, firms can arbitrage the systematic mispricing between the debt and equity markets. They conjecture that the impact of securitization of senior bank debt in LBO deals may have fueled the second buyout boom, which lasted through the first half of 2007, while growth in the junk bond market may have fueled the buyout boom of the 1980s.

Kaplan and Stein (1993) present evidence that is consistent with high-yield bond investors providing extremely favorable terms to private equity investors in the 1980s buyout wave. Kaplan and Strömberg (2009) also note that the credit market turmoil in late 2007 and early 2008 suggests that extremely favorable terms from debt investors may have helped fuel the buyout wave from 2005 through mid-2007. Axelson et al. (2009) present an agency-based theory arguing that the compensation structures of private equity funds provide incentives to take on more debt than is optimal for the individual firm. Axelson et al. (2010) find evidence that is consistent with the hypothesis that credit market conditions may drive the debt financing of LBOs rather than the relative benefits of leverage for the particular firm. Finally, Demiroglu and James (2010) as well as Ivashina and Kovner (2010) find that more prominent private equity funds apparently can obtain cheaper loans and looser covenants than other lenders. Overall, these results are consistent with the availability of debt financing and the credit market conditions affecting the cyclicality in the private equity market.

SUMMARY AND CONCLUSIONS

Overall, the empirical evidence supports the notion that private equity firms create value for their portfolio companies that transition from public to private status. LBO transactions have positive impacts on management incentives, corporate governance, and operating performance. They also reduce the tax obligations of portfolio firms that go private by substantially increasing their leverage. Finally, firm values and valuation multiples significantly increase from the time of the buyout until a subsequent exit event. These gains are also reflected in the high investor returns generated for private equity investors.

Operating gains and productivity improvements for the buyouts in the second private equity wave from 1995 to 2007 are much more modest than those reported for the public-to-private transactions in the first wave during the 1980s. However, since most of the new empirical results are largely based on LBOs completed before 2006, more research is needed to understand the economic impact of private equity on firms going private near the end of the second private equity wave. This latest wave went bust with the turmoil in credit markets and the ensuing global economic recession. Thus, future research on this topic is important given the increased frequency of large public-to-private transactions.

High returns to private equity investors may not be sustainable under less favorable credit and equity market conditions. Even though the LBOs of the second wave are not as highly levered as their counterparts from the late 1980s, the effect of the "great recession" on firm cash flows and valuation multiples will affect the overall value created by private equity firms in the most recent wave of public-to-private LBO transactions. Research should also evaluate the impact of general market conditions and the availability of debt financing on future harvesting (exit) opportunities and investor commitments to private equity.

DISCUSSION QUESTIONS

1. How can the cyclicality of private equity activity be explained?
2. How is the structure of private equity deals likely to evolve after the end of the latest private equity boom?

3. What are some of the potential sources of value creation in public-to-private LBO transactions?

4. How do private equity firms that focus on LBOs differ from venture capital firms in the way they create value for their portfolio companies?

REFERENCES

Acharya, Viral V., Moritz Hahn, and Conor Kehoe. 2010. "Corporate Governance and Value Creation: Evidence from Private Equity." Working Paper, Stern School of Business, New York University.

Amess, Kevin, and Mike Wright. 2007. "The Wage and Employment Effects of Leveraged Buyouts in the UK." *International Journal of the Economics of Business* 14:2, 179–195.

Andrade, Gregor, and Steven N. Kaplan. 1998. "How Costly Is Financial (Not Economic) Distress? Evidence from Highly Leveraged Transactions That Became Distressed." *Journal of Finance* 53:5, 1443–1493.

Axelson, Ulf, Tim Jenkinson, Per Strömberg, and Michael Weisbach. 2010. "Leverage and Pricing in Buyouts: An Empirical Analysis." Working Paper, Swedish Institute for Financial Research.

Axelson, Ulf, Per Strömberg, and Michael Weisbach. 2009. "Why Are Buyouts Levered? The Financial Structure of Private Equity Firms." *Journal of Finance* 64:4, 1549–1582.

Bargeron, Leonce, Frederik Schlingemann, René Stulz, and Chad Zutter. 2007. "Why Do Private Acquirers Pay So Little Compared to Public Acquirers?" Working Paper, Fisher College of Business, The Ohio State University.

Bayar, Onur, and Thomas J. Chemmanur. 2010. "IPOs versus Acquisitions and the Valuation Premium Puzzle: A Theory of Exit Choice by Entrepreneurs and Venture Capitalists." *Journal of Financial and Quantitative Analysis*. Forthcoming.

Bergström, Clas, Mikael Grubb, and Sara Jonsson. 2007. "The Operating Impact of Buyouts in Sweden: A Study of Value Creation." *Journal of Private Equity* 11:1, 22–39.

Boucly, Quentin, David Sraer, and David Thesmar. 2009. "Job Creating LBOs." Working Paper, University of California–Berkeley and HEC Paris.

Cao, Jerry, and Josh Lerner. 2009. "The Performance of Reverse Leveraged Buyouts." *Journal of Financial Economics* 91:2, 139–157.

Chemmanur, Thomas J., and Paolo Fulghieri. 1999. "A Theory of the Going-Public Decision." *Review of Financial Studies* 12:2, 249–279.

Chemmanur, Thomas J., Shan He, and Debarshi Nandy. 2010. "The Going-Public Decision and the Product Market." *Review of Financial Studies* 23:5, 1855–1908.

Cornelli, Francesca, and Oguzhan Karakas. 2008. "Private Equity and Corporate Governance: Do LBOs Have More Effective Boards?" *World Economic Forum: The Global Economic Impact of Private Equity Report 2008*, 65–84.

Cotter, James F., and Sarah W. Peck. 2001. "The Structure of Debt and Active Equity Investors: The Case of the Buyout Specialist." *Journal of Financial Economics* 59:1, 101–147.

Davis, Steven J., John Haltiwanger, Ron S. Jarmin, Josh Lerner, and Javier Miranda. 2008. "Private Equity and Employment." Working Paper, Harvard University and University of Chicago.

Demiroglu, Cem, and Christopher M. James. 2010. "The Role of Private Equity Group Reputation in LBO Financing." *Journal of Financial Economics*. Forthcoming.

Gertner, Robert, and Steven Kaplan. 1996. "The Value Maximizing Board." Working Paper, University of Chicago.

Guo, Shourun, Edith S. Hotchkiss, and Weihong Song. 2010. "Do Buyouts (Still) Create Value?" *Journal of Finance*. Forthcoming.

Harris, Richard, Donald S. Siegel, and Mike Wright. 2005. "Assessing the Impact of Management Buyouts on Economic Efficiency: Plant-Level Evidence from the United Kingdom." *Review of Economic and Statistics* 87:1, 148–153.

Holmstrom, Bengt, and Steven Kaplan. 2001. "Corporate Governance and Merger Activity in the U.S.: Making Sense of the '80s and '90s." *Journal of Economic Perspectives* 15:2, 121–144.

Ivashina, Victoria, and Anna Kovner. 2010. "The Private Equity Advantage: Leveraged Buyout Firms and Relationship Banking." Working Paper, Harvard Business School.

Jensen, Michael. 1986. "Agency Costs of Free Cash Flow, Corporate Finance and Takeovers." American Economic Review 76:2, 323–329.

Jensen, Michael. 1989. "Eclipse of the Public Corporation." *Harvard Business Review* 67:5, 61–74.

Jensen, Michael. 1991. "Corporate Control and the Politics of Finance." *Journal of Applied Corporate Finance* 4:2, 13–33.

Jensen, Michael, and William Meckling. 1976. "Theory of the Firm: Managerial Behavior, Agency Costs and Ownership Structure." *Journal of Financial Economics* 3:4, 305–360.

Jensen, Michael, and Kevin J. Murphy. 1990. "Performance Pay and Top Management Incentives." *Journal of Political Economy* 98:2, 225–64.

Kaplan, Steven. 1989a. "The Effects of Management Buyouts on Operating Performance and Value." *Journal of Financial Economics* 24:2, 217–254.

Kaplan, Steven. 1989b. "Management Buyouts: Evidence on Taxes as a Source of Value." *Journal of Finance* 44:3, 611–632.

Kaplan, Steven. 1989c. "Campeau's Acquisition of Federated: Value Destroyed or Value Added." *Journal of Financial Economics* 25:2, 191–212.

Kaplan, Steven. 1991. "The Staying Power of Leveraged Buy-outs." *Journal of Financial Economics* 29:2, 287–313.

Kaplan, Steven. 1994. "Campeau's Acquisition of Federated: Post-Bankruptcy Results." *Journal of Financial Economics* 35:1, 123–136.

Kaplan, Steven. 1997. "The Evolution of U.S. Corporate Governance: We Are All Henry Kravis Now." *Journal of Private Equity* 1:1, 7–14.

Kaplan, Steven, and Antoinette Schoar. 2005. "Private Equity Performance: Returns, Persistence, and Capital Flows." *Journal of Finance* 60:4, 1791–1823.

Kaplan, Steven, and Jeremy Stein. 1993. "The Evolution of Buyout Pricing and Financial Structure in the 1980s." *Quarterly Journal of Economics* 108:2, 313–358.

Kaplan, Steven, and Per Strömberg. 2009. "Leveraged Buyouts and Private Equity." *Journal of Economic Perspectives* 23:1, 121–146.

Lerner, Josh, Morten Sorensen, and Per Strömberg. 2008. "Private Equity and Long-Run Investment: The Case of Innovation." Working Paper, Stockholm School of Economics.

Leslie, Phillip, and Paul Oyer. 2009. "Managerial Incentives and Value Creation: Evidence from Private Equity." Working Paper, Stanford University.

Lichtenberg, Frank, and Donald Siegel. 1990. "The Effects of Leveraged Buyouts on Productivity and Related Aspects of Firm Behavior." *Journal of Financial Economics* 27:1, 165–194.

Metrick, Andrew, and Ayako Yasuda. 2010. "The Economics of Private Equity Funds." *Review of Financial Studies*. Forthcoming.

Ofek, Eli. 1994. "Efficiency Gains in Unsuccessful Management Buyouts." *Journal of Finance* 49:2, 637–654.

Opler, Tim, and Sheridan Titman. 1993. "The Determinants of Leveraged Buyout Activity: Free Cash Flow versus Financial Distress Costs." *Journal of Finance* 48:5, 1985–1999.

Renneboog, Luc, Tomas Simons, and Mike Wright. 2007. "Why Do Firms Go Private in the UK?" *Journal of Corporate Finance* 13:4, 591–628.

Shleifer, Andrei, and Robert Vishny. 1991. "The Takeover Wave of the 1980s." *Journal of Applied Corporate Finance* 4:3, 49–56.

Singh, Harbir. 1990. "Management Buyouts: Distinguishing Characteristics and Operating Changes Prior to Public Offering." *Academy of Management Journal* 11:1, 111–129.

Smith, Abbie J. 1990. "Capital Ownership Structure and Performance: The Case of Management Buyouts." *Journal of Financial Economics* 27:1, 143–164.

Strömberg, Per. 2008. "The New Demography of Private Equity." *World Economic Forum: The Global Economic Impact of Private Equity Report 2008*, 3–26.

Toms, Steven, and Mike Wright. 2005. "Divergence and Convergence within Anglo-American Corporate Governance Systems: Evidence from the US and UK 1950–2000." *Business History* 47:2, 267–295.

Weir, Charlie, Peter Jones, and Mike Wright. 2008. "Public to Private Transactions, Private Equity and Performance in the UK: An Empirical Analysis of the Impact of Going Private." Working Paper, Nottingham University Business School and Robert Gordon University.

ABOUT THE AUTHOR

Onur Bayar is an Assistant Professor of Finance at the University of Texas at San Antonio. Professor Bayar's research interests are in corporate finance with an emphasis on capital structure, security issues, IPOs, M&As, and entrepreneurial finance. Professor Bayar received a BS in Industrial Engineering from Bogazici University, an MS in Industrial Engineering from the University of Pittsburgh, an MS in Finance from Carnegie Mellon University, and a PhD in Finance from Boston College.

CHAPTER 24

International Takeovers and Restructuring

RITA BISWAS
Associate Professor of Finance, University at Albany–SUNY

INTRODUCTION

Despite the global economic downturn during 2008 and 2009, one set of corporate activities continues to grow: mergers and acquisitions (M&As). According to *Bloomberg Businessweek* (2010), more than 2,034 cross-border transactions were announced by the end of the first quarter of 2010. The total deal value exceeded $249 billion, which is more than double the corresponding figure for the first quarter of 2009. Exhibit 24.1 shows the global distribution of cross-border activity from 2007 to the first quarter of 2010 across four key regions: the United States, Europe, Asia (excluding Japan), and Japan. In general, both the number of deals and deal values have been declining since 2007, but signs of recovery in global M&A markets for almost all regions emerged during the first quarter of 2010. However, while cross-border deals in the United States, Europe, and Japan declined between 2008 and 2009, a few large deals in the category of outward acquisitions from Asia caused both the value of outbound deals and total deals to increase between 2008 and 2009 in the Asian category.

Many reasons exist for the current trend in M&As. First, companies now recognize that to thrive and remain competitive they must be global in scale and scope, and technological progress in the current era makes such expansion feasible. Second, the formation of the euro-zone, privatization of certain economies, deregulation of specific industries, and market liberalization in various parts of the world have given rise to a wave of consolidation across borders in regions beyond the United States, Western Europe, and Japan. The distribution of commercial power has shifted from this tripolar system to a wider multipolar world. In fact, a striking feature in this current wave of cross-border M&A activity is the increasing presence of acquirers from emerging markets. During the month of March 2010, the $10.7 billion bid for Zain Africa by India-based telecom provider Bharti Airtel and Norwegian fertilizer producer Yara International's proposed acquisition of U.S.-based Terra Industries are examples of this phenomenon. However, as Exhibit 24.2 shows, even as recently as 2008, the top 10 mega-deals in cross-border acquisitions did not involve emerging markets in general.

Exhibit 24.1 Cross-Border M&A Activity from 2007 to the First Quarter of 2010

Panel A. United States

United States	Outbound		Inbound		Total U.S. Cross-border	
Rank Date	Value ($ Mil)	Number of Deals	Value ($ Mil)	Number of Deals	Value ($ Mil)	Number of Deals
2007	409,152.7	2,701	445,010.6	2,639	854,163.3	5,340
2008	158,906.6	2,259	382,606.7	2,153	541,513.3	4,412
2009	127,411.5	1,746	97,531.6	1,859	224,943.1	3,605
2010	46,933.7	660	107,738.4	659	154,672.1	1,319
Total United States	742,404.4	7,366	1,032,887.3	7,310	1,775,291.8	14,676

Panel B. Europe

Europe	Outbound		Inbound		Total Europe Cross-border	
Rank Date	Value ($ Mil)	Number of Deals	Value ($ Mil)	Number of Deals	Value ($ Mil)	Number of Deals
2007	382,226.9	2,438	372,769.4	2,428	754,996.3	4,866
2008	356,461.4	2,241	205,447.6	2,265	561,909.0	4,506
2009	87,178.5	1,540	239,969.9	1,919	327,148.4	3,459
2010	94,824.0	523	73,365.1	714	168,189.1	1,237
Total Europe	920,690.8	6,742	891,551.9	7,326	1,812,242.8	14,068

Panel C. Asia Excluding Japan

Asia (Excluding Japan)	Outbound		Inbound		Total Asia Cross-border	
Rank Date	Value ($ Mil)	Number of Deals	Value ($ Mil)	Number of Deals	Value ($ Mil)	Number of Deals
2007	156,307.2	1,206	122,289.1	1,757	278,596.3	2,963
2008	88,761.6	1,040	101,768.7	1,827	190,530.3	2,867
2009	120,635.7	1,007	71,618.4	1,581	192,254.1	2,588
2010	55,942.2	441	21,890.5	479	77,832.7	920
Total Asia (excluding Japan)	**421,646.6**	**3,694**	**317,566.7**	**5,644**	**739,213.4**	**9,338**

Panel D. Japan

Japan	Outbound		Inbound		Total Japan Cross-border	
Rank Date	Value ($ Mil)	Number of Deals	Value ($ Mil)	Number of Deals	Value ($ Mil)	Number of Deals
2007	28,951.7	352	36,197.6	338	65,149.3	690
2008	64,256.6	405	11,268.5	247	75,525.1	652
2009	32,623.3	353	7,325.1	255	39,948.4	608
2010	13,124.0	129	3,683.4	89	16,807.4	218
Total Japan	**138,955.5**	**1,239**	**58,474.6**	**929**	**197,430.2**	**2168**

Source: This exhibit shows the outbound and inbound cross-border M&A activity during 2007 to the first quarter of 2010 by aggregate deal value and the number of deals for the United States, Europe, Asia, and Japan. Thomson Financial.

439

Exhibit 24.2 Top 10 M&A Deals Worth More Than $10 Billion Completed in 2008

RANK	VALUE ($ Bil)	TARGET COMPANY	TARGET COUNTRY	INDUSTRY OF THE ACQUIRED COMPANY	ACQUIRER	BIDDER COUNTRY	INDUSTRY OF THE ACQUIRING COMPANY
1	52.2	Anheuser-Busch Cos Inc	United States	Malt beverages	InBev NV	Belgium	Malt beverages
2	23.1	Fortis Bank Nederland (Holding) NV	Netherlands	Banks	Netherlands national government	Netherlands	National government
3	17.9	Altadis SA	Spain	Cigarettes	Imperial Tobacco Overseas Hldgs Ltd	United Kingdom	Investors
4	17.6	Reuters Group PLC	United Kingdom	News syndicates	Thomson Corp	United States	Information retrieval services
5	16.3	Imperial Chemical Industries PLC	United Kingdom	Paints and allied products	Akzo Nobel NV	Netherlands	Paints and allied products
6	16.0	Intelsat Ltd	Bermuda	Communications services	Serafina Holdings Ltd	United Kingdom	Investors
7	15.0	OCI Cement Group	Egypt	Cement, hydraulic	Lafarge SA	France	Cement, hydraulic
8	14.9	Scottish & Newcastle PLC	United Kingdom	Malt beverages	Sunrise Acquisitions Ltd	Jersey	Investors
9	14.3	Endesa Italia	Italy	Electric services	E ON AG	Germany	Electric services
10	14.3	Rio Tinto PLC	United Kingdom	Gold ores	Shining Prospect Pte Ltd	Singapore	Investors

Source: This exhibit shows the 10 largest cross-border deals in 2008. The industries of the acquirer and the target illustrate the motives for these mergers, ranging from synergistic economies of scale, product and geographical diversification, to strategic fit. Of the 10 motives, four are for investment purposes. Data from UNCTAD Cross-Border M&A Database (www.unctad.org/fdistatistics) and United Nations (2009).

Why does acquiring firms abroad make sense even during a severe economic downturn? Compared to the period 2006 to 2007, market capitalizations of firms around the world dropped 40 percent to 70 percent during the period 2008 and 2009. This makes the price for entering an industry via an acquisition much cheaper. Thus, target firms, which were previously too costly, are now within budgetary reach. Because many firms are in desperate need of capital infusions, this need provides acquirers with strategic opportunities. Finally, firms with marginal financing alternatives have been driven from the global market for corporate control, leaving stronger but fewer competitors with solid cash positions.

Substantial value potential and other strategic opportunities may be present in pursuing cross-border acquisitions. Yet, compared to domestic acquisitions, such deals have greater inherent risks and challenges because of their large size and greater variability between bidding firms and target firms. Thus, before making the aggressive, strategic play of an international acquisition, firms need to understand the range of issues involved in cross-border takeovers.

This chapter highlights the motives underlying international takeovers and discusses the differences between domestic and international acquisitions. These issues range from picking a target firm based on strategic value to integrating the operations of the target firm postacquisition so as to realize the projected synergistic value. The chapter has the following organization. The next section discusses the wide range of factors motivating firms for making international acquisitions while the section following it presents the intricacies of the issues unique to foreign takeovers. The current status of the empirical evidence on cross-border takeovers is then presented, followed by a brief summary and conclusions.

FACTORS MOTIVATING INTERNATIONAL TAKEOVERS

Firms can expand abroad either by making a *de novo* entry or acquiring an existing firm. Since the 1990s, international acquisitions have become the dominant mode of foreign direct investment (FDI). Strategically, this is because a merger or an acquisition provides access to an infrastructure and a customer base in the foreign country more easily than starting a new enterprise. Acquiring an existing brand name in a foreign country can also give a strong business edge by providing the acquirer with a reputation and goodwill in the foreign market in the shortest possible time. Thus, international acquisitions provide ready access to foreign markets. The motives for international acquisitions as a preferred mode of foreign expansion are discussed below. Some of the discussion also applies to the *de novo* entry method of foreign expansion.

Several major forces at the macro-level and industry-specific or firm-specific level drive international acquisitions. Some factors relate to the acquiring firm's corporate strategy and could be aggressive or defensive strategies, depending on whether the firm is an industry leader or a follower. Other factors relate to the firm's financial well-being and could be more tactical than strategic in nature. Finally, some factors could be generated from conditions in the home country "pushing" firms to expand abroad, while others could be based on conditions in the host country "pulling" firms into their country. The discussion now turns to these drivers of international acquisitions, focusing on the firm-level and industry-level factors followed by country-level factors.

Inputs: Lower Cost and Availability

The classical theory of FDI, which includes foreign acquisitions, is that firms go abroad in search of lower cost inputs (Dunning, 1993). Despite the recent phenomenon of globalization and technological innovation, markets for the factors of production remain segmented to a large extent. The implication is that labor and capital cost differentials across national borders are sufficiently wide enough to make pursuing global sourcing of these inputs worthwhile. Wages continue to be lower in relatively labor-abundant, developing countries such as Mexico, India, and China. By contrast, borrowing costs continue to be lower in relatively capital-abundant, developed countries such as the United States and Germany. A related motive for a firm's foreign expansion is to acquire natural resources, such as copper or iron ore, which may be uniquely available in certain countries.

Technological Innovation and Dedicated Skills

This motivating factor encompasses both technical knowledge and specialized skill sets. Technical knowledge could be intangible assets such as patents or copyrights on certain manufacturing processes. Specialized skill sets could include intangible assets related to intellectual property or specific expertise in certain types of software use. For instance, pharmaceutical companies could have the scientific knowledge of manufacturing a particular drug while financial firms could have a unique lending technique.

This motivation can work in two ways. First, a firm can have a technological capability that has been copied by competitors in the home market but is transferable across borders and so can continue to provide the firm with a competitive edge in a foreign market. A cross-border acquisition could provide an expeditious mode of entry into the foreign market for the firm to continue exploiting its technological capability to achieve monopoly advantage. This would be the "push factor" related to technology and would most likely apply to acquirers from developed countries buying targets in less developed countries (Caves, 1982a, 1982b).

The technology-related "pull factor" would apply to situations where firms in less developed economies need to acquire the technological knowledge to improve their competitive positions both at home and abroad. For example, China's phenomenal growth in FDI into developed foreign markets from 1991 to 2007 is attributed primarily to this phenomenon of technology sourcing and has led to productivity increases at home (Zhao, Liu, and Zhao, 2010).

Market Expansion and Diversification

Four major market-related factors motivate foreign acquisitions: the first two deal with corporate strategy while the latter two involve the acquirer's financial stability and profitability. The first motivating factor involves instances in which a firm finds the product market in its home country approaching saturation and, therefore, acquires firms in foreign countries to make a rapid expansion into untapped markets.

The home market saturation could be due to such factors as the maturation of the economy, demographic changes, and industry structure changes. Generally, firms from developed countries are likely to acquire targets in less developed countries when driven by this "push factor."

The second factor involves a potential "gap" in the market for a particular product in a specific country. For instance, Procter & Gamble and Kimberly-Clark both spotted the absence of local diaper producers in the Latin American and Asian markets in the late 1980s and early 1990s. Both firms soon filled this gap by expanding into these markets as a result of this "pull factor."

The third market-related reason for firms acquiring targets in foreign countries is because they want to diversify their sales revenue stream through geographical diversification. If the home economy is in a down-cycle and the firm also has a market in a country experiencing an up-cycle, its consolidated revenue stream will become less volatile. In general, acquirers motivated by this factor could be from both developed and developing countries and could expand into both developed and developing countries, as long as the host (foreign) country's business cycle has a low correlation with the home country's business cycle.

Fourth, larger firms in the home market may be more competitive because they keep costs low by producing on a larger scale and reaping economies of scale. Medium-sized firms may want to produce on this larger scale with lower unit costs but may find selling the increased quantities difficult in the competitive home market. This would drive them to seek alternative outlets overseas so as to enable their larger scale of operations to be profitable.

Industry Structure: Market Share and Market Power

The nature of the product market and structure of the industry in the home country often play a key role in driving firms to expand overseas. If the home market is highly competitive with little opportunity for product differentiation, firms may be forced to expand abroad to increase market share. If, however, the firm has a relatively inelastic demand for its uniquely positioned product at home, it is less likely to venture into riskier foreign markets.

A related factor is a firm's market power in its home market. This also relates to the nature of the firm's management team. The management team may want to establish a monopolistic or at least an oligopolistic position in its product market, either due to hubris or for profit-seeking reasons. If the structure of the home market forces the firm to be a price-taker, foreign expansion may provide the only way for managers to engage in empire building. If the management team is relatively less risk-averse, it may be willing to be the first to enter uncharted territory. Although the risks may be high, the firm may be able to earn monopoly rents in the new foreign market because it will be a price-setter in the foreign market.

Customer Retention

Global businesses have global customers. If a firm's clients expand abroad, the firm may need to follow suit. This is especially true in the financial services industry. Each financial institution develops a distinctive package of financial services for its client, and this highly differentiated product gives the financial institution a competitive edge. To preserve this edge over the longer term, a financial institution needs to follow its customer, even abroad. For instance, when German multinationals started expanding into the United States, Deutsche Bank acquired Bankers Trust to retain its customers from home. Another dimension of this motivating factor is gaining customers through the supply chain. If an important downstream client starts manufacturing its product in a foreign location, the supplier might find that following the customer to the foreign location is profitable in the long term. This is especially true for the automobile manufacturing industry and auto parts suppliers. For instance, when Honda Motor Company expanded their operations into China, one of Honda's suppliers, Japanese electronics maker Omron Corporation, followed Honda into China to retain Honda's business.

Vertical Integration and Quality Control

In large manufacturing industries such as the automobile or shipbuilding industries, manufacturing firms often acquire firms upstream to maintain quality control of their inputs. The foreign suppliers may have the lowest costs, but adequate processes for maintaining quality may not be in place. In such instances, a roll-up acquisition (acquiring a firm up the supply chain) could be cost effective for the manufacturer. The next section turns to some country-level factors that motivate international acquisitions.

Regulations, Entry Barriers, and Other Institutional Controls

Differences in regulations between the home country and the host country, trade barriers, and capital controls can play important roles in motivating international acquisitions. Profit-seeking firms try to circumvent such growth impediments in home country sales and exports to foreign countries by engaging in foreign acquisitions.

Generally, due to more funds being allocated to research and development (R&D) in the developed countries, the negative externalities of certain manufacturing processes or the detrimental effects of certain products often become evident in these countries, and corporations are subject to restrictive regulations as a result of such research. Further, with law and order also being relatively more organized in these countries, enforcement of regulations is stricter. Under these circumstances, firms from developed countries seek markets in less developed countries where such regulations are slower to be adopted, and even when adopted, they are rarely enforced with complete stringency. The tobacco industry is a glaring example of this phenomenon. After regulators placed more restrictions on the manufacture and sale of tobacco products in the United States, American cigarette makers began selling the excess products into less regulated non-U.S. markets and moving their manufacturing to Europe, Latin America, and Asia.

The same is true regarding environmental protection laws. Manufacturing processes that violate the more stringent laws of the United States are often acceptable in other parts of the world, particularly in developing countries. Firms frequently acquire smaller competitors in these countries to avoid their home country's regulations and fines.

Regulations and government policy in the host country may also be a driver of international acquisitions. Host countries might have certain requirements such as zoning laws or local labor and local bank financing, which may be a deterrent for *de novo* entry. Acquiring existing facilities in such markets provides a legal and efficient means of avoiding these requirements.

Most countries have regulations prohibiting firms from consolidation acquisitions that might lead to monopolistic practices in a particular industry. Firms facing regulatory constraints against lateral expansion at home may consolidate across borders and thus increase their global market share without raising antitrust concerns at home.

Trade barriers, in the form of quotas and tariffs, are often in place to protect certain domestic industries. While several bilateral and multilateral treaties as well as regional free trade zones exist today, firms still see such barriers as binding constraints and use international acquisitions as a means of circumventing them.

Similarly, certain less developed countries often impose capital controls on short-term repatriation, especially during times of financial turmoil. For instance, during the Asian financial crisis of 1997, Malaysian premiere Mahathir Mohammed imposed controls on the repatriation of short-term investment, fearing the exacerbation of the volatile Malaysian ringgit. In such instances, receiving immediate payments for exports and licensing arrangements may become uncertain. In this case, acquiring a firm in the host country may prove beneficial in the long term. That is, revenues can be plowed back into the firm and repatriated only when controls are lifted or after they qualify as returns on long-term investments.

Tax Arbitrage and the Exchange Rate Advantage

Corporate income tax rates are not homogeneous across countries. Firms often acquire targets in countries with lower tax rates and manage reported earnings by transferring profits across subsidiaries through holding company structures. However, similar to trade treaties, bilateral tax treaties exist between most developed countries. Current global technology allows sufficient information sharing to make this motive less important.

A more powerful financial motive for international acquisitions is the expected long-term exchange rate differential between the home and host countries. Firms would rather export from depreciating or soft currency environments in order to price their products more competitively. If the need to shift production to the host country is immediate, based on the future outlook of the exchange rate, an acquisition rather than a *de novo* entry would make sense. The drawback is that such a move is irrevocable in the short run and hence the quality of the forecast is critical.

Another exchange rate–related advantage involves the repatriation of profits. Firms usually have some flexibility as to when they want to convert their foreign profits into their home currency and often make some conversion gains in the process. Further, multinational corporations with manufacturing facilities spanning multiple countries can use production capacity to hedge against exchange rate risk. Finally, firms acquire targets in host countries with weak currencies so that they can be on a "discount sale" relative to domestic targets.

Political and Economic Environment

Well-run firms located in less developed countries often face insurmountable institutional challenges when attempting organic growth within their country. Such
firms have a strong motive to merge with firms in developed countries with more
stable economic and political environments that permit firms to realize their full
growth potential.

ISSUES TO CONSIDER IN INTERNATIONAL TAKEOVERS

In 1999, KPMG (1999) published the results of a study indicating that only 17 percent of all international acquisitions created value, while 53 percent of international
acquisitions destroyed value. In attempting to determine the causes of this poor
track record of postacquisition success of international acquisitions, Rottig (2007)
states that several studies establish that cultural differences and cultural distance
are the main causes. However, his own study demonstrates that the real culprit is
not the cultural differences *per se* but the management of these differences during
the postacquisition stage. The same reasoning applies to all the issues related to
the additional complexities of cross-border acquisitions listed below. The fact that
differences exist in the global marketplace should not be a problem for successful
postacquisition integration. Thus, management should engage in careful planning
around these differences to enhance the probability of success of the merger or acquisition. As Rottig notes, understanding the micro- and macro-characteristics that
distinguish the country in which the bidding or target firm resides is instrumental
to a merger's eventual success.

Given institutional barriers and other imperfections in factor and product
markets, foreign expansion is not the same as a firm expanding within its home
country. The dynamics of the core M&A activities of target identification, due
diligence, valuation, and integration still remain the same. Yet, acquirers need
to consider more varied issues at the international level. Such issues contribute to
additional uncertainty about the ultimate outcome of the merger. Although some of
these issues may present additional challenges throughout the acquisition process,
these challenges can prove to be opportunities if the acquirer considers them at the
appropriate time and in the proper manner.

Target Search and Identification Stage

A typical merger or acquisition, domestic or cross-border, proceeds through the
following three broad phases: (1) target search and identification, (2) execution of
the transaction, and (3) integration of the target into current operations. Below is
a discussion of the issues that the acquirer should consider at each stage when
planning, executing, and integrating a cross-border acquisition.

Strategic Context

The discussion on motives for foreign expansion through acquisitions outlines the
various strategic benefits a firm can achieve if successful, including geographical
diversification, market share expansion, and product complementarities. A key

motivating factor is determining the strategic gap that the potential target can fill, both from the home market's and host country's perspective. In the international context, the challenge may be precisely establishing the strategic context. The acquiring firm needs to initially perform a thorough country-, industry-, and firm-level analysis of the potential market. This analysis for cross-border mergers entails two problems. First, in assessing the market potential, the acquirer needs to account for economic and social factors such as per capita income levels, stability and distribution, consumption patterns, demographic profiles, cultural habits, and religious taboos. Second, information on these variables may not be easy to obtain, especially in a developing host country where both superior quality data as well as sufficient quantities of historical data are scant.

Finkelstein (1999) suggests developing a framework of evaluation criteria and then maintaining focus on the specific criteria throughout the process. He suggests that acquiring firms should consider the following questions before the merger or acquisition. First, how are synergies going to be created, and when will they be realized? Second, why would this acquirer be better than other potential acquirers for this particular target? Third, would this firm be better off as a result of the merger through a stronger competitive position, lower cost structures, and greater capabilities? Sell-side considerations would primarily focus on whether this merger presents the best exit strategy for the firm.

Selecting from a Global Set

With the recent globalization of markets, deregulation of certain industries, and privatization of some economies, the universe from which potential merger partners can be selected has exploded. As data earlier presented in Exhibit 24.1 show, corporate cross-border acquisition strategists must be aware that the deal-making universe is now much larger than previously. This can be a double-edged sword. While a wider and deeper pool of firms exists from which to select across any type of market, the number of competing bidders is also increasing. This implies that acquirers should not only be more prepared to succeed but also achieve a higher level of preparation in a timelier manner. Further, as is evident from Exhibit 24.1, firms must now plan for competing acquirers from emerging markets, which is definitely not the typical scenario, even as recently as the beginning of the 2000s.

Transaction Execution Stage

In a recent survey conducted by Accenture (2008), managers rated three areas of M&A transaction execution as more challenging for cross-border mergers when compared with domestic mergers. As Exhibit 24.3 shows, these areas are legal and regulatory compliance, integrating local management, and conducting due diligence. In the transaction execution stage, complications arise because several consents and approvals have to be obtained, including foreign investor approvals, exchange control approvals, local antitrust compliance approvals, and tax-related approvals. Further, these approvals may have to be cleared both at the federal level of the host country as well as the state level of the host country. If multiple jurisdictions are involved, several government approvals may be required.

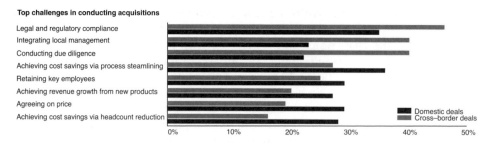

Exhibit 24.3 Top Challenges in Conducting Acquisitions
Note: This exhibit shows the relative importance of various factors cited as challenges encountered by managers conducting domestic and cross-border acquisitions, based on a survey conducted by Accenture in 2008.
Source: Accenture.

Vehicle and Form of Acquisition

The first set of structural decisions in M&A transactions includes the choice of the acquisition vehicle (i.e., who should be the buyer?) and the form of the acquisition (i.e., what is going to be bought, shares or assets?). In deciding who should be the buyer, the acquiring company needs to determine which entity will be buying the target firm: the acquiring entity itself, its domestic subsidiary, or a newly created or preexisting subsidiary in the target country. The acquirer often bases the decision on the regulatory complexity of the target's country. For instance, foreign acquirers buying a U.S. target could choose to execute the acquisition via a "C" corporation, a limited liability company, a partnership, or a holding company.

The "C" corporation is easy to set up because prior government approvals are not required and no restrictions for foreign ownership exist, except in certain industries such as the defense or energy sectors. This could also be the preferred vehicle for acquiring targets in Commonwealth countries as they follow common law and recognize the corporation form. The advantage of limited liability companies is that they can sell the shares freely to the participating investors and the target firm can operate as a subsidiary. This form could be the preferred vehicle for civil law-abiding countries as limited liability companies would be consistent with local laws in such countries.

A partnership is easy to set up and can afford some tax advantages for partners from countries with bilateral tax treaties with the United States. The holding company has the advantage of providing the flexibility of profit and loss transfers across sister subsidiaries for tax management purposes and having a subsidiary in place for future acquisitions. The type of entity acquiring the foreign target (a partnership or a holding company) determines the tax implications. Often the structure that works best from a business perspective may not be the best from a tax perspective. Thus, early planning and coordination among all involved divisions are keys to designing the optimal deal structure.

Regarding the form of the acquisition, the deal may be structured as a stock purchase or an asset purchase. With either choice, the deal may be structured as a taxable transaction or a tax-free restructuring. For cross-border acquisitions, share purchase is the preferred method due to its simplicity. Under this method, all the benefits and risks associated with the target's business are effectively transferred to the acquirer at closing. If closing is to be deferred due to pending regulatory approvals, such as merger control clearances or a time delay between signing and closing, a purchase price adjustment mechanism is available for any value changes occurring during this period. The key document in this case is the sale and purchase agreement (SPA). In general, fewer transfer documents are required under this method, and transfer taxes are kept at a minimum. One disadvantage is that unforeseen tax liabilities or liens on assets may be revealed postclosing. To avoid this, an acquirer often includes an indemnification clause to protect its interests against any prior tax liabilities revealed during the due diligence process or not disclosed in the purchase agreement.

An asset purchase is procedurally more complicated due to the fact that each of the separate assets, including transactions or trading relationships, need to be transferred. These assets could be located in several jurisdictions and obtaining clearance and consent from the different jurisdictions in order to comply with all local laws could prove cumbersome and time-consuming. However, the asset purchase method provides greater flexibility and selectivity. This method is especially useful in cases where the target has liabilities that cannot be identified or quantified easily or where the target has immovable assets that the acquirer does not want.

Transactional and Strategic Tax Issues

Tax-related factors in cross-border mergers need to be considered at three levels. First, depending on the structure of the transaction deal itself, different tax implications may exist for the target company's shareholders. Second, managing tax due diligence in a cross-border merger can be challenging and expensive. For example, concepts, standards, and agreement norms could differ between countries. Additionally, documents could be in languages foreign to the acquiring firms' management. Third, strategic tax planning is an important value driver.

With respect to the transaction deal structure and payment method, the acquirer may buy the target firms' shares or assets in three ways. Under the first method, target firm shareholders would receive the shares of the acquiring firm in exchange for all of their assets and liabilities or shares. In the United States, the acquirer would set up a U.S. subsidiary, which would merge with the target according to U.S. laws. The entire stock-exchange transaction would be nontaxable for all shareholders. In cross-border mergers, a big obstacle to the feasibility of this method is the problem of *flowback*, which is the unwillingness of target firm shareholders to hold the acquiring company's shares, as the acquiring company is domiciled in a foreign country. Since the merged firm is not going to be indexed in the target firm's country, indexers have little incentive to hold the acquirer's shares and prefer to sell them, lowering the share price of the acquirer for some period of time. However, with careful planning and coordination, flowback can be managed with appropriate target country investor education and by convincing major target firm shareholders to hold the acquirer's shares. In the United States, when a share purchase is made and the foreign acquirer sets up a U.S. shell subsidiary firm to merge with the target, the transaction is termed a tax-free *reverse triangular merger*.

When the target firm's shareholders relinquish their shares or assets and liabilities in exchange for debt or cash, the transaction is a taxable event, as the target shareholders realize gains or losses on the merger transaction. When the exchange is primarily cash for most of the target shareholders and shares for the few who prefer the acquirer's shares, the transaction (called a *forward triangular merger*) is taxable and executed through a local subsidiary of the foreign acquirer. Finally, transactions may also be structured in a *hybrid* way, such that some target shareholders receive nonvoting preferred stock in exchange for their common stock and pay no taxes on the transaction, while others receive cash in exchange for their common stock and do pay taxes on the transaction.

Taxes are not the only consideration when bidding firms are trying to select the method of payment in an acquisition. Hansen (1987), Eckbo, Giammarino, and Heinkel (1990), and Moeller, Schlingemann, and Stulz (2007) develop models of private information available to bidding and target firms' management. In particular, they examine the respective firms' intrinsic value and the role this plays in the acquirer's choice of stock exchange versus cash as the medium of payment. If an acquirer's stock is overvalued, the acquirer tends to choose stock as the medium of exchange. Likewise, if a high degree of asymmetric information exists between the acquirer and the target firm, as is usually the case in cross-border acquisitions, the acquirer uses cash to deter competing bids (Chemmanur, Paeglis, and Simonyan, 2009). Consistent with this theory of asymmetric information, Officer, Poulsen, and Stegemoller (2009) find that acquiring firm shareholders gain when they use the stock exchange method of payment for hard-to-value targets. John, Freund, Nguyen, and Vasudevan (2010) find support for this theory when considering private targets in cross-border acquisitions.

When managing tax due diligence, all valuation analyses should typically be conducted on an after-tax basis. Tax risks, including multijurisdictional tax constraints, should be considered when performing the valuation analysis. Specifically, the acquiring firm should address the following tax-related questions before structuring a cross-border deal:

1. Does the target firm have an organizational structure that can serve its business needs and handle tax, finance, and treasury functions on a global basis? If so, to what extent does this structure complement the acquiring firm's existing strategy?
2. Would the host country's legal, accounting, and tax regime allow for regular repatriation of cash, and if so, how efficiently?
3. What is the target company's effective income tax rate, and how does it compare with the acquiring firm's tax rate and with that of its competitors?
4. Does the target company have any cash, and if so, is it local or overseas? Does its treasury strategy complement the acquiring firm's strategy? Are there any legal constraints on dividends or intracompany transfers and transfer pricing?
5. Has the target firm complied with all local reporting structures, or has it been audited or fined recently?

Finally, concerning strategic tax planning, international tax structuring can be used in certain cases to the acquiring firm's competitive advantage. Integrated operational strategies, such as identifying activities to be conducted in low-tax jurisdictions, allocating global income to minimize local, state, federal, and international tax liabilities, and using a centralized offshore treasury function may all serve to reduce the consolidated postmerger effective tax rate. Acquiring firms may also analyze alternative structures to minimize or defer income tax, transfer tax, and capital tax and to accelerate or use favorable tax attributes of the target firm. Further, they can use tax-efficient methods of disposition for unwanted assets. Acquirers expecting dividend streams from the target firms should structure with a view toward withholding tax requirements in the host country and should consider the possibility of using a subsidiary located in a country that has a favorable tax treaty network so as to minimize the dividend tax as they cross borders.

Cross-Border Valuation-Related Considerations

The broad framework of discounted cash flow (DCF) analysis used for valuing domestic target firms is also applicable to valuing a foreign target with several adjustments. The basic DCF valuation formula is:

$$V_0 = \sum_{t=1}^{\infty} \frac{CF_t}{(1+r)^t} \tag{24.1}$$

where V_0 = the value of the firm at $t = 0$; and CF_t = the free cash flows expected from the target firm in the future, discounted at the weighted average cost of capital, r.

Short-term and long-term transactions in commodities and financial markets across national borders are governed by a set of equilibrium relationships called *international parity conditions*. Under assumptions of perfect and efficient markets, arbitrage drives interest rates, exchange rates, and prices to the point where there are no more profit-seeking incentives, hence, the term "parity" or equilibrium conditions (Lipson, 2009).

The specific issues to be considered for cross-border valuation are related to answering various questions. Some of these issues entail making adjustments to the cash flows while others require making adjustments to the cost of capital. First, in which currency should the valuation analysis be conducted? The primary choices include estimating the cash flows in the target country's currency and using a weighted average cost of capital (WACC) denominated in that currency or converting the estimated cash flows to the bidder's home currency using a series of forward exchange rates and discounting at the home currency WACC. If markets were perfect and all the parity conditions held true, both approaches would give the same results. However, in reality there could be reasons for preferring one approach over the other. Free cash flows, which are derived from earnings before interest but after taxes (EBIAT) by deducting noncash expenses and adding any capital expenditures and additions to net working capital, are generated in the local currency. If exchange rates in the host country are expected to be volatile, then using a series of appropriate forward exchange rates (based on the purchasing power parity, for instance) to convert the cash flows to the home currency would be preferable, thereby incorporating the exchange rate volatility explicitly into the analysis. On the other hand, if the acquisition is being financed with local currency sources of capital, keeping the estimated cash flows in the local currency and discounting at the local currency WACC would make sense.

Second, how should the appropriate components of the cost of capital be computed? Several approaches are possible. If cash flows are going to be converted to the home currency, then the analyst can use the WACC of the acquiring company to discount the cash flows. If the cash flows are going to remain in the target country's currency, then a target currency WACC needs to be used for discounting, but it does not have to be constructed in that currency.

Sometimes, using the acquirer's home currency WACC and converting it to the host country's currency makes sense. A practical reason for using this approach is that data on the host country's capital markets are difficult to obtain. Risk-free government securities and reliable market indices or consistent market risk premiums may be unavailable. One approach would be to use international parity conditions and deflate the home currency WACC (usually with the gross domestic product [GDP] deflator) and then reinflate it at the expected rate of inflation for the target country to obtain the target currency denominated WACC.

An alternative approach is to construct the target currency WACC from each of its components. For the proportions of debt and equity capital, the best approach is to use the long-term target capital structure of the acquired firm, if it is to be maintained as an ongoing concern. For the pretax cost of debt, the cost of borrowing should be used, and if market rates are unavailable, the acquirer's cost of debt should be used, appealing to the interest rate parity to convert it to the target firm's cost of debt. For computing the after-tax cost of debt, the best approach is to use the higher of the corporate tax rates, either of the acquirer or the target.

Analysts often use the capital asset pricing model (CAPM), a standard method used for determining shareholders' required rate of return from their equity investments, to compute the cost of equity. Again, two approaches are available to apply this model depending on the target country's capital markets. If the target firm is in a developed country with globally integrated capital markets, then some common assumptions are that investments are made globally and the systematic risk is measured relative to a global index. The beta would be relative to a world market index such as the Morgan Stanley Capital Index. However, if the target firm is in a less developed country with segmented equity markets, a preferred approach is to apply the CAPM with the target country's market index, and the beta of the target firm is calculated relative to this domestic market index (Kennedy, 2002).

Third, which country's tax rate should be used for estimating the after-tax future cash flows and for determining the after-tax cost of debt? Corporate tax rates vary widely across countries and so do other rules regarding, for instance, the frequency of payments during the year and foreign tax credit allowances (Froot, 1997). Generally, multinational corporations (MNCs) are chartered in one home country where they submit, at least once a year, a consolidated set of financial statements according to the accounting principles of that country. MNCs also have to abide by the tax regime of this country of domicile. Generally, under the "worldwide tax credit system," firms pay taxes on their entire worldwide income and receive credit against foreign-source income only for any foreign taxes paid. Under the "territorial tax exemption system," firms do not pay taxes on their foreign source income in their country of domicile. Instead, they pay taxes to the foreign government for their foreign source income. Using the higher of the two country's tax rates is appropriate under the worldwide tax credit system, but using the tax rate of the target country is preferred in the territorial tax exemption system.

Fourth, how should the timing and amount of the cash flows be recognized— when the cash flows are realized or when they are available for repatriation?

Although cash flows generated by the target firm may be plowed back into the target itself, remitted to a sister subsidiary, or blocked for transfers back to the home country due to capital controls, they typically should be recognized as they are earned. Just as retained earnings are included in cash flows while valuing domestic acquisition targets, likewise, in cross-border acquisitions, all cash flows should be included, whether they are distributed to the shareholders immediately or not.

Fifth, how should foreign exchange risk be identified, measured, and taken into account? Foreign exchange risk arises when unanticipated changes in the exchange rate affect a firm's cash flows. When a firm acquires a target in a foreign country, there can be multiple sources of foreign exchange risk. In the narrowest sense, if the acquirer has committed to a certain transaction to be settled in the future in a foreign currency and the exchange rate changes in the interim, the acquirer faces *transaction exposure*. One approach to estimating the future cash flows uses a series of estimated forward rates to convert the foreign currency cash flows to the home currency. Any unanticipated changes in the exchange rates will affect the forecasted cash flows. So, depending on the volatility of the target country's exchange rates, either the cash flows have to be adjusted or a premium has to be added to the discount rate. The exchange rates can also move in favor of the acquirer, but the concern is with downside risks.

Next, the acquirer has to submit annually a consolidated statement of accounts in the home currency. Targets acquired in foreign locations may generate the same magnitude of local currency cash flows year to year, but if exchange rates change unexpectedly, then *translation* gains or losses may occur when these cash flows are converted to the home currency for reporting purposes.

Finally, the long-term strategic viability of a target firm's operations, and hence its synergistic contributions to the acquirer, may change with time if the target country's exchange rate changes in an unanticipated manner over the long term, subjecting the acquirer to *economic exposure*. There are several ways to manage such foreign exchange exposures (Eun and Resnick, 2009). Ex ante, especially if the risks are nondiversifiable and not captured by the target's beta, a premium should be added to the discount WACC when conducting the initial valuation of the target. Ex post, the acquiring firm may use financial hedging to manage the foreign currency exposures.

Sixth, how should political risk be identified, measured, and taken into account? When unanticipated political events affect the cash flows that the acquiring firm expects to earn from the target firm, the acquirer is exposed to political risk. As in the case of foreign exchange risk, this source of risk can have a substantial impact as the political events can range from a *coup d'état* to a democratic and peaceful regime change, resulting in nonapproval of previously negotiated acquisitions, expropriation of assets, disruption of operations, capital controls on repatriation of earnings, and inconvertibility of the local currency (Wan and Wong, 2009). Ex ante, the acquiring firm should conduct a thorough macroeconomic and sociopolitical analysis. Examples of early warning indicators of political unrest include a recent political regime change, the political minority growing in popularity, economic and financial crises, and a discordant neighboring country (Eiteman, Stonehill, and Moffett, 2008). Rather than purchasing expensive insurance against political risk, strategic methods of managing this risk may be cheaper and more effective.

Such methods include hiring local labor, using multiple source borrowing (including from local financial institutions), engaging the local community, and contributing to the local infrastructure. If the firm purchases insurance, then it should deduct the premium costs from the estimated cash flows rather than making any adjustments to the discount rate.

Finally, what are some additional secondary synergistic effects and special risks of an acquisition, and how should these be incorporated into the valuation analysis? In some instances, local governments may provide subsidies in various forms or concessionary loans to attract foreign investors. In other instances, capital controls could prevent the acquirer from repatriating earnings from a previously acquired target, but the target now being considered could use some of that locked capital. All of these secondary synergistic effects have a positive impact on the value of the target being considered. As such, analysts should factor these effects into the cash flows estimation rather than into the discount rate as they are likely one-time or limited time effects. Likewise, analysts may need to account for some special risks when their firms seek to acquire targets in less developed countries. Unanticipated macroeconomic volatility, sudden regulatory changes, severe devaluations of the local currency and hyperinflation, poorly defined property rights, and weak enforcement can all lead to less than expected cash flows. While adding a premium to the discount rate to account for all of these risks is easy, this can lead to errors in valuation because it masks the true nature and magnitude of the risks (Froot, 1997). Incorporating these risks in the cash flows forces managers to recognize these risks more explicitly and more precisely, thereby enhancing the precision of the valuation analysis.

Integration Stage

Academics and practitioners continue to be concerned about the high failure rate of M&As. On average, 50 percent of domestic acquisitions and 70 percent of cross-border acquisitions fail to produce the intended results (Capron, 1999). Studies show that the problems besetting M&As include the lack of a compelling strategic rationale, unrealistic estimates of the potential synergies, and the payment of inflated merger premiums (Aguilera and Dencker, 2004). These generic problems with domestic acquisitions are compounded in cross-border acquisitions due to differences in languages, national cultures, social norms, ethical standards, political influences, and regulatory hurdles. The discussion now turns to the issues unique to cross-border acquisitions within the integration stage.

Role of Human Resources and Culture
Survey results in the human resource management field show that 70 percent of target firm executives experience acculturative stress postmerger and depart from the firm within five years of the completion of the acquisition (Krug and Aguilera, 2005; Cartwright and Schoenberg, 2006). One set of causes for the executives' merger-related stress involves the integration stage and the gross negligence of human resources and culture during this stage of the acquisition process.

Based on a longitudinal study of the U.S.-based firm First Automotive and four of its European target firms, Quah and Young (2005) propose a phased approach for postacquisition integration and management. They identify the level of integration, postacquisition changes and the timing of such changes, cultural influences, and employee behavior in the target firm as the key factors interacting and influencing the outcome in the integration stage. They recommend that successful integration should be given at least five to seven years to complete, starting with planning the integration as well as executing and implementing it. As such, acquirers should use a sequential, evolutionary approach to reorganize internal management processes. Recommended success strategies for the integration stage are conducting thorough audits of management personnel, providing clear communication of the objectives of each stage and the overall acquisition, and retaining the existing management for at least three years. When replacing existing management, a focus should be on local recruits so as to preserve the local culture of the acquired firm and to maximize postmerger customer retention.

Barmeyer and Mayrhofer (2008) maintain that in cross-border acquisitions, the integration stage is crucial to the success of the merger because cultural differences exacerbate organizational differences. Early in the process, the acquirer needs to decide whether the approach should be convergent or divergent. If convergent, the strategy should be one of harmonization, but if divergent, the strategy should be one of plurality and intercultural compromises. Based on their in-depth analysis of the successful melding of Spanish, French, and German cultures to form the EADS group, Barmeyer and Mayrhofer emphasize the importance of allowing an interculture to emerge from the national cultural differences in cross-border acquisitions.

EMPIRICAL EVIDENCE

As with domestic acquisitions, event study methodology shows that the majority of the empirical evidence associated with cross-border acquisitions results in abnormal returns accruing to acquiring firms' shareholders and/or the target firms' shareholders. Although no single comprehensive study documents evidence spanning several countries and several decades, the general consensus is that target firms' shareholders gain significant positive returns varying from 20 to 40 percent when acquired by foreign acquirers (Harris and Ravenscraft, 1991; Cheng and Chan, 1995; Moeller and Schlingemann, 2005). The evidence on acquirers is mixed, but most studies find shareholders of bidding firms do not make any significant gains (Eckbo and Thorburn, 2000; Walker, 2000). Danbolt (2004) notes that the abnormal returns accruing to the target firms' shareholders are sensitive to the method of payment, the degree of investor protection in the target country, and the extent of geographical and industry diversification resulting from the merger.

SUMMARY AND CONCLUSIONS

Cross-border M&As continue to be on the rise despite the recent economic downturn. Some new features characterize the cross-border acquisitions of the twenty-first century. For example, an increasing number of acquirers are now from less developed countries with private equity and sovereign wealth funds as major sources of financing for such acquisitions. Strategic and tactical synergistic gains continue to motivate these acquisitions. Specifically, firms continue to acquire targets abroad in the quest for lower costs, better technology, wider and deeper markets, and tax and regulatory efficiencies. The cross-border acquisition process is much more complex than domestic acquisitions. In the target identification stage, the feasible set of targets is much larger and selecting the target that satisfies the right strategic fit is difficult. In the transaction execution stage, selecting the appropriate form and vehicle of acquisition in structuring the deal and the tax due diligence must also take into consideration various trade-offs. The valuation of the cross-border cash flows involves complexities such as deciding the currency in which the analysis should be conducted, which firm's cost of capital should be used, and how foreign exchange risk and political risk should be accounted for in the valuation analysis. However, not all acquisitions result in being value-enhancing despite using sophisticated valuation techniques and foreign exchange and political risk assessment. Current research has identified the integration stage and the human resource and cultural aspects of that stage as the leading causes of merger failures. Thus, future research on the success of cross-border acquisitions should focus on this area.

DISCUSSION QUESTIONS

1. Why do M&As make sense for firms even during economic downturns?
2. Explain whether international acquisitions are an effective means of expanding market share and market power.
3. Explain whether foreign acquisitions are an effective means of arbitraging regulatory and other institutional controls.
4. What factors should be used to determine the choice of the currency in the valuation analysis? Under what circumstances would one method be preferred over another?
5. How can an acquiring firm manage the various sources of foreign exchange risk arising from a cross-border acquisition?

REFERENCES

Accenture. 2008. *Achieving Value Faster*. London: Accenture Mergers and Acquisitions, Merger Integration Services.

Aguilera, Ruth V., and John C. Dencker. 2004. "The Role of Human Resource Management in Cross Border Mergers and Acquisitions." *International Journal of Human Resource Management* 15:8, 1355–1370.

Barmeyer, Christoph, and Ulrike Mayrhofer. 2008. "The Contribution of Intercultural Management to the Success of International Mergers and Acquisitions." *International Business Review* 17:1, 28–38.

Bloomberg Businessweek. 2010. "M&A Creeps Higher on Cross-Border, Hostile Deals." April 1, Bloomberg L.P.

Capron, Laurence. 1999. "The Long Term Performance of Horizontal Acquisitions." *Strategic Management Journal* 20:11, 987–1018.

Cartwright, Susan, and Richard Schoenberg. 2006. "Thirty Years of Mergers and Acquisitions Research: Recent Advances and Future Opportunities." *British Journal of Management*, 17:S1, S1–S5.

Caves, Richard E. 1982a. "Multinational Enterprises and Technology Transfer." In Alan M. Rugman, ed. *New Theories of the Multinational Enterprise*, 254–279. London: Croom Helm Ltd.

Caves, Richard E. 1982b, *Multinational Enterprise and Economic Analysis*. Cambridge: Cambridge University Press.

Chemmanur, Thomas J., Imants Paeglis, and Karen Simonyan. 2009. "The Medium of Exchange in Acquisitions: Does the Private Information of Both Acquirer and Target Matter?" *Journal of Corporate Finance* 15:5, 523–542.

Cheng, Louis T. W., and Kam C. Chan. 1995. "A Comparative Analysis of the Characteristics of International Takeovers." *Journal of Business Finance and Accounting* 22:5, 637–657.

Danbolt, Jo. 2004. "Target Company Cross-border Effects in Acquisitions into the U.K." *European Financial Management* 10:1, 83–108.

Dunning, John H. 1993. *Multinational Enterprises and the Global Economy*. Reading, MA and Wokingham, United Kingdom: Addison Wesley.

Eckbo, B. Espen, Ronald M. Giammarino, and Robert L. Heinkel. 1990. "Asymmetric Information and the Medium of Exchange in Takeovers: Theory and Tests." *Review of Financial Studies* 3:4, 651–675.

Eckbo, B. Espen, and Karin S. Thorburn. 2000. "Gains to Bidder Firms Revisited: Domestic and Foreign Acquisitions in Canada." *Journal of Financial and Quantitative Analysis* 35:1, 1–25.

Eiteman, David K., Arthur I. Stonehill, and Michael H. Moffett. 2008. *Multinational Business Finance*. New York: Addison-Wesley Pearson.

Eun, Cheol S., and Bruce Resnick. 2009. *International Financial Management*. New York: Irwin/McGraw-Hill.

Finkelstein, Sydney. 1999. "Safe Ways to Cross the Merger Minefield." In *Financial Times Mastering Global Business: The Complete MBA Companion in Global Business*, 119-123. London: Financial Times Pitman Publishing.

Froot, Kenneth A. 1997. *Cross Border Valuation*. Cambridge, MA: Harvard Business School Publishing.

Hansen, Robert G. 1987. "A Theory for the Choice of Exchange Medium in Mergers and Acquisitions." *Journal of Business* 60:1, 75–95.

Harris, Robert, and David. Ravenscraft. 1991. "The Role of Acquisitions in Foreign Direct Investment: Evidence from the U.S. Stock Market." *Journal of Finance*, 46:3, 825–844.

John, Kose, Steven Freund, Duong Nguyen, and Gopala K. Vasudevan. 2010. "Investor Protection and Cross-Border Acquisitions of Private and Public Targets." *Journal of Corporate Finance* 16:3, 259–275.

Kennedy, Robert E. 2002. "Project Valuation in Emerging Markets." Harvard Business School Case Note 0-720-077. Cambridge. MA: Harvard Business School Publishing.

KPMG. 1999. *Mergers and Acquisitions: Global Research Report 1999*. London: KPMG.

Krug, Jeffrey A. and Ruth V. Aguilera. 2005. "Top Management Team Turnover in Mergers and Acquisitions." In Sydney Finkelstein and Cary Cooper, (eds.), *Advances in Mergers and Acquisitions* 4, 121–149. Bingley, United Kingdom: Emerald Group Publishing Limited.

Lipson, Marc. 2009. "Parity Conditions in International Markets." University of Virginia Case Note YV 2538. Charlottesville, VA: Darden Business Publishing.

Moeller, Sara B., and Frederick P. Schlingemann. 2005. "Global Diversification and Bidder Gains: A Comparison Between Cross Border and Domestic Acquisitions." *Journal of Banking and Finance* 29:3, 533–564.

Moeller, Sara B., Frederik P. Schlingemann, and René Stulz. 2007. "How Do Diversity of Opinion and Information Asymmetry Affect Acquirer Returns?" *Review of Financial Studies* 20:5, 2047–2078.

Officer, Micah S., Annette Poulsen, and Michael Stegemoller. 2009. "Target-firm Information Asymmetry and Acquirer Returns." *Review of Finance* 13:3, 467–493.

Quah, Penelope, and Stephen Young. 2005. "Post Acquisition Management: A Phases Approach for Cross-Border M&As." *European Management Journal* 23:1, 65–75.

Rottig, Daniel. 2007. "Successfully Managing International Mergers and Acquisitions: A Descriptive Framework." *International Business: Research, Teaching and Practice* 1:1, 97–118.

United Nations. 2009. *World Investment Report*. New York and Geneva: United Nations Conference on Trade and Development.

Walker, M. Mark 2000. "Corporate Takeovers, Strategic Objectives and Acquiring-Firm Shareholder Wealth." *Financial Management* 23:1, 53–66.

Wan, Kam-Ming, and Ka-Fu Wong. 2009. "Economic Impact of Political Barriers to Cross-Border Acquisitions: An Empirical Study of CNOOC's Unsuccessful Takeover of Unocal." *Journal of Corporate Finance* 15:4, 447–468.

Zhao, Wei, Ling Liu, and Ting Zhao. 2010. "The Contribution of Outward Direct Investment to Productivity Changes Within China, 1991–2007." *Journal of International Management* 16:2, 121–130.

ABOUT THE AUTHOR

Rita Biswas joined the School of Business at University at Albany—SUNY in 1990. Professor Biswas has published in the areas of international financial markets and financial institutions in journals such as the *Financial Review*, *Journal of Financial Services Research*, *Review of Futures Markets*, *Global Finance Journal*, *Journal of International Financial Markets, Institutions and Money*, and others. Professor Biswas' teaching interests are in financial management, M&As, and international financial markets. She has won several undergraduate and graduate teaching awards, is a frequent teacher in Executive MBA programs worldwide, and is a visiting faculty member at the Frankfurt School of Finance and Management, Germany. Professor Biswas received a BA and MA in Economics from Calcutta University, an MS in Economics from the University of Rochester, and a PhD in Finance from Texas A&M University.

PART VI

Special Topics

CHAPTER 25

Joint Ventures and Strategic Alliances: Alternatives to M&As

TOMAS MANTECON
Assistant Professor of Finance, University of North Texas

JAMES A. CONOVER
Professor of Finance, University of North Texas

INTRODUCTION

When a firm decides to expand the boundaries of its operations, it frequently has a menu of different options. These alternatives can be classified by the degree of control of the new operating assets. A firm can acquire full ownership of the assets, share ownership with other firms in alliances or partial acquisitions, or enter into arm's-length contracts with a third party. This chapter focuses on the choice between mergers and acquisitions (M&As) and alliances. An alliance is broadly defined as a contractual relationship in which several independent partners share tangible or intangible assets. Gomes-Casseres (1996, p. 34) defines an *alliance* as "any governance structure to manage an incomplete contract between separate parties in which partner has limited control." The realm of alliances includes equity alliances managed in a joint venture (JV) by an independent board of directors, and nonequity alliances that expand a wide range of contractual collaborations including technology, research and development (R&D), manufacturing, materials supply or marketing, and licensing.

The economic relevance of M&As can be conjectured from observing the more than $38 trillion (in 2009 constant dollars) in acquisitions during the period 1990 to 2008, as compiled by the Securities Data Company's (SDC) Mergers and Acquisitions Database. This figure, however, underestimates the magnitude of this market because as many as 56 percent of SDC M&A deals do not report a dollar value and SDC is extensive, not comprehensive.

The importance of alliances is more difficult to quantify because partners do not report the value of the assets involved in the agreement, some of which are intangibles and thus difficult to value. Sebastian (1995, p. A1) reproduces the findings of a study by Coopers & Lybrand showing that "55 percent of the nation's faster growing companies are involved in an average of three alliances." The growing number of alliances has lead some researchers to propose that a firm is no longer a valid unit of analysis to study competition because firms now do not

461

compete with other firms; instead, "constellations" of firms compete against each other (Gomes-Casseres, 2005).

The economic significance of M&A and alliances is paralleled by a large body of academic research that expands across many disciplines, including management, economics, finance, accounting, sociology, and marketing. Summarizing exhaustively each of the hundreds of interdisciplinary studies on M&As and alliances would be fruitless. The goal of this chapter is to provide for entrepreneurs and scholars a manageable number of dimensions that are important in the decision to acquire assets or to share ownership of assets in an alliance.

The remainder of the chapter has the following organization. The decision to ally or acquire is framed by presenting the relative importance of M&As and alliances during the period from 1990 to 2008. Important costs and benefits of sharing ownership and full integration, as well as the choice between equity and nonequity alliances, are outlined. A separate section is dedicated to cross-border deals because of the special characteristics of these transactions. Existing evidence on wealth creation for each alternative is reviewed. Before concluding, future research is suggested to settle unresolved questions about the decision to expand the boundaries of the firm with M&As or by sharing control in alliances.

The Preferred Choice

To gain an overall perspective for the size of the market for corporate control, Exhibit 25.1 presents SDC's total number of reported M&As (deals that result in more than 50 percent control of the target) and alliances. SDC reports 339,792 acquisitions and 108,928 alliances from 1990 to 2008, involving 214 countries. The market for corporate assets appears to follow the patterns of global economic activity. For example, both M&As and alliances increase steadily until 2000, decreasing in the early 2000s, and then again decreasing in 2008 in the middle of the global economic crisis. Exhibit 25.1 also shows that the relative importance of alliances declined from around 50 percent in the early 1990s to less than 25 percent of the number of M&A deals in 2008.

Exhibit 25.1, columns (7)–(10), shows SDC reported M&A activity for the three industries that have the greatest amount of reported activity. Alliances are more concentrated in a few industries than M&As. For instance, in 2008, 42.94 percent of the deals occurred in the business services, wholesale, and trading industries, although these industries only accounted for 17.57 percent of total market capitalization of U.S. exchange-listed firms. This observed concentration of alliances is consistent with prior studies that highlight the economic importance of alliances for specific industries. For instance, Lerner and Merges (1998) suggest that throughout much of the 1990s, biotechnology firms relied more on funding from alliances than the next three most common sources of financing combined.

Two questions arise from the data overview in Exhibit 25.1. What explains the preference for control inferred from the larger number of M&A deals? What factors determine the choice between alliances and M&As?

This chapter analyzes these questions from the perspective of an entrepreneur (who wants to expand a business) and evaluates the costs and benefits of the decision to acquire or to ally. The chapter also focuses on costs because both alternatives are treated as complementary, so higher costs of one alternative will

Exhibit 25.1 Activity of M&As and Alliances during the Period 1990 to 2008

Year (1)	M&A (2)	Alliances (3)	JVs (4)	% of Alliances to M&A (5)	% of JVs to Total Alliances (6)	Industries with the Largest Number of Alliances (7)	% of Total (8)	Industries with the Largest Number of M&As (9)	% of total (10)
1990	7,658	3,317	1,804	43.31	54.39	Business Services Trading Wholesale	38.38	Banking Business Services Wholesale	26.21
1991	10,196	5,918	3,066	58.04	51.81	Business Services Wholesale Trading	36.56	Business Services Banking Wholesale	24.97
1992	10,029	3,046	909	30.37	29.84	Wholesale Business Services Pharmaceutical Products	43.53	Business Services Banking Wholesale	24.66
1993	10,423	6,831	2,998	65.54	43.89	Wholesale Business Services Electronic Equipment	37.02	Business Services Banking Wholesale	24.41
1994	12,262	82,23	4,401	67.06	53.52	Wholesale Business Services Electronic Equipment	32.15	Business Services Wholesale Banking	25.85

(*Continued*)

Exhibit 25.1 (*Continued*)

Year (1)	M&A (2)	Alliances (3)	JVs (4)	% of Alliances to M&A (5)	% of JVs to Total Alliances (6)	Industries with the Largest Number of Alliances (7)	% of Total (8)	Industries with the Largest Number of M&As (9)	% of total (10)
1995	15,025	8,983	5,704	59.79	63.50	Business Services Wholesale Electronic Equipment	27.46	Business Services Wholesale Banking	26.02
1996	16,145	5,212	2,899	32.28	55.62	Business Services Wholesale Telecommunications	32.60	Business Services Wholesale Trading	18.47
1997	18,820	6,767	3,437	35.96	50.79	Business Services Wholesale Electronic Equipment	32.74	Business Services Wholesale Trading	27.11
1998	21,411	7,858	2,880	36.70	36.65	Business Services Trading Telecommunications	40.12	Business Services Real State Wholesale	29.79
1999	22,742	8,777	3,010	38.59	34.29	Business Services Trading Telecommunications	48.02	Business Services Wholesale Trading	32.22
2000	24,400	10,502	3,390	43.04	32.28	Business Services Telecommunications Trading	59.51	Business Services Telecommunications Wholesale	39.01

Year							
2001	19,049	6,996	36.73	31.25	Business Services, Telecommunications Trading	52.03	Business Services Trading Wholesale	35.24
2002	16,838	5,065	30.08	34.85	Business Services Trading Computers	46.31	Business Services Trading Wholesale	32.39
2003	17,775	4,872	27.41	18.68	Business Services Trading Wholesale	60.35	Business Services Trading Wholesale	30.94
2004	19,983	4,129	20.66	20.00	Business Services Wholesale Trading	60.73	Business Services Trading Wholesale	31.73
2005	22,915	4,883	21.31	26.21	Business Services Computers Trading	57.00	Business Services Trading Wholesale	31.75
2006	24,606	4,777	19.41	29.39	Business Services Computers Trading	56.15	Business Services Trading Real Estate	31.88
2007	25,742	5,606	21.78	38.83	Business Services Trading Computers	46.17	Business Services Trading Real Estate	31.95
2008	23,773	5,389	22.67	37.74	Business Services Wholesale Trading	42.94	Business Services Trading Real Estate	31.95

This exhibit presents SDC's number of reported M&As (deals that result in more than 50 percent control of the target) and alliances during the period 1990 to 2008. Separate analyses for JVs as a special type of alliance are also presented. The industry classification follows Fama and French (1997).

justify the adoption of the other choice. The next section integrates different views about the entrepreneur's decision that include transaction costs, internalization, organizational learning, social embeddedness, and real options. The chapter then presents sections on costs of integration, joint ventures and nonequity alliances, cross-border deals, and wealth creation. The final section provides a summary and conclusion.

THE COSTS OF SHARING OWNERSHIP

When compared with an acquisition, alliances provide an opportunity for sharing costs, risks, and knowledge. Exhibit 25.1 shows, however, that firms seem to prefer full control than to ownership sharing. A reason for the preference for full control can be the low rate of success in alliances. For instance, Das and Teng (2000) report that less than half of alliances perform satisfactorily and that alliances, in general, are less successful and less stable than organizations controlled by one firm. Berg, Duncan, and Friedman (1982) among others suggest that sharing ownership is the desired organizational structure only when no other alternative is available. Why do so many alliances fail? In other words, what are the costs from sharing ownership?

Organizational Instability and Coordination Problems

Some problems stem from the lack of control combined with divergent goals in alliances. In the sample of alliances from Exhibit 25.1, 89 percent of the alliances are owned by two partners and 65 percent are equally owned. This governance structure can be unstable because it creates a situation similar to the "prisoners' dilemma" in which the partners may choose to not cooperate when they perceive opportunistic behavior by the other partner.

Joint ownership structures imply required veto power for both partners during the negotiations in order to reach agreements. Consensus-building can slow the speed of adaption to new competition and lack of control increases the cost of coordinating activities, a fundamental explanation for the hierarchical structure of firms (Porter, 1990). The instability of alliances can also be due to changes in a parent firm's governance, strategic goals, competitive environment, and relative bargaining power of the partners that occurs over time (Inkpen and Beamish, 1997).

Appropriation of Partners' Intangible Capital

The common explanation behind the creation of alliances is to facilitate the exchange of knowledge among partners. Knowledge-sharing, however, is a double-edged sword. It can be used not only to increase the value of the collaboration, but also to appropriate the other partner's intangible capital. This opportunistic behavior by partners in alliances, dubbed "learning races," is one of the fears preventing firms from entering into alliances and explains the preference for the internalization of assets in a firm (Gulati and Singh, 1998). Prior studies show that the risk of expropriation is more relevant for firms that compete in the same industry (Oxley and Sampson, 2004), when firm-specific knowledge, proprietary knowledge, and marketing resources are highly valuable (Reuer and Koza, 2000).

Costs of sharing ownership can be reduced by full acquisitions, but opportunistic behavior can also be mitigated by repeated interactions among partners. Strategic alliances create networks that promote trust among participants. In turn, trust reduces the fear of expropriation and fosters learning and know-how transfers (Gulati, 1995; Zaheer, McEvily, and Perrone, 1998; Kale, Singh, and Perlmutter, 2000). Robinson and Stuart (2007) report that better networked firms in alliances between pharmaceutical firms and biotechnology research rely less on equity to reduce opportunistic behavior.

COSTS OF INTEGRATION

Full ownership solves issues of instability and opportunistic behaviors among partners. However, it also requires larger investments and does not benefit from risk-sharing or cooperation between independent partners. This section provides an analysis of an extensive body of literature on the costs of hierarchical ownership structures.

Integration of the Assets of the Target (or "Indigestibility")

Assets that a company acquires from a different organization may need to be reshaped to fit into the acquiring firm's structure. While presenting a complete list of the costs needed to integrate assets is difficult, these costs are likely to increase with the target's size, firms in different lines of business, and firms with different organizational cultures that impede the assimilation of human capital. The acquiring firm also needs to consider the cost to dispose of the target firm's undesired assets. These costs are higher when the market for these assets is illiquid, the costs of terminating duplicated, and unnecessary labor contracts are elevated.

Hennart and Reddy (1997) show that the integration of assets is preferred by managers when the desired assets are not commingled with other assets. Prior research also indicates that when these integration costs are high, either a partial acquisition (Chari and Chang, 2009) or an alliance with the target firm that involves only the desired asset can be a superior alternative to expanding the firm's boundaries (Hennart, 1991).

Valuation Uncertainty

In the presence of high levels of uncertainty, an alliance or partial acquisition can be a preferred mechanism to acquire assets because it mitigates the risk of bad acquisitions and increases the value of the transaction (Balakrishnan and Koza, 1993; Reuer and Koza, 2000). Uncertainty about future cash flows increases with the presence of information asymmetry between buyers and acquirers. Cash flow uncertainty should be lower when the acquirer and the target firm compete in similar markets as buyers have more expertise in valuing assets similar to their own operations.

A joint venture (JV) can be a mechanism to exchange information conducive to an eventual acquisition in the presence of high levels of valuation uncertainty (Mantecon and Chatfield 2007; Mantecon, 2009). Consistent with this transitional perspective of JVs, buyers gain more in acquiring assets shared in a JV with other partners, and these gains are positively associated with the degree of uncertainty.

Other forms of sharing ownership such as partial acquisitions can also be a desired structure to gain access to assets in the presence of uncertainty. Buyers may decide to acquire a noncontrolling interest in the target to gain information on the target and to reduce potential free-riding problems or managerial resistance in a follow-on acquisition. Partial acquisitions can be a faster method of entry than JVs because they do not demand the creation of a new entity. Partial acquisitions are also easier to unwind by selling the ownership share, where the dissolution of a JV requires negotiations among partners (Inkpen and Beamish, 1997; Chen and Hennart, 2004).

Alignment of Incentives

The integration of acquired assets inside an existing firm may have negative effects on the incentives of the employees managing the assets. Managerial motivation can be hampered in acquisitions because the assets are integrated into the parent firm and the target is not subject to market discipline (Williamson, 1985; Pisano, 1989). Information production about the target's assets declines and the link between compensation and performance is clouded due to difficulties in isolating the performance of divisions within a firm.

Capital allocation within a firm can have a detrimental effect on employees and firm value. Lack of transparency, combined with self-interest, can lead divisional managers to misrepresent the true value of their divisions in order to attract capital (Milgrom and Roberts, 1988).

Even in the absence of agency problems, the allocation of capital can result in misaligned incentives. Managers seeking to increase firm value will allocate capital to the most profitable divisions (Robinson, 2008). This "winner-picking" leads managers of less productive divisions to exert less effort because they know that capital will be shifted from their divisions to the most profitable divisions. This is especially problematic in projects that have a low probability of success but potentially high payoffs.

Choosing alliances in which to undertake risky projects is an enduring trend in the academic literature. In a survey of chief executive officers (CEOs), Berg et al. (1982) report that risk-sharing is the main reason for creating a JV. Robinson and Stuart (2007) and Robinson (2008) find that alliances cluster in inherently risky industries, and firms use alliances to conduct operations that are riskier than internally organized projects. Palia, Ravid, and Reisel (2008) report similar findings.

JOINT VENTURES OR NONEQUITY ALLIANCES

Equity JVs can be distinguished from nonequity alliances in that a new entity is created with separate boards of directors formed by the partners, usually according to the contribution to the JV. Column (6) in Exhibit 25.1 shows alliances are more frequent than JVs and the relative importance of JVs has declined over the years. After 1997, managers created only one JV for every three nonequity alliances.

The larger proportion of alliances may reflect the higher costs of forming a new independent unit, which may not be necessary for smaller projects. As summarized in the next few paragraphs, a large body of academic literature analyzes the benefits brought about by JV collaborations.

Equity Sharing in Joint Ventures Reduces Opportunistic Behaviors

The asset contribution in a JV acts as a hostage and reduces opportunistic behaviors (Williamson, 1979). Both partners are forced to collaborate because they are penalized if the value of the JV decreases. Sharing of assets in a JV also reduces "hold-up" problems that occur in other unilateral contractual solutions (Johnson and Houston, 2000).

Previous studies also show that the administrative structure created by equity JVs increases the control of technology transfer and increases collaboration (Balakrishnan and Koza, 1993). The independent JV board of directors induces cross-monitoring, which reduces opportunistic behaviors, enforces each partner's rights in conflict resolution, and facilitates dealing with unforeseeable contingencies (Pisano, 1989; Oxley, 1997). Creating an independent entity can also increase information produced about JV operations, and partners have auditing rights that are unavailable in other nonequity alliances (Osborn and Baughn, 1990).

Joint Ventures Promote Cooperation and Knowledge-Sharing

A main reason for creating JVs is that they are superior vehicles for learning than nonequity contractual collaborations (Oxley and Wada, 2009). According to Kogut (1988), JVs are organizational embedded entities that encourage knowledge transfer. From this perspective, equity joint ventures have advantages over nonequity collaborations in that they involve the creation of a common identity with its unique culture that facilitates the exchange and generation of ideas. The close collaboration among teams favors the spontaneous exchange of tacit knowledge, which increases in value with project complexity.

Equity-Sharing in Joint Ventures Reduces Valuation Uncertainty

The reduction in uncertainty brought about by equity JVs can be analyzed from two different perspectives depending on the type of uncertainty being considered. First, buyers face uncertainty about asset quality. The target's willingness to share ownership in assets acts as a positive signal about asset quality. Second, both parents face uncertainty about the future feasibility of a project. A JV allows both partners to limit their initial investment and grants the option to expand later if uncertainty is resolved favorably. An extensive body of research considers the option characteristics of JVs (e.g., Kogut, 1991).

Both perspectives suggest that JVs are more valuable in the presence of high levels of valuation uncertainty. Examples include projects with both high expected payoffs and high chances of failure; when the assets are difficult to value (for instance, intangible assets); when high levels of asymmetric information are present between buyers and sellers; and when a partner lacks the experience needed to value the assets.

CROSS-BORDER DEALS

Differences in legal systems and in social and business norms can influence the choice between M&A and alliances for a firm that decides to expand its business to a different country. This section expands the discussion of the costs of internationalization and sharing control to these cross-border deals. Also discussed are cross-border deals as analyzed in the literature that considers the cross-border relative importance of the method of ownership and the cross-border factors affecting the decision to ally or acquire separately.

The Relative Importance of M&As, Nonequity Alliances, and Joint Ventures

Exhibit 25.2, Column (1), shows that the percentage of cross-border acquisitions during the period 1990 to 2008 is stable at about 30 percent of total M&A deals. Column (2) reports that the percentage of cross-border alliances to cross-border M&As ranges between 50 percent and 70 percent. The percentage of cross-border JVs to cross-border M&As, reported in column (4), is larger than the percentage of nonequity alliances. This result contrasts with the larger number of nonequity alliances compared to JVs reported in Exhibit 25.1 and highlights the relevance of JVs in cross-border deals. Restrictions in foreign direct investment (FDI) probably explain, at least partially, the larger relevance of ownership-sharing in cross-border deals. Some countries prohibit or limit the ownership by foreign companies (usually to less than 50 percent). This is not only in undeveloped or underdeveloped or emerging economies but also in Organisation for Economic Co-Operation and Development (OECD) countries (for instance, restrictions on foreign ownership in airlines in the European Union and North America and in the telecommunications industry in Japan). Restrictions on operating a business in a foreign country include limitations on having foreign nationals as workers, managers, or board members.

Columns (5)–(10) present the *Index of Economic Freedom* for the country where the target assets are located. This index measures freedom of a country's economic activity with higher values for countries with higher freedom. Published by *The Wall Street Journal* and the Heritage Foundation since 1995 for 162 countries, it combines statistics from the International Monetary Fund, World Bank, and the Economist Intelligence Unit. Alliances are associated with lower levels of the index than M&As and equity JVs exhibit the lowest levels of the index. Results in Exhibit 25.2 suggest that firms prefer alliances over complete acquisitions in cross-border acquisitions. A preference also exists for equity alliances in countries with higher investment risk.

Exhibit 25.2 Cross-Border M&A and Alliances Activity in the Period 1990 to 2008

Year	Cross-Border Deals				Average Index of Economic Freedom					
	% C-B M&As to Total M&As (1)	% C-B Alliances to C-B M&As (2)	% C-B Non-JVs to C-B M&As (3)	% C-B JVs to C-B M&As (4)	C-B M&As (5)	Domestic M&As (6)	C-B Alliances (7)	Domestic Alliances (8)	C-B JVs (9)	Domestic JVs (10)
1990	29.65	68.02	59.10	75.11	76.25	79.17	72.19	79.10	76.49	70.82
1991	24.78	70.83	62.65	77.93	74.47	76.37	71.10	79.01	75.75	69.65
1992	22.81	62.22	54.19	78.42	73.92	76.72	70.81	79.10	74.81	66.46
1993	23.79	65.12	53.37	79.93	73.55	77.64	66.12	77.40	72.84	61.60
1994	25.29	64.68	51.64	76.03	73.51	77.58	65.15	77.48	73.82	61.50
1995	25.73	64.41	47.78	73.96	73.13	77.11	65.50	76.90	74.27	63.01
1996	37.86	63.18	49.47	74.32	73.24	77.54	66.68	77.33	73.73	63.47
1997	25.95	59.34	46.76	71.54	73.20	77.87	67.89	77.81	73.82	64.46
1998	26.79	57.30	50.31	69.33	73.20	77.81	68.20	77.12	71.52	64.69
1999	29.21	53.41	46.06	67.17	72.88	76.85	70.19	78.15	72.82	67.33
2000	31.99	53.05	48.20	63.24	73.24	76.16	70.58	76.74	71.82	69.03
2001	30.66	58.55	54.07	68.41	72.36	75.79	68.22	76.20	69.85	66.17
2002	26.29	60.03	37.32	80.42	72.36	76.12	64.87	76.20	68.82	61.28
2003	25.60	54.37	50.30	72.15	72.40	76.05	67.98	78.19	72.03	62.40
2004	26.61	55.27	51.12	71.95	72.46	76.30	67.04	78.51	70.47	62.55
2005	28.96	56.11	50.14	73.06	72.14	76.03	66.26	77.79	70.56	62.46
2006	30.06	54.07	47.21	70.67	72.11	76.02	66.00	77.84	70.90	62.44
2007	31.40	59.72	51.80	72.31	72.21	75.72	63.41	75.23	68.51	60.63
2008	29.68	63.54	57.95	72.85	71.64	74.39	63.72	74.20	67.42	61.23

This exhibit shows the cross-border (C-B) M&A and alliances based on data compiled by SDC during the period 1990 to 2008. The exhibit also presents separate analyses for JVs as a special type of alliance. The Index of Economic Freedom measures freedom of a country's economic activity with higher values for countries with higher freedom.

Factors Affecting the Decision to Acquire or to Ally in Cross-Border Deals

Alien institutions magnify the costs of internationalization and sharing control described above. The list of factors that increase the risk in cross-border acquisitions includes differences in the legal system, protection of property rights, expropriation, political uncertainty, and social and business norms. These factors are broad, interrelated, and country-specific, and their influence in international deals has spawned a large body of research (Teece, 1985; Chari and Chang, 2009). The next section expands the previous discussion on the costs of sharing ownership and internalization for the specific characteristics involved in cross-border deals.

The Costs of Sharing Ownership in Cross-Border Deals

The costs of sharing ownership may be magnified by different regulations and cultural norms that increase organizational instability or coordination among partners located in different countries. Differences in legal norms can also increase the risks of appropriation of intangible capital in cross-border deals.

Organizational Instability and/or Coordination Problems
Sharing control in cross-border deals increases the difficulty of coordinating worldwide operations, setting intrafirm price transfers, and optimizing taxes. Full ownership permits multinational firms to set transfer prices for tax regimes in different countries to reduce the final tax bill (Kant, 1990). Full integration also facilitates the coordination of worldwide operations. Desai, Foley and Hines (2004) report that liberalized ownership restrictions and changes in the Tax Reform Act of 1986 impose tax penalties on JVs, thus reducing shared ownership. These results suggest that firms prefer whole ownership of foreign subsidiaries because hierarchical structures favor coordination between parent and affiliate trades and facilitate both technology transfer and tax joint planning.

Appropriation of Partners' Intangible Capital
A main reason some host countries require shared ownership of FDI is to acquire knowledge from foreign partners. Reducing possibilities for opportunistic behavior in cross-border acquisitions argues for internationalization when entering different geographic markets (e.g., Reich and Mankin, 1986; Kogut and Singh, 1988; Hennart and Reddy, 1997). Potential buyers may prefer sharing ownership or entering into alliances in countries with low levels of corporate governance, protection of property rights (Ethier and Markusen, 1996), and development in their legal system (Mansfield, 1994).

Costs of Integration in Cross-Border Deals
The costs of integration may be higher in cross-border deals due to institutional or cultural dissimilarities between targets and acquirers. Additionally, costs of integrating assets located in a different country could be subject to higher levels of valuation uncertainty.

Integration of the Assets of the Target

Integration of assets is complicated by the different institutions and cultures among the parties. Many studies analyze different institutions and cultural aspects that affect the choice of entry and performance of acquisitions. For instance, Barkema and Vermeulen (1998) find greater cultural distance is associated with a propensity for partly owned acquisitions relative to complete acquisitions. Javorcik and Wei (2009) report sharing ownership increases with the corruption level in a country. Authors often find differences between buyers and targets increase the cost of full integration and call for sharing the ownership of the assets. A foreign firm can benefit from the host country partner's knowledge about how to manage employees in a different local labor market and how to conduct business and navigate the rules and regulations of a different legal system (Kogut and Singh, 1988).

A firm acquiring foreign targets should consider potential postacquisition costs derived from divesting unnecessary assets. Lack of liquidity in the market for corporate assets, presence of asymmetries of information, and legal regimes with poor investor protection rights can reduce divested asset values (La Porta, Lopez-de-Silanes, Shleifer, and Vishny, 2002). Also, managers of firms involved in cross-border acquisitions should analyze foreign labor market regulations for the targeted assets. Rigid labor market regulations that increase the cost of terminating contracts tied to undesired assets should be impounded in the premium paid for the for the target (Krishnan, Hitt, and Park, 2007) and can affect the entry strategy in foreign markets.

Valuation Uncertainty

Differences in legal and cultural norms between countries are likely to increase valuation uncertainty. As a consequence, partial ownership structures such as JVs are proposed as mechanisms to reduce uncertainty risk (Gomes-Casseres, 1996; Inkpen and Beamish, 1997). For instance, Chen and Hennart (2004) find that ex ante valuation problems and ex post opportunism by targets explain the propensity of Japanese acquirers to opt for less than full ownership of U.S. target firms.

Managers might use JVs as a mechanism to reduce country investment risk when the final goal is a complete acquisition. Mantecon (2009) shows that foreign firms can benefit from the exchange of information inside a joint venture before the acquisition of assets located in countries with higher levels of investment risk.

DO M&As OR ALLIANCES CREATE MORE VALUE FOR SHAREHOLDERS?

Evaluating the performance of M&As or alliances is a difficult task. Lack of disclosure usually impedes observing the performance of assets integrated in a firm and partners typically do not provide individualized measures of alliances performance. Researchers are obliged to use indirect measures of the performance of M&As and alliances. Many researchers analyze changes in firm value around the announcement (usually in 1- to 5-day windows around the announcement). This event study analysis relies on the joint assumptions that prices are unbiased measures of future cash flows and that stock prices react quickly to public announcements.

A secondary approach to measure performance is to analyze the long-run stock and operating performance during an arbitrary period following the event (usually 3 or 5 years). This measure also has shortcomings. First, it may not reflect the performance of M&As or alliances because isolating the impact of the event from other corporate decisions before the announcement or during the period of study is difficult. From a methodological point of view, some long-run results disappear when alternative methodologies and measures of risk are used, casting doubt on the overall benefits from these studies.

Gains to Buyers in M&As

Event study analysis shows significant gains to targets in M&As whereas acquirers experience small or negative returns (Jensen and Ruback, 1983). The evidence regarding buyers' gains in cross-border acquisitions is inconclusive. Some studies suggest that global diversification is associated with a reduction in firm value (Denis, Denis, and Yost, 2002), and others report that buyers benefit in cross-border deals (Freund, Trahan, and Vasudevan, 2007).

Researchers have analyzed a multitude of factors that affect the returns to acquirers. Arguably, the most important are the size of the acquirer, method of payment, and public or private status of the target. Smaller buyers gain more than larger buyers (Moeller, Schlingemann, and Stulz, 2005); buyers gain more in cash than in stock acquisitions (Hansen, 1987) and more in the acquisition of private targets than in the purchase of public firms (Chang, 1998).

Analysis of stock returns in the years following the acquisitions challenges the assumptions under the event study methodology: Markets seem to underreact to announcement of M&As, and prices do not always reflect fundamental value. Several studies find poor stock performance for acquirers during the years following stock acquisitions and positive returns (although small and only weakly significant) in cash deals (Loughran and Vijh, 1997). However, Savor and Lu (2009) consider the possibility that prices are overvalued at the announcement of the acquisition. Taking into account the endogeneity of payment method and acquirer performance, the authors find that buyers also experience gains in acquisitions when they use stock as the method of payment.

Studies of the postoperating performance of mergers also yield inconclusive results. Some studies find no evidence of improvement in operating or productivity performance (Ghosh, 2001), and others find improvements in operating performance after mergers (Healy, Palepu, and Ruback, 1992).

Gains to Partners in Alliances

The preference for full control and the poor performance of alliances do not predict better performance for buyers in alliances when compared to buyers in M&As. Robert A. Lutz, retired vicechairman of Chrysler Corp., articulated the pessimism about alliances when commenting on the Renault and Nissan alliance: "They might as well take $5 billion in gold bullion, put it in a huge container, spray-paint the word 'Nissan' on the side, and drop it into the middle of the Pacific Ocean"

(Naughton, Miller, and Thornton, 1999, p. 37). Rating agencies and analysts argued that a clash of cultures and the nationalistic and patriotic behaviors would impede collaboration and lead to the failure of the Renault and Nissan alliance (Treece and Farhi, 1999).

Whether the negative perception about alliances corresponds to reality is unclear. The Renault and Nissan alliance turned out to be extremely successful, and event study methodology suggests that alliances increase the partners' shareholder wealth (McConnell and Nantell, 1985; Chan, Kensinger, Keown, and Martin, 1997).

Consistent with the reasons behind choosing alliances, Chan et al. (1997) find that partners experience larger gains in horizontal alliances in the high tech industry. The gains of JVs are also larger in the presence of potential hold-up problems (Johnson and Houston, 2000) and in the presence of higher degrees of valuation uncertainty and country investment risk (Mantecon, 2009).

Assessment of the long-run stock or operating performance of alliances is intricate because alliances are usually small relative to the parents' size. Also, a firm may have several alliances, increasing the difficulty of separating the performance of the alliance from the performance of the parent.

A commonly used measure for the success of alliances is their duration. For instance, Pisano (1997) finds that in the biotechnology industry many more partnered or collaborative projects are terminated than are internally developed projects, suggesting that full control is more stable than alliances. However, the duration of a JV may indicate that one of the partners has acquired the desired information from the JV (Habib and Mella-Barral, 2007). A short-lived alliance could have transmitted valuable knowledge while the alliance was alive, and the parents may have learned from failed alliances (Das and Teng, 2000). The termination of an alliance can be due to strategic changes in one of the partners that are unrelated to alliance performance.

Some studies use survey data to measure performance. For example, Kale, Dyer, and Singh (2002) use managerial assessments of alliances based on surveys. Interestingly, they find a high correlation between this measure and event study results. Other analyses employ detailed information on alliances and compare alliances with full integration of assets and arm's-length contracts. Since these studies are industry-specific, they cannot be generalized to the overall alliance phenomenon. The evidence from these studies is also inconclusive. Palia, Ravid, and Reisel (2008) report that projects in the movie industry (developed internally and externally) perform similarly. However, Gomes-Casseres, Hagedoorn, and Jaffe (2006) explore alliances as a mechanism for sharing technological knowledge and find that knowledge flows are greater inside firms than with arm's-length relationships outside the firm.

Comparing the Gains of Buyers in M&As and Partners in Alliances

The discussion in prior sections suggests that the choice between M&As and alliances depends on the characteristics of the transaction. Thus, there is no reason, a priori, to expect differences in risk-adjusted performance between these two alternatives to acquire assets.

Several studies suggest similarities between acquirers' gains in M&As and alliances. Results from event studies suggest similar gains for buyers in M&As and partners in nonequity alliances and JVs (McConnell and Nantell, 1985; Chan et al., 1997). Firms with small market capitalization experience larger gains when they acquire assets and when they partner with another firm in alliances. The main difference for event studies is that gains in M&As accumulate to targets but both partners experience positive abnormal returns around the announcement of JVs (Slovin, Sushka, and Mantecon, 2007). Thus, buyers seem to fare better in JVs than in M&As.

Contrary to the findings in McConnell and Nantell (1985), Slovin et al. (2007), using JVs in which both partners are listed, find that the combined gains to partners in M&As are larger than the combined gains to JVs. Yet, the gains created by JVs experience larger gains than the acquisition of asset sales. Gomes-Casseres et al. (2006) report similar rankings as they find that knowledge flows are greater inside firms than in alliances but greater in alliances than between firms in arm's-length relationships.

Future Research

The evidence presented in this chapter is only a small fraction of an extensive body of research. However, the relatively few studies in the field of finance probably results from the lack of prices and disclosure about the contracts that govern alliances. Thus, further research is likely to occur when new databases on alliances contracts become available.

Several questions may merit future research to understand the choice between M&As and alliances. Prior studies offer a rich number of dimensions to consider in the decision on how to acquire assets. However, the evidence on which of these alternatives is more beneficial to potential buyers is inconclusive. An entrepreneur facing the choice between an M&A and a strategic alliance should consider different factors and choose the appropriate strategy. Thus, similar risk-adjusted returns are likely from the two alternatives. However, event studies show that a buyer fares better in an alliance than in an acquisition. Future research can try to explain this apparent contradiction. One possible explanation is that the market for M&As is more competitive than the market for alliances, which is driven by private negotiations and consensus among parties. A second explanation, also discussed below, is that researchers are not using the correct measure of risk to compare M&As with alliances. A third explanation is that managers do not accurately evaluate the impact of the different factors that affect the decision. A final explanation is that managers can extract more private benefits from integrating the firm (Dyer, Kale, and Singh, 2004). For instance, whereas an M&A increases the resources under managerial control, a JV is an independent unit jointly controlled with a partner firm.

Theoretical models and empirical research suggest that alliances are more prevalent in the presence of valuation uncertainty and project risk. Thus, the measure of risk used to estimate excess returns should differ for M&As and alliances. The higher rate of failure in alliances can be a natural consequence of the high level of risk in these enterprises and not due to the cost of ownership sharing. Future research should explore how to measure the different degrees of risk in alliances and M&As and its implications for the value created by alliances.

SUMMARY AND CONCLUSIONS

The large number of academic studies on M&As and alliances reflects the complexity of these choices. An entrepreneur faced with the option to either acquire or ally faces many dimensions that affect the decision.

Full control of the assets remains the preferred choice to expand the boundaries of firms. As Berg et al. (1982, p. 12) note, alliances still appear as the "last-ditch" effort to acquire assets when the costs of integration are too high. The main factors associated with establishing alliances are the presence of valuation uncertainty, indigestibility costs, country investment risk (including many institutional and cultural factors), asset specificity, and project risk. These factors are highly correlated and difficult to separate.

Equity JVs are generally less common than other alliances, suggesting that they are more costly to form, operate, and unwind than other alliances and contractual arrangements. Joint ventures, however, are more common than nonequity alliances in cross-border deals and very common for firm entry in countries with low levels of economic development. The governance in JVs can also be useful to reduce opportunistic behaviors and to foster information exchange. Finally, JVs appear to be an effective transitional mechanism to exchange information and ascertain the value of the assets before a full acquisition. These arguments suggest that firms may prefer equity JVs over other alliances in the presence of higher levels of uncertainty, risk, opportunistic behaviors, and need for knowledge exchange.

Existing empirical evidence does not provide a clear answer on which alternative (an acquisition or an alliance) is more beneficial for an entrepreneur facing the decision to acquire assets. Whereas event study analysis suggests that an alliance is associated with larger gains, long-run performance studies cast doubts on the results from event studies and offer contradictory results.

From the perspective of a policy maker with the goal of increasing social welfare, the empirical evidence suggests that M&As create more aggregate wealth than alliances. A few recent studies seem to suggest that the flow of information is also large inside firms, with JVs occupying second place behind full integration but before arm-length transactions. However, the scenarios in which alliances may be more beneficial (uncertainty and risky projects) highlight the importance of alliances in innovation and in expanding local firms to new markets.

The future of the role of alliances and M&As in the market for corporate control is unclear. Even though papers on alliances commonly note that these arrangements have increased over time and occupy an increasing role in the economy, the relative importance of alliances has remained stable or has even experienced a decline in relative importance since 1990. As Desai et al. (2004) suggest, increasing disclosure, information production, and globalization can be expected to reduce uncertainty and coordination costs, and consequently, the need for alliances. However, increasing technological complexities may require knowledge-sharing by several independent teams. Information production can also increase transparency and reduce the chance of opportunistic behaviors, inducing cooperation. The growing need for cooperation among independent units, facilitated by continuous enhancements in technology and information production, can result in a future increase in the relative importance of ownership sharing in alliances networks versus full integration.

DISCUSSION QUESTIONS

1. Evidence indicates three M&A deals for every alliance, suggesting a preference for control. What are the reasons an entrepreneur looking to acquire assets may prefer an acquisition over an alliance?
2. When will management prefer an alliance over an M&A?
3. Joint ventures are less common than other alliances. What are the costs and benefits associated with joint ventures?
4. Looking at existing evidence about M&As and alliances, which strategy is associated with larger wealth creation?

REFERENCES

Balakrishnan, Srinivasan, and Mitchell P. Koza. 1993. "Information Asymmetry, Adverse Selection and Joint-Ventures: Theory and Evidence." *Journal of Economic Behavior and Organization* 20:1, 99–117.

Barkema, Harry G., and Freek Vermeulen. 1998. "International Expansion through Start-Up or Acquisition: A Learning Perspective." *Academy of Management Journal* 41:1, 7–26.

Berg, Sanford V., Jerome Duncan, and Philip Friedman. 1982. *Joint Ventures and Corporate Innovation.* Cambridge, MA: Oelgeschlager, Gunn, and Hain.

Chan, Su Han, John W. Kensinger, Arthur J. Keown, and John D. Martin. 1997. "Do Strategic Alliances Create Value?" *Journal of Financial Economics* 46:2, 199–221.

Chang, Saeyoung. 1998. "Takeovers of Privately Held Targets, Methods of Payment, and Bidder Returns." *Journal of Finance* 53:2, 773–784.

Chari, Murali D. R., and Kiyoung Chang. 2009. "Determinants of the Share of Equity Sought in Cross-Border Acquisitions." *Journal of International Business Studies* 40:8, 1277–1297.

Chen, Shih-Fen S., and Jean-Francois Hennart, 2004. "A Hostage Theory of Joint Ventures: Why Do Japanese Investors Choose Partial over Full Acquisitions to Enter the United States?" *Journal of Business Research* 57:10, 1126–1134.

Das, T. K., and Bing-Sheng Teng. 2000. "Instabilities of Strategic Alliances. An Internal Tensions Perspective." *Organization Science* 11:1, 77–101.

Denis, David J., Diane K. Denis, and Keven Yost. 2002. "Global Diversification, Industrial Diversification, and Firm Value." *Journal of Finance* 57:5, 1951–1979.

Desai, Mihir A., Fritz C. Foley, and James R. Hines, 2004. "The Costs of Shared Ownership: Evidence from International Joint Ventures." *Journal of Financial Economics* 73:2, 323–374.

Dyer, Jeffrey H., Prashant Kale, and Harbir Singh. 2004. "When to Ally and When to Acquire." *Harvard Business Review* 82:7-8, 108–115.

Ethier, Wilfred J., and James R. Markusen, 1996. "Multinational Firms, Technology Diffusion and Trade." *Journal of International Economics* 41:1-2, 1–28.

Fama, Eugene, and Kenneth R. French, 1997. "Industry Costs of Equity." *Journal of Financial Economics* 43:2, 153–193.

Freund, Steven, Emery A. Trahan, and Gopala K. Vasudevan. 2007. "Effects of Global and Industrial Diversification on Firm Value and Operating Performance." *Financial Management* 36:4, 143–161.

Ghosh, Aloke. 2001. "Does Operating Performance Really Improve Following Corporate Acquisitions?" *Journal of Corporate Finance* 7:2, 151–178.

Gomes-Casseres, Benjamin, 1996. *The Alliance Revolution: the New Shape of Business Rivalry.* Cambridge, MA: Harvard University Press.

Gomes-Casseres, Benjamin, 2005. "How Alliances Reshape Competition." Oded Shenkar and Jeffrey J. Reuer (eds.), *Handbook of Strategic Alliances*, 39–54. Thousand Oaks, CA: Sage Publications.

Gomes-Casseres, Benjamin, John Hagedoorn, and Adam B. Jaffe. 2006. "Do Alliances Promote Knowledge Flows?" *Journal of Financial Economics* 80:1, 5–33.

Gulati, Ranjay. 1995. "Does Familiarity Breed Trust? The Implications of Repeated Ties for Contractual Choice in Alliances." *Academy of Management Journal* 38:1, 85–112.

Gulati, Ranjay, and Harbir Singh. 1998. "The Architecture of Cooperation: Managing Coordination Costs and Appropriation Concerns in Strategic Alliances." *Administrative Science Quarterly* 43:4, 781–814.

Habib, Michael A., and Pierre Mella-Barral. 2007. "The Role of Knowhow Acquisition in the Formation and Duration of JVs." *Review of Financial Studies* 20:1, 189–233.

Hansen, Robert G. 1987. "A Theory for the Choice of Exchange Medium in Mergers and Acquisitions." *Journal of Business* 60:1, 75–95.

Healy, Paul M., Krishna G. Palepu, and Richard S. Ruback. 1992. "Does Corporate Performance Improve after Mergers?" *Journal of Financial Economics* 31:2, 135–175.

Hennart, Jean-Francois. 1991. "The Transaction Costs Theory of Joint Ventures: An Empirical Study of Japanese Subsidiaries in the United States." *Management Science* 37:4, 483–497.

Hennart, Jean-Francois, and Sabine Reddy. 1997. "The Choice between Mergers/Acquisitions and Joint Ventures: The Case of Japanese Investors in the United States." *Strategic Management Journal* 18:1, 1–12.

Inkpen, Andrew C., and Paul W. Beamish. 1997. "Knowledge, Bargaining Power, and the Instability of international Joint Ventures." *Academy of Management Review* 22:1, 177–202.

Javorcik, Beata S., and Shang-Jin Wei. 2009. "Corruption and Cross-Border Investment in Emerging Markets: Firm-Level Evidence." *Journal of International Money and Finance* 28:4, 605–624.

Jensen, Michael C., and Richard S. Ruback. 1983. "The Market for Corporate Control: The Scientific Evidence." *Journal of Financial Economics* 11:1-4, 5–50.

Johnson, Shane, and Mark B. Houston. 2000. "A Reexamination of the Motives and Gains in Joint Ventures." *Journal of Financial and Quantitative Analysis* 35:1, 67–85.

Kale, Prashant, Jeffrey H. Dyer, and Harbir Singh. 2002. "Alliance Capability, Stock Market Response, and Long-Term Alliance Success: The Role of the Alliance Function." *Strategic Management Journal* 23:8, 747–767.

Kale, Prashant, Harbir Singh, and Howard Perlmutter. 2000. "Learning and Protection of Proprietary Assets in Strategic Alliances: Building Relational Capital." *Strategic Management Journal* 21:3, 217–237.

Kant, Chander. 1990. "Multinational Firms and Governance Revenues." *Journal of Public Economics* 42:2, 135–147.

Kogut, Bruce. 1988. "Joint-Ventures: Theoretical and Empirical Perspectives." *Strategic Management Journal* 9:4, 319–332.

Kogut, Bruce. 1991. "Joint Ventures and the Option to Expand and Acquire." *Management Science* 37:1, 19–33.

Kogut, Bruce, and Harbir Singh. 1988. "The Effect of National Culture on the Choice of Entry Mode." *Journal of International Business Studies* 19:3, 411–432.

Krishnan, Hema A., Michael A. Hitt, and Daewoo Park. 2007. "Acquisition Premiums, Subsequent Workforce Reductions and Post-Acquisition Performance." *Journal of Management Studies* 44:5, 709–732.

La Porta, Rafael, Florencio Lopez-de-Silanes, Andrei Shleifer, and Robert Vishny. 2002. "Investor Protection and Corporate Valuation." *Journal of Finance* 57:3, 1147–1170.

Lerner, Josh, and Robert P. Merges. 1998. "The Control of Technology Alliances: An Empirical Analysis of the Biotechnology Industry." *Journal of Industrial Economics* 46:2, 125–156.

Loughran, Tim, and Anand M. Vijh. 1997. "Do Long-Term Shareholders Benefit from Corporate Acquisitions?" *Journal of Finance* 52:5, 1765–1790.

Mansfield, Edwin. 1994. "Intellectual Property Protection, Foreign Direct Investment and Technology Transfer." Working Paper 19, World Bank and International Finance Corporation.

Mantecon, Tomas. 2009. "Mitigating Risks in Cross-Border Acquisitions." *Journal of Banking and Finance* 33:4, 640–651.

Mantecon, Tomas, and Robert R. Chatfield. 2007. "An Analysis of the Disposition of Assets in a Joint Venture." *Journal of Banking and Finance* 31:9, 2591–2611.

McConnell, John J., and Timothy J. Nantell. 1985. "Corporate Combinations and Common Stock Returns: The Case of Joint Ventures." *Journal of Finance* 40:2, 519–536.

Milgrom, Paul, and John Roberts. 1988. "An Economic Approach to Influence Activities in Organizations." *American Journal of Sociology* 94:3, S154–S179.

Moeller, Sara B., Frederik P. Schlingemann, and René M. Stulz. 2005. "Wealth Destruction on a Massive Scale? A Study of Acquiring-Firm Returns in the Recent Merger Wave." *Journal of Finance* 60:2, 757–782.

Naughton, Keith, Karen Lowry Miller, and Emily Thornton. March 8, 1999. "Nissan? Drive Carefully, Mr. Schrempp." *Business Week* 37:3619, 37.

Osborn, Richard N., and C. Christopher Baughn. 1990. "Forms of Interorganizational Governance for Multinational Alliances." *Academy of Management Journal* 33:3, 503–519.

Oxley, Joanne E. 1997. "Appropriability Hazards and Governance in Strategic Alliances: A Transaction Cost Approach." *Journal of Law, Economics and Organization* 13:2, 387–409.

Oxley, Joanne E., and Rachelle C. Sampson. 2004. "The Scope and Governance of International R&D Alliances." *Strategic Management Journal* 25:8-9, 723–749.

Oxley, Joanne E., and Tetsuo Wada. 2009. "Alliance Structure and the Scope of Knowledge Transfer: Evidence from US-Japan." *Management Science* 55:4, 635–649.

Palia, Darius, S. Abraham Ravid, and Natalia Reisel. 2008. "Choosing to Co-Finance: Analysis of Project-Specific Alliances in the Movie Industry." *Review of Financial Studies* 21:2, 483–511.

Pisano, Gary P. 1989. "Using Equity Participation to Support Exchange: Evidence from the Biotechnology Industry." *Journal of Law, Economics and Organization* 5:1, 109–126.

Pisano, Gary P. 1997. "R&D Performance, Collaborative Arrangements, and the Market for Know-How: A Test of the 'Lemons' Hypothesis in Biotechnology." Working Paper 97-105, Harvard Business School.

Porter, Michael E. 1990. *The Competitive Advantage of Nations.* New York: Free Press.

Reuer, Jeffrey J., and Mitchell P. Koza. 2000. "Asymmetric Information and Joint Venture Performance: Theory and Evidence for Domestic and International Joint Ventures." *Strategic Management Journal* 21:1, 81–88.

Reich, Robert B., and Eric D. Mankin. 1986. "Joint Ventures with Japan Give Away Our Future." *Harvard Business Review* 64:2, 78–86.

Robinson, David T. 2008. "Strategic Alliances and the Boundaries of the Firm." *Review of Financial Studies* 21:2, 649–681.

Robinson, David T., and Toby E. Stuart. 2007. "Network Effects in the Governance of Strategic Alliances." *Journal of Law Economics and Organization* 23:1, 242–273.

Savor, Pavel G., and Qi Lu. 2009. "Do Stock Mergers Create Value for Acquirers?" *Journal of Finance* 64:3, 1061–1097.

Sebastian, Pamela. 1995. "A Special Background Report on Trends in Industry and Finance." *The Wall Street Journal*, April 20, A1.

Slovin, Myron, Marie Sushka, and Tomas Mantecon. 2007. "Analyzing Joint Ventures as Corporate Control Activity." *Journal of Banking and Finance* 31:8, 2365–2382.

Teece, David J. 1985. "Multinational Enterprise, Internal Governance, and Industry Organization." *American Economic Review* 75:2, 233–238.

Treece, James, B., and Stephane Farhi. 1999. "Renault Goes for Broke with Nissan Bid: Problems Abound; Culture Is Big One." *Automotive News* March 22, 43.

Williamson, Oliver E. 1979. "Transaction Cost Economics: The Governance of Contractual Relations." *Journal of Law and Economics* 22:2, 233–261.

Williamson, Oliver E. 1985. *The Economic Institutions of Capitalism.* New York: Free Press.

Zaheer, Akbar, Bill McEvily, and Vincenzo Perrone. 1998. "Does Trust Matter? Exploring the Effects of Interorganizational and Interpersonal Trust on Performance." *Organization Science* 9:2, 141–159.

ABOUT THE AUTHORS

Tomas Mantecon is an Assistant Professor of Finance at the University of North Texas. His areas of interest include joint ventures, mergers and acquisitions, and initial public offerings. He has published several articles in the *Journal of Banking and Finance* emphasizing empirical analysis of finance theories about joint ventures and alliances. He has also taught international business in both San Sebastian and Bilbao, Spain. Professor Mantecon received a BA in Economics from the University of Oviedo in Spain; a Master in Financial Economics from ICADE University in Madrid, Spain; a Master in International Management from Thunderbird School of Global Management; and a Ph.D. in Finance from Louisiana State University.

James Conover is a Professor of Finance at the University of North Texas. Professor Conover's research interests are in corporate finance, empirical methods, and derivatives. His refereed articles appear in *Research in Finance, Journal of Real Estate Literature, Financial Analysts Journal, Journal of Financial Transformation, Financial Services Review, Journal of Applied Finance, Journal of Information Technology, Journal of Investing, Quarterly Review of Economics and Finance, Journal of Financial and Quantitative Finance, Financial Practice and Education, Advances in International Accounting, Review of Quantitative Finance and Accounting,* and *Oil and Gas Tax Quarterly.* Professor Conover received a B.S. from Cornell University, followed by an M.S. and a Ph.D., both from Texas A&M University.

CHAPTER 26

Fairness Opinions in M&As

STEVEN M. DAVIDOFF
Associate Professor of Law, University of Connecticut School of Law

ANIL K. MAKHIJA
David A. Rismiller Professor of Finance, Fisher College of Business,
The Ohio State University

RAJESH P. NARAYANAN
Charles Clifford Cameron Associate Professor of Finance,
Ourso College of Business, Louisiana State University

INTRODUCTION

In evaluating a merger or acquisition (M&A) proposal, boards frequently seek to determine that the consideration to be paid or received is "fair from a financial point of view" to shareholders. For such a purpose they obtain a "fairness opinion" from a financial advisor. Typically, the investment banks advising on the merger render the opinion, although other entities that specialize in valuation may also be called upon to provide one as well.

The chapter begins with a summary description of the fairness opinion's procedures and content to highlight how its form and structure result from concerns regarding liability associated with delivering the opinion. This description clarifies that a fairness opinion is not an appraisal of target value. Instead, it is the opinion of the advisor that the consideration is within a range of values that would be deemed "financially" fair, although the opinion does not detail how various valuation analyses are combined to arrive at a judgment of fairness, nor does it provide an explanation as to what would constitute fairness in the considered context. The chapter then proceeds to explain how Delaware corporate law and a Delaware Supreme Court ruling in the case of *Smith v. Van Gorkom* (1985) combined to institutionalize fairness opinions within the M&A calculus by making it a de facto, if not legal, requirement for all targets to obtain fairness opinions.

The chapter next reviews the criticisms of fairness opinions in the legal literature that stem from inherent subjectivity and the lack of established standards in preparing opinions, as well as the conflicts of interest associated with the provision of fairness opinions by investment bankers whose compensation is dependent on the deal's success. It also discusses some proposed remedies. The majority view in this literature is critical of the fairness opinion's ability to provide value to shareholders. Yet, arguments in the literature suggest that the true value of fairness opinions may lie in the financial valuation analyses underlying the opinion. These actual analyses provide a basis for investment bankers to bargain over transaction price, or otherwise provide support for the price being paid when there is no competitive bidding for an asset. Ultimately, whether fairness opinions add value or are a "legal" tax on corporate control transactions is an empirical question.

The chapter then reviews the empirical evidence available in the finance literature. This review reveals that a complete and consistent view of the value of fairness opinions is yet to emerge. Importantly, it reveals the difficulties associated with testing for the value of fairness opinions when there is very little cross-sectional variation in the opinions (all observed opinions are "fair" ones), or their providers (the majority of opinions are provided by investment bank advisors). Despite the identified shortcomings of fairness opinions, the widespread use of fairness opinions raises the question as to why the market continues to rely on them. The chapter concludes by raising several possibilities whose merits can only be ascertained with future research.

INSTITUTIONAL DETAILS

In a corporate control transaction, a fairness opinion is typically provided to a board, or a committee thereof, at the time of its consideration of the relevant transaction. The fairness opinion is usually delivered orally at this meeting by the investment bankers in attendance and confirmed in a subsequent, written letter addressed to the board from the investment bank. This two- or three-page letter sets forth the transaction terms, as well as the qualifications and assumptions underlying the investment bank's fairness determination. In fact, this is the letter's primary purpose—to manage and restrict the investment bank's liability for rendering the opinion. The laundry list of qualifications and assumptions is the bulk of the text. At the letter's end is one sentence wherein the fairness of the transaction at hand is opined. In a corporate control transaction, this is a statement that the consideration paid or received in the transaction is "fair from a financial point of view" to a specified party. The party is dependent upon the form and posture of the transaction, but the opinion is typically directed to the party receiving or paying the transaction consideration. For example, in an opinion delivered to a target board considering the transfer of corporate control through a corporate sale, the opinion would be directed toward the corporation's selling stockholders (Davidoff, 2006, 2008).

A fairness opinion is not an appraisal. It does not specify a set value or presume to be a determination of price (Kennedy, 2001). Instead, a fairness opinion is the opinion of a financial or other advisor that a specified transaction is within a range of values encompassing financial "fairness." A more specific definition of fairness in these circumstances is almost never proposed or spelled out (Chazen, 1981). The definition of fairness varies in context and, in each instance, is subject to debate among practitioners and academics. In a corporate control transaction, one definition of fairness from a target's perspective is a minimum range of values that the corporation's unaffiliated stockholders could otherwise receive in a board-run auction process conducted in a fair, open, and equivalent manner. However, the definition of fairness depends upon the recipient as well as the transaction and its unique characteristics. To date, there is no agreed-upon standard definition among academics, practitioners, or standard-setters of what fairness is in any circumstance (Elson, Rosenbloom, and Chapman, 2003).

Liability concerns have driven the fairness opinion structure and form. Investment banks have eschewed definitional fairness since elaboration provides further facts and conclusions upon which to challenge the opinion's validity or preparation or to otherwise assert under the federal securities (and other disclosure-based laws) that it is a statement of fact rather than opinion. The qualification and assumptions are crafted responses designed in part to restrict or obviate past court attempts to broaden the courts' ability to review a fairness opinion analysis, as well as the scope of an investment bank's duty to the relevant corporation's stockholders. Even the addressee—the board—is a source of liability concern. The board, rather than stockholders, is the addressee in order to provide a legal argument that stockholders cannot rely upon the opinion. Ultimately, while a full review of the fairness opinion form is beyond the scope of this chapter, some claim that these caveats and omissions eat up much of the worth of any fairness opinion (Davidoff, 2006). Recent evidence of this came from the Lazard fairness opinion to Bear Stearns shareholders with respect to the fairness of the consideration initially offered by J. P. Morgan. In that opinion, Lazard was able to conclude that J. P. Morgan's $2 a share price was fair, since Lazard assumed that the only alternative transaction was a bankruptcy where the equity holders received nothing (see Bear Stearns Companies Inc. *Definitive Proxy Statement*, 2008).

A fairness opinion delivered orally or in writing by the preparer at a board meeting is almost always, at least in a corporate control transaction, accompanied by a "board book." The board book details the underlying analyses conducted by the opiner used to arrive at and conclude financial fairness. The "meat" of the investment banker's work lies here. A well-advised board will review this book in connection with their receipt of a fairness opinion and question the bankers as to their derivation of fairness. The fairness opinion's meaning and worth, if any, lies in these actual analyses.

There are a number of different underlying valuation analyses upon which a fairness opinion can rest and which are set forth in this "board book." The most common and accepted techniques are discounted cash flow, comparable companies, premium, break-up, and liquidation analysis. The preparer of a fairness opinion will typically utilize a weighted combination of these to arrive at a fairness conclusion. However, in the investment banking community, no uniform, specific, and objective guidelines exist explaining the exact mix and weight to assign to each of these methods to arrive at fairness.

Each of the techniques is also prone to subjectivity. There is, however, no standard-setting or other body guiding these or other preparation decisions. This lends itself to valuation approach differences in each application and among institutions as each of them develops its own individual approach. For instance, Shaked and Kempainen's (2009) analysis of fairness opinions and the related proxy statement's description of the underlying analyses illustrate the considerable variation in the valuation techniques used and the assumptions underlying each valuation approach. They point out that the inadequate information available to shareholders regarding the inputs and valuation approaches used increases the difficulty for shareholders to determine if the board actually made the right decision.

LEGAL ORIGINS

Cain and Denis (2009) analyze a sample of 582 negotiated public transactions during the period from 1998 to 2005. They find that targets disclosed receiving a fairness opinion in 96 percent of transactions and acquirers in 28 percent of transactions. The ubiquitous use of fairness opinions by targets stems from the vagaries of Delaware corporate law. This is a fairly recent development. Before 1985, the role and necessity of the fairness opinion in a corporate control transaction was a legal uncertainty. These opinions existed solely as an investment banking product. This is not to say that legal practitioners perceived these opinions as valueless in aiding board decision making and satisfying a board's fiduciary duties. They did see such utility and routinely advised their obtainment. The need for a fairness opinion was not, at this time, recognized by the Delaware courts as an integral (or indeed any) part of the corporate control transaction process, and, before 1985, fairness opinions were rarely mentioned in Delaware jurisprudence.

The Delaware Supreme Court issued its opinion in *Smith v. Van Gorkom* (1985). The court found the board of the Trans Union Corporation to have breached its duty of care by approving the acquisition of a corporation (in a cash-out merger) in a manner that was not the product of an informed business judgment. The court held that the board's failure to obtain anything more than a "rough" and unquestioned estimate of possible value from the corporation's chief financial officer did not satisfy this explicated duty. More was required, and any reading of the opinion suggested that a fairness opinion was not necessarily this requirement. Rather, a target board, as part of its greater duty of care in a corporate control transaction, was now obligated to duly inform itself of its corporation's sale value through a well-prepared financial analysis. The fairness opinion would become institutionalized due to other entwinements of Delaware law.

The transforming actor was Delaware statute 8 Del. C. § 141(e). This provision of the Delaware General Corporation provides that directors are "fully protected in relying in good faith . . . upon such information, opinions, reports or statements presented to the corporation by any of the corporation's officers or employees or by any other person as to matters the member reasonably believes are within such other person's professional or expert competence." The directors in *Van Gorkom* had claimed reliance on this statute based upon the advice of the corporation's chief executive and chief financial officers. The court rejected this defense in those circumstances but did strongly imply that obtaining a thoroughly prepared valuation study or a fairness opinion not only would satisfy the board's duty of care and to be duly informed as to corporate value but also would establish sufficient basis to rely on 8 Del. C. § 141(e). Later Delaware court opinions would provide further support for this inference, particularly with respect to fairness opinions.

The majority of U.S. publicly listed corporations are organized in the State of Delaware and governed by its laws. Moreover, the law of Delaware carries enormous weight in corporate law matters in the other states. Thus, in the aftermath of *Van Gorkom*, the fairness opinion became a de facto if not legal requirement throughout the United States for targets in a corporate control transaction.

THE LEGAL LITERATURE

The subjectivity inherent in picking and choosing the underlying analyses for a fairness opinion as well as the differing techniques used to prepare fairness opinions have led them to be criticized in the legal literature. Bebchuk and Kahan (1989) criticize fairness opinion practice for two fundamental faults. First, they cite the discretion inherent in the preparation of these opinions. Bebchuk and Kahan segment this into "definitional" and "measurement" problems. The "definitional" problem posited by the authors is the lack of any meaningful explanation in these opinions as to what constitutes a fair price. The "measurement problem" constitutes the subjectivity in the valuation techniques underlying fairness opinions. Bebchuk and Kahan's criticism of fairness opinions for subjectivity and definitional vagueness are echoed in work by Carney (1992), Elson (1992), and Davidoff (2006).

Carney (1992) and Elson (1992) also argue that, as a valuation mechanism, a fairness opinion is inherently defective and market mechanisms should be preferred. Elson asserts that the market is the true and correct arbiter of price, and the fairness opinion is an unnecessary and valueless substitute. Elson (p. 1002) asserts that fairness opinions are "as necessary to valuation analysis as is the appendix to the human digestive system . . . [and] [o]ther than producing profits for the investment banking industry, it produces no benefit for the shareholders." Referring to the preference of market mechanisms, Carney (p. 528) states that fairness opinions are a "costly tax that legal rules impose on business transactions." Carney (p. 525) also posits that they "exist for two reasons: a judicial belief in the determinacy of value, and legal rules that shelter the business judgment of a board when based on reliance on the opinions of experts." He further suggests that the real function of fairness opinions is to serve to encourage directors to take reasonable risks.

In contrast, Davidoff (2006) highlights the subjectivity inherent in fairness opinions and the lack of set valuation standards but also notes that these faults are commonly known in the marketplace. Davidoff asserts that these opinions may be valued for other purposes. A fairness opinion's value may be in the underlying analysis and the tool it provides investment bankers to bargain over transaction price. Davidoff also argues that fairness opinions themselves are a poor substitute for market mechanisms such as auctions and competitive bidding situations. The opinions, however, can substitute for the market mechanisms when they are unavailable such as in freeze-out acquisitions by controlling shareholders.

For all of these reasons, legal commentators who have considered the issue have almost uniformly called for a repudiation of *Van Gorkom*'s financial analysis requirement. They view *Van Gorkom* as imposing an unnecessary transaction tax on the system by creating a de facto obligation for target boards to obtain a fairness opinion when considering a corporate control transaction. Fischel (1985) derisively refers to investment banks as "the biggest winners" after *Van Gorkom* due to the decision's effect on fairness opinion practice.

No consensus exists on a post-*Van Gorkom* legal regime for fairness opinions. Bebchuk and Kahan (1989) argue that courts should still consider fairness opinions provided certain measurement mechanisms are given weight. Davidoff (2006) echoes this call but asserts that courts should only rely on fairness opinions when market mechanisms are unavailable. Both Carney (1992) and Elson (1992) think

that courts should not rely at all on fairness opinions due to the superiority of market mechanisms. Elson et al. (2003, p. 7) back away from this position and assert
that fairness opinions can add value provided there are standards "to guide investment banks in their due diligence and pricing of transactions." Oesterle (1992),
Elson et al. (2003), and Davidoff (2006) all call for investment banks to self-regulate
by setting their own fairness opinion standards. To date, investment banks have
not made any move to do so, most likely because a universal requirement already
exists that targets provide fairness opinions. Improved fairness opinions might be
sought out more frequently by acquirers if such standards were set, but investment banks most likely see the costs of establishing these superior standards and
adhering to them as greater than the extra possible revenue.

A second strand of legal literature focuses on the liability of investment banks,
presuming that by providing some recourse for ill-prepared fairness opinions,
fairness opinion practice will become more disciplined. Giuffra (1986) and Fiflis
(1992) argue for heightened liability for investment banks to the target or the
target's shareholders for the rendering of negligent fairness opinions. Thomas and
Hansen (1992) reject heightened liability for investment banks since they believe
it will not improve investment bank practice but will raise costs to companies
as investment banks raise fees and seek increased indemnification in response
to greater liability exposure. To date, courts have generally agreed with Thomas
and Hansen and have been quite wary of accepting theories that allow target
shareholders to sue investment banks on negligence, agency principles, or other
grounds.

Bebchuk and Kahan (1989), Elson (1992), and Davidoff (2006) also cite the
potential conflicted nature of investment banks as further devaluing fairness opinions. Bebchuk and Kahan note that many fairness opinions fees are premised upon
the success of the transaction. Investment banks also cross-sell other products in
connection with the delivery of a fairness opinion and desire repeat business. All of
these factors incentivize bankers to rule fair transactions favored by management.
Cleveland (2006) argues that these conflicts are further distorted by cognitive biases of investment bankers including behavioral biases such as the overconfidence
bias, availability bias, and self-serving bias.

Conflicts can be mitigated by full disclosure. Moreover, the familiarity of a company's regular investment bankers with the company can facilitate the financial
analysis underlying the fairness opinion. Investment banks also regularly provide conflicted advice in M&As due to their general success fee—the fact that the
fairness opinion is also based on these conflicts should not be surprising. Nonetheless, Bebchuk and Kahan (1989) argue that these conflicts make fairness opinions
without preset measurements and standards inherently unreliable.

Other academics offer different remedies for the perceived conflicts problem.
Elson et al. (2003) maintain that due to these conflicts, when an investment bank
representing a target receives a success fee, the board should obtain a fairness
opinion from a second investment bank for a set fee. Oesterle (1992) argues that
where a board uses a conflicted investment bank to hide its own opportunism, it
should be used as evidence against the board for breach of its own fiduciary duties.
Cleveland (2006) contends that the existing apparatus can handle these conflicts
by allowing directors to rely on fairness opinions only if the directors themselves
have scrutinized and adequately questioned the underlying analysis.

THE FINANCE LITERATURE

Given the size of the transactions in the market for corporate control, determining whether board-sought fairness opinions are in the board's best interests is important for both bidder and target shareholders. Despite the importance of this issue, limited empirical evidence is available on the matter. To date, only Kisgen, Qian, and Song (2009) have published a study and only a few working papers exist on the subject. The following discussion presents the current state of knowledge on the value of fairness opinions by reviewing the published paper and two recent working papers by Cain and Denis (2009) and Makhija and Narayanan (2009).

Using a sample of 1,509 M&A transactions over the period 1994 to 2003, Kisgen et al. (2009) examine two hypotheses: the legal protection only hypothesis and the transaction improvement hypothesis. Under the legal protection only hypothesis, fairness opinions serve only to provide legal protection to managers and board members. Under the transaction improvement hypothesis, fairness opinions provide value to shareholders because they can help prevent an undesirable M&A deal, or lead to improved negotiations that result in better terms for shareholders. Kisgen et al. find that, despite 80 percent of the targets obtaining fairness opinions, these opinions have no noticeable impact on deal premiums or the probability of deal completion. Contrary to the transaction improvement hypothesis, these findings suggest that fairness opinions do not provide value to target shareholders. However, on the acquirer side the authors find that 37 percent of the acquirers who obtain fairness opinions pay premiums for targets that are on average 4.3 percent lower. Paid deal premiums are even lower if acquirers obtain multiple fairness opinions. Furthermore, the use of a fairness opinion by an acquirer improves the chances of deal completion. These findings on the acquirer side support the transaction improvement hypothesis.

Kisgen et al.'s (2009) analysis of shareholder returns surrounding the merger presents findings that are difficult to reconcile with those observed on deal premiums and outcomes. When targets obtain fairness opinions, they observe no material effect on announcement-period returns. However, when acquirers obtain fairness opinions, announcement period returns are a significant 2.3 percent lower. Furthermore, the authors find these announcement period returns to be lower when acquiring shareholders perceive that the investment banker's interests are not aligned with theirs. A fairness opinion carries with it a level of certification from the issuing investment banker because investment bankers are unlikely to stake their reputation on "low-quality" deals (ones with greater probability of wealth destruction for shareholders). Consistent with this view, the interests of lower-tiered advisors do not appear to be aligned with those of acquirers' shareholders. When acquirers obtain fairness opinions from investment bankers with lower reputations, there is a higher probability of deal completion, higher premiums paid to targets, and significantly lower announcement period returns to bidders. In a similar fashion, when the investment banker providing the fairness opinion is compensated through a fee contingent upon deal completion, acquiring shareholder returns are lower. Thus, despite evidence on improvement in deal terms when acquirer boards seek fairness opinions, acquirer shareholders discount such opinions, which contradicts the transaction improvement hypothesis. Instead, their evidence appears to favor the legal protection only hypothesis since self-serving managers are likely to have sought this defensive tactic. Chen and Sami (2006) also find a similar negative effect on acquirer stock and interpret it as evidence of the use of fairness opinions to reduce potential litigation risk.

Cain and Denis (2009) explicitly examine the valuation analyses underlying the fairness opinion reported in the merger proxy statement for 582 negotiated mergers announced between 1998 and 2005 for evidence on valuation biases that would favor deal advisors. Using data on high and low target valuations produced by the various valuation techniques underlying fairness opinions on both sides of the deal, they compare the average target valuation against the offer price and thus determine the extent of "bias" in the fairness opinions provided by investment bankers. Although the authors do not observe any bias associated with target fairness opinions, they find that fairness opinions sought by acquirers are optimistically biased in that the valuations underlying the opinion are significantly higher than the offer price (by 20 percent on average). Additionally, Cain and Denis find the bias to be lower when top-tier investment banks provide the fairness opinion and when the advisor has a prior relationship with the firm. They report two other findings. First, the bias does not vary based on whether investment bankers are paid contingent fees. Second, neither does the bias vary based on whether the valuations are performed by unaffiliated investment banks (without the alleged conflicts faced by advisors in the deal) or by affiliated advisors. Cain and Denis interpret their evidence to be consistent with advisors delivering valuations that favor the completion of deals.

To determine whether stockholders incorporate the bias in their evaluation of the merger, Cain and Denis (2009) examine how the bias is related to stock price reactions at (1) the announcement of the merger when valuations underlying the fairness opinion are still not public, and (2) the date the merger proxy is mailed, when the valuation analyses become public. They find that at the announcement of the merger, acquirer cumulative abnormal returns (CARs) are positively related to valuation biases underlying both target and acquirer fairness opinions. The authors interpret this correlation as evidence that investment banks incorporate publicly available information into their valuation analyses. At the proxy mailing date, acquirer CARs are positively related to biases, but only those found in the valuations underlying the target fairness opinion. Cain and Denis interpret this finding to imply that fairness opinions sought by acquirer boards do not reveal any incremental information about target values to acquiring shareholders. Instead, the incremental private information provided by fairness opinions, if any, arises when target-sought fairness opinions indicate that they are paying less to acquire the target. Their evidence thus corroborates the findings of Kisgen et al. (2009) in some aspects, but additionally suggests that the disclosure of the valuation analyses underlying the fairness opinions (at least those on the target side) provides incremental information to the market.

Makhija and Narayanan (2009) point out that the deal (merger) premium and the fairness opinion do not arise independently in the merger process. They maintain that investment bankers use the analysis underlying a fairness opinion to negotiate a merger premium that would get the deal done and one that they can ratify as fair. As a result, shareholders do not observe "unfair" opinions as the merger premium is renegotiated until the investment banker can render a "fair" opinion. This, they argue, is consistent with the observation that fairness opinions are always "fair" and are predominantly provided by deal advisors. Thus, what shareholders observe is a proposed merger premium always ratified as "fair" by the deal advisor. This implies that the value of a fairness opinion to shareholders cannot be ascertained by studying the impact of fairness opinions on deal premiums or completion probabilities (as they are jointly determined). Moreover, it implies that the identity of the fairness opinion provider is insufficient to determine whether the fairness opinion suffers from conflicts of interest because the merger advisor and the fairness opinion provider are often the same.

Consequently, Makhija and Narayanan (2009) contend that, in the case of targets where a fairness opinion is almost always obtained by the board, shareholders can assess the merger based only on other salient features of the process that generated the fairness opinion. These features include the quality of board governance, managerial and advisor incentives, and the reputation of the advisor. In the case of acquirers, where fairness opinions are less frequently obtained, the decision made by the board to obtain a fairness opinion can be of informational value to shareholders. Therefore, Makhija and Narayanan's approach to the problem is to study the stock price reaction to the merger premium ratified by a fairness opinion using the deal as a unit of analysis and how this response is moderated by the other contextual variables. Thus, their experimental design focuses on shareholders' reactions to the adequacy of the merger premium ratified by a fairness opinion, rather than the stock price reaction to the use of fairness opinions themselves.

Examining 1927 deals from 1980 to 2004, Makhija and Narayanan (2009) find that both target and acquiring shareholders' evaluation of the proposed merger premium is negatively influenced when the board obtains a fairness opinion from the deal advisor. Further examination of target shareholder reactions reveals that the reputation of the deal advisor ratifying the merger premium as "fair" mitigates this unfavorable reaction, while incentives faced by boards and management that aggravate conflicts with shareholders exacerbate it. Acquiring shareholders react unfavorably to proposed merger premiums when boards seek a fairness opinion from the deal advisor, as compared to instances where the proposed merger premiums are not ratified by a fairness opinion. This pattern on the acquirer side remains irrespective of the reputation of the advisor, the structure of the advisor's deal (success) fees, the nature of the board, and management stake. Altogether, Makhija and Narayanan interpret their findings as being consistent with the criticism that boards and investment banks use fairness opinions to further their own interests at an expense to shareholders, with shareholders being cognizant of such incentives.

SUMMARY AND CONCLUSIONS

Although some criticize fairness opinions for their subjectivity, a lack of set standards, and the inherent conflict regarding the investment banks providing them, the literature has failed to produce empirical evidence that is capable of addressing a more fundamental question—why does the market still rely on fairness opinions structured and prepared in this manner? While the portrayal of fairness opinions as a regulatory tax paid by shareholders in part explains the widespread use of fairness opinions by targets, fairness opinion fees can number in the millions of dollars. If fairness opinions are worthless due to subjectivity, why do boards not ask for more disciplined fairness opinions in order to obtain value for their money? Also, what explains the use of fairness opinions by acquirers? Possible answers are that fairness opinions (1) do not matter, (2) do have value in nonmarket transactions, and (3) as currently provided, do add value for bargaining purposes over transaction price, as a market signaling mechanism, or for the information content a fairness opinion's underlying analysis provides. Further research is needed to fully characterize the economic value of fairness opinions.

DISCUSSION QUESTIONS

1. How can fairness opinions provide value to shareholders in M&As?
2. How can fairness opinions destroy shareholder value in M&As?
3. What mechanisms can protect shareholders against the conflicts of interest associated with fairness opinions?
4. Would requiring firms to seek fairness opinions from entities specializing in valuation and not advising on the deal effectively mitigate the conflicts of interest facing investment banks?

REFERENCES

Bear Stearns Companies Inc. 2008. *Definitive Proxy Statement on Schedule 14A*, at 40, April 28.

Bebchuk, Lucian Arye, and Marcel Kahan. 1989. "Fairness Opinions: How Fair Are They and What Can Be Done About It?" *Duke Law Journal*, 27–53.

Cain, Matthew D., and David J. Denis. 2009. "Do Fairness Opinion Valuations Contain Useful Information?" *AFA 2008 New Orleans Meetings Paper*. Available at http://ssrn.com/abstract=971069.

Carney, William J. 1992. "Fairness Opinions: How Fair Are They and Why We Should Do Nothing About It?" *Washington University Law Quarterly* 70, 523–540.

Chazen, Leonard. 1981. "Fairness from a Financial Point of View: Is 'Third-Party Sale Value' the Appropriate Standard?" *Business Lawyer* 36, 1439.

Chen, Lucy H., and Heibatollah Sami. 2006. "Does the Use of Fairness Opinions Impair the Acquirers' Abnormal Returns? The Litigation Risk Effect." Working Paper, Arizona State University.

Cleveland, Steven J. 2006. "An Economic and Behavioral Analysis of Investment Bankers When Delivering Fairness Opinions." *Alabama Law Review* 58, 299–348.

Davidoff, Steven M. 2006. "Fairness Opinions." *American University Law Review* 55, 1557–1625.

Davidoff, Steven M. 2008. "Fairness Opinions: Thoughts, Perspectives and Legal Doctrine." In Wolfgang Essler and Sebastian Lobe, eds. *Fairness Opinions*, 221–233. Stuttgart, Germany: Schäffer-Poeschel.

Elson, Charles M. 1992. "Fairness Opinions: Are They Fair or Should We Care?" *Ohio State Law Journal* 53, 951–970.

Elson, Charles M., Arthur H. Rosenbloom, and Drew G. L. Chapman. 2003. "Fairness Opinions—Can They Be Made Useful?" *Securities Regulation and Law Reporter* 35:46, 1–8.

Fiflis, Ted J. 1992. "Responsibility of Investment Bankers to Shareholders." *Washington University Law Quarterly* 70, 497–521.

Fischel, Daniel R. 1985. "The Business Judgment Rule and the Trans Union Case." *Business Lawyer* 40, 1437–1455.

Giuffra, Robert J. 1986. "Investment Bankers' Fairness Opinions in Corporate Control Transactions." *Yale Law Journal* 96, 119–141.

Kennedy, Michael J. 2001. "Functional Fairness—The Mechanics, Functions and Liabilities of Fairness Opinions." In *Handling High-Tech M&As in a Cooling Market: Ensuring That You Get Value.* PLI Corp. Law & Practice, Course Handbook Series No. B-1255.

Kisgen, Darren J., Jun "QJ" Qian, and Weihong Song. 2009. "Are Fairness Opinions Fair? The Case of Mergers and Acquisitions." *Journal of Financial Economics* 91:2, 179–207.

Makhija, Anil K., and Rajesh P. Narayanan. 2009. "Fairness Opinions in Mergers and Acquisitions." Working Paper, Fisher College of Business, The Ohio State University.

Oesterle, Dale A. 1992. "Fairness Opinions as Magic Pieces of Paper." *Washington University Law Quarterly* 70, 541–561.

Shaked, Israel, and Stephen Kempainen. 2009. "A Review of Fairness Opinions and Proxy Statements: 2005–2006." *Journal of Applied Finance* 19:1/2, 103–128.

Smith v. Van Gorkom. 1985, 488 A.2d 858 (Del. 1985).

Thomas, Randall S., and Robert G. Hansen. 1992. "A Theoretic Analysis of Corporate Auctioneers' Liability Regimes." *Wisconsin Law Review*, 1147–1191.

ABOUT THE AUTHORS

Steven M. Davidoff is an Associate Professor of Law at the University of Connecticut School of Law. His research focus includes M&As, deal theory, alternative markets, and jurisdictional competition. Professor Davidoff graduated from the Columbia University School of Law where he was a Harlan Fiske Stone Scholar and received a bachelor's degree from the University of Pennsylvania, cum laude with honors. He has a master's degree in finance from the London Business School.

Anil K. Makhija is the Rismiller Professor of Finance at the Fisher College of Business, The Ohio State University. His research and teaching interests are in the field of corporate finance and focus on issues relating to capital structure, corporate governance, and utilities. Professor Makhija earned his Bachelor in Technology (Chemical Engineering) from the Indian Institute of Technology, New Delhi, an MBA from Tulane University, and a Doctorate in Business Administration (Finance) from the University of Wisconsin–Madison.

Rajesh P. Narayanan is an Associate Professor of Finance and holds the Charles Clifford Cameron Professorship at the Ourso College of Business, Louisiana State University. Professor Narayanan's research interests are in the areas of financial markets and institutions. He received his Bachelor in Technology (Mechanical Engineering) from Bharatiar University, an MBA from Southern Illinois University, and a PhD (Finance) from Florida State University.

CHAPTER 27

How Initial Public Offerings Affect M&A Markets: The Dual Tracking Phenomenon

ROBERTO RAGOZZINO
Assistant Professor of Strategic Management, University of Texas at Dallas

JEFFREY J. REUER
Blake Family Endowed Chair in Strategic Management and Governance,
Purdue University

INTRODUCTION

In June 2004, AOL placed a $435 million bid to acquire Advertising.com, a major buyer of online pop-up advertising. While interesting in its own right, that announcement might not have stood out from the more than a hundred other statements describing merger and acquisition (M&A) activity in the high-technology sector in the first six months of the year. However, the fact that Advertising.com had recently filed to go public made this deal noteworthy and suggestive of a broader phenomenon connecting initial public offerings (IPOs) and M&As. As another illustration, in mid-2002, eBay bid $1.5 billion to purchase PayPal, a privately held company with cutting-edge technology in antifraud online payments. In this transaction, the two companies had been discussing an acquisition before September 28, 2001, the date on which PayPal announced that it had filed to go public. Interestingly, since its IPO on February 14, 2002, the company had experienced gains of about 77 percent, and eBay eventually put in a bid to acquire PayPal at a price that was roughly 20 percent higher than the highest amount sought by the company during the previous negotiations.

Defining Dual Tracking

Dual tracking occurs when a company files a registration statement to go public, also called an S-1, and then later gets acquired in the M&A market. This phenomenon can be further divided into private dual tracking and public dual tracking. The former occurs when the acquisition materializes before the IPO takes place, that is, when the filing firm is still closely held. Besides the instance of Advertising.com, the acquisitions of Borden Chemical by Apollo Management, Brightmail by Symantec, and Noveon by Lubrizol are other cases of private dual tracking. To give a sense of the economic importance of private dual tracking, while only about 5 percent of early IPO withdrawals were acquired in the late 1980s, that figure rose to 27 percent by the end of 1990s (Lian and Wang, 2007).

While evidence does not exist on the motives of private firms to carry out an IPO, withdraw from this process, and complete a sale, such statistics are suggestive of overlooked connections between IPOs and M&As. By contrast, public dual tracking happens when, as in the case of PayPal, the target firm sees the public offering through and then gets bought out shortly after the IPO. Because more research exists on this type of dual tracking, the chapter focuses on this area.

Dual tracking hardly seems like a sound hedge for the firm seeking to go public and feeling unsure about its chances of being bought out. Besides the considerable investment in terms of required managerial time, IPOs come with a hefty price tag that averages 14 percent of the total proceeds raised. These substantial costs can make the IPO economically unviable if the market responds weakly to the offering. Why then would a company move forward with the costly and highly uncertain proposition of an IPO, instead of actively seeking a partner, or overcoming the obstacles that stand in the way of a successful negotiation with an existing suitor? What is the link between the going public event and the M&A markets that can make dual tracking attractive to a buyer or seller? These questions challenge the current wisdom on IPOs because market participants traditionally view going public as a vehicle for entrepreneurial firms to raise needed growth capital, as well as lucrative conduits for entrepreneurs or other investors such as venture capitalists (VCs) to exit.

The dual tracking phenomenon therefore broadens the scope of IPOs and raises the possibility that undergoing this process can bring about consequences for the firm and its stakeholders that span far beyond the traditional IPO boundaries. This phenomenon also challenges executives and academics to think through the merits of IPOs and acquisitions together and consider the benefits of staging these decisions, rather than considering IPOs or acquisitions in isolation or in simpler go/no-go terms (Reuer and Shen, 2004). The fact that preliminary evidence shows that dual tracking typically yields a 24 to 26 percent premium for firms over their single-tracking counterparts (Brau, Sutton, and Hatch, 2010) makes this possibility all the more interesting.

The remainder of the chapter has the following organization. First, as the underlying problems that lead to dual tracking, adverse selection and the economics of bargaining under asymmetric information in M&A are discussed. After offering a summary of the known remedies to adverse selection, attention turns to the central question of the chapter—dual tracking. Next, a discussion of the signaling properties of IPOs helps to shed light on the link between IPOs and M&As, and last, we present the implications of dual tracking as a tool to deal with the hazards of adverse selection.

FRAMING THE DETERMINANTS OF DUAL TRACKING

The performance record of M&As to date has been rather poor and the empirical evidence shows that, on average, 44 percent of all acquisitions are subsequently divested (Kaplan and Weisbach, 1992). The root causes for such a dismal record can be found in such issues as managerial hubris, overestimation of the synergies stemming from a deal, the challenges of postmerger integration, and the erroneous valuation of the acquired company. These concerns are important, though in practice they are connected with each other as incorrect target selection or appraisal difficulties can later lead to postmerger integration difficulties. The problem of valuing targets and carrying out negotiations appears to be one of the main rationales for dual tracking. At a basic level, much of the probability of successful due diligence for acquirers rests with their ability to gather as much information as possible on the target firm. Ideally, if the buyer knows as much about the seller as the seller does, the transaction would clear at a price that fully reflects the value of the seller. Unfortunately, this scenario rarely unfolds and acquirers are often faced with information asymmetry, which in turn gives rise to an economic problem known as adverse selection.

Describing adverse selection by drawing from the seminal example used by Akerlof (1970) may be useful. Akerlof uses the market for used cars as the backdrop of his explanation for causes of market failures and develops a simplified reality in which cars can either be of good quality or "lemons." To the extent that the buyer cannot tell the two apart, the sellers of lemons have an incentive to misrepresent the value of their cars and demand the same price as the sellers of the good cars. Consequently, absent appropriate remedies, the expected value of a car for a buyer is always below the full asking price, and the buyer either risks overpaying for a vehicle or walks away and the market does not clear. Among the remedies Akerlof discusses are warranties and money-back guarantees, which allow the good-quality sellers to distinguish themselves from their counterparts. Information asymmetry is not only detrimental to buyers but also to sellers of good-quality assets. Without costly remedies, sellers cannot credibly convey the true value of their good-quality assets to the market, thus being forced to offer discounted prices as a consequence.

Although Akerlof's (1970) example is the market for used cars, this fundamental logic can be extended to several other markets (e.g., Spence, 1974; Stiglitz, 2000) including the M&A market. Evidence suggests that adverse selection is one of the key determinants of failure in acquisitions (e.g., Higgins and Rodriguez, 2006). But if sellers in the used-car market have warranties or opportunities to build reputations as remedies to information asymmetry, what can prospective M&A targets do in order to convey their value to buyers, and how can acquirers cope with the challenges presented by asymmetric information? The ensuing section discusses a few ways to address the adverse selection problem in an acquisition. The discussion points out that while these solutions reduce asymmetric information and its consequences in M&As, they also present distinct trade-offs that make them attractive under specific sets of circumstances.

Known Remedies to the Adverse Selection Problem in M&As

Perhaps the most widely used method to reduce the adverse selection risk for acquirers is to make variable payments in which the payment a seller receives is a function of its subsequent performance. For instance, instead of paying for the target in cash, the acquirer could use stock as a currency for the exchange. The willingness by the target to accept stock triggers two related useful outcomes.

First, the willingness of sellers to accept a contingent payment conveys that the seller believes in its resources and capabilities. Second, using stock shifts part of the overpayment risk from the less informed buyer to the better informed seller. This method is more efficient. The usage of stock payments can therefore be valuable to bidders that are purchasing firms that are more difficult to value, such as private targets, and that have little familiarity or history together with the acquiring firms (e.g., in the form of prior collaborative agreements) (Reuer and Ragozzino, 2008).

However, when buyers offer stock as a medium of exchange in acquisitions, they often create the belief both in the target and the investment community that their stock is overvalued because the buyer has a natural incentive to use stock for consideration in M&As when its stock is overvalued. This explains why the market often responds negatively and buyers obtain negative returns when they announce acquisitions with stock rather than cash payments. In other words, just as information asymmetries can exist between buyers and sellers in the M&A market regarding the target's assets, there can also be information asymmetries between managers and shareholders in the acquiring firm regarding the acquiring firm's value. These latter information asymmetries introduce a cost of using stock to address the former problem.

A second potential remedy to adverse selection in acquisitions is the use of contingent earnouts (e.g., Ragozzino and Reuer, 2009). Like stock payments, contingent earnouts offer substantial benefits for acquirers seeking to minimize their exposure to overpayment risk. With earnouts, acquirers do not pay for the target entirely upfront, but commit to making future payments contingent upon the seller's ability to deliver upon certain future performance goals. Thus, if the seller cannot meet certain performance targets, the acquirer makes no further payments in excess of the initial disbursement. The case of the eBay's acquisition of Skype in 2005 serves as an example. In addition to the initial outlay of $2.6 billion in cash, eBay committed itself to paying $1.5 billion by 2009, if Skype had managed to meet certain performance goals that were agreed upon at the completion of the deal.

As with stock payments, the contingent nature of earnouts reduces buyers' overpayment risk and signals the value of targets to acquirers. However, as before, earnouts also present distinct disadvantages. First, they cause a necessary delay in the integration of the target resources because keeping the target separate in order to measure its future performance and determine whether payouts need to be made is imperative. Whenever high levels of integration play an important part in the value creation logic of a deal (e.g., scope economies from cross-selling or efficiencies from sharing back-office functions), earnouts are unlikely to be appropriate, compared to the case when the buyer wants the target firm management to stay and operate on an autonomous basis. Second, although earnouts reduce the adverse selection risk for buyers upfront, they also bring about the risk of moral hazard after the deal takes place, as the target management may try to inflate its performance to increase the chances of additional payments before contract expiration (Kohers and Ang, 2000; Datar, Frankel, and Wolfson, 2001). For instance, buyers might reduce expenses in areas such as maintenance, research and development (R&D), or other areas that would serve the long-term interests of the business.

A third remedy to the adverse selection problem in M&As is for acquirers to stage their investments, rather than engaging in acquisitions immediately. For instance, an acquirer may choose to enter into an alliance or a joint venture with a target firm and then, if more information on the value of the underlying firm becomes available, buy out its partner in the future. This solution offers the opportunity for buyers to experiment with the target on a piecemeal basis before the takeover step is taken. As an example, in 1988 Whirlpool acquired a 53 percent stake in Royal Philips Electronics in order to understand the strength of the dealer network. Whirlpool ended up acquiring the remaining 43 percent of the venture in 1991 in light of what it had learned about the investment. As another illustration, Cisco often uses equity alliances as a stepping-stone to acquisitions. Recent academic research shows that alliances can be useful to manage the risks of adverse selection and that equity markets tend to respond more positively to alliance announcements of deals characterized by asymmetric information than otherwise (Balakrishnan and Koza, 1993; Reuer and Koza, 2000).

Alliances can also be useful in signaling the value of a firm to another investor. For example, when a biotechnology firm obtains its first alliance agreement with a pharmaceutical company, it often receives a lower payment than in subsequent alliances. This is partly because the firm is effectively reimbursing the pharmaceutical firm for the information costs it bears associated with due diligence. The biotechnology firm benefits from the signal to other investors such as VCs or the equity markets, and is therefore able to recoup this reimbursement in the form of higher subsequent valuations (Nicholson, Danzon, and McCullough, 2005). Despite their effectiveness, alliances and joint ventures also have certain drawbacks such as limiting the access to the target's assets and requiring shared decision making by partners, making their use less suitable for some investments and requiring greater control and coordination of assets.

The Link between IPOs and Acquisitions

Having framed the problem of adverse selection in M&As and outlined some of the remedies available to acquirers to reduce their exposure to this problem, the chapter can now begin to link IPOs and acquisitions and explain how the former offers direct and indirect information on the target's assets that can facilitate exchanges and help M&A markets to clear. The chapter also provides evidence showing that certain IPOs can help buyers to circumvent the information asymmetry problem and avoid some of the disadvantages of the other remedies that are discussed above (i.e., stock payments, contingent earnouts, and alliances/joint ventures). Although adverse selection is a widely recognized problem in acquisitions, it is bound to be even more salient when the target firm is a startup company. Entrepreneurial firms that are considering an IPO typically have short histories and as private firms, the little codified information available on them may be difficult to obtain. Further, the value of these firms is often tied to their intangible assets and growth prospects instead of their established assets, which makes the due diligence process all the more challenging for acquirers. Thus, the importance of the topic is amplified as it pertains to a category of targets that have greater information asymmetries and adverse selection risk.

The most straightforward way in which IPOs can ease acquirers' due diligence and valuation problems is by causing the filing firm to disclose information in a credible manner such as through the course of registration. In addition to this information, once the firm becomes listed, prospective acquirers can also use its stock price as a starting point for bidding, as the price represents the unbiased investment community's aggregate judgment of the firm. Clearly, none of this information is available for single tracking firms, which turn into acquisition targets without ever starting the IPO process. Therefore, based on the differences in information availability characterizing single and dual tracking firms, due diligence for single tracking firms may be more challenging for buyers. Consequently, a greater incidence of acquisition activity should be observed for IPO firms than comparable private firms. Indeed, the evidence suggests that newly public firms attract M&A suitors at a greater rate than other firms (e.g., Pagano, Panetta, and Zingales, 1998).

There are, however, other important but less tangible ways by which IPOs alleviate the information asymmetry problem in M&As. First, recognizing that firms filing an S-1 are not a random sample of the overall population of their startup peers is important. Rather, a selection process takes place such that only the most promising firms are the ones that can take on the costs and risks of going public. In this sense, the simple separation of firms with concrete IPO aspirations from others works as a weeding mechanism by which acquirers can begin to distinguish the likely good-quality prospects from the "lemons." Thus, all else being equal, a reasonable assumption is that buyers prefer prospective targets that can undergo an IPO from one without such capabilities. Put differently, by initiating and seeing through the IPO process, newly public firms effectively signal their value to the investment community in ways that lower quality firms cannot replicate. Recalling the example of the used car market described by Akerlof (1970), by attaching a warranty to the vehicle, not only do good sellers provide buyers peace of mind but they also signal that they are confident in the asset's value. In contrast, low-quality sellers will be unable to imitate this signal and their identity will be so revealed. Interestingly, the act of filing to go public is a powerful tool for sellers as well. In fact, anecdotal evidence shows that the threat of an IPO can increase the incentive by existing prospective acquirers to accelerate a deal, and it often results in better terms for sellers. Using one of the examples mentioned earlier as an illustration, when Advertising.com informed AOL that it had filed an S-1 because of the uncertainty surrounding the takeover, AOL ended up speeding up the deal and eventually paying a higher price that matched the target's initial demand.

Second, in addition to the self-selection process that leads firms to file for an IPO, IPOs present heterogeneous characteristics that can offer additional screening tools for acquirers. In other words, not only does the act of going public hold potentially valuable signals for acquirers but so does the manner in which firms structure their IPOs. David Langstaff, the chief executive officer (CEO) of Veridian Corp., an IT security firm acquired by General Dynamics in 2003, discussed the need to make the right "first impression" when going public by deciding on which exchange to list, which investment banker to use for the IPO, and which analysts would cover the firm once the offering had taken place.

IPO Signals as Remedies to the Information Asymmetry Problem in M&As

Recent research has identified at least three IPO features that have a direct impact on the likelihood of a post-IPO acquisition: (1) the presence of a venture capitalist at the time of the offering, (2) the reputation of the lead underwriter in the deal, and (3) the magnitude of the underpricing on the first day of the IPO. Each of these characteristics and findings in recent research is discussed below.

Venture Capitalist Backing
Besides injecting capital into a startup, VCs add value by taking membership in the firm's board of directors, assisting in the formulation and implementation of strategic plans, contributing their network of relations, and hiring key personnel (Megginson and Weiss, 1991; Brav and Gompers, 1997). However, startups can find that obtaining VC support is challenging, as venture capitalist firms tend to be very discerning about the businesses in which they invest. Megginson and Weiss, for instance, report that VCs fund less than 1 percent of the proposals they receive. Given their expertise and selectivity, one would expect that the mere presence of a VC in a startup could be a strong signal of the quality of the funded firm, not only for investors considering the firm's stock as a possible addition to their equity portfolios at the time of the IPO, but also to prospective acquirers.

Based on this simple logic, research has attempted to determine whether firms with the benefit of VC backing are more likely to be acquired shortly after going public than their counterparts. Indeed, a recent paper by Ragozzino and Reuer (2007) finds that firms backed by VCs are almost twice as likely to be bought out in M&A markets within the first five years of the IPO as firms without VC backing, and even more so within the first year of the IPO. The authors contend that the positive signal embedded in the presence of a venture capitalist extends well after the IPO for at least two reasons. First, VCs retain ownership in funded firms well after the IPO date. Summarizing research in the area, Gompers and Lerner (2004) report that the typical distribution occurs nearly 20 months after the firm goes public and that VCs hold an average ownership in the funded firm of about 34 percent before its IPO and let go of only about 10 percent of that ownership after the offering is consummated. Second, VCs rely heavily on the accumulation of reputation capital, which limits their incentive for opportunistic behavior and window-dressing to maximize the proceeds at the time of the IPO (Gompers, 1996).

In addition to increasing the likelihood of a post-IPO acquisition, studies also show that VC backing affects the characteristics of the acquirer as well as the governance choices implemented by a firm seeking to access the target's assets. In a cross-industry study of U.S. IPO and acquisition activity between 1993 and 2002, Ragozzino and Reuer (2011) find that venture-backed startups are more likely to be bought by acquirers situated at greater distances than firms not backed by VCs. More precisely, they report that buyers pick off the VC-backed firms located an average of 1,381 miles from the target, while buyers acquire non-VC-backed firms located an average of less than 800 miles away. Since geographic distance is a powerful indicator of the information asymmetry problem that arises in economic exchanges (e.g., Coval and Moskowitz, 1999, 2001; Garmaise and Moskowitz, 2004; Malloy, 2005; Bae, Stulz, and Tan, 2005; Grote and Umber, 2006), VC backing works as a remedy to this problem and therefore reduces the natural localization of M&A markets. In a related paper, Ragozzino and Reuer find that when firms are VC backed, they are more likely to be acquired after their IPO. In contrast, when firms are not VC backed, the lack of signal leads to a joint venture instead. Tying this finding with the earlier discussion of the adverse selection remedies, this additional result suggests that prospective acquirers can use the signal of VC backing as an alternate way to reduce their exposure to information asymmetry, without suffering the downsides of choosing intermediate governance solutions in lieu of acquisitions. Alternatively stated, the signal operates as a substitute for carrying out an alliance and enables the firm to proceed with an acquisition.

The Reputation of the IPO Lead Underwriter

Another IPO characteristic that contributes to the dual tracking phenomenon is the reputation of the lead bank underwriting the offering. Paralleling the discussion on VCs, investment banks place much emphasis on their reputation or reputational capital, so their decision of which companies to take public can affect their credibility in future deals. Any incentive to rake up every and any startup with IPO ambitions and behave opportunistically when presenting the client to investors is reduced by the short-term fears of lawsuits and even more importantly by the marred reputation and lost future business that would result (Carter and Manaster, 1990). Thus, while investment banks have different objective functions from VCs, the associations between reputable investment banks and issuing firms carry similar implications: Prominent lead underwriters can function as signals of a newly public firm's quality and help prospective acquirers differentiate between better targets and less attractive ones.

Academic research has developed a way to rank investment banks' reputations based upon their position over time in IPO tombstones (e.g., Loughran and Ritter, 2004). Researchers have also studied these ranks in conjunction with the dual tracking phenomenon, in order to determine whether the effects of information asymmetry can in fact be mitigated by the signal provided by the lead underwriter's reputation. Indeed, the association of a startup with a prominent investment bank has been reported to be directly linked with a greater likelihood of post-IPO acquisition, particularly when the startup goes public without the support of a VC (Ragozzino and Reuer, 2007). As such, not only might signals substitute for other remedies to the adverse selection problem, but also evidence suggests that alternative signals can substitute for one another. As in the case of the VC signal, the reputation of the lead investment bank also affects the geographic distance separating the acquirer from the newly public firm. Comparing a sample of 212 U.S. IPOs that were subsequently acquired in M&As, Ragozzino and Reuer (2011) find that the average distance in a deal involving targets with highly reputable underwriters was about 1,400 miles, much higher than the less than 1,000 miles for targets whose IPO was underwritten by less reputable banks.

As a final illustration, the reputation of the underwriter has also been strongly associated with a greater likelihood of an acquisition over a joint venture after the IPO. Therefore, the information signal embedded in a public offering led by a reputable bank can help to reduce the effects of information asymmetry for buyers. As above, this suggests that the investment bank signal enables the firm to proceed with an acquisition rather than implement a joint venture to address this problem. Thus, this signal also substitutes for the type of investment used to tap into the target's assets.

Underpricing

While both the involvement of a VC and a highly reputable underwriter are signals related to the association of the IPO firm with key financial intermediaries, underpricing is a market-based signal. For the sake of clarity, *underpricing* is defined as the returns experienced by a newly public firm at the closing of the first day of the IPO (e.g., Habib and Ljungqvist, 2001; Aggarwal, Krigman, and Womack, 2002). Therefore, underpricing is effectively money left on the table by an issuing firm and as such it can represent a significant indirect cost of going public. For example, first-day returns averaged 18 percent for the United States since the 1960s and were considerably larger during the late 1990s (e.g., Draho, 2004). Given the economic importance of underpricing and theoretical interest, the finance literature has devoted much attention to it. Covering the details of this vast body of work is clearly beyond the scope of this chapter, so the goal is to offer the basic notions that explain why underpricing might affect dual tracking and then report recent findings that corroborate this idea empirically.

Early discussions of the signaling properties of underpricing can be traced back several years, when research noted that by discounting their shares on the day of the IPO, high-quality firms can signal their value to outsiders, positioning themselves to obtain future benefits in subsequent secondary offerings (e.g., Ibbotson, 1975; Allen and Faulhaber, 1989; Grinblatt and Hwang, 1989; Welch, 1989). Because underpricing is a costly signal, low-quality issuers cannot replicate this strategy, enabling investors to tell them apart from better firms (e.g., Beatty and Ritter, 1986).

More recent research attempts to investigate the signaling effects of underpricing beyond the context of IPOs. For example, Demers and Lewellen (2003) find that underpricing can be a powerful marketing tool for high-technology firms. In their work, newly public firms with large underpricing experienced significantly greater Web traffic to their sites than firms with less underpricing. More to the point of dual tracking, Ragozzino and Reuer (2011) find that underpricing directly affects the average geographic distance separating buyers and newly public sellers in acquisitions and, following the logic previously laid out, this finding provides evidence of the signaling benefits of underpricing. Related work also reports some evidence that underpricing affects the likelihood of post-IPO acquisitions, but unlike the cases of VC-backing and underwriter reputation, these effects tend to dissipate quickly within one year of the initial public offering (Ragozzino and Reuer, 2007). Combined, this set of findings indicates that the decision to discount share prices on the day of the IPO can have ramifications that extend beyond the financing outcome obtained by a firm through its offering.

While this chapter has focused attention on these signals as illustrations, targets can signal their value in many other potential ways. Some of these ways are more financial in nature and are closely connected to the IPO context (e.g., lockups), while others apply more to other publicly held firms in general (e.g., capital structure and dividend policies). Further, firms can signal value to outsiders in many other means. Many of these signals apply to firms other than IPO firms but are also available to newly public companies (e.g., alliances, board composition, characteristics of top management teams, competitive actions. and announcements). Future investigations should examine how IPO firms and others might signal their quality in the M&A market, the degree to which these signals substitute for other potential remedies to adverse selection (e.g., earnouts), when firms might prioritize certain signals over others, and whether various signals work as substitutes.

THE IMPLICATIONS OF DUAL TRACKING

This section examines the implications in a world with and without dual tracking.

A World without Dual Tracking

The discussion of dual tracking so far highlights that this phenomenon presents distinct benefits for both sides of an acquisition. For their part, buyers routinely face uncertainty and information-gathering costs in M&As. Often these firms choose to proceed with a deal, even when facing the possibility of overpaying for a target. Because information asymmetry is at least partially responsible for acquisition failures (e.g., Fishman, 1989; Eckbo, Giammarino, and Heinkel, 1990), transactions carried out in the face of information asymmetry should be avoided or their inherent risks minimized. Although acquirers can choose to protect themselves from the hazards of adverse selection and introduce contingency clauses in a deal, or otherwise stage their investments to reduce their exposure to asymmetric information, these remedies involve compromises for both sides of the deal. Namely, they reduce the acquirer's ability to extract value from a deal by raising transaction costs and limiting the manner in which synergies can be created.

Equally importantly, these remedies require the willingness from targets to bear additional costs to signal their value, thereby gaining credibility with the buyer. For instance, with earnouts the seller may not obtain the projected future performance goals specified in the contract, and this result may not necessarily be endogenously driven. Such events as the introduction of a superior product by a competitor and the deterioration of macroeconomic conditions could affect the target performance, consequently also reducing the likelihood of the conditional payments contemplated in the earnout. Thus, unless a complete contract is designed at the time of the execution of the acquisition, earnouts can lead to ex post disagreements and even litigation. Not surprisingly, these considerations often cause sellers—even good-quality sellers—to shy away from earnouts. In fact, these deals typically amount to about 3 percent of the total acquisitions in the United States (Kohers and Ang, 2000), although this percentage increases significantly when the information asymmetry between the parties is high. For instance, earnouts are used in 6 percent of all transactions when the acquirer comes from an industry that is unrelated to the target's industry and in almost 13 percent when the acquirer has no prior M&A experience (Ragozzino and Reuer, 2009).

Similar to earnouts, stock payments require the seller to put its trust in the buyer because both will be residual owners of the combined entity after the acquisition is consummated. As previously mentioned, the mere fact that buyers would offer stock as a medium of payment for a deal rather than cash could be suggestive of the overvaluation of their equity. Paradoxically, then, while addressing information asymmetry for buyers, stock payments may introduce the same problem for the seller in an acquisition and this could cause sellers to discount the acquirer's shares, thus making negotiation more challenging and a successful transaction less likely. Hansen (1987) documents this interesting reciprocal information asymmetry dilemma, which is known as the "double lemons" problem.

Staged investments bring about perverse incentives of their own. Besides keeping buyers from unrestricted access to the target's resources, joint ventures also keep both firms' objective functions distinct. Often times setting common goals, sharing ownership, and forming a joint board of directors are insufficient steps in keeping parties moving in the same direction. The evidence shows that shifting conditions and motivations can eventually lead to the joint venture's dissolution (e.g., Park and Russo, 1996). Thus, firms can use cooperative agreements such as joint ventures and more broadly strategic alliances as precursors to acquisitions. This occurs only to the extent that full integration can be delayed and the acquirer does not eventually receive less than anticipated.

The above discussion leads to two fundamental conclusions about M&As in a world without dual tracking. First, various remedies are available to the problems presented by asymmetric information when moving from Akerlof's (1970) setting of used car markets to M&A markets, yet each of these remedies offers some important downsides. Second, firms apparently use each of these remedies as substitutes, perhaps in light of the different costs that each of them presents to buyers and sellers.

A World with Dual Tracking

Dual tracking therefore offers another way for acquirers to reduce their exposure to information asymmetry. As emphasized above, when a firm contends with information asymmetries in M&A markets, one means of reducing this problem is through target selection policies that help reduce overpayment risk. Specifically, just as an acquirer might want to prioritize targets that are geographically proximate or possess familiar resources and capabilities, the firm might go forward with a newly public target rather than a comparable private business. Dual tracking therefore facilitates target search and selection can help address information asymmetries when conducting M&As. As noted above, IPO firms also vary considerably with respect to the potential signals they send to acquirers. Thus, a buyer might also want to prioritize a target that was backed by a VC or associated with a reputable underwriter even if the target remains difficult to appraise and price.

Turning to the sell side, dual tracking holds a substantial amount of upside for high-quality targets whose value is hard to discern. Although contingent payment structures may be available as ways for targets to signal their value, these remedies also introduce new uncertainty in the deal. In contrast, dual tracking allows targets to offer important signals on quality while also limiting the acquisition costs. This is true because the costs of such signals as VC presence and underwriter reputation are often not created with a post-IPO acquisition in mind. However, their effects directly impact the likelihood of a deal as many as five years after the IPO. This also suggests that firms lacking these characteristics will need to consider other means of addressing information asymmetries in order to obtain a better offer price from a potential acquirer.

While dual tracking can yield buyers and sellers certain benefits, there can be important drawbacks to following this strategy, particularly for entrepreneurial firms. For example, IPOs bring with them substantial fees, averaging one-eighth of the total proceeds, so this cost might be prohibitive for many private firms. This is precisely what separates high-quality firms from others. Also, dual tracking can be risky because outcomes of the IPO are tied to many factors that are not directly related to the underlying quality of the issuing firm such as macroeconomic conditions and the cyclicality of IPO markets. Further, an ill-conceived IPO may send a negative signal to the market and ultimately hurt, rather than improve, the chances of a post-IPO acquisition for an aspiring target.

There are other broader potential drawbacks of going public to buyers and sellers. The ideas presented in this chapter are built around the notion that the firm going public enhances its visibility and credibility through the IPO, and the information that is produced and disseminated during this process spills over into the M&A market and facilitates such transactions because their efficiency is enhanced. However, informational spillovers may happen not only with respect to IPOs and M&A markets, but also across IPOs and other markets. These downsides of IPOs have not yet been investigated. For example, greater information on the IPO target and validation by the equity markets might lead direct competitors to imitate its technology or encourage firms from other industries to enter into its product-market space. On the one hand, if the IPO conveys the firm's commitment to a technology or product as well as its new financial wherewithal, this might deter some firms from competitive engagement. On the other hand, to the extent that other firms receive positive market signals about the prospects for the IPO firm's products or technologies, imitation or substitution risks might arise. As another example, information from IPO markets might spill over from equity markets to labor markets, resulting in the firm's inability to retain key talent and associated human capital profits.

Ironically, one of the potential downsides of IPOs before acquisitions is rooted in the key benefits of visibility and credibility that IPO firms enjoy when going public. For instance, when signals are available on the IPO firm, these signals are not only beneficial in reducing the overpayment risk of the focal acquirer but also are available to other potential bidders and can reduce their overpayment risk. Thus, these signals can increase the potential competition for a given IPO firm in the M&A market. This would appear to be beneficial to the target, as multiple bids might have a positive effect on the premium offered for the transaction. However, this situation might also create contracting problems because acquirers must engage in certain efficiency-enhancing activities (e.g., integration planning and sharing information with the target firm), and these firms will either not engage in such activities or will lose such deal-specific investments if another firm acquires the target. Buyers will therefore be willing to make these investments as long as they are compensated for them if the target sells to, or even pursues, another bidder. For example, termination fees are routinely used in acquisitions and acquirers also negotiate options on the target's stock if another bidder emerges, driving up its valuation. In the context of IPO firms' acquisitions, such termination payment provisions are more likely to be negotiated when signals are disseminated on the target firm. Granting termination fees and lockup options to an acquirer is more costly to a target expecting to have alternative buyers, so buyers will need to compensate the target for these foregone opportunities by offering a higher acquisition premium. Thus, IPOs can have important consequences for competition in M&A markets, contracting problems, and the negotiation of termination provisions and prices (Wu and Reuer, 2010).

SUMMARY AND CONCLUSIONS

Dual tracking raises the possibility that the decisions made by firms in the context of IPO markets will have material and direct consequences on the outcomes they experience in an entirely separate context—the M&A market. Little research has linked IPOs and M&As. In fact, the finance literature has largely ignored other vehicles to address the adverse selection problem in acquisitions such as strategic alliances and joint ventures (Higgins and Rodriguez, 2006). An important opportunity exists for scholars to begin thinking about these corporate events as connected and to investigate the conditions that cause firms to choose one, the other, or a combination of them. Not only would research in this direction help explain the evolutionary path of firms, but also it would be valuable in examining how financial choices such as IPOs have important consequences for the firm's activities in other markets that determine firm value. In order to develop a more complete picture of the dual tracking phenomenon, more research needs to be directed to the question of how newly public sellers and their acquirers capture value under different circumstances. On an even broader level, given that many acquisitions fail and yet they continue to be the preferred method of corporate growth the world over, the questions above brought about by dual tracking become even more compelling for M&A academics and practitioners alike.

DISCUSSION QUESTIONS

1. What is the theoretical link between IPOs and M&As that helps to explain the dual tracking phenomenon?

2. How can IPOs and their characteristics help to reduce the effects of adverse selection?

3. What other instruments are available to buyers to address information asymmetries in acquisitions and make a deal happen?

4. In what ways can dual tracking help not only buyers but also sellers of newly public firms?

5. What are some potential downsides to sellers in pursuing a dual tracking strategy?

REFERENCES

Aggarwal, Rajesh K., Laurie Krigman, and Kent L. Womack. 2002. "Strategic IPO Underpricing, Information Momentum, and Lockup Expiration Selling." *Journal of Financial Economics* 66:1, 105–137.

Akerlof, George A. 1970. "The Market for 'Lemons': Qualitative Uncertainty and the Market Mechanism." *Quarterly Journal of Economics* 84:3, 488–500.

Allen, Franklin, and Gerald R. Faulhaber. 1989. "Signaling by Underpricing in the IPO Market." *Journal of Financial Economics* 23:2, 303–323.

Bae, Kee-Hong, René M. Stulz, and Hongping Tan. 2005. "Do Local Analysts Know More? A Cross-Country Study of the Performance of Local Analysts and Foreign Analysts." Working Paper 11697, National Bureau of Economic Research, Cambridge, MA.

Balakrishnan, Srinivasan, and Mitchell P. Koza. 1993. "Information Asymmetry, Adverse Selection, and Joint Ventures." *Journal of Economic Behavior and Organization* 20:1, 99–117.

Beatty, Randolph, and Jay R. Ritter. 1986. "Investment Banking, Reputation, and the Underpricing of Initial Public Offerings." *Journal of Financial Economics* 15:1–2, 213–232.

Brau, James C., Ninon K. Sutton, and Nile W. Hatch. 2010. "Dual-track Versus Single-Track Sell-Outs: An Empirical Analysis of Competing Harvest Strategies." *Journal of Business Venturing* 25:4, 389–402.

Brav, Alon, and Paul A. Gompers. 1997. "Myth or Reality? The Long-Run Underperformance of Initial Public Offerings: Evidence from Venture and Nonventure Capital-Backed Companies." *Journal of Finance* 52:5, 1791–1821.

Carter, Richard, and Steven Manaster. 1990. "Initial Public Offerings and Underwriter Reputation." *Journal of Finance* 45:4, 1045–1067.

Coval, Joshua D., and Tobias J. Moskowitz. 1999. "Home Bias at Home: Local Equity Preference in Domestic Portfolios." *Journal of Finance* 54:6, 2045–2073.

Coval, Joshua D., and Tobias J. Moskowitz. 2001. "The Geography of Investment: Informed Trading and Asset Prices." *Journal of Political Economy* 109:4, 811–841.

Datar, Srikant, Richard Frankel, and Mark Wolfson, M. 2001. "Earnouts: The Effects of Adverse Selection and Agency Costs on Acquisition Techniques." *Journal of Law, Economics, and Organization* 17:1, 201–238.

Demers, Elizabeth, and Katharina Lewellen. 2003. "The Marketing Role of IPOs: Evidence from Internet Stocks." *Journal of Financial Economics* 68:3, 413–437.

Draho, Jason. 2004. *The IPO Decision: Why and How Companies Go Public.* Cheltenham, United Kingdom: Edward Elgar.

Eckbo, Espen B., Ronald M. Giammarino, and Robert L. Heinkel. 1990. "Asymmetric Information and the Medium of Exchange in Takeovers: Theory and Tests." *Review of Financial Studies* 3:4, 651–675.

Fishman, Michael J. 1989. "Preemptive Bidding and the Role of the Medium of Exchange in Acquisitions." *Journal of Finance* 44:1, 41–57.

Garmaise, Mark J., and Tobias J. Moskowitz. 2004. "Confronting Information Asymmetries: Evidence from Real Estate Markets." *Review of Financial Studies* 17:2, 405–437.

Gompers, Paul. 1996. "Grandstanding in the Venture Capital Industry." *Journal of Financial Economics* 42:1, 133–156.

Gompers, Paul, and Joshua Lerner. 2004. *The Venture Capital Cycle.* Boston: MIT Press.

Grinblatt, Mark, and Chuan Y. Hwang. 1989. "Signaling and the Pricing of New Issues." *Journal of Finance* 44:2, 393–420.

Grote, Michael H., and Marc P. Umber. 2006. "Home Biased? A Spatial Analysis of the Domestic Merging Behavior of US Firms." Working Paper, Goethe-Universität Frankfurt am Main.

Habib, Michael A., and Alexander P. Ljungqvist. 2001. "Underpricing and Entrepreneurial Wealth Losses in IPOs: Theory and Evidence." *Review of Financial Studies* 14:2, 433–458.

Hansen, Robert G. 1987. "A Theory for the Choice of Exchange Medium in Mergers and Acquisitions." *Journal of Business* 60:1, 75–95.

Higgins, Matthew J., and Daniel Rodriguez. 2006. "The Outsourcing of R&D through Acquisitions in the Pharmaceutical Industry." *Journal of Financial Economics* 80:2, 351–383.

Ibbotson, Roger G. 1975. "Price Performance of Common Stock New Issues." *Journal of Financial Economics* 2:3, 235–272.

Kaplan, Steven N., and Michael S. Weisbach. 1992. "The Success of Acquisitions: Evidence from Divestitures." *Journal of Finance* 47:1, 107–138.

Kohers, Ninon, and James Ang. 2000. "Earnouts in Mergers: Agreeing to Disagree and Agreeing to Stay." *Journal of Business* 73:3, 445–476.

Lian, Qin, and Qiming Wang. 2007. "The Dual Tracking Puzzle: When IPO Plans Turn into Mergers." Available at http://ssrn.com/abstract=899983.

Loughran, Tim, and Jay Ritter. 2004. "Why Has IPO Underpricing Changed over Time?" *Financial Management* 33:3, 5–37.

Malloy, Christopher J. 2005. "The Geography of Equity Analysis." *Journal of Finance* 60:2, 719–755.

Megginson, William L., and Kathleen A. Weiss. 1991. "Venture Capitalist Certification in Initial Public Offerings." *Journal of Finance* 46:3, 879–903.

Nicholson, Sean, Patricia M. Danzon, and Jeffrey McCullough. 2005. "Biotech-Pharmaceutical Alliances as a Signal of Asset and Firm Quality." *Journal of Business* 78:4, 1433–1464.

Pagano, Marco, Panetta, Fabio, and Luigi Zingales. 1998. "Why Do Companies Go Public? An Empirical Analysis." *Journal of Finance* 53:1, 27–64.

Park, Seung H., and Michael V. Russo. 1996. "When Competition Eclipses Cooperation: An Event History Analysis of Joint Venture Failure." *Management Science* 42:6, 875–890.

Ragozzino, Roberto, and Jeffrey J. Reuer. 2007. "Initial Public Offerings and the Acquisition of Entrepreneurial Firms." *Strategic Organization* 5:2, 155–176.

Ragozzino, Roberto, and Jeffrey J. Reuer. 2009. "Contingent Earnouts in Acquisitions of Privately-Held Targets." *Journal of Management* 35:4, 857–879.

Ragozzino, Roberto, and Jeffrey J. Reuer. 2011. "Geographic Distance and Corporate Acquisitions: Signals from IPO Firms." *Strategic Management Journal*, forthcoming.

Reuer, Jeffrey J., and Mitchell P. Koza. 2000. "Asymmetric Information and Joint Venture Performance: Theory and Evidence for Domestic and International Joint Ventures." *Strategic Management Journal* 21: 81–88.

Reuer, Jeffrey J., and Roberto Ragozzino. 2008. "Adverse Selection and M&A Design: The Roles of Alliances and IPOs." *Journal of Economic Behavior and Organization* 66:2, 195–212.

Reuer, Jeffrey J., and Jung-Chin Shen. 2004. "Sequential Divestiture through Initial Public Offerings." *Journal of Economic Behavior and Organization* 54:2, 249–266.

Spence, Michael B. 1974. *Market Signaling: Informational Transfer in Hiring and Related Screening Processes.* Cambridge, MA: Harvard University Press.

Stiglitz, Joseph. E. 2000. "The Contributions of the Economics of Information to Twentieth Century Economics." *Quarterly Journal of Economics* 115:4, 1441–1478.

Welch, Ivo. 1989. "Seasoned Offerings, Imitation Costs, and the Underpricing of Initial Public Offerings." *Journal of Finance* 44:2, 421–449.

Wu, C.-W., and Jeffrey J. Reuer. 2010. "Termination Agreements in M&A Contracting." Working Paper, Purdue University.

ABOUT THE AUTHORS

Roberto Ragozzino is an Assistant Professor of Business in the Organization, Strategy and International Management group at the University of Texas at Dallas. His research involves M&As and strategic alliances with an emphasis on how these corporate events apply to entrepreneurial ventures. Professor Ragozzino's recent work investigates how going public affects entrepreneurial firms' growth and opportunities in the aftermaths of their IPO. His work has appeared in several scholarly journals such as the *Strategic Management Journal*, *Journal of International Business Studies*, *Journal of Management*, and *Journal of Management Studies*, among others. He has also published in practitioners' outlets such as the *Financial Times* and the *Journal of Applied Corporate Finance*. Professor Ragozzino is on the editorial board of several journals. He received a BBA and an MS in Finance from Georgia State University in 1997 and 1998, respectively, and a Ph.D. in Business Policy and Strategy from The Ohio State University in 2004.

Jeffrey J. Reuer is the Blake Family Endowed Chair in Strategic Management and Governance at the Krannert School of Management at Purdue University, where he is also the Area Coordinator. Before joining Purdue, he was the Boyd W. Harris, Jr. Distinguished Scholar and Professor of Strategic Management at the Kenan-Flagler Business School, University of North Carolina. Professor Reuer has also taught in executive education programs at Harvard Business School, Duke University, INSEAD, and the Indian School of Business. His current research investigates the design and performance of alliances and M&As, alliance governance, the roles IPOs play in acquisition markets, and the performance implications of firms' growth options. The results of his work have appeared in the top scholarly journals in strategic management as well as in practitioner-oriented articles and research briefings in the *Harvard Business Review, MIT Sloan Management Review, Financial Times, Journal of Applied Corporate Finance,* and *Long Range Planning.* He serves as an Associate Editor of the *Strategic Management Journal* and as a Consulting Editor for the *Journal of International Business Studies.*

CHAPTER 28

The Diversification Discount

SEOUNGPIL AHN
Associate Professor, Sogang University

INTRODUCTION

Using a strategic perspective of firm growth and following the product life cycle theory, diversification spurs the growth of a firm. The Boston Consulting Group (BCG) matrix method illustrates the importance of the creation of this internal capital market to nurture the fast-growing divisions as opposed to seeking capital through the external capital market. Under the BCG-type logic, firms are encouraged to take a diversification strategy at a certain point of time within a firm's growth stages: The firm constructs a portfolio of businesses that combines both high-growth, cash-needy business units and low-growth, cash-rich units.

Does the internal capital market exist? Before discussing the efficiency of the internal capital market, there is a need to establish that the headquarters of a diversified firm is involved with the active reallocation of resources across divisions. Investigating the reliance of divisional investment on other divisions' cash flows, Shin and Stultz (1998) find that the amount of cash flows that are available in other divisions greatly affects a division's investment. As a result, investment by divisions of diversified firms is less sensitive to their own cash flows than investment of comparable single-segment firms. Similarly, Lamont (1997) examines diversified firms operating in the oil industry and finds interdependence between one division's investment and the other divisions' cash flows. Using internal funds, a division of a diversified firm would be able to invest in profitable projects regardless of its own cash flow. This evidence indicates that the headquarters of a diversified firm gathers resources from all divisions and reallocates them across divisions.

Are internal funds cheaper than external financing? Myers and Majluf (1984) and Hubbard (1998) contend that information asymmetry poses deadweight costs in a firm seeking external financing. When external financing is costly, the creation of an internal capital market relaxes the firm's financial constraints and increases the amount of capital available for investment. In this vein, Williamson (1975) documents that the creation of an internal capital market may be value enhancing, if headquarters could mitigate financial constraints through a winner-picking process. Stein (1997) argues that headquarters is better informed about the growth opportunities of divisions than outside investors. When headquarters actively engages in a winner-picking process, the internal capital market creates value by reducing the underinvestment problem associated with external financing. Diversification also affects firm value through its impact on the amount of capital available for investment. Having internal capital markets, diversified firms may face fewer financial constraints than focused firms. Lewellen (1971) posits that diversified firms have higher debt capacity than focused firms, through the coinsurance effect across imperfectly correlated divisions. This higher debt capacity relaxes financial constraints for diversified firms, leading to higher firm value. Therefore, looking at the positive side of diversification, an internal capital market can relax financial constraints when external financing is costly.

However, agency theory suggests that managers may take a diversification strategy, driven by managerial incentives to increase private benefits (e.g., Jensen, 1986; Stulz, 1990; Denis, Denis, and Sarin, 1997). Managers of a diversified firm may easily waste resources in larger firms with broader operational scopes. These incentives include empire building (Jensen, 1986), risk reduction (Amihud and Lev, 1981), overconfidence (Roll, 1986), increased value of managers' human capital (Shleifer and Vishny, 1989), and inertia (Bertrand and Mullainathan, 2003). These managerial incentives imply that agency conflicts drive some diversification decisions and that diversification itself is a form of overinvestment.

Additionally, diversification complicates organizational structure and causes double layers of agency problems: one between headquarters and outside shareholders and another between headquarters and divisional managers. In a diversified firm, headquarters draws resources from all divisions and then redistributes them across divisions. Value-maximizing headquarters will make an efficient resource allocation decision by redirecting resources from cash-rich divisions to the fast growing divisions. However, this cross-subsidization often becomes poorly exercised when headquarters does not have perfect oversight over the growth opportunities of each division. Divisional managers have incentives to inflate growth perspectives of their divisions to extract more resources from the headquarters.

Given this rent-seeking behavior of divisional managers and the information problem of headquarters, the internal capital market works inefficiently as headquarters allocates more funds to divisions with low-growth opportunities and less to divisions with high-growth opportunities. Scharfstein (1998) and Scharfstein and Stein (2000) show that managers of divisions with less valuable assets are more willing to engage in rent-seeking and socialism in capital budgeting, leading to cross-subsidization in which divisions with less valuable assets get more resources than their efficient share of the capital budget. Further, Rajan, Servaes, and Zingales (2000) document that the distortion of investment is exacerbated as the diversity of divisional growth opportunities increases.

Weighing these potential benefits and costs of diversification, the net effect of diversification on firm value could be positive or negative. The essence of the debate on the diversification discount is whether this valuation impact of diversification is positive or negative. Much literature suggests that this net effect of diversification is, on average, detrimental to firm value. That is, diversified firms are generally traded at a discount relative to their imputed value as a sum of stand-alone values (Lang and Stulz, 1994; Berger and Ofek, 1995; Scharfstein, 1998; Rajan et al., 2000; Scharfstein and Stein, 2000). This panel data evidence is supported by event studies, in which the literature on corporate refocusing provides consistent evidence. Ahn and Denis (2004), Gertner, Powers, and Scharfstein (2002), and Dittmar and

Shivdasani (2000) document that diversified firms are valued less than focused firms, and refocusing is value-enhancing by eliminating inefficiency in diversified firms. These findings suggest that the creation of internal capital markets causes inefficient capital allocation among divisions and leads to the value discount for diversified firms.

Yet, ample evidence exists to the contrary. Chevalier (2000) and Whited (2001) argue that measurement errors can explain the empirical results supporting the inefficient investment hypothesis. Studies by Hyland (1999), Campa and Kedia (2002), and Maksimovic and Phillips (2002) contend that the relationship between diversification and value is not necessarily causal but the result of an endogenous decision to diversify by these firms. Further, the observed diversification discount results from endogenous self-selection behavior by low-valued firms and shows little relation to diversification itself. Graham, Lemmon, and Wolf (2002) show that at least part of the diversification discount is attributable to the discount that existed before diversification. Çolak and Whited (2007) reexamine the improvement of investment efficiency following spinoffs and divestitures with heteroscedasticity-consistent econometric methods. They criticize the evidence from the corporate refocusing literature by showing that matched firms that share the similar characteristics with refocusing firms also improve investment efficiency, even though they never undergo refocusing.

These streams of the literature indicate that measurement errors in estimating the value of diversification and biases in incorporating a firm's endogenous decision to diversify are the reasons diversified firms appear to be valued lower than comparable focused firms, even though diversification does not destroy firm value. However, more recent research indicates that some of these criticisms against the existence of the diversification discount are biased. Recently, Santalo and Becerra (2008) find that the instrumental variable approach that is used in Campa and Kedia (2002) causes a positive bias in estimating the value of diversification. After properly adjusting for the industry composition of diversified firms and focused firms, diversified firms are still valued at discount.

Given these ongoing debates, the impact of diversification on firm value is inconclusive at best. Rather, the existing evidence suggests that other important aspects of diversification are yet to be explored. For example, the value of diversification is perceived differently depending on the types of firms, industry conditions, and the time period. The number of diversified firms and the proportion of diversified firms in an industry change over time. Which factors are responsible for the changes in the nature of diversification? How are these changes related to the mergers and restructuring waves in the past? How useful is excess value in sorting out the value of diversification and predicting dismantling of failed conglomerates? What firm and industry characteristics and economic environments spur growth through diversification? How and when does diversification fail?

The goal of this chapter is to provide a synthesis of the literature on the theory and empirical evidence involving the diversification discount. The remainder of the chapter has the following organization. The next section explains how the value of diversification is measured in the academic literature, which is followed by a discussion of the debate on the diversification discount based on cross-sectional evidence. Following that is a section on the time-series pattern of the diversification discount. The next to last section discusses international evidence on the diversification discount, implications of this research, and future research directions. The final section summarizes and concludes.

MEASURING THE EFFECT OF DIVERSIFICATION ON FIRM VALUE

How does corporate diversification affect firm value? Examining market reactions on the announcement of diversifying mergers and acquisitions (M&As) provides a way of determining whether the market views on diversifying M&As are harmful or beneficial to acquiring firms. To date, academic evidence is inconclusive. The conglomerate merger wave that swept the United States in the late 1960s seems to have offered a way to circumvent underdeveloped public capital markets, allowing mature firms to invest in fast-growing businesses that would otherwise be starved of cash. During the 1960s, bidder announcement returns were generally positive for acquisitions that lead to diversification.

Companies making diversifying M&As saw a marked increase in their share price, with the best performing mergers being those in which cash-rich companies bought cash-constrained ones (Matsusaka, 1993; Hubbard and Palia, 1999). This may also explain why conglomerates are valued higher in emerging markets with less efficient capital markets (Khanna and Rivkin, 2001). Recently, however, some have challenged the idea of value creation through diversification. When investors within well-developed capital markets hold well-diversified portfolios of stocks, corporate diversification is at best unnecessary and even value-destructive because it may cause inefficient decision making inside the firm. The evidence on the 1980s and 1990s bidder returns, therefore, is at best mixed (e.g., Morck, Shleifer, and Vishny, 1990; Kaplan and Weisbach, 1992; Hyland, 1999; Graham et al. 2002).

Another way of measuring the valuation impact of corporate diversification is to estimate "excess value." Excess value is the value of a diversified firm, relative to the imputed value from comparable single-segment firms operating in the same industries of the diversified firm's divisions. Excess value can be computed using segment asset-weight as follows:

$$\text{Excess Value} = \left(\frac{MV}{Assets}\right)_d - \sum_{j=1}^{n}\left(\frac{MV}{Assets}\right)_j^{ss} \times \frac{Segment\ Assets_j}{Assets} \qquad (28.1)$$

$(MV/Assets)_d$ is the market value of a diversified firm divided by book value assets of the firm. $Segment\ Assets_j$ is the end-of-the-year assets of segment j (j =1 to n), where n is the number of divisions within a diversified firm. $(MV/Assets)_j^{ss}$ is the median (or average) market-to-assets ratio of stand-alone firms operating in the same industry of segment j. The second part of the right-hand side of the equation is known as imputed value. The *imputed value* is the estimated value of a diversified firm if each division of the firm operates as a stand-alone firm. Excess value is therefore designed to capture the valuation impact of diversification compared to the sum of stand-alone values. Without altering the inference, excess value can be measured with segment sales weights, and different industry matching methods can be used.

In theory, excess value can be positive or negative. Thus, a diversified firm could trade at a premium or a discount. During the 1980s and 1990s, various studies such as Berger and Ofek (1995) reported that companies with several lines of businesses were worth between 8 and 18 percent less than comparable stand-alone focused firms. Further, Rajan et al. (2000) find that this diversification discount is greatest in firms whose business lines have very different growth opportunities to each other.

Given this large economic magnitude of the diversification discount, the puzzle remains why many large public U.S. firms still pursue diversification strategy. This leads to the diversification debates, which are discussed next.

DEBATES ON THE DIVERSIFICATION DISCOUNT

The effect of the corporate diversification on firm value remains controversial and is still not completely understood despite numerous studies. Much of the previous research documents a "diversification discount" showing that conglomerates are valued less than comparable focused firms. Two views help to explain this "diversification discount" phenomenon. One view is that diversification is value destructive. Academics put forward various reasons for why the discount first came into existence. Perhaps the opacity of conglomerates made investors and analysts wary. Divisional managers might spend their time and effort lobbying headquarters for additional resources rather than doing their jobs. Top management might allow healthy business units to cross-subsidize faltering divisions, either out of socialism or in an attempt to build empires at the shareholders' expense. Berger and Ofek (1995), Comment and Jarrell (1995), and Rajan et al. (2000) show that diversified firms, on average, allocate capital inefficiently. This inefficient internal capital market hypothesis suggests one specific reason for corporate break-ups. Namely, if the internal capital market does a poor job of allocating investment capital and the inefficiency in capital allocation leads to the value discount, break-ups of diversified firms will remove the inefficiency and the discount in diversified firms.

This view implies that the measured discounts represent disequilibrium, which will be eventually resolved through the dismantling of diversified firms. When external and internal disciplinary mechanisms work properly, any value loss that is directly associated with diversification will be subsequently eliminated by these disciplinary forces. Consistently, many document the trend of break-ups by diversified firms. Comment and Jarrell (1995) find a trend toward focus during the late 1980s. Kaplan and Weisbach (1992) report that, following large acquisitions, almost 44 percent of target companies are divested in the later period. Mitchell and Lehn (1990) also discover that poorly performing firms are more likely to be the target of acquisitions themselves. Lang and Stulz (1994) observe that the diversification discount gradually decreased from 1986 through 1990. According to Berger and Ofek (1996), the diversification discount increases the possibility of bust-up takeovers. Ahn (2009) also finds that excess value measures correctly predict the survivorship of the diversification strategy.

Recent empirical papers provide evidence consistent with the inefficient internal capital market hypothesis. The refocusing literature including Dittmar and Shivdasani (2000), Gertner et al. (2002), and Ahn and Denis (2004) also documents that markets value diversified firms less than focused firms and that refocusing restores the value loss by eliminating the inefficiency presented in diversified firms. Gertner et al. examine changes in investment allocations in spun-off divisions and report that investment in the division is more sensitive to their growth opportunities following the spin-off. Ahn and Denis further find that spin-offs create value by improving investment efficiency. Similarly, Dittmar and Shivdasani examine how the divestiture of a division affects investment in the parent firm's remaining divisions. They find that increased investment in underinvesting segments is associated with a reduction in the diversification discount.

Despite the evidence from corporate restructuring in the 1980s and early 1990s, diversification remains surprisingly common. This creates a puzzle about why firms still diversify and remain diversified when diversification itself leads to lower value. Even after the wave of divestitures in the late 1980s and early 1990s, over half of the assets owned by U.S. public companies are owned by diversified firms. In this regard, some challenge the view that diversification itself causes the diversification discount.

The argument is that diversification does not destroy value, but a discount in diversified firms is observed because of measurement errors in computing excess value. The observed diversification discount is also attributable to self-selection behavior of firms that choose to diversify. Whited (2001) and Villalonga (2004a, 2004b) contend that the average excess value is estimated with a downward bias and, after correcting for the estimation error, the average excess value does not differ from zero. Common practice in testing the efficiency of internal capital markets is to examine the sensitivity of a segment's investment to the segment's growth opportunity (Shin and Sultz, 1998; Scharfstein, 1998). Shin and Sultz document that after controlling for segment growth opportunity, investment of a segment is sensitive to the other segments' cash flows. They argue that the sensitivity of investment to other segments' cash flows indicates that headquarters is actively engaged in capital allocation. Scharfstein and Rajan et al. (2000) further demonstrate that the active capital allocation by headquarters results in overinvestment in divisions with poor growth opportunities and underinvestment in divisions with good growth opportunities. In their tests, these authors proxy the growth opportunity of a division by that of stand-alone firms operating in the same industry because the market value of divisions within a conglomerate is unobservable.

However, Whited (2001) contends that measurement-error problem in the proxy of true segment growth opportunities distorts the existing evidence on the inefficient capital allocation within a conglomerate. She argues that the remaining portion of true segment growth opportunity, which is not captured by the industry average (median), is positively correlated with other segments' cash flows. This yields spurious results of inefficient cross-subsidization. Villalonga (2004a) maintains that the diversification discount is the result of inaccurate matching with focused firms. Using more accurate business data from the Business Information Tracking Series (BITS) database, she identifies comparable stand-alone firms that most closely resemble the segments of diversified firms and shows that diversified firms actually trade at a premium.

Lamont and Polk (2001) argue that the diversification discount may reflect differences in expected returns and cash flows among diversified versus focused firms. Given the same level of cash flows, the market discounts diversified firms over focused firms because diversified firms have higher expected returns.

As expected, Lamont and Polk find that diversified firms that are discounted have higher subsequent returns than premium firms. They also estimate the proportion of diversification discount (around 50 percent) that can be explained by the rational expected return phenomenon. Lamont and Polk conclude that a part of the diversification discount is attributable to the differences in expected returns.

Others, including Chevalier (2000), Campa and Kedia (2002), and Graham et al. (2002), find that at least part of the diversification discount is attributable to the discount that existed before diversification. These authors also find that endogenous diversification behavior leads to the observed negative correlation (and not causality) between diversification and value. They point out that the observed diversification discount is the result of endogenous selection behavior by low-valued firms and has nothing to do with diversification itself. Campa and Kedia analyze the diversification discount in self-selection models, which endogenize a firm's decision to diversify and refocus with instrumental variables representing the firm's characteristics, industry conditions, and macroeconomic indicators. They argue that the excess value measure overestimates the diversification discount among diversifying firms and underestimates the discount among refocusing firms. The evidence suggests that excess value is a noisy measure and, therefore, it might misclassify firms as discount firms when their diversification is not value-destroying and as premium firms when their diversification is value-destroying.

After examining the investment patterns of merging firms in the years before their merger, Chevalier (2000) also finds that cash flow of independent firms is correlated with each firm's investments before the firms undertook a diversifying merger. She argues that because no cross-subsidization is possible before the merger occurs, the positive sensitivity of investments to the other segments' cash flows in a conglomerate is due to the correlation of investment to cash flow, instead of indicating cross-subsidization.

In sum, critics against inefficient diversification provide logic for the persistence of diversification strategy. However, such logic contradicts the evidence from the corporate refocusing literature. Although diversification could be the result of a firm's optimal behavior in response to the changes in the firm's industrial and economic environment, evidence from restructuring suggests that some failed firms do not initiate restructuring until they are forced to do so (e.g., Denis et al., 1997; Ahn and Walker, 2007).

Some also challenge arguments grounded in measurement errors and the endogenous nature of the diversification decision. Recently, Santalo and Becerra (2008) found that industry composition of diversified firms and focused firms affects the average diversification discount. Specifically, they report a negative relationship between excess value and the number of focused firms used to match with segments of diversified firms. As a result, the industry matching technique used in Berger and Ofek (1995) results in a downward bias on the average excess value, while the self-selection model in Campa and Kedia (2002) yields a positive bias on the estimated average excess value.

How can the contradicting evidence in these empirical studies be reconciled? Using theoretical models, Matsusaka (2001), Maksimovic and Phillips (2002), and Gomes and Livdan (2004) attempt to reconcile the evidence. In Matsusaka's model, firms facing decreasing profitability in their existing business are in search of a good match for the firm's organizational capabilities and diversification is the result of the search process. The search process is costly, and diversified firms may trade at discounts before they finally find a good match after a trial-and-error process. In Gomes and Livdan's model, diversified firms are worth less than focused ones at any given point in time, but the diversification decision is a rational reaction to constraints in the growth of their core businesses. This means that diversification may be a rational and value-increasing reaction to firm growth. In the value-maximizing neoclassic approach proposed by Maksimovic and Phillips, the survival of successful diversified firms and the refocusing of unsuccessful diversified firms are modeled. They find that the majority of mergers and selloffs are driven by efficiency considerations and the surviving diversified firms grow efficiently across the industries in which they operate.

Is excess value an adequate measure in identifying firms that are successful and unsuccessful in their diversification strategy? The debate on the diversification discount is overwhelmingly focused on whether excess value is, on average, positive or negative. Villalonga (2003) provides an excellent summary on the debate. While this is an important issue in detecting the overall effect of a corporate diversification strategy, it does not reveal much about whether certain types of firms should operate in different lines of businesses or reduce their scope of operations. In theory, diversification has the potential to increase or destroy firm value. Anecdotally, some diversified firms have performed well while others have not. What makes the benefits of diversification outweigh the costs of diversification in some firms but not in other firms? Arguably, the value of corporate governance is conditional on firm characteristics, industry and economic conditions, and the degree of capital market development. The creation of internal capital markets gives an advantage to certain firms to capitalize on growth opportunities, while it is more detrimental to firm value in other circumstances.

The diversification discount may be caused by poor investment decisions and reluctance to cut off subsidiaries to poorly performing divisions. Therefore, the poor performance of diversified firms is the manifestation of agency problems and the failure of corporate governance structure, rather than the issue of diversification. The value of diversification is not static over time and across firms and industries. This aspect of diversification is not well documented and understood. The next section examines some of these issues.

THE DYNAMIC PATTERN IN THE DIVERSIFICATION DISCOUNT

Ahn (2009) documents the time-series pattern in excess value from 1980 to 2003. The diversification discount was substantially higher during the period from 1980 to 1986, but it was mostly eliminated during the period from 1987 to 1998. Diversified firms trade at substantial discount again in the period from 1999 to 2003. Ahn also documents that the diversification discount is positively correlated with the number of diversified firms existing within the particular time period. That is, the diversification discount increases as many firms diversify, and the discount is relatively low as many firms undo their diversification subsequently.

Similarly, Servaes (1996) finds a significant diversification discount during the 1960s but not during the early and mid-1970s. Lang and Stulz (1994) and Comment and Jarrell (1995) document a trend toward refocusing during the second half of the 1980s and a corresponding decrease of the diversification discount. Campa and Kedia (2002) also report similar time patterns over the period from 1978 to 1996. The trends of refocusing can be attributable to the relaxation of antitrust laws in the early 1980s (Shleifer and Vishny, 1991), product market competition (Liebeskind and Opler, 1994), and reversals of prior diversification mistakes (Jensen, 1993). However, these explanations fail to describe the resurgence of diversification in the 2000s.

Interestingly, the dynamic pattern of the diversification discount coincides with the periods of merger waves during the early 1980s and the late 1990s (Mitchell and Mulherin, 1996; Andrade, Mitchell, and Stafford, 2001; Moeller, Schlingemann and Stulz, 2005). This time pattern of the diversification discount suggests that many firms diversify during the same time period in response to industry shocks and that merger waves are followed by subsequent exits of unsuccessful diversified firms.

In economic Darwinism, poorly performing conglomerates will eventually refocus if their diversification strategy causes poor performance. Firms successful in their diversification stay diversified, those unsuccessful in their diversification exit, and this cycle repeats when another shock arrives. In the absence of market frictions, firms choose to have an optimal scope of operation, and a diversification discount is observed. However, when nontrivial transaction costs must be made to make adjustments to the current organizational structure, firms may temporarily have suboptimal structures. Nonetheless, diversified firms are temporarily valued lower than focused firms, as the restructuring might be delayed. Therefore, the observed diversification discount reflects switching costs, such as managerial incentives and a social consideration. This argument is similar to the costly search model proposed by Matsusaka (2001).

The restructuring process is not necessarily timely for two reasons. First, as mentioned above, managers of diversified firms may resist restructuring even if refocusing is optimal. The failure of governance system would also cause a temporarily higher discount for diversified firms (Berger and Ofek, 1999). The presence of antitakeover defenses may diminish the effectiveness of the external discipline as well. Jensen (1993) argues that restructuring through hostile takeovers could take two or three years, while voluntary restructuring through internal control mechanisms could take up to 10 years in some cases, such as General Mills' restructuring during the 1980s. Second, compared to the market for financial assets, the market for physical assets is illiquid. Schlingemann, Stulz, and Walkling (2002) document that the liquidity of the market for corporate assets is an important factor in determining which segments of a firm are divested. The liquidity of the market for corporate assets may deter diversified firms from quickly refocusing, even though their managers would like to do so. The liquidity problem in the market for corporate assets may delay the restructuring process when many firms restructure their assets at the same time (Pulvino, 1998).

The survival of successful diversified firms and the refocusing of unsuccessful diversified firms are similar to the value-maximizing neoclassic model proposed by Maksimovic and Phillips (2002). Yet, they implicitly assume that the entire process of diversification and refocusing is timely and efficient. However, if firms reverse their diversification immediately whenever diversification is value-decreasing, there will be no time-series fluctuations in the diversification discount over time. Therefore, the observed dynamic pattern of diversification discounts may indicate the delay in the corporate refocusing process following merger waves.

As in the case with studies on merger waves, the link between merger waves and the diversification discount is the least explored area. Ahn (2009) documents that the value of diversified firms fluctuates in response to merger and restructuring waves. Two issues are related to the efficiency of the entire process. The first issue is whether the initial decision to diversify is ex-ante efficient. The results generally do not support an agency view that managerial objectives drive diversification at the shareholders' expenses. This agency view, however, contradicts the return of the diversification discount and the increase in the number of diversified firms starting from the late 1990s. If diversification is value-decreasing, diversified firms and the discount should be completely eliminated. As Gomes and Livdan (2004) argue, some agency models fail to explain why diversified firms exist at all when diversification is ex-ante inefficient. Grounded in the agency theory, Berger and Ofek (1999) predict that the diversification discount will be eliminated as diversified firms are forced to be dismantled. They show that managerial objectives drive some diversification and, as a result, firms are forced to refocus. However, the number of these cases seems small relative to the entire universe of diversified firms.

The evidence of forced refocusing does not necessarily contradict the claim that the initial decision to diversify is efficient on average. Although the ex-ante decision to diversify may be efficient on average, some diversification could be ex-ante inefficient or turn out to be a failure ex post. Nevertheless, these unsuccessful firms could follow their value-losing diversification strategies, unless they are forced to refocus. A firm's inertia makes reversing existing strategies difficult, once they are already set in place. If the restructuring process on failed diversification is timely, a diversification discount and its time-variant pattern should not be observed. The dynamic pattern of the diversification discount over time suggests that the correction process is slow and value-losing diversified firms may stay for a while until they are eventually disciplined. An endogenous, self-selection story assumes that the correction process is voluntary and instant. Therefore, reconciling this with the observed dynamic pattern in the diversification discount is difficult.

Mitchell and Mulherin (1996), Andrade et al. (2001), and Harford (2005) argue that the merger waves are an efficient way of reallocating assets to the best users of the assets. Among diversifying mergers, Kaplan and Weisbach (1992) contend that, although diversifying acquisitions are more likely to be divested than related acquisitions, little evidence suggests that the diversified acquisitions are unsuccessful because selling prices of the divested units are higher than purchasing prices. Consistent with this view, Ahn and Denis (2004) find that the value loss from diversification is completely restored through spin-offs. These studies imply that diversification is a costless attempt because the failure of diversification can be recovered through refocusing at any time. However, the argument is misleading because it does not take into account opportunity costs that might have been forgone by delaying the restructuring of unsuccessful diversification.

INTERNATIONAL EVIDENCE ON THE DIVERSIFICATION DISCOUNT

Although evidence indicates that corporate diversification is value-destroying for U.S. firms, whether this discount exists under different institutional environments at the international context is unclear. Lins and Servaes (1999) examine the valuation effects of industrial diversification for firms in Germany, Japan, and the United Kingdom. They find a diversification discount of 10 to 15 percent for firms in Japan and the United Kingdom but not for firms in Germany. Differences in corporate governance practice apparently yield different valuation effects of diversification in these countries. The results suggest that the effect of diversification on firm value varies across countries. In particular, firms located in emerging capital markets may gain from corporate diversification. Given the greater level of information asymmetry and other market imperfections, firms in these economies would benefit from the creation of an internal capital market. According to Stein (1997), the more severe the asymmetric information, the higher the cost of external financing over internal financing is. Corporate diversification in this case allows firms to overcome constraints in external capital markets. As a result, an internal capital market can allocate resources more effectively than external capital markets.

Arguably, diversification itself is attributable to higher information asymmetry in a diversified firm. Because growth perspectives and operating activities of an individual business unit within a diversified firm are not clearly identifiable to outside investors, a common perception is that diversified firms are subject to larger information asymmetry than focused firms. Thus, the benefits of internal capital market might be completely offset by higher information problems in diversified firms. In this regard, Krishnaswami and Subramaniam (1999) argue that one benefit of corporate breakup is to mitigate information problems in a conglomerate. To the contrary, Thomas (2002) studies the magnitude of information asymmetry in diversified firms compared to focused firms and finds that diversification does not necessarily exacerbate the information problem. Therefore, the information problem is less likely to completely eliminate the benefits of an internal capital market that overcome external market frictions.

For the valuation effects of diversification in emerging markets, Lins and Servaes (2002) study the costs and benefits of corporate diversification in seven emerging markets, namely, Hong Kong, India, Indonesia, Malaysia, Singapore, South Korea, and Thailand. Comparing the value of diversified firms and focused firms for each country, they find that diversified firms are valued lower than focused firms in these countries. Further, the authors show that the diversification discount is related to the ability of controlling managers to expropriate small shareholders. Therefore, the benefits of the internal capital market are at least partially attenuated with the costs of expropriation of minority shareholders' interests.

There is, however, evidence to the contrary. Taking into account the typical underdevelopment of external markets in developing economies, Khanna and Rivkin (2001) contend that diversified corporate structures in emerging markets create considerable opportunities to create value for shareholders. For instance, business groups can use resources from existing operations to start a new business, which carries substantial risk that is hardly recognized and priced incorrectly by the external capital market. In these circumstances, business groups can substitute for the role of venture capital, which is not readily available in emerging markets. The severe market imperfections and the problems associated with information asymmetries that prevail in the external capital markets of emerging markets make using internal capital markets look more attractive. Khanna and Palepu (2000) investigate the effects of corporate diversification on firm value for Indian firms. Keister (1998) reports that business groups in China show better performance and productivity than nongroup firms. Investigating 14 emerging markets, Khanna and Rivkin (2001) conclude that group-affiliated firms generally outperform unaffiliated firms.

Although industrial diversification has decreased over the decades, there has been a substantial increase in global diversification for U.S. firms. Does this trend of globalization suggest efficient deployment of knowledge and management skills internationally? Using the method of Berger and Ofek (1995), Denis, Denis, and Yost (2002), who compare the value of globally diversified firms to the value of locally operating firms, find that global diversification is also associated with lower firm value. Therefore, as is the case with industrial diversification, geographical diversification leads to the inefficient cross-subsidization of less profitable business units and lower firm value.

SUMMARY AND CONCLUSIONS

For decades, the value of corporate diversification has interested academics, investors, and managers. The finding that diversified firms, on average, trade at a substantial discount compared to focused firms ignited the debates on diversification discount. Given that diversification destroys firm value, how can the popularity of a diversification strategy be explained today? Agency problems, measurement errors in computing the diversification discount, and the self-selection hypothesis partially explain the observed diversification discount. Although diversification could result from a firm's optimal behavior in response to the changes in its industrial and economic environment, evidence from restructuring suggests that some failed diversification does not necessarily correct the problem until firms are forced to do so. Therefore, diversification has an adverse impact on firm value, at least for some firms. The question is whether an excess value measure can capture this adverse impact of diversification. Apart from the debate on whether excess value is, on average, positive or negative, excess value appears to be able to correctly identify firms that are successful and unsuccessful in their diversification. Thus, excess value is a meaningful measure.

The value of diversification is conditional on firm characteristics, industry conditions, and the degree of the capital market development. Which specific characteristics of these conditions define success and failure of a diversification strategy and how they are related to the measure of the value of diversification are unclear. These areas remain largely unexplored in the diversification discount literature.

DISCUSSION QUESTIONS

1. Some view emerging capital markets as inefficient in allocating resources for firms having good growth potential. Discuss the potential benefits and costs of corporate diversification for firms located in an emerging capital market.

2. Some argue that the observed diversification discount is attributable to measurement errors and self-selection bias. This implies that firms, on average, make the right decisions involving diversification. Reconcile this argument with the fact that many firms have an ineffective corporate governance system and managers typically hold only a small share of equity ownership.

3. From the perspective of outside investors, what are the potential merits of investing in a well-diversified firm instead of holding a portfolio of similar focused firms? Discuss the implications of the diversification discount for outside investors.

4. Product market competition in domestic and international market should drive out potential inefficiency in an organizational structure. If this view is true, what would be the proportion of diversified firms and focused firms depending on industry structure?

REFERENCES

Ahn, Seoungpil. 2009. "The Dynamics of Diversification Discount." *Asia-Pacific Journal of Financial Studies* 38:2, 277–310.

Ahn, Seungpil, and David J. Denis. 2004. "Internal Capital Markets and Investment Policy: Evidence from Corporate Spinoffs." *Journal of Financial Economics* 71:3, 489–516.

Ahn, Seoungpil, and Mark D. Walker. 2007. "Corporate Governance and the Spinoff Decision." *Journal of Corporate Finance* 13:1, 76–93.

Amihud, Yakov, and Baruch Lev. 1981. "Risk Reduction as a Managerial Motive for Conglomerate Mergers." *Bell Journal of Economics* 12:2, 605–617.

Andrade, Gregor, Mark Mitchell, and Erik Stafford. 2001. "New Evidence and Perspectives on Mergers." *Journal of Economic Perspectives* 15:2, 103–120.

Berger, Philip G., and Eli Ofek. 1995. "Diversification's Effect on Firm Value." *Journal of Financial Economics* 37:1, 39–65.

Berger, Philip G., and Eli Ofek. 1996. "Bustup Takeovers of Value-destroying Diversified Firms." *Journal of Finance* 51:4, 1175–1200.

Berger, Philip G., and Eli Ofek. 1999. "Causes and Effects of Corporate Refocusing Programs." *Review of Financial Studies* 12:2, 311–345.

Bertrand, Marianne, and Sendhil Mullainathan. 2003. "Enjoying the Quiet Life? Corporate Governance and Managerial Preferences." *Journal of Political Economy* 111:5, 1043–1075.

Campa, Jose M., and Simi Kedia. 2002. "Explaining the Diversification Discount." *Journal of Finance* 57:4, 1731–1762.

Chevalier, Judith. 2000. "Why Do Firms Undertake Diversifying Mergers? An Examination of Investment Policies of Merging Firms." Working Paper, University of Chicago.

Çolak, Gönül, and Toni Whited. 2007. "Spin-offs, Divestitures, and Conglomerate Investment." *Review of Financial Studies* 20:3, 557–595.

Comment, Robert, and Gregg A. Jarrell. 1995. "Corporate Focus and Stock Returns." *Journal of Financial Economics* 37:1, 67–87.

Denis, David J., Daine K. Denis, and Atulya Sarin. 1997. "Agency Problems, Equity Ownership, and Corporate Diversification." *Journal of Finance* 52:1, 135–160.

Denis, David J., Daine K. Denis, and Kevin Yost. 2002. "Global Diversification, Industrial Diversification, and Firm Value." *Journal of Finance* 57:5, 1951–1979.

Dittmar, Amy, and Anil Shivdasani. 2000. "Divestitures and Divisional Investment Policies." *Journal of Finance* 58:6, 2711–2744.

Gertner, Robert, Eric Powers, and David Scharfstein. 2002. "Learning about Internal Capital Markets from Corporate Spin-offs." *Journal of Finance* 57:6, 2479–2506.

Gomes, Joao, and Dmitry Livdan. 2004. "Optimal Diversification: Reconciling Theory and Evidence." *Journal of Finance* 59:2, 507–535.

Graham, John R., Michael L. Lemmon, and Jack G. Wolf. 2002. "Does Corporate Diversification Destroy Value?" *Journal of Finance* 57:2, 695–720.

Harford, Jarrad. 2005. "What Drives Merger Waves?" *Journal of Financial Economics* 77:3, 529–560.

Hubbard, R. Glenn. 1998. "Capital-market Imperfections and Investment." *Journal of Economic Literature* 36:1, 193–225.

Hubbard, R. Glenn, and Darius Palia. 1999. "A Reexamination of the Conglomerate Merger Wave in the 1960s: An Internal Capital Market View." *Journal of Finance* 54:3, 1131–1152.

Hyland, David. 1999. "Why Firms Diversify: An Empirical Examination." Working Paper, University of Texas at Arlington.

Jensen, Michael C. 1986. "Agency Costs of Free Cash Flow, Corporate Finance, and Takeovers." *American Economic Review* 76:2, 323–329.

Jensen, Michael C. 1993. "The Modern Industrial Revolution, Exit, and the Failure of Internal Control Systems." *Journal of Finance* 48:3, 831–880.

Kaplan, Steven N., and Michael S. Weisbach. 1992. "The Success of Acquisitions: Evidence from Divestitures." *Journal of Finance* 47:1, 107–138.

Keister, Lisa A. 1998. "Engineering Growth: Business Group Structure and Firm Performance in China's Transition Economy." *American Journal of Sociology* 104:2, 404–440.

Khanna, Tarun, and Krishna Palepu. 2000. "Is Group Affiliation Profitable in Emerging Markets? An Analysis of Diversified Indian Business Groups." *Journal of Finance* 55:2, 867–891.

Khanna, Tarun, and Jan W. Rivkin. 2001. "Estimating the Performance Effects of Business Groups in Emerging Markets." *Strategic Management Journal* 22:1, 45–74.

Krishnaswami, Sudha, and Venkat Subramaniam. 1999. "Information Asymmetry, Valuation, and the Corporate Spin-off Decision." *Journal of Financial Economics* 53:1, 73–112.

Lamont, Owen. 1997. "Cash Flow and Investment: Evidence from Internal Capital Markets." *Journal of Finance* 52:1, 83–109.

Lamont, Owen, and Christopher Polk. 2001. "The Diversification Discount: Cash Flows Versus Returns." *Journal of Finance* 56:5, 1693–1721.

Lang, Larry H. P., and René M. Stulz. 1994. "Tobin's q, Corporate Diversification, and Firm Performance." Journal of Political Economy 102:6, 1248–1280.

Lewellen, Wilbur G. 1971. "A Pure Financial Rationale for the Conglomerate Merger." *Journal of Finance* 26:2, 521–537.

Liebeskind, Julia P., and Tim C. Opler. 1994. "Corporate Diversification and Agency Costs: Evidence from Privately Held Firms." Working Paper, The Ohio State University.

Lins, Karl, and Henri Servaes. 1999. "International Evidence on the Value of Corporate Diversification." *Journal of Finance* 54:6, 2215–2239.

Lins, Karl, and Henri Servaes. 2002. "Is Corporate Diversification Beneficial in Emerging Markets?" *Financial Management* 31:2, 5–31.

Maksimovic, Vojislav, and Gordon M. Phillips. 2002. "Do Conglomerate Firms Allocate Resources Inefficiently Across Industries? Theory and Evidence." *Journal of Finance* 57:2, 721–767.

Matsusaka, John G. 1993. "Takeover Motives during the Conglomerate Merger Wave." *RAND Journal of Economics* 24:3, 357–379.

Matsusaka, John G. 2001. "Corporate Diversification, Value Maximization, and Organizational Capabilities." *Journal of Business* 74:3, 409–431.

Mitchell, Mark L., and Kenneth Lehn. 1990. "Do Bad Bidders Become Good Targets?" *Journal of Political Economy* 98:2, 372–398.

Mitchell, Mark L., and J. Harold Mulherin. 1996. "The Impact of Industry Shocks on Takeover and Restructuring Activities." *Journal of Financial Economics* 41:2, 193–229.

Moeller, Sara B., Frederick P. Schlingemann, and René M. Stulz. 2005. "Wealth Destruction on a Massive Scale? A Study of Acquiring-firm Returns in the Recent Merger Wave." *Journal of Finance* 60:2, 757–782.

Morck, Randall, Andrei Shleifer, and Robert W. Vishny. 1990. "Do Managerial Objectives Drive Bad Acquisitions?" *Journal of Finance* 45:1, 31–48.

Myers, Stewart C., and Nicholas S. Majluf. 1984. "Corporate Financing and Investment Decisions When Firms Have Information That Investors Do Not Have." *Journal of Financial Economics* 13:2, 187–221.

Pulvino, Todd C. 1998. "Do Asset Fire-sales Exist? An Empirical Investigation of Commercial Aircraft Transactions." *Journal of Finance* 53:3, 939–978.

Rajan, Raghuram G., Henri Servaes, and Luigi Zingales. 2000. "The Cost of Diversity: The Diversification Discount and Inefficient Investment." *Journal of Finance* 55:1, 35–80.

Roll, Richard. 1986. "The Hubris Hypothesis of Corporate Takeovers." *Journal of Business*, 59:2, 197–216.

Santalo, Juan, and Manuel Becerra. 2008. "Competition from Specialized Firms and the Diversification-performance Linkage." *Journal of Finance* 63:2, 851–883.

Scharfstein, David S. 1998. "The Dark Side of Internal Capital Markets II: Evidence from Diversified Conglomerates." Working Paper, MIT Sloan School of Management.

Scharfstein, David S., and Jeremy C. Stein. 2000. "The Dark Side of Internal Capital Markets: Divisional Rent Seeking and Inefficient Investments." *Journal of Finance* 55:6, 2537–2564.

Schlingemann, Frederik P., René M. Stulz, and Ralph A. Walkling. 2002. "Divestitures and the Liquidity of the Market for Corporate Assets." *Journal of Financial Economics* 64:1, 117–144.

Servaes, Henri. 1996. "The Value of Diversification during the Conglomerate Merger Waves." *Journal of Finance* 51:4, 1201–1225.

Shin, Hyun-Han, and René M. Stulz. 1998. "Are Internal Capital Markets Efficient?" *Quarterly Journal of Economics* 113:2, 531–552.

Shleifer, Andrei, and Robert W. Vishny. 1989. "Management Entrenchment: The Case of Manager-specific Investments." *Journal of Financial Economics* 25:1, 123–140.

Shleifer, Andrei, and Robert W. Vishny. 1991. "The Takeover Wave of the 1980s." *Journal of Applied Corporate Finance* 4:3, 49–56.

Stein, Jeremy C. 1997. "Internal Capital Markets and the Competition for Corporate Resources." *Journal of Finance* 52:1, 111–133.

Stulz, René M. 1990. "Managerial Discretion and Optimal Financing Policies." *Journal of Financial Economics* 26:1, 3–27.

Thomas, Shawn. 2002. "Firm Diversification and Asymmetric Information: Evidence from Analysts' Forecasts and Earnings Announcements." *Journal of Financial Economics* 64:3, 373–396.

Villalonga, Belén. 2003. "Research Roundtable Discussion: The Diversification Discount." *FEN-EducatorSeries*. Available at http://papers.ssrn.com/sol3/papers.cfm?abstract_id=402220.

Villalonga, Belén. 2004a. "Diversification Discount or Premium? New Evidence from the Business Information Tracking Series." *Journal of Finance* 59:2, 479–506.

Villalonga, Belén. 2004b. "Does Diversification Cause the "Diversification Discount?" *Financial Management* 33:2, 5–27.

Williamson, Oliver E. 1975. *Market and Hierarchies: Analysis and Antitrust Implications.* New York: Collier and Macmillan Publishers.

Whited, Toni M. 2001. "Is It Inefficient Investment That Causes the Diversification Discount?" *Journal of Finance* 56:5, 1667–1692.

ABOUT THE AUTHOR

Seoungpil Ahn is an Associate Professor at the Sogang Business School, Sogang University, Korea. Before joining the school, he served on the faculty at Concordia University and the National University of Singapore. Professor Ahn has published a wide range of papers on corporate diversification, refocusing, and corporate governance in such journals as the *Journal of Financial Economics*, *Journal of Corporate Finance*, and *Journal of Banking and Finance*. He currently serves as an associate editor for numerous finance journals. Professor Ahn has taught courses on corporate finance, valuation, and M&As at both undergraduate and graduate levels. He received a BA in Business Administration and an MS in Finance from Pusan National University, and an MBA and a PhD both from the Krannert School of Management at Purdue University.

CHAPTER 29

Partial Acquisitions: Motivation and Consequences on Firm Performance

PENGCHENG ZHU
Assistant Professor of Finance, University of the Pacific

SHANTANU DUTTA
Assistant Professor of Finance, University of Ontario Institute of Technology

INTRODUCTION

During the last few decades, corporate merger and acquisition (M&A) activities has experienced a tremendous increase along with academic interest in studying the topic. Based on the Security Data Corporation (SDC) Platinum database, the worldwide M&A transaction value increased 10 times from about US$280 billion in 1990 to about US$2.7 trillion in 2007. The number of deals also rose from about 4,000 in 1990 to 17,000 completed transactions in 2007. Most studies focus on complete acquisitions in which the acquiring firm buys majority ownership in the target firm, resulting in the delisting of the target firm from the public market. Yet, researchers have paid less attention to partial acquisitions despite their importance. The purpose of this chapter is to provide a review of some major studies on partial acquisitions and to summarize the key findings in the literature.

Partial acquisitions are corporate ownership transactions in which the acquiring firm only acquires part ownership of the target firm. The target firm thus remains an independent entity in the public market. Researchers use different criteria to define partial acquisitions. Some studies such as Choi (1991) and Akhigbe, Martin, and Whyte (2007) only consider the acquisitions of nonmajority controlling ownership (i.e., usually less than 50 percent ownership in the target firm), while others such as Chen and Hennart (2004) use a much higher threshold. Some other studies focus on toehold acquisitions where the acquiring firm acquires less than 5 percent ownership. This chapter uses the terms *partial acquisitions*, *block ownership purchase*, and *toehold acquisitions* interchangeably.

The partial acquisition sample provides unique insights for corporate M&A research, particularly from the target firm's perspective. Studying partially acquired target firms provides a way to directly observe the impact of the acquisition on target firm value and performance as the target firm continues listing on the public market after the partial acquisition. It also allows opening the "black box" of the corporate integration process by tracking the target firm's organizational and policy changes. This can provide direct evidence of the disciplinary and monitoring function in corporate control transactions. Further, firms may choose partial acquisitions over full acquisitions for reasons of distinct strategy. Thus, studying partial acquisitions can not only help to improve understanding of M&A theory but also provide useful strategic alternatives to the practitioners in the takeover market. Finally, this chapter provides a review of the evidence on cross-border partial acquisitions, which have become an important mode of entry into international markets.

The chapter reviews partial acquisition studies in four ways. First, it introduces the motivation of undertaking partial acquisitions. Second, it summarizes the short-term and long-term consequences of partial acquisitions on target firm performance. Third, the chapter discusses the factors that may explain the impact of partial acquisitions on target firm performance. Finally, the chapter provides a review of several studies that investigate financial policy changes after partial acquisitions. It offers additional evidence of the monitoring effect brought by the acquiring firms and provides further explanation about why partial acquisitions affect target firm performance.

MOTIVATION OF PARTIAL ACQUISITIONS

Similar to full acquisitions, partial acquisitions can be used to achieve synergy gains and maximize shareholders' value. Roy (1985, 1988) challenges the conventional wisdom that only full acquisitions can maximize the acquiring firm's gain. He separates the bidder's synergy from the target firm's synergy and shows that acquiring less than 100 percent ownership can sometimes maximize the acquirer's gain. Synergy gains can arise from the traditional ways of efficiency enhancement such as revenue improvement and cost reduction. Gains can also result from introducing an external block shareholder who can increase the monitoring power over the target management team and improve the governance mechanism in the target firm. Thus, a poor performing management team is under threat of replacement (Choi, 1991) and suppressed firm value is improved in a better governed environment.

Some propose using partial acquisitions as a solution to the "free rider" problem in corporate takeovers. For example, Grossman and Hart (1980) consider a takeover model in which the target company is owned by atomistic shareholders who consider themselves as having negligible impact on a takeover outcome. Their model suggests that these shareholders would free-ride on their fellow shareholders, rejecting any tender offer unless the acquiring firm offers the full acquisition benefits. As a result, potential bidders have no incentive to attempt any acquisition as they would not benefit from a successful takeover. Grossman and Hart suggest using toehold acquisitions in which the acquiring firm only acquires a small portion of the target firm's ownership before the full acquisition. In order to avoid paying the full premium to acquire these shares, the acquiring ownership must be less than 5 percent so that the acquisition does not trigger a disclosure to the regulatory authority and public investors as required by the Securities and Exchange

Commission (SEC) in the United States. With the increase in target stock price after the public announcement of the acquisition, the pre-acquisition ownership in the target firm can yield sufficient returns to the acquiring firm to cover the administrative cost of the acquisition. This provides an incentive to the acquiring firm to participate in the takeover market and keep the market running efficiently.

Another motivation for using partial acquisition is to facilitate full acquisition and to help the bidding firm win a takeover battle. Stulz, Walkling, and Song (1990) and Betton and Eckbo (2000) find that prior partial ownership may benefit bidders as it helps to deter rival bidders and increases the bidder's chance of winning a full acquisition. Bulow, Huang, and Klemperer (1999) show that the acquiring firm with prior ownership in the target firm becomes more aggressive in the takeover battle. As the bidding price increases, the value of the toehold ownership also increases, which provides more bargaining power to the acquiring firm and leads to a more aggressive bidding offer. Having block ownership in the target firms also reduces the likelihood of management resistance to a full takeover (Jennings and Mazzeo, 1993; Betton and Eckbo, 2000).

Empirical studies report consistent evidence that partial acquisitions facilitate subsequent full acquisitions. For example, Mikkelson and Ruback (1985) find that 26 percent of partially acquired targets are subsequently taken over by a firm or third party within three years of the initial position. Choi (1991) reports that approximately 16 percent of targets involved in toehold bids are subsequently taken over or have an ownership change within a year of the initiation of the toehold position. Singh (1998) concludes that toeholds increase the probability of a full takeover and the price paid for the remaining shares. Using a sample of tender offers, Betton and Eckbo (2000) find that the probability of a successful single-bid takeover increases with the size of the prior partial ownership position. Akhigbe et al. (2007) also find that partial acquisitions involving corporate bidders are more likely to result in full acquisitions.

Managers can use partial acquisitions to mitigate the asymmetric information in cross-border transactions. In a typical corporate takeover transaction, the acquiring firm usually has less knowledge about the target firm's value than the target firm's owner does (Balakrishnan and Koza, 1992; Reuer and Koza, 2000). Such information asymmetry exists in both ex-ante screening of cross-border M&A targets and ex-post enforcement of cross-border M&A contracts (Chen and Hennart, 2004). Due to asymmetric information, self-interested target firms' owners have the incentive to misrepresent the value of their firms (Ravenscraft and Scherer, 1987). Thus, the acquiring firms must incur extra costs (sometimes prohibitive) to identify poor-quality firms and guard against target firm's misrepresentations.

The acquiring firm also needs to deal with ex-post opportunism in the integration process. Without an effectively binding mechanism, the target firm may not transfer the full value of the intangible assets and management expertise to the acquiring firm, resulting in an unsuccessful integration. Chen and Hennart (2004) propose that partial acquisitions can create a hostage effect that facilitates ex-ante screening of targets and ex-post enforcement of takeover contracts. Specifically, the willingness of the sellers to accept partial acquisition signals ex-ante quality of their firms, and the remaining equity posts a bond to restrain them from committing ex-post opportunism. Accordingly, Chen and Hennart use a sample of 114 Japanese firms acquiring U.S. firms to test the hostage hypothesis. They find that the target firms subject to higher information asymmetry are more likely to be partially taken over.

Finally, in the international business literature, partial acquisitions are considered one of the important foreign market entry modes available to the multinational corporations. Policy makers in foreign governments can also use partial divestment as a means to privatize state-owned enterprises and attract foreign investment. Acquiring firms use partial acquisition to penetrate the foreign market. Acquiring partial ownership allows the acquiring firm to align interests with the foreign target firm and control the foreign expansion risk (Chari and Chang, 2007). It also helps the acquiring firm gain access to the target firms' important strategic resources, such as the market share, distribution channel, brand name, and human capital. Partial ownership serves as an important stepping-stone for the acquiring firm in entering the foreign market and creates unique value for shareholders of the multinational corporation (Jakobsen and Meyer, 2007).

Some investors express concern that firms using partial acquisitions may be motivated to obtain the target firms' intercorporate perquisites. The corporate perquisites may take the form of "financial market" transactions such as partial acquirers forcing the target firms to adopt a high dividend policy to take advantage of the intercorporate dividend exclusion rule. Such action, however, may be harmful to the remaining target shareholders who may prefer capital gains (Shleifer and Vishny, 1986). Corporate perquisites may also involve "product market" transactions where partial acquirers may seek benefits such as favorable terms for intercorporate product purchases, technology sales, and the division of distribution channels or marketing areas (Rosenstein and Rush, 1990). Further, some partial acquirers are considered "corporate raiders" that are detrimental to the long-term value of the target firm. However, empirical evidence does not support these criticisms of partial acquisitions (e.g., Mikkelson and Ruback, 1985; Holderness and Sheehan, 1985; Choi, 1991). Empirical studies find that partial acquisition accompanied by ownership transfer usually improves target firm performance and value in both the short-term and long-term. The next section provides more detailed reviews of the consequence of partial acquisition on firm performance and value.

Exhibit 29.1 summarizes the five main motivations of undertaking partial acquisitions. Firms use partial acquisitions to create synergy values. Acquiring partial ownership in the target firm can also solve the shareholder "free-ride" problem and facilitate the full acquisition. In cross-border acquisitions, the acquiring firm

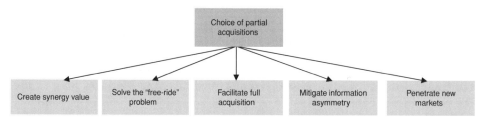

Exhibit 29.1 Motivation for Undertaking Partial Acquisitions
Note: This exhibit summarizes the five main motivations for undertaking partial acquisitions.

acquires partial ownership in the target firm to mitigate the information asymmetry and to penetrate a new foreign market.

CONSEQUENCES OF PARTIAL ACQUISITIONS

This section summarizes the impact of partial acquisitions on the performance of target firms. It reviews the impact of acquisition announcements on the short-term stock prices of target firms based on event study evidence. Finally, the chapter summarizes the consequence of partial acquisitions on the operating variables and long-term stock performance of target firms.

Impact of Partial Acquisition on Firm Short-Term Performance

To examine the short-term impact of partial acquisition on shareholder value, many studies use event study methodology to test partial acquisition announcement effects. Most studies find that such announcements have a positive impact on the target firm's stock price. In one of the first empirical tests of partial acquisitions, Madden (1981) finds significantly positive abnormal returns accruing to the target firms during the month of the partial acquisition announcement.

Mikkelson and Ruback (1985) measure the announcement effect on stock prices of a corporate investment of 5 percent or more of another company's equity securities. Based on a sample of 473 partial acquisitions reported to the SEC from 1978 to 1980, they find that both acquiring and target firms gain significant and positive abnormal returns for the initial announcement of partial acquisitions.

For the three years following the initial partial acquisitions, Mikkelson and Ruback (1985) classify the follow-up investment events into four outcomes: (1) a completed takeover, (2) a repurchase of the investment position by the target firm, (3) a completed takeover by another firm, and (4) a sale of shares in the public market. Their evidence shows that if the partial acquisition ends up as a completed takeover, the acquiring firm gains zero total abnormal returns. If the partial acquisition results in a target repurchase, the sale of shares, or a takeover by a third party, both the acquiring and target firms gain positive total abnormal returns. In the case of the target repurchase, the target firm experiences negative abnormal returns on the repurchase date, but this negative return is offset by the positive return on the initial acquisition announcement. Therefore, regardless of the investment outcome (including a target repurchase), the authors find that the partial acquisition typically increases the target firm's shareholder wealth. Their results also show that the average total valuation effect on the target firm appears to be negative when no outcome occurs in the three years following the initial announcement. Mikkelson and Ruback also split the sample by frequent acquirers (also referred to as "corporate raiders") and infrequent acquirers. They find that the value impact on the target firm is the same in both samples. Thus, this finding does not support the argument that frequent acquirers may take advantage of the target firm at the expense of the target firm's other shareholders (i.e., the "raiding" effect).

Unlike Mikkelson and Ruback (1985) who study intercompany partial acquisitions, Holderness and Sheehan (1985) examine partial acquisitions made by six influential individual investors who are "corporate raiders." These investors may reduce the wealth of fellow stockholders by raiding target firms and transferring corporate assets to themselves. The study measures the stock price changes associated with the first public announcement of the partial acquisition made by any of the six investors between 1977 and 1982. Contrary to the corporate raiding hypothesis, Holderness and Sheehan find that, on average, stockholders of target firms earn statistically significant positive abnormal returns upon the public announcement of such partial acquisitions.

Holderness and Sheehan (1985) also follow the investors' activities in the target firms for the two years following their initial stock purchases. They classify the target firms into four groups: (1) target firms that are successfully reorganized (whether by the investor or by a third party), (2) firms where a reorganization effort failed within those two years, (3) target firms that repurchase at least some of the investors' shares, and (4) all other target firms not experiencing any of these events in the two years. Their evidence shows that no matter what eventually happens to the target firm within two years, target firm stockholders, on average, earn positive returns. Thus, the study does not support the raiding hypothesis for these influential investors. When the acquiring firm withdraws the reorganization effort, target firm stockholders suffer wealth losses, although the total valuation (including the initial announcement returns) is positive. For the acquiring firms, the results are mixed. The announcement return is positive and significant when initially announced, but in a longer event window, the return becomes negative and insignificant. Although the study rejects the raiding hypothesis, it does not provide evidence that the increased shareholders' values in the target firms are due to the improvement of management quality based on the effort of the six activist investors. Another explanation simply could be that the six investors are good at selecting undervalued target firms.

An implication of these studies is that partial acquisitions create values to target firm shareholders. But how do partial acquisitions compare to full acquisitions? Comment and Jarrell (1987) compare the acquisition premium paid for partial and full acquisitions from a sample of 210 cash tender offers in the United States between 1981 and 1984. They find that partial tender offers pay lower premiums than full tender offers (i.e., any-or-all offers or two-tier offers) because the acquiring firm only gains the nonmajority controlling ownership in the target firm.

Similarly, Amoako-Adu and Smith (1993) compare the gains to target shareholders in complete tender offers resulting in delisting of the target firm stock with those in partial tender offers. Based on a sample of 160 Canadian target companies listed on the Toronto Stock Exchange between 1977 and 1989, the authors find that partial acquisitions create value for target firm shareholders upon the public announcement. However, their evidence also shows that complete tender offers provide larger gains to target shareholders than those obtained in partial acquisitions. Amoako-Adu and Smith attribute the value difference to the cost of being a public firm. The cost includes servicing shareholders, preparing financial reports and shareholder meeting circulars, and spending management time on meeting with dispersed shareholders. Taking a company private reduces the agency costs of equity, particularly the expenses of settling differences between controlling and minority shareholders, proxy fights, and potential class suits. Therefore, the expectation is that complete tender offers create more value than do partial acquisitions, which do not lead to privatization.

Some studies focus on the acquiring firm's perspective by investigating how partial acquisitions affect the acquiring firm's value. Further, does the acquisition affect the shareholders' and debt holders' value differently? Datta and Iskandar-Datta (1995) study 63 large partial acquisition announcements in the United States between 1982 and 1990. They examine the wealth effect on both the acquiring firm's bondholders and shareholders. The authors show that bondholders experience significant losses, while stockholders experience normal returns. Partial acquisitions are value-neutral from a firm-level perspective. Datta and Iskandar-Datta also conduct a cross-sectional analysis focusing on the financing method (cash, stock, or debt) in the acquisitions. The financing variables are significant in explaining both bondholder and shareholder wealth but have opposite effects on the two types of security holders. Thus, the authors suggest that a wealth redistribution effect (i.e., wealth transfer from debt holders to shareholder holders) exists in the partial acquisitions, which are related to the financing method used in the acquisitions.

The literature concludes that partial acquisitions increase the target firms' short-term value, especially those experiencing reorganization and corporate control transfer after the partial acquisitions. However, target firm shareholders do not obtain more benefits in partial acquisitions than in full acquisitions. There is no evidence that the acquiring firm or individual investor raids the target firm and transfers wealth from the target firm to the acquirer. Evidence shows that acquiring firms in partial acquisitions generally do not gain any short-term economic benefits. The acquiring firm's shareholders are at best value neutral in the partial acquisitions, and wealth redistributions may occur from the bondholders to the shareholders in the acquiring firm. The next section provides a review of studies that examine the long-term impact of partial acquisitions on firm performance.

Impact of Partial Acquisitions on Firm Long-Term Performance

Announcement returns in event studies rely on market expectations and sometimes investors' sentiments. Although short-term studies reflect an optimistic view of the partial acquisitions, a need exists to understand the real impact of partial acquisitions on target firms' fundamentals, such as operating performance and shareholders' value, in a longer time horizon.

Based on a sample of 62 U.S. target firms between 1973 and 1981, Eyssell (1989) examines the partial acquisition effects on firm operating performance. The target firms in the sample have experienced at least six separate partial acquisitions by a unique bidder in the sample period. The acquiring firm must obtain at least 15 percent of the target's outstanding shares in each partial acquisition. To examine the performance change in the partial target firms, Eyssell develops a control sample consisting of 62 firms matched to the target firms on the basis of firm size and industry membership. No control firms are involved in any acquisition activity during the sample period. Using year-end financial data surrounding the partial acquisitions, the author calculates 20 representative measures of the target firms' pre-event and postevent liquidity, profitability, operating expenses, financial leverage, asset utilization, and dividend policy. Eyssell examines the five years before and after the initial purchase of the target firm's ownership and compares the same ratios in the control firms in the corresponding time window. Although most studies find that the target firms gain abnormal returns upon the announcement of takeover bids, Eyssell finds few significant changes in the financial operating performance or other financial characteristics in partially acquired firms. The study concludes that the sources of the observed takeover premiums in partial acquisitions are not detectable in the financial statement data of the target firms.

Rosenstein and Rush (1990) reach a contradictory conclusion by examining the long-term stock performance of partially acquired target firms. Based on a sample of 51 industrial firms' partial acquisitions between 1980 and 1984, they find that the risk-adjusted monthly stock returns of partially acquired firms are significantly lower than those of control group firms in the five years following the partial acquisitions. Further, Rosenstein and Rush report that partially acquired firms do not demonstrate abnormally poor performance before the acquisition.

The empirical results become more mixed when Sudarsanam (1996) finds contrasting results based on a sample of 228 U.K. companies during the period 1985 to 1992. He tracks the stock market valuation of the targets for three years following the partial acquisitions. His results show a significant improvement of long-term stock performance in the partially acquired target firms.

FACTORS AFFECTING PARTIAL ACQUISITIONS AND TARGET FIRM PERFORMANCE

Given the mixed results on the long-term performance of partial acquisitions, examining the cross-sectional variation of the performance and identifying the determinant factors of the performance variation are important. This section reviews several such factors studied in the literature, such as external and internal corporate control change, the identity and motivation of acquiring firms, and information asymmetry.

Governance and Control Change after Partial Acquisitions

In order to explain the inconsistent long-term performance result in partial acquisitions, some studies track the corporate control changes in the target firm after the partial acquisitions and relate such changes to the impact on firm performance and value. For example, Choi (1991) examines the valuation consequences of control-related events after partial acquisitions. He also extends the research of Mikkelson and Ruback (1985), which focuses on external control transfer mechanisms such as divestitures and takeovers. He tests the proposition that partial acquisitions facilitate value-enhancing international control transfers such as management turnover and proxy fights. Based on a sample of 322 public announcements of partial acquisitions between 1982 and 1985, Choi finds that takeovers, proxy fights, and management turnovers systematically follow partial acquisitions, which exhibit abnormal increases in share value. Negative abnormal returns for the targets precede partial acquisitions, implying that poor performance and/or management inefficiency encourages partial acquisitions that are likely to be followed by value-enhancing control transfers. Choi also shows that the absence of control transfer events lowers target share price. This result augments the findings in Holderness and Sheehan (1985), which are unable to distinguish between the management quality improvement effect and the undervaluation effect in the partial acquisition. Choi clearly shows that the value enhancement in the target firm results from the monitoring role of the partial acquirers rather than from the acquirers' expertise in selecting the undervalued targets.

Akhigbe, Madura, and Spencer (2004) also highlight the monitoring role played by the partial acquirers in the target firm. They examine the long-term stock performance of 330 partially acquired U.S. firms between 1980 and 1998 and during the three years after the partial acquisitions. Although they find that the firms experience insignificant valuation effects (buy and hold abnormal returns), the cross-sectional analysis shows that the long-term performance effects are more favorable when the partial target has more growth opportunities and a lower degree of financial leverage, and the partial acquirer is within the same industry and closer in size to the partial target. Akhigbe et al. contend that these factors are related to the control power of the partial acquirer. They believe the initial announcement effect reflects the perceived benefits of improved monitoring in the partially acquired firm.

Torabzadeh and Dube (2007) analyze a sample of 206 partial acquisitions of publicly listed U.S. firms from 1995 to 2000. They focus on the effects of CEO turnover on the postacquisition changes in the target firms' stock and operating performance. According to their evidence, target firms that retain their pre-acquisition CEO show a significant deterioration in operating and share performance after the acquisition compared to those target firms that do not retain their CEO. The authors also observe a substantial increase in CEO compensation for the sample that retains their CEO, as compared to the latter sample that hires a new CEO. Torabzadeh and Dube conclude that the disciplinary effort contributed by the acquiring firm improves the long-term performance of the partially acquired firm.

Identity of Acquiring Firms

The inconsistent findings of the long-term studies might result from the mix of different types of acquiring firms participating in the partial acquisitions. Since acquiring firms have different motivations in the transactions, they may choose to exercise different monitoring power in the target firms. The acquiring firm's monitoring effort should have a direct impact on the long-term performance of the target firm. Therefore, some studies focus on the different roles that various acquiring firms play.

Bethel, Liebeskind, and Opler (1998) document the causes and consequences of significant share purchases of large U.S. corporations during the 1980s. They classify partial acquirers into three groups: activist, financial, and strategic acquirers. The activist acquirers are those who announce their intention of influencing firm policies. The financial acquirers include banks, pension funds, money managers, and individuals who are only motivated by portfolio investment purposes. The strategic acquirers are nonfinancial investors who are unopposed by the target management.

Based on a sample of 224 block purchases of 425 *Fortune* 500 companies from 1980 to 1989, Bethel et al. (1998) find that activist, financial, and strategic investors target the stock of firms that are performing poorly and that these investors do not appear to be deterred by standard antitakeover defenses. Particularly, activist investors are likely to purchase blocks of stock in more diversified firms. These results are consistent with the view that the market for partial corporate control helps reverse inefficient diversification. The authors also find that block purchases by activist investors are followed by increases in the rate of asset divestitures, share repurchases, and management turnover and decreases in the rate of mergers and acquisitions. Moreover, activist block share purchases are followed by a two-year increase in operating profitability and abnormal stock price appreciation. Taken as a whole, Bethel et al.'s study suggests that the market for partial acquisition plays an important role in limiting agency costs due to the separation of ownership and control in large U.S. corporations.

Bethel et al. (1998) find that financial and strategic investors also target underperforming firms but do not systematically target highly diversified firms. In contrast to firms that experience activist block share purchases, firms targeted by financial and strategic investors do not undergo extensive operational changes and experience smaller ex-post improvements in profitability. The evidence shows that activists contribute most to the improvement of corporate governance and performance of the target firms.

Park, Selvili, and Song (2008) draw a similar conclusion based on a U.S. sample of 264 partial acquisitions between 1997 and 2000. They find the three-day cumulative abnormal returns on activist and strategic block purchases are significantly higher than those for financial block purchases. The authors maintain that the value added by activist blocks reflects monitoring benefits brought to the target firm, whereas the value added by strategic blocks reflects both synergy and potential monitoring benefits. According to their results, the acquiring firms that do not have current or potential business relationships with the target firm produce a larger positive market reaction. Further, the acquiring firms having a seat on the target's board of directors tend to achieve a larger positive market reaction. Park et al.'s study suggests that activist blockholders bring monitoring benefits to the targets of partial acquisitions and that these monitoring benefits are economically significant. The extent of monitoring depends on acquirer and target characteristics, such as block size, business ties with the target firm, presence of any previous outside block, and managerial ownership in the target firm.

Activist Financial Institutions

Although the studies by Bethel et al. (1998) and Park et al. (2008) show no significant contribution from the financial acquirers, debate still exists on the role that financial institutions play in exercising monitoring power and improving performance in the partially acquired firm. Clifford (2008) studies the partial acquisitions by hedge funds and their activist monitoring effect to improve target firms' performance. Based on 197 unique hedge fund families, he finds that firms targeted by hedge funds for active monitoring purposes earn larger positive short-term abnormal returns than firms targeted by hedge funds for passive investment purposes. His results also show that firms targeted by activists experience a large, positive increase in operating efficiency (measured by return on assets) in the year following the acquisition by the hedge fund. Indirect evidence suggests that a reduction in assets drives this result more so than an increase in cash flows. The evidence also shows that hedge funds pursuing activist strategies employ organizational structures that enable them to mitigate liquidity constraints in their investment portfolio. Thus, hedge funds with longer lock-up and redemption notification periods are more likely to initiate activist campaigns. These results are consistent with the view that the relatively costless redemption of shares by a financial intermediary's investors such as mutual funds shareholders may reduce the ability or incentive of the fund manager to engage in lengthy activist battles. Finally, the study reveals that hedge funds earn larger holding period returns on their active blocks than their passive blocks. The average annual return to activist holdings is 8 percent to 21 percent larger than the returns to passive holdings, indicating that activist shareholders may use higher returns to mitigate the cost of their monitoring effort.

Yet, Greenwood and Schor (2007) question the real value brought by the financial partial acquirers to the target firm. They examine long-horizon stock returns around investor activism in a comprehensive sample of 980 public filings by portfolio investors between 1993 and 2006. The authors find that the announcement returns and long-term abnormal returns surrounding investor activism are high for the subset of targets that are acquired ex post, but not detectably different from zero for firms that remain independent a year after the initial partial acquisition. Firms that are targeted by activists are more likely to get acquired than those in a control sample. The results suggest that hedge funds' short investment horizons make them better suited to identifying undervalued targets and prompting a takeover than at fixing corporate strategy or tackling long-term corporate governance issues. Greenwood and Schor argue that ex-post partial acquisition takeovers are the only way to create value for the target firm. Due to the short investment time horizon, hedge funds can contribute little value to the governance improvement in the target firm.

Klein and Zur (2006) explore the valuation impact on target firms from a slightly different aspect. They examine a sample of 194 partial acquisitions made by hedge fund activists between 2003 and 2005. Their evidence shows that the market reacts favorably to the announcement of these partial acquisitions. Unlike Bethel et al.'s (1998) study, which reports that activist block holders target for underperforming firms, Klein and Zur find that hedge funds are more likely to invest in healthy, profitable firms. They also report that in more than 60 percent of the instances, hedge fund activists are successful in getting existing management to acquiesce to their demands such as gaining representation on the firm's board, enacting a change in strategic operations, repurchasing shares by the firm, scuttling an existing merger proposal, or being acquired by another firm.

Klein and Zur (2006) find that hedge fund activists do not improve the accounting performance of firms in the year after the initial purchase. In fact, earnings per share, return on assets, and return on equity decline in the fiscal year after the partial acquisition. Yet, the authors find that one-year buy-and-hold abnormal returns are higher for the hedge fund target firm than the control firms. The hedge funds appear to extract cash from the firm through increasing the debt capacity of the target firm and paying themselves higher dividends. The latter result, coupled with the positive stock price reaction surrounding the acquisition announcements, suggests that stockholders perceive benefits to reducing agency costs associated with excess cash and short-term investments. Examining proxy fights and threats accompanying the activist campaign suggests that hedge fund managers achieve their goals by posing a credible threat of engaging the target in a costly proxy solicitation contest. Apparently, hedge funds target firms that are rich in cash and short-term investments and have low debt capacities. After gaining control of the firm, hedge funds increase the debt load of the firms, reduce the cash on hand, and pay out increased dividends to the shareholders. These findings are consistent with Jensen's (1986) free cash flow hypothesis, which suggests that firms can control agency costs by reducing free cash flows.

Asymmetric Information Environment

Kang and Kim (2008) examine a sample of 799 partial acquisitions in the United States between 1990 and 1999. They find that geographically proximate block acquirers are more likely than remote block acquirers to be involved in postacquisition governance activities in targets. Specifically, acquirers located close to the targets are more likely to have their representatives on the target's board and replace poorly performing target management after block share purchases. Kang and Kim argue that information advantages that arise from geographic proximity provide blockholders with strong incentives to actively monitor target managers, fostering corporate governance activities in targets. The acquiring firms at further physical distance face higher monitoring costs because of extra communication and transportation costs. Thus, these acquiring firms have lower incentive to exercise active monitoring power in the partial target firms.

According to Kang and Kim (2008), targets that are close to the acquirers experience significantly higher abnormal announcement returns and better postacquisition operating performance than those targets that are far away. The positive valuation effects are more pronounced when the targets are smaller and riskier, have a higher level of research and development investments, and experience worse past performance or have higher insider ownership. Thus, the authors argue that the benefits of monitoring are likely to be more valuable for targets that have greater information asymmetries. Kang and Kim suggest that geographically proximate investors are better able to exploit their informational advantage when local firms have an opaque information environment. Since geographically proximate block acquirers face lower monitoring costs associated with their governance activities, the authors' findings also suggest that such a cost advantage incentivizes the block acquirers to pursue more active governance in targets, which in turn benefit the target shareholders.

Kang and Kim (2010) examine the impact of asymmetric information on the target firm performance based on a sample of 268 partial acquisitions of U.S. firms by foreign firms during the period between 1981 and 1999. They find that compared to domestic partial acquirers, the foreign partial acquirers are less likely to engage in governance activities of U.S. targets.

In particular, the extent of governance activities by foreign investors, such as the threat of hostile takeovers, proxy fights, expression of opposition to or attempts to amend antitakeover provisions, seeking representatives on the target's board, and asset downsizing, are negatively related to the information asymmetry proxies, such as the geographic distance, cultural distance, acquisition experience, and language difference between the acquiring and target country. Compared to domestic acquirers, the results confirm the view that foreign acquirers are more subject to information asymmetry and less likely to engage in active monitoring

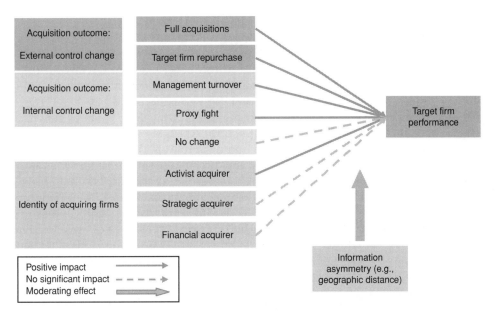

Exhibit 29.2 Factors Affecting Partial Acquisition and Target Firm Performance

Note: This exhibit shows the determinant factors of the target firm performance in partial acquisitions, which are classified into three broad categories: external corporate control change, internal corporate control change, and the identity of acquiring firms. Under each category, the exhibit lists the specific factors and shows their impact on target firm performance.

and governance restructuring in the target firm. Using the event study method, Kang and Kim (2010) find that the abnormal returns for U.S. targets in cross-border partial acquisitions are negatively related to the information asymmetry variables. This result suggests that information asymmetry reduces the monitoring power of the partial acquirers and weakens the partial acquisition impact on target firm performance.

Exhibit 29.2 summarizes the key factors that affect the long-term performance of the target firm. The factors are classified into three broad categories: external corporate control change, internal corporate control change, and the identity of acquiring firms. Under each category, the exhibit lists specific factors and indicates their impact on target firm performance. The exhibit shows that partially acquired firms experience improved performance when they are subsequently taken over by full acquisitions or their shares are repurchased by the target firm. Target firms that experience internal corporate control changes, such as management turnover or a proxy fight, also have better firm performance. However, no significant performance change is observed if the target firm does not have external or internal corporate control change. Further, depending on the motivation of the acquiring firms, the activist acquirers have the most positive effect on target firm performance. Strategic and financial acquirers do not add consistent and significant value to the target firms. Evidence suggests that the closer the geographic distance or the less asymmetric information between the acquiring and target firms, the stronger is the monitoring power of the acquiring firm in the partial acquisition, which leads to better target firm performance.

SUBSEQUENT FINANCIAL POLICIES AFTER
THE PARTIAL ACQUISITIONS

Using a partial acquisition sample permits direct observation of the target firm's postacquisition policy changes. It reveals insights about the integration process and also sheds light on the interrelated monitoring relationships between the target and acquiring firms. Spencer, Akhigbe, and Madura (1998) examine how the degree of control imposed by the partial acquirer affects subsequent financial policies enacted by the partial target. Based on a sample of 215 partial acquisitions between 1980 and 1993, the authors examine three types of financial policies after the partial acquisitions: acquisitions, divestitures, and dividends. The subsequent acquisition sample consists of 86 partial targets announcing acquisitions between 1980 and 1993. The authors find that the abnormal return is not significantly negative for the partial target, while the partial acquirer's stock experiences positive and insignificant valuations. Their results also show that the acquisitions of related firms in the same industry create value for the partial target and acquiring firm. According to Spencer et al., this finding suggests that the market recognizes the monitoring effect of the partial acquirer on the acquisition decisions of the partial target.

Subsequent divestiture samples show that the partial target and acquiring firms both lose when the target firm divests a related business, while the partial target firm gains when divesting a nonrelated business. For the dividend increase events, both partial target and acquiring firms gain abnormal returns. For the dividend decrease cases, only partial target firms experience negative abnormal returns, which suggests that dividend reduction does not signal information about the partial acquirer. In the cross-sectional analysis, Spencer et al. (1998) find that the measures of the acquiring firm's monitoring ability have a positive impact on the announcement effect of the subsequent events (e.g., the percentage owned by the partial acquirer of the target, the presence of the partial acquirer on the board of directors of the target, and managerial ownership of the partial acquiring firm).

The results of the Spencer et al. (1998) study imply that the market not only interprets the actions of the partial target to revalue the target but also assesses how these actions may affect the partial acquirer. The study also suggests that a partial acquirer must be cognizant of its monitoring influence on its partial target. If the partial acquirer fails to effectively monitor the partial target's decisions (e.g., the partial target buying an unrelated firm), it too may share negative effects on its stock price. Further, Spencer et al.'s evidence shows that the acquiring firms with better monitoring capabilities can benefit both acquiring and target firms after partial acquisitions.

Akhigbe, Madura, and Spencer (2001) examine three other target firm financial events after a partial acquisition: seasonal equity financing, stock repurchase, and debt financing. Based on 92 partial acquisitions between 1975 and 1993, they find that some financing strategies send similar signals for both the partially acquired firms and their partial acquirers. For example, subsequent decisions by the partially acquired firm suggesting positive information about the firm's future cash flows (e.g., stock repurchase) produce positive share price reactions for the partial acquirer and target. Equity offerings by the partially acquired firm produce a significant negative share price reaction for both the partial acquirer and target firm, whereas debt offerings result in positive valuation effects for only the partial target firm. Based on cross-sectional analyses, the valuation effects of the partially acquired firms resulting from their financing strategies are conditioned on the monitoring power of the partial acquirer. When the acquiring firm is part of the same industry as the target firm, has more managerial ownership, and is better performing, investors respond more favorably to financing policies by the partial target firm.

Akhigbe et al. (2001) also examine the market reaction to the sale of target firm stocks after the partial acquisition. They find a strong, positive investor reaction when the partial acquirer sells its shares in the partial target firm to a third party and a corresponding negative reaction when it sells its shares in the open market. This provides further evidence of the importance the market places on the monitoring influence of a partial acquirer.

SUMMARY AND CONCLUSIONS

This chapter provides a synthesis of some important findings on partial acquisitions in the academic literature over the past 30 years. It focuses on the motivations for undertaking partial acquisitions as well as short-term and long-term consequences of the partial acquisition on firm performance. Moreover, the chapter summarizes several key factors identified in the literature that may explain the impact of partial acquisitions on firm performance. These factors include postacquisition governance and control change, acquiring firm identity and motivation, and the external information environment. Most studies reach a similar conclusion. Namely, target firms benefit from the increased monitoring power brought by the acquiring firms and postacquisition performance is positively related to the acquiring firms' monitoring efforts. The impact of the subsequent financial policies in the partial targets also reflects the interrelated monitoring relationship between the target and acquiring firms.

DISCUSSION QUESTIONS

1. How does a partial acquisition differ from a full acquisition? What are the benefits of studying partial acquisitions?
2. What are the motivations behind a partial acquisition?
3. Discuss how a partial acquisition may affect future firm performance and shareholder value.
4. Discuss some important factors that may affect partial acquisitions and target firm performance.

REFERENCES

Akhigbe, Aigbe, Jeff Madura, and Carolyn Spencer. 2001. "Financing Decisions and Signalling by Partially Acquired Firms." *Journal of Financial Research* 24:1, 99–118.
Akhigbe, Aigbe, Jeff Madura, and Carolyn Spencer. 2004. "Partial Acquisitions, Corporate Control, and Performance." *Applied Financial Economics* 14:12, 847–857.

Akhigbe, Aigbe, Anna D. Martin, and Ann Marie Whyte. 2007. "Partial Acquisitions, the Acquisition Probability Hypothesis, and the Abnormal Returns to Partial Targets." *Journal of Banking & Finance* 31:10, 3080–3101.

Amoako-Adu, Ben, and Brian Smith. 1993. "Comparative Study of Complete Tender Offers and Partial Acquisitions." *Journal of Banking and Finance* 17:6, 1097–1110.

Balakrishnan Srinivasan, and Mitchell P. Koza. 1992. "Information Asymmetry, Adverse Selection and Joint Venture: Theory and Evidence." *Journal of Economic Behavior & Organization* 20:1, 99–117.

Bethel, Jennifer E., Julia Porter Liebeskind, and Tim Opler. 1998. "Block Share Purchases and Corporate Performance." *Journal of Finance* 53:2, 605–634.

Betton, Sandra, and B. Espen Eckbo, 2000. "Toeholds, Bid Jumps, and Expected Payoffs in Takeovers." *Review of Financial Studies* 13:4, 841–882.

Bulow, Jeremy, Ming Huang, and Paul Klemperer. 1999. "Toeholds and Takeovers." *Journal of Political Economy* 107:3, 427–454.

Chari, Murali D. R., and Kiyoung Chang. 2007. "Minority Acquisitions as a Strategy to Mitigate International Acquisition Risks." Academy of Management Conference Proceedings. Available at www.iusb.edu/~sbres/randd/final/chari2007.pdf.

Chen, Shih-Fen, and Jean-Francois Hennart. 2004. "A Hostage Theory of Joint Ventures: Why Do Japanese Investors Choose Partial over Full Acquisitions to Enter the United States?" *Journal of Business Research* 57:10, 1126–1134.

Choi, Dosoung. 1991. "Toehold Acquisitions, Shareholder Wealth, and the Market for Corporate Control." *Journal of Financial and Quantitative Analysis* 26:3, 391–407.

Clifford, Christopher P. 2008. "Value Creation or Destruction? Hedge Funds as Shareholder Activists." *Journal of Corporate Finance* 14:4, 323–336.

Comment, Robert, and Gregg A. Jarrell. 1987. "Two-tier and Negotiated Tender Offers: The Imprisonment of the Free-riding Shareholder." *Journal of Financial Economics* 19:2, 283–310.

Datta, Sudip, and Mai E. Iskandar-Datta. 1995. "Corporate Partial Acquisitions, Total Firm Valuation and the Effect of Financing Method." *Journal of Banking & Finance* 19:1, 97–115.

Eyssell, Thomas H. 1989. "Partial Acquisitions and Firm Performance." *Journal of Economics and Business* 41:1, 69–88.

Greenwood, Robin, and Michael Schor. 2007. "Investor Activism and Takeovers." Working Paper, Harvard Business School.

Grossman, Sanford J., and Oliver D. Hart. 1980. "Takeover Bids, the Free-Rider Problem, and the Theory of the Corporation." *Bell Journal of Economics* 11:1, 42–64.

Holderness, Clifford G., and Dennis P. Sheehan. 1985. "Raiders or Saviors? The Evidence on Six Controversial Investors." *Journal of Financial Economics* 14:4, 555–580.

Jakobsen, Kristian, and Klaus E. Meyer. 2007. "Partial Acquisition: the Overlooked Entry Mode." In John Dunning and Philippe Gugler, eds. *Foreign Direct Investment, Location and Competitiveness, Volume 2 (Progress in International Business Research)*, 203–226. Oxford: Elsevier Science.

Jensen, Michael C. 1986. "Agency Costs of Free Cash Flow, Corporate Finance, and Takeovers." *American Economic Review* 76:2. 323–329.

Jennings, Robert H., and Michael A Mazzeo. 1993. "Competing Bids, Target Management Resistance, and the Structure of Takeover Bids." *Review of Financial Studies* 6:4, 883–909.

Kang, Jun-Koo, and Jin-Mo Kim. 2008. "The Geography of Block Acquisitions." *Journal of Finance* 63:6, 2817–2858.

Kang, Jun-Koo, and Jin-Mo Kim. 2010. "Do Foreign Investors Exhibit a Corporate Governance Disadvantage? An Information Asymmetry Perspective." *Journal of International Business Studies*, forthcoming.

Klein, April, and Emanuel Zur. 2006. "Hedge Fund Activism." ECGI Working Paper 140/2006.

Madden, Gerald P. 1981. "Potential Corporate Takeovers and Market Efficiency: A Note." *Journal of Finance* 36:5, 1191–1196.

Mikkelson, Wayne H., and Richard S. Ruback. 1985. "An Empirical Analysis of the Interfirm Equity Investment Process." *Journal of Financial Economics* 14:4, 523–553.

Park, Yun W., Zekiye Selvili, and Moon H. Song. 2008. "Large Outside Blockholders as Monitors: Evidence from Partial Acquisitions." *International Review of Economics and Finance* 17:4, 529–545.

Ravenscraft, David J., and Frederic M. Scherer. 1987. *Mergers, Sell-offs, and Economic Efficiency.* Washington, D.C.: Brookings Institute.

Reuer, Jeffrey J., and Mitchell P. Koza. 2000. "Asymmetric Information and Joint Venture Performance: Theory and Evidence for Domestic and International Joint Ventures." *Strategic Management Journal* 21:1, 81–88.

Rosenstein, Stuart, and David F. Rush. 1990. "The Stock Return Performance of Corporations that Are Partially Owned by Other Corporations." *Journal of Financial Research* 13:1, 39–51.

Roy, Asim. 1985. "Partial Acquisition Strategies for Business Combinations." *Financial Management* 14:2, 16–23.

Roy, Asim. 1988. "Optimal Acquisition Fraction and a Theory for Partial Acquisitions." *Journal of Business Finance & Accounting* 15:4, 543–555.

Shleifer, Andrei, and Robert W. Vishny. 1986. "Large Shareholders and Corporate Control." *Journal of Political Economy* 94:3, 461–488.

Singh, Rajdeep. 1998. "Takeover Bidding with Toeholds: The Case of the Owner's Curse." *Review of Financial Studies* 11:4, 679–704.

Spencer, Carolyn, Aigbe Akhigbe, and Jeff Madura. 1998. "Impact of Partial Control on Policies Enacted by Partial Targets." *Journal of Banking & Finance* 22:4, 425–445.

Stulz, René M., Ralph A. Walkling, and Moon H. Song. 1990. "The Distribution of Target Ownership and the Division of Gains in Successful Takeovers." *Journal of Finance* 45:3, 817–833.

Sudarsanam, Sudi. 1996. "Large Shareholders, Takeovers and Target Valuation." *Journal of Business Finance & Accounting* 23:2, 295–315.

Torabzadeh, Khalil, and Sema Dube. 2007. "Motives for Partial Acquisition: Evidence from the Effects of CEO Change on the Performance of Partially Acquired U.S. Target Firms." *Corporate Ownership & Control* 4:4, 103–111.

ABOUT THE AUTHORS

Pengcheng Zhu is an Assistant Professor of Finance at the Eberhardt School of Business at the University of the Pacific, Stockton campus. His research focuses on cross-border mergers and acquisitions, corporate governance, and emerging market finance. He has published in such journals as *Corporate Governance: An International Review, Journal of Educational & Behavioral Statistics, Journal of Modern Applied Statistical Methods, Canadian Investment Review,* and *Advances in Quantitative Analysis of Finance and Accounting.* Professor Zhu is a recipient of the Barclay Global Investor Canada Research Award in 2006. Before joining the faculty at the University of the Pacific, he taught at the Sprott School of Business, Carleton University. He also worked as a business analyst in a global management consulting firm in Canada. Professor Zhu received his Ph.D. from Carleton University and is a Chartered Financial Analyst (CFA).

Shantanu Dutta is an Assistant Professor of Finance at University of Ontario Institute of Technology (UOIT). Previously, he taught at St. Francis Xavier University,

Nova Scotia, and Assumption University, Bangkok, as a full-time faculty member. Before his career in academe, he served as a Finance Manager and Project Controller at Lafarge, a world leader in construction materials. Professor Dutta's research focuses on corporate governance, mergers and acquisitions, market efficiency, dividend policy, and technology management. He has published in *Journal of Banking & Finance, Global Finance Journal, Canadian Investment Review, International Journal of Theoretical and Applied Finance, International Journal of Managerial Finance, International Journal of Technology Transfer*, and *International Journal of Global Energy Issues*. He has also participated and presented papers at many scholarly conferences. Professor Dutta received the Barclay Global Investor Canada Research Award in 2006.

Answers to End-of-Chapter Discussion Questions

CHAPTER 2   MERGER WAVES

1. Motives for individual mergers include agency-related and hubris-driven motives as well as efficiency and market power/collusion–based motives. Agency and hubris–driven mergers should result in wealth losses for bidding shareholders and, due to the lack of synergies, would not create value overall. If the wealth loss from bidder shareholders is purely transferred to target shareholders, the combined net value creation would be zero. If the merger involves additional costs, the net value creation could be negative.

   More efficiency-based reasons include economies of scale and/or scope and the possibility of creating market (pricing) power through horizontal merger in a concentrated industry. In these cases, the combined net value creation is positive, but the premium paid determines how much of it bidder shareholders capture (resulting in positive bidder announcement return).

2. Some behavioral hypotheses are market driven, such as Shleifer and Vishny (2003), where overvalued equity directly leads managers to use equity as currency to acquire the real assets of targets. In others, the high valuation creates uncertainty for target managers as to whether the premium represents true synergies or misvaluation.

   In the neoclassical view, the rising stock market reflects aggregate economic activity as well as capital liquidity, both of which contribute to increasing merger activity. Thus, rising stock prices do not cause the merger activity but reflect the same underlying forces that cause the activity.

3. There are many ways to use international data to examine the causes of merger waves. First, using international data would potentially be a good test of the behavioral hypotheses in the following way. If global merger activity in an industry is more correlated than are the stock valuations across different markets, this result would tend to be consistent with neoclassical explanations of merger activity. Similarly, one might look at whether firms in high-value stock markets are buying firms in low-value stock markets, as the behavioral view would suggest. One could further test for valuation effects caused by relative currency appreciation that could affect merger activity.

4. More than one explanation exists for merger activity. These explanations do not have to be mutually exclusive. The existence and prevalence of neoclassically motivated mergers increases the likelihood of observing one of the other motives. If there were not good reasons to merge, then managers with bad motives could not pool with efficiency-increasing deals. Consequently, a bid would be revealing of agency problems and would not be approved. Consequently, an increase in efficiency-driven merger

activity actually facilitates a simultaneous increase in nonefficiency–driven activity. In this way, clustering of merger activity for efficiency reasons can provide sufficient transaction volume to camouflage the agency or misvaluation–driven deals.

CHAPTER 3   TAKEOVER REGULATION

1. Although takeover regulation is mainly seen as a mechanism to facilitate efficient corporate restructuring, it is also an important tool in terms of mitigating conflicts of interest among diverse companies' constituencies such as management, shareholders, and other stakeholders. Takeover regulation not only curbs conflicts of interest related to transfers of control, but also has a more general impact on the agency problems between management and shareholders, minority and majority investors, and other stakeholders. As such, it constitutes an important element of a corporate governance system.

    When companies have dispersed ownership, the primary role of takeover regulation is to facilitate corporate takeovers that restrain opportunistic managerial behavior. Small shareholders cannot effectively monitor the management due to coordination problems and have to rely on external monitoring via the market for corporate control. Part of the takeover activity focuses on poorly performing firms and aims at replacing poorly performing management.

    For companies with concentrated ownership, takeover regulation could function as a corporate governance device aimed at protecting minority shareholders' interests. Concentration of ownership and control can serve as an alternative mechanism that can mitigate the conflicts of interest between management and shareholders. However, the presence of controlling shareholders may also be associated with their potential opportunistic behavior toward minority shareholders. Overall, takeover regulation can have various provisions that perform corporate governance functions both in the case of a transfer of control and in the case of governance of ordinary corporate activities.

2. The mandatory bid rule provides the minority shareholders with an opportunity to "exit the company on fair terms" once a large shareholder reaches a certain level of ownership. The rule imposes a duty on the acquirer to make a tender offer to all shareholders once the acquirer has accumulated a certain percentage of the shares.
    * The mandatory bid requirement is justified on the grounds that, following the acquisition of a large block of shares, the remaining shares in the hands of minority shareholders may become illiquid and their value may plunge on the market. Anticipating this, shareholders may feel pressure to accept any offer the acquirer makes, even when the offer undervalues the company. The mandatory bid rule ensures that all shareholders have the opportunity to sell their shares to the acquirer at a fair price, thereby protecting the target's shareholders from being pressured by the acquirer to sell their shares at unfavorable terms.
    * Although the mandatory bid requirement may mitigate the problem of expropriation of the target company's incumbent shareholders by the acquirer, it also decreases the likelihood of value-creating restructuring. This mainly occurs because the rule makes control transactions more expensive and thereby discourages acquirers from making a bid in the first place.

3. The major takeover regulation provisions in the Unites States include the following:
    * No mandatory bid requirement
    * *Two-tier takeovers (as opposed to the equal treatment principle).* In contrast to the equal treatment requirement, takeover transactions in many individual states in the United States, including Delaware, can be structured as a two-tier offer consisting of two parts. In the first-tier offer, the acquirer pays a premium above the market price for a controlling block, whereas in the second tier, the terms are less favorable.

- *Appraisal right.* All state laws in the United States grant shareholders appraisal rights that allow them not to tender shares and, after the tender has closed, demand the controlling shareholder to purchase their shares at a fair price, which is typically determined by the court.
- *Freeze-out right.* This is similar to the squeeze-out right in Europe. The right grants a majority blockholder compulsory purchase power over the minority's shares, no matter whether the majority was acquired or not. The fair price in the freeze-out purchase is typically set by statute or by an outside expert and, in many cases, is determined as the average of past market prices.
- *Ownership and control disclosure.* Disclosure rules oblige companies to inform regulators and public investors when one of the shareholders accumulates a substantial share block in the company. In the United States, the minimum ownership disclosure threshold is 5 percent.
- *Allowable antitakeover measures such as a poison pill.* Poison pills are allowable antitakeover measures in the United States and, particularly, in Delaware. Regulators allow managers to adopt poison pills at their own discretion whenever they consider doing so is necessary.
- *Management discretion over takeover defense measures.* Delaware allows management to install antitakeover devices such as a poison pill following its own judgment and without asking shareholders' consent. Recently, an increasing number of U.S. companies have amended their articles of incorporation to require management to obtain shareholders' ratification for the antitakeover devices.
- *Mandatory bid rule.* The rule imposes a duty on the acquirer to make a tender offer to all the shareholders once it has accumulated 30 percent of the shares. The acquirer has to offer the target shareholders a cash alternative if it makes an equity offer.
- *Equal treatment principle.* The principle requires controlling shareholders, the management, and other constituencies to treat all shareholders within each individual class of shares equally. In the context of the mandatory bid, the U.K. equality principle requires the price to be equal to the highest price paid for pre-bid purchases.
- *Squeeze-out right.* The rule gives the acquirer the right to force minority shareholders who hold out in a tender offer to sell their shares to the acquirer at the same price as the tender offer. The squeeze-out rule in the United Kingdom applies after the acquirer has accumulated 90 percent of the equity.
- *Sell-out right.* If shareholders tender 90 percent of shares, the remaining shareholders can require the acquirer to buy out their shares at a fair price to exit the company. The sell-out price is typically the same as the price paid in the tender offer.
- *Ownership and control disclosure.* Disclosure rules oblige companies to inform regulators and public investors when one of the shareholders accumulates a substantial share block in the company. In the United Kingdom, the minimum ownership disclosure threshold is 3 percent.
- *Management neutrality.* The City Code in the United Kingdom imposes a requirement for the target company's board neutrality with respect to takeover offers, preventing the board of directors from taking actions that may frustrate a potential bid. The board should remain neutral and limit the use of antitakeover devices unless the shareholders at a general meeting approve an antitakeover strategy and only after the announcement of the bid.
- *Antitakeover measures only when takeover bid is made.* The City Code on Takeovers and Mergers in the United Kingdom prohibits management from taking any actions against a takeover without shareholder consent and limits the number of allowable antitakeover tactics to virtually none. Poison pills are forbidden in the United Kingdom.

- *Poison pills.* A poison pill refers to those types of takeover defense measures that effectively block an acquisition attempt or force the acquirer to pay a substantial premium to the target's shareholders. A well-known type of poison pill is a shareholder rights plan that grants the incumbent target's shareholders the exclusive right to buy a company's newly issued equity at a substantial discount. The right is conditional upon acquiring a certain percentage of shares by an outside investor. For example, a typical shareholder rights plan enables shareholders to exercise the right after an outside investor has acquired more than 15 percent of the target company's shares. In this case, the rights-holders become eligible to buy more of the company's shares at a lower than market price. An additional equity issue, in the wake of a takeover, dilutes the share block accumulated by the acquirer and makes the acquisition more costly and often virtually impossible. Therefore, many view the poison pill as a highly effective antitakeover device.

  Another form of a poison pill consists of "golden shares." A golden share grants a decisive vote that allows its holder to veto corporate decisions and overrule the voting outcome of all other shareholders. A government typically holds golden shares and implements its veto power through clauses in the company's articles of incorporation.

- *Changes in capital structure and asset sell-offs and spin-offs.* Companies can prevent a takeover by making a major change in their capital or assets structure. For instance, a company can take on more debt and use the borrowed funds to buy back its shares. A company may also engage in a leveraged buyout to prevent an unwanted takeover by using the borrowed money to buy back all of its shares and go private. Increased debt may make a company less attractive as a takeover target because an acquirer would ultimately have to pay out these debts. Not all companies can afford such defense tactics due to the limited access to and high costs of debt financing.

- *Voting rights restrictions.* Deviation from the "one-share-one-vote" principle by means of voting restrictions such as shares with multiple voting rights, non-voting shares, and voting caps represents effective antitakeover measures that discourage potential acquirers from making a takeover offer. Voting caps set a limit on the number of votes that a single shareholder can control, independent of the size of the shareholdings.

CHAPTER 4   CORPORATE GOVERNANCE AND M&AS

1. The two levels of corporate governance could be complements or substitutes in influencing firms' acquisition decisions. A complementary relationship may result if stronger investor protection at the country level needs to be invoked by independent boards or independent institutional investors to keep managers from making shareholder value-reducing acquisitions. A substitutive relationship is also likely if strong firm-level governance is especially valuable in countries with poor investor protection and accounting disclosure practices.

2. Corporate governance may play an even more important role in cross-border acquisitions than in domestic ones. Cross-border acquirers face major challenges because they must contend with unfamiliar political, regulatory, and industry conditions, limited and opaque information about potential targets, and foreign legal, cultural, and social norms. Consistent with these difficulties, Eckbo and Thorburn (2000) and Moeller and Schlingemann (2005) find that acquirers perform significantly worse in cross-border deals than in domestic deals.

3. As documented by Bliss and Rosen (2001), Grinstein and Hribar (2004), and Harford and Li (2007), acquiring chief executive officers (CEOs) often receive large bonuses and equity grants following the consummation of mergers even when their shareholders are worse off as a result of the transactions. These payouts are so substantial that they dwarf the incentives provided by CEOs' preexisting stock and option ownership, ultimately rendering these preexisting incentives ineffective.

4. The financial crisis of 2008 to 2009 highlights the importance of making better decisions that deliver shareholder returns in the long run. With this emphasis taking a front and center position in current discussions of governance and compensation reform, the relationship between corporate governance mechanisms and acquisition performance could become more pronounced, at least in the immediate aftermath of the crisis and possibly in the long run as well.

CHAPTER 5   ETHICAL AND SOCIAL ISSUES IN M&AS

1. Some of the main ethical issues that have been raised regarding M&As include:
   - The effect that M&As have on the various stakeholders such as the local community, workers, suppliers, shareholders, and creditors. Some ethicists believe that the only stakeholders who need to be considered are shareholders, whereas others believe that all stakeholders need to be considered.
   - The effect that M&As have on competition. Some contend that M&As are anticompetitive and move the industry in question closer to monopoly. However, studies generally indicate that M&As do not increase industrial concentration. Further, increases in industrial concentration are not necessarily bad. Some M&As actually cause competition to increase, especially in cases where a strong company rescues a weak company that might otherwise go bankrupt.
   - Fiduciary duty breaches. Corporate officers and directors sometimes make decisions that are in their own self-interest rather than in the interest of the corporation. They often resist a hostile takeover to protect their own jobs instead of protecting the shareholders.
   - Use of poison pills. A common belief is that the use of poison pills constitutes unethical conduct because it prevents or increases the costs of M&As. Studies show that most M&As are in the best interest of shareholders, so taking actions to prevent them does not benefit shareholders.
   - Greenmail. A general belief is that paying predators to go away using corporate assets is unethical. If a merger or acquisition would be good for the shareholders, which is generally the case, then using corporate assets to pay predators to go away works against the interests of the shareholders.
   - Golden parachutes. Golden parachutes can be ethical or unethical depending on how they are structured. If the effect of a golden parachute is to reduce or eliminate the incentive for top managers to act against the interests of the shareholders, they are a good thing. If golden parachutes act like a poison pill or dissipate corporate assets, then they are a bad thing.
   - Insider trading. Although widely considered to be unethical, insider trading is ethical in some cases. Insider trading makes markets work more efficiently, which in turn makes the practice ethical according to utilitarian ethical principles. However, the practice is unethical if a fiduciary duty is breached or if property or contract rights are violated. One problem in determining whether a particular action is unethical is that the property rights in information are not always clearly defined.

- Compensating stakeholders who are harmed as a result of a merger or acquisition. Some ethicists believe that certain stakeholders other than shareholders should be compensated if they are harmed as the result of a merger or acquisition. Other ethicists believe that a corporation has no duty to anyone other than shareholders. Justifying using corporate assets to compensate anyone who is not a party to the transaction (buyers or sellers of shares) is difficult.

2. Ethicists and others use several different and sometimes conflicting sets of ethical principles to resolve ethical issues regarding M&As. One set of principles is the utilitarian approach. Utilitarian ethics hold that an act or policy is good if the result is the greatest good for the greatest number, if the gains exceed the losses, or if the result is a positive-sum game. The main strength of the utilitarian approach is that it is a widely used ethical system and many people believe that it is a fair system.

   Utilitarian ethics has several deficiencies. First, maximizing more than one variable at the same time is impossible. One may try to maximize either the good or the benefit to the greatest number but not both at the same time. Second, accurately identifying and measuring gains and losses to various groups may not always be possible. Third, comparing interpersonal utilities is impossible. Finally, the utilitarian approach ignores rights because it is a consequentialist philosophy. The end justifies the means. If rights have to be violated to achieve the goal, they should be violated according to the utilitarian approach.

   By contrast, rights-based ethics avoids the structural deficiencies of utilitarian ethics. Rights-based ethics does not require calculating gains or losses or identifying affected groups. All that is needed is to determine whether anyone's rights have been violated. Any act or policy that violates even one person's rights is unethical. The problem with rights-based ethics is that it is an incomplete ethical system. Determining whether certain acts or policies are unethical is impossible under this system. Rights-based ethics provides no tools to analyze whether non-rights-violating behavior such as prostitution, taking drugs, or other victimless crimes is ethical.

   Duty-based ethics, such as Kantian ethics, asks whether a duty (such as a fiduciary duty) has been breached. If the answer is yes, then the act is unethical. One weakness in duty-based ethics is that it does not tell whether acts or policies that do not involve breaches of duty constitute unethical conduct. Some utilitarians would consider a breach of duty as one negative result that must be compared to the positive results. Utilitarians would attempt to balance the good with the bad, whereas Kantians would not. Kantians would focus their attention only on whether a duty has been breached.

3. Corporate officers, directors, and managers have a duty to do what is in the best interests of the shareholders. Sometimes, however, they take actions that are in their own best interests. For example, if a merger would likely result in the manager being fired, many managers would try to prevent the merger from being successful even if it is to the detriment of the shareholders. Managers place their own interests above those of the shareholders. Whether a breach of fiduciary duty can be justified ethically depends on which set of ethical principles is being applied. When applying Kantian (duty-based) ethics, the answer is that such conduct is always unethical. When applying rights-based ethics, breaches of fiduciary duty always constitute unethical conduct because they violate an implied or explicit contract between the shareholders and the managers to act in the best interests of the shareholders. When applying utilitarian ethics, the answer is less clear. Some utilitarians would merely view such breaches as a negative in the utilitarian calculus, something that must be weighed against some other positive aspects of the act or policy.

4. Those who argue that M&As should be regulated usually contend that regulation is necessary to ensure that all stakeholders are treated fairly and are protected or that

competition is not adversely affected. Those who oppose regulation of M&As believe that shareholders generally benefit from them. Studies tend to support this position, although not all M&As benefit shareholders. The problem involves the difficulty of knowing whether M&As benefit shareholders until after the fact. Advocates of no regulation also believe that the only stakeholders whose welfare needs to be considered are shareholders. Evidence generally suggests that M&As do not have an adverse effect on competition and may even strengthen it if a strong firm rescues a weak firm. Another argument in favor of not regulating such activity is the belief that all acts between or among consenting adults should be unregulated.

CHAPTER 6   THEORETICAL ISSUES ON MERGERS, ACQUISITIONS, AND DIVESTITURES

1. The quicker the second stage event occurs, the higher is the likelihood of a sell-off, especially if the parent's share in the initial public offering is relatively small.

2. Roll's (1986) hubris theory asserts that overconfidence leads managers to overestimate their abilities to identify and estimate potential synergies. Hubris may cause managers to overpay for the target firm and hence experience a winner's curse that increases the probability of failure. According to Goel and Thakor's (2010) CEO envy hypothesis, when CEO compensation increases with firm size and market value, CEO envy can cause mergers even if the initial trigger is idiosyncratic. Similar to the hubris hypothesis, the more envious CEOs are likely to overpay for the target firm.

3. In the Shleifer and Vishny (2003) model, managers of the bidding firm have private information about the degree of misevaluation and seek arbitrage profits via M&As. This permits the overvalued bidding firms to exchange expensive equity for relatively less expensive equity of target firms. In the Rhodes-Kropf and Viswanathan (2004) model, managers of the bidding firm have private information about the value of their firm as well as the potential value of the merged firm. But managers of the target firm cannot distinguish between systematic and firm-specific errors. This is why target firms rationally accept offers from overvalued acquirers.

4. A common explanation for this finding is that a firm's cost of capital decreases during a market expansion, leading to higher stock market valuation.

5. A focused divestment creates corporate value by eliminating peripheral activities while maintaining the core strategy. The rationale is that the market may be undervaluing the firm because of a lack of synergy between the parent firm and the subsidiary. The consequence is less complexity and information asymmetry and optimal pricing.

6. Khan and Mehta (1996) show that a firm divests via a sell-off when the subsidiary is experiencing low growth and stable earnings but prefers a spin-off when the subsidiary has high growth prospects and uncertain earnings.

CHAPTER 7   THE SHORT-TERM AND LONG-TERM PERFORMANCE OF M&AS

1. The finance literature offers three major reasons for the positive returns of target firm shareholders after the announcement of a merger or a takeover attempt: synergy, agency problems, and multiple bidders and bargain power. First, the synergy motive is based on the assumption that managers of both bidding and target firms desire to maximize

shareholder wealth. Otherwise, they would not engage in takeover activity unless both sets of shareholders gained. Second, the M&A literature indicates that acquiring firms look for targets that are currently poorly managed but have a strong potential for future gains. Such poor management is generally termed an agency problem. Once these target firms are acquired, stock returns for target firms increase in anticipation of disciplinary actions taken against target managers who perform poorly. Third, the possibility of multiple bidders for a target firm may lead to a price war among the potential acquirers. Further, target firms could adopt various antitakeover strategies to resist a takeover attempt. In such instances, bidding firms need to pay higher premiums, which would lead to increased gains for the target firm's shareholders.

2. The M&A literature focuses on various firm-specific and deal-specific factors that may result in abnormal returns. Some important factors are discussed below.
   - *Target type (public or private).* Bidders acquire targets for a better price when they buy a private (nonpublic) firm, as compared to a public firm, resulting in a better return for the shareholders of acquiring firms. Financial economists generally attribute such an outcome to the liquidity constraints of private targets. Further, shareholders of private firms are more likely to remain in the merged firm as blockholders and provide better monitoring of management actions.
   - *Methods of payment (cash vs. stock).* A bidder may use stock as the medium of exchange if the board believes that its firm's shares are overvalued. Alternatively, if the firm is confident about its current valuation, the board may offer cash in order to send a positive signal to the market. As a result, the market will view a cash offer more favorably than a stock offer.
   - *Cash reserves.* Cash reserves can provide a valuable source of funds for investment opportunities. Firms often accumulate much more cash than they require. Excessive cash reserves insulate managers from being monitored by the external market forces. Managers with an empire-building objective might use this extra cash in poor investment activities, such as nonproductive acquisitions, rather than distributing it to the shareholders. As a result, a high level of cash reserves in an acquiring firm is likely to generate a low level of abnormal returns.
   - *Relative size.* Acquiring a relatively large target is likely to be a more important economic event for the acquirer than acquiring a relatively small target. A larger relative size could result in more synergy and a positive effect. Alternatively, managing a larger target company could be more difficult, resulting in a negative effect. Also, as the size of a target increases, the target may have more bargaining power, which could result in the acquisition becoming more expensive for the acquiring firm.

3. Long-term studies on M&As typically report that acquiring firms experience significantly negative abnormal returns over one to three years after the merger. Such results are controversial because they contradict the notion of market efficiency and the goal of M&A activities. The following reasons illustrate this point. First, neoclassical economic theory assumes that managerial activities should lead to the maximization of shareholders' wealth. Therefore, M&A activities should not lead to wealth destruction of the acquiring firms' shareholders in the long run. Second, according to the efficient market hypothesis, the market should immediately digest the full impact of an acquisition surrounding the announcement date. Therefore, finding long-term stock return underperformance even three years after an acquisition is surprising.

Various studies examine this issue and find that results of long-term performance studies vary substantially regarding methodological choice and M&A characteristics. Some studies show that after resolving the methodological inconsistencies, long-term stock return performance disappears. Fama (1998) terms the long-term abnormal return results "chance results." Nonetheless, some studies still report long-term stock return underperformance. Such studies posit that market participants may require a long time before they realize the full effect of some complex corporate activities such as M&As. Hence, reporting of long-term abnormal returns for acquiring firms is not entirely surprising.

CHAPTER 8 STANDARD VALUATION METHODS FOR M&AS

1. Balance sheet–based methods are commonly used to evaluate a firm. These methods consider that a firm's value lies basically in its balance sheet. Because they determine the value from a static viewpoint, balance sheet–based methods do not take into account the company's possible future evolution and ignore the time value of money. Some of the more common methods are book value, adjusted book value, and liquidation value. Another type of method is based on a firm's income statement. They seek to determine the company's value through the size of its earnings, sales, or other indicators. For example, a common practice is to perform quick valuations of cement companies by multiplying their annual production capacity (or sales) in metric tons by a ratio (multiple); to value parking lots by multiplying the number of parking spaces by a multiple; and to value insurance companies by multiplying annual premiums by a multiple. Third, discounted cash flow (DCF) methods seek to determine a firm's value by estimating the cash flows it will generate in the future and then discounting them at a discount rate matched to the riskiness of these flows.

2. The most conceptually correct valuation method is based on cash flow discounting. This is because DCF methods seek to determine the firm's value by estimating its future cash flows and then discounting them at a rate reflecting the riskiness of these flows. Both economic theory and common sense support such methods.

3. There is no correct number for the market risk premium. For example, in his review of 150 textbooks on corporate finance and valuation published between 1979 and 2009, Fernandez (2009) finds that the authors of these books recommend an equity premium between 3 percent and 10 percent.

4. The term equity premium designates four different concepts. First, the *historical equity premium* refers to the historical differential return of the stock market over treasuries. Second, *expected equity premium* is the expected differential return of the stock market over treasuries. Third, *required equity premium* is the incremental return of a diversified portfolio (the market) over the risk-free rate required by an investor, which is used to calculate the required return to equity. Finally, the *implied equity premium* is the required equity premium that arises from assuming that the market price is correct.

CHAPTER 9 REAL OPTIONS AND THEIR IMPACT ON M&AS

1. Traditional capital budgeting methodology often uses net present value (NPV). However, expected NPV fails to adequately capture elements of managerial flexibility related to the opportunity to grow, delay, scale down, or abandon projects, exchange resource inputs, and incorporate learning or uncertainty resolution. Further, traditional capital budgeting that uses the cost of capital does not consider any flexibility that may arise regarding financing options. That is, the M&A may affect debt capacity, among other things. Failure to consider these additional elements may result in mispricing of the transaction for both the acquirer and the target firm.

2. In a corporate context, a real option refers to a decision point whereby the manager has the flexibility to change the course of action. By contrast, financial options represent the opportunity to buy or sell underlying assets in financial markets. An acquiring firm works to structure a deal with additional decision points over the life of the deal. For instance, the acquirer may gain the right to acquire additional assets at some point in time. In the context of real options, acquiring firms can actually gain from uncertainty because option values are based, in part, on timing and volatility.

3. The first type of real options is a growth option where firms may exploit synergies that affect the growth options of both the acquiring and the target firm. A second type is a flexibility option that allows for further adjustment in a variety of managerial practices such as marketing, manufacturing, and financing. The third type of real option is a divestiture or abandonment option, which can serve to limit downside losses to the acquiring firm.

4. There are several ways to structure a stock-for-stock M&A transaction. With a switching option, the acquirer can switch between alternate purchase considerations. Another framework is to use an exchange ratio swap, which is basically holding a cap and selling a floor with an identical strike price. With the collar type, managers can negotiate a range within which the deal may fluctuate. A fourth type is the ratchet or cliquet option, which includes a series of consecutive forward start options. The first option is active immediately, and then the second becomes active after the expiration of the first option.

5. *Competitive real options* are options that are exercised unilaterally by the parties with the objective of increasing the payoff for individual parties. Such options are modeled as competitive games and can also have agency features. An analogy is claiming a share of a fixed pie. *Cooperative options* are options exercised jointly by the parties to maximize the total deal value. These do not involve claiming but focus on creating value. Such collaborative real options fall within the boundaries of risk-sharing contracts. For example, typical M&A transactions may include or have the opportunity to enter into future research and development (R&D) joint ventures. A substantial part of target value may arise from the dynamics of such ventures.

CHAPTER 10   THE LAW AND FINANCE OF CONTROL PREMIUMS AND MINORITY DISCOUNTS

1. If someone such as an analyst is valuing a controlling block and if control has value, that value is already reflected in the prices of that controlling block. So, when valuing a controlling block, there is no need to apply a control premium. However, if the person is valuing a minority stake, the answer depends on why and for whom the person is valuing the minority stake. If the person is valuing the minority stake in an appraisal for a Delaware court, the current practice is to apply a control premium to control for the implicit minority discount. The Delaware courts have held that the prices of all publicly traded equity reflect a minority discount and therefore are less than the intrinsic value of the shares. However, this view is contrary to the efficient market hypothesis and is not held by most financial economists.

2. Although the empirical evidence is mixed, most of the results pertain to large, publicly traded firms that trade in liquid, well-regulated markets. Such markets are characterized by a relatively high level of transparency where minority shareholders are more likely to be able to use legal remedies to project their rights. Nagar, Petroni, and Wolfenzon (2010) study closely held firms that are private or illiquid and, therefore, operate in an environment that is not characterized by a high level of transparency.

They find that firms with a controlling shareholder and dispersed minority ownership significantly underperform relative to firms with no controlling shareholder and dispersed ownership. The authors attribute this difference to the majority controlling shareholder experiencing benefits of control at the expense of the minority.

3. The implicit minority discount implies that all equity prices are undervalued. However, if it were known that all equity prices reflect a minority discount and are less than their pro-rata share of the intrinsic value of the firm, trading would immediately eliminate such a discount. Therefore, no need exists to adjust for an implicit minority discount in a reasonably efficient market.

4. According to Delaware General Corporate Law § 262(h), the minority shareholders are entitled to the going-concern value of the firm, excluding any benefits anticipated to result from the acquisition.

5. In a squeeze-out merger, the law compels minority shareholders to sell their shares and to do so without the benefit of a third-party, arms-length transaction. Therefore, as a matter of equity, the law grants minority shareholders appraisal rights in squeeze-out mergers and requires the courts to see that such shareholders receive fair value for their shares.

CHAPTER 11   CROSS-BORDER VALUATION EFFECTS IN DEVELOPED AND EMERGING MARKETS

1. In many ways, motivations for cross-border M&As are similar to those of domestic M&As. Cross-border M&As are a channel to enable firms to take advantage of economies of scale and scope, synergy effects, and foreign market conditions such as lower labor costs. Entering a market in a foreign country can be full of obstacles such as conforming to the foreign government's regulations and laws, assessing a new customer base, dealing with new suppliers and employees, and setting up new distribution networks. Therefore, acquiring an already established firm with the existing infrastructure and know-how in place can be a much easier way to enter the new market than starting from scratch.

    Another reason for cross-border M&As is obtaining new technology that is unavailable in one's own country. Because technological innovations are typically patented, the only way to obtain them is through buying the patent-holding firm. Other motivations for cross-border M&As might stem from regulatory restrictions such as high tariff barriers for imports or legal barriers in entering certain sensitive industries such as defense, banking, and telecommunications. By engaging in M&As with a firm in the country with these regulations, the acquiring firm can sidestep these adverse regulations.

2. Cross-border M&As often involve multiple complex steps that are subject to fees. Before the merger, firms incur transaction costs due to legal expenses, banker fees, accounting fees, and advisor fees that are all necessary to conduct the merger. The other portion of the cost lies in the restructuring and integration after the merger is effective. Those costs involve stock option adjustments and implementing payroll, accounting, and information systems. Additional challenges and complications include different political systems in the target and acquirer nations. Also, adverse political developments might affect the success rate of the merger. Sometimes these costs add up to an amount that the acquirer firm is unwilling to pay and the deal can fall apart without realization. Other times, an M&A deal might go through but the acquirer and target firms realize that the

match does not realize the expected synergy gains in the long run. The Daimler-Chrysler merger is an example of a failed M&A transaction.

3. Acquisitions in emerging markets often raise questions of whether a target firm in the emerging market can enforce financial contracts as well as protect investors. Acquirers from developed markets going into emerging markets are particularly keen on protecting their intangible assets such as brand names and knowledge, which can be accomplished only with majority control. With control, acquirers from developed markets can improve corporate governance practices such as legal and accounting standards in the target that is located in an emerging market. Industries extensively using intangible assets have proprietary technologies that parent companies are unwilling to share unless they own the majority of the target and have better contract-enforcing mechanisms. Having majority control is a way to enable the acquirer to transfer its corporate governance onto the target firm and therefore protect the intangible assets that change hands during the transaction.

4. In a way, emerging market firm–initiated cross-border M&A deals into developed markets are not that different from cross-border deals initiated by firms in developed markets. Firms seek new markets and technology. The recent trend of emerging market firm acquisitions shows, however, that those acquirers are particularly seeking already established brands in the Western market. One of the major differences is that emerging market firms are targeting natural resources firms. Other differences are reflected in the restructuring processes in the target firms after the M&A occurs. Not surprisingly, emerging market firms implement changes in the target that are complementary to their comparative advantage, for instance, redirecting labor-intensive production from the developed market target to the relatively cheaper emerging market parent location.

CHAPTER 12   SOURCES OF FINANCING AND MEANS OF PAYMENTS IN M&AS

1. The sources of takeover financing comprise the way an acquiring firm raises capital to fund an acquisition of another company. Financing sources can be classified into three general categories: internally generated funds, equity issues, and debt issues including issues of bonds or loan notes and borrowing from a bank. Many acquiring companies use more than one source to finance their takeovers. The means of payment is what the acquiring firm is actually offering to the target's shareholders in exchange for their shares. This can be equity of the acquiring (or combined) firm, cash, loan notes, or their combination. Despite being closely related, the takeover financing sources and means of payment do not always coincide. Financing the takeover with internally generated funds or with debt implies that the acquisition is entirely paid with cash. Debt-financed acquisitions may also involve payment with loan notes. In contrast, equity financing may be used in acquisitions fully paid with equity, with cash and equity, or entirely with cash. An acquiring firm may either directly exchange the shares from a seasoned equity offering for the shares of the target firm (in all-equity and cash-and-equity offers) or sell its new shares and use the proceeds to pay for the acquisition (all-cash payment). When the acquirer issues debt and equity, it may pay for the target firm's shares with a combination of cash (and loan notes) and equity or with cash (and loan notes) only.

2. The vast body of theoretical and empirical literature documents that market imperfections induce systematic corporate preferences for specific sources of financing. These

imperfections can be partitioned into two dominant categories that explain financing preferences: cost of capital factors and agency-related issues. The former explanation upholds that market imperfections or institutional rigidities, such as information asymmetries, legal protection of shareholders and creditors, or taxes, may disproportionally affect the costs of debt and equity capital. The latter explanation endorses that a firm issues specific securities to mitigate agency problems among its management, shareholders, and creditors.

3. Strategic considerations, such as the need to diversify the risk of overpayment for the target, the risk of a change in the firm's control structure, and the risk of the bid's failure, generally drive the acquirer's decision on the payment method.

   The risk of overpayment for the target (due to information asymmetries between acquirer and target) is an important determinant of the means of payment in corporate takeovers (Hansen, 1987). In particular, high uncertainty about the true value of the target firm induces the acquirer to pay with its own equity rather than cash. Capital participation in the combined firm makes the target shareholders share the risk of potential downward revaluations after the takeover's completion.

   Another determinant is the threat of control change. Acquiring firms prefer cash to equity payment when they are vulnerable to the threat of control change. Faccio and Masulis (2005) document that a threat of a change in the corporate control structure, for instance, by means of voting power dilution or the emergence of an outside blockholder, may discourage acquirers from paying for the acquisition with equity.

   Still another determinant of the means of payment in corporate takeovers is the risk of the bid's failure. First, an equity payment is less likely to be offered in cross-border takeovers. The target shareholders may be reluctant to accept an equity offer from a foreign acquirer if the latter's shares are not traded in the target's country. Also, the regulation in the target's country may impose restrictions on foreign equity investments. Second, offers increase the probability of the bid's success in tender offers, mandatory bids, competing bids, and hostile takeovers, and are hence preferred by bidders in such types of transactions. Third, the incumbent owners of an unlisted target are more likely to accept a cash payment, as their primary incentive to sell the firm is frequently to cash out. Therefore, equity bids are also least likely when the target firm is unlisted or closely held.

4. The dominant explanation is that investors consider a seasoned equity offering as a signal that the acquirer's shares are overpriced and hence adjust the share price downward when equity financing is announced (Myers and Majluf, 1984). Managers attempt to time equity issues to coincide with surging stock markets or even with the peak of the stock market cycle (Baker, Ruback, and Wurgler, 2004). Shleifer and Vishny (2003) and Rhodes-Kropf and Vishwanathan (2004) contend that overvalued acquirers use equity to buy real assets of undervalued (or less overvalued) targets to take advantage of the mispricing premium over the longer term when the overvaluation will be corrected. The market may also interpret an equity payment as a negative signal about uncertainty with respect to the target firm's quality and potential takeover synergies. If the quality of the acquired assets is more uncertain, the acquirer is likely to pay with equity in order to share with the target's shareholders the risks of being unable to realize the expected synergies.

5. A growing body of literature advocates that regulation is an important determinant of corporate financing decisions. La Porta, Lopez-de-Silanes, Shleifer, and Vishny (1998), Levine (1999), and Djankov, McLiesh, and Shleifer (2007) argue that regulation affects the terms at which financiers are willing to provide firms with funds. When a regulatory

environment protects the providers of funds against expropriation by corporate management, external finance may be available at lower costs. Specifically, strong creditor protection assumes that lenders can more easily force repayment, take possession of collateral, or even gain control over the firm. This results in lower creditor risks and hence in lower costs of borrowing. Similarly, strong shareholder protection increases the relative attractiveness of equity financing. Better legal investor protection facilitates the use of external sources of financing.

The importance of a regulatory environment in takeover financing decisions is supported by data. Martynova and Renneboog (2009) show that acquisitions financed by equity (relative to those financed by cash) are more likely in countries with stronger protection of shareholder rights. This is consistent with the prediction that strong shareholder protection reduces the cost of equity capital and, hence, increases the attractiveness of equity as a source of financing. Also, when the creditor rights protection is high, acquirers prefer debt over equity financing. These results suggest that the legal protection of shareholders and creditors affects the costs of debt and equity capital and thereby induces systematic corporate preferences for the most appropriate (less expensive) source of financing.

6. Myers (1977) argues that the conflicting interests of shareholders and creditors may encourage firms to issue equity rather than debt to raise external funds. In his view, the wealth-maximizing preferences of shareholders dictate that managers undertake a project only if its expected benefits exceed the payments to debtholders. This may lead to underinvestment because managers may forego positive NPV investment projects if the expected benefits from the projects are sufficient to repay debt only, while leaving the shareholders' pockets empty. To minimize the scope of underinvestment, firms with high-quality projects may limit leverage and avoid further borrowing. As such, firms with high growth potential are more likely to issue equity to finance acquisitions.

CHAPTER 13   CULTURAL DUE DILIGENCE

1. Organizations maintain their existing cultures through four related processes: attraction, selection, socialization, and attrition. In general, potential employees will be attracted to organizations whose cultures reveal values that are similar to their own. Similarly, organizations are likely to choose employees who fit with the organization's personality and are likely to meld seamlessly with existing employees. Finally, those employees whose personalities, values, and work style preferences are not aligned with those of the organization are likely to be less engaged, happy, or committed to work and more likely to seek employment elsewhere.

Organizations often attempt to socialize new hires to shape the way these employees come to know the policies, norms, values, and expectations embedded in the existing culture. By carefully introducing essential aspects of culture to new members, organizations attempt to reinforce the core values and expectations for work. Some common methods in the socialization process offer new employees a realistic job preview, an orientation program, role models in the organization, and several specific requirements that must be met before one becomes part of the group. Organizations can change their cultures by changing leadership and policies that specify expectations for performance and stakeholder interaction.

2. Organizations reveal cultural preferences in various tangible ways including symbols (e.g., a company's logo or images used in marketing material), physical structures, language (e.g., jargon, slogans, slang, and common expressions), stories (e.g., anecdotes

about important moments in the organization's history), rituals (e.g., daily, weekly, or monthly routines that occur), and ceremonies (e.g., formal events and celebrations). Culture can also be revealed in less tangible ways, including the existence of implied norms and expectations for behavior (e.g., participation in "voluntary" organizational functions).

3. Person-organization fit indicates the extent to which a person's own personal values and personality align with those of an organization. When a person's preference for detail and precision, for example, is similar to the demands for a particular job, that person has a high level of "fit" with the job. Although fit is a strong indicator of a person's willingness to maintain membership in an organization, it is a weak predictor of an individual's job performance, which often depends on skill, training, resources, leadership, and support. While strong cultures tend to foster high levels of loyalty among employees who come to personally identify with the organization's core values, these same cultures are likely to alienate others who are not naturally inclined to exhibit similar preferences.

4. Organizations can ensure that newcomers will fit into the organization through a process of socialization in which new members develop relationships with existing members, acquire important information about the organization, and "learn the ropes" for how to carry out common functions. The process of socialization increases the likelihood that employees will come to understand and appreciate the traditions, core values, and expected norms of behavior that characterize an organization's typical operating environment. Essentially, socialization allows employees to (1) gather knowledge that is important for one's own specific job and for the successful functioning of the organization; (2) learn heuristics for decision making and problem solving; and (3) appreciate the organization's mission, vision, and strategic purpose. Whereas most firms can enhance and enforce cultural traditions by hiring new employees that "fit" with an organization's personality, firms involved in mergers, acquisitions, or complicated partnerships might pay particular attention to the processes by which new members are socialized. This is an important process for increasing the rate of long-term success for newcomers.

5. Walker (1998) offers a succinct and powerful guideline for integrating distinct cultures. To increase the chances for success, Walker recommends that senior managers (1) celebrate small and incremental victories during the integration process; (2) acknowledge value in past practices; (3) involve employees in managing the integration process; (4) identify ingrained behaviors that might become obstacles; (5) communicate details about the integration process; and (6) provide a clear rationale for the merger. Senior managers may also enhance commitment to the merger by establishing relationships built on trust, using training and socialization to enforce core values and expectations, and respecting both individual and temporal aspects of the integration process.

CHAPTER 14   NEGOTIATION PROCESS, BARGAINING AREA, AND CONTINGENT PAYMENTS

1. If the Chief Financial Officer (CFO) had not been through this negotiation process, an initial step could be to read several books and articles about the process to get different views on how to react to a proposal and how to conduct the negotiating process. The CFO could share materials with other members of the top management team. The CFO

could also organize a retreat for the top management team dedicated to rehearsing a hypothetical negotiation of the sale of the company. At the retreat, the CFO could present issues that are likely to be involved in an acquisition and discuss how to deal with each issue. The CFO could also involve an investment banker in this retreat and hire an expert at negotiation to coach the team on how to negotiate a deal.

2. A company goes to great lengths to keep confidential the fact that it is engaged in discussions to acquire another company. Some actions to prevent information leaks include the following:
   - Use code names for the project.
   - Limit knowledge of the discussions to as few people as possible.
   - Use outside consultants, investment bankers, accounting firms, and others to gather and analyze information about the potential seller.
   - Have team meetings at off-site locations.
   - Have written policies and guidelines pertaining to the confidentiality of this kind of information and prohibiting trading on inside information.
   - Have standard responses to inquiries about possible discussions that are taking place, such as "We do not disclose any discussions we are having about acquisitions and frequently engage in preliminary discussions of potential acquisitions."

3. There should be a single point of contact for any conversations with media representatives. If the press calls a member of the team, the call should be referred to the designated person immediately and without any comment. If the rumor is true, but a deal is not probable yet, the contact person can make the standard comment described above, namely, "We do not disclose any discussions we are having about acquisitions and frequently engage in preliminary discussions of potential acquisitions." If the deal is close to being probable and the rumor reflects accurate knowledge of the likely terms, confirming the discussions may be wise. The nondisclosure agreement with the seller may require the buyer to consult with the seller before making such disclosure.

4. Often, the management team for a seller has not previously been involved in an acquisition. The team has not gone through the thought process involved in the many issues that will be negotiated. As a result, the team has never given in-depth thought to the trade-offs that can be made among the issues or considered the priority or value of each issue in the overall context of a deal. When faced with these issues in the real-time environment of negotiating a deal, the management team may not adequately consider the choices that may be available to achieve its objectives or the consequences of trade-offs it may make on the various issues. By rehearsing a typical negotiation, the team can be educated on the alternatives and interaction among the issues and predict how the buyer will react to different approaches to reaching agreement on all of the issues. Often in the real-time environment of negotiations of this type, important issues are decided in minutes. Yet, if these issues had been considered beforehand, the outcome could have been much more beneficial to the seller's shareholders.

CHAPTER 15 MERGER NEGOTIATIONS: TAKEOVER PROCESS, SELLING PROCEDURE, AND DEAL INITIATION

1. The fact that the bid premium is, on average, the same for the two sales procedures suggests that negotiations are as competitive as auctions. This can be understood using

the two-stage takeover process introduced by Betton, Eckbo, and Thorburn (2009). In their model, the process starts with a one-on-one negotiation in which the target and the acquirer bargain under the shadow of an auction. Aktas, de Bodt, and Roll (2010) go a step further and emphasize that the first-stage negotiation takes place under the threat of an auction because the target always has the option to leave the negotiation table and start a competitive selling procedure. The threat of an auction during negotiations potentially explains why the bid premium in negotiated deals is, on average, identical to the bid premium in auctions. Potential competition acts as a latent factor that positively affects the bid premium in one-on-one negotiations.

Moreover, according to Boone and Mulherin (2007), choosing an auction versus a negotiation in a given takeover reflects a trade-off between competition and information costs. Ex-post targets seem to adopt, on average, the most efficient selling procedure, given their situation, asset specificity, and the economic environment in which the deal takes place.

2. The private component of the takeover process involves 7 steps:
   - The process starts with the initiation of the deal (whether it is by the target or the acquiring company).
   - After the initiation, the parties retain financial and legal advisors to provide professional advice regarding the deal.
   - With the help of these advisors, the target company chooses the selling procedure, which can range from a formal auction among multiple bidders to a negotiation with a single bidder.
   - The next step of the process is the signing of confidentiality and standstill agreements by potential bidders and the start of the initial due diligence.
   - Bidders then provide indications of interest. They propose a range of possible prices for the target. The bidders with the best possible prices are invited for additional due diligence.
   - After the additional due diligence, the remaining bidders submit formal private bids.
   - The private takeover process results in a merger agreement between the bidder with the highest offer and the target. This agreement includes the offer price (or the premium above a given market price for the target), the method of payment (proportion of cash and stock payment), and various protection devices for the acquirer such as termination fees.

3. The five factors that help explain the choice of selling method are as follows.
   - *Sensitive competitive information.* According to Hansen (2001), targets are more willing to limit the number of bidders when sensitive competitive information could be disclosed or when targets in R&D-intensive industries are expected to resort to more negotiations.
   - *Relative size of the asset being sold.* Auctions are more suited for relatively small targets and negotiations are more suited for relatively large strategic transactions with great potential for value creation (Boone and Mulherin, 2009; Subramanian, 2009).
   - *Acquirer size:* Large and well-known firms are more reluctant to participate in competitive auctions (Aktas, de Bodt, and Roll, 2010).
   - *Number of potential bidders:* Researchers argue that the likelihood of an auction is related to the potential depth of the bidder pool (e.g., Klemperer, 2002; Subramanian, 2009).
   - *Asset specificity or complexity:* Researchers contend that auctions are a better choice when the exchanged asset can be precisely specified (Subramanian, 2009) and/or is less complex (Betton, Eckbo, and Thorburn, 2008).

4.

A. Deal Characteristics	
Acquirer	McClatchy
Target	Knight Ridder
Deal value	$ 4.57 billion
Form	Merger
Payment method	60.075% Cash – 39.925% Stock
Offer price	$ 40 in cash + 0.5118 McClatchy Class A stock
Termination fees	$ 171.9 million
B. Investment Banks	
Acquirer	Credit Suisse Securities
Target	Goldman Sachs – Morgan Stanley
C. Takeover Process	
Selling procedure	Auction
Date of initiation	November 14, 2005
Initiating party	Target
Number of contacted bidder(s)	34
Confidentiality	21
Indications of interest	11
Private bids	1
Public bids	1
Announcement date	March 13, 2006
Completion date	June 27, 2006

CHAPTER 16   POSTACQUISITION PLANNING AND INTEGRATION

1. Jemison and Sitkin (1986) propose that the acquisition should be conceived as a process. Conceiving the acquisition as a process implies that it does not end with closing the deal but can last several years after it, depending on how the integration process unfolds. The reason for adopting a process perspective is to recognize the importance of what happens after signing the deal, namely, the integration process. Such a process is necessary because the presence of a fit between the two organizations does not in itself ensure successfully exploiting the expected benefits. Therefore, if any change occurs within the expected deadline for value creation, this could change the potential price that the acquirer is willing to pay.

2. The integration process is generally conceived as the process through which the acquiring company organizes the interaction with the target company and implements changes in order to exploit the expected synergies and forecasted cash flows. Haspeslagh and Jemison (1991) define the integration as the process through which the merging companies become one entity. If handled carefully and effectively, this process allows the merging companies to learn to work together and cooperate in transferring strategic

capabilities. The integration process is not a unitary process but involves two distinct processes: task integration, which deals with asset rationalization, and the human integration, which deals with employees' acculturation. Task integration involves capabilities transfer from one company to the other and resource sharing between the two companies. Task integration may also include the rationalization of activities through downsizing and asset sales. This most likely occurs in the case of an "overcapacity" M&A, and through this process, management can exploit synergies. Human integration refers to the process of building a shared identity among the employees of the merging companies.

3. Leadership is essential to effectively manage the integration process, because this process is often surrounded by great uncertainty and a leadership vacuum. Given the complexity of such a process, several people are likely to lead the process. Top management is responsible for defining the integration model, appointing the integration manager, and approving the manager's choices such as the transition team leaders' appointments. The integration manager is responsible for running the integration process. Finally, transition team leaders are responsible for undertaking specific integration tasks under the integration manager's supervision.

4. An integration leader should have the ability to guide people toward an intended change and to gain commitment within the integration team. Also, this individual should have a networking capability to ease the permeability of the merging companies' boundaries. To facilitate interaction among people, the integration manager should have both communication and relational skills. Others need to view this person as having the legitimacy to serve as integration leader.

   The integration leader performs different roles during the integration process. The first role the integration leader will perform is labeled "organizational maverick." It consists of promoting a cooperative atmosphere between integration teams. To achieve this end, leadership and communication skills are essential. The second role is labeled "transformational leader." Again, leadership and the ability to gain commitment play key roles for a transformational leader. As the integration process unfolds, the third role performed by the integration leader is as an organizational buffer to allay concerns, pressures, and political factors that can harm the effectiveness of integration teams. Performing this role requires legitimacy, networking capability, and communication skills. The fourth role is that of network facilitator. Performing this role means that the integration leader needs to promote cooperation and creativity within and among teams, spread the results of team cooperation, and promote creativity within teams.

5. Integration mechanisms are the tools available to the acquirer to foster task and human integration. Each of the seven integration mechanisms is intended to achieve one or more goals.
   - *Restructuring*: Allows for rationalizing assets through the accumulation/stabilization of similar activities and the combination/timing of flows of related activities.
   - *Formal planning*: Allows for reducing ambiguity and uncertainty thorough the formal preadjustment of activities.
   - *Management information system*: Improves the communication process through budgeting and reporting systems standardization.
   - *Transition teams*: Consist of members from both organizations in order to leverage the coordinative integration efforts. Transition teams help provide and communicate new information.
   - *Socialization*: Improves the coordination within merging companies and creates a common culture.
   - *Mutual consideration*: Reduces resistance and possible sources of conflicts and creates a more favorable climate toward the intended changes.

- *Human resources systems*: Reduce employee resistance by dealing with job design, rewards systems, personnel policies, and career planning.

    These tools require communication to foster integration and change. Open communication between the merging companies is a way to reduce ambiguity about the future.

6. There is no single metric to measure M&A performance. The research question at hand and the setting under investigation should guide the choice of an M&A performance metric. To identify a suitable measure for M&A performance according to the research question and the kind of deal under investigation, the M&A scholar should answer such questions as the following: What is M&A performance? When is M&A performance measured? What is the unit and level of analysis for M&A performance?

    Clearly specifying the first question refers to the meaning attached to the label "M&A performance." M&A performance can be conceived as both financial and nonfinancial performance. Moreover, M&A performance can be measured using different types of measurement, along different dimensions, and using different indicators.

    Regarding the second question, M&A scholars should be aware that M&As are process events, meaning that they unfold over time. The implication of the process nature of M&As is that measuring M&A performance after five days produces a different understanding of performance, as compared with measuring it after three years.

    The third question deals with the unit of analysis and the level of analysis for M&A performance. The unit of analysis could be the acquiring or the target company. Because these units of analysis reflect conflicting interests, M&A scholars should clearly specify for whom they are measuring performance. Other possible units of analysis could be the investment banks and business consulting firms. The level of analysis could be at the organizational level, as in the case of the acquiring or the target firms, or at the individual level of analysis, as in the case of employees.

CHAPTER 17   ORGANIZATIONAL AND HUMAN RESOURCE ISSUES IN M&AS

1. This statement may not always be true. Some contend that the greater the organizational fit, the higher is the probability of success of acquisition integration. The central argument of the process school of M&As is that the acquisition process itself, independent of strategic and organization fit, may affect the acquisition outcome under some conditions. The integration process, being a part of the acquisition process, may create barriers. Examples of such process-based barriers are activity segmentation, escalating momentum, expectational ambiguity, management style misapplication, determinism, and choice of the integration approach. Barriers may not occur in every acquisition, but their frequency varies with the circumstances. Some barriers are insurmountable. The best the managers can do is to understand these barriers to know how they might affect a particular event.

2. Research under this theme can be broadly classified into two parts: integration as a decision-making process and integration as a merging of two different organizational cultures. Researchers who view integration as a decision-making process posit that better outcomes are associated with the characteristics of the process that are used to make and implement integration decisions. Some researchers examine the impediments of the integration decisions, while others see them as the choice of a particular integration approach. Scholars also examine how the irrationality of decision making, in terms of

politicizing the integration issues in the situation of ambiguity and confusion, stymie the progress of integration. From the strategic standpoint, integration decisions are seen as characterized by a high degree of intrafirm linkage ambiguity. Researchers also advocate that human integration mediates the relationship between task integration and acquisition outcome. Another view states that value in M&As is created through the knowledge transfer between the merging firms. As a result, scholars examine the patterns of knowledge transfer and identify the factors that facilitate knowledge transfer under different integration approaches.

Another stream of research views organizational integration as a process of merging two different organizational cultures. As a result, some studies focus either on the acculturation process (modes of acculturation) or on the factors (autonomy removal) that affect the degree of acculturation. Some studies also document how cultural clash during the integration period affects employees' attitudes and behaviors. Last, a few studies suggest ways to reduce the cultural clash either by increasing interaction or by clarifying and addressing the actual cultural differences in a meaningful way.

3. The social integration literature contributes to an understanding of employee group behavior in M&As. Based on social identity theory, this school of thought recognizes that cooperation is necessary and the creation of a postmerger organizational identity is desirable. Researchers identify that premerger identity, sense of continuity, and future expected benefits are the three most important predictors of postmerger identification. Several studies find a positive relationship between the pre- and postmerger organizational identification. Sense of continuity is conceptualized in terms of uncertainty, perceived threat, and trust by the researchers. Uncertainty and perceived threat both affect postmerger identification negatively. Trust between the merging firms is positively related to postmerger identification. Some also suggest that observable and projected continuity are both important to establish an overall sense of continuity. Studies find that future expected benefits of a merger, such as better opportunities and team performance, are correlated positively with the postmerger identification.

The justice literature, with its domain in the legal and political studies, provides a basis for understanding the effects of the integration decision-making process on people's behavior. In an M&A context, this suggests that distributive and procedural justice applied in various people-related decisions (e.g., new pay structures, promotions, allocation of new roles, and termination decisions) during the postacquisition integration can be related to the M&A outcome in terms of goal achievement and postmerger identification. However, the above relationship is not simple. There could be complex interplay among the equity distributive rule, equality distributive rule, and procedural justice rule because some contextual factors, such as the relative power of parties and the nationalities of the merging firms, play an important role in the above relationship.

CHAPTER 18   TAKEOVER STRATEGIES

1. In large firms with dispersed ownership, owners (shareholders) may not have sufficient incentives to monitor the employees (managers). If an individual owner chooses to monitor managers, that owner has to bear the costs of monitoring including information gathering, analysis, and forcing managers to undertake shareholder value-maximizing actions. However, all owners share the benefits of such monitoring even if some of them choose not to be involved with the monitoring activities. This creates free-rider problems where some owners can take advantage of the actions of other owners without bearing any costs. In the case of potential targets, free-riding problems arise, for example, when owners need to expend resources in analyzing bids or even seeking potential bidders, negotiating with the acquirers, and complying with the regulatory requirements. The

benefits of successfully completing the takeover process accrue to all target shareholders, though the costs are borne only by those shareholders who are actively involved in the takeover process. Therefore, such free-rider problems in target firms can create inefficiencies, including delays and a lack of interest on the part of target shareholders to engage in negotiations.

Rational acquirers can anticipate such problems in target firms and take action to mitigate them. One possible approach is to undertake a minority ownership in the target, called a "toehold," before launching the takeover bid. Since acquirers become a shareholder in the target, they can play an active role in takeover negotiations and mitigate inefficiencies. Alternatively, acquirers can impose (often implicitly) threats of post-takeover dilution through mechanisms such as unfair transfer pricing schemes, target asset disposal, and compensation to acquirer managers. Such measures can cause target shareholders to take an active interest in the takeover process to protect firm value and mitigate delays and value losses.

2. Stock-for-stock acquisitions are more likely to qualify for tax-free status under section 368 of the Internal Revenue Code, in which case target shareholders need not pay capital gains tax on the payment received (acquirer's shares) until they actually sell the shares. In the absence of the tax-free status, target shareholders are liable for taxes immediately upon completing the deal. If acquirers structure the takeover as a stock exchange offer, they can avoid having to compensate target shareholders for their tax liability, which would arise from, for example, a cash offer that is not tax-free. However, a stock exchange offer is subject to adverse market reaction when the takeover is announced. Therefore, the acquirer would need to carefully consider the timing and disclosures related to acquisition announcement. Thus, taxes can have several direct or indirect effects on the acquirer's takeover strategies.

3. In the business press and among practitioners, much is made of the distinction between friendly and hostile takeover offers. A common assumption is that friendly takeovers are initiated with a view to unlock synergistic gains between the two firms, while hostile takeovers seek to remove inefficient target management and improve firm performance. Consequently, a general belief is that friendly offers have a greater likelihood of being welcomed by the target firm and, thus, are more likely to succeed. However, academic studies such as Schwert (2000) cast doubt on such distinctions and suggest that the supposed differences between the two kinds of offers are difficult to establish empirically. Often what appears to be a friendly takeover ex post started as a hostile bid. Therefore, the friendly versus hostile distinction could be more semantic than substantial.

4. In general, equity issues are associated with information asymmetries between issuers and investors (Myers and Majluf, 1984). Specifically, acquirer managers are more likely to use their own stock as compensation when they believe the stock is overvalued. Consistent with this argument, the market punishes equity issues in general and stock-for-stock acquisition announcements in particular. However, other considerations include taxes, desired capital structure (leverage), dilution of control rights, market conditions, ease of transaction, and registration requirements with the Securities and Exchange Commission. In addition to stock returns at announcement, the method of payment has also been linked to post-takeover performance consequences. Empirical studies generally find that stock-for-stock deals tend to underperform cash deals over several years after the acquisition.

5. Acquirers often use collars in conjunction with floating rate stock exchange offers where the number of acquirer shares to be given to the target shareholders is not fixed but depends on the actual share prices prevailing at the time of deal completion. Therefore, predicting the final exchange ratio at the time of the merger announcement is impossible, because it depends on the relative movement in acquirer and target stock prices. In

such cases, target shareholders could demand protection against adverse movements in stock prices that would dilute their control rights in the merged firm. Collars specify the upper and lower bounds around the exchange ratio within which the deal is to be realized. Thus, collar offers can be viewed as insurance for target shareholders against unanticipated variations in the acquirer's stock price.

Yet, termination or breakup fees offer protection to the acquirers against deal failure. Acquirers have to expend substantial resources to identify and evaluate potential targets. Further, during negotiations acquirers may be required to disclose nonpublic information to target firms. In such situations, acquirers would have to bear a high cost if the target begins to seek rival bidders and the deal fails. By imposing termination fee provisions, acquirers hope to dissuade targets from "shopping around" and to expedite deal completion. Thus, termination fees are a bonding mechanism that makes the takeover process more efficient from the acquirer's point of view.

6. Toehold share ownership is a minority stake purchased by the acquirer in a potential target before the acquirer launches a full-scale bid. Toeholds presumably benefit acquirers in several ways. First, they allow the acquirer to assume an insider position by becoming a shareholder in the target firm. Thus, the acquirer hopes to influence the decision-making process within the target firm and secure better terms. Second, target shares prices typically increase after a takeover announcement in anticipation of a bid premium. Such announcements may also attract rival bidders. If the acquirer is eventually unsuccessful in winning the target, its toehold purchase allows it to realize a profit upon selling those shares and thus earn a return on its investment.

CHAPTER 19   DEFENSE STRATEGIES IN TAKEOVERS

1. Before the beginning of the crisis, many corporations abandoned preventive anti-takeover provisions in their corporate bylaws due to strong shareholder pressure. That alone could have led to an increasing number in hostile takeovers. However, the financial crisis caused even stronger pressure on the hostile takeover market. Many economically challenged corporations got weaker during the crisis and thus became easy targets for financially strong corporations. Additionally, decreasing corporate valuations, low stock prices, and historically low interest rates allowed healthy companies to impose hostile takeovers on weakened target firms. Because most of these companies had abandoned preventive anti-takeover strategies and lacked the financial means for remedial defense tactics, their shareholders ran the risk of being exploited by the bidding companies. Thus, politicians called for stronger shareholder protection in order to prevent bidding companies from exploiting the shareholders of financially distressed companies.

2. Stockholder A would prefer short-term value maximization. Therefore, the stockholder would prefer an anti-takeover provision because it would lead to a highest possible takeover premium. The threat of triggering a poison pill could increase the takeover premium, the same way a competing bidder in the form of a white knight would increase the premium. For stockholder B, the goal clearly has to be long-term value maximization. Thus, the stockholder would want either efficient management to work undisturbed from hostile takeover attempts or inefficient management to be replaced by a bidder for a fair price.

The goal for stockholder A is short-term value maximization. Target companies usually see strong short-term stock movements after the announcement of a planned takeover. Next to the economic validity of the deal (e.g., the use of synergies), takeovers usually involve a premium over the current stock price, which target shareholders receive for their shares. This premium is reflected in the price increase of the targets' shares. Stockholder A would hence benefit from a takeover announcement. Thus, any kind of preventive anti-takeover provisions would harm stockholder A because these provisions would defer potential bidders from engaging in takeover attempts and would result in lost premiums. However, stockholder A should also be interested in maximizing the takeover premium. This can be done if the target company has certain provisions in place that strengthen the target's bargaining position. A stronger bargaining position allows the target to negotiate the premium with the bidder. The result should be higher premiums for the stockholders. Any kind of anti-takeover provision can enhance a target's bargaining position. Therefore, the question cannot be answered conclusively. The trade-off is between the maximization of the premium through better negotiating, which is supported by anti-takeover provisions, and the risk of deferring a potential bidder through anti-takeover provisions.

3. Both remedial and preventive anti-takeover strategies generally facilitate management entrenchment. Such strategies allow management to defend against acquiring companies, which, in most cases, aim at replacing the target company's management. However, some strategies allow for longer-term entrenchment than other strategies.
   - *Staggered boards.* Such boards prevent a bidder from replacing the whole board at once. Yet, especially for a persistent bidder, staggering a board only defers a replacement. However, empirical evidence shows that from 1996 to 2000, not a single takeover attempt succeeded against a staggered board of directors. This finding alone could imply that a staggered board of directors is a very useful entrenchment tool for management. This is why shareholder activist groups have most recently begun to call for an abandonment of these tactics.
   - *Poison pills.* Some studies conclude that the market views poison pills as a means to entrenchment. Empirical evidence finds that slight stock decreases occur when firms announce the adoption of poison pills, implying that shareholders do not value the enactment of poison pills. Other studies show that companies in which managers do not hold any shares usually enact poison pills. Based on these empirical findings, a possible conclusion is that poison pills serve as a tool for management entrenchment. However, the many positive aspects of poison pills, such as putting a company up for auction and gaining a better bargaining position, actually benefit shareholders. Thus, possible management entrenchment might be acceptable considering such benefits.
   - *Golden parachutes.* Golden parachutes can support management entrenchment. To forego having to pay large lump sum payments, shareholders and bidders often choose not to "lay off" a target's management.
   - *Jonestown defense.* This tactic facilitates entrenchment only in the short term. If a target sells all assets and successfully averts the takeover, the target company will have lost most, if not all, of its economic value.
   - *Greenmail.* The use of greenmail facilitates entrenchment. Because the acquirer mainly wants to make profits by reselling the shares to the company, a hostile company would not want to replace target management.
   - *White knight.* Using a white night facilitates entrenchment. A white knight is usually a "friendly" company that allows the target's management to stay in office. Target management would not choose a white knight whose intention would be to replace the managers.
   - *Pac-Man.* The Pac-Man defense facilitates entrenchment. Buying the potential bidder retains the target's management board and prolongs its tenure.

4. An unregulated market would mean that all anti-takeover tactics are allowed. The market for corporate control actually serves as a sort of a control mechanism to replace inefficient management or to force managers to work efficiently and maximize corporate value. If all companies had the opportunity to defend against hostile takeovers with

all means possible, management would have fewer incentives to work efficiently. That is, the threat of being taken over and being replaced would be strongly reduced. In this respect, shareholders would be harmed. A second disadvantage for shareholders is that they would not get paid premiums for their shares in case of a takeover. However, shareholders could benefit if target companies can defend against hostile bids that do not pay an adequate amount of money for the company. The same rationale goes for "putting a company up for auction." If a target can fend off a "bad" deal, it may be able to find a "better" bidder. If legislation forbade all anti-takeover provisions, shareholders could be assured that corporate managers would have to work efficiently and maximize firm value. On the other hand, the shareholders would run the risk of being "bought out" of the company by a hostile bidder at unfavorable terms.

CHAPTER 20   THE IMPACT OF RESTRUCTURING ON BONDHOLDERS

1. The basic principal-agent conflict between shareholders and managers arises from management trying to extract both pecuniary and nonpecuniary benefits from the firm, while transferring some or all of the cost incurred to the outside shareholders. An important source of such benefits may be managerial empire building. Empire building is closely tied to the argument that managers prefer building less risky, diversified firms with lower leverage, so that they can reduce the uncertainty of their human capital investment in the firm, thus lowering the probability of bankruptcy and employment risk. To that end, the risk preferences of managers are closely aligned with those of creditors but in direct conflict with those of shareholders.

2. The principal-agent conflict between creditors and shareholders can give rise to several agency problems in the context of the firm. The asset substitution problem captures the fact that shareholders may expropriate creditor wealth without affecting total firm value by substituting low-risk assets with high-risk ones. Claims dilution may also significantly damage the interests of existing creditors. These problems are anticipated by creditors, who price their debt accordingly, transferring the ensuing costs to the firm itself. Bondholders may also write protective covenants into the bond indenture, while private lenders respond through increased monitoring and continuous renegotiation of the debt contract. Keeping debt maturity short also mitigates the agency costs of debt.

3. *Portfolio restructuring* makes disposals from and additions to a firm's businesses such as through asset sales, spin-offs, equity carve-outs, or M&As. *Financial restructuring* changes the firm's capital structure, for example, through leveraged buyouts (LBO), leveraged recapitalizations (LR), share repurchases, or employee stock ownership plans (ESOP). Finally, *organizational restructuring* represents a change from a functional to a business-unit design. These restructurings often occur simultaneously or sequentially at any one time.

4. Corporate restructuring and portfolio refocusing in particular are often preceded by public-to-private transactions. These transactions are typically referred to collectively as leveraged buyouts (LBOs), as they are almost exclusively financed with massive leverage. The majority of LBOs are management led, but firms can be taken private by a variety of entities: the incumbent management (management buyout, MBO), outside management (management buyin, MBI), employees (employee buyout, EBO), or institutional investors and private equity firms (institutional buyout, IBO).

   LBO firms typically provide strong incentives for managers to maximize firm value by offering them considerable equity stakes, as well as contain managerial agency problems by boosting leverage and concentrating ownership. Better expectations of firm performance tend not to compensate creditors for the huge risk effect of the leverage increase.

5. Evidence on how restructuring affects bondholders is often inconclusive or conflicting. In *portfolio restructuring*, spin-offs and asset sell-offs reduce bondholder wealth by expropriating collateral and increasing cash flow volatility (unless subsequent improvements in operating performance are large enough to compensate). M&As reduce or leave bondholder wealth unchanged except under specific conditions, which implies that shareholders try to reverse any reduction in default risk in the combined firm. In *financial restructuring*, new debt issues do not reduce bondholder wealth unless motivated by cash flow shortfalls, but bondholders respond negatively to new bank loans. New equity issues tend to increase bondholder wealth, though negative signaling effects can dominate. The impact of security exchanges is unclear due to strong signaling implications. Executive stock options reduce bondholder wealth, reflecting the realignment of managerial and shareholder interests at the expense of creditors. Leveraged buyouts reduce bondholder wealth and conflicting evidence exists on the impact of leveraged recapitalizations. The impact of dividend changes and share repurchases is ambiguous, reflecting strong signaling effects.

CHAPTER 21   BEHAVIORAL EFFECTS IN M&AS

1. Neoclassical theory assumes that rational managers who act in informationally efficient financial markets drive M&As. When both managers and investors act rationally, motives such as lowering costs and increasing profits will drive merger activity. Because managers do not display cognitive biases and investors can adequately assess the implications of a merger, mergers should display performance improvements. Thus, one of the rationality assumption consequences is that economic reasons motivate activity in the market for corporate control and thus lead to measurable postmerger performance improvements.

2. Merger waves can occur under both the neoclassical paradigm and behavioral explanations. The classic view stipulates that industry shocks such as innovation and industry regulation give rise to merger waves. The assumption is that economic reasons motivate mergers. Neoclassical theories emphasize that economic, technological, and regulatory shocks to an industry environment generate merger activity. In response to these shocks, firms both inside and outside a particular industry typically embark on an M&A asset reallocation process. As firms simultaneously react to identical shocks and compete for the most suitable asset reallocations, merger activity clusters in time, leading to merger waves.

    Overconfidence cannot explain merger waves, because there is no logical reason to presume that a large number of executives simultaneously suffer from hubris. However, merger waves can exist under the assumption of chief executive officer (CEO) rationality. For instance, this can occur when merger waves end and when the ex-post experience of recent adopters is sufficiently poor, deterring the remaining firms from adoption ex ante. Thus, merger waves and the underperformance of merger wave late entries are consistent with managerial rational behavior but not with late movers making the wrong decision.

    While overconfidence cannot explain merger waves, the market timing approach to merger waves can. The market timing approach stipulates that highly valued firms face incentives to lock in excess value by acquiring undervalued firms. Thus, market timing is a form of arbitrage conducted by rational CEOs in informationally inefficient markets.

3. The main reason for the superior performance of cash-financed acquisitions is believed to lie in the market-timing approach to M&As. The basic argument is that management's perception of a company's valuation drives acquisitions. If managers believe that their firm is overvalued, they will seek to preserve some of the excess value for shareholders by purchasing relatively undervalued equity with their overvalued stock. Shleifer and Vishny's (2003) model advances a behavioral rationale for both the occurrence of M&As (i.e., to capitalize on temporary equity misvaluations) and the mode of acquisition payment (i.e., equity for overvalued bidders). In essence, the model describes managers as being rational when identifying inefficiencies in asset prices and acting to capitalize on these inefficiencies.

Consequently, high value-to-book firms purchase low-valuation firms. Thus, overvalued firms (or more precisely, firms where managers believe that the equity is overvalued) will prefer equity-financed deals. In anticipation of falling equity prices in the postmerger period, investors have a clear preference for cash over stock-financed deals. This is because cash-financed deals will not be the subject of market-timing considerations by the CEO.

4. Agency theory varies from behavioral finance in one important aspect. The main difference is that corporate governance relies on the presence of managerial moral hazard or opportunism. This is different from the assumption that inflated takeover valuations and underperforming deals are by-products of hubris. In other words, agency theory views managers as opportunistic, while the behavioral school believes that managers engage in good faith mismanagement.

Nonetheless, some corporate governance aspects can be linked to behavioral effects in mergers. Executive compensation provides a good example of this. If higher CEO pay packages inadvertently provide positive feedback to CEOs (that is, serving as a sign of success), higher CEO pay will most likely boost CEO confidence. Another fair assumption is that the highest paid CEOs in an industry suffer from inflated senses of self-worth. Next to absolute levels of pay, the dispersion of pay across the industry or board is likely to breed managerial overconfidence. Stressing the behavioral consequences of CEO pay on overconfidence offers a behavioral approach that can explain why managers overinvest in the market for corporate control.

CHAPTER 22 FINANCIAL RESTRUCTURING

1. While tax burdens on dividends were heavier relative to capital gains before the mid-1980s, the risk of violating the antimanipulative provisions of the Securities Exchange Act of 1934 deterred most corporations from repurchasing shares (Grullon and Michaely, 2002). Indeed, after the Securities and Exchange Commission adopted Rule 10b-18 in 1982, which provided a safe harbor to repurchasing corporations, repurchase activity experienced an upward structural shift. Just one year after the approval of Rule 10b-18, the aggregate amount of cash spent on share repurchase programs tripled. Since then, the level of share repurchase activity in the United States has been at record highs.

2. Bagnoli, Gordon, and Lipman (1989) show that stock repurchases serve as a defense against takeover by signaling management's private information regarding firm value. Additionally, Bagwell (1991a) shows that when shareholders possess heterogeneous valuations, the shareholders who are willing to tender in a repurchase are systematically those with the lowest valuations. Therefore, repurchase programs skew the distribution of the remaining shareholders toward a more expensive pool, raising the cost of takeover. Billett and Xue (2007) argue that open-market repurchases affect the takeover process differently than tender offers. While tender offers are an effective defense in the midst

of takeover battles, open-market repurchases may deter unwanted bids, preempting would-be acquirers from bidding in the first place.

3. Dual-class firms are virtually immune to hostile takeovers. The typical dual-class firm issues two classes of common stock: a publicly traded "inferior" class of stocks with one vote per share and a nonpublicly traded "superior" class of stock with 10 votes per share. Almost without exception, the class of shares with superior voting rights sells at a premium over the class with inferior voting rights. The most common voting structure is 10:1, in which the superior class has 10 votes per share and the inferior class has one vote per share. On average, the insiders of dual-class firms own a majority of the voting rights (about 60 percent) and a large minority of the cash flow rights (about 40 percent). The other forms of antitakeover protection are no match for the power of dual-class stock.

4. DIP financing is a court-approved financing available to firms filing Chapter 11. Such financing is made possible by the "automatic stay" provision of bankruptcy law and the ability of the court to grant super-priority status to the DIP lender. The borrower has to pay off DIP loans completely before emerging from Chapter 11. According to Dhillon, Noe, and Ramirez (2007), about half the firms filing for Chapter 11 obtain DIP financing. The market perceives an announcement of DIP financing as a good signal. More specifically, Dahiya, John, Puri, and Ramirez (2003) find that the DIP-financed firms, relative to non–DIP-financed firms, are both more likely and are quicker to emerge from Chapter 11, have a shorter reorganization period, and are quicker to liquidate. Dhillon et al. find evidence of a positive stock price reaction to DIP announcements. Firms employing DIP financing also have more successful reorganizations.

CHAPTER 23   GOING PRIVATE AND LEVERAGED BUYOUTS

1. Private equity activity is subject to boom and bust cycles, which are driven by the level of interest rates relative to earnings and stock market values. This especially applies to larger public-to-private transactions. From the summer of 2007, interest rates on buyout-related debt have increased substantially. Consequently, firms have had difficulty raising buyout debt. The recession has also had a negative effect on corporate earnings. In this setting, private equity activity, particularly large public-to-private transactions, is likely to be relatively low.

2. A likely expectation is that private equity firms will make investments with lower levels of leverage due to less favorable conditions in debt markets and the lower availability of debt financing. Whether the securitization markets for senior bank debt used in buyout deals will revive again is questionable. With less leverage available, cross-sectional differences in the performances of private equity firms may become more important and visible. Some scholars and practitioners predict that private equity firms will be more likely to take minority equity positions in public or private companies rather than buy the entire company. This would imply that large public-to-private LBOs may occur less frequently in the near future.

3. In public-to-private LBO transactions, private equity firms buy public companies, fix them, and then exit (sell their equity holdings). Most research papers that studied LBOs in the 1980s contend that private equity firms mitigate managerial agency problems, thereby creating value by improving management and operating efficiency. These papers emphasize three mechanisms: (1) increased managerial incentives through concentrated equity ownership, (2) the disciplining effect of greater debt on managers,

and (3) enhanced governance and monitoring by private equity firms. More recent empirical results suggest that post-1980s public-to-private transactions may differ from those of the 1980s in how they create value for both private equity investors and the portfolio companies in which they invest. Empirical studies of investor returns at the private equity fund level or the portfolio company level in post-1980s public-to-private transactions show that high returns to private equity investors cannot be solely attributed to improvements in operating performance after going private. For instance, Guo, Hotchkiss, and Song (2010) document that increases in industry and market valuation multiples and tax shield benefits of debt are each as important in explaining the realized returns to capital as changes in operating performance.

4. Recent empirical evidence suggests that buyout funds are more scalable than venture capital (VC) funds and that past success has a differential impact on the terms of their future funds. The scalability of their business allows buyout firms to sharply increase the size of their funds and the size of the capital managed per partner or professional while keeping the number of companies per partner and per professional fairly constant. This is not the case for VC firms. Metrick and Yasuda (2010) argue that the crucial difference between buyout firms and VC firms derives from the fact that a manager's skills in a buyout firm can add value to extremely large companies, whereas a VC manager's skill can only add value to small companies.

CHAPTER 24   INTERNATIONAL TAKEOVERS AND RESTRUCTURING

1. When the economy slows down as it did during the period from 2008 to 2009, many firms go into bankruptcy or exit the industry for fear of being too close to bankruptcy. Firms remaining in the industry lose value. Some firms have excess cash due to a slowdown in business and fewer investment opportunities. The fact that potential targets are now available at lower values and well-functioning firms have financial slack makes acquisitions a good way for entering an industry. Further, target firms, which were previously too expensive for acquirers, now fall within their budgetary reach. During times of recession, many firms need capital infusions, making them prime candidates for acquisition targets. This need for capital infusion provides bidding firms with strategic opportunities for making acquisitions. Finally, during economic downturns, firms with marginal or weak financing alternatives are driven from the global market for corporate control, leaving behind stronger but fewer competitors with solid cash positions to make the acquisitions.

2. International acquisitions often provide an effective means of expanding market share. The determining factor is the nature of the product market and the structure of the industry in the home country market. This is especially true for firms in developed countries. By contrast, firms in advanced countries face sophisticated, mature, and close-to-saturation markets. Further, the home market is highly competitive with little opportunity for differentiating the firm's product, forcing a firm to expand abroad to increase its market share. If, however, the firm manages to maintain a differentiated product at home and faces a relatively inelastic demand curve, it has less of an incentive to venture into foreign markets. Moreover, foreign expansion is associated with certain risks not present in the home market.

Similarly, foreign acquisitions also give the firm's managers an opportunity to establish their desired degree of market power. This factor has much to do with the nature of the firm's management team. For instance, the management team may want to establish a monopolistic (or at least an oligopolistic) position in its product market, either due to hubris or for profit-seeking reasons. If the structure of the home market forces the firm to be a price-taker, foreign expansion may be the only way for managers to engage in empire building. If the management team is relatively less risk-averse, it may be willing to be the first to enter uncharted territory. Although the risks may be high, a firm may be able to earn monopoly rents in the new foreign market because it will be a price-setter in the foreign market.

3. Cross-border acquisitions can be an effective means of arbitraging regulatory and other institutional controls. Specifically, differences in regulations between the home country and the host country, trade barriers, and capital controls can play important roles in motivating international acquisitions. Profit-seeking firms may engage in foreign acquisitions to circumvent such institutional growth impediments in home country sales and exports to foreign countries.

   Generally, in developed and politically stable countries with sound legal systems, the negative externalities of certain manufacturing processes or the detrimental effects of certain products are often apparent. In these countries, corporations are subject to more restrictive regulations. Further, with law and order being relatively more organized in these countries, implementation and enforcement of regulations is stricter. Under these circumstances, firms from developed countries often find selling their products in the markets in less developed countries advantageous. In developing countries, regulations are slower to be adopted, and even when adopted, they are rarely enforced with complete stringency. The pharmaceutical and tobacco industries are examples of this phenomenon. A similar arbitrage opportunity is available concerning environmental protection laws. Manufacturing processes that violate the more stringent laws of the United States are often acceptable in other parts of the world, particularly in developing countries. Firms often acquire smaller competitors in these countries to avoid the home country's regulations and fines.

   Regulations and government policy in the target firm's country or host country may also be a driver of international acquisitions. Host countries might have certain requirements such as zoning laws or local labor and local bank financing, which may be a deterrent for *de novo* entry. Acquiring existing facilities in such markets provides a legal and efficient means of avoiding these requirements.

   Most countries have regulations prohibiting firms from consolidation acquisitions that might lead to monopolistic practices in a particular industry. Firms facing regulatory constraints against lateral expansion at home may consolidate across borders and thus increase their global market share without raising the antitrust flag at home.

   Trade barriers, in the form of quotas and tariffs, are often in place to protect certain domestic industries. While several bilateral and multilateral treaties, as well as regional free trade zones, exist today, firms still see such barriers as binding constraints and use international acquisitions as a means of circumventing them.

   Similarly, certain less developed countries often impose capital controls on short-term repatriation, especially during times of financial turmoil. In such instances, receiving immediate payments for exports and licensing arrangements may become uncertain. In this case, acquiring a firm in the host country may prove beneficial in the long term. That is, revenues can be plowed back into the firm and repatriated only when controls are lifted or after they qualify as returns on long-term investments.

4. One of the key decisions related to valuing cash flows in cross-border acquisitions is the decision about the currency of analysis. In the discounted cash flow (DCF) analysis used for valuing the cross-border cash flows, the numerator and denominator of the DCF formula need to be in the same currency. In other words, the cash flows and the WACC need to be in the same currency—either both should be

in the acquirer's home currency or both could be in the host country or target's currency.

Under the first approach, the cash flows are generated in the target's currency. A series of forward exchange rates needs to be developed and used to convert all cash flows to their home country counterparts. The WACC is usually already available through the acquiring firm's home country operations. Under the second approach, the cash flows remain in the host or target country's currency, but the acquirer's WACC is converted to the currency of the cash flows to be consistent.

If markets were perfect and all of the parity conditions held true, both approaches would give the same results. In practice, however, there could be reasons for preferring one approach over the other. Free cash flows, which are derived from earnings before interest but after taxes (EBIAT) by deducting noncash expenses and adding any capital expenditures and additions to net working capital, are generated in the local currency. If exchange rates in the host country are expected to be volatile, then using a series of appropriate forward exchange rates (based on the purchasing power parity, for instance) to convert the cash flows to the home currency would be preferable, thereby incorporating the exchange rate volatility explicitly into the analysis. On the other hand, if the acquisition is being financed with local currency sources of capital, keeping the estimated cash flows in the local currency and discounting at the local currency WACC would make sense.

5. Foreign exchange risk arises when unanticipated changes in the exchange rate affect a firm's cash flows. When a firm acquires a target in a foreign country, there can be multiple sources of foreign exchange risk. There are three different sources of risk. In the narrowest sense, if the acquirer has committed to a certain transaction to be settled in the future in a foreign currency and the exchange rate changes in the interim, the acquirer faces *transaction exposure*. One approach to estimating the future cash flows uses a series of estimated forward rates to convert the foreign currency cash flows to the home currency. Unanticipated changes in the exchange rates will affect the forecasted cash flows. So, depending on the volatility of the target country's exchange rates, either the cash flows have to be adjusted or a premium has to be added to the discount rate. The exchange rates can also move in favor of the acquirer, but the concern is with downside risks.

The second source of foreign exchange risk is related to accounting reporting requirements. According to most countries' accounting standards, every firm has to submit, once a year, a consolidated statement of accounts in the home currency. In other words, the financials of all subsidiaries, domestic and foreign, have to be consolidated with the parent firm's financials and reported in the parent firm's currency. Since this process is done on an annual basis, even if all else remains equal and just the exchange rate changes between one of the foreign subsidiaries' currencies and the parent firm's currency, foreign exchange exposure would result. This is *translation exposure*.

Specifically, targets acquired in foreign locations may generate the same magnitude of local currency cash flows year to year, but if exchange rates change unexpectedly, then translation gains or losses may occur when converting these cash flows to the home currency for reporting purposes.

Finally, the long-term strategic viability of a target firm's operations, and hence its synergistic contributions to the acquirer, may change with time if the target country's exchange rate changes in an unanticipated manner over the long term, subjecting the acquirer to *economic exposure*. Ex ante, especially if the risks are nondiversifiable and not captured by the target's beta, a premium should be added to the discount WACC when conducting the initial valuation of the target. Ex post, the acquirer can use financial hedging with forwards, futures, options, and swaps and other derivatives to manage the foreign currency exposures.

CHAPTER 25   JOINT VENTURES AND STRATEGIC ALLIANCES: ALTERNATIVES TO M&AS

1. Alliances are frequently equally owned by two parents. Lack of control increases the cost of coordinating activities, and consensus-building among partners can slow the speed of adaption to changes in competition. The difficulty in finding a consensus and changes in the partners' strategic goals (after the formation of the alliance) can explain the high rate of alliance failures and the preference for full control. Firms may also prefer full ownership in the presence of potential opportunistic behaviors by the partners trying to appropriate strategic know-how from each other. An alternative explanation for the prevalence of full control is that managers can extract more private benefits by integrating the firm. Whereas M&As increase the resources under managerial control, a joint venture (JV) is an independent unit jointly controlled with a partner firm.

2. When compared with an acquisition, the main benefits of alliances are derived from sharing costs, risks, and knowledge. Sharing ownership in an alliance can reduce some problems associated with full asset integration. A firm may prefer an alliance over a merger in the presence of high costs to integrate the acquired assets and divest undesired assets. In the presence of high levels of uncertainty, an alliance may be preferred because the exchange of information inside the alliance mitigates the risk of bad acquisitions. Management should also choose alliances when integration has a detrimental impact on the effort exerted by the employees managing the acquired assets. These costs are especially relevant in projects with a low probability of success but potentially high payoffs.

3. An equity JV can be distinguished from other alliances in that a new entity is created with a separate board of directors. A JV may be more costly to create and to unwind than a nonequity alliance, and many smaller projects may not justify these higher costs. Joint ventures can reduce opportunistic behaviors because the assets contributed to a JV act as hostages. An independent board of directors induces cross-monitoring among partners, facilitates conflict resolution, and makes dealing with unforeseeable contingencies easier. The information exchange inside a JV can also reduce valuation uncertainty and can facilitate learning. A JV can also be an effective transitional mechanism to exchange information and to ascertain the value of the assets before a full acquisition. These arguments suggest that firms may prefer equity JVs over other alliances in the presence of higher levels of uncertainty, risk, potential for opportunistic behaviors, and need for knowledge exchange.

4. Lack of disclosure usually impedes observing the performance of assets integrated in a firm, and partners usually do not provide individualized measures of alliance performance. Event study analysis shows significant gains for M&A targets, whereas acquirers experience small or negative returns. Results using this methodology also indicate that alliances are associated with an increase in shareholder wealth. Long-term analyses of M&As and alliances yield inconclusive results and call for further research. Studies comparing M&As and alliances show larger combined gains for buyer and target firms in M&As than for partners in alliances. The gains for alliance partners are similar to the gains for M&A buyers. However, the gains in M&As accumulate for targets, but both partners experience positive abnormal returns around the announcement of alliances.

CHAPTER 26   FAIRNESS OPINIONS IN M&AS

1. When the board of directors auctions the assets, competitive bidding establishes a price for the assets. However, when the merger is negotiated or is a freeze-out acquisition,

there is no market mechanism to establish price. In such instances, fairness opinions can provide value when the underlying analyses that the investment banker providing the opinion performs help negotiate suitable considerations or prevent mergers with inadequate considerations from taking place.

2. A fairness opinion can be used by the board, management, or deal advisor to pursue their interests at the expense of shareholders. Managers may seek to enter into mergers or pursue acquisitions that enhance their private benefits from controlling a larger enterprise (such as higher pay and prestige) even if the transaction is not in the best interest of the shareholders. Board members may acquiesce to management wishes to retain their board positions. Investment banks advising on the deal may want to ensure a continued relationship with management and hence opine favorably to ensure that the deal goes through and they stand to collect deal contingent fees.

3. An independent board with the requisite expertise can ensure that the merger or acquisition is in the best interest of the shareholders by rigorously questioning the investment bankers over the analyses underlying their opinion before accepting it. To ensure that the deal advisor is not opining to get the deal done, the board could employ another investment bank to make the case against the transaction.

4. There is no guarantee that independent entities will not be favorably disposed to supplying "fair" opinions to self-serving management and captured boards. Faced with the possibility that management may engage in "opinion shopping," independent boards may seek to accommodate management. Deal advisors may be better informed than other market participants about the firm's intrinsic value (at least on the target side) and thus benefits may result from having them provide opinions.

CHAPTER 27   HOW INITIAL PUBLIC OFFERINGS AFFECT M&A MARKETS: THE DUAL TRACKING PHENOMENON

1. IPOs produce effects that go beyond their purpose of raising capital. Filing to go public and structuring the IPO in certain ways can lead to the phenomenon of dual tracking. With dual tracking, newly public firms can signal their value through IPOs, and an acquisition follows shortly after or even immediately before the IPO occurs.

2. Besides the information disclosure required by the filing process, the ties of newly public firms with prominent institutional figures, such as venture capitalists and top investment banks, can also offer indirect information on the quality of the underlying firm. Studies show that underpricing (defined as the firm's first-day returns upon going public) have information signaling properties. Together, these items allow prospective acquirers to reduce their exposure to adverse selection and therefore increase the likelihood of a post-IPO acquisition.

3. Acquirers can protect themselves from the hazards of information asymmetry by introducing contingencies in acquisitions such that the seller is effectively taking on the "burden of the proof." For instance, by paying in stock, sellers lack the incentive to misrepresent their value, because they will remain as partial owners of the combined entity after the acquisition is consummated. Similarly, contingent earnouts, which consist of conditional payments made to the seller only if the latter can deliver certain performance objectives in the future, also allow buyers to circumvent the risks of information asymmetry. Last, acquirers can stage their investments and enter into joint ventures as precursors to acquisitions and decide to buy out their partners once more information becomes available. While effective, the instruments above present unique

downsides that must be considered by acquirers vis-à-vis the acquisition's goals and timing requirements.

4. Adverse selection is a predicament not only for buyers but also for good-quality sellers who are willing to disclose their value truthfully, but are unable to do so due to information asymmetry. To the extent that dual tracking helps to reduce information asymmetry, it helps both buyers and sellers to find an accord, helping M&A markets to clear.

5. If sellers purposely sought to be dual tracked, they would face the substantial costs and risks of IPOs as well as the challenges of M&A negotiations. The existing evidence suggests that dual tracking facilitates post-IPO acquisitions and that sellers obtain higher premiums than single tracking firms. Thus, firms considering this two-stage exit strategy should reconcile their objectives against a broad set of considerations such as the existence of suitors before filing, the IPO cycle, and the firm's ability to attract key institutional figures as they go public.

CHAPTER 28   THE DIVERSIFICATION DISCOUNT

1. Some contend that the potential benefits of the internal capital market are greater for firms in emerging capital markets compared to developed capital markets. Under a poorly functioning external capital market, an internal capital market can allocate resources more effectively than external capital markets. However, the potential costs of inefficiency would also be greater for diversified firms in these markets. Given that minority shareholders' rights are not well protected in emerging markets, diversified firms in these markets might misuse the increased resources. Therefore, weighing the incremental benefits and costs of the internal capital market in emerging markets, the net effect of diversification is not necessarily positive.

2. Given the failure of some corporate governance systems and the lack of managers' incentive alignment, managers often make poor diversification decisions. If so, poor diversification results in lower firm value. However, this diversification discount suggests disequilibrium that the market will eventually resolve. Therefore, some diversified firms might trade at a discount at a certain time, but diversified firms on average and over the long run would not trade at a discount.

3. In a perfect market, no value is added for corporate diversification, and individual investors can easily construct portfolios of similarly focused firms. However, given market frictions, corporate diversification might be beneficial to outside investors. A corporation can often borrow at a cheaper rate than individuals and invest in diversified operations. A firm has informational advantages about its growth opportunities of new projects, compared to external investors. Investors can reduce transaction costs by trading in diversified firms instead of developing a similar portfolio of focused firms. Given these potential benefits of investing in diversified firms, outside investors should net these benefits against a diversification discount. If the diversification discount is less severe, investing in diversified firms may be more beneficial to outside investors than developing a comparable portfolio consisting of focused firms.

4. Given that diversification, on average, leads to inefficient capital allocation, product market competition provides an incentive for a firm to eliminate this inefficiency. Therefore, more focused (diversified) firms should be observed in highly (less) competitive industries. However, agency theory suggests that managers may pursue unwise diversification even if it is harmful for a firm's survival.

CHAPTER 29   PARTIAL ACQUISITIONS: MOTIVATION AND CONSEQUENCES ON FIRM PERFORMANCE

1. Partial acquisitions are corporate ownership transactions in which the acquiring firm only acquires part of the target firms' ownership. The target firm remains as an independent entity in the public market after the partial acquisitions. In a full acquisition, the acquiring firm gains the target firm's complete ownership, the target firm becomes a subsidiary of the acquiring firm, and the acquisition results in the target firm's delisting from the public market. The partial acquisition sample provides a unique opportunity for researchers to study the impact of acquisitions on the target firms and provides useful insights about the integration process after the acquisitions.

2. In certain situations, bidding firms use partial acquisitions to maximize the synergy gains. Particularly, partial acquisitions introduce an external blockholder that improves the monitoring power and the governance mechanism in the target firm and thus creates value for the shareholders. Another use of partial acquisitions is to mitigate the free-rider problem in corporate takeovers. Acquiring a small portion of the target firm's ownership provides necessary incentives to the acquiring firms to undertake competitive takeovers and to keep the takeover market running efficiently. Some firms use partial acquisitions to win the final takeover battle and to acquire full ownership in the target firm. The acquiring firm usually has more bargaining power and faces less resistance from the target management team after the partial acquisitions. Thus, partial acquisitions increase the chances that the acquiring firms will win the takeover battle. Partial acquisitions may also be useful in mitigating the asymmetric information problem, controlling foreign expansion risk, and facilitating the penetration into foreign markets in the cross-border deals.

3. Empirical results generally show a positive impact of partial acquisitions on target firm performance. Based on the event study method, the announcement of partial acquisitions can result in increases in both the target and the acquiring firm's stock price in the short term. Evidence shows that target firm performance is only positive and significant if the partially acquired firm experiences major restructuring changes after the acquisition. This suggests that the improved performance in the target firm is because of the increased monitoring power and reorganization effort brought by the acquiring firm instead of its expertise in selecting undervalued target firms. In the long term, the impact of partial acquisitions on the target firm performance is mixed. This is due to the contextual differences in various partial acquisitions and the necessity to control for these determinant factors in studying the impact of partial acquisition on long-term firm performance.

4. Several factors may affect partial acquisitions and target firm performance. First, the changes in the target firm's governance and control directly affect its long-term performance. Firms undergoing internal governance changes, such as management turnover and proxy fights, experience positive and significant improvement in long-term stock and operating performance. Second, long-term performance is conditional on the acquiring firm's identity and motivation. Evidence shows that an activist acquiring firm that wants to make restructuring changes in the target firm tends to improve the target firm's long-term performance. However, there is mixed evidence about the roles played by the strategic and financial acquirers. Specifically, research indicates that because financial acquirers tend to have short investment horizons, they may not have incentives to alter the operation and governance structure in the target firm. Therefore, the fundamental value and performance of the target firm is not expected to improve after these acquisitions.

Asymmetric information moderates the impact of partial acquisitions on target firm performance. Evidence shows that the target firm benefits more from partial acquisitions when there is less information asymmetry between the target and the acquiring firm. For example, geographic proximity reduces information collection costs and thus increases the monitoring power of the acquiring firm. In cross-border acquisitions, acquiring firms have a stronger motivation and greater ability to monitor the target firm when they have a common culture and language with the target firm and more acquisition experience in the target country. Evidence also suggests that acquiring firms with less information asymmetry can perform an active governance role in disciplining target firms' management. Accordingly, target firm performance is improved due to the monitoring and governance changes.

Index

Note: Page numbers followed by *e* refer to exhibits.